GREAT EVENTS FROM HISTORY

Great Events from History

Worldwide
Twentieth Century Series

Volume 2
1945-1971

Edited by
FRANK N. MAGILL

Associate Editor
Edward P. Keleher

SALEM PRESS, Incorporated
Englewood Cliffs, New Jersey

LIBRARY OF CONGRESS CATALOG CARD NUMBER: 72-86347

Complete Set: ISBN   0-89356-116-9
Volume 2:   ISBN   0-89356-114-2

FIRST EDITION
First Printing

PRINTED IN THE UNITED STATES OF AMERICA

LIST OF EVENTS IN VOLUME TWO
Worldwide Twentieth Century Series

INITIALS IDENTIFYING CONTRIBUTORS OF SIGNED ARTICLES

A.C.R.	Anne C. Raymer	J.R.B.	John R. Broadus
A.G.G.	Alan G. Gross	J.R.H.	John R. Hanson, II
A.M.	Anne Millbrooke	J.R.P.	John R. Phillips
A.O.B.	Anita O. Bowser	J.R.S.	Jane R. Shoup
B.F.	Barry Faye	J.S.A.	J. Stewart Alverson
C.C.H.	Cabot C. Holmes	J.W.P.	James W. Pringle
C.E.C.	Charles E. Cottle	L.H.D.G.	Leonard H. D. Gordon
C.K.	Clive Kileff	L.R.M.	Lincoln R. Mui
C.W.J.	Charles W. Johnson	L.S.	Leon Stein
C.W.T.	Carol Whyte Talabay	M.G.	Manfred Grote
D.D.D.	Daniel D. DiPiazza	M.S.S.	Margaret S. Schoon
D.F.P.	Doris F. Pierce	M.W.B.	Meredith William Berg
D.W.T.	David W. Talabay	P.A.	Paul Ashin
E.A.Z.	Edward A. Zivich	P.D.M.	Paul D. Mageli
E.F.	Elizabeth Fee	P.M.	Paul Monaco
E.G.D.	E. Gene DeFelice	P.R.P.	Philip R. Popple
E.P.K.	Edward P. Keleher	R.A.G.	Roger A. Geimer
F.B.C.	Frederick B. Chary	R.E.	Rand Edwards
G.J.F.	George J. Fleming	R.H.S.	Richard H. Sander
G.R.M.	George R. Mitchell	R.J.C.	Ronald J. Cima
G.R.M.	Gordon R. Mork	R.L.L.	Richard L. Langill
H.H.B.	Henry H. Bucher, Jr.	R.R.	Richard Rice
J.A.B.	James A. Berlin	S.L.	Saul Lerner
J.C.C.	John C. Carlisle	S.V.D.	Stuart Van Dyke, Jr.
J.C.N.	John C. Neeley	T.A.B.	Terry Alan Baney
J.D.R.	John D. Raymer	T.D.	Tyler Deierhoi
J.G.U.	Jonathan G. Utley	T.D.C.	Thomas D. Crouch
J.H.	Jean Harber	T.M.S.	Thomas M. Smith
J.H.M.	John H. Morrow, Jr.	T.R.K.	Thomas R. Koenig
J.J.H.	James J. Herlan	V.N.	Victor Namias
J.L.C.	Jack L. Calbert	W.S.	Walter Schultz
J.M.F.	Jonathan M. Furdek		

GREAT EVENTS FROM HISTORY

DIGITAL COMPUTERS AND THE INFORMATION REVOLUTION

Type of event: Technological: onset of information processing, automation, and the information revolution
Time: 1945 to the present
Locale: The United States and Europe

Principal personages:

JOHN VON NEUMANN (1903-1957), a European-educated mathematician who enunciated the "stored program" concept

ALAN M. TURING (1912-1954), a British logician and mathematician who wrote seminal pioneering papers on the logical properties and potentialities of the computer

JOHN PRESPER ECKERT (1919-   ), an American electrical engineer

JOHN W. MAUCHLY (1907-   ), an American physicist, who with J. P. Eckert first successfully reduced the theory of the computer to electronic machine practice by designing and building ENIAC

JAY W. FORRESTER (1928-   ) and

ROBERT R. EVERETT (1921-   ), American electrical engineers who designed and built the first control computer ("Whirlwind")

Summary of Event

In the beginning of the information revolution a few key men were involved, but as the computer gradually became a part of the everyday life of industrialized nations, the broad social and economic developments eclipsed the personal contributions. The computer emerged first as a theoretical design concept in the 1930's as a result of the creative activity of such innovators as Leslie Comrie and Alan Turing in Britain and Howard Aiken, John Atanasoff, Claude Shannon, and George Stibitz in the United States. Then in the early 1940's, the first electronic digital machine, ENIAC (Electronic Numerical Integrator And Computer), came into being at the University of Pennsylvania to produce urgently needed ballistics calculations for the United States Army. ENIAC's switching circuits and eighteen thousand vacuum tubes, installed in a large room for ease of experimental access, were designed and built during World War II by a research and development team led by a physicist, John W. Mauchly, and an electrical engineer, John Presper Eckert.

By 1945 the machine was ready for experimental testing, but in the meantime extensive theoretical research into the logical and the electrical engineering principles of the computer was being pursued at the

ENIAC project, at the Massachusetts Institute of Technology, at the Institute for Advanced Study (IAS) in Princeton, and elsewhere. Fruitful conversations involving Eckert, Mauchly, and the IAS mathematician John von Neumann culminated in a famous, extremely influential theoretical paper that Neumann issued in June, 1945, the "First Draft of a Report on the EDVAC" (Electronic Discrete Variable Automatic Computer). It showed how data and processing instructions could efficiently be intermixed and stored in the machine. EDVAC became operational as a unit in 1951.

It was typical of the early state of the art that ideas from the EDVAC paper should be incorporated by Turing in 1945 in a less widely known but more powerfully generalized and visionary paper, "Proposals for Development . . . of an Automatic Computing Engine." Hindsight shows that Turing's paper was so ahead of its time, describing in abstract, logical detail how complex and powerful the computer actually would become, that experts shortsightedly saw it as even more fanciful than the extravagant, five million dollar unorthodox design project the United States Navy and the Air Force were to support at MIT during the next five years, Project Whirlwind.

While ENIAC (1943-1946) spawned EDSAC (Electronic Delay Storage Automatic Calculator) (1947-1949) in Great Britain, IAS (1946-1952) at the Institute for Advanced Study, and UNIVAC (Universal Automatic Computer) (1948-1951) at the Bureau of the Census, "Whirlwind" (1945-1951) trained a generation of American computer designers and programmers who spread out into the emerging computer industry of the 1950's, accelerating computer design progress. The prospects of putting computers to work at a wide variety of tasks indicated a marketing future so attractive that large corporations, such as Radio Corporation of America (RCA), International Business Machines (IBM), Sperry-Rand, and General Electric became involved. The scientific usefulness of the computer became eclipsed by its promising economic value to industrialized society, as the United States assumed world leadership in computer design and applications.

During the first thirty years of its existence, the electronic digital computer acquired four major features that determined its technical, economic, and social future:

(1) *Basic Design Principles.* A complete computer was required to perform five essential functions: information input; output; incredibly swift, electronic, binary, calculating, and logical processing operations; the storage and retrieval of data, instructions, and processed information in internal "memory banks"; and the centralized control and correlation of all the numerous and simultaneous electronic operations going on within the computer, in order to produce the coherent new information delivered by the output devices.

(2) *Uses.* Many early policymakers and fund managers had regarded the computer as primarily a mathematical instrument invaluable to fundamental mathematical and scientific research of all kinds. Neumann's prestige was an important influence

here. But others were impressed by the practical potential of the computer, and they saw it as a center of information and control for, say, coordinating the combat operations of destroyers and aircraft in antisubmarine warfare or regulating air traffic at a busy airport or controlling complex, delicate manufacturing processes or assisting banking and commercial operations. Reliability and accuracy were far more crucial in these "real time" situations than in carrying out academic research, and they imposed expensive quality standards on hardware components. The "Whirlwind" computer, designed and built by a research and development team led by two erstwhile MIT graduate students, Jay W. Forrester and Robert R. Everett, was the first of the successful high-speed, high-reliability computers. It became the prototype of a continent-wide air defense computer that the federal government asked the International Business Machines corporation to build to Project Whirlwind's specifications. IBM capitalized on this opportunity, together with its merchandising experience, to pull ahead of Philco, Eckert and Mauchly, and other firms and thus gain a leading share in what would become a multibillion-dollar industry in less than half a century.

(3) *Software.* Although the computer might appear to "think," it could not. It was and remained a machine that had to be instructed to undertake its every action. The technique of writing these instructions was immediately seen as an important key to multiplying the operations and the uses of the computer. As a result, there arose the profession of computer programmers whose most sophisticated function was creating "software," that is, elaborate instructional programs that translated the rational instructions of human operators (who need not know how the computer worked) to the basic, painstaking, blow-by-blow level of instruction needed to make all programmable computers work. (Partial computers, such as digital watches, automatic elevator controls, or pocket calculators of the simpler type, did not use software, since their functions were predetermined by the design of their hardware.) During the first twenty-five years of the computer era, a supportive industry of software consultants developed innumerable programs of increasing complexity and power, calling these "compilers," "interpreters," and "languages" (for example, "Fortran," "Algol," "Basic") and devising them in order to expand the capacity of human operators to make more versatile use of the computer.

(4) *Hardware.* From its inception the computer was never a machine of standard hardware design. Obsolescence, dramatic advances in design, and radical changes in the materials and techniques of construction dominated computer engineering and manufacture. The perfection of the transistor during the 1950's rendered the vacuum-tube pioneers obsolete. The metallic "printed circuit" replaced the original soldered-wires assembly, and when molecular-scale, microminiaturized circuits were developed during the 1960's, computers grew even smaller. The long-range trend was toward faster, more compact machines of larger and larger

capacity. Speed of calculation rose from thousandths of a second to millionths during the 1950's and 1960's and to billionths by the 1970's.

Increasing complexity and versatility dominated hardware design progress, while unit and operating costs steadily shrank. The result of this trend was a rapid spread of computer use in banking, commerce, telephonic and television communications, travel reservations, engineering, manufacturing, research, education, and diverse military and civil government operations. Whereas at the start only institutions and corporations could afford to lease and use computers, by the end of the first thirty years, private personal use was spreading as the public bought computerized toys and games, ovens, radios, television recorders, pocket calculators, and built-in automotive-engine ignition, fuel-injection, and trouble-shooting and repair circuits, to name but a few. Some saw these as the opening years of an Information Revolution in which increasing numbers of people began to appreciate the consequences of increased control of their social, financial, and personal affairs—a control made possible, perhaps inevitable, by the computer's talent for increasing both the sheer quantity and the organization of information.

In these opening decades of the computer era, the uses outweighed the abuses, even while an uneasy, rising awareness began to spread among users and citizens that the character of personal and corporate life was undergoing changes so profound that their precise nature and consequences could not readily be anticipated.

Pertinent Literature

Mowshowitz, Abbe. *The Conquest of Will: Information Processing in Human Affairs*. Reading, Mass.: Addison-Wesley, 1976.

The first part of the title expresses the author's deep concern over the approaching hurricane of social consequences that he sees being generated by an increasingly sophisticated, powerful, and pervasive computer technology. It is not the computer as such, but rather the information technology the computer provides that perennially threatens to engulf mankind by making it easier for individuals to acquiesce in the alienation of responsibility. The result is a conquest of personal will that is likely to allow power to become so concentrated in pyramidal corporate and state organizations that a devastating loss of personal freedom and responsibility will ensue. While the computer itself is no monster, the history of tyrants shows that we may expect some individuals to so exploit the powers of the computer to sort, process, and generate information that it will be easier than ever for them to confront, affront, and violate human dignity, self-respect, democratic ideals, and man's equally long-standing talent for constructive personal action that has civilized him and shaped the highest and best of human values.

Examining the contemporary and

pending state of the computer art that has made the machine so useful, Mowshowitz describes its ability to coordinate diversity and thereby enhance organized activity in economic and political affairs. He reviews its ready assistance to corporate decisionmaking, to teaching and education and indoctrination, to health care, and to the welcome performance of those unavoidable routine jobs required by any society. But such transformations as have already set in will be dwarfed by those he sees ahead: the computer will become as ubiquitous as the telephone and the water faucet, and far more useful; the heightened interaction between men and machines will further transform the character of work, increasing the hazards of alienation and anomie as the traditional values attached to work disintegrate; problems of human identity and personal uncertainty will multiply, and a facile solution will be to impose greater social control in centralized form.

Mankind will need first to arm itself as rapidly and thoroughly as possible with the particulars of what the computer can and cannot be expected to do, and Mowshowitz shows how this can be done. Men will have to face up to the fact that the computer's terrifying potential for invasion of privacy (political surveillance or credit ratings, for example) will not vanish if ignored. The encouragement computerized information offers to increasingly arbitrary police action by a few in the name of the state will have to be assessed and counteracted. Smashing computers will not suffice to remove this danger.

Mowshowitz regards the political balance between the individual's right to participate in the exercise of political power and the government's inclination to act autonomously in decisionmaking as a very delicate balance maintained only in the minority of democratic republics in the world. The exercise of power, he notes, is enhanced by the acquisition of esoteric knowledge, and information restricted to computer databanks not accessible to the citizens is just such knowledge. We may well witness, he says, "the emergence of powerful forms of political control disguised as interactive systems" of information. There will be rule by experts who, while they need not be sinister, power-hungry men, might nevertheless be neither wise nor worthy enough to rule.

The spreading use of the computer as a simulator (of war games, of market behavior, of organizational crises that must be solved by administrators, and so forth) reveals how typical are both the allure and the limitations of information processing. The truth of the matter is that "operations research" and "systems analyses" techniques used in simulations, although readily computerized and impressively technical, cannot be expected to eliminate unwise or unjust decisions. Where information enhances power, those who traffic in power first and social accountability second can be expected to seek that information and control its use. The opportunities for use, misuse, and abuse of simulation information are legion in a society as heavily committed to planning as are those of the twentieth century. Such opportunities are not automatically reduced by more sophisticated and erudite simulation programs run on more powerful computers.

The book is less frantic in its appraisal than these excerpted impressions might suggest, and it contains a superb bibliography. The author points out that the selection and organization of information always reflects built-in biases, and computerized information is no exception. There will still be the problems of who is to decide what biases are built into the databanks, the processed information, and the simulations. How corruptive of acute judgment the biases may be will still be a matter that *people* must take under advisement, as always. Mowshowitz is confident that the strengths and the frailties of information processing can be understood without requiring us to master the technical intricacies of the computer. The way will be long, tortuous, and by no means easy. But first there must be the persisting will, and the computer's powers must not be permitted to seduce it.

Pylyshyn, Zenon W., ed. *Perspectives on the Computer Revolution.* Englewood Cliffs, N.J.: Prentice-Hall, 1970.

The historical emergence of the computer and the subsequent technical, economic, political, social, intellectual, philosophical, and moral opportunities and problems that the computer has generated are the subject of this book. It is an anthology of selections from thirty-five authors of all degrees of persuasion: Neumann, Turing, Samuel Butler, John R. Pierce, Margaret Mead, Norman Cousins, Jacques Ellul, and Herbert Simon, to name only a few.

Pylyshyn framed three overarching themes that he felt would put the computer and the Information Revolution in perspective. First, there are insights into the development of computer science offered by participants and observers, and these contemplate both the technical developments of representative computers themselves and their technical potential as regarded by experts at the time. The reader is made privy to some of the basic theoretical ideas associated with machine design, with the nature of automata, and with the important promise of software programs. It one wishes to know how and why algorithms are so important to computer science, as well as what they are, he may parse the technical formulas and diagrams of B. A. Trakhtenbrot's article, but most of the articles in the book require no specialized expertise from the reader for their comprehension.

Pylyshyn's second theme is "Man and Machine," and here several writers examine what we mean by "machine intelligence," while others examine the potentiality for confrontation between man and machine, and still others examine practices and possibilities that suggest partnership is equally likely. As wide as the world is, it seems likely that we may have both partnership and confrontation today and in the years to come. The artist or the composer who uses the computer as a creative medium may not be at such odds with the machine as are the hapless victims in Jack Williamson's "With Folded Hands," which depicts the suffocating solicitude of robots for their masters' welfare. In another version of this book, the robots open up undreamt-of vistas for humans to explore. Pylyshyn's selections show that we are far from being restricted solely to either alternative, yet these remain matters for our thoughtful concern.

The third theme moves to a wider view, of "Society and Machine," and considers the implications for educational policies and practices, for social control, and for the kinds of automatic control, feedback, and functionally modified control that are adaptable to manufacturing processes, to traffic-glutted freeways, and to all sorts of activities that would yoke man and machine together, *en masse*, in "automated cybernation" (which the experts explain is a technically redundant phrase in several senses). Pylyshyn's anthology, like Mowshowitz's analysis, offers illuminating pictures of where we have been, how computer technology and the Information Revolution have begun to take shape, and whither these developments may be taking us.
— *T.M.S.*

Additional Recommended Reading

Aiken, Howard. "Proposed Automatic Calculating Machine" (c. 1937), in *Spectrum*. I, no. 8 (August, 1964), pp. 62-69. Excellent description on the state of the art of automatic calculating machines.

Carpenter, B. E. and R. W. Doran. "The Other Turing Machine," in *The Computer Journal*. XX, no. 3 (August, 1977), pp. 269-279. Describes prescient 1945 proposal for a stored-program computer; includes bibliography.

Chase, George C. "History of Mechanical Computing Machinery," in *Proceedings of the Association for Computing Machinery*. (1952), pp. 1-28. Excellent survey with sixty illustrations, from the abacus to Aiken's Mark I, detailing the historical technical base from which the digital computer "took off."

Eames, Charles and Ray Eames. *A Computer Perspective*. Edited by Glen Fleck. Cambridge, Mass.: Harvard University Press, 1973. Pictorial, informative book version of elaborate IBM Exhibit with historical narrative by Glen Fleck.

Redmond, Kent C. and Thomas M. Smith. "Lessons from Project Whirlwind," in *Spectrum*. XIV, no. 10 (October, 1977), pp. 50-59. Describes technical contributions to computer progress in early pioneering years.

Rosen, Saul. "Electronic Computers: A Historical Survey," in *Computing Surveys*. I, no. 1 (March, 1969), pp. 7-36. Starts with ENIAC, concludes with commercial time-sharing systems by GE, RCA, Control Data, *et al*; eighty-three-item bibliography.

Serrell, R., M. M. Astrahan, G. W. Patterson and I. B. Pyne. "The Evolution of Computing Machines and Systems," in *Proceedings of the IRE*. (May, 1962), pp. 1039-1058. Contains large bibliography arranged chronologically from 1914, 1921, 1938, 1946-1961.

PUBLIC AWARENESS OF ENVIRONMENTAL DANGERS

Type of event: Sociological: public appreciation of threats to health and to the environment
Time: 1945 to the present
Locale: The United States

BARRY COMMONER (1917-), environmentalist and author of *The Closing Circle*, *Science and Survival*, and *The Poverty of Power*

RACHEL LOUISE CARSON (1907-1964), popularizer of the dangers of insecticides and author of *Silent Spring*

PAUL RALPH EHRLICH (1932-), popularizer of population threat, advocate of "zero population growth," and author of *The Population Bomb*

Summary of Event

The modern environmental movement emerged after World War II as a consequence of four major issues that attracted wide public concern in the 1960's and 1970's. Chronologically, the first of these issues to attract considerable public support was the threat of open-air nuclear testing. Initially disturbed about the terrible effects of atomic weapons on Hiroshima and Nagasaki, nuclear scientists were also greatly troubled about continued nuclear testing after World War II that eventually led to the development of the hydrogen bomb.

These atomic scientists discerned that open-air testing of nuclear weapons resulted in high fallout levels in the North Temperate Zone where most of the world's population live. The fallout resulted in concentrations of strontium 90 in milk and in bone splinters remaining in ground and other types of meat. Scientists were equally concerned about concentrations of radioactive iodine in thyroid glands. While government estimates of these nuclear tests, such as *The*

Effects of Nuclear Weapons (published jointly in 1957 by the Atomic Energy Commission and the Department of Defense), were invariably optimistic, scientists and the press continually criticized government reports and spokesmen.

Fallout became a political issue in the 1956 United States presidential campaign. Although he lost the election to Dwight D. Eisenhower, Adlai Stevenson's publicity of the issue generated much scientific and popular attention. Two years later, Dr. Barry Commoner and his colleagues established at Washington University in St. Louis, Missouri, the St. Louis Comittee for Nuclear Information. This organization attempted to provide the public with nontechnical information concerning the effects of fallout on human populations. All of this publicity and public concern bore fruit in 1963 in the negotiation and ratification by the United States and the Soviet Union of a Limited Nuclear Test Ban Treaty. This document put an end to atmospheric nuclear

542

testing by these nations, although it did not prevent nonsignatories, particularly France and Communist China, from continuing open-air nuclear testing.

A second major issue that eventually attracted enormous public attention was population growth. Following World War II, important scholars pointed out the dangers to all mankind of continued exponential population growth exceeding world food supplies. As examples, Aldous Huxley's *Brave New World Revisited* (1958) and Harrison Brown's *The Challenge to Man's Future* (1954) clearly dramatized this danger. These arguments attracted limited popular attention and remained mostly academic and intellectual concerns until 1968, when Paul Ehrlich published his book *The Population Bomb*.

Publication of this book followed Ehrlich's trip to India, where he was traumatized by the magnitude of the population and the terrible social and economic problems of the Indian people. Ehrlich attributed these difficulties to the sheer numbers of people that India had to sustain. *The Population Bomb* was Ehrlich's panicked reaction to his Indian experiences. The lesson that Ehrlich attempted to teach in this book, as well as in subsequent publications, was that population growth was the source of all other environmental problems, such as environmental pollution. Population growth was so rapid that economic and social chaos and disaster would inevitably result unless something drastic were done immediately. Ehrlich's only solution to what he regarded as an explosive growth of population was "zero pop-

ulation growth." If the world's population growth could be stopped, the survival of mankind was possible. Otherwise, Ehrlich predicted Malthusian disaster.

Ehrlich's book was enormously successful. Along with the efforts of various groups seeking population reduction, it popularized the term "zero population growth" and contributed significantly to public awareness in the United States and elsewhere of such issues as abortion, the use of contraception, and sex education in the public schools.

The third source of the modern environmental movement was the publication in 1962 of Rachel Carson's book, *Silent Spring*. This exceedingly popular work described the ways in which DDT and other pesticides had seeped into the food chain causing real dangers both to life within the food chain and to human beings. Prior to World War II, arsenic had been the most widely used insecticide in the United States; each year many people died because of improper handling of the chemical. The discovery in 1939 that DDT could effectively kill insects was greeted with much enthusiasm, especially since DDT made possible military operations in the South Pacific during World War II. After World War II, DDT was enthusiastically adopted by the American farm community. Rachel Carson's book, a direct attack on DDT and other insecticides, was so effective in documenting the dangers of DDT (because it does not dissipate quickly but remains potent and dangerous for many years) that this substance was soon taken off the market.

While one aspect of the environmental movement since World War II was the danger from environmental pollution, another involved saving the environment in the sense of preserving the wilderness. In the 1950's and 1960's, the American public became increasingly aware of the destruction of the wilderness by those seeking economic and other antiwilderness goals. Thus in 1950 environmentalists were shocked to hear of the threat to Dinosaur National Monument by the proposed construction of Echo Park Dam. Mounting a massive propaganda effort, the environmentalists fought against those who sought the dam for irrigation and storage purposes on the Colorado River. Finally, after years of political fighting, the Echo Park Dam proposal was defeated in 1956; the environmentalists had scored a major triumph. Having gained much popular support, wilderness advocates pressed for additional legislation.

From 1957 to 1964 the Congress of the United States debated creation of a national wilderness bill to establish long-range planning of wilderness preserves. The Wilderness Act that emerged in 1964 established the Wilderness System and methods for its administration. The Wilderness Act represented clear recognition by the Congress of the United States of the importance of the wilderness as a part of a national environmental program. All problems were not resolved, however. In the late 1960's, environmentalists had to fight to prevent damage to the Grand Canyon as a result of the Central Arizona Project, a massive irrigation construction. Environmentalists were finally successful in September, 1968. Moreover, in October, President Lyndon Johnson signed a bill establishing the National Wild and Scenic Rivers System. Here was legislation reflecting both public and governmental awareness of environmentalism.

Altogether these four issues—nuclear fallout, population growth, the use of insecticides, and the preservation of wilderness—led to other issues and generated an environmental movement that won wide public support in the United States and in Western Europe. Adopted by many young people, environmentalism became one of the props of the so-called "youth revolution" of the late 1960's and early 1970's. Popular as an issue among antiestablishmentarian young people who used it to attack contemporary society, environmentalism was equally popular among all ages of consumers.

Environmentalism generated an enthusiasm that was dramatically expressed on Earth Day, April 22, 1970, in a universal outpouring of sentiment that involved many American people in national celebration of environmentalism. The event was the highpoint of popular awareness of threats to the environment and an appreciation of ecology, the science of the interrelatedness of life forms on the earth. In the meantime, the Congress of the United States had also come to recognize the importance of this issue in a series of legal enactments, such as the National Environmental Policy Act (1969), the Clean Air Act (1970), the Toxic Substances Act (1976), and others, and the enforcement of these laws by such agencies as the Environmental Protection Agency and other federal, state, and local regulatory organizations. Clearly, by the early 1970's environmentalism had been established as one of the foremost public concerns of the post-World War II period.

Pertinent Literature

Commoner, Barry. *The Closing Circle: Nature, Man and Technology*. New York: Alfred A. Knopf, 1971.

One of the most important surveys of environmental problems since World War II is Barry Commoner's *The Closing Circle*. Starting with a description of Earth Day, 1970, Commoner contends that the event was a national recognition of environmental crisis. He then probes the sources of such crisis. Believing the ecosphere, "the earth's thin skin of air, water, and soil, and the radiant solar fire that bathes it," about to collapse from environmental damage and abuse, Commoner asks why.

The Closing Circle began as an attempt to describe and illustrate the concept of ecology. Emphasizing the interrelatedness of all life, Commoner describes what scientists have regarded as the origin of life on earth—the development and evolution of a primordial chemical soup into the many forms of life. The principles to be derived from Commoner's depiction of the origin of life are: (1) "the reciprocal interdependence of one life process on another"; (2) "the mutual, interconnected development of the earth's life system and the nonliving constituents of the environment"; and (3) "the repeated transformations of the materials of life in great cycles, driven by the energy of the sun."

Given these concepts, Commoner illustrates their operation and establishes what he refers to as the "laws" of ecology. He maintains that (1) "Everything is connected to everything else," (2) "Everything must go somewhere," (3) "Nature knows best," and (4) "There is no such thing as a free lunch." Having identified what he regarded as the principles of biological development and his rather crude "laws" of ecology, Commoner clearly indicates a theme of his book—that human societies which seek wealth and the exploitation of the environment are in fundamental conflict with biological and environmental requirements and needs.

In describing and detailing the nature of this conflict, Commoner devotes much of his book to a history of environmental problems since World War II; for example, he traces the problem of nuclear fallout from World War II until the 1963 Limited Test Ban Treaty. Most significantly, he describes how both human life and the environment were allowed to be damaged and endangered before adequate knowledge made scientists aware of the consequences of nuclear testing. He makes a plea for adequate public information and the testing of potentially hazardous substances before they are allowed into the environment.

Commoner again illustrates how technological changes were allowed to endanger human life and the environment in his description of air pollution since World War II. The high compression automobile engine was manufactured to increase the profits of automobile companies. Yet this type of engine generated, in combination with necessary mixtures of gasoline, air pollution that was most conspicuous as smog on the West Coast and endangered health in urbanized America.

The author also describes the dangers of excessive nitrate fertilization of crops and use of biohazardous insecticides. Eutrophication caused the aging and damaging of bodies of water, such as Lake Erie. Moreover, insecticide seepage into lakes and rivers has contributed to water pollution. Again, the justification used at the time was increased yields and profits regardless of the consequences.

Commoner argues that one characteristic of human life on earth has historically been the fact of growth, while the earth's resources have remained finite. Air and water pollution are signs that the ability of the earth to cleanse itself has been overtaxed and that the ecosystem is breaking down. He speculates about the growth of environmental damage since World War II, viewing this period as one of fundamental technological and economic changes. These changes, such as suburban growth, nuclear energy, chemical insecticides, fertilizers, high technology automation, electrical appliances, and detergents, all had a particularly burdensome effect on the environment. American affluence supported and made these changes possible, and the desire for profit on the part of manufacturers provided the stimulus. All Americans have sought a continually increasing Gross National Product that has turned American technology and industry into a threat to the environment and to man. "The new technology is an economic success— but only because it is an ecological failure."

Modern technology has had certain features which explain, for Commoner, why it has been very successful in accomplishing its carefully defined and limited goals. The problem, however, has been that, in subdividing its concerns into small, manageable parts, technology has made no effort to see the entire picture in context or to understand the social or environmental consequences of a technological innovation. Such reductionism has also affected science, which undertook all types of experiments and research without investigating their social or environmental effects. Reductionism has isolated scientists and technologists from society. What Commoner recommends is a benefit-to-risk computation on each scientific or technological innovation. Such a computation would make those engaged in research fully aware of the consequences of their work. Similarly, Commoner believes that the public must be made fully aware of the consequences of their actions, such as the dangers of excessive population growth.

Commoner is convinced of the importance of providing adequate information to give the public an awareness of the present environmental crisis. Otherwise catastrophe could well result. He believes that the environmental crisis involves the very survival of humanity. In view of such a dangerous situation, the author believes that free enterprise should be required to attain a "no-growth" condition in order to reduce the strain on the environment. In advocating limits to growth, Commoner hopes to substitute social goals for the profit motive as the central objective of the economy and of politics. He advocates a fundamental reorientation of the world's and America's value systems.

Kahn, Herman, *et al. The Next 200 Years: A Scenario for America and the World.* New York: William Morrow and Company, 1976.

Barry Commoner's *The Closing Circle* is illustrative of much recent environmental literature in advocating major changes in society to avert environmental catastrophe. Some advocates of environmentalism have been far less fearful of catastrophe and far more willing to retain the *status quo*. An important volume reflecting this view is Herman Kahn's *The Next 200 Years*, produced by the Hudson Institute as a bicentennial description of the past two hundred years of United States national life and a projection of the next two hundred years.

The book is written from the view that projections of continual exponential growth of population, energy utilization, raw material use, drain on food supply, and environmental pollution were misleading. The worldwide catastrophe that environmentalists contemplate and about which many people have felt panic, will probably not happen. Kahn and his Hudson Institute associates argue that the history of the past two hundred years has manifested exponential growth in all of these areas, but that during the next two centuries, the rate of this growth will decline significantly. Graphic depiction of population growth, consumption of food,

energy, and raw materials, and pollution growth from 1776 to 2176 will be an "S" curve. This will all happen if there is little or no additional regulation of free enterprise and business or if present regulation is limited or reduced. If business were given freedom to expand as much as desired, all of mankind's major problems would be eliminated or solved. While Barry Commoner and other environmentalists argue that the world's major problems can only be solved by limiting growth, the Kahn study maintains that these problems can only be solved if growth is unhampered.

The Hudson Institute study holds that the rate of population growth slowed in industrial countries because of a rising standard of living. If the entire world were industrialized, the resulting rise in living standards would reduce population growth and the world population by 2176 would stabilize itself at "approximately 15 billion, give or take a factor or two." This population would be satisfactorily sustained if growth were allowed to continue.

In the field of energy utilization, the Kahn study argues that the world is rapidly using up its fossil fuels. As this short-term supply was coming to an end, however, nuclear fission could be employed as an intermediate-term power source until long-term energy sources are developed. Such long-term sources included geothermal, solar, nuclear fusion energy, and wind, wave, and tide power. Kahn believes that the transition to long-term energy sources can only take place if business is allowed to develop these sources freely. If it is, by the end of the twenty-second century the world will have adequate energy for all of the needs of a population of fifteen billion. Although the period leading to the twenty-second century might produce some hardships, by that century the world could have inexhaustible energy supplies.

The Kahn study also discounts the dangers projected from the exhaustion of raw materials. First, many substitutes for raw materials are and will be available. Second, many resources can be recycled again and again and will be if there is a need. As materials are recycled, their use will be greatly extended. Third, present technology permits rather limited extraction of minerals. The future will bring new technologies which will permit mining in areas where it is presently impossible and will allow for more efficient use of minerals than at present. Indeed, Kahn holds that there might be some difficulty for the industrial nations in the short-term, but in the long-term world mutual interdependence will evolve and eliminate shortages. All of this will be possible only if industry is permitted to expand and to develop new technologies that will provide raw materials for a population of fifteen billion.

Similarly, food supplies will satisfactorily sustain the population of the twenty-second century if business can continue to grow. Tillable acreage will be expanded, multiple cropping will take place, yields will increase, and unconventional agricultural methods will be employed. Kahn does not anticipate the Malthusian scenario of population growth exceeding food supply.

In the area of environmental pollution, Kahn claims to support the environment. He criticizes excessive regulation from the Environmental Protection Agency and other regulatory bodies. Like Barry Commoner, he agrees that technologies should be evaluated on a risk-to-benefit basis. He stresses the idea that it is appropriate to subject the population to risk if the benefit outweighs that risk. He also suggests a new land use policy that would permit some lands to be regarded as "junk" and used by industry for anything they wish, as long as other properties are protected from pollution. While Kahn cannot see catastrophe in the future, he is uncertain as to whether pollution will be a problem in the twenty-second century.

The Hudson study projects a future in which the major problems presently besetting mankind will all be solved by the twenty-second century. A future population of fifteen billion would be prosperous and have most of their material needs provided. Given these prospects, the major problem that Kahn and his associates see for the future is boredom. The future might well be violent and unhappy precisely because the age-old problems of mankind would be solved and leisure would weigh too heavily   on all people. — *S.L.*

Additional Recommended Reading

Nash, Roderick. *Wilderness and the American Mind*. New Haven, Conn.: Yale University Press, 1973. An excellent, definitive survey of the wilderness movement through American history which focuses particularly on the nineteenth and twentieth centuries.

Carson, Rachel Louise. *Silent Spring*. Boston: Houghton Mifflin Company, 1962. Traces the dangers to life and the environment of continuous use of insecticides and fertilizers; this work significantly attracted public attention to environmental issues.

Ehrlich, Paul. *The Population Bomb*. New York: Ballantine Books, 1968. Highly emotional description of the dangers of population growth; this work attracted wide public interest in the late 1960's and early 1970's and made "zero population growth" a significant national issue.

Meadows, D., *et al. The Limits to Growth*. New York: Universe, 1972. Based on a computer study of the future, this work is one of the more interesting environmental studies advocating limits to growth.

Rienow, Robert and Leona Rienow. *Moment in the Sun*. New York: Ballantine Books, 1969. An interesting and comprehensive survey of the entire range of environmental problems confronting the United States.

Commoner, Barry. *Science and Survival*. New York: The Viking Press, 1963. Interesting description of the nature of science and technology showing how scientific research and technological progress have caused health problems and environmental damage and urging that the public become informed about such dangers.

Neuhaus, Richard. *In Defense of People*. New York: The Macmillan Company, 1971. Severe criticism of environmentalists from the view that limiting growth will permanently keep the poor in poverty; contends that saving people is more important than saving trees.

Maddox, John. *The Doomsday Syndrome*. New York: McGraw-Hill Book Company, 1972. Excellent critical assessment of environmental movement in which the environmentalists are taken to task for their immoderate demands, passionate convictions, logical fallacies, and lack of humor.

THE RISE OF THE MEGALOPOLIS

Type of event: Sociological: scattering of urban population
Time: 1945 to the present
Locale: Northeastern seaboard, Great Lakes region, California coast, and Florida

Summary of Event

Along the Northeastern seaboard of the United States from Boston to Washington, D.C., there is almost continuous urban development. Each city within this area—including Boston, New York City, Philadelphia, Baltimore, and Washington, D.C.—is surrounded by tier upon tier of suburbs. In addition to such cities with populations of half a million or more, there are numerous other cities of considerable size such as Hartford and New Haven, Connecticut; Providence, Rhode Island; Newark and Trenton, New Jersey. Between these urbanized areas there are small and medium-sized cities with concentrations of population in areas between the established cities. This same process of multiple metropolitan centers expanding until they form a carpet of urbanization is occurring along the Great Lakes, the California coast, and the east and west coasts and central zone of the Florida peninsula. The urbanized areas expand until they touch and then surround and engulf formerly isolated independent cities to form a megalopolis.

Although the term "megalopolis" was first used by the French geographer Jean Gottmann in 1957, the explosion of cities and overreaching of boundaries began to take place soon after the end of World War II in 1945. The United States had been in a long upward spiral of increased urbanization, but the growth of the suburban areas was greatly accelerated after World War II by the demand for housing by the returning servicemen, many of whom had married during the war or shortly thereafter. There was a high demand for housing from the general population as well because few new houses had been built during the war and because there had been high employment and high wages during wartime. Many people, therefore, were able to afford new or improved housing. Home financing insurance, which made it easier to buy a house, was available through the Federal Housing Administration and the Veterans' Administration. The policy of the federal government gave preference to the purchase of new houses rather than the rehabilitation of older homes in central cities. Thus, the desire for a private home and available financing contributed to the powerful outflow and overflow from established urban nuclei. From 1950 to 1960, the population outside the central cities grew by more than eighteen million, while the population in the central cities increased by only a little more than six million. These figures dramatize the rapid growth of suburban areas in contrast with the central cities.

This suburban growth after World War II was different from the suburban growth of earlier eras because it was shaped by the privately owned automobile as the primary mode of transportation. As long as suburban-ites depended upon railroads to travel to the central city, suburban growth was concentrated around railroad sta-tions; but with the widespread own-ership of the automobile, new hous-ing development could occur anywhere in the metropolitan area. Scattering of new housing develop-ments over a wide area is the essential feature of the megalopolis, and, not surprisingly, the prevalence of the private automobile parallels the emergence of the megalopolis. In 1930 there were only twenty-six mil-lion cars and trucks registered in the United States. However, between 1955 and 1965 the number of motor vehicles increased by twenty-four million to a total of eighty-five mil-lion. In 1977 alone, 11.2 million mo-tor vehicles were sold.

The government responded to this increased importance of the auto-mobile and the new pattern of living by building more roads and high-ways. In 1956 the interstate highway program was begun. It was to provide 46,000 miles of expressways when completed.

The dispersal of urbanization cre-ated demands for the transportation and distribution of goods and services over a wide area. Trucks, using the road and highway system, had the advantage of flexibility over fixed rail transportation in meeting this de-mand. Just as suburbs of an earlier era had clustered around railroads, businesses and manufacturing plants were located near the major termi-nals and intersections of railroads or around important waterways and ports. With the upsurge in truck transportation, businesses and indus-tries were free to move from the cen-tral city into the suburbs or to indus-trial parks in unincorporated areas.

The use of truck transportation was not the only reason for business and industry to move away from estab-lished dense population centers. Often new technology necessitated modern-ization of plant and equipment, which sometimes required more floor space and land. Suburban land was more available and usually less costly than that in the heart of the cities. During the same period a communications revolution removed the need for a business to be located in proximity to other businesses. The result of these forces was many new facilities beau-tifully landscaped and located in or near a new town or suburb where it was easier to attract better-trained employees. The suburban share of manufacturing jobs was increasing, and by 1970 most of the cities with populations in excess of one million in the East and Midwest were declin-ing in population and manufacturing jobs.

Not all social and economic groups were able to participate in the migra-tion to suburbia and beyond. Older people, families with limited eco-nomic resources, blacks, and other minorities tended to be left in the old inner city areas or the decaying first ring of suburbs while the younger middle- and upper-income groups moved to the suburbs. As the social and economic problems of the inner cities mounted, they stimulated fur-ther flight.

The social and economic problems of the older cities on the Atlantic sea-board and around the Great Lakes may be a factor in the shift of capital, investment, and people to the Sun Belt. This is contributing to the rise of megalopolises in Florida and in California.

Planners, architects, and students of the city view the megalopolis differently. One group sees the megalopolis as the destruction of the city and favors regional planning, which would restore order to the urban growth, conserve the environment, and create a more social and humane way of life. Others who accept the megalopolis as the natural evolution of urban living find it varied, exciting, and stimulating. Their chief concern is to minimize frustrations and inconveniences, and they look upon improved technology as the way to achieve this goal.

Pertinent Literature

Gans, Herbert J. *The Levittowners*. New York: Pantheon Books, 1967.

Herbert Gans is both a sociologist and planner. He has written numerous articles about popular culture and the mass media. In 1962 *The Urban Villager*, a study of the life of poor Italian-Americans in Boston, was published.

In *The Levittowners* Gans reports the results of the study which he made during the first two years after Levittown, New Jersey, was built by Levitt and Sons. Levittown was the real name of the town at the time of the study, but its name has since been changed to Willingboro. It is seventeen miles from Philadelphia. Gans was one of the first to move to Levittown and buy a house; he went there to research the development of a new town. This book is a result of his observations as a participant in the community and its affairs, his interviews with other residents, and two sets of questionnaires. His motivation for the research was a desire to analyze criticism directed toward suburbs and suburban life.

This criticism was harsh, diverse, and well publicized. A major criticism was that suburbs were monotonous in appearance and not aesthetically pleasing. The sameness of the physical characteristics of the homes was thought to be matched by the homogeneity of the people who lived there. Critics claimed these conditions stifled individuality and created deadening conformity. The implication was that suburbs were a dull place to live and that people who lived there were deprived of the cultural advantages available in large cities. Boredom was thought to be so serious that many women suffered severe emotional and mental illness.

In addition to the criticism which centered around the visual sameness and the low quality of life, there was criticism which focused upon the wastefulness of land, the ugliness of the general landscape, and the overall damage to the environment resulting from the endless sprawl of suburbs. Although the evidence in Gans's study addresses the question of the quality of life in the suburb, he rejects the charge of wasteful use of land. He sees no reason to restrict present use of land in the name of future generations because there is no way to know the preferences of future generations. He is not alarmed by the development of the megalopolis and, in fact, expects the development of suburbs to continue as the children of the children of the postwar baby boom marry and form families. The main factor which will limit the extension of suburban development is the length of time people are willing to spend commuting, and there are two developments which may reduce even this limitation. The first is the development of high-speed mass transportation which will extend the distance without substantially increasing commuting time. Also, as it becomes more and more possible to find employment in the suburbs, the commuting time from the suburb to the central city is no longer a limiting factor in the location of new suburbs. Gans does not view urban sprawl as a serious problem but sees the development of many different suburbs over a wide area as a means of providing variety and flexibility. The only difficulty he acknowledges with the expansion of the suburbs into a megalopolis is the development of many local governments concerned only with their local problems. He favors some type of regional government to deal with issues that cannot be satisfactorily dealt with by the local suburban governments.

Although Gans addresses these criticisms of ever-increasing suburban sprawl and the megalopolis, his study is concerned more directly with the criticism that suburbs are monotonous and force conformity upon their residents, making life boring and unsatisfactory. Levittown appears to justify this criticism, since its houses were mass-produced in only three different styles. However, the three styles were mixed within the block, which, according to Gans, William Levitt considered a daring thing to do. Gans says Levitt was opposed to city planners and was convinced that to sell houses, he simply had to build houses worth their price. Indeed, Gans found that a new community is not shaped by the founder, the builder, the city planner, or the aspirations that lead the residents to the community: he concludes that it is the population mix that shapes the community. People are initially motivated by the house and family life, and it is only after they have lived in the community that they form ideas about community institutions. Through a process of struggle and compromise in which minority desires are often pushed aside, the community emerges.

Just as Gans rejects the idea that the builder or city planner originates the community, he denies that there is greater homogeneity in the suburbs than in city neighborhoods. Although taken as a whole, a large city is diverse in social class and racial and ethnic composition, people live in neighborhoods, which tend to be islands of homogeneity. Even though Levittown was made up predominantly of lower-middle-class families, it did have working-class and upper-middle-class people. Gans found the uniformity of physical appearance did not bother the residents, and as time went along, they made changes and additions which made the houses more distinctive to their owners. Likewise, what appeared to be undue conformity to the outsider was to the

Levittowner the natural process of borrowing ideas and acting out a lifestyle that was pleasing. By and large, people were satisfied with their lives, and only a small proportion was unhappy with life in the suburb. Those who were most unhappy were people who had been a part of a large extended family in Philadelphia and now found it too expensive to call and visit as much as they desired. Since the suburb was designed more for the young adults and children, those who found the suburb dull or boring were most often adolescents and older people. The adolescents sometimes felt there was "nothing to do," and some older people felt left out. Yet other older people became active in community affairs or developed a satisfactory role as pseudoparents for the younger families. All in all, Gans finds little to support the popular criticism of suburbs and looks favorably upon the development of more suburbs.

Mumford, Lewis. *The Urban Prospect.* New York: Harcourt, Brace and World, 1956.

Lewis Mumford has written extensively about cities. *The Culture of Cities* (1938) established his reputation as a worldwide authority on cities; *The City in History* (1961) is another major work. *The Urban Prospect* is a collection of essays written and published from 1952 to 1968, years which coincide with our recognition of and concern over the rise of the megalopolis. In these essays Mumford expresses his strong distaste for the megalopolis and recommends alternative urban forms.

Historically, Mumford sees two Americas: the America of settlements and the America of migrations. The first migration was the clearing of the land across the continent and the foundation of the first settlements. The second migration occurred with the rise of factories and the movement of people from the rural areas in this country and from Europe into the established cities. The third migration occurred with the full flowering of the Industrial Revolution in the last quarter of the nineteenth century and the emergence of great financial centers and huge corporations. This produced great concentrations of people in cities such as New York City and Chicago, but it was accompanied by the movement from small and medium-sized cities to submetropolitan areas as well. The fourth migration came in this century and is the result of a technological revolution. This migration has dispersed population, and in its most extreme manifestation, has produced the megalopolis.

The technological revolution of the fourth migration includes changes of technology in transportation, communications, and energy. The automobile is central to the dispersal of population, but the new means of communication and entertainment also tend to make families more isolated and independent. These mobile, self-contained families are forces against the development of cities, which are an organic whole where people of all ages lead meaningful and rewarding lives which mutually reinforce one another. But Mumford believes there is a special "technology of megalopolis" which operates strongly against the human condition. Mass production, the computer, and systems analysis are key elements of the "technology of megalopolis" and impel structures, whether office buildings or housing developments, too large and insensitive to the human condition. This technology makes it financially more profitable to build large housing subdivisions that he considers aesthetically dreary and socially monotonous. Many urban renewal projects demonstrate that the "technology of megalopolis" is designed to meet the needs of building contractors, real estate developers, and government officials rather than the people who will live in them.

Mumford does not accept the megalopolis produced by this new technology as a true city but calls it anticity; he sees it as a random scattering of the population. It lacks the unity necessary for a city and is incapable of performing the nurturing of life that a true city provides. Mumford's idea of the city is influenced by Ebenezer Howard, who published *Garden Cities of Tomorrow* in 1898. Although the idea of garden cities is now well known, to Mumford it was more important that Howard proposed a new image of the modern city and an organic method of handling its continued growth. City size would be limited and population growth accommodated by the creation of new towns which would be self-contained, including industry, commerce, and professional services. This is a concept different from the residential suburb that is dependent upon a central city for jobs as well as most of the other necessities of life. There would be numerous cities grouped around a larger city of approximately 350,000. A green belt around each of the towns would help it maintain its own identity as well as provide accessible recreation areas and visually pleasing open space. The outside rings around cities would be connected to the central city by rapid transit systems. To Mumford it was important that the individual cities, which he called containers, be built to a human scale and have coherence. He believes the Howard method of nucleating and integrating urban functions can be applied to the existing metropolitan centers.

Mumford believes that our great metropolitan centers need not inevitably dissolve into megalopolises; rather, through a system of regional planning carried out under the authority of the state, disorderly metropolitan growth could be controlled. Since cities are not separate from the land surrounding them but are a part of it, the planning for cities can only take place within the regional matrix. He recognizes and desires to maintain the great benefits that come from diversity and high density, but congestion and long-distance commuting could be avoided with proper regional planning.

In proposing regional planning, Mumford is aware of the practical political problems that in the past have separated planning from authority to act, so that too often plans have been a waste of paper. As a solution, he proposes regional development authorities with power to plan and with control over capital investment and corporate actions. He also suggests it might be necessary to have regional legislatures to check possible abuse by the regional planning authorities.

Mumford dislikes the sprawl of the megalopolis and its failure to perform the basic integrative functions which he thinks are essential to a city, but he also dislikes the congestion in the center of the metropolitan area, which he feels downgrades the essential human qualities and produces emptiness, violence, and related pathology. He is careful as he reviews the problems of the riots and general turbulence of the large cities in the late 1960's to warn that many of the ills of the city are the result of ills in the society as a whole, and rearrangement of the urban setting should not be expected to cure all the ills of central cities. He remains confident, however, that his basic idea of regional planning with the orderly dispersal of the population in small units around a central city with green belts to define them clearly would contribute to a solution of the problems which beset society. After this had been accomplished, there could be experimentation with additional procedures to cure the remaining ills.
— *D.F.P.*

Additional Recommended Reading

Goldston, Robert. *Suburbia: Civic Denial.* New York: The Macmillan Company, 1970. A careful examination of the growth of suburbia on the Northeastern seaboard until it developed into the formless megalopolis so hostile to human life that it calls for new attention to regional planning.

Klebanow, Diana, Franklin L. Jonas and Ira M. Leonard. *Urban Legacy.* New York: New American Library, 1977. A history of the dynamic impact of cities on the social, economic, and political development of American society from the colonial period to the present, recounted in a readable and thorough manner.

Gruen, Victor. *The Heart of Our Cities.* New York: Simon and Schuster, 1964. An architect-planner analyzes the functions of cities, discusses the ills of the sprawl of the anticity, and offers solutions based on his practical experience.

Jacobs, Jane. *The Death and Life of Great American Cities.* New York: Random House, 1961. Attacks contemporary practices in urban planning because they destroy the diversity of mixed use, which is necessary for safety and vitality in urban areas.

Mumford, Lewis. *The City in History: Its Origin, Its Transformations, and Its Prospects.* New York: Harcourt, Brace and World, 1961. One of the best-known writers about urban life presents a classical treatment of the historical development of cities.

THE "THIRD WORLD'S" STRUGGLE FOR EQUALITY

Type of event: Political: effort of emerging nations to secure complete acceptance within the family of nations
Time: 1945 to the present
Locale: Underdeveloped countries of Asia, Africa, and Latin America

Summary of Event

The expression "Third World" has in the past twenty-five years become the generally accepted way of referring to the mass of relatively underdeveloped countries of Asia, Africa, and Latin America whose populations constitute a majority of the human race. These nations have fought since the end of World War II, when many of them were still under European control, to attain equality with the industrialized world in terms of both their standard of living and their political power in the international arena.

The goal of the first phase of this struggle was the attainment of political independence from the European colonial empires of Asia and Africa. Nationalist leaders insisted that only by cutting their political bonds with Europe could the colonized peoples regain their dignity and achieve the economic development that the West had promised to bring. They frequently appealed to world opinion as a means of applying pressure to the colonizing governments to accede to their demands for independence; they were subsequently to use this method with much skill to draw attention to the problems that the Third World nations faced. Alternatively, some independence leaders perfected methods of guerrilla warfare that were to continue to be used in the fight against foreign rulers. By 1962 most

of Europe's colonies had successfully reached their goal, with the important exception of Portugal's colonies in southern Africa, which were to become the focus of major liberation movements in the 1970's.

During the 1950's, the most rapid route to political and economic equality with the West was believed by Third World leaders of Asia and Africa to be "solidarity" among their peoples, through which they could more effectively attack the multitude of problems besetting them and exert more pressure on the advanced nations of both capitalist and Communist worlds. The edifice of Afro-Asian solidarity was constructed on the twin pillars of neutrality toward the two dominant powers—the United States and the Soviet Union—and friendship between the two largest Third World nations, India and China. Underdeveloped nations of Latin America did not generally identify themselves with this Afro-Asian bloc until much later, in part because of the dominating presence of the United States. This ideal of Afro-Asian solidarity was embodied in a series of Afro-Asian Peoples Solidarity Conferences beginning in 1957, but the Bandung Conference of 1955 is probably the best-known expression of this ideology. There the leaders of twenty-nine countries, some of them still colonies, laid the foundation for joint action at the United Nations and, by their unanimity and moderation, helped gain their nations some of the international recognition they desired. This approach to development began to falter in the 1960's, however, in part because of the border war between India and China in 1962 and the growing radicalization of some members of the group; a separate African bloc began to form in the United Nations from about 1960, and by 1963 thirty-four of 113 members of that body were African. A renewed emphasis on solidarity and cooperation among Third World nations has characterized the 1970's, though there is a new recognition of the necessity to accept diversity among them in cultural, political, and economic affairs.

The emphasis in the Third World's fight for equality has, in the years since the war, shifted from politics to economic development and better terms of trade for Third World exports. These two fronts in the struggle for equality should not be separated artificially, however: the struggle to raise the standard of living of their people, for instance, is part and parcel of the struggle of Third World nations for equal status on the international scene.

Political leaders of Asia and Africa have generally been attracted to the idea of centralized planning, as exemplified in the Communist-bloc nations, while those of Latin America have generally adhered more closely to capitalistic free market principles in the development of their countries. Whatever their orientation on this issue, these leaders have been almost unanimous in emphasizing the development of heavy industry as the best way to achieve economic equality with the West. Rather dramatic gains were made in this area during the 1960's, when the First United Nations Development Decade's goal of raising output by five percent was far exceeded. Though rapid industrialization remains the kingpin of the developmental process, this is now seen to be a part of an integral process involving light industry and agriculture as well as heavy industry.

In their attempt to attain greater equality with the industrialized world, most Third World nations have tried to diversify their economies and reduce their dependence on the export to the industrialized world of primary products (minerals, oil, and so forth) for foreign exchange earnings. This dependence on single export products has often adversely affected development plans which are financed with such export earnings, since these earnings have fluctuated with changes in the international prices of these exports and have decreased with the economic slowdown in the West in the 1970's. Recently the major oil exporting nations of the Third World have banded together in an organization (OPEC) to establish a uniform high price for this natural resource as a means of acquiring funds for development. It remains unclear, however, whether producers of other primary products can form cartels as the OPEC nations have done to obtain fairer and more stable prices for their exports.

The United Nations Conference on Trade and Development (UNCTAD), under pressure from Third World nations, has formulated a number of proposals for attaining a more equitable distribution of the world's wealth which rely largely on the generosity and enlightened self-interest of the developed nations. At two meetings in 1964 and 1968, UNCTAD proposed not only guaranteed prices for primary products exported by the Third World but a voluntary tax on the rich nations of the globe and the granting of preferences to goods produced in the Third World. Sympathy for the developmental needs of the Third World has been expressed by the major Western trading nations and Japan at meetings since the late 1950's, but few concrete proposals have emerged; the rise of protectionist sentiment in the West in the 1970's has put the attainment of these goals even further in doubt.

An issue that has focused much of the world's attention on the problem of inequality in the years since World War II is that of apartheid in South Africa. Though ostensibly a domestic issue, the fight to bring this system to an end is viewed by many Third World leaders as a microcosm of the broader struggle for political, social, and economic equality in the world. It is seen, particularly by other African nations, as a test case of the West's willingness to make sacrifices to help a Third World people attain equality in their own country. Despite a 1962 United Nations General Assembly vote calling on all member states to cut off relations with South Africa, the United States, Great Britain, and other developed nations have increased their trade and investment in South Africa, fundamental facts which reaffirm to Third World leaders that their nations still have far to go in their struggle for equality.

Pertinent Literature

Bairoch, Paul. *The Economic Development of the Third World Since 1900.* Translated by Lady Cynthia Postan. Berkeley: University of California Press, 1975.

This survey of the Third World's attempt to attain economic equality with the West by the Belgian economist Paul Bairoch is one of the best available. It surpasses other such studies both in its chronological breadth and in the large number of cases it considers. One of Bairoch's major contributions is to differentiate among the countries constituting the underdeveloped world according to the specific problems they face; implicitly he questions the very notion of a Third World with monolithic characteristics.

Bairoch defines economic development as increasing per capita income. He argues that to achieve this goal the nations of the Third World must follow essentially the same sequence as was followed by the nations of the industrialized West. The key to the West's economic "take-off" lies in the growth of per capita output in the agricultural sector during the eighteenth and nineteenth centuries, which was a consequence of both the enclosure movement and improved farming techniques. This expanded production fostered the growth of

England's internal market, which in turn encouraged the growth of light industries to provide for the needs of this market. Comparing the West's historical experience with the situation of the underdeveloped world today, Bairoch finds that per capita agriculture production in the latter is fully fifty percent lower than that of Europe at a comparable stage of the Industrial Revolution. Moreover, the increases in productivity that have occurred have been wiped out as a result of the tremendous growth of population in the Third World, a growth far more rapid than that experienced by Europe during the initial stages of industrialization.

Most underdeveloped nations have not attempted to follow the route taken by the West, however, but have chosen instead to emphasize the development of extractive industries (oil, minerals, and so on) and heavy industry. The author points out the numerous pitfalls of the former, such as the fact that, since most extractive industries are foreign-owned, few of the profits benefit the inhabitants of the exporting country. Furthermore, the reorientation of lines of communication toward export points discourages the development of the internal markets that are necessary if these countries are to develop. Finally, Bairoch cautions that underdeveloped countries that rely heavily on extractive industries are in essence mortgaging their own futures, for, by the time these nations have developed industries that can use them, only the most inaccessible resources will remain, necessitating a massive investment in advanced technology to remove what is left.

The dramatic growth of manufacturing industry in the Third World has been largely the result of the expansion of heavy industry, which has been emphasized in part because of the prestige associated with this sector of the economy. But even this growth is somewhat deceptive, since the almost complete absence of these industries until recent decades has made even a slight growth seem substantial. The effects of this industrialization, Bairoch notes, are not as widely distributed as was the case during the West's industrialization because of the smaller labor force required to run and maintain modern machinery. The restricted effect of this industrialization is reinforced by the fact that more than ninety percent of the capital equipment used in the underdeveloped world is imported, while in the West this machinery was almost all of local origin. This statistic is particularly alarming when one considers the important part played by the manufacture of capital equipment in the economic "take-off" of the West. Finally, it seems that a limit has nearly been reached in the growth of light industry in the Third World, since growth up to now has been dependent upon the process of "import substitution," the replacement of goods formerly imported from the West by domestically produced goods, a process that is nearly completed unless some way of expanding the internal market is found.

Bairoch is not content merely to describe the Third World's struggle for economic equality since 1900: he also prescribes what he believes are the best means of achieving this goal. To attain the key goal of expanding per capita agricultural output, he favors the redistribution of agriculture land, especially in Latin America; the expanded use of advanced technology and fertilizers; and the growth of the area under cultivation where possible. For any of these devices to be successful a strict birth control policy must be instituted to prevent gains in productivity from being wiped out. Second, these nations must create industrial enterprises that favor general economic development, rather than creating very modern industries with very limited effects on the economy at large. To achieve the level of economic development desired by these nations while avoiding the undesirable consequences of growth as experienced by the West, Bairoch believes that it is necessary for the state to play a much larger role in planning than it did at a comparable stage of the West's development. He concedes, however, that few of the present governments of the Third World have the desire or the ability to institute the necessary programs.

Gurley, John G. *China's Economy and the Maoist Strategy*. New York: Monthly Review Press, 1976.

The People's Republic of China has occupied a somewhat ambiguous position in many discussions of the Third World. Because of its close relationship with the Soviet Union before their break in 1960 it was often excluded from such discussions, just as was Latin America because of its close relationship with the United States. But in terms of the level of economic development of China after the conclusion of the revolution in 1949 and the problems of illiteracy, disease, and poverty its people shared with those of Africa and the rest of Asia, it too, along with Latin America, must be considered part of the Third World. Increasingly, since the end of the cultural revolution and the beginning of its diplomatic thrust outward, it has become both a model and a threat to other underdeveloped nations. Gurley tries to explain the nature of China's success, analyzing the Maoist strategy of development on its own terms and suggesting to what extent aspects of this model might be applied to other nations.

Gurley begins by contrasting the capitalist approach to development to the Marxist-Leninist alternative worked out in China during the last three decades. The former method, followed in variously modified forms throughout most of the Third World, fundamentally relies on individual initiative, the profit motive, and determination of what is to be produced by market forces. National output is the standard by which economic development can best be measured, according to this outlook.

Maoists disagree with both the means and ends associated with the capitalist position. They criticize the results of capitalist development in the Third World, even where it has been most successful. For instance, it has led to the creation of ultra-modern cities immersed in backward agricultural regions and has sharpened the contrasts between wealth and poverty found in these countries. Communist China, on the other hand, has since its break with the Soviet Union emphasized a more balanced approach to development. It has encouraged the growth of agriculture as much as industry, light industry as much as heavy industry. It has sought to eliminate the stark contrasts between cities and agricultural regions, rich and poor, that characterize many Third World countries. Even the very aim of development is dramatically different for the Chinese: while they agree with other nations that it is important to raise the standard of living of their people, China's leaders believe that the best way to do this is to provide their people with the means to realize their full human potential; no one should be left behind in the process of development. They particularly oppose the idea that development is best encouraged by increasing specialization and division of labor: all must become as familiar as possible with the entire production process and will, thereby, become better able to perform each individual task. The profit motive on which the capitalist system depends for much of its drive is discouraged as much as possible and more socially oriented virtues are cultivated in its place.

Whatever the attitude in the West toward the Maoist approach to development, the "basic overriding economic fact about China," as Gurley notes, "is that for twenty years it has fed, clothed, and housed everyone, has kept them healthy, and has educated most." This fact alone makes the Maoist approach worthy of attention, but China's ability to find employment for the vast majority of her people, the relative absence of inflationary pressures, the success of her family-planning program, and the steady increases in output in recent years have all enhanced the prestige of the Chinese system. Consequently China can begin to make her weight felt in the international arena to an extent rare among Third World countries.

Gurley concludes his study by asking if any of the elements of this Chinese model might be used by other nations which are struggling to attain economic and political equality with the developed world. He points out, first of all, that there are powerful forces in the Third World which have opposed, and are likely to continue to do so, any thoroughgoing plans for economic development, since economic development disturbs a society's equilibrium and creates new classes of people who compete with the old order. Thus, despite much discussion of development by leaders of the Third World, there is quite often no serious intention behind it. A second problem is that individual elements taken from the Chinese model as a whole might prove ineffectual in an alien environment. The rural industrialization program successfully carried out in China, for example, would not be likely to succeed in other societies governed by different values where it would conflict with the urban-industrial sector's need for cheap rural labor. Consequently, Gurley believes that the Chinese model can only be transferred successfully to countries that already have a socialist mode of production. China is more likely to be a model of revolutionary strategy and tactics in these countries before it becomes a model for economic development.

It is for this reason that China represents both a model and a threat to present-day leaders of the Third World. — *R.E.*

Additional Recommended Reading

Albertini, Rudolf von. *Decolonization*. Garden City, N.Y.: Doubleday & Company, 1971. A comparison of the nationalist movements in British and French colonies and European responses to them.

Dumont, René and B. Rosier. *The Hungry Future*. New York: Frederick A. Praeger, 1969. A warning of imminent danger of famine in the underdeveloped world if effective action is not taken at once.

Myrdal, Gunnar. *The Asian Drama*. New York: Pantheon Books, 1968. Advocates comprehensive state planning of all facets of life as the most rapid solution of the problem of poverty in Asia.

Nkrumah, Kwame. *Neo-colonialism*. New York: International Publishers, 1965. A call by an African leader for African nations to work together to obtain better treatment from the more developed world.

Rhodes, Robert I., ed. *Imperialism and Underdevelopment: A Reader*. New York: Monthly Review Press, 1970. A radical critique of Western policies toward Third World nations, who are blamed for their continuing problems.

Sachs, Ignacy. *The Discovery of the Third World*. Cambridge, Mass.: MIT Press, 1976. Examines the growing awareness in the West of what is now called the Third World and analyzes present-day Western stereotypes of the area.

WORLDWIDE ATTEMPTS AT NUCLEAR DISARMAMENT AND NONPROLIFERATION

Type of event: Diplomatic: international peace efforts
Time: 1945 to the present
Locale: The United Nations and the world

Principal personages:
DEAN GOODERHAM ACHESON (1893-1971), Under-Secretary of State of the United States
DAVID ELI LILIENTHAL (1899-   ), Chairman of the Tennessee Valley Authority
BERNARD MANNES BARUCH (1870-1965), United States Representative to the United Nations Atomic Energy Commission
DWIGHT DAVID EISENHOWER (1890-1969), thirty-fourth President of the United States, 1953-1961
ANDREI A. GROMYKO (1909-   ), Soviet Union's Representative to the United Nations

Summary of Event

Toward the end of World War II, the United States contemplated the future of atomic energy in the world, having been responsible for the first detonation of an atomic device at Alamogordo, New Mexico on July 16, 1945, and the dropping of two atomic bombs on Japan in August, 1945. Realizing the potential of the bomb's vast destructive capabilities and realizing also that the present technological monopoly would not last, the government began devising a system for the international control of atomic weapons. The American plan was based upon a tripartite declaration enunciated on November 15, 1945, by England, Canada, and the United States which described the atomic bomb as a "means of destruction hitherto unknown, against which there can be no adequate defense. . . ." The declaration held that only the "prevention of war" offered genuine protection to civilization. It recommended the immediate establishment of a United Nations Commission to prepare agreements aimed at utilizing atomic energy solely for peaceful purposes.

Dean Acheson, then Under-Secretary of State, and David Lilienthal, chairman of the Tennessee Valley Authority, were assigned the task of carrying out the provisions of the Declaration. They prepared a proposal which was presented to the newly formed United Nations Atomic Energy Commission on June 14, 1946, by the U.S. representative to that body, Bernard Baruch, elder statesman and adviser to President Harry Truman. The proposal which is now known as the "Baruch Plan" provided for the creation of an international authority to control the use of atomic energy for peaceful purposes. The plan also provided for the eventual elimination of all atomic weapons. It also specified that the Security Council of the United Nations have no veto of the Authority's findings and operations. On June 19, 1946, Andrei Gromyko, the Russian representative to the United Nations, effectively decimated the American plan by offering a counterproposal which would prohibit the use, stockpiling, and manufacture of atomic weapons. It was his position that nuclear disarmament should take precedence over control (at the time the United States had an atomic monopoly). Moreover, he insisted that the Security Council's veto be retained. The debate that followed crystalized the issues, which were not resolved in subsequent disarmament negotiations in the United Nations.

With the rejection of the Baruch proposal by the Soviet Union, the United States sought temporarily to protect its monopoly by severely restricting the export of any nuclear technology. However, this did not prevent Great Britain from exploding its first atomic bomb in October, 1952, and Russia its first hydrogen bomb in August, 1953. Russia had previously detonated an atomic bomb in 1949. The United States had also detonated a hydrogen bomb in 1952. The nuclear arms race was seriously under way.

Recognizing that any chance for the development of civilian nuclear power under pervasive international control was lost in the stalemated disarmament discussions in the United Nations, and believing that failure to share nuclear technology would likely accelerate nuclear development on a nationalistic basis and thereby en-

hance the risk of nuclear proliferation, President Dwight D. Eisenhower felt compelled to take some action. In an address delivered before the United Nations on December 8, 1953, he outlined his "Atoms for Peace" proposal. It was his idea to extend the benefits of nuclear technology to all countries in return for their guarantees that such assistance would be used for peaceful purposes only.

Unfortunately, in nuclear technology there is no difference between a peaceful atom and a military atom; it was understood, therefore, that some safeguards were required. Consequently, the International Atomic Energy Agency (IAEA) with headquarters in Vienna was created in 1957 to monitor civilian activities. Under this safeguard system, regular detailed reports are given by each member nation of its civilian nuclear activities. To verify these reports international inspectors are granted access to all nuclear facilities to assure that there is no diversion of materials from civilian to military use. The agency's inspection-control system is not ironclad, however, in that current international rules permit a country to possess nuclear explosive material without violating IAEA standards.

On March 25, 1957, the European Common Market countries—France, West Germany, Italy, the Netherlands, Belgium, and Luxembourg—created the European Atomic Energy Community (ERATOM), whose main purpose is to facilitate for its members the development and integration of nuclear industries for peaceful purposes. These countries, although signatories of the IAEA, retain regulatory administrative powers over their own fissionable materials and are not restricted by IAEA safeguards. The United States supported ERATOM as a regional cooperative enterprise, hoping that a supranational organization of this kind would help prevent the proliferation of nuclear weapons. France, however, in February, 1960, became the fourth nation to detonate a bomb. Technically, the International Atomic Energy Agency and the European Atomic Energy Community were not instituted to prevent nuclear weapons proliferation but were formed instead to promote cooperation in the peaceful uses of atomic energy. Nonetheless, they are regarded as a part of the nonproliferation system because of the safeguards they provide to prevent the diversion of fissionable materials from peaceful civilian use to the manufacture of weapons. Similarly, the bilateral Strategic Arms Limitations Talks between the Soviet Union and the United States, referred to as SALT I (1969-1972) and SALT II (1974-1979) are attempts to implement provisions of the Nuclear Nonproliferation Treaty (NPT). They tend also to stabilize a state of deterrence between the two superpowers.

The Nuclear Nonproliferation Treaty was approved by the U.N. General Assembly on June 4, 1968; the treaty entered into force in 1970 and now has ninety-nine members who agree to accept IAEA safeguards on all of their peaceful nuclear facilities. While the treaty does not impose this duty on nuclear-weapon countries, the United States has voluntarily offered to enter into such an arrangement and thereby has been instrumental in inducing other nations to adhere to the agreement. This offer by the United States to bring its nuclear facilities, not having direct national security significance, under international safeguards was first made on December 2, 1967, by President Lyndon Johnson and has been endorsed by all succeeding administrations.

One of the difficulties of the Nuclear Nonproliferation Treaty is that it has not prevented nonsignatory states, namely, Brazil, Spain, and India, from obtaining nuclear material and technology. On May 18, 1974, India set off a "peaceful" nuclear device and became the world's sixth nuclear power. China had exploded a bomb in 1964 and France a hydrogen bomb in 1968. Other nations are reported to have technological capabilities and materials to defuse nuclear weaponry. These developments took place despite the many international efforts to control proliferation, efforts which resulted in a number of bilateral and multilateral arrangements.

In addition to the 1968 Nuclear Nonproliferation Treaty, the treaties of note are: The Antarctic Treaty (1959), which committed the United States, the Soviet Union, and sixteen other states to a ban on the stationing of nuclear weapons in Antartica; the "Hot Line" Agreement (1963) between the Soviet Union and the United States to reduce the possibilities of a miscalculated nuclear attack; the Limited Test Ban Treaty (1963) between the United States, the Soviet Union, and the United Kingdom, prohibiting nuclear tests in outer space, above ground and under water, approved by an overwhelming majority of the members of the United Nations; the Outer Space Treaty (1967) banning emplacement of nuclear weapons in outer space or on other celestial bodies; the Treaty of Tlatelolco (1968) banning emplacement of nuclear weapons in Latin America; the Seabed Arms Control Treaty (1971) prohibiting nuclear weapons in the sea depth; the Convention on Biological Weapons (1972) prohibiting the development, production, and stockpiling of bacteriological or toxin weapons; and the Threshold Test Ban Treaty (1974) limiting underground nuclear weapons tests to a yield of 150 kilotons with no limitations on underground nuclear tests for peaceful purposes.

There have been many attempts to reduce international tension by limiting and reducing armaments. Even though progress has been slow, each effort can be viewed as an expression to strengthen the presumption against proliferation and world annihilation. The consensus is that these efforts must continue if humankind is to survive its own destructive capabilities.

Pertinent Literature

Epstein, William. *The Last Chance: Nuclear Proliferation and Arms Control.* New York: The Free Press, 1976.

William Epstein, a Canadian, has been officially associated with the United Nations' efforts in arms control and disarmament for a period of more than twenty-five years. In this volume he presents readable, useful, and comprehensive information and analysis of the various aspects and ramifications of the nuclear proliferation issue. He regards the nuclear arms race as the most important problem facing the world and admits that the problem is enormously difficult of solution. He emphasizes that if the international system which was erected to prevent the proliferation of nuclear weapons fails, human survival is in doubt.

Epstein traces initial world disarmament efforts from 1945, when the United States detonated the first atomic bomb, to the year 1963, when the Treaty Banning Nuclear Tests in the Atmosphere, in Outer Space and Under Water was concluded. He points out that in the following decade, and in fairly rapid succession, there were more than a dozen important multilateral or bilateral agreements for arms and limitation control. He claims that in this brief time span sanity prevailed among nations. Important international accords were entered into, such as the 1968 Treaty on the Limitation of Anti-Ballistic Missile Systems. However, in 1974, when India exploded what it claimed was a "peaceful" nuclear device, there was a resumption of nuclear testing by various nuclear powers followed by abortive attempts to halt either the quantitative or qualitative strategic nuclear arms race. The international realization was that a major change had taken place. India's bomb had been put together with material taken from a civilian research reactor. This meant that many countries, including those that were unstable, could now readily procure nuclear bombs.

That same year also marked the advent of an energy crisis and a quadrupling of oil prices which created interest around the world in buying and building nuclear power reactors. This activity, coupled with the desire of nuclear supplier countries to sell nuclear materials, equipment, technology, and reactors for both exchange and profit, increases the possibility, according to Epstein, of world annihilation. He explains that power reactors are a source of plutonium, which is useful in the manufacture of bombs. Since plutonium can be easily separated from used reactor fuel, there is nothing to prevent any state, organization, criminal, or terrorist group from acquiring plutonium stockpiles and producing bombs. His fear is that easy access could result in an unintended nuclear war ignited by accident, miscalculation, nervous impulse, or unauthorized behavior. He suggests a safeguard that would require supplier nations to demand that all spent fuel be returned to the supplier state for reprocessing or for storing or be sent to some internationally operated and safeguarded plant. He feels that if reprocessing were done at cost or without charge this would induce countries not to acquire or use their own reprocessing systems. Furthermore, he would require nuclear suppliers to refrain from exporting nuclear material, equipment, or technology to any nonnuclear country that has or that acquires any reprocessing plant under national control. He would also encourage supplier countries to adopt a national and international security system which would prevent the theft of nuclear explosive materials. In addition, he would impose sanctions against those nations who violated the rules of the Nonproliferation Treaty.

The Nonproliferation Treaty, Epstein believes, is in need of tighter controls. In an article-by-article analysis of each of the treaty's provisions, he offers some thought-provoking recommendations to cure what he perceives to be the document's defects. Among other things, he would provide security assurances to nonnuclear states that have no nuclear weapons. He would ban all underground nuclear weapons tests. Peaceful nuclear explosions, however, could be carried out only when authorized under a special international regime. He would also have the superpowers begin immediate negotiations to reduce their long-range bombers with a view to their elimination, and he would insist that superpowers unilaterally pull back and reduce tactical nuclear weapons in Central Europe. He would further recommend that the NATO and Warsaw Pact powers begin immediate negotiations to limit their weapons deployment.

The possibility of imminent nuclear disaster outlined in Epstein's well-written book convinces readers to contemplate seriously their "last chance" prospects. Appended to "The Last Chance" text is a Chronology of the Development of Nuclear Weapons and of Arms Control Measures. Appended also are copies of three treaties: The Treaty Banning Nuclear Weapon Tests in the Atmosphere, in Outer Space and Under Water; the

Treaty for the Prohibition of Nuclear Weapons in Latin America; and the Treaty on the Nonproliferation of Nuclear Weapons.

Myrdal, Alva. *The Game of Disarmament: How the United States and Russia Run the Arms Race.* New York: Pantheon Books, 1977.

This is an excellent book that describes in detail and with ample documentation the plight of the nonaligned nations and their futile attempts within the United Nations Committee system to effect disarmament agreements.

Myrdal is Swedish and has had a brilliant diplomatic career covering a twenty-five-year period. During twelve of those years, she served as Sweden's Minister of Disarmament to the United Nations and participated in multilateral disarmament negotiations. She speaks, therefore, with authority, crucial concern, and personal involvement. Her motivation for writing is to present the view of the majority of mankind whose position, she believes, has not been adequately heard. Reasoning about armaments and disarmament, she contends, has become encapsulated in a bipolar model involving only the United States and the Soviet Union. Although the United Nations provides the platform from which all nations may speak out against the threat of superpower hegemony, the collective voice of all has been overruled by both of the superpowers, whose "game play" is to thwart all serious disarmament efforts and whose motive is to increase their own military stature at the expense of everyone's safety.

Myrdal contends that there has always been a "secret and undeclared collusion between the superpowers in spite of their outwardly often fierce disagreements." Neither wishes to be restrained by effective disarmament measures. She points to the many lost opportunities for disarmament in the postwar period and holds the superpowers primarily responsible. Both sides, she alleges, have presented from time to time grandiose schemes for disarmament, but have carefully built into each new arrangement certain conditions which each knew the opposite party either could not or would not accept. Those conditions that were acceptable were the ones that would not appreciably alter their plans of action.

Nonaligned countries, Myrdal discloses, have long been dissatisfied with the lack of practical results of disarmament discussions in the United Nations and have repeatedly called for a world disarmament conference to dramatize the urgency of the issue. It is Myrdal's belief that such a conference should be initiated and called immediately. (A special session of the United Nations General Assembly was held May 23-June 28, 1978, devoted to disarmament.) The author recommends, however, that certain substantive conditions be imposed on the superpowers and cleared in advance of the conference to avoid failure.

The first condition would be a "no first use" oath or one that would have the superpowers pledge not to commence any act of nuclear warfare; the second would be their commitment not to attack any nuclear-weapons-free country with nuclear weapons. For the conference Myrdal suggests an agenda based on the various proposals of merit made in the course of previous negotiations in the Geneva Disarmament Committee and the General Assembly of the United Nations. These include a deescalating of nuclear weapons toward minimum deterrents; a comprehensive test ban including total cessation of further development of weapons, strategic and tactical; a prohibition of production of cruel antipersonnel weapons, characterized as causing "unnecessary suffering"; demilitarization of oceans; and the elimination of foreign bases with withdrawal of tactical nuclear weapons from foreign territories and prohibition of passage through foreign territorial seas. It is Myrdal's belief that cutting off not only the quantitative but the qualitative continuation of all arms races would not only establish a reign of security in the world but would also divert innovative capacities from military to peaceful purposes.

The Game of Disarmament is designed as an appeal to morality and rationality. The message it contains is convincingly stated and easily comprehended. The message is that we must disarm to survive. — *A.O.B.*

Additional Recommended Reading

Barnaby, Frank and Ronald Huiske. *Arms Uncontrolled*. Cambridge, Mass.: Harvard University Press, 1975. Contains statistical data on world armament levels.

Burns, Richard Dean. *A Bibliography*. Santa Barbara, Calif.: American Bibliographical Center/Clio Press, 1978. Considered to be the most comprehensive bibliography on arms control and disarmament available.

Cox, Arthur Macy. *The Dynamics of Détente: How to End the Arms Race*. New York: W. W. Norton and Company, 1976. *Détente* is considered in depth and is recommended as a worthwhile activity to help eliminate the possibilities of war.

Gompert, David C., Michael Mandelbaum, Richard L. Garwin and John H. Barton. *Nuclear Weapons and World Politics: Alternatives for the Future*. New York: McGraw-Hill Book Company, 1977. Each of the four authors outlines a nuclear alternative and examines the values, goals, premises, and implications of the regime.

Jensen, Lloyd. *Return from the Nuclear Brink*. Lexington, Mass.: Lexington Books, 1974. Provides a concise and readable account of the Nuclear Nonproliferation Treaty; makes the point that NPT provisions are distinctly favorable to established nuclear powers and suggests that "threshold" nations are the category crucial to the immediate future of the treaty.

Nash, Henry T. *Nuclear Weapons and International Behavior*. Amsterdam: A. W. Sikthoff International Publishing Company, 1975. Shows how the balance of power, alliance, and warfare all have been changed by nuclear weaponry and contends that the behavioral changes can prove to be beneficial for mankind by bringing about a more stable environment.

Quester, George H. *Offense and Defense in the International System*. New York: John Wiley and Sons, 1977. The relationship between offense and defense as a question of military strategy is provided, based on the premise that peace is more likely when defenses are the most formidable.

INFLATION AND LABOR UNREST

Type of event: Economic: strike wave by organized labor to raise wages
Time: 1945-1948
Locale: The United States

Principal personages:

JOHN LLEWELLYN LEWIS (1880-1969), President of the United Mine Workers during the post-World War II period

HARRY S TRUMAN (1884-1972), thirty-third President of the United States, 1945-1953

WALTER PHILIP REUTHER (1907-1970), emerging national leader of the United Auto Workers following World War II

PHILIP MURRAY (1886-1952), second President of the Congress of Industrial Organizations (CIO), 1940-1952

HENRY AGARD WALLACE (1888-1965), Progressive Party presidential candidate in the 1948 election

Summary of Event

In examining the crisis in labor relations following World War II, the historian is confronted not by a single dramatic event but by a long chain of interrelated developments. Clearly, the origins or causes of postwar labor conflict are traceable to the war years themselves. Government intervention during the war forestalled many of the aims of the emerging labor movement. With the end of various government controls over industrial relations in 1945, labor was intent on catching up in areas delayed by the war, especially in the wage field. As a result, a truly massive strike wave shook the country following war's end. The key industrial sectors of the economy felt strike activity. The strikes occurred against the backdrop of reconversion—shifting from war-oriented to peacetime industrial production. In addition, the labor movement was still far from united in the immediate postwar period. The

strikes and labor's internal dissension provided enemies of the labor movement with enough evidence to restrict labor severely through amendment of the federal labor legislation inherited from the 1930's.

Government intervention in industrial relations during the war had been clearly necessary to ensure uninterrupted production of war matériel. Regulation of the labor movement fell to the War Labor Board. The Board helped several unions of the Congress of Industrial Organizations (CIO), most notably the United Steel Workers and the United Auto Workers, to achieve employer recognition. Yet, the Board set a relatively severe restriction on wage increases in its "Little Steel" wage award in 1942. The pattern set in that decision involved tens of thousands of steel workers employed by Bethlehem, Inland, Republic, and Youngstown. It regulated wages in such a way as to prevent the wartime abundance of overtime work from raising actual levels of take-home pay in basic industries. Still, despite the efforts of the Office of Price Administration (OPA), prices rose thirty-three percent during the war; inflation was severe enough to provoke highly controversial strikes *during* the war, in spite of the "no-strike" pledges of most wartime union leaders. John L. Lewis, President of the United Mine Workers, led his key mineworkers out on strike in 1943 despite recrimination from government and fellow unionists. If even an occasional major walkout could take place during the war, what might be in store for the country following the lifting of wartime restrictions? Workers felt the inflation throughout the war, and, following the war, labor was poised for strike action on economic issues. The end of government price and wage controls following victory over Japan in August, 1945, brought on the massive strike wave.

In 1945 and 1946, the United Steel Workers struck United States Steel, Lewis' Mine Workers struck the coal industry, the United Auto Workers, led by Walter P. Reuther, struck General Motors and Ford, and the United Electrical Workers struck General Electric. The overwhelming issue was wages. With the end of price controls, the inflationary spiral set in the war years soared to unprecedented heights. The unions were determined to help their members keep up with prices by negotiating wage increases. The strikes were marked in some cases with picketline violence reminiscent of the tumultuous 1930's.

The unions won hardfought settlements, but the price of battle was heavy indeed. John L. Lewis and his union were heavily fined for defying back-to-work injunctions. In fact, a bill authorizing *peacetime* seizures of coal mines by the government passed easily during the strike crisis.

Ironically, as the unions effectively flexed their political and economic strength, several forces were already hard at work to diminish labor's power. Union organizational drives met increased opposition, not only from employers, but now also from the public. This was particularly true with the ill-fated "Southern Drive" launched by the CIO in 1947, an abortive attempt to organize industries in the traditionally antiunion South.

Not only organizational drives met the chilling effect of postwar conservatism. The Cold War with the Soviet Union complicated already existing divisions within the labor movement. Since the CIO's formation in the 1930's, industrial unions had waged an often bitter competitive struggle against the craft unions of the American Federation of Labor (AFL). The breach between the rival federations was still wide in the period 1945-1948, and, within the CIO itself, factional differences between non-Communist and pro-Communist organizations led to further weakness. The CIO Communists, despite their often aggressive approach to union activity, retained their devotion to Soviet aims following the war, and, for a brief time, they successfully attained CIO affiliation with the Soviet-backed World Federation of Trade Unions. However, the rapid development of the Cold War isolated the

Communist unionists from their fellow workers and from American public opinion as a whole. The Communists opposed the Marshall Plan to aid in the reconstruction of devastated Western Europe, while most CIO affiliates backed the proposal. The 1948 presidential election found the Communist-leaning CIO unions backing the independent left-liberal Progressive candidate, Henry Wallace. Philip Murray, CIO President, and the wide majority of CIO affiliates and members stood behind Harry S Truman's candidacy. By 1948, the CIO began the process of expelling many of the Communist-led unions, creating intraorganizational conflicts and bitterness.

The strike wave, coupled with labor's internal divisions, led to disaster for the union, given the country's postwar swing toward conservatism. Intense business lobbying by organizations such as the National Association of Manufacturers began to achieve results favorable to employers. In 1947, the Taft-Hartley Act was passed over President Truman's veto. Consisting of a series of severe limitations on union activity, the Taft-Hartley Act also included strict anti-Communist oaths for union officers. With the passage of Taft-Hartley, a distinct period of labor history came to a close. Organizational gains had been checked and membership began to level off or decline. Unions were subject to a variety of charges accusing them of unfair labor practices. During 1948, government intervention was employed to halt strikes in the coal, railway, and steel industries. The militant activism of 1945 and 1946 met the conservative reaction of 1947-1948, and as a result the peaks in labor unrest began to level off.

Pertinent Literature

Seidman, Joel. *American Labor from Defense to Reconversion*. Chicago: University of Chicago Press, 1953.

Joel Seidman has been one of the keenest of academicians in recent decades to study American trade unionism. Long active on the industrial relations faculty of the University of Chicago, Seidman wrote this book while a young instructor at Chicago. The author admits at the onset to a viewpoint that is sympathetic to democratic trade unionism, a sympathy that in no way damages the excellent balance in his narrative. He is true to the historian's craft, basing his account on solid primary sources. Most importantly, Seidman has chosen a topic which has been given very little scholarly attention. His book stands out as the single most influential account of labor in the 1940's.

Seidman begins his account with a chapter describing the labor movement as it emerged from the 1930's. He next traces major events during the prewar defense buildup; discussions of the war years and the postwar turmoil comprise most of the volume.

Seidman's book captures a sense of historical continuity essential to understanding labor's postwar turmoil. The author presents a detailed assessment of government wartime intervention in labor relations, with particular care to present the effects of government wage policy on earnings during the war and on aspirations for postwar wage increases. He describes the reactions of labor groups to wartime restrictions, and the participation of labor leaders such as Sidney Hillman of the Clothing Workers in government agencies during the war. For Seidman, the roots of postwar disorders lay in the war years, especially in the rise of wartime inflation.

Seidman gives a fine narrative account of the postwar strike wave. All of the color and controversy of strike leaders such as John L. Lewis and Walter Reuther are present. In addition, Seidman unravels the complex attempts of government and the courts to stay the labor disorder and relates the culmination of these attempts with the passage of the Taft-Hartley Act.

Seidman writes here of a crucial period in the history of American labor. Much of the current "stagnation" of organized labor as a social force dates from the late 1940's, and the impact of measures such as Taft-Hartley is very much in evidence today. Any student of labor history and current industrial relations should give this volume his attention.

Millis, Harry A. and Emily Clark Brown. *From the Wagner Act to Taft-Hartley: A Study of National Labor Policy and Labor Relations*. Chicago: University of Chicago Press, 1950.

The authors of this ponderous volume possess excellent academic and practical credentials. The late Dr. Harry A. Millis served as a arbitrator of labor disputes during the 1930's. Trained as an economist, Millis served as Chairman of the National Labor Relations Board (NLRB) between 1940 and 1945. Established by the National Labor Relations Act of 1935, the Board heard cases involving union organization campaigns through the tremendous upsurge of union growth during the 1930's and 1940's. Emily Clark Brown served as an operating analyst for the NLRB between 1942 and 1944, and was a member of the Vassar faculty when she completed the volume.

For readers interested in post-World War II labor unrest, the coauthors present a definitive study of government reaction as reflected in the NLRB and the move toward adoption of Taft-Hartley. Millis and Brown offer an account that is simply exhaustive. The detailed narrative description of NLRB decisions proves invaluable for nonattorneys interested in the operation of government labor policy in the crucial years between 1935 and 1948. In effect, the book is totally based on primary legal sources. Millis and Brown, despite their active participation on the NLRB staff, are objective in discussing the Board's first years of operation. They give more than adequate coverage of conservative criticisms of the Board—criticisms that led to Taft-Hartley.

In sum, the volume provides an important reference for studying the singularly important role of government in postwar labor matters. Much of the turmoil and issues of postwar labor are reflected through the cases handled by the NLRB and so ably described by Millis and Brown in their work. — *E.A.Z.*

Additional Recommended Reading

DeCaux, Len. *Labor Radical: From the Wobblies to CIO, a Personal History.* Boston: Beacon Press, 1970. An account by a one-time editor of the *CIO News* of postwar labor from a leftist participant-observer standpoint.

Dubofsky, Melvyn and Warren Van Tine. *John L. Lewis.* New York: Quadrangle Books, 1977. Authors Dubofsky and Van Tine present a masterful, comprehensive biography of by far the most tumultuous leader of labor following World War II.

Boyer, Richard and Herbert Morais. *Labor's Untold Story.* New York: Banner Press, 1970. Boyer and Morais present exciting narrative accounts of the postwar strikes, but interpret the strikes from a Communist-oriented viewpoint.

Lens, Sidney. *The Crisis of American Labor.* New York: A. S. Barnes, 1961. A detailed description of post-World War II labor unrest spiced by the author's independent leftist critique of postwar labor leaders.

Paradis, Adrian A. *Labor in Action: The Story of the American Labor Movement.* New York: Julian Messner, 1975. Paradis gives his readers a straightforward, factual, and compact account of labor unrest following World War II.

THE BATTLE OF GERMANY

Type of event: Military: concluding battle in the European theater of World War II
Time: January-May, 1945
Locale: Nazi Germany

Principal personages:

ADOLF HITLER (1889-1945), Chancellor and Führer of Germany, 1933-1945

FIELD MARSHAL KARL RUDOLF GERD VON RUNDSTEDT (1875-1953), German Commander in Chief on the Western Front to March 10, 1945

FIELD MARSHAL ALBERT KESSELRING (1887-1960), German Commander in Chief on the Western Front, appointed to succeed Rundstedt on March 10, 1945

SIR WINSTON LEONARD SPENCER CHURCHILL (1874-1965), Prime Minister of Great Britain, 1940-1945

GENERAL DWIGHT DAVID EISENHOWER (1890-1969), Supreme Commander of the Allied Expeditionary Force

FIELD MARSHAL BERNARD LAW MONTGOMERY (FIRST VISCOUNT MONTGOMERY OF ALAMEIN) (1887-1976), Commander of the Allied Twenty-first Army Group

GENERAL OMAR NELSON BRADLEY (1893-1979), Commander of the Allied Twelfth Army Group

JOSEPH STALIN (IOSIF VISSARIONOVICH DZHUGASHVILI) (1879-1953), Dictator of the Soviet Union, 1924-1953

MARSHAL GEORGI KONSTANTINOVICH ZHUKOV (1895-1974), Commander of the First White Russian Front

MARSHAL KONSTANTIN K. ROKOSSOVSKI (1896-1968), Commander of the Second White Russian Front

MARSHAL IVAN STEPANOVICH KONEV (1897-1973), Commander of the First Ukrainian Front

Summary of Event

The beginning of 1945 saw Adolf Hitler's Third Reich on the verge of total defeat. Hitherto distant battlefronts in Normandy and Russia had now converged on the borders of the German homeland. In the West, British, American, and Canadian forces, under the supreme command of General Dwight David Eisenhower, were slowly pushing the Germans back from the bulge which they had created in the front in mid-December, 1944, when they launched their surprise offensive in the Ardennes region of Belgium and Luxembourg. His troops and armor seriously mauled, Hitler, on January 8, reluctantly authorized Field Marshal Karl von Rundstedt, Commander in Chief in the West, to withdraw toward the West Wall (Siegfried Line), the extensive fortifications which the Germans had constructed along their western frontier before the war. On the following day, Hitler received from his intelligence officers yet another in a series of ominous reports about the grave threat to his eastern flank; namely, the heavy build-up of Soviet forces on the Vistula river. The Russians, according to the reports, would soon launch a massive offensive against the Reich from their positions on the Vistula which they had held since August, 1944. The Führer, however, refused to take these warnings seriously, despite the loss of most of the Balkans during the fall of 1944 to rapidly moving Soviet armies which now stood only 120 miles from Vienna.

On January 12, just three days after Hitler received the latest warning about the Soviet build-up, ten Russian armies, organized into "fronts" (Soviet army groups), surged across the Vistula, quickly overrunning the weakly held German line of defense. Spearheaded by the forces of Marshal Georgi Zhukov, Commander of the First White Russian Front, and Marshal Ivan Konev, Commander of the First Ukrainian Front, the Russian drive made spectacular gains all along the section of front stretching from East Prussia to the Carpathian Mountains. Zhukov's forces took Warsaw on January 17, while those of Konev penetrated the German frontier in Silesia just three days later. To the north, the Second White Russian Front under the command of Marshal Konstantin Rokossovski swept to the Gulf of Danzig, and by January 26 had isolated all German forces in East Prussia. Zhukov, meanwhile, crossed the Reich frontier into Pomerania and Brandenburg, and on January 31 his advance units reached the Oder river—just forty miles from Berlin. Early in February, Konev overran most of Silesia in a successful effort to bring his forces up even with those of Zhukov. By the end of that month, the Russian drive had lost its momentum, thus giving the Germans time to bring up reinforcements with which to stabilize the Eastern Front along the Oder and Neisse rivers. Many of these reinforcements, however, were drawn from German units holding the Western Front, where the Battle of the Rhineland had already begun.

Eisenhower had decided to clear the entire left bank of the Rhine before attempting to cross that last great barrier to the German heartland. This decision was consistent with his "broad front" strategy, which contrasted sharply with the views of Field Marshal Bernard Law Montgomery, the British Commander of the Allied Twenty-first Army Group. Montgomery wanted to launch a single powerful striking force across the Rhine, past the Ruhr Valley industrial complex, and on to Berlin. Eisenhower's views prevailed, and the Battle of the Rhineland began on February 8. The major obstacle to the Allied advance was the heavily fortified West Wall, which guarded the major approaches to the Rhine along most of its length. Throughout February and March the Allied forces, composed of three army groups, pressed steadily forward. Montgomery's Twenty-first Army Group and General Omar Bradley's Twelfth Army Group cleared the lower and middle Rhineland respectively by mid-March. On March 7, an American unit fighting under Bradley's command became the first Allied combat force to cross the Rhine when it seized a bridge at Remagen which the Germans had failed to destroy. Exploiting this spectacular success, the Americans promptly established a bridgehead on the east bank. Three days later, Hitler replaced Rundstedt with Field Marshal Albert Kesselring as Commander in Chief in the West. In the south, meanwhile, where German resistance was much heavier, part of Bradley's forces joined with the Sixth Army Group to wipe out German opposition in the Saar Basin. Hence, by March 25, all organized German resistance west of the Rhine had ended.

Already the Allies had begun to cross the Rhine in force to deliver the final blow to Hitler's tottering Reich. Montgomery's forces surged across the lower Rhine on March 23-24, while other crossings took place at several points farther south. On March 26, American units broke out of the Remagen bridgehead and the great dash of Allied armies into the German heartland was under way. Eisenhower's plan called for Montgomery's forces on the north and those of Bradley on the south to encircle the Ruhr Valley in a giant pincer movement. The two forces met east of the Ruhr on April 1, thus sealing off the area from the rest of the Reich and tearing a two hundred-mile breach in Germany's disintegrating Western Front, which Kesselring could not close. Some 325,000 German troops were taken prisoner on April 18, when the Ruhr pocket finally collapsed.

The collapse of Germany as a whole was now at hand. American forces reached the Elbe river on April 11, where Eisenhower ordered them to halt. In late March, British Prime Minister Winston Churchill had urged Eisenhower to take Berlin so as to deny this prize to Joseph Stalin, whose forces were preparing to launch a final drive on the Reich capital from their positions on the Oder-Neisse front. Eisenhower rejected Churchill's plea, citing the heavy casualties it would cost to seize Berlin, half of which in any event was to be turned over to Russia under the Allied agreements on the postwar division of Germany. Instead, in keeping with his "broad front" military strategy, Eisenhower decided to concentrate on the destruction of German military forces in the north and south of the Reich. In the south, rumor had it that the Nazis were going to fortify a "National Redoubt" in the Bavarian and Austrian Alps from which they would make a last bitter stand. Consequently, Eisenhower, solely on the basis of military considerations, left Berlin to the Soviets, who, on April 16, launched their planned offensive against the capital. By April 25, the day that advance American and Soviet units met on the Elbe, Berlin was surrounded. Hitler committed suicide in the ruins of the Reich Chancellery in Berlin on April 30, just two days before the city fell to the Russians. The Western Allies, in the meantime, had pushed into northern Germany to seal off Denmark in order to prevent German forces from withdrawing into that country for a last-ditch stand. In the south, where the "National Redoubt" proved to be a myth, American forces overran Bavaria and even pushed into western Czechoslovakia. On May 7, representatives of the German High Command signed the instruments of surrender. World War II in Europe had come to an end.

Pertinent Literature

Toland, John. *The Last 100 Days*. New York: Random House, 1966.

John Toland has written several books on World War II, including *Battle: The Story of the Bulge*; *Adolf Hitler*; and the Pulitzer Prize-winning *The Rising Sun: The Decline and Fall of the Japanese Empire*. *The Last Hundred Days*, like the author's other books, is based on numerous interviews with eyewitnesses to or participants in the events the author describes. For this book, Toland also consulted more than two hundred manuscripts prepared by German officers for the United States Department of the Army. Toland writes in an easy, narrative style, and makes considerable though judicious use of historical flashbacks and anecdotal material. He further enlivens his book with colorful descriptions of the Allied and Axis leaders whose decisions during the last days of the war helped to shape the character of the postwar period that followed.

Toland builds his story around the four major developments that ultimately brought World War II in Europe to a close. These include the great Red Army offensive launched in January, 1945; the drive of the Western Allies across the Rhine and into the German heartland and the controversy surrounding the decision of General Eisenhower not to take Berlin; the historic meeting on the Elbe river of American and Red Army units that cut Nazi Germany in two; and, finally, the Nazi surrender. Three wartime leaders, as Toland observes, did not live to see the end of the conflict. President Franklin D. Roosevelt died on April 12; before the end of that month Adolf Hitler committed suicide; and Benito Mussolini, the Italian Dictator, was summarily shot by partisans.

Toland begins his book with a vivid description of what he calls "the greatest offensive in military history," one that dwarfed even the number of men involved in the D-Day landing in Normandy in June, 1944. On January 12, 1945, some three million Soviet troops, organized into four "fronts," launched an offensive against 750,000 poorly equipped Germans along a four hundred-mile front running through the center of Poland from the Baltic Sea to the Carpathian Mountains. German resistance crumbled all along the front as the Soviet tide surged forward. By the end of January, units of the Red Army had crossed the prewar German frontier, pushing deeply into East Prussia, Brandenburg, and Silesia. The difficulties faced by the German army in trying to hold some kind of defensible front were made more acute by the waves of German civilians who fled westward to escape the looting, murder, and raping of an avenging Red Army. Toland describes the frantic and unsuccessful efforts of SS personnel to destroy all the evidence, at the notorious Auschwitz concentration camp, of the Nazi mass extermination of Jews that was carried out there during the war. When Soviet troops finally liberated this huge complex at the end of January, only 5,000 prisoners were left, the healthier ones having been sent to other camps in the West to prevent their liberation. The Soviet forces continued their advance unchecked until mid-February, when their overstretched supply lines and a stiffening German defense forced them to halt their drive on the Oder river about forty miles from Berlin. Propaganda Minister Paul Joseph Goebbels did his best to strengthen German resolve by publicizing the decisions reached by Great Britain, the United States, and the Soviet Union at the recently concluded Yalta Conference to dismember Germany and to force her to pay heavy reparations.

While the Yalta Conference was taking place early in February, the British, American, and Canadian forces launched the offensive that would clear the left bank of the Rhine and enable them to cross the river at numerous points by the end of March. Toland, in describing the progress of this offensive, devotes considerable attention to the controversy that arose between Prime Minister Churchill and General Eisenhower over the latter's decision at the end of March to leave the capture of Berlin to the Russians. Eisenhower reasoned that because his own forces, which had just crossed the Rhine, were still almost three hundred miles from Berlin, the Red Army would undoubtedly get there first. He would,

therefore, use his strength to surround the Ruhr area and then launch attacks designed to secure his northern flank at Lübeck and his southern flank in Bavaria and Austria to wipe out the supposed National Redoubt. The attacks on the southern flank, Toland feels, may also have been motivated by his desire to transfer the initiative to American generals— among them Omar Bradley and George S. Patton—who felt that their talents had not been fully utilized since the Battle of the Bulge. Eisenhower, then, by the close of March, no longer considered Berlin an important objective, either militarily or politically.

Churchill vehemently disagreed with Eisenhower on both counts. Militarily, the fall of Berlin would, in his estimation, seriously weaken the German will to resist in other parts of the Reich. Politically, he felt that to leave Berlin to the Russians would only serve, in his words, to "strengthen their conviction, already apparent, that they have done everything" of significance to win the war. Toland, concurring with Churchill's views, states that by mid-April there was nothing standing between the American forces on the Elbe and the city of Berlin except a few isolated German units and General Eisenhower.

Elsewhere in the book, Toland describes in detail the historic link-up on the Elbe between American and Russian units on April 25. Contrary to popular belief, the meeting of American and Russian troops at Torgau was not the first of that day. Several hours earlier an American patrol had made contact with a contingent of Russian soldiers near the village of Strehla, some twenty miles up-stream from Torgau. A week after the Americans and Russians met on the Elbe, German troops began to surrender in large numbers. In the course of examining the protracted nature of the German surrender during the first week of May, 1945, Toland provides some lively portraits of the soldiers of all the armies and their reaction to the cessation of hostilities.

Pogue, Forrest C. "The Decision to Halt at the Elbe," in *Command Decisions*. Edited by Kent Roberts Greenfield. Washington, D.C.: U.S. Government Printing Office, 1960.

Forrest C. Pogue, combat historian with the First United States Army during World War II, offers a view on General Eisenhower's attitude toward the capture of Berlin which differs sharply from that expressed by John Toland in *The Last Hundred Days*. Pogue strongly defends Eisenhower's decision to halt his forces at the Elbe rather than to push on to Berlin and Prague. That decision, Pogue states, was made solely for military reasons and not out of political considerations, as some observers have suggested.

General Eisenhower, according to the author, was schooled in a military tradition which held that commanders should concentrate on gaining military victory and leave political decisions to their civil superiors. From the time he was appointed to lead the invasion of Normandy, Eisenhower was operating under a directive which called only for military action against Germany. Consequently, Eisenhower did not allow the political decision reached by Great Britain, the United States, and the Soviet Union on the postwar division of Germany into zones of occupation to influence his military plans for the final conquest of the country.

Eisenhower, to be sure, did concur with Omar Bradley's assessment at the time that it would be sheer folly for the Western Allies to pay the price of the 100,000 casualties it would cost to take the Berlin area when in any case it would have to be turned over the the Russians as part of their previously designated zone of occupation. This view, however, did not contradict Eisenhower's basic position of keeping military planning separate from the Big Three's decision to divide Germany, because by March 28, 1945, Berlin, in his judgment, had ceased to be a major military objective. Pogue defends Eisenhower's judgment on Berlin by pointing out that he genuinely believed (as did many others) that the Nazis were going to fortify the National Redoubt and that consequently he should conserve his forces for a quick drive into that area. Furthermore, Eisenhower wanted to avoid as many casualties as possible in order to facilitate the redeployment of the maximum number of troops to the Pacific theater of the conflict. — *E.P.K.*

Additional Recommended Reading

Eisenhower, Dwight D. *Crusade in Europe*. Garden City, N.Y.: Doubleday & Company, 1948.

Montgomery of Alamein, Field Marshal. *Memoirs*. Cleveland, Oh.: World Publishing Company, 1958.

Churchill, Winston S. *The Second World War*. Vol. VI: *Triumph and Tragedy*. Boston: Houghton Mifflin Company, 1953.

Bradley, General Omar N. *A Soldier's Story*. New York: Holt, Rinehart and Winston, 1951. Four memoirs of the leading participants in the Battle of Germany which provide good descriptions of the bitter fighting on the Western Front during 1945.

Ryan, Cornelius. *The Last Battle*. New York: Simon and Schuster, 1966. An engrossing narrative account of the Soviet assault on Berlin in the spring of 1945.

Wilmot, Chester. *The Struggle for Europe*. New York: Harper & Row Publishers, 1952. One of the best histories of World War II, in which the author provides three informative chapters on the Battle of Germany.

GENERAL MacARTHUR ADMINISTERS THE RECONSTRUCTION OF JAPAN

Type of event: Military: occupation of a defeated country
Time: September 2, 1945-April 28, 1952
Locale: Japan

Principal personages:
GENERAL DOUGLAS A. MACARTHUR (1880-1964), Supreme Commander for the Allied Powers
SHIGERU YOSHIDA (1878-1967), Prime Minister of Japan, 1946-1947 and 1948-1954
JOSEPH DODGE, leader of the Dodge Mission
GENERAL MATTHEW BUNKER RIDGWAY (1895-   ), Supreme Commander for the Allied Powers
HARRY S TRUMAN (1884-1972), thirty-third President of the United States, 1945-1953

Summary of Event

War in the Pacific officially ended on September 2, 1945. The seven-year military occupation which followed was the first time in history Japan was invaded. The revolutionary reforms of the Occupation had a great impact on subsequent Japanese history. There were some failures and misunderstandings, but America's role in reshaping Japanese society was unique. Expecting a harsh military rule, the Japanese encountered a constructive Occupation; anticipating treachery and hatred, Americans found openness and cooperation.

Japanese militarism led to disaster. Over two million servicemen had been killed or wounded since 1937, cities were reduced to rubble, factories were heavily damaged and lacked raw materials, and transportation was disrupted. The population was underfed, disillusioned, and apprehensive. The Potsdam Declaration of July 26, 1945, required unconditional surrender. In the words of the Emperor's broadcast on August 15, Japan had to "bear the unbearable." Failing in war, the Japanese people were open to change and receptive to new leadership.

That leadership was provided by General Douglas MacArthur, Supreme Commander for the Allied Powers (SCAP). MacArthur was the ideal man to head the Occupation. He had a strong sense of history, a dramatic public image, and supreme confidence that Americans could create a democratic Japan. There is disagreement over what role MacArthur had in specific reforms, but little doubt that he dominated and set the tone for the entire Occupation. The SCAP acronym soon came to mean the Occupation in general. MacArthur's power was near absolute. Directives from the thirteen-nation Far Eastern Commission in Washington were broad, and the Allied Coun-

584

cil in Tokyo, consisting of an American, Commonwealth, Chinese, and Soviet representative, had little influence. A staunch Republican favorite in a Democratic administration, MacArthur could order revolutionary change without being labeled a radical.

MacArthur did not allow Soviet policy to interfere as in Germany. In Germany, military government ruled, but in Japan SCAP worked through a reconstructed Japanese government. Military teams in the prefectures were assigned to see that reforms were carried out.

Policies reflected the American view that political, economic, and social reforms were essential to create a peaceful and democratic Japan. Traditionally, in Japan it was believed that the military allied with *zaibatsu* (economic conglomerates) manipulated the hierarchical social system centering on the Emperor and the state Shintō religion. Reforms were designed to destroy this "feudal" system and its values. The goal was a total restructuring of society.

SCAP policy had indigenous support. Politicians, intellectuals, and the moderate left were glad to see a reaffirmation of the liberal trends of the 1920's. Retention of most reforms was due to this substantial popular support.

MacArthur demanded constitutional change, but the draft presented to SCAP in February, 1946, was judged a modest revision of the 1889 Meiji Constitution. The Government section of SCAP under the command of General Courtney Whitney quickly produced a draft which was presented to the Japanese on February 19. It

was ultimately approved with minor revisions by the Diet in November, 1946.

The new constitution, which went into effect May 3, 1947, was clearly an American document, despite its claim to represent "the freely expressed will of the Japanese people." The Emperor became a "symbol of the state" with ceremonial duties, as he had denied all claims to divinity on January 1, 1946. The right to maintain military forces and resort to war was denied. Prewar nonparliamentary organs of state such as the Privy Council, the military services, and advisers to the Emperor were abolished. Human rights were guaranteed. A British-style Cabinet chosen by the majority party or coalition in the Diet became the new focus of political power. Diet members were to be chosen by an electorate expanded to include all over twenty years of age, including, for the first time, women. Increased powers of taxation, police, and schools were delegated to local government. "The result," writes Japan specialist Peter Duus, "was a curious hybrid between British style parliamentarianism and American federalism." Other measures were taken to destroy militarism. The empire was liquidated and 6.5 million overseas Japanese were repatriated. In addition to the dismantling of the military services, paramilitary and ultranationalist organizations were disbanded and Shintō disestablished. Political prisoners were released and the repressive Home Ministry abolished. Education was liberalized and nationalism expunged from textbooks. War crime trials were held, and seven, including Hideki

Tojo, were executed in December, 1948. About 200,000 former military officers, high officials, and business leaders were purged from public life.

SCAP felt that economic and social changes were essential. Both industry and agriculture were targets for reform aimed at redistribution of wealth on a more equitable basis. *Zaibatsu* holding companies were banned and the fortunes of *zaibatsu* families seized. Conglomerates were separated into their component industries and banks, and antimonopoly laws were passed. In agriculture, the forty-six percent tenancy rate reinforced poverty, hierarchy, and authority in the villages. Under strong SCAP pressure, a revolutionary land reform was passed in October, 1946. The government purchased all land held by absentee landlords and all other landlord holdings above a certain size, selling it to farmer tenants on easy terms. Because of inflation, former owners received virtually nothing. Land reform amounted to confiscation and tenancy dropped to ten percent.

Despite his Republicanism, MacArthur ordered creation of a strong union movement, seeing it as essential for democracy. The prewar union movement revived with vigor, with 6.5 million members by 1949. However, SCAP policy towards unions shifted in 1947, when MacArthur forbade a threatened general strike by government railway employees on February 1.

In 1947, SCAP turned from reform to reconstruction as the Japanese government under Shigeru Yoshida was given ever-increasing power. Plans for further industrial deconcentration where shelved. In 1949, the Dodge Mission was sent to Japan to study requirements for complete economic recovery. Joseph Dodge, a conservative Detroit banker, forced a drastic deflationary policy which caused mass unemployment. Political protest followed and SCAP carried out a second purge, this time of "reds." A police force was organized in 1950. It became the National Self-Defence Force, in contradiction to Article Nine of the Constitution which forbade a reconstructed military. When the Korean War broke out in June, 1950, United States spending helped stimulate Japan's first postwar economic boom and provided Japan with one more object lesson. In April, 1951, MacArthur was dismissed by Truman because of disagreement over war policy, thus reasserting civilian power over the military. General Matthew Ridgway directed the final year of Occupation. A peace treaty was signed in San Francisco on September 8, 1951, ending the Occupation on April 28, 1952.

MacArthur's direction of the Occupation was remarkably successful given the bitterness of war and the disparities of American and Japanese culture. Despite some reverses since 1952, the constitution and many other reforms have had a lasting and radical impact.

Pertinent Literature

Kawai, Kazuo. *Japan's American Interlude*. Chicago: University of Chicago Press, 1960.

This well-written interpretive study is not a detailed history of the Occupation, but rather an attempt to weigh the impact of selected reforms on postwar Japan. It is still the best volume on the period. Kawai shows how reforms that built upon indigenous trends made the greatest impact. Programs which took no account of Japanese history and society were resented and rejected after 1952. On the whole, Kawai argues, the Occupation was surprisingly successful.

In Chapter One, Kawai explains why the Japanese were so cooperative with their recent enemies and receptive to change. The thoroughness of defeat and their unpreparedness for it left them disillusioned with the goals of militarism. Some argue that "situational ethics" left no rules for defeat. In addition, Japan had experienced a hundred years of Western influence, and individuals harbored few personal animosities toward Americans. Japan saw international relations as a hierarchy and accepted an inferior position. Liberal trends of the 1920's, thwarted by militarism, quickly reemerged. Finally, there was no realistic course other than cooperation.

MacArthur, by his calm landing at Atsugi before Japanese troops were disarmed, showed both personal courage and trust, traits to which the Japanese warmly responded. They came to see the Occupation primarily as MacArthur, secondarily as American, and only remotely as an Allied operation. Occupation policies were usually sound and benevolent, administered in the early years with a missionary zeal from MacArthur on down.

Kawai sees reforms as falling into two categories, negative and positive. He quickly covers the former, which focused on demilitarization, and analyzes in detail positive reforms which aimed at rebuilding a new Japan. Change would certainly have followed defeat in war, but the "induced revolution" allowed MacArthur to shape the direction of that change.

Chapter Four deals with the 1947 constitution. Kawai argues that SCAP went too far in imposing a solution which was obviously an American and not a Japanese creation, leaving it open to future attacks as an alien document. Popular sovereignty, appealing as it is, had no roots in the popular consciousness nor in Japanese constitutional theory. The author agrees, with most scholarship, that retaining the Emperor as a national symbol was wise, drawing a useful analogy to the American flag. He notes that rights of assembly, a free press, liberty, and pursuit of happiness found in the American Bill of Rights were supplemented by protection of academic freedom and collective bargaining.

Much of the book deals with political power and its transformation by the Occupation. Political decentralization, following American federalism, had neither roots nor logic in a country of Japan's size and homogeneous nature. Programs decentralizing police and strengthening local government had little lasting impact. The most important political change, according to Kawai, was clearly placing power in the Diet. Cabinet leadership now prevails, the Cabinet acting as an "executive committee of the

Diet." There was an irony in that SCAP imposed democracy from above. Of all the prewar power groups, the bureaucracy was least changed by Occupation reforms, but postwar bureaucrats had to form alliances with the political parties, tempering their power.

Although Americans believed "you cannot teach democracy to a hungry people," economic recovery was delayed until 1949, partly because no early plans had been made to rebuild Japan. The initially ambitious deconcentration plans came under attack by Washington and the American business community, perhaps remembering the New Deal trust-busting zeal of the 1930's. The number of *zaibatsu* firms to be dissolved fell from 1,200 to 325, then to thirty and nineteen. In the end, only nine corporations were disbanded by the Occupation as the Cold War shifted policy. Japan was seen as the "workshop of Asia" after China fell into the Communist camp in 1949.

Kawai contends that SCAP failed most in reforming education through ignorance of Japanese conditions, and by focusing on administrative and structural changes, neglecting the content and spirit of postwar education. Elementary texts were revised, but university standards were debased in a misdirected attempt to install American-style mass higher education. Although an attempt was made to revise the curriculum to allow independent thought and to create values supportive of democracy and personal rights, Kawai feels that this was only partly successful.

Japanese journalism, despite Occupation censorship, eventually emerged as a strong influence for democracy and a watchdog against renewed authoritarianism. Kawai finishes by noting the substantial social changes in postwar Japan. The democratic trends he cites have continued since the publication of his book. Concluding, he claims "the Occupation for all its shortcomings must be judged on balance as a magnificent success."

Yoshida, Shigeru. *The Yoshida Memoirs: The Story of Japan in Crisis.* Translated by Kenichi Yoshida. Boston: Houghton Mifflin Company, 1962.

If MacArthur embodied American idealism, Shigeru Yoshida, Prime Minister of Japan, 1946-1947 and 1948-1954, represented Japanese pragmatism. Yoshida had been a pro-Western career diplomat before the war. He saw no alternative but to cooperate with SCAP, although he thought that many political and civil reforms were excessive. A political autocrat, Yoshida favored business and distrusted labor. His main goal was independence and economic reform, not social and political change. Because he was the Prime Minister for most of the Occupation, his personality dominated Japanese postwar politics just as MacArthur dominated SCAP. His personal account of those critical years is clearly biased, but it reveals many interesting insights from the Japanese point of view.

Yoshida was particularly suited to leadership during the Occupation. His long prewar diplomatic experience in dealing with foreigners was invaluable, and he was known to favor British and American ties. In April, 1945, he had been arrested by military police for planning peace negotiations. Because of this and his earlier pro-Western attitude, Yoshida was acceptable to SCAP. He escaped the purges to enter politics and lead the Liberal Party. His political reign from 1946 to 1954, broken only by a brief and unsuccessful Socialist Party government led by Katayama Tetsu, was so powerful that he was called "one-man" Yoshida.

His memoirs make it clear that Yoshida, like many prewar liberals, was a conservative in the new postwar political climate. He thought Mac-Arthur had "a genuine understanding of the country," but worried about policies advocated by young "New Dealers" whom he felt were using Japan as a testing ground for radical reform. Although he knew overt resistance was impossible, Yoshida used bureaucratic rivalries within SCAP to cast doubt on reforms judged too far-reaching. The fact that the Occupation lasted only six years and eight months was due to the generally cooperative front the Japanese presented: "My policy . . . was to say whatever I felt needed saying, and to accept what transpired."

As a career bureaucrat and an agent of Japanese business interests, Yoshida was particularly disturbed by the 1945-1947 policy of encouraging unionism and toleration of Communism, his *bête noire*. Although he criticized the blanket purge of those associated with militarism as ". . . arbitrary standards based upon a misreading of history," he was only too glad to use the "reverse course"

after 1947 to justify suppression of the Communists in 1950 to purge leftists from the press, industry, and government. His government was also able to dismiss 260,000 unruly employees of the government-run railways by citing the Dodge Plan for fiscal reform and a balanced budget.

Yoshida also makes clear Japanese misgivings over the 1947 Constitution, a topic he covers in considerable detail. Although MacArthur wisely realized the importance of retaining the Emperor, much of the Constitution was "revolutionary" to Yoshida. The great haste with which it was drafted and presented to the Japanese was due to "impulsiveness common to military people of all countries." Nevertheless, Yoshida argues that the Constitution was not entirely a *diktat* since minor revisions were made by the Japanese government.

Japanese concerns over the new education and police systems are also discussed. As with other reforms, the reservations and bargaining of Japanese officials make clear the external impetus of reform. Following the independence achieved in 1952, Yoshida and other conservatives worked to undo reforms they considered too radical: police were again centralized, some control of educational curriculum maintained, and disruptive leftist activity curtailed. It is significant, however, that these all caused considerable opposition in the Diet as well as popular protest.

Yoshida reveals how receptive conservative forces were to the so-called "reverse course." It began, in his view, with a speech made by Secretary of the Army Kenneth C. Royall in January, 1948, pointing out the need to rebuild Japan. Japanese officials were able to use the Cold War conflict to ease the burdens of defeat and ameliorate many of the "idealistic" features of the first two years of the Occupation. A final Yoshida victory was the American refusal to write SCAP reforms into the 1951 Peace Treaty, thus avoiding making them permanent.

Taking a strong anti-Communist line was more than a mere artifice for Yoshida. His memoirs reveal a deep and long-abiding distrust of the left. Although this book needs to be balanced with others, it provides important information concerning the most important events of the time, and reveals clearly the outlook of the leading Japanese political figure. — *R.R.*

Additional Recommended Reading

Dore, Ronald P. *Land Reform in Japan*. London: Oxford University Press, 1959. A detailed analysis of the history and impact of one of the most important Occupation reforms, written in a lucid style and supported by ample statistics.

Martin, Edwin M. *The Allied Occupation of Japan*. Stanford, Calif.: Stanford University Press, 1948. A brief quasiofficial account of the early Occupation, rather idealistic in tone.

Fearey, Robert A. *The Occupation of Japan, Second Phase: 1948-1950*. New York: The Macmillan Company, 1950. The sequel to the study cited above, written by a career diplomat with extensive firsthand knowledge of Japan.

The MacArthur Memorial. *The Occupation of Japan: Proceedings*. Norfolk, Va.: The MacArthur Memorial, 1975-1978. A valuable series based on annual scholarly seminars on various aspects of the Occupation, including both research papers and commentary by many participants in the Occupation.

Minear, Richard H. *Victors' Justice: The Tokyo War Crimes Trial*. Princeton, N.J.: Princeton University Press, 1971. A critical study of the Tokyo War Crime Trials and their context in international law.

Sheldon, Walt. *The Honorable Conquerors: The Occupation of Japan, 1945-1952*. New York: The Macmillan Company, 1965. The story of the Occupation told from numerous human-interest accounts and anecdotes.

Tsurumi, Kazuko. *Social Change and the Individual: Japan Before and After Defeat in World War II*. Princeton, N.J.: Princeton University Press, 1970. A pioneering sociological study of the social changes caused by the defeat of Japan and the Occupation.

Wildes, Harry Emerson. *Typhoon in Tokyo: The Occupation and Its Aftermath*. New York: The Macmillan Company, 1954. An interesting and detailed account partly based on the author's experiences, giving an authentic flavor to the period.

THE PARIS PEACE CONFERENCE

Type of event: Diplomatic: peace conference to settle terms of treaties with Axis powers
Time: July 29, 1946-February 10, 1947
Locale: Paris

Principal personages:
JAMES FRANCIS BYRNES (1879-1972), United States Secretary of State, 1945-1947
GEORGES BIDAULT (1899-   ), Foreign Minister of France, 1944-1951
ERNEST BEVIN (1884-1951), Foreign Secretary of Great Britain, 1945-1951
VYACHESLAV MIKHAILOVICH MOLOTOV (SKRYABIN) (1890-   ), Soviet Commissar for Foreign Affairs

Summary of Event

During the summer of 1945, shortly after the defeat of Nazi Germany, the Big Three wartime allies—the United States, the Soviet Union, and Great Britain—met in the Potsdam Conference to consider the many problems arising from the outcome of the war. It was agreed at Potsdam to establish a Council of Foreign Ministers whose task would be the drafting of the peace treaties, first with Italy, Rumania, Bulgaria, Hungary, and Finland, and eventually with Germany. No draft treaty, however, was ever prepared for Germany because of the sharp differences between the Western Powers and the Soviet Union over the future of that country.

Between December, 1945, and July, 1946, the Council of Ministers negotiated the terms of the treaties to be presented to the peace conference. The Council of Ministers included James F. Byrnes, the United States Secretary of State, and foreign ministers Vyacheslav M. Molotov of the Soviet Union, Ernest Bevin of Great

Britain, and Georges Bidault of France. Bidault played a relatively minor role in the proceedings. The deliberations of the foreign ministers were marked by a growing enmity between the Western Powers and the Soviet Union as both sides feared the other was seeking to gain undue advantage. Finally, by midsummer, after many disagreements, the Council of Ministers had drawn up virtually complete drafts of the peace treaties for each of the five minor Axis Powers. The task of the peace conference was to be that of accepting, rejecting, or amending articles within the draft treaties. Thus, as in the First Paris Peace Conference in 1919 after World War I, the peacemaking in 1946 was also dominated by a "Big Four."

The second Paris Peace Conference formally opened on July 29, 1946. Twenty-one allied nations, including the Big Four, were represented at Paris. In addition, representatives of the five enemy states were invited to present their views to

591

plenary sessions of the conference. Most of the work of the peace conference, which consisted of reviewing the draft treaties, was handled by various commissions. By October 7, the commissions had their completed reports ready to submit to the plenary conference. In the week that followed, the five treaties were approved, and on October 14, the conference adjourned. The Big Four, however, had decided in advance that the Council of Ministers must agree after the peace conference upon the final terms of the treaties as accepted by the conference as a whole. This accomplished, the five treaties were signed in Paris on February 10, 1947, by representatives of the Axis states and representatives of all the Allied states which had participated in the peace conference, with the exception of the United States. Secretary Byrnes signed for the United States in Washington, D.C., on January 20, the day before he left office.

Of the five separate peace treaties concluded with each of the ex-belligerent nations, the most extensive, and perhaps the most important, was with Italy. Italy was forced to pay $100,000,000 in reparations to the Soviet Union and $260,000,000 to be divided between Greece, Yugoslavia, Albania, and Ethiopia. Her armed forces were ordered limited, and she was stripped of her African empire, including Libya, Ethiopia, Eritrea, and Italian Somaliland. The independence of Albania was also guaranteed by the treaty. For the time being, however, the matter of Trieste and the surrounding area, long contested by Yugoslavia and Italy, was not resolved; a compromise solution was

found only in 1954.

The Italian Treaty provided a model for the peace treaties concluded with Finland, Hungary, Rumania, and Bulgaria. All four states were obliged to limit strictly their armed forces and to make reparations payments to various of their neighbors, including the Soviet Union and other Eastern European countries. Territorially, Finland lost several areas to the Soviet Union, notably the Petsamo district with its valuable mineral deposits and its outlet to the Arctic Sea. Hungary returned to its borders of January, 1938, with the exception of a small area ceded to Czechoslovakia. Rumania accepted the loss of Bessarabia and northern Bukovina to the Soviet Union, which that power had seized in June, 1940. In addition, Rumania was forced to recognize the loss of the southern Dobrudja to Bulgaria, which also dated from 1940.

In some ways, the Paris Peace Conference of 1946-1947 harkened back to the peace settlements after World War I. Indeed, these post-World War II treaties did reaffirm the general territorial sovereignty of the Eastern European states created after 1919. This time, however, there was not even lip-service paid to the notion of the "self-determination of peoples." Soviet influence in the area was growing apace, even as the final documents were being readied for signatures. The swift evolution of three of the states involved—Rumania, Hungary, and Bulgaria—into Soviet satellites greatly diminished those clauses implicit in the Paris Peace Treaties which were intended to avoid such actions. Within a short time, both Great Britain and the United States protested violations of the three governments against the "human rights" clauses of the Paris treaties, but their protests came to naught. More positive, of course, from the Western point of view, were the settlements with Finland and Italy. The former provided the basis for strengthening Finnish independence and national sovereignty in spite of her geographical proximity to the Soviet Union. The Italian Treaty established the basis for a generally stable, if somewhat fragile, Italy to develop a partnership with the West, and the basis for resolution of her long-standing territorial disagreements with Yugoslavia.

Unlike the settlements that followed other wars, those that came in the wake of World War II seem, to some extent, to be both piecemeal and stillborn. A peace with Japan was handled as an entirely separate matter, and peace with Germany has not yet been formally concluded, whereas a settlement with Austria emerged only in 1955 and then under surprisingly agreeable conditions. If the Paris Peace Conference harkened back to the peace conference following World War I, it also provided a kind of bridge between the initial chill in East-West relations in 1945-1946 and the emergence in earnest of a Cold War after 1948.

Pertinent Literature

Opie, Redvers, *et al. The Search for Peace Settlements.* Washington, D.C.: The Brookings Institution, 1951.

This study surveys the overall problem of the search for peace settlements after World War II. It includes chapters on the preludes to peace: the Atlantic Charter; the Dumbarton Oaks, Yalta, and Potsdam conferences; and the post-Potsdam strategies. Individual sections deal with each of the nations over which the Paris Conference deliberated: Italy, Finland, and the so-called "Satellite States." The remainder of the book is devoted to consideration of the problems of peace settlements with Austria, Germany, Japan, and Korea.

The book takes as its opening premise the notion "that the negotiations of a peace settlement by a coalition of nations is a laborious and time-consuming process." Hence, the problems of obtaining peace after World War II is put into a proper historical context. It was not merely the struggle between the two superpowers, the United States and the Soviet Union, and the emerging Cold War between the East and West that complicated matters. Peace settlements are inevitably difficult. Parallels to the earlier peace settlements after major conflicts, such as the Napoleonic Wars and World War I, are established. One of the unique complicating factors of the post-World War II treaties was the insistence on political clauses by certain negotiating parties, such as those which guaranteed the "enjoyment of human rights and of fundamental freedoms" to all persons "without distinction as to race, sex, language, or religion." The

Congress of Vienna of 1814-1815 had pursued a single-minded goal based substantially on the traditional search for "balance of power" on the Continent. After World War I, this pursuit still prevailed, and, at heart, the notion of a League of Nations was a step beyond "balance of power" toward "collective security." The authors conclude that immediately after World War II, the Allies were "relatively free from commitments" and "well-furnished with general agreements on principles." The results, however, as of the book's publication were minimal: there had been no general settlement of the problems of peace.

A chapter devoted to Soviet purposes and actions argues that the Soviet policy of cooperation with and neutrality toward Germany in 1939 undermined the U.S.S.R.'s later wartime alliance with Great Britain and the United States. Hence, when Germany invaded Russia in June, 1941, the Soviet-British cooperation which ensued was grounded in an abiding sense of mistrust and suspicion. This situation was not significantly altered with the entry of the United States into the war at the end of the year. The details of the various wartime conferences—the Atlantic Charter Meeting, the Moscow Conference, Cairo, Teheran, Dumbarton Oaks, and Potsdam—had little to do directly with the Paris Peace Conference, the authors point out.

The Italian Treaty that emerged from the Paris Conference is given the most detailed treatment. The status of Italy, having abandoned its Axis partnership, is considered, in general, with sympathy. The authors point out that Italy suffered signifi-cant losses, both in material and personnel, only after she turned against Germany and when, as a cobelligerent, she and the Allies fought their way up the peninsula. Omitted here is any reference to the Soviet position of vengefulness toward Italy at the Conference because of the role her troops had played on the German eastern front between the summer of 1941 and her unconditional surrender to Anglo-American forces in September, 1943. At the Conference itself conflict arose over descriptive terminology depicting Italy's role in the war. Her representatives objected strongly to phrases such as "war of aggression" and "her share of responsibility for the war." Italian requests to participate in settlements with Germany and Japan, against whom she had fought for a year and a half, were denied categorically.

The treaty with Italy is regarded as a "model" for the treaties concluded with the other nations (Bulgaria, Finland, Hungary, and Rumania), even though Italy's position as of 1946-1947 was different from that of the others because of her presumed position in the sphere of Western influence.

The basic territorial provisions of that settlement reestablished the Italian boundaries of January 1, 1938. Italian conquests of Ethiopia and Albania were voided; Italy lost her overseas colonies and ceded certain islands in the Mediterranean to Greece, Albania, and Yugoslavia respectively. She had to agree to certain modifications of the Franco-Italian border; these were considered to be of strategic importance for French national defense. In settling the Yugoslav-Italian border question, the free territory of Trieste was created from former Italian territory. On the issue of the Tyrol, the Council of Foreign Ministers had already agreed earlier that the area would remain under Italian sovereignty, although guarantees would have to be made regarding the "equal treatment" of Austrians living in the area. The authors find most striking in the Italian Treaty the political provisions, primarily the ones modeled on the agreement of the Foreign Ministers of the Allied nations in Moscow in 1943 relating to the guaranteeing of basic liberties such as freedom of expression, the press, religious worship, and the like.

It was in regard to the economic clauses of the Italian Treaty that the United States was most active in seeking amelioration of the terms. Soviet demands in this regard would have given the U.S.S.R. substantial control over the Italian economy for purposes of reparations payments. Eventually, agreements were reached under Western pressure for the Soviets to supply certain raw goods to Italy (on commercial terms) since those would be necessary to assure reparations deliveries. Actually, the reparations payments agreed on by the Conference were renegotiated

upwards at the Council of Foreign Ministers' meeting in New York in November, 1946. Italy's final reparations were thus extended to a sum of $360,000,000.

The position of the nation states which had been satellites of Germany (Bulgaria, Finland, Hungary, and Rumania) was substantially different from that of Italy. By 1946 all except Finland were under Soviet military occupation and their economies were likewise dominated by the Soviet Union. The treaties with all four were drawn up at the same time and were substantially similar in all regards. The United States was not a party to the Finnish Treaty, and the settlement with that nation differed from the others in omitting two clauses: one pertaining to the withdrawal of Allied forces (as Finland was not occupied) and the other to navigation rights on the Danube (which affected the other three countries, but not Finland).

In territorial settlements, Bulgaria, which since the war's end had proven most agreeable to cooperating with the Soviet Union, received the most favorable treatment. She did, however, have to give up Serbian territory to Yugoslavia and territory in Western Thrace to Greece, both parcels having been obtained by her after 1941.

Kovrig, Bennett. *The Myth of Liberation.* Baltimore, Md.: The Johns Hopkins University Press, 1973.

The literature available in English on the Paris Peace Conference of 1946-1947 is sparse. In his treatment of East-Central Europe in United States diplomacy since 1941, Bennett Kovrig places those aspects of the set-

tlement as applied to Bulgaria, Hungary, and Rumania in a broad and informative context. The effort here treats the Peace Conference as a pivotal affair in the emerging Cold War.

The United States, France, and

Great Britain, as Kovrig points out, pursued the attempt to "ameliorate political conditions in East-Central Europe" at the Conference, in spite of the fact that Soviet refusal to withdraw its armies of occupation minimized any such effort. This refusal, tied to the Soviet delay in undertaking negotiations on the German and Austrian questions, was a precipitating difficulty for the Paris Peace Conference.

The one compromise which the Western delegations extracted from the Soviets before the Conference commenced formally concerned Trieste. The Conference itself showed in its early days the division of West and East into sides of support. The United States, France, and Great Britain "championed Italy and a relatively uncontroversial Finland," while the Soviet Union adopted a position of relative support for Rumania and Bulgaria, in concert with the representatives of Poland and Czechoslovakia.

In dealing with Hungary, Bulgaria, and Rumania, the question of "restoration of, or compensation for" Allied property led to a split between the United States and Great Britain, which finally ended in compromise. Actually, the Soviet Union had sided with the United States on this matter.

The complex intertwined questions of minority peoples and territorial settlements in East-Central Europe as addressed by the Conference are considered. While the Conference approved a proposal by the United States delegation to mandate Hungarian-Czechoslovakia negotiations, Korvig concludes that the Americans basically wanted to be rid of the complex questions posed by ethnicity and territorial sovereignty in East-Central Europe. Hence, although each of the treaties signed with Germany's former allies included military and political causes, the factor of Soviet military occupation of Hungary, Rumania, and Bulgaria rendered these meaningless.

Kovrig cites claims that the entire settlement, as formally sealed on February 10, 1947, was made with "little joy" and "supreme indifference." In his treatment of the Paris Peace Conference the author points out the weaknesses of American policy, its inconsistencies and purposelessness, and consequently, Secretary of State James Byrnes's "failure."

While the "peace settlements" of the Paris Conference nominally disposed of the formal issues of what to do with Germany's defeated allies, they created the tactical basis for the Cold War. Hence, they were not only ineffective in many ways, but, in fact, widened the growing East-West split. In particular, the end of the Conference did not stabilize the political situation in Hungary, but led rather to the liquidation of a predominantly anti-Communist government there.
— *P.D.M.*

Additional Recommended Reading

Collier, David S. and Kurt Glaser, eds. *The Conditions for Peace in Europe: Problems of Détente and Security.* Washington, D.C.: Public Affairs Press, 1969. A variety of articles whose emphasis is on the situation as of the late 1960's, with numerous references to the post-World War II settlements in Europe.

Graebner, Norman A. *Cold War Diplomacy: American Foreign Policy, 1945-1960.* Princeton, N.J.: D. Van Nostrand Company, 1962. Deals extensively with the East-West split, which found one of its origins in the disagreements arising out of the Paris Peace Conference.

Hogye, Michael. *The Paris Peace Conference of 1946: Role of the Hungarian Communists and of the Soviet Union.* New York: Mid-European Studies Center, 1954. One of the best detailed studies in English treating the actual thinking behind the East bloc position at the Conference.

Lukacs, John A. *The Great Powers and Eastern Europe.* New York: American Book Company, 1953. Lukacs investigates the Eastern European question broadly, giving much insight into the Peace Conference and its background as well as its results.

Wolfers, Arnold, ed. *Changing East-West Relations and the Unity of the West.* Baltimore, Md.: The Johns Hopkins University Press, 1964. Wolfers considers the problem of Western unity into the early 1960's, with numerous references to the immediate post-World War II settlements in Europe.

DISCOVERY OF THE DEAD SEA SCROLLS

Type of event: Religious: discovery of ancient manuscripts with far-reaching historical and archaeological implications
Time: 1947-1967
Locale: Khirbet Qumran and nearby caves located in the Judean desert of Palestine/ Jordan near the western and northwestern shores of the Dead Sea

Principal personages:

MUHAMMAD ADH-DHIB, Bedouin shepherd who discovered the first cave with scrolls in 1947

ARCHBISHOP ATHANSIUS YESHUE SAMUEL, the Syrian Metropolitan of St. Mark's monastery in Jerusalem who acquired several of the Dead Sea Scrolls in 1947

E. L. SUKENIK (1889-   ), Professor of Palestinian Archaeology at the Hebrew University of Jerusalem who was the first to authenticate and date some of the Dead Sea Scrolls which he acquired in 1947

G. LANKESTER HARDING (1901-   ), Director of Antiquities of the Hashemite Kingdom of Jordan, who, between 1949 and 1956, systematically explored the area west of the Dead Sea in search of additional scrolls

ROLAND DE VAUX (1903-   ), Catholic priest and Director of the École Biblique et Archéologique de Jerusalem, who worked with G. L. Harding in exploring the area west of the Dead Sea

YIGAEL YADIN (1917-   ), son of E. L. Sukenik, professor of archaeology, and Israel's leading archaeologist who acquired the *Temple Scroll* in 1967

Summary of Event

In the spring of 1947, a young Bedouin shepherd, Muhammad adh-Dhib, discovered eleven ancient leather scrolls in a cave located in the cliffs above the northeastern corner of the Dead Sea, an area of the Judean desert which at that time was part of the Kingdom of Jordan. (Following the proclamation of the State of Israel in 1948, Jordan seized Judea during the ensuing Arab-Israeli War; Israel occupied Judea in 1967 during the Six-Day War with the Arabs.) Muhammad divided the scrolls with two other Bedouins who shared in the discovery. Together the three shepherds eventually went to the market town of Bethlehem to sell the scrolls. Two of the Bedouins went on to Jerusalem where they sold their share of the scrolls to Archbishop Yeshue Samuel, the Syrian Metropolitan of St. Mark's monastery. The third shepherd, meanwhile, sold his scrolls to a Bethlehem merchant who in turn sold them to E. L. Sukenik, Professor of Palestinian Archaeology at the Hebrew University of Jerusalem. In

1955, Archbishop Samuel sold the scrolls, which he had brought to the United States, to a representative of the Hebrew University, Yigael Yadin, the son of E. L. Sukenik and, like his father, a professor of archaeology at that institution. Yadin flew the scrolls to the Hebrew University where they were reunited with those purchased by his father eight years before.

The eleven so-called Dead Sea Scrolls embrace seven distinct manuscripts. Through the collective work, originally of Sukenik and subsequently of other authorities, the eleven scrolls have been authenticated as having been written in the period from roughly the second century B.C. to the time of the unsuccessful Jewish revolt against Rome (A.D. 66-70), when its armies occupied much of ancient Judea in force. These manuscripts, together with numerous scroll fragments discovered in other nearby caves, were written variously in Hebrew and Aramaic. They included portions of practically all of the books of the Old Testament, Apocrypha (books excluded from the Jewish and Protestant versions of the Old Testament), prayers, hymns, commentaries, and rules, the most important set of which is *The Manual of Discipline*.

Between 1949 and 1956, the systematic archaeological exploration of the area west of the Dead Sea was carried out by G. Lankester Harding, Director of Antiquities of the Hashemite Kingdom of Jordan, and Father Roland De Vaux, Director of the École Biblique et Archéologique de Jerusalem. The two men thoroughly explored the original cave and more than two hundred others, finding in many of them numerous additional fragments of scrolls, pieces of pottery, coins, and other evidence of human occupancy. Most of these caves are located in the vicinity of Khirbet (Arabic for "ruin") Qumran, itself less than a mile south of the original cave, and in the ravine of Wadi Murabbaat some ten miles farther south. The excavations at Khirbet Qumran revealed four distinct phases of occupation from the Iron Age (eighth to seventh century B.C.) to the use of the ruins by Jewish insurgents in the second revolt against Rome that was crushed in A.D. 135. Significantly, Harding and De Vaux uncovered a monastery built by a religious-monastic sect, the Community of the Covenant, which occupied Khirbet Qumran between 200 B.C. and A.D. 68. They found evidence that many of the Dead Sea Scrolls were copied by members of the sect in the monastery and, in times of danger, were hidden in the caves surrounding Khirbet Qumran. A particularly rich find of scrolls, or fragments thereof, was made in 1952, including two copper scrolls. Four years later, after considerable difficulty, the two scrolls were unrolled. They provided lists of gold and silver treasures, apparently hidden from the Romans, with directions as to where they could be found.

Major discoveries were also made in the caves at Wadi Murabbaat. The biblical manuscripts found there date from the first and second centuries A.D. These manuscripts were very important in that, unlike those at Khirbet Qumran, they indicate that the Hebrew Bible had reached its final form by about the end of the first one third of the second century A.D.

The older Khirbet Qumran biblical manuscripts revealed a scriptural text that was still evolving. Among the other documents found in the Wadi Murabbaat caves were a Hebrew papyrus of the seventh century B.C., the earliest yet known, and records from the second Jewish Revolt against Rome, A.D. 132-135. These records are highly significant as they reveal new and precise information about the revolt and its leader Bar Kokhba.

Subsequent to the Harding-De Vaux explorations of 1949-1956, additional documents were discovered. Between 1962 and 1964, papyri fragments dated 375-335 B.C. were found in a cave north of ancient Jericho where they had been left by the Samarians fleeing before the armies of Alexander the Great in 331 B.C. These fragments comprise the earliest extensive group of papyri to have been found in Palestine. In 1963-1964, valuable fragments of biblical writings were discovered in the ancient citadel of Masada where in A.D. 73 the Jewish Zealots made their last stand against the Romans. Finally, in 1967, Yigael Yadin, Israel's foremost archaeologist, revealed the existence of the *Temple Scroll* which he had been tracking down for seven years. Yadin so named the scroll because much of it contained directions for building a Temple to serve the monastic sect at Khirbet Qumran.

The discoveries of the Dead Sea Scrolls stand among the greatest finds in the history of modern archaeology. Broadly speaking, the contents of the scrolls shed much light on the religious and political life of the Jewish people in the centuries just before and after the time of Christ. In addition, the documents are of great importance for the understanding of early Christianity. The biblical scrolls antedate the earliest extant Hebrew text by about a thousand years. Fragments of the Isaiah text discovered at Wadi Murabbaat are in complete agreement with the current biblical text, thus confirming the authenticity of later Hebrew texts.

Equally important are the non-biblical manuscripts, in particular *The Manual of Discipline* and the *Temple Scroll*, since they reveal much about the lives and thought of the men who lived at Khirbet Qumran, the monastic group mentioned above which called itself the Community of the Covenant. The ideas of this group are strikingly similar to those of the Essenes who, according to ancient writers, lived on the western shore of the Dead Sea. Some authorities have gone so far as to equate the holy men in the Community of the Covenant with the Essenes and to attribute to the Essenes many of the Dead Sea Scrolls.

Still other writers are struck by the resemblance between the ideas and practices of the Essenes and the early Christians in such matters as brotherly love, the immortality of the soul, and liturgy. The view of these writers that the Essenes comprise a transitional group between Judaism and Christianity is rejected by other authorities, however. These interpreters also point out that definite proof is lacking that the Essenes occupied the Khirbet Qumran monastery. Hence, the debate on the authorship and contents of the Dead Sea Scrolls continues, and more scrolls may be discovered in the future.

Pertinent Literature

Burrows, Millar. *The Dead Sea Scrolls*. New York: The Viking Press, 1955.

Millar Burrows, a leading authority on biblical theology, has written one of the great pioneer works on the discovery of the Dead Sea Scrolls. In 1947, the year the first scrolls were found, Burrows was in Palestine conducting field trips to study the land's archaeology and historical geography. This activity was one of his duties as Director of the American School of Oriental Research in Jerusalem during that year. His field trips took him through that part of the Judean desert where many of the caves containing the ancient manuscripts were located. In fact, as he relates on the first page of his book, had he and his party only known it when they went down to the northwestern shore of the Dead Sea late in October, 1947, they could have walked to the cave where the first of the scrolls had been discovered several months before. The cave, however, would not be thoroughly explored until 1949.

In its overall scope, Burrows' study is divided into six major areas. Part One covers the initial discovery in 1947 and those made during the early 1950's. Parts Two and Three deal respectively with the ages of the manuscripts and the dates of their composition. Next, the author discusses the monastic community of Khirbet Qumran, its history, beliefs, and role in composing the Dead Sea Scrolls. Burrows concludes his study with an analysis of the importance of the Dead Sea Scrolls and a translation of selections from several of the manuscripts.

Burrows opens his study with a detailed chapter describing the discovery of the eleven major scrolls and their contents. No one will ever know for sure just how or exactly when the Bedouin shepherd, Muhammad adh-Dhib, happened to stumble upon the cave in which the scrolls were hidden; it was probably in February or March of 1947 that he found the scrolls. One account says Muhammad was searching for a lost sheep or goat when he found the cave; another story has it that he and one or two companions took refuge in the cave during a thunderstorm. In any event, Muhammad and his friends discovered the scrolls, made of leather and wrapped in linen cloth, protruding from one of several jars that they found in the cave. Apparently aware that these scrolls might be of some value, the Bedouins went to Bethlehem to sell them. Burrows describes in detail how the scrolls finally came into the hands of their new owners, Archbishop Samuel and Professor E. L. Sukenik, by the end of 1947.

According to the author, these scrolls, all of which were reunited at the Hebrew University in 1955, embrace six (some writers say seven) distinct manuscripts. The largest and oldest of the scrolls contains the complete Old Testament Book of the prophet Isaiah. When unrolled, the leather scroll, made of strips sewed end to end, is about one foot wide and twenty-four feet long. The Hebrew text of the scroll is written in the square or Aramaic alphabet. According to Burrows, the forms of the letters in the Isaiah manuscript and the other scrolls found in the cave resemble those found in Palestinian inscriptions about the first century before Christ. The text, however, is not as clearly or beautifully written as that of the scroll containing the *Commentary of Habakkuk*, which is a historical commentary of the Old Testament Book of Habakkuk.

The third and one of the most important of the six manuscripts is *The Manual of Discipline*, contained in two of the eleven scrolls. The author supplied this title himself after first reading the text in Jerusalem in March, 1948. It contains the rules and regulations by which the monastic sect living on the west shore of the Dead Sea was governed. Burrows was struck by the general similarity of these ordinances and those found in the manual of discipline of the Methodist Church; hence the title. The original title, if there was one, has been lost because the beginning of the scroll has been damaged.

The remaining three manuscripts include the *Lamech Scroll*, the *War of the Sons of Light with the Sons of Darkness*, and the *Thanksgiving Psalms* contained in four scrolls. An eleventh scroll contained an incomplete text of Isaiah, which some authorities count as a distinct manuscript, for a total by this reckoning of seven manuscripts. The *Lamech Scroll*, because of its brittle condition, was not unrolled for several years and then only after the publication of Burrows' book. Now known as the *Genesis Apocryphon*, this manuscript contains apocryphal accounts in Aramaic about some patriarchs in Genesis such as Noah and Abraham and other biblical personalities including Sarah and Lamech. The scroll of the *War of the Sons of Light with the Sons of Darkness* gives directions for the conduct of an actual or eschatological war between members of the Qumran sect and their enemies. Although Burrows accepts the view that this sect was more closely related to the Essenes than to any other known group, he stops short of asserting that the two were one and the same.

Wilson, Edmund. *The Dead Sea Scrolls, 1947-1969.* New York: Oxford University Press, 1969.

Edmund Wilson wrote more than twenty books on a wide variety of subjects, including *To the Finland Station*, *The Cold War and Income Tax*, and *The Duke of Palermo and Other Plays*. His book on the Dead Sea Scrolls consists of a reprinting of the chapters of his first account of the subject, published in 1955, and new material which relates further discoveries in the 1960's. As part of the research for both books, Wilson conducted expeditions to the area where the scrolls were found. Wilson's latest book on the subject thus provides a complete picture of scholarly activity on the Dead Sea Scrolls from the discovery of the first manuscripts in 1947 to the revelation of the *Temple Scroll* twenty years later.

In his account, Wilson subscribes to the school of thought which holds that the monastic sect at Khirbet Qumran and the Essenes were one and the same. It was this group, he believes, that was responsible for writing the scrolls which were discovered in 1947. As proof of this, Wilson cites, among other pieces of evidence, the descriptions which the ancient Jewish historian, Josephus, gives of the Essenes. Josephus' summary of the Essene rule of life tallies almost exactly with that given in the *Manual of Discipline* scrolls.

The discovery, then, of the Dead Sea Scrolls has shed much light on the Essene sect, how they lived and what they believed. The scrolls enforce what is already known about the Essenes from the writings of Josephus and other ancient authors. Living on the western shores of the Dead Sea, the Essenes comprised a monastic order of men who were governed by a strict moral code which prepared them for eternal life with God.

Wilson describes in some detail the leader of the sect, known as the Teacher of Righteousness, which may have been a general title that was given to a succession of messiahs. The teacher is also referred to in the Dead Sea Scrolls as The Elect One and The Righteous One. Wilson cites one authority, M. Dupont-Sommer, Professor of Semitic Languages and Civilization at the Sorbonne, as stating that the Teacher of Righteousness was in some respects an exact prototype of Jesus.

Indeed, Wilson points out that some authorities believe there is a direct line of continuity between the Essene sect and early Christianity. These writers are impressed by the apparent similarity between the Teacher of Righteousness and Jesus, as indicated above; the sacred meal of the Essenes and the Last Supper; and the emphasis of the Essene sect and Christianity on a strict moral life in the preparation for eternal life. Wilson concludes that the monastery of Khirbet Qumran is, perhaps more than Bethlehem or Nazareth, the cradle of Christianity.

The author also provides some interesting details on the *Temple Scroll* which Professor Yigael Yadin revealed in 1967. He had known of the existence of this scroll for several years and managed to acquire it under still secret circumstances in 1967 at the time of the Arab-Israeli Six-Day War. The scroll unrolled to four feet longer than the complete Isaiah scroll, heretofore the longest known. Written, according to Wilson, by a member of the Essene sect, the scroll is unique among Hebrew religious writings in that it purports to be a message communicated not through a prophet but directly by God himself. The text of the scroll provides, among other things, a set of rules for services in the Temple. Because almost half of the scroll is occupied with plans for building the Temple, Professor Yadin named it the *Temple Scroll*. Together with the scrolls discovered earlier, it sheds still more light on the Essene community.
— *E.P.K.*

603

Additional Recommended Reading

Wilson, Edmund. *The Scrolls from the Dead Sea*. New York: Oxford University Press, 1955. Wilson's first book on the scrolls.

Roth, Cecil. *The Dead Sea Scrolls: A New Historical Approach*. New York: W. W. Norton and Company, 1965. An examination of the historical origins and backgrounds of the Dead Sea Scrolls.

Ploeg, J. van der. *The Excavations at Qumran: A Survey of the Judean Brotherhood and Its Ideas*. London: Longmans, Green, 1958. Interesting study which accepts as highly probable the view that the sect at Khirbet Qumran and the Essenes were one and the same.

Burrows, Millar. *More Light on the Dead Sea Scrolls: New Scrolls and New Interpretations*. New York: The Viking Press, 1958. An update of Burrows' earlier study.

Mansoor, Menahem. *The Dead Sea Scrolls: A College Textbook and a Study Guide*. Grand Rapids, Mich.: Eerdmans, 1964. A very useful summary of the discovery of the Dead Sea Scrolls and other manuscript fragments through the early 1960's.

THE PARTITION OF INDIA

Type of event: Political: creation of two new nations
Time: August 15, 1947
Locale: South Asian subcontinent

Principal personages:
MOHAMMED ALI JINNAH (1876-1948), President of the All-India Muslim League, 1935-1947; and the founder of Pakistan
JAWAHARLAL NEHRU (1889-1964), leader of the Indian National Congress, the main opponent of the Muslim League
MOHANDAS KARAMCHAND GANDHI (1869-1948), leader of the Indian National Congress
LORD LINLITHGOW (VICTOR ALEXANDER JOHN HOPE) (1887-1951), Viceroy of India during crucial period, 1936-1943
SIR RICHARD STAFFORD CRIPPS (1889-1952), head of important mission to India, 1942
LORD LOUIS MOUNTBATTEN (FIRST EARL MOUNTBATTEN OF BURMA) (1900-1979), Viceroy of India at time of partition

Summary of Event

On August 15, 1947, what had been for more than one hundred years British India, the "jewel" in the imperial crown, became independent. But the British did not leave behind them the peaceful, unified India envisioned by hopeful observers as little as ten years before; instead, they departed a subcontinent wracked by communal fighting and divided between two hostile new states, a secular but predominantly Hindu India and an avowedly Muslim Pakistan. How this situation came to be is largely the story of the rise to supremacy in Muslim politics of the All-India Muslim League under the leadership of Mohammed Ali Jinnah in the years 1935 to 1947.

Jinnah had returned to India in 1935 after a five-year absence in England to prepare the ailing Muslim League for the important 1937 elections. But these elections were a disaster both for the League and for Jinnah personally, since the League failed to back up its claim to be the sole spokesman for the Muslim community. In particular, the important Muslim politicians of the two Muslim majority areas, such as Fazl al-Haq of Bengal and Sir Sikander Hayat Khan of the Punjab, rejected Jinnah's leadership and sought their fortunes in cooperation with non-Muslim parties.

Following a major grassroots reorganization, the League entered into an intensified rivalry with the Indian National Congress, centering on the latter's claim to represent all Indians in their struggle against British rule. Jinnah attempted to discredit the Congress ministries which held power in six provinces by charging them with improprieties and discrimination

605

against Muslims, thus raising Muslim fears of life in an independent India dominated by the Congress.

The outbreak of World War II and the unilateral declaration of war against Germany on India's behalf by the Viceroy, Lord Linlithgow, gave a great boost to the League's position. In the wake of this declaration, Congress ministries across the country resigned, creating a political vacuum and making the support of the League even more important to the beleaguered imperial government. Jinnah suddenly found himself on an equal footing with Jawaharlal Nehru and Mohandas Gandhi, the Congress leaders, in British counsels, which in turn raised his stature in the Muslim community.

Having obtained the bargaining power he had long sought, Jinnah set out to provide the League with a clear political goal which would attract to it the unmoved masses of the Muslim majority provinces. At the Lahore meeting of the League in early 1940 Jinnah asserted that "Mussalmans are a nation according to any definition of a nation, and they must have their homelands, their territory, and their state." The delegates at this meeting passed a resolution declaring the creation of "Pakistan" ("Land of the Pure"), an independent Muslim state, to be the final goal of the League's activities.

Neither the British nor even the Congress rejected this resolution outright, and both expressed their unwillingness to force any group to join a future Indian union which it found unacceptable. The Cripps mission of 1942 gave further encouragement to the League. Sir Richard Stafford Cripps, who headed the mission, indicated that the British would accept an independent Muslim state if solid support for this notion existed in the two Muslim majority areas.

At the end of the war the new Labour government's announcement of the first provincial elections since 1937 gave the League the opportunity to demonstrate its new-found strength at the polls. Its campaign was based wholly on the demand for Pakistan and an appeal to the religious sentiments of the Muslim masses. This strategy worked superbly, winning the League 439 of 494 seats reserved for Muslims in the provincial assemblies and all thirty Muslim seats in the Central Legislative Assembly. Most importantly, the League proved for the first time that it had mass support in both Bengal and the Northwest.

Several months later a cabinet mission headed by Lord Pethwick-Lawrence arrived in India. It ultimately announced a plan for the transfer of power which, as a concession to Muslims, called for the formation of a very loose federation of Indian states. After initially agreeing to the plan, the two parties fell into a dispute over the Congress's claim that it, too, had the right to represent Muslims. In response Jinnah declared August 16, 1946, to be "direct action day," which led to the "Great Calcutta Killing"— large-scale rioting in which more than four thousand people were killed. Thousands more were killed as rioting spread to neighboring areas.

In October, 1946, the Muslim League decided to participate in the Executive Council, which the Congress leaders had already joined, but only to obstruct its proceedings. Two months later the League boycotted a Constituent Assembly called by the British. Meanwhile, massive killing spread to the Punjab, where Sikh desires for autonomy complicated the communal picture.

In a last-ditch effort to break the stalemate, the new British Prime Minister, Clement Attlee, announced his country's intention of transferring power in India by June, 1948. Simultaneously, Lord Mountbatten was chosen to replace Lord Wavell as Viceroy and was assigned the task of preparing a plan for the transfer. But even these actions failed to bring about a compromise.

Finally, in March, 1947, the Congress hierarchy began to realize that the only alternative to extended civil war was agreement to the League's demands. In May, they recommended the partition of the Punjab. The goal of the Congress now became to limit the new Muslim state to as small an area as possible—to a "maimed, mutilated, and moth-eaten" Pakistan, as Gandhi called it.

Lord Mountbatten himself now came to see partition as the only solution to the impasse. On June 3, he announced that he had obtained cabinet approval of a plan to transfer power in India to two separate Hindu and Muslim states and that the date of the British departure had been moved up to mid-August, 1947.

Thus, at midnight on August 14, 1947, Mohammed Ali Jinnah and Lord Mountbatten became the first Governor-Generals of independent Pakistan and India, respectively. But partition did not immediately bring tranquillity: before the subcontinent returned to a state of peace, more than 200,000 people were killed as Hindus fled their homes in Pakistan and Muslims theirs in India. The bitter legacy of partition has been a series of wars and threats of war between India and Pakistan which has prevented the two nations from devoting their energies wholly to the pressing task of improving the lot of their impoverished people.

Pertinent Literature

Philips, C. H. and Mary Doreen Wainwright, eds. *The Partition of India: Policies and Perspectives, 1935-1947*. Cambridge, Mass.: MIT Press, 1970.

The All-India Muslim League moved in the short span of ten years from a small, moribund group of office-seekers and landlords, largely from the United Provinces, to a mass movement dominant throughout Muslim India and able to thwart the will of both the Congress and the imperial government. Two basic orientations have emerged from the debate on the question of how this transformation took place and how the state of Pakistan came to be a reality.

The first view, for the most part identified with the Muslim League and the powerful group of *ulema*, or Muslim scholars, within it, maintains that the Muslims and Hindus who have shared the same land for more than a thousand years have *always* formed two nations. This is the view asserted by Jinnah in his Lahore speech of 1940: "[Hindus and Muslims] neither intermarry nor interdine together and, indeed, they belong to two different civilizations which are based mainly on conflicting ideas and conceptions." Consequently, the unity that India experienced under British hegemony was totally artificial and had to end when the British departed. The League's role between 1937 and 1947, then, was simply to give a political expression to these deep-seated differences, and the partition was the natural and inevitable outcome of a thousand years of Hindu-Muslim relations.

The opposing position is that partition was not inevitable, that the roots of Pakistan were far shallower than the Muslim League maintained, and that the partition, therefore, tore apart a potentially viable political entity. The proponents of this second view cite as evidence for their case the fact that not until the 1945 elections could the League claim the support of most Muslims in the two Muslim majority areas. The creation of Bangladesh in 1971 out of what had been Eastern Pakistan is used as retrospective evidence against the unity of the Muslim community which, the League argued, was the foundation for the creation of Pakistan.

This second view is basically that of C. H. Philips, editor of the present volume. Philips believes that a detailed examination of the events of the decade before independence and of the views of various groups participating in the events will yield the clearest understanding of why partition occurred. A wide range of opinions is represented by the contributors to this collection, and the reader will find that the passions generated by partition continue to affect the way people view the events of the period.

For a number of contributors, Ali Jinnah is the main instigator of partition. For Khalid Sayeed, the most extreme representative of this group, Jinnah was driven by a desire to accumulate power in his own hands, and the movement for the creation of Pakistan was simply a means of obtaining this end. More benevolently, another group of contributors stress Jinnah's supreme skills as a logician and political tactician, and they see him as simply taking advantage of the opportunities offered by the Congress and by the British. For them the demand for Pakistan was chiefly a ploy for assuring that attention would be paid to other Muslim demands and was not taken seriously in itself until the Muslim masses fervently took up the cry and made it impossible for Jinnah to back down from his demand.

Jinnah's rivals in the Indian National Congress, primarily Nehru and Gandhi, are also attacked by several contributors. They note that the reluctance of Congress leaders to denounce the notion of Pakistan altogether encouraged Jinnah to press his demands. The Congress' decision to withdraw from the provincial ministries after Lord Linlithgow's unilateral declaration of war and the "Quit India" campaign of 1942 are generally condemned for discrediting the Congress in British eyes and removing prominent party leaders from the political stage, thus providing Jinnah with unexpected opportunities to improve the status and power of the League.

As for the British, they are variously accused of encouraging Muslim separatism, as a counterbalance to the Congress and as a means of prolonging the necessity of their own rule, and of frustrating it. The British, as the editor points out, did not give high enough priority to working out a compromise between the two parties, thinking that perhaps decades remained before independence would be granted, and British involvement in World War II merely reinforced this neglect.

Generally speaking, the contributors to this volume are more concerned with apportioning blame for partition than with arriving at an objective historical understanding of how and why partition occurred. However, the book remains a valuable collection of the views traditionally held on this subject and contains a detailed chronology of the events of the period.

Hardy, Peter. *The Muslims of British India*. Cambridge: Cambridge University Press, 1972.

Professor Peter Hardy offers a different perspective on partition from those presented above. While in no way accepting the League's position, he does show that there were deep historical and cultural reasons for the success of the Muslim League in the period after 1935. He attempts to debunk the League's myth of Muslim solidarity by stressing the historical diversity of backgrounds, interests, and religious beliefs within the Indian Muslim community. For example, the landlords and office-holders of the United Provinces who formed the original core of the League were often members of former Mughal military and bureaucratic families, while the vast majority of Muslims, far humbler than the former group, were located in the Northwest and Bengal and were descended from lower caste Hindu converts to Islam. A more recent division was that between Western-educated, often secularist Muslims and conservative members of the *ulema*, whose position was increasingly threatened by British intrusions into education.

How, then, did these various groups come to see themselves as, first and foremost, Muslims? Hardy believes that British rule was basically responsible for this development. While rejecting the notion that the British had a deliberate policy of "divide and rule," he holds that the way the British divided up Indian society for administration purposes greatly influenced the way that Indians came to see themselves. The explanation of this division, however, has more to do with British culture, with its emphasis on religious categories, than with any "natural order" of Indian society. The way in which the British distributed rewards and punishments was based on this division, and in time Indians learned to manipulate this system for their own benefit, thereby reinforcing it.

Toward the end of the nineteenth century, and especially after 1906, Indians were given a larger, albeit still limited, voice in their government. The Indian National Congress, which Muslims saw as a predominantly Hindu-oriented body, became ever more insistent in its demands for more self-government. Muslims, fearing that increasing self-government would mean domination of their minority community (twenty-four percent of the total population) by Hindus, saw continuation of British rule as the best safeguard of their interests. It became apparent, however, that there was no turning back the progress of the constitutional clock and that Muslims, too, would have to organize politically. In response to the British announcement of further constitutional reforms, a delegation of Muslims met with the Viceroy in 1906 to request that separate electorates be established for Muslim representatives in the new plan, and that Muslims be given a "fair share" of seats which would take into account not only numerical strength, but also Muslim political and military importance.

The British looked favorably on these requests because they saw Muslims as a loyal counterweight to the increasingly nationalistic Congress and because they felt that Muslims, as a natural estate, deserved to be represented. The Muslims received their separate electorates, and once this system had been established it was in the interest of Muslim politicians to maintain and reinforce it; thus, they saw issues more and more in Muslim terms.

But these matters were primarily the concern of the small minority of politically conscious Muslims, and it is clear that Pakistan would never have come into existence without the involvement of the Muslim masses. Hardy shows that only when this group of politicians allied with Muslim religious leaders, with their tremendous influence over the community, did Muslim politics become truly popular. This occurred for the first time during the Khilafat movement, which began before World War I and ended with the abolition of the Caiphate by Kemal Atatürk after the war. This movement, whose aim was to force the British to preserve the integrity of the Caliphate against the maneuverings of the Western imperialist powers, stimulated a level of religious emotion among the Muslim masses unrivalled until the movement for Pakistan in the late 1930's and 1940's. Hardy sees the latter movement as a chiliastic religious movement rather than a pragmatic political one. It was all things to all people, a panacea for the ills of all classes of Muslims. Lord Acton's observation that "[nationalism] was appealed to in the name of the most contradictory principles of government, and served all parties in succession because it was one in which all could unite" applies as much to Pakistan as to the European nationalisms to which he referred. This interpretation is strengthened by the breakup of the alliance between the Western-educated intelligentsia and the conservative *ulema*, which had been the secret of the League's success, soon after the attainment of independence. But Hardy fails to explain why this appeal to Muslim religious sentiment received the response it did among the masses, and the answer to this question may provide the key to the problem of India's partition.　　— *R.E.*

Additional Recommended Reading

Moon, Penderel. *Divide and Quit.* Berkeley: University of California Press, 1962. An eyewitness account of partition disorders in a Muslim state by a member of the Indian Civil Service; includes a valuable detailed study of party politics in Punjab prior to and during World War II.

Robinson, Francis. *Separatism Among Indian Muslims: The Politics of the United Provinces' Muslims, 1860-1923.* Cambridge: Cambridge University Press, 1974. A generally unsympathetic treatment of the growth of Muslim feeling in the core area of India.

Ali, Chaudhri Muhammad. *The Emergence of Pakistan.* New York: Columbia University Press, 1967. A study favorable to the Muslim League which argues that partition was carried out to Pakistan's disadvantage because of the favoritism of Mountbatten.

Menon, V. P. *The Transfer of Power in India.* Princeton, N.J.: Princeton University Press, 1957. A detailed study by a high official in the Indian Administration of the political developments of the last years of colonial rule; slights intellectual, social, and economic changes leading to partition.

Hodson, H. V. *The Great Divide: Britain, India, Pakistan.* London: Hutchinson, 1969. A thorough and generally favorable account of the Viceroyalty of Lord Mountbatten which argues that the solution finally adopted to the Hindu-Muslim conflict was the only one possible.

Wolpert, Stanley. *A New History of India.* New York: Oxford University Press, 1977. A good general survey of Indian history which fills in the background to the controversy stirred by the Muslim League and narrates the course of the partition agitation.

INVENTION OF THE TRANSISTOR

Type of event: Scientific: development of electronics technology
Time: December 23, 1947
Locale: Bell Telephone Laboratories at Murray Hill, New Jersey

Principal personages:
   LEE DE FOREST (1873-1961), inventor of the three-element
      vacuum tube
   MERVIN KELLY, Director of Research at Bell Telephone Lab-
      oratories
   WILLIAM BRADFORD SHOCKLEY (1910-   ), physicist at Bell
      Telephone Laboratories, and co-winner of the Nobel Prize
      in 1956 for invention of the transistor
   JOHN BARDEEN (1908-   ), physicist at Bell Telephone Lab-
      oratories, and co-winner of Nobel Prize in 1956 for inven-
      tion of the transistor
   WALTER HOUSER BRATTAIN (1902-   ), physicist at Bell
      Telephone Laboratories, and co-winner of Nobel Prize in
      1956 for invention of the transistor

Summary of Event

The invention of the transistor in December, 1947, revolutionized the fledgling electronics industry and paved the way for a postwar explosion in communications technology. The invention of the transistor was also one of the most significant productions of industrial scientific research laboratories, first established by the electrical and chemical industries, to organize and direct the process of scientific research towards the needs of the sponsoring corporations.

The Bell Telephone Laboratories, which produced the transistor, were first established in 1925 to serve the research and development interests of their co-owners, the American Telephone and Telegraph Company and the Western Electric Company. The Bell Laboratories (Bell Labs) were systematically organized into research sections, each concentrating on various aspects of the communi-

cations industry. Their primary corporate goal was the improvement and expansion of existing communications equipment.

Before the invention of the transistor, the expansion of the telephone system was limited by the use of the vacuum tube. The main problem in sending telephone messages over long distances was that the current carrying the voice lost its strength as it traveled, so that the message became increasingly faint. The invention of the three-element vacuum tube in 1906 by a young inventor, Lee De Forest, had permitted the amplification and reamplification of the voice signal; with further improvements, the vacuum tube had made possible the first transcontinental telephone call between New York and San Francisco in 1915.

By 1936, Mervin Kelly, Director of research at the Bell Labs, had become concerned about the limitations of the vacuum tube. The tube had serious drawbacks: it was fragile, bulky, gave off too much heat, and consumed too much electrical power. Because the tubes did not last very long, circuits using a great many of them were too costly to operate and maintain.

Kelly approached a young physicist working at the Labs, William Shockley, with the problem of finding a cheap and efficient replacement for the vacuum tube. Shockley had been working on semiconductors, which he thought might have the potential for amplifying electrical currents. (Semiconductors have properties intermediate between those of insulators, such as glass, and conductors, such as copper, and they are capable of picking up electrical signals.) Shockley began exchanging ideas with Walter Brattain, another young Bell physicist, who had also been working with semiconductors. World War II interrupted their research, however, and it was not until late 1945 that they were able to return to the problem.

After the war, they were joined by John Bardeen, one of Bell Labs' theoretical physicists. The three decided to begin their investigations with germanium and silicon, two semiconductor solids that had been widely used during the war for signal detection.

Shockley and Brattain tried to understand why the semiconductors allowed current to flow through them at points of contact with certain other metals. Shockley felt that the electrical fields set up by the current at these points of contact might be made to control the amount of current flowing through the semiconductor. If so, a small electrical charge at the contact point could be made to generate a large current in the semiconductor. This could provide the amplifier they sought.

The team's first experimental device consisted of a tiny slab of germanium mounted close to, but insulated from, a piece of metal. It failed, and continued to fail, although many design changes were tried.

Following this failure, John Bardeen developed a theory explaining the peculiar movements of electrons on the surface of a semiconductor. In an absolutely pure state, a crystal of germanium does not carry an electrical current, because of the stability of the electron-sharing pattern between germanium atoms. If an impurity is present, however, this electron-sharing pattern is altered. Depending upon the atomic structure of the impurity, various numbers of electrons are freed to migrate whenever an electrical charge reaches the crystal. This electron movement allows the electrical current to flow across the germanium without changing its structure.

When Bardeen had formulated the solid-state theory, Brattain began experiments to confirm it. Months of experimenting went by as the team pursued what Shockley came to call the "creative failure methodology." On November 17, 1947, the last phase of discovery began. Following the suggestion of a colleague, Robert B. Gibney, Shockley, Brattain, and Bardeen tried generating an electrical current perpendicular to the semiconductor. They set their germanium crystal in contact with two wires two-thousandths of an inch apart. When the current reached the semiconductor, it amplified over forty times. The "transistor effect" had been discovered.

By December 23, 1947, the three men were ready to demonstrate a working model to their colleagues. Their little device looked primitive. Bardeen had pressed two tiny strips of gold leaf, to act as contacts, onto a germanium crystal, which he then put on top of a piece of metal. This was the first transistor, called a "solid-state" device because it had no movable parts. It could amplify an electrical current more efficiently than the vacuum tube.

For six months the invention was kept a secret while improvements were made and patents drawn up. On July 1, 1948, Bell Labs reported the discovery. The unheralded announcement went virtually unnoticed by the general public. After an initial period of concern over the cost involved in switching production technology, the electronics industry responded with a considerable degree of excitement.

In 1952, when Bell first offered the developed transistor in a licensing arrangement, all the major vacuum tube manufacturers took out licenses and soon began producing transistors. Realizing the potential of the device for military electronic equipment, the Department of Defense began to sponsor further research, development, and production of transistors. Additional private capital was invested in the field, and, within a few years, a variety of new types of transistors had been developed for application in all forms of electronic communications: from computers and telephones, radios and tape recorders, remote-control equipment and military sensing devices, to hearing aids and pacemakers. All electronic products could now be made much smaller, could run on much less power, and could be made much more cheaply; a new technology and a new industry were built on the tiny germanium crystal.

Pertinent Literature

Noble, David F. *America by Design: Science, Technology, and the Rise of Corporate Capitalism.* New York: Alfred A. Knopf, 1977.

This important work sets out to analyze, rather than simply to describe, the development of modern technology in the context of corporate capitalism. Noble rejects the notion of a technological determinism which opposes technology, as an autonomous force, to society, as a human construct. He argues that this view constitutes a mystification of technology, and that, ironically, it became widespread just when the technological process as a whole first came under the control of human authority, in the shape of modern corporate capital. In reality, he argues, technology is always a social process, and modern industrial technology is a fundamental social development that needs to be understood in its historical context.

Noble shows how the modern corporation and modern technology developed together; the corporations, by bringing science as a productive force into industry, provided the conditions for their own unlimited growth. The twentieth century technological revolution was, thus, a creature of industry, and not a process that occurred in a social vacuum. Science was linked to the service of capital through a new class of professional managers and engineers; by contrast, the new technology bound the worker more closely to his task and further removed the labor process from his control.

In the first part of his book, Noble traces the late nineteenth century wedding of science to industry. Unlike older industries, which had developed from a basis in traditional crafts, the new chemical and electrical industries of the 1880's were based on scientific discoveries in chemistry and physics. They were soon to set the patterns of production and management for modern industry as a whole.

Through consolidation, patent monopoly, and merger, the new science-based industries came to be dominated by a few giant corporations. The professional engineers had gained a monopoly over the practice of scientific technology; the giant corporations in turn employed the engineers in management positions to direct the process of technological development.

In the second part of his book, Noble describes in detail the institutions established to carry out the program of corporate-directed technology, the reorganization of research, of education, and finally, of the labor

process itself, under "scientific management." Here, he provides the historical framework for understanding the development of the Bell Telephone Laboratories as one of the first organized research laboratories in industry.

Since its beginning, the telephone industry had depended on research. The American Telephone and Telegraph Company (the parent of Bell Labs) had first conducted applied research in several scattered laboratories; in 1907, these were combined to form the engineering department of their manufacturing subsidiary, the Western Electric Company. The industry soon found, however, that their initial policy of restricting research to questions of immediate practical utility was self-defeating. They could not rely on the process of spontaneous and sporadic individual invention to solve major technological problems; they needed fundamental scientific research.

The Bell Labs were established in 1925 to serve this need. Once begun, they grew rapidly, and, by 1930, had an annual budget of more than twenty million dollars. They were bigger and had more money than any university in the country; university scientists were easily attracted by their almost unlimited research funds, and by 1937, Bell Labs had their first Nobel Prize-winner.

Noble describes the way in which the research at the Labs was systematically organized and controlled, with almost military precision. The old system of paying bonuses to employees for patented inventions was dropped, as encouraging the scientific worker to work for himself rather than for his employer. Bell preferred the "group" or "systems" method of research, whereby a particular problem was broken down into its elements and divided up between a group of specialists, who then worked cooperatively towards the solution.

One method of controlling scientific workers was to foster a spirit of cooperation among researchers, second only to a spirit of loyalty to the corporation. An inventor no longer had an individualistic pride in, and reward for, his invention; instead, he had security and a good, regular salary check. Indeed, he had little choice in the matter, as it was now almost impossible for an isolated inventor to compete with the huge corporate laboratories. Even small and medium sized firms could hardly compete, and the patent system, supposedly established to insure the rights of the individual inventor, guaranteed the increasing concentration of economic and technological power in the hands of the corporate giants.

The invention of the transistor, a tribute to the success of the large industrial research laboratory, was a product of the economic power of AT&T; only a giant corporation could have afforded to pay for research on such a grand scale. Yet as Noble shows, it was also the guarantee of their future power, since they were thus able to control a huge new market. Noble argues clearly and convincingly that the development of modern technology and the concentration of economic power in large corporations are mutually reinforcing, and that each generates the other. He provides a powerful analytic framework, going far beyond most recent debates about technological progress, and future writers on technology will find his arguments difficult to ignore.

Brooks, John. *Telephone: The First Hundred Years*. New York: Harper & Row Publishers, 1975.

John Brooks's history of the telephone, in large part a history of the American Telephone and Telegraph Company, is a very refreshing change from the frequently dull and self-congratulatory tomes which usually pass as corporate histories. The story is fascinating and forthrightly told in a vivid and vigorous style. Brooks seems to enjoy the fire and politics of great corporate struggles, and, indeed, they do constitute some of the most dramatic confrontations of the twentieth century. AT&T, he tells us, is the richest corporation on the face of the earth; it has battled with, and vanquished, a multiplicity of smaller rivals; has been threatened with, but escaped, bankruptcy; has survived depressions, scandals, and even a government seizure of its property; and it has successfully withstood two major antitrust suits, emerging from the fray more powerful than ever.

With rare bravery, AT&T executives agreed to open their corporate files and offices to Brooks, having initially been satisfied that he began research with no special prejudice against the company. He has used his freedom well, and his attitude towards the company and its executives is sometimes curious, sometimes admiring, and often critical.

Brooks makes it quite clear, for example, that the company has consistently protected its stockholders, while granting its employees all the burdens and few rewards. Between 1925 and 1929, the average weekly earnings of Bell employees rose from $26 to $29; in the same period, stockholders made a profit of more than fifty percent on their investments. Selling stock widely and keeping wages low, AT&T had become, by 1929, the first corporation in history to gross more than one billion dollars in revenues. Their stock was considered so safe, it was "the first choice investment for widows and orphans." Faced with the Depression, AT&T chose to hold its dividend steady at nine dollars, and to cut its payroll by twenty percent. The entire brunt of Depression was let fall on labor, and capital investments did not suffer.

The company sponsored its own unions; in 1932, employees were asked to spend their evenings and weekends, without pay, canvassing for new telephone subscribers. Apparently, many did so. Then, between 1929 and 1935, the company eliminated 70,000 jobs by converting to dial phones. Not until the Wagner Act of 1935 did employees have the right to form their own unions, and even then, top management was only narrowly dissuaded from defying the law.

This is only one of many corporate issues, struggles, failures, and successes that Brooks delineates with insight and sometimes with humor. He describes the long battles over federal regulation, from the first serious attack on the telephone companies in 1934, by the newly established Federal Communications Commisssion, to the suit filed against AT&T under the Sherman Antitrust Act in 1949. This suit was finally settled in AT&T's favor in 1956, thanks to the support of the Department of Defense. By this time, the Bell System was so heavily involved in the production of atom bombs, guided missiles, and radar systems, that, had the suit against AT&T succeeded, the entire weapons program of the United States would have been badly damaged.

Brooks also describes the internal politics of AT&T, the struggles over presidential succession, and the different management styles and policy decisions of the chief executives. He explains why the "democratization" of ownership by selling shares to more than half a million small stockholders had effectively served to centralize decision-making power. He describes the impact of World War II in increasing the demand for long distance telephone services, to the point where the resources of the existing technology were strained to their limits. Then, the ending of the war brought an even greater demand for telephone services. Fortunately, the invention of the transistor in 1947 meant that the telephone system could continue to expand almost indefinitely.

Brooks's description of the invention of the transistor is brief but useful, and he quotes directly from the scientists involved. In his account of the history of AT&T, however, technological innovations play a minor role as compared to the battles over politics, policies, and prices. This book is a useful counter and correc-

tive to the myopic vision of some his- the development of techniques, and
tories of technology which see only never their context. — *E.F.*

Additional Recommended Reading

Kelly, Mervin J. "The First Five Years of the Transistor," in *Bell Telephone Magazine*. XXXII (Summer, 1953), pp. 73-86. Kelly explains the early types of transistor design and their applications.

Mabon, Prescott C. *Mission Communications: The Story of Bell Laboratories*. Murray Hill, N.J.: Bell Telephone Laboratories, 1975. This official history of the Bell Labs, by an ex-Vice-President of the American Telephone and Telegraph Company, mixes useful information with heavy doses of public relations.

Fagen, M. D., ed. *A History of Engineering and Science in the Bell System: The Early Years, 1875-1925*. Murray Hill, N.J.: Bell Telephone Laboratories, 1975. A weighty and encyclopedic history of early telephone technology by members of the technical staff of Bell Telephone Laboratories.

Bruce, Robert V. *Bell: Alexander Graham Bell and the Conquest of Solitude*. Boston: Little, Brown and Company, 1973. A lively and scholarly biography of the inventor of the telephone.

Sampson, Anthony. *The Sovereign State of I.T.T.* New York: Stein and Day, 1973. A fascinating account of the international deals of the International Telephone and Telegraph Company, from cooperation with Nazi Germany to the overthrow of Allende's Chile.

Schiller, Herbert I. *Mass Communications and American Empire*. New York: A. M. Kelley, 1969. An analysis of the relationship between communications technology and American power.

Pool, Ithiel de Sola, ed. *The Social Impact of the Telephone*. Cambridge, Mass.: MIT Press, 1970. A collection of sociological and historical essays from a symposium series at MIT, funded by AT&T.

Duerig, W. H. and J. F. Jenkins, *et al. Notes on Transistor Physics and Electronics*. Silver Spring, Md.: Applied Physics Laboratory, The Johns Hopkins University, 1953. A set of lecture notes on transistor physics and electronics for those interested in the technical aspects of the subject.

Gregor, Arthur. *Bell Laboratories: Inside the World's Largest Communications System*. New York: Charles Scribner's Sons, 1972. A popular, illustrated, history of the Bell Laboratories.

Brooks, Harvey. *The Government of Science*. Cambridge, Mass.: MIT Press, 1968. A collection of essays on science, technology, and public policy.

Dupré, Joseph Stefan and Stanford A. Lakoff. *Science and the Nation: Policy and Politics*. Englewood Cliffs, N.J.: Prentice-Hall, 1962. An analysis of the relationship between industrial, military, and university-based scientific research.

PUBLICATION OF THE KINSEY REPORTS

Type of event: Scientific: significant studies on human sexuality
Time: 1948 and 1953
Locale: The United States

Principal personages:

ALFRED CHARLES KINSEY (1894-1956), Professor of Zoology,
Director of the Institute for Sex Research at Indiana University, and principal author of the Reports

WARDELL B. POMEROY (1913-   ), a principal author of
the Reports, and the primary interviewer

CLYDE E. MARTIN, principal statistician for the two Kinsey
Reports

PAUL H. GEBHARD (1917-   ), one of the authors of the
volume on the female, now Director of the Institute for
Sex Research

Summary of Event

When *Sexual Behavior in the Human Male* (Kinsey, Pomeroy, Martin;
Philadelphia: Saunders) was published in 1948, it was the result of
many years of intensive interviewing
by Alfred C. Kinsey and his staff at
the Institute for Sex Research at Indiana University. Eighteen thousand
men and six thousand women were
questioned in strict anonymity about
their sex lives. The resulting compi-
lations of information when published amazed, amused, and vaguely
outraged the American public. Sex
as a topic for general discussion has
never been the same.

Dr. Kinsey might have, at first
glance, been the least likely type of
person to produce the first definitive
information on human sexuality. He
was a zoologist by training, known
for his meticulous study of gall wasps,
a shy scientist who had married the
first girl he ever dated. Indiana, the
state in which the Institute for Sex
Research is located, was an especially

conservative location to foster such
controversial inquiries.

Alfred C. Kinsey was an assistant
professor of zoology with a Bachelor's degree from Bowdoin College
in zoology and psychology and a Doc-
torate from Harvard in zoology and
botany when he joined the staff at
Indiana University in 1920. For many
years he concentrated on teaching,
writing general biology textbooks,
and attempting to collect and study
all of the different types of gall wasps
in existence. When, in 1938, the
University began a course on marriage for its students, Kinsey coordinated the several professors who
taught the course as well as taking
responsibility for the sections relating
to the clinical aspects of sex. Four
years later, he founded the Institute
for Sex Research.

As he prepared his lectures, he discovered that very little was actually
known about human sexual behavior
aside from the biological principles

619

of reproduction. Since he could find no sizable body of scientific knowledge from which to draw information, he began to gather it himself. Dr. Kinsey's early questionnaires about sexual behavior were addressed to his students and others in the University community, but as patterns began to develop in his information, he realized that a more thorough interviewing technique and population sample might net more reliable and generally applicable results.

Kinsey therefore developed a set of five hundred questions covering a broad spectrum of behavior, of which approximately three hundred were asked in each interview, depending upon the direction in which the interviewer felt it would be most fruitful to proceed. Rather than taking a random sample of the population at all levels and conditions, Kinsey chose to collect "100% samples," or interviews, with all of the members of a particular group. Such groups might have included entire small towns, all of the members of a fraternity, or all of the members of a civic or social organization. He believed that by taking all of the members of diverse groups he would be just as likely to cover the range of possible answers as he would in a more random sample. After gathering as much information as he could at Indiana University, Kinsey branched out first to nearby Indianapolis, then to Chicago, and finally to other areas of the country. He noted the responses to his memorized questions in a type of shorthand of marks made on graph paper, which assured those being interviewed of the confidentiality of the information which they volunteered.

Wardell B. Pomeroy was the other principal interviewer with Kinsey. Clyde E. Martin, whose principal role was as statistician to the project, was also trained as an interviewer, as was Paul Gebhard, who joined the research for the publication of the second volume.

When *Sexual Behavior in the Human Male* was published, ten years after Kinsey's research began, it was hailed as a most important work and as a major piece of research. Many responses to it from professionals in the field were soundly analytical, many laudatory, some concerned about sampling techniques and the consequent validity of the information. There were many other reactions by both professionals and laymen that were considerably less analytical and far less laudatory, the writers often alarmed at the possibility that the Kinsey publication would subvert the practice of a custom, religion, or law of which they were particularly fond. The influence of this latter group was often considerable, and their vehemence attracted the attention of many.

Although many members of the general public talked about the Kinsey findings, a relatively small proportion actually read the whole work. Many who did at least read excerpts from it had little scientific, sociological, or statistical expertise with which to assess the findings. A great number, however, formed their opinions on hearsay or patterned them after one of the more vocal analysts.

After many articles had been published and many questions raised, a committee was appointed by the

American Statistical Association to study the validity of Kinsey's methodology. In a study that was published in final form in 1954, they found that although there was some general weakness in his method, the data were still of significant importance.

Nonetheless, the debate by both the qualified and the unqualified as to whether or not the publication of such information would undermine the morals of young people or spell the doom of marriage as an institution continued. One thing, therefore, that the publication did do from the very start was to bring to the attention of the general populace their previous lack of concrete information on the subject of sex. Until the publication of the Kinsey Report, sexual behavior was not often the subject of casual conversation in polite circles. However, the same year in which the report on the male was published, Cole Porter, the popular composer, quoted some of Kinsey's statistics in lyrics of "Too Darn Hot" from his musical *Kiss Me Kate*:

> According to the Kinsey Report
> Every average man you know
> Much prefers to play his favorite sport
> When the temperature is low.

In less than a year Dr. Kinsey's dry statistical study had made its way into American popular culture as well as to the bestseller list.

When in 1953 the Institute for Sex Research published *Sexual Behavior in the Human Female* (Kinsey, Pomeroy, Martin, Gebhard; Philadelphia: Saunders), the reaction was notably less rational than it had been five

years earlier. The appearance of this volume had been eagerly awaited since the publication of the first. As a consequence, the Institute was besieged by writers, reporters, and the generally curious for months before publication. Kinsey and his staff gave advance press releases to a select group of journalists, carefully explaining the data to them so that they could better explain it to the public.

Although *Sexual Behavior in the Human Female* appeared on the bestseller list soon after publication, the American public was not ready to accept much of what Kinsey had recorded. There seemed to be a definite gap between what American women did and what the myth of the All-American Girl purported that she did.

Outside support of Kinsey's sex research had begun with a small grant from the National Research Council's Committee for Research on Problems of Sex, followed by larger ones from the Rockefeller Foundation. Much of this support was withdrawn after publication of *Sexual Behavior in the Human Female*, because the disclosures contained therein were less well tolerated by the general public. Pressure was placed on the Rockefeller Foundation in the form of a Congressional investigation into their spending practices and the Foundation support was subsequently withdrawn.

Although Alfred Kinsey died in 1956, the Institute for Sex Research, under the direction of Paul Gebhard, continued to collect information and publish studies. The Institute has received support from the National Institute for Mental Health as well as other groups, as the value and validity of their inquiries to the advancement of scientific knowledge have come to be taken for granted.

Sexual Behavior in the Human Male and *Sexual Behavior in the Human Female* had great scientific as well as social impact. They were the first thorough descriptions of the sexual behavior of a large number of individuals. The research exposed many variations and differences in behavior from one person or social group to another. It has also spurred further research into particular aspects of human sexuality, notably the work by William H. Masters and Virginia E. Johnson, codirectors since 1958 of the Reproductive Biology Research Foundation in St. Louis, Missouri.

Pertinent Literature

Ernst, Morris Leopold and David Loth. *American Sexual Behavior and the Kinsey Report*. New York: Greystone, 1948.

When *Sexual Behavior in the Human Male* was published, a great amount of discussion began. Ernst and Loth in this volume attempt to reach the segment of the population that was less well prepared to evaluate the Report and its impassioned critics. Ernst had written many legal and social treatises and Loth had published several biographies. Their writing talents combined to produce a popular, careful, if occasionally simplistic explication of some of the more important points covered by Kinsey. Since much of the previous research in the field of sexual behavior had not come to the attention of the general populace, many people were wary of Dr. Kinsey and his study; they were under the impression that his was an isolated and unusual interest in a subject that perhaps should not have been discussed.

The authors begin by considering the findings in the light of previous research, emphasizing that Kinsey's work, though of historical significance, was part of a natural progression of inquiry. They also emphasize, in this regard, that while Kinsey did much of the work himself, there was an entire team of interviewers involved in the project.

Approaching the more substantive questions slowly, Ernst and Loth make the crucial distinction for the layman between the word "in" and the word "of" in scientific parlance. They emphasize that a book entitled *Sexual Behavior in the Human Male* indicates that the information presented therein is selective, while the same title using the word "of" would indicate an all-inclusive study of the topic. While this may seem to be a minor point, it is the basis for their recurring theme throughout the remainder of the volume, that the statistics put forth by Alfred Kinsey are just a beginning point for further research. In each of their subsequent chapters, the authors discuss some of the Kinsey findings, but also attempt to define areas in which interpretation is difficult because so much more research needs to be done.

Reading the Ernst and Loth book through the perspective of time reveals in its painstakingly calm if not almost patronizing tone the abysmal ignorance of and emotional over-reaction to sexual matters that must have been the norm for the general reader at the time. The authors spend many paragraphs exhorting their readers to keep open minds about the findings, emphasizing thereby that the popular reaction in the year in which both this book and *Sexual Behavior in the Human Male* were published was wont to be more hysterical than rational.

The largest part of *American Sex-* *ual Behavior and the Kinsey Report* is a chapter by chapter discussion of the sexual behavior reported by Kinsey. They emphasize that Kinsey's study has disclosed that normal behavior covers a wide range. Such concerns may now seem to be of little consequence, but the greatest value of the Ernst and Loth volume to those considering the impact of the publication of the Kinsey Reports is found in the social and emotional progress that has been made through the open discussion proposed here.

Deutsch, Albert, ed. *Sex Habits of American Men: A Symposium on the Kinsey Report.* New York: Prentice-Hall, 1948.

In an early attempt to assay the impact and import of *Sexual Behavior in the Human Male* (1948), Deutsch has collected papers from representatives of various fields. He begins the volume with an introduction of the Kinsey project and a laudatory assessment of its importance. He reviews the most important facts and figures from the Report itself in an attempt to give the discussions included in the volume a solid reference point for those readers who have not read the entire Report.

Deutsch, a newspaper columnist, pays particular attention to describing Kinsey and his associates as individuals as well as researchers. His discussion of Kinsey's interviewing techniques, and especially of how Kinsey could gain the total confidence of a complete stranger in such a situation, have great impact as Deutsch confesses to having been interviewed himself. He also emphasizes the scientific nature of the study by explaining some of the statistical hurdles that had to be overcome and by disclosing the ongoing nature of the research.

Other authors in this volume also provide the reader with discussions of the social and ethical implications, even though such considerations were not part of Kinsey's studies.

Robert J. Havighurst, Professor of Education at the University of Chicago, in his essay "Cultural Factors in Sex Expression" analyzes the Kinsey findings by social group, delving into some of the likely causes for their differences in sexual behavior.

In "Psychiatric Issues in the Kinsey Report," Robert P. Knight, Clinical Professor of Psychiatry at Yale Medical School, gives general approval to the Report as a statistical frame of reference for professionals in other fields. He does argue over the validity of the data because they were drawn primarily from the memory of those being interviewed, which, he emphasizes, might not always be accurate. Knight voices a prevalent belief among many who contributed to this and other volumes in lauding the open discussion resulting from the Kinsey studies, that the work will foster healthier attitudes toward sex.

Joseph K. Folsom, Professor of Sociology at Vassar, analyzes selected data for their sociological implications in the hope of pointing toward some general trends, while a very different point of view is presented by Clyde Kluckhohn, Professor of Anthropology at Harvard. The latter discussion concerns American Indian cultures and the correlation of their sexual behavior with the findings of the more white, Anglo-Saxon, Protestant interviewees of Kinsey. He also includes a general overview of previous studies of sexual behavior in American culture.

A final pertinent selection from this compilation is the article by Leo Crespi, Assistant Professor of Psychology at Princeton and Associate Director of the Princeton Office of Public Opinion Research. Crespi addresses the question of the validity of Kinsey's methods, but, taking a different point of view from many other statistical inquiries, emphasizes that the sample in question was experimental in nature and certainly not final.

This is not a strictly laudatory volume, although most of those represented would agree that the findings were a positive step forward in a relatively neglected field. The responses from the various disciplines often conflict in emphasis if not greatly in substance. — *M.S.S.*

Additional Recommended Reading

Cochran, William Gemmell, *et al. Statistical Problems of the Kinsey Report on Sexual Behavior in the Human Male*. Washington, D.C.: American Statistical Association, 1954. The purpose of this report was to examine Kinsey's methodology in the areas of sampling, interviewing, and measurement.

Geddes, Donald Porter, ed. *An Analysis of the Kinsey Reports on Sexual Behavior in the Human Male and Female*. New York: E. P. Dutton, 1954. Essays in response to both the first and second Kinsey Reports are included in this volume.

Himelhoch, Jerome and Sylvia Fava, eds. *Sexual Behavior in American Society: An Appraisal of the First Two Kinsey Reports*. New York: W. W. Norton and Company, 1955. A collection of essays prepared by experts in various fields relating to sex research which is amplified by a bibliographical essay by Leo P. Chall on the "Reception of the Kinsey Reports in Periodicals of the United States" and a summary of the Report by the committee appointed to review the statistical methods used for the first Kinsey Report.

Pomeroy, Wardell B. *Dr. Kinsey and the Institute for Sex Research*. New York: Harper & Row Publishers, 1972. Written by one of the founding associates of the Institute for Sex Research, this biography of Alfred C. Kinsey concentrates on the personal dedication and great dynamism that propelled the Institute staff through uncharted waters in their research.

Christenson, Cornelia V. *Kinsey, A Biography*. Bloomington: Indiana University

Press, 1971. Written by a former research associate of Kinsey at the Institute for Sex Research, this biography concentrates on the man behind the myth, giving good insights into the characteristics and habits which suited him so admirably for the role he played in the history of sex research.

THE COMMUNIST *COUP* IN CZECHOSLOVAKIA

Type of event: Political: Communist takeover of the Czech government
Time: February 20-25, 1948
Locale: Prague, Czechoslovakia

Principal personages:
EDUARD BENEŠ (1884-1948), President of Czechoslovakia, 1945-1948
KLEMENT GOTTWALD (1896-   ), Czech Communist Party chief; Czech Prime Minister, 1946-1948; and President of Czechoslovakia, 1948-1953
JOSEPH STALIN (IOSIF VISSARIONOVICH DZHUGASHVILI) (1879-1953), Dictator of the Soviet Union, 1924-1953
JAN GARRIGUE MASARYK (1886-1948), Czech Foreign Minister and the son of the President-Liberator of Czechoslovakia, Tomáš Masaryk

Summary of Event

From the Battle of White Mountain in 1620 to the end of World War I, the territories comprising modern Czechoslovakia were constituent parts of the Habsburg Empire. By the mid-nineteenth century, an educated Czech bourgeoisie and industrial proletariat had emerged which desired the same privileges held by the Germans and the Hungarians within the Dual Monarchy. These were not granted, and when World War I broke out, the Czech national leader, Tomáš Masaryk, openly sided with the Allied Powers, demanding the creation of an independent state. The Allied victory and the disintegration of the Habsburg Empire enabled this dream to become reality.

In the Europe of the Great Powers, the security of a small state is always in jeopardy. Its continued existence generally depends either on the firm patronage of a Power, such as England provided for Holland and Belgium, or an impregnable geographic position as in the case of Switzerland and Sweden. Without the latter, Czechoslovakia opted for the former, signing a mutual security pact with France in 1924. Internally, Czechoslovakia was a democracy, permitting the free competition of all political parties. The Communists won slightly more than ten percent of the votes.

The assumption of power in Germany by Adolf Hitler threatened the future of this dynamic little country. Hitler was ambitious to dominate all of Eastern Europe. Since there were three million Germans living in the border areas of Czechoslovakia, the German leader demanded the inclusion of these lands in the Third Reich. As these areas were heavily fortified and mountainous, however, their loss meant that Czechoslovakia would be completely defenseless. This conflict came to a head in September, 1938, at the Munich Conference, when France, supported by Great Britain, refused to honor her treaty and agreed to the German annexation of the border territories. The independence and integrity of Czechoslovakia were not important enough to the French to risk war. Abandoned by her ally, the Prague government allowed Hitler to move in peacefully, and six months later he occupied all the Czech lands, while setting up a puppet state in Slovakia.

The dismemberment of Czechoslovakia made a lasting impression on her President, Eduard Beneš, the successor to Tomáš Masaryk. Even though he set up Czechoslovakia's wartime provisional government in London, he came to the conclusion that the West could not be relied on to defend his country. An alliance with the Soviet Union would therefore be absolutely essential. As a result, diplomatically, Beneš became dependent on Joseph Stalin, the Soviet Dictator.

While Beneš had been in London, the Czech Communist Party leaders spent the war in Moscow. Here their already close ties to the Soviet leadership were strengthened and those Communists most acceptable to the Russians succeeded the best. Inside Czechoslovakia, the tightly knit Communist Party organization, combined with the determined Russian military effort, enabled the Communists to play a much greater role in the Resistance than they had in prewar politics. As in all countries occupied by the Germans, the war served as a catalyst to radicalize the population, minimizing class distinctions and stimulating demands for greater social justice. Both the internal and external situation, then, made the Communist Party much stronger than it had been before the war.

In 1945, Beneš traveled to Moscow to negotiate the membership of the new government of Czechoslovakia with the Communists. Here he had to acknowledge the gains they had made by granting them such important ministries as the Interior, which controlled the police; Agriculture, which distributed the lands expropriated from the Sudeten Germans, and Information. The Prime Minister and Minister of Defense were both Communist sympathizers. Furthermore, Beneš agreed to set up National Committees to run local government until elections could be held. Since Czechoslovakia was liberated by the Russians, these National Committees became dominated by the Communists. Finally, the Trade Unions which had been divided among the parties before the war were now united, a million members strong, under Communist leadership. In 1945, then, the Communist Party assumed a dominant position in the country, neutralizing the army and the police, gaining control of local government, and winning peasant support. Nevertheless, a democratic regime was installed. Its survival depended on the ability of the non-Communists to solidify their support and on the maintenance of good will between the wartime allies, the Soviet Union, Great Britain, and the United States.

This alliance, however, did not hold together. At first, it appeared as if it might. In November, 1945, the Soviet Army evacuated the country, and in 1946, free elections were held, with the Communists winning thirty-eight percent of the vote. As a result, Communist leader Klement Gottwald became Prime Minister in a new coalition cabinet. International tensions, meanwhile, developed between the Soviet Union and the Western Allies on a whole series of fronts, ranging from China in the Far East to Iran and Turkey in the Middle East to Germany and Eastern Europe in the West. In June, 1947, the American Secretary of State, George Marshall, announced a plan to help Europe recover economically. The Russians interpreted this move as an American way of buying friends in Europe and refused to allow Czechoslovakia to participate. They also decided it was time to solidify their control over their neighbors. The newly established Cominform (Communist Information Bureau) criticized the Czech Communists for not proceeding with the socialization of their country as rapidly as the other East European Communists. Elections in Czechoslovakia were set for May, 1948, and a recent poll showed the Communists had lost about ten percent of their support. The Soviet pressure and their slipping popularity made it imperative to assume complete power before the elections.

In September, 1947, three booby-trapped boxes of perfume were sent by an important Communist official to non-Communist ministers, including the Foreign Minister, Jan Masaryk, son of Tomáš Masaryk. None of these bombs exploded. In November, the Slovak Communists set up a showdown in the Slovak regional government which led to a partial resignation of the leaders of the Slovak Democrat Party. Then, in February, 1948, a great Trade Union Congress was called which was to ask for fur-

ther nationalization of industry and expropriation of land. Simultaneously with this Congress, the Minister of Interior abruptly replaced eight non-Communist police commanders with Communists. The matter of police control was an extremely sensitive issue, one of the vital keys of power, and a majority of ministers in the Cabinet voted to rescind this order. When the Minister of Interior refused to obey this decision and was supported by Prime Minister Gottwald and the Communist Party, the twelve non-Communist ministers in the cabinet resigned in protest. They hoped that President Beneš would be able to step in, but he was unable to convince the Communists to back down.

In the meantime, Prague was filled with militant delegates to the Trade Union Congress, arms were passed out to workers' militia groups, Communists in the ministries of the twelve resigned ministers assumed power, and a number of arrests were made. The democrats stood by helplessly as these events took place. Between February 20 and February 25, a *coup* occurred in which the Communist Party gained control of the state and the street. On February 25, Beneš, faced with the prospect of civil war or a possible Russian invasion, and unable to rely on either the army or the police, accepted the twelve resignations and approved a new government completely dominated by the Communists. Using the strong position they had won in 1945, under pressure from Moscow on the one hand and fearful of the elections on the other, the Communists pushed the democratic ministers out of the government and with a show of force in the streets of Prague, forced Beneš to approve the creation of a new regime. An extensive purge occurred immediately afterwards with thousands of jobs switching hands. On March 10, Jan Masaryk, the Foreign Minister, was killed when he jumped— or was pushed—from his office window. In the May elections victory resulted for the single list of the Communist-dominated National Front. Beneš resigned as President on June 7, and a week later Gottwald succeeded him as head of state. A Communist dictatorship now reigned supreme in hapless Czechoslovakia.

The repercussions of the Prague *coup* have been twofold. Internationally, the determination of the West to resist further Communist encroachments was strengthened, resulting in the Berlin Airlift and the NATO alliance. Second, the domestic politics of the West European countries with significant Communist parties, France and Italy, were affected, as the danger of allowing Communist representation in the government had been made clear. Even thirty years later in these countries there is a lack of confidence that the Communist Party would obey the rules of democratic government if it were permitted to administer the major institutions of the state.

Pertinent Literature

Zinner, Paul. *Communist Strategy and Tactics in Czechoslovakia, 1918-1948.* New York: Frederick A. Praeger, 1963.

Zinner's work is a well-reasoned, balanced, and scholarly account of the Communist takeover in Czechoslovakia. As such, it is useful in pointing out two contradictory aspects of the Party. In a historical section, Zinner describes the development of Moscow's domination over the Czech Communists in the 1920's and 1930's, a phenomenon similar to what occurred in other European Communist parties. By the postwar period, as a result, Stalin had considerable control over what happened in Prague. On the other hand, Zinner goes on to show the genuine support which the Communists enjoyed in Czechoslovakia. Millions of workers, peasants, and intellectuals believed that a Communist regime would secure the brightest future, and the Com-

munists, as a result, were the strongest political force in the country. The Prague *coup* of 1948, then, was a combination of the ambitions of Russian foreign policy and the revolutionary impulse of a significant proportion of the Czech population.

Prior to World War I, Marxism in Europe was represented by the Social Democratic parties. In general, these parties included both a reformist and a revolutionary wing, with the former predominating. The success of the Bolsheviks in Russia brought this ideological conflict to a head because the Soviets demanded allegiance to their revolutionary principles. The result was a split, as the revolutionary Marxists broke off to form Communist parties. In Czechoslovakia, reformist Marxism was very strong, and the split did not come until 1921. Even so, the new Communist Party was not revolutionary enough for Moscow, and it was severely criticized in the Comintern, the international Communist organization. Russian pressure and invective led to two left-ward movements, one in 1925 and the second in 1929, when a leadership under Klement Gottwald was elected which completely adhered to the Soviet line. The increasingly radical ideological tone took its toll on the moderate Czech working class, for membership dropped from 350,000 in 1921 to 24,000 in 1929, climbing to 75,000 during the 1930's. The Party did continue to poll about 750,000 votes at each election, ten percent of the electorate, but only controlled six percent of organized labor.

As explained, the Munich crisis and the war altered this situation dramatically. By the end of 1945, Party membership had reached a million and at the time of the *coup* it was a million and a half. Since three million Germans were expelled from the country, an enormous amount of land was available for distribution, and the Communist control of the Ministry of Agriculture meant it was able to direct this bonanza. Its standing with the peasantry naturally increased proportionally. Finally and most importantly, the unification of the trade unions by the Germans during the war enabled the Communists to gain undisputed ascendency over the more than two million members. In a country of 12,000,000 these numbers were important and are reflected in thirty-eight percent of the vote won in the 1946 elections.

Despite this position of strength, the Czech Communist Party did not decide to take over the government on its own. The pressure came from Moscow, and when the decision was made, Valerian Zorin, Russian Deputy Foreign Minister came to direct and coordinate activity. All the Communist trump cards were played during the *coup* itself. The Minister of Defense, Communist sympathizer Ludvik Svoboda, kept the troops neutral. The police, directed by Communist Minister of Interior Vaclav Nosek actively aided the Party. The Trade Union Congress was worked into a revolutionary fervor, and for good measure, the Communists organized a peasants' congress for February 29. This mobilization of the masses emphasized the weakness of the democratic ministers, for they were unable to counter with massive demonstrations of their own supporters. Only a group of five thousand students marched in their favor. Furthermore, the Communist Party organized workers' militia groups to patrol the streets of Prague, and on February 25, twelve thousand arms were distributed. In the countryside, action committees were set up to remove non-Communists from their positions, and a number of the resigned ministers were prohibited entry to their offices. It was this manifestation of overwhelming power and complete control which forced Beneš to accede to the Communist demands. The virtue of Zinner's book is his demonstration that hand in hand with the pressure from Moscow and the extralegal measures went an enormous amount of actual popular support.

The Communist Coup in Czechoslovakia

Sterling, Claire. *The Masaryk Case*. New York: Harper & Row Publishers, 1968, 1969.

If Zinner's study underlines the solid base supporting the Communist Party, this gripping work by journalist Claire Sterling delves into the disturbing brutality used by the Party to gain its ends. Well-written and skillfully organized, *The Masaryk Case* focuses on the death of Czech Foreign Minister Jan Masaryk on the night of March 9, 1948. Woven into this story is a description of the "Prague Spring" of 1968, when the author's investigation is carried out, an analysis of the Prague *coup* of 1948, the immediate background to Masaryk's death, and a smattering of Czech history going back to Jan Hus. It is her brilliant and suspenseful unraveling of the Masaryk case, though, which is the heart of this interesting book.

Masaryk himself was a flawed hero. The son of the President-Liberator of Czechoslovakia, the distinguished professor Tomáš Masaryk, Jan was a poor student who never graduated from college and was shipped off to the United States at age twenty to build a life for himself. After World War I, with his father in the president's office, Jan entered the Foreign Service, and in 1925 was appointed Ambassador to Great Britain. Since he had more of a reputation as a playboy than as a political mind, his elevation caused a certain amount of resentment. He stayed at this post until 1938, when he was unable to convince the English to go to war in order to save his country. During World War II, he was named Foreign Minister in Beneš' government-in-ex-

ile in London, where he became its principal spokesman, broadcasting week after week into occupied Czechoslovakia. Here he made a name for himself, gaining a great deal of popularity as he encouraged his countrymen to hold out against the German occupier. After liberation, he retained the post of Foreign Minister in the coalition government. He tried to maintain friendship with the West, but found his hands increasingly tied by the Russians, especially in the decision to reject the Marshall Plan. He did not resign with the twelve democratic ministers on February 20, 1948, and stayed in the Communist-dominated government, apparently out of loyalty to Beneš. His position was becoming intolerable, however.

On the morning of March 10, Masaryk was found dead, lying in the courtyard of the Foreign Ministry underneath the bathroom window of his third floor residential apartment. His heel bones were shattered, and the head was closest to the wall, an extremely rare position for someone to land in who has jumped, because of the distribution of body weight. The police doctor's report stated, " . . . The rectum is soiled with excrement. Otherwise there are no marks on the body that would point to violence." The apartment upstairs was in a great state of disorder, with tables and lamps knocked over, sheets pulled off the bed, and pillows were found in the bathroom. About a dozen cigarette butts of different brands were in the ashtray. Within six hours, the government announced that Masaryk had committed suicide and the case was closed. Although a number of Czech *émigrés* insisted that Masaryk had been murdered, the facts never went beyond these simple ones.

During the "Prague Spring" of 1968, though, the case was officially reopened, and Sterling began an investigation of her own. The police doctor and a major in the security forces allegedly responsible for the murder had both died under suspicious circumstances within six months of Masaryk. The butler, with twenty-eight years of service with the Masaryks, said that he had never seen Jan's room in the state in which it was found on March 10, and Masaryk's nieces reported that he was unhappy, but not morbidly depressed in the days preceding his death. Furthermore, there were a number of indications that Masaryk had made plans to flee, including notes sent out to the West and conversations with Beneš. Since the President's house was apparently bugged, there was every possibility that both the Czech and Russian secret services were aware of his plans, giving them a motive to silence a man whose resistance from the West could be extremely embarrassing and even dangerous. It was very easy to enter the Foreign Ministry, which was not well-guarded; and to complete Sterling's line of reasoning, she shows that there was a group of Czech security agents directly controlled by the Russian NKVD. Therefore, in addition to the odd position of the body and the disarray of the bedroom, there were both motive and method for murder, with little evidence pointing towards suicide.

Sterling then went to London, where she questioned Scotland Yard's chief doctor. Although he could not talk in an official capacity, he made a number of interesting statements. In forty years, he had never come across a suicide who lost control of his sphincters before death, a fact confirmed by the chief physician of the Italian criminal division. Loss of sphincter control was also much rarer in moments of great terror than one might imagine. There was one form of death, however, in which this loss was rather common, death by suffocation. Naturally enough, Sterling remembered the two soiled pillows found in the bathroom. As a result, she concludes that two Czechs, acting under Russian orders, broke into Masaryk's apartment late during the night of March 9, and tried to convince him to kill himself (hence the dozen cigarette butts). This tactic failed, so a violent struggle broke out; Masaryk was wrestled into the bathroom where he was pinned down in the bathtub and murdered by forcing the pillows over his face. He was then thrown out the window to make it look like suicide. This exciting book makes clear the lengths to which the Communists were willing to go in order to rule Czechoslovakia. — *S.V.D.*

Additional Recommended Reading

Bruce-Lockhart, Robert H. *Jan Masaryk*. New York: Philosophical Library, 1950. A personal memoir by an important British diplomat who knew Masaryk from the 1920's to his death.

Friedman, Otto. *The Break-up of Czech Democracy*. London: Victor Gollancz, 1950. A brief account of the Communist takeover by a pro-Western Czech.

Korbel, Josef. *The Communist Subversion of Czechoslovakia, 1938-1948: The Failure of Coexistence*. Princeton, N.J.: Princeton University Press, 1959. A comprehensive study of the activities of the Communists written by the Czech Ambassador to the United Nations who resigned in 1948.

Ripka, Hubert. *Czechoslovakia Enslaved*. London: Victor Gollancz, 1950. An insider's viewpoint by one of the twelve democratic ministers.

Rohan, Bedrich. *What Happened in Czechoslovakia*. Prague: Orbis, 1948. An account written by a Communist, including many speeches and documents of the Communist Party.

PROCLAMATION OF AN INDEPENDENT JEWISH STATE

Type of event: Political: affirmation of nationhood
Time: May 14, 1948
Locale: Palestine

Principal personages:
THEODOR HERZL (1860-1904), the founder of Zionism
DAVID BEN-GURION (1886-1973), first Prime Minister of the State of Israel
CHAIM WEIZMANN (1874-1952), a principal modern proponent of Zionism and first President of the State of Israel
COUNT FOLKE BERNADOTTE AF WISBORG (1895-1948), United Nations mediator, murdered by Jewish terrorists

Summary of Event

With the Proclamation of an Independent Jewish State on May 14, 1948, for the first time since the destruction of the Temple and the dispersion of the Jews, Jewishness became a nationality as well as a religion. By the law of return every Jew had a right to Israeli citizenship. Thus the State of Israel had become a solution to the problem of the Jews whose history since the dispersion had been one of trauma and tragedy. In medieval England the Jews had been expelled; in fifteenth century Spain they had endured the same fate. In most cases, Jews could not achieve political equality in the lands where they settled, and they lacked a land which they could call their own and to which they could return.

With the coming of the Enlightenment and the French Revolution, it seemed, at least to Western European Jews, that the promise of full emancipation would soon be fulfilled. This emancipation would solve the problem of the Jews because they would cease to be a separate nation, even theoretically, and would merely be citizens of a particular country to whom they owed full political allegiance: Frenchmen or Germans who happened to be Jews. Judaism would thus become no more than a religion.

In the East, the Jews had a different problem. In Russia or Poland there was no hope of emancipation. Relentless anti-Semitism, official and unofficial, dogged Jewish footsteps. In this atmosphere of constant oppression and cyclical pogroms, the idea of Zion, a land to which Jews could return, had its authentic birth in the writings of Theodor Herzl (1896). It would be a land where Hebrew was the spoken language, a land sustained by Jewish laborers and farmers as well as Jewish professionals. At first this country was not necessarily Palestine, although, of course, Palestine had a certain mythic attraction. South America was suggested; a country in Africa was under serious consideration. In the meantime Palestine was settled with Jews and land was bought against the possibility that Palestine would be Zion.

At last, during World War I, it

seemed possible to negotiate an agreement with the British for a Jewish homeland in Palestine. This led to the Balfour Declaration of 1917. The tone of the Declaration was moderate:

> His Majesty's Government view with favour the establishment in Palestine of a national home for the Jewish people, and will use their best endeavours to facilitate the achievement of this object, it being clearly understood that nothing shall be done which may prejudice the civil and religious rights of existing non-Jewish communities in Palestine, or the rights and political status enjoyed by Jews in any other country.

After the war, Britain was given Palestine as a mandate under the League of Nations, raising the hopes of Jews that they would have a homeland at last. Then, in a series of White Papers (1922, 1930, 1939), Britain made clear its intention of renouncing in fact the promises of the Balfour Declaration. Moreover, the accession after World War II of the Labour Party, which had previously been sympathetic to Jewish interests, provided no discontinuity with the anti-Zionist policies of Winston Churchill's government that was in power during most of the war. It was clear that Britain saw its national interest as aligned to the Arab cause. Britain in fact demonstrated its desire to give up its mandate, something it did in May of 1948, leaving the Jews to the mercy of invading Arab armies.

The history of the mandate had emphasized the Jewish folly of relying on Britain, or any one power, to guarantee the safety of a Jewish national home; Nazi Germany had likewise underlined their folly in relying on the nations of the world in concert. Hitler's solution to the Jewish problem made no distinction between emancipated Western Jews and unemancipated Eastern ones; his "final solution" made a mockery of such distinctions by dictating the murder of *all* Jews. In the 1930's World Jewry could see that the survival of European Jews depended on mass immigration to Palestine and to friendly states. This humanitarian imperative, however, was rejected by Britain and by those countries, like the United States, where Jews might conceivably have found a home. Faced with Hitler's hatred on the one hand, and world indifference on the other, World Jewry realized the absolute need for a Jewish homeland, a sovereign state where Judaism was not only a religion, but a nationality.

At the end of World War II, the British and the Arabs maintained their opposition to this solution. Well before the British withdrew their mandate, in 1948, it was clear that the Arabs would not accept the 1947 United Nations partition of Palestine. In the face of Arab raids intended to disrupt communications, British support of the Arab cause, and their own lack of arms, Palestinian Jewry attempted to defend its virtually indefensible borders and to survive. In the midst of this struggle, and faced with the possibility of imminent destruction by invading Arab armies, they proclaimed the birth of Israel on May 14, 1948, with David Ben-Gurion as Prime Minister and Dr. Chaim Weizmann, the venerable leader of the world Zionist movement, as President.

The proclamation of an independent Israel was the signal for a combined attack by the Arab states. After initial setbacks and mixed success, the Israelis were able to create a national army and to arm it, to an extent, with modern weapons. As a result of these efforts, the tide of battle gradually turned, and, by the end of 1948, Israeli forces spearheaded through Southern Palestine and even into Egypt itself. In a later thrust, an Israeli column drove down to the Red Sea, securing the port of Eilat. During one of several ceasefires, Count Folke Bernadotte Af Wisborg, the United Nations mediator, was assassinated by Zionist terrorists. Finally, by July, 1949, armistice agreements were signed with the Arab states. As subsequent wars have demonstrated, however, the state of Israel continues to be unacceptable to neighboring Arab states. Only by the assertion of sovereignty, backed by force of arms and international diplomacy, has Israel continued to exist as a state.

Pertinent Literature

Lorch, Netanel. *The Edge of the Sword: Israel's War of Independence.* New York: G. P. Putnam's Sons, 1961.

The Edge of the Sword is a military history of the first Arab-Israeli War—Israel's War of Independence—written by a man who was an officer in Israel's Defense Army at the time of the conflict. The book concentrates on the strategy and tactics of the war, but tries to place these matters in a political and global context. Inevitably, the story of the war is told from the Israeli point of view.

The book is mainly a narrative about the progress of the war. By 1947 the British were no longer supportive of the Jewish state. The Arabs, of course, had never accepted this idea. It was no surprise, therefore, when they refused to accept the United Nations partition of Palestine, promulgated November 29, 1947. As the British rapidly concluded their mandate, the Arabs raided with the intent of disrupting Jewish communications. This was a good strategy, since the Partition made those lines of communication very tenuous, and in fact the borders of the proposed "Jewish State" were not viable or defensible. In these raids, the Arabs were helped by British sympathy and even, on occasion, by British aid.

However, it was soon possible for the Jews to take the initiative. In April-May of 1948, Operation Nachshon opened the road to Jerusalem, and captured Tiberius, Haifa, Safed, and Jaffa. In the midst of this operation, the State of Israel was proclaimed, setting off, on the night of May 14, an invasion of five regular Arab armies and a host of guerrilla fighters. From this time until June 11—the date of the first truce—it was the Arab intent to overwhelm the infant state by a war of lightning speed. In this they did not succeed. The first truce ended on July 9 and was followed by a period of fighting until October 22, when there was a second ceasefire. On December 22, fighting resumed. As 1948 wore on, Israeli victories became more numerous and Israeli military superiority ever clearer. On January 7, 1949, there was another, more permanent cease-fire which led to extended armistice negotiations. Finally, on July 20, the last of the Armistice Agreements was signed between the Jews and Arabs, ending the War of Independence.

Inconclusive fighting, truce, armistice—these terms typify the difficulties in mediating this conflict. The United Nations was dealing with two peoples at total loggerheads. The Israeli insistence on defensible borders was understandable, as was the Arab feeling that Israel ought not to exist at all. Such quarrels, in fact, cannot be mediated. The first mediator, Count Folke Bernadotte Af Wisborg, was murdered by Jewish terrorists. His successor, Ralph Bunche, was seemingly more successful. Still, all of his efforts were only able to bring forth an armistice, not a real peace. In fact, to this day there is no real peace between Israel and the Arab States. Israel's borders have become more and more defensible—but as a result of conquest, not mediation.

While it is well to avoid the pro-Israeli bias of the book, it nevertheless seems necessary to note the audacity of those who first affirmed the state of Israel, a nation without armed forces and without defensible borders, threatened on all sides but the sea by hostile armies. Coupled with the audacity of national affirmation is the fact of survival in this war, despite large handicaps. The reasons for this survival are not entirely clear, but several factors ought to be mentioned. First, the Arabs lacked unified command and were perhaps overconfident. Also, two truces prolonged the war, which may well have been to Israel's advantage, since during the prolongation the Israelis transformed the Haganah into Zahal, a national army, at the same time incorporating or suppressing the terrorist Irgun and the Stern group. Moreover, there was time to obtain weapons and equipment for this force (weapons and equipment that the Arabs largely had at the beginning of the conflict). A final factor, perhaps, was the realization on the part of the Israelis that defeat must be equated with destruction. The Arabs could survive defeat, but not the Jews. It was their last chance.

Halpern, Ben. *The Idea of the Jewish State*. Cambridge, Mass.: Harvard University Press, 1969.

The Idea of the Jewish State is an intellectual history of Zionism, the search for a spiritual and political homeland for the Jewish people. In this carefully thought-out and well-documented study, Ben Halpern traces the history of the Zionist idea from its beginnings in early nineteenth century Christian proto-Zionism to the present-day creation and defense of the State of Israel. In tracing this history, the author highlights the problem of the Jewish people since the dispersion (Diaspora), and the anomaly of Israel as a national state.

Zionism had its vague beginnings in traditional Judaism and Christian proto-Zionism. Traditionally, Zion was an idea, a symbol of hope to all Jews. It was not and was never meant to be a real place or country. Christian proto-Zionists felt Zion should be a place, but got nowhere in convincing European nations to found a Jewish state.

Only with the advent of Theodor Herzl was Zionism welded into an international political movement. Even so, the movement had its Jewish enemies; traditional Jews never wavered in their opposition to political Zionism. Western Jews felt that the solution to the problem of the Jews was full emancipation in their particular countries, not immigration to another land; they believed that Zionism, in its insistence that Jewishness was a nationality, retarded emancipation and encouraged anti-Semitism. Only when Hitler united World Jewry by his implacable hatred was it clear to everyone concerned that the Jews did indeed need a national homeland.

In Halpern's history, one of the persistent themes is that since the Diaspora there has always been a problem of the Jews. Surely it is one of the great tragic ironies of history that a people at the fountainhead of Western culture, a people who have contributed so much to that culture, have endured a fate of discrimination, oppression, and mass murder. The two rational solutions to the problem—emancipation and the creation of the Jewish state—always had seemed within the realm of probability. But the first was not to be, since after the Holocaust it was impossible for any Jew to believe wholly in emancipation, and the second came into being only in the face of Arab hatred and world indifference.

Furthermore, the state of Israel itself is an anomaly having continual problems with the international community and World Jewry. Unlike most nationalist movements, Zionism is not concerned with minority rights within a larger political context, such as the minority rights of the Basques in Spain. On the contrary, the Jews were a dispersed people, finally forced to assert their ownership of a country where they had only tenuous historical rights, and neighboring enemies with competing claims. Little wonder, then, that the international community represented first by the League of Nations and then by the United Nations, could not solve the problem of Israel. The proclamation of the sovereignty of Israel was therefore not an assertion of right in defiance of other possible solutions, but a decision made in the face of the failure of all other possible solutions.

Despite its status as a Jewish state, Israel continues to have problems with World Jewry. It relies on the financial and moral support of World Jewry, especially of American Jews, but it remains a bastion of orthodox Judaism—Conservative and Reform—to which the majority of American Jews adhere. In addition, Israel, as a small state jockeying for position in the community of nations, has very limited powers as a defender of Jews. For instance, by permitting unlimited Jewish immigration it can be a refuge to Soviet Jews who are allowed to emigrate, but it cannot defend effectively the rights of those who remain in the Soviet Union. Finally, the founding of the State of Israel has not halted anti-Semitism; in fact, it has in many cases exacerbated   it. — *A.G.G.*

Additional Recommended Reading

Ben-Gurion, David. *Israel: A Personal History*. New York: Funk and Wagnalls, 1971. A personal account of the conflict by Israel's first Prime Minister.

Collins, Larry and Dominique Lapeirre. *O Jerusalem!* New York: Simon and Schuster, 1972. A minute-by-minute account, based on numerous interviews, of the fight for Jerusalem.

Hertzberg, Arthur, ed. *The Zionist Idea: A Historical Analysis and Reader*. Garden City, N.Y.: Doubleday & Company, 1959. A reader containing excerpts from Zionist precursors in the mid-nineteenth century through Herzl and others and on to more modern documents.

Keller, Werner. *Diaspora: The Post-Biblical History of the Jews*. New York: Harcourt, Brace and World, 1969. A chronicle of the achievements in politics, philosophy, the arts, and other spheres of human endeavor of the Jews of Europe, Africa, and Asia.

EXPULSION OF YUGOSLAVIA FROM THE COMINFORM

Type of event: Diplomatic: severance of ties between the Communist bloc and a member state
Time: June 28, 1948
Locale: Eastern Europe

Principal personages:

JOSEPH STALIN (IOSIF VISSARIONOVICH DZHUGASHVILI) (1879-1953), Dictator of the U.S.S.R., 1924-1953

JOSIP BROZ TITO (1892-   ), Marshal of the Yugoslav Army, Prime Minister of Yugoslavia, 1945-1953

GEORGI DIMITROV (1882-1949), Prime Minister of Bulgaria, 1946-1949

ENVER HOXHA (1908-   ), General Secretary of the Albanian Communist Party, 1943-

STRETEN ZHUYOVICH-TSRNI, Stalinist agent on Yugoslav Communist Party Central Committee

ANDREYA HEBRANG, a member of Yugoslav Communist Party Central Committee, accused Stalinist agent

Summary of Event

In 1945 Joseph Stalin appeared to have no more loyal ally and devoted Communist supporter than Josip Broz Tito, the leader of Yugoslavia's wartime resistance. Marshal Tito had become the leader of Yugoslavia's Communist Party with Stalin's sponsorship in the 1930's. Now after the war Tito quickly began to turn the Yugoslavia he led into a socialist state modeled on the Soviet Union, and became one of the most vociferous antagonists of Moscow's former Western allies in the growing postwar rift among the victors. There was even some talk of Yugoslavia's becoming a constituent republic of the U.S.S.R.

However, relations between Moscow and Belgrade were not as smooth as they appeared. For one thing, Stalin's support of Tito's movement during the war was less than the Yugo-

slav leader had desired. For many months the Soviet Union had acquiesced as the Allies backed Tito's non-Communist resistance rivals in the Balkan country. Marshal Tito, with some justice, believed that he himself had earned the backing of the United Nations in spite of, not because of, Moscow's actions. Second, by the famous percentages agreement worked out for Eastern Europe by Stalin and British Prime Minister Winston Churchill in Moscow in 1944, Soviet influence in Yugoslavia was to be shared with the West on a fifty-fifty basis. Even if neither side intended this agreement to have the significance which it had at first glance, when news of it was leaked in the Western press, Tito felt that Stalin had betrayed him.

On the other hand, Stalin did not trust Tito, despite the latter's genuine loyalty to Moscow and Communist ideology. The Soviet leader was more interested in creating a worldwide base of support with Communist parties dependent upon him personally. Tito had too much potentiality for independence, since, as the leader of a popular movement he had come to power without the aid of the Red Army. Precisely for this reason Stalin was unable to establish the kind of relationship between Moscow and Belgrade that he was able to bring about in other Eastern European capitals under Communist control.

One of the instruments which Stalin planned to use to control these new allies was the Communist Information Bureau (Cominform), established, ironically, in Belgrade in September, 1947. Members included Yugoslavia, Bulgaria, Poland, Hungary, Rumania, Czechoslovakia, and, of course, the Soviet Union. (Albania, whose Communist Party and government was linked to Yugoslavia, was not a member, but Italy's Communist Party participated.) Another method of Kremlin control was a series of binational economic agreements with the new governments of Eastern Europe—agreements heavily weighted in favor of the Soviet Union, although providing a minimum framework for economic cooperation in the region.

Stalin, seeking to monitor Tito's position in Yugoslavia, found agents among the latter's associates, including Streten Zhuyovich-Tsrni and, according to some authorities, Andreya Hebrang, two members of the inner circles of the Yugoslav Communist Party's Central Committee. Meanwhile, Soviet economic penetration, cultural domination, and political interference caused a sharp reaction in Belgrade. In January, 1948, Tito demoted the accused Stalin agent Hebrang from his position as Chairman of the Economic Planning Commission. This, together with other signs of Yugoslav resistance and stubbornness, caused Stalin to launch an active but nonpublic, campaign against Tito the next month. Moscow refused to conclude a trade treaty which Tito wanted; moreover, the Kremlin ordered the recall of Soviet military and civilian advisers from Yugoslavia. The Yugoslav Communist Party's Central Committee for its part resolved to resist the Soviet pressure.

Throughout the spring of 1948, Belgrade and Moscow exchanged communications justifying their positions in the still secret dispute. If there was any intention on either side to heal the rift by this correspondence, it was a dismal failure, since the exchange had quite the opposite effect and made the break irreparable. Moscow accused Belgrade of being both Trotskyist and Menshevik at the same time—that is, practicing both left-wing and right-wing deviations from Communism. Tito proclaimed Yugoslavia's loyalty and accused Stalin of interfering in his country's internal affairs.

Moscow also forced the other countries of the Cominform to denounce Tito's deviation. While the Kremlin's efforts were completely successful in this regard, there appears to have been some reluctance on the part of Georgi Dimitrov, the Prime Minister of neighboring Bulgaria and, because of his famous defiance of the Nazis at the Reichstag fire trial in 1933, an outstanding Communist hero in his own right. Tito and Dimitrov were proposing a Balkan confederation, to which Stalin gave nominal support but in fact mistrusted because of its potential as competition in the East European Communist sphere. On June 28, the Cominform officially expelled Yugoslavia for its "unsocialist behavior," condemning in particular the recent arrests of Hebrang and Zhuyovich-Tsrni. The date of the expulsion is especially noteworthy, as both the Serbian national holiday, commemorating the fourteenth century defeat of the country by Ottoman Turkey, and the anniversary of the assassination of Archduke Franz Ferdinand of Austria by a Serb nationalist in 1914.

That summer at the Yugoslav Communist Party Congress Tito brought the dispute into the open, and a three-front war of nerves began between Yugoslavia on one side and the Soviet Union and her allies on the other. On the economic front the Cominform countries began to break off their trade agreements with Belgrade. This in fact began with Albania, the one Communist–ruled state which was not in the Cominform.

Albania's leader, Enver Hoxha, however, aligned himself with Stalin in order to overthrow Yugoslav control of his party and country. Territorial disputes between these two Balkan nations made Belgrade's confrontation with Albania in many ways even more hostile and lasting than that with Moscow.

On the political front, the Cominform countries began to sponsor anti-Tito Yugoslav Communists, inviting them to conferences in their countries, and pointing them out as martyrs of genuine Socialism. On the military front, Yugoslavia suffered minor territorial incursions on its Albanian and Bulgarian borders, but while the country prepared for a major Soviet invasion, none came about.

Tito weathered this ostracism by turning partially to the West and by developing a more "liberal" brand of socialism at home. His defiance of Stalin also gained him national support. After Stalin died in 1953, Tito continued his independent path and indeed became a leader of the "nonaligned bloc." He resumed relations with the Soviet Union and yet continued as one of the world's most influential statesmen.

Pertinent Literature

Dedijer, Vladimir. *The Battle Stalin Lost: Memoirs of Yugoslavia, 1948-1953*. New York: The Viking Press, 1970.

Vladimir Dedijer is a former colonel in the Yugoslav partisan movement, an associate of Tito, and former Director of Information in Yugoslavia's postwar government; he is also a professional historian. These facts alone make this work an important contribution to the study of the Moscow-Belgrade split—not so much because of any startling revelations it contains, for much of the ground covered has been presented many times before, but because it gives a Yugoslav inside view of occurrences by an author with the critical ability to evaluate these events. We must hasten to recognize that this does not necessarily mean an impartial view, for Dedijer does not claim impartiality. He has been a semiofficial chronicler and apologist scholar for Tito's brand of socialism, and among his works is an authorized biography of the Yugoslav leader.

The Battle Stalin Lost originated as a series of articles written for the Slovenian press (in Yugoslavia) warning of the dangers of neo-Stalinism in the Soviet Union after the 1968 Czechoslovak invasion. Dedijer's major purpose in this volume is to show that Yugoslavia's socialism is the true form and that Stalin's was deviant.

Despite the subtitle it is not really a memoir of those years; it is the history of the split with some anecdotes and tales of Dedijer's personal experiences before, during, and after the years under consideration. Dedijer professes to be a loyal Titoist, which he is. He also professes that he, along with Tito, Milovan Djilas, Eduard Kardelj, Aleksandur Rankovic, and other members of Tito's inner circle, were loyal Stalinists as well. He records their shock when they first learned that Stalin regarded them as dissidents who had committed some unknown crime against socialism. There was further shock when they realized that in order to defend themselves they would have to oppose not some recognizable enemy—Fascists or capitalists—but the motherland of socialism itself. Nevertheless, Tito made the commitment, and

his followers stood by him.

The author traces the sources of the conflict back to the purges of the 1930's in which many Yugoslav Communists suffered. Then during the war there was another great dispute between Moscow and Tito's partisan headquarters as to whether the Yugoslav Communists should put aside their revolutionary goals and join with the Serbian monarchist resistance simply to drive out the Fascist invaders. Stalin desired this course of action, but Tito vehemently opposed it, believing that success could come only if the partisans fought the former Yugoslav ruling class along with the foreign occupiers.

After the war it became apparent that Stalin wished to gain control over Yugoslavia principally through economic means. Dedijer recounts the establishment of joint Soviet-Yugoslav corporations in the Balkan country and describes in detail how their contracts favored the Soviets. He points to the proposed Soviet-Yugoslav bank as being particularly dangerous to Yugoslav postwar recovery. When the Yugoslavs resisted, Stalin used all methods at his command short of war to bring Tito down— economic blockade, public humiliation before the Communist movement, ideological denunciation, espionage and infiltration, and so forth.

Dedijer believed that Stalin wanted to destroy Tito as the first step in his drive to bring all of the Eastern European Communist governments under his control. By dealing with the strongest leader, he would render the rest easier to master. In fact, though Tito resisted, the other parties were not in so fortunate a position, and in the wake of the Soviet-Yugoslav conflict a series of purges raged through the Cominform parties. Dedijer indicates that Tito did receive confidential support from Communist leaders both in the East, particularly Bulgaria's Dimitrov, and in the West, for example, France's Maurice Thorez and Italy's Palmiro Togliatti. Even in the Soviet Union's Communist circles, Dedijer claims that Tito had admirers. He recalls that when Tito visited Moscow after Stalin had died, his former friend Marshal Kiment Voroshilov exclaimed to him, weeping, "What a dunce I am. What stupidities I had to mouth at Stalin's orders! How ashamed I am! Forgive me, please."

In the final analysis, Dedijer believed, Stalin did not invade the country because of the risk of world war; but he gives full credit for Tito's victory to the backing he received from Yugoslav people of all nationalities within the country.

Campbell, John C. *Tito's Separate Road: America and Yugoslavia in World Politics.* New York: Harper & Row Publishers, 1967.

This volume was published for the prestigious Council on Foreign Relations as one of its "Policy Book Series" whose purpose is to inform the American public on world affairs. The author of the present volume is a distinguished scholar of the diplomacy of Southeast Europe; he is a former state department official and, at the time of writing *Tito's Separate Road*, was a senior fellow of the Council.

The book is far more extensive than its subtitle implies. In fact, it is a general description of the consequences of Tito's independent Communist path in Europe and in the world at large. The underlying theme of the book, however, is an examination of past American relations with Yugoslavia since 1948 and Professor Campbell's recommendations in 1967 of what future American policy towards Tito should be.

Campbell views the split between Tito and Stalin as resulting from Tito's refusal to bend to Stalin's will. "The fact remains that he was kicked out [of the Cominform] because, as the record shows, he would not take orders. It was his defiance that brought about the split." Furthermore, Campbell concludes that this was a daring act. There was no guarantee that Tito would be able to maintain this rebellion against the "fatherland of socialism." However, the decision of the United States to support Tito in his struggle against the Kremlin was an important factor in sustaining Yugoslavia's independence. This policy, originating with the Truman Administration, was continued in that of Eisenhower. Even though John Foster Dulles, the Republican Secretary of State in the 1950's, was staunchly anti-Communist and regarded neutrality in the Cold War as immoral, the benefits to American policy of having a dissident Marxist in Eastern Europe were so great that support for Tito continued.

Campbell traces the maintenance of Tito's independent path even after the death of Stalin and its resulting effect on Yugoslavia and Eastern Europe. He analyzes particularly the advantages that Tito's rebellion had for the United States, and he praises the wisdom of diplomats in supporting the Yugoslav leader. The author examines Tito's role as a leader of the nonaligned or Third World, viewing this as a consequence of the split. He also examines the effect of the split on the other countries of Eastern Europe. Campbell believes that Tito's defiance of Moscow in 1948 was one of the principal reasons that several of the countries of the region were later able to lessen their ties with the Soviet Union. He sees the independent stance of Rumania in the 1960's as a particularly cogent example of a nation directly benefiting from Tito's example.

Campbell also examines some of the effects of Titoism on Yugoslavia's domestic policies. He notes that there exist some economic stagnation and political repression, but that Belgrade's detachment from Moscow has allowed for economic experimentation, some of which even has spread to other countries, notably, for a time, to Poland in the late 1950's. Yugoslavia's most troublesome domestic problem, however, remains national rivalry and hostility among the peoples who make up the state. Campbell believes that the force of Tito's reputation and personality has up to the time of his writing (1967) kept this potentially dangerous issue from causing a major upheaval, but that Tito's successors will have a more difficult, but not unsolvable task.

Campbell concludes that the interests of the United States lie in the futher support of Yugoslavia's independence, particularly through trade. Furthermore, he writes that the Yugoslav policy of the United States and of her European allies should be part of an overall strategy for bringing Eastern Europe into the European community of nations. He recommends three main lines of policy. First, we must pursue greater unity in Western Europe. Second, the nations of the West should seek all sorts of cultural and economic ties with those of Eastern Europe. Finally, efforts at *détente* with those countries, including the Soviet Union, should not cease. Campbell sees Yugoslavia as occupying a key place in putting this strategy into practice precisely because of the country's divergence from Moscow in 1948. — *F.B.C.*

Additional Recommended Reading

Farrell, R. Barry. *Jugoslavia and the Soviet Union, 1948-1956: An Analysis with Documents*. Hamden, Conn.: Shoe String Press, 1956. A scholarly examination of the events with copies of the most important documents translated into English.

Wolff, Robert Lee. *The Balkans in Our Time*. New York: W. W. Norton and Company, 1967. Contains a good readable account of the events placed in the context of the twentieth century history of the Balkans.

Adamic, Louis. *The Eagle and the Roots*. Garden City, N.Y.: Doubleday & Company, 1952. Although this book does not deal with the post war period, it is a readable, sympathetic account of Tito's life, particularly during World War II, by a popular

Slovenian-American author and follower of Tito.

Armstrong, Hamilton Fish. *Tito and Goliath*. New York: McGraw-Hill Book Company, 1974. A popular account by a British author who has written several books about the Balkans.

Auty, Phyllis A. *Tito: A Biography*. New York: McGraw-Hill Book Company, 1970. A scholarly biography by one of Britain's most respected authorities on modern Yugoslavia.

Ulam, Adam B. *Titoism and the Cominform*. Cambridge, Mass.: Harvard University Press, 1952. An analysis by one of America's foremost scholars of Communist ideology.

Rusinow, Dennison. *The Yugoslav Experiment, 1948-1974*. Berkeley: University of California Press, 1977. A recent analysis of the results of Tito's separate path by an expert scholar and observer of contemporary Yugoslavia.

THE CREATION OF THE FEDERAL REPUBLIC OF GERMANY AND THE GERMAN DEMOCRATIC REPUBLIC

Type of event: Diplomatic: shaping of postwar Germany
Time: September 21 and October 7, 1949
Locale: Bonn and Berlin

Principal personages:

LUCIUS DU BIGNON CLAY (1897-   ), General and military governor of the American occupation zone, 1947-1949

JAMES FRANCIS BYRNES (1879-1972), United States Secretary of State, 1945-1947

KONRAD ADENAUER (1876-1967), Chancellor of the Federal Republic of Germany and Chairman of the Christian Democratic Union, 1949-1963

THEODOR HEUSS (1884-1963), President of the Federal Republic of Germany and Chairman of the Free Democratic Party, 1949-1959

WALTER ULBRICHT (1893-1973), head of the ruling Socialist Unity Party of East Germany

Summary of Event

The formal establishment of the Federal Republic of Germany (FRG) and the German Democratic Republic (GRD) occurred on September 21 and October 7, 1949, respectively. The creation of these two separate German states was the ultimate consequence of the Cold War between the United States and the Soviet Union which evolved soon after the defeat of Nazi Germany. The division of Germany came to symbolize the division of the world into Eastern and Western blocs and represented one of the most serious threats to world peace.

At the close of World War II, the Allied Powers had concerned themselves only in a limited way with the future of Germany. In effect, they had decided to divide the prewar territory of the German Reich into eight separate parts. The most important were the four zones of occupation. The capital city of Berlin was given separate special status, placed under four-power control and divided into four occupation sectors. East Prussia was divided, the northern half given to the Soviet Union and the southern half placed under Polish administration, along with all the territory east of a line formed by the Oder and the western Neisse rivers. In addition, the Saar region was given special status and placed under French control. Regarding the control machinery for the occupation zones, it was stipulated that each Allied commander in chief would function as military governor in his respective occupation zone. Matters of common concern to all of occupied Germany were to be dealt with by an Allied Control Council. These arrangements were intended to be temporary, pending more detailed and permanent agreements for the uniform political and economic administration of Germany. However, such agreements never materialized.

At the Potsdam Conference in the summer of 1945, the victorious Allies reiterated their intentions for defeated Germany. These included complete disarmament and demilitarization; the eradication of all vestiges of Nazism and the restructuring of German political life along democratic lines; the destruction of the industrial cartels and monopolies; and the extraction of reparations. At this time, major differences regarding the future of Germany between the United States and Great Britain on one side and the Soviet Union on the other were already apparent. Disagreement over the issue of reparations was the major reason for the failure to reach a permanent agreement on all of occupied Germany. The United States and Great Britain were becoming apprehensive about Soviet power extending deep into central Europe, and they envisioned a revived Germany serving as a barrier to the expansion of Communism. Conversely, the Soviet Union was unwilling to relinquish its claim to participate in the determination of policies regarding the western zones and to face the prospect of having the resources of that area turned against it. In the end, it was agreed that each occupying power could draw reparations from its own zone and the Soviet Union, in view of the greater industrial wealth in the western zones, would receive from these zones an additional twenty-five percent of the industrial equipment considered unessential for the German peace economy. The provisions were highly ambiguous and the subject of considerable polemics between the occupying powers. A major item of contention was whether the Soviet Union's share of reparations should be derived from the removal of plants existing at the end of the war or from current production. The United States refused to allow payments from current production.

The functioning of the Allied Control Council came to an end when the Soviet commandant walked out of the Control Council on March 20, 1948, and shortly thereafter the Soviet Military Administration began to impose a blockade on Berlin. As the hostilities and suspicions between the powers mounted, the Soviets used their control over the western military and civilian traffic to and from Berlin to retaliate for what they considered hostile acts. In this case, it was the introduction into West Berlin of the German mark, the new currency of the western zones. On July 24, the Soviets halted all rail and road traffic with the West. The Berlin blockade was the most serious crisis of the evolving Cold War. The United States responded by supplying the daily needs of the western sectors through the most massive airlift in history, for a period of eleven months. The consequence was the definite split of Berlin. The sobering crisis also had the effect of ending the stubborn French opposition to the creation of a West German government. Moreover, the path was clear for twelve nations to respond to the United States initiatives and to negotiate the North Atlantic Pact, signed on April 4, 1949.

The United States and Great Britain had already agreed to an economic fusion of their zones as early as December, 1946. The area, known as Bizonia, was to become self-sustaining in three years and thus reduce occupation costs. With the assistance of selected German leaders, an administrative machinery was established in Frankfurt. By 1947 an Economic Council was in existence, the members of which were selected by the popular branches of the newly established provincial legislatures within Bizonia. This body could adopt and promulgate ordinances, with the approval of an Anglo-American Bipartite Board. Soon an executive committee and a German high court were added to the Economic Council. Thus, the organs of a central German government were gradually emerging for the American and British zones. The growing split between the Soviet Union and the three western Allies ultimately induced France to join in the establishment of a central German government for all three western zones.

The United States had been on public record since September, 1946, when Secretary of State James F. Byrnes declared that the United States would grant the German people the right to manage their own affairs, as soon as they were able to do so in a democratic manner. This matter was more deliberately taken up at the meeting of the Council of Ministers in London, in February, 1948. In addition to the three western Allies, Belgium, the Netherlands, and Luxembourg were participating in the deliberations. At this time, basic agreement on the fusion of the three western zones was achieved. As the four-power control apparatus had come to a complete standstill in mid-1948, the western Allies proceeded with specific trizonal arrangements. The heads of the various German provincial governments were empowered by the military governors to convene a constituent assembly for the purpose of drafting a democratic, federal constitution. The German assembly, apprehensive about finalizing the division of Germany and desirous to give the formal arrangements a kind of provisional status, called itself "Parliamentary Council" and the new constitution came to be referred to as "Basic Law." The composition of the Parliamentary Council reflected the proportionate strength of the political parties. Konrad Adenauer, the Chairman of the Christian Democratic Union (CDU), was elected the presiding officer.

On May 23, 1949, the Basic Law was formally adopted. The Allies approved it with some reservations and negotiated for the arrangements paving the way for civilian control. Residual occupation powers were exercized by a new Allied High Commission. Following the first postwar elections, the new Parliament convened in Bonn for its inaugural session on September 7, 1949. A federal convention elected Theodor Heuss, the Chairman of the Free Democratic Party (FDP), as Federal President. Heuss then nominated Konrad Adenauer for Federal Chancellor. Adenauer was elected by the Parliament with a one-vote margin and formed a coalition government. Thus, all the basic arrangements being attended to, the Federal Republic of Germany was officially launched in a formal ceremony on September 21, 1949.

The Soviet Union strongly and bitterly protested the establishment of the West German state. However, in its zone fundamental societal changes had begun to be implemented, with the objective of eliminating all aspects of capitalism and creating a socialist society. The Soviet Military Administration had for some time permitted the formation of German central organs. These were controlled by the Communist-dominated Socialist Unity Party (SED), under the effective leadership of Walter Ulbricht. The Soviet Union was, therefore, able to follow suit quickly in the formal division of Germany. It authorized the drafting of a constitution for an East German state. On October 7, 1949, a so-called German People's Council convened in Berlin and voted unanimously to transform itself into the provisional People's Chamber of the German Democratic Republic and adopted the new constitution, thereby formally launching the GDR.

Pertinent Literature

Gimbel, John. *The American Occupation of Germany: Politics and the Military, 1945-1949.* Stanford, Calif.: Stanford University Press, 1968.

John Gimbel's excellent study of the implementation of American policies toward occupied Germany enhances an understanding of the developments leading up to the creation of the two German states. The reader is made aware of the broad range of interests and objectives pursued by the United States. The American military government was directed to follow through with the punitive measures agreed to in the wartime conferences and at Potsdam. Denazification, demilitarization, and democratization of the Germans were high on the list of priorities. At the same time, concern over national security increased and led to the determination to contain the spread of Communism. An economically rehabilitated Germany was to help deflect the perceived dangers. Gimbel notes that certain American interests were left unstated, but they may have assumed a higher priority than those officially enumerated. His study suggests, contrary to many tracts covering this period of American foreign policy, that there was a substantial continuity of American interests underlying the course of United States postwar policies toward defeated Germany.

The book traces the American occupation policies from the Potsdam Conference in 1945 to the establishment of the FRG. In exploiting the records and documents of the American military government, the various German provincial archives, and the parliamentary library in Bonn, Gimbel is able to point out discrepancies between the official policy and the views of those who were to carry it out. General Lucius D. Clay, the able and strong-willed military governor, tried to fulfill the chiefly punitive provisions of secret army directives and the Potsdam Agreement. However, the German realities gradually led him to press the top policy makers in Washington for revisions and to further German economic rehabilitation. Indeed, some of these very policy makers were shocked by the unbelievable destruction they encountered when they first set foot on German soil and became sympathetic to Clay's demand for a more flexible occupation policy. Clay clamored particularly for freedom of action to get German industries back into production and to prevent widespread hunger and unrest among the German people. Clay succesfully pressured for a reassessment and clarification of the original terms set for occupied Germany. He knew exactly what he wanted and how to get it, and, thus, had a tremendous impact on the shaping of United States postwar policies in Germany.

Clay's initiatives included halting the dismantling operations of German industrial plants and repudiating any further payments to the Soviet Union out of the American zone. He saw to the convening of a German provincial council, composed of the ministers-president of the various newly established provincial governments in the American zone. By the end of 1946, his program to establish a degree of local and provincial self-government, based on elections, constitutions, and the principle of political responsibility, had progressed significantly. Gimbel recalls the intense public interest in Germany,

which was seen as the key to European stability. Clay's analysis of the German problem had a direct bearing on the Marshall Plan. The denazification program, initially assuming a high priority, gradually came to be criticized as an impediment to economic recovery. Denazification, once pressed by the American military governor as a precondition for economic rehabilitation, was to come to a speedy conclusion as a precondition for economic recovery by March, 1948.

Gimbel provides some insight into the emerging German party-political scene. Fights between the two largest parties, the CDU and the Social Democratic Party (SPD), led by Kurt Schumacher, slowed and stalled the work for the creation of bizonal agencies. German leaders had serious reservations about the proposed central government. Understandably, they were also most reluctant to bring about a permanent split of Germany. The real momentum toward a West German government was touched off by the Berlin blockade. Clay succeeded in obtaining German cooperation for the creation of the bizonal governmental organs, which were to serve as a "magnet" for the remainder of occupied Germany to rally around and designed, in particular, to break French intransigence regarding a central West German government. At last, the London meeting of the Council of Foreign Ministers in 1948 prepared the groundwork for the creation of the FRG.

Hartmann, Frederick H. *Germany Between East and West: The Reunification Problem*. Englewood Cliffs, N.J.: Prentice-Hall, 1965.

The main portion of this slim volume focuses on the problems caused by the division of Germany and the numerous diplomatic attempts made by the Four Powers to settle some of the key issues. The analysis of the negotiations is preceded by a helpful, concisely written coverage of the background and the origin of the German problem. Frederick Hartmann believes very strongly that the German problem constitutes the most serious threat to world peace. Potential conflict over Germany would involve the American and Soviet forces directly, he writes, and it would mean all-out war with all the most devastating weaponry. A particularly volatile element of the German problem has been the special status of Berlin, which exists as an enclave about one hundred miles deep in East Germany. He reviews the two major crises which have involved this city, each entailing the extreme danger of escalating conflict between the superpowers.

With the benefit of hindsight and the knowledge of the signing of the Four Power agreement on Berlin in 1971 and the subsequent formal accommodations between the two German states, it can be said that Hartmann's analysis of the German problem is slightly overdrawn. The urgency in his argument that Germany must be reunited in order to avert disaster has lost credibility. He infers from the limited public opinion poll data on the subject of national unity and the proclamations of West German leaders that a strong will for reunification exists, and that a continued frustration of this will can only mean instability and conflict in the future.

The West German government,

especially under the leadership of Willy Brandt, initiated effective new policies toward the East. It faced the realities and agreed to a *de facto* recognition of the GDR. Brandt and his supporters hoped to mitigate the harsh impact of the division of the nation on the people. In this they were to some extent successful, for the German-German negotiations brought about some relief by easing the travel restrictions for West Germans into East Germany and by providing for the rejoining of separated families. Today, the two German states no longer merely exist side by side; they are formally dealing with each other. Typically, two German ambassadors reside in the many capitals across the globe. For all intents and purposes, the German problem seems solved. Clearly, the division of Germany no longer represents a major peril to world peace.

Nevertheless, the German national question, as such, is still open and continues to motivate the governments in Bonn and East Berlin, albeit in different ways. Only in this limited sense have Hartmann and countless other writers on the subject been right. The question of the nature of the German nation has been one of the most ardently argued topics in Germany. The GDR regime has declared the concept of the all-German nation to be dead. It insists that there are two fundamentally different German nation-states, the "socialist" GDR and the "bourgeois" FRG, each with its own distinct national consciousness. As contacts between the two states have increased, the SED has become acutely concerned about the "eroding" impact on "socialist gains." Consequently, they seek to impose the strictest demarcation between the two peoples.

The West German government, on the other hand, insists that there continue to be special bonds between the two states, that they cannot be exactly like two foreign countries in their relations with each other. The official position of the FRG is "two states within one nation." It can be argued that the West German efforts regarding normalization of affairs were designed to preserve a consciousness of belonging to one German nation, to prevent the complete estrangement between the people of the two states. Meanwhile, it appears that strong nationalistic aspirations attributed to the German people since World War II were largely exaggerated. The initial resigned acceptance of the postwar realities seems to give way to a positive willingness to live with the *status quo*. — *M.G.*

Additional Recommended Reading

Dornberg, John. *The Two Germanys*. New York: The Dial Press, 1974. Contains sharply drawn profiles of postwar leaders of the two countries.

Kolko, Gabriel. *The Politics of War: The World and United States Foreign Policy, 1943-1945*. New York: Random House, 1968. An analysis of Allied wartime diplomacy and its impact on the division of Germany.

Kuklick, Bruce. *American Policy and the Division of Germany*. Ithaca, N.Y.: Cornell University Press, 1972. An excellent work on the developments leading up to the division of Germany and the emergence of the two German states.

Merkl, Peter H. *The Origin of the West German Republic*. New York: Oxford University Press, 1963. A detailed study of the origin of the FRG.

Pounds, Norman J. G. *Divided Germany and Berlin*. New York: D. Van Nostrand, 1962. A useful general work dealing directly with the division of Germany.

Prittie, Terence. *Germany Divided: The Legacy of the Nazi Era*. Boston: Little, Brown and Company, 1960. A thoughtful, well-documented analysis of the complexities and problems of the divided nation.

PROCLAMATION OF THE PEOPLE'S REPUBLIC OF CHINA

Type of event: Political: formation of a Communist government in China
Time: October 1, 1949
Locale: Peking, China

Principal personages:

MAO TSE-TUNG (1893-1976), Chairman of the Chinese Communist Party, 1949-1976

CHIANG KAI-SHEK (1887-1975), leader of the Nationalist Party

SUN YAT-SEN (1866-1925), father of the Chinese Revolution

CHOU EN-LAI (1898-1976), a founder of the Chinese Communist Party and first Vice-Chairman

Summary of Event

On the afternoon of October 1, 1949, Mao Tse-tung, a leader of the Communist Party in China since its beginnings in 1921, stood on a platform at Tien An Men (Gate of Heavenly Peace) Square in Peking and officially proclaimed the establishment of the People's Republic of China (PRC). Months of careful preparation had preceded this event, which symbolically marked the start of an extraordinary experiment in social reorganization and national revival. For the largest country in Asia, containing approximately one fourth of the world's population, it marked the end of civil war, hyperinflation, foreign domination, illiteracy, and postwar disillusionment. In his proclamation, Mao forcefully made known China's future position with respect to the rest of the world.

Just before his formal assumption of power, Mao had declared that his nation would never again be insulted and had demanded that China be treated with full respect by other governments. For more than a century prior to 1949, China had enjoyed neither peace at home nor respect abroad. The weakness of the Manchu Dynasty (1644-1911) led to its despoiling and dismemberment by foreign powers. Widespread encroachments on Chinese national sovereignty were made first by the British in the Opium Wars (1839-1842), then by the French, Germans, and Russians (1844-1860), who sought major spheres of interest in China and special commercial concessions. The first war with Japan (1894-1895) resulted in the loss of Taiwan and the Pescadores Islands. The abortive Chinese Boxer Uprising (1898-1900) protesting foreign incursions and exploitation ended with Western powers and Japan occupying Peking.

The overthrow of the decadent Manchu regime in 1911 and the establishment of a Republic by Chinese revolutionary forces was followed by two decades of civil war, in the course of which Chinese warlords in search of personal advantage fragmented the country and subjected the peasants to autocratic rule. In 1931 Japan invaded Manchuria and transformed it into a vast military base. There were also Japanese thrusts into Inner Mongolia and North China. As the second war with Japan (1937-1945) ended and the Japanese capitulated to Allied forces, friction between the Nationalists (Kuomintang) and the Communists became more pronounced; civil war broke out with renewed fury. The Communist victory in 1949 reestablished national unity (except for Taiwan) for the first time since 1911.

Almost from its formation in 1921, the Chinese Communist Party had competed with nationalist groups for leadership of the country. In 1923, however, the Chinese Communists, under a directive of the Soviet Union, cooperated with the Kuomintang, then led by Sun Yat-sen. Known as the father of the Chinese Revolution, Sun Yat-sen hoped that the Allied powers would come to China's aid after World War I; when they did not, he turned to Russia for help. He died in 1925 without realizing his goal of unification and was succeeded by Chiang Kai-shek, who had the immediate task of solving policy disputes within the ranks of his party, curbing the power of the warlords, and dealing with Communist infiltration of the Kuomintang.

In 1927, Chiang launched a series of successful raids against the Communists and their sympathizers. Those Communists who could escape went into hiding in scattered areas throughout the countryside, where they continued to wage guerrilla warfare. Beginning in 1931, Chiang conducted extermination campaigns against Mao's base of operation in Southeast China. Mao barely withstood these attacks and eventually was forced to make a precarious six-thousand-mile circuitous trek by foot with his force of some 100,000 into the hills of Shensi. This fighting retreat, known as the "Long March," began on October 16, 1934, and lasted more than a year. It subjected the participants to great deprivation and cost countless lives. The experience is viewed by Chinese Communists as an exploit of great heroism and historical significance. The survivors of the March became the core of both the Communist Party and the Red Army. Leaders who emerged from the epic ordeal included not only Mao Tse-tung, but also Chu Teh, Chou En-lai, Lin Piao, and P'eng Teh-hauai.

Upon the outbreak of war with Japan in 1937, the Communists, motivated by patriotic considerations, at first cooperated with the Nationalists to fight the common enemy. Motivated also by a desire to advance their own political interests, they used the time beginning in 1940 to augment their own forces; by so doing they again came into conflict with the Nationalists. During most of the war, therefore, there was a three-way struggle among the Nationalists, the Communists, and the Japanese.

When World War II ended, it was hoped that a way might be found to resolve the differences between the warring political factions in China, and that peace, reconstruction, rehabilitation, and unification would follow. Chiang and Mao met on several occasions to discuss common problems; a solution to the grave economic crisis facing China had to be found. The United States was willing to extend badly needed financial aid, but only on condition that there be no civil war. Toward that end, President Harry S Truman sent his Chief of Staff, General George C. Marshall, to China as a special envoy to seek some form of national integration by peaceful and democratic means. The result of this effort was a ceasefire agreement signed on January 10, 1946, by representatives of the Kuomintang and the Communist Party, and the calling of a Political Consultative Conference (PCC) to which delegates from various major political groups, not merely Communists and Nationalists, convened in Chungking for the purpose of forming a coalition government. Since neither the Kuomintang nor the Communist Party was seriously committed to the agreement and each believed the other could be defeated, this effort to establish a new government was short-lived. Marshall's mission had failed. Meanwhile, the other political groups joined either the Nationalists or the Communists, so that the fighting that ensued became a two-way confrontation.

For a time, it appeared that Chiang would be able to defeat the Communists. Armed with heavy military equipment supplied by the United States, his troops spread across China and Manchuria and managed to dislodge the Communists from various strongholds, including their capital at Yenan. The Nationalist victories were merely temporary, however, for even though they were able to seize and hold cities and towns, they could neither destroy the determined and well-disciplined Communist forces nor capture the loyalty of the peasantry, who were being propagandized not only by promises of a new coalition government guaranteeing land reform and fundamental freedoms but also by an effective Communist political campaign which denounced the corruption of the Nationalist government and portrayed Chiang Kai-shek as a lackey of Western imperialism.

Moreover, the Communists were able to increase their forces by equipping the newly indoctrinated peasants with Japanese weaponry captured by the Russians in Manchuria at the end of the war and turned over to the Chinese Liberation Army. Mao also held out the promise that the Communists, once they had gained power, would gradually transform the economy and work for the control of capitalism, not its elimination. This promise won the sympathies of many urban industrial people not directly involved in counterrevolutionary activities. Assurances were also given that Sun Yat-sen's "Three Principles of the People"—nationalism, democracy, and livelihood—were not in conflict with Communist goals. A further promise was that once the Kuomintang and the "reactionary landlord, the compradors, and the bureaucracy" were defeated, a peaceful development into a higher stage of socialism could come into being and a "New Democracy" would result. These statements tended to weaken whatever organized resistance remained to a Communist takeover.

By 1948 the Communists began

defeating the Nationalists in open battles. On April 22, 1948 Yenan was recovered; and in the fall of that same year, Mukden, the metropolis of Southern Manchuria, surrendered to Mao's forces after a bitter siege. The loss of this base marked the beginning of the end of Kuomintang supremacy. Mao opened an all-out offensive that resulted in his forces capturing Shanghai, Nanking, and Hankow; Peiping was surrendered without a fight. After a succession of fierce battles, extensive losses, and deepening apathy, Chiang's troops increasingly deserted to the Communist camp, taking with them their American military equipment.

In August, 1949, with much of China now in Communist hands, the United States Department of State issued a White Paper disavowing any responsibility for the impending Nationalist defeat and stressing that the heavy losses were entirely due to the negligence and miscalculations of high commanding officers—not to the lack of United States assistance. The paper was severely criticized by Mao as a "counterrevolutionary document which openly demonstrates United States imperialist intervention in China." Unable to check Communist advances, and no longer able to count on support from the United States, Chiang Kai-shek and the Kuomintang fled to the island of Taiwan. All of mainland China was finally under Communist control.

When it had become apparent that the collapse of the Nationalist government was imminent, the Communist Party issued its first call for the creation of a new government. On May 1, 1948, invitations were extended to all democratic groups and persons who opposed Kuomintang actions and policies, American imperialism, feudalism, and bureaucratic capitalism. A conference was held in Manchuria on November 25, 1948, and a Preparatory Committee, whose responsibility was to convene a People's Congress and formulate plans for a democratic coalition government, was selected. The Committee, composed of 134 delegates representing twenty-three political organizations, met first in June and again in September, 1949. Twenty-one persons were ultimately selected from this group to constitute a Standing Committee. Mao Tse-tung was elected Chairman and Chou En-lai Vice-Chairman. The Committee chose to designate the proposed new organization as the Chinese People's Political Consultative Conference (CPPCC), a title of some significance since it carried a multiclass appeal and incorporated the term "people," on which Mao's doctrinal system was predicated.

In 1940, when Mao had visualized a political system for postrevolutionary China, he had spoken pointedly of "the people." In 1949, when total victory was a certainty, he indicated that "at the present stage in China the people are the working class, the peasantry, the petty bourgeoisie, and the national bourgeoisie." Unlike orthodox Marxists, who regard "national bourgeoisie" as enemies of the people, Mao saw the practical necessity of tolerating this group at least until such time as China's backward economy could be raised to a higher level.

The CPPCC met for the first time

on September 21, 1949, with 588 voting delegates who were affiliated with various political groups from various geographical regions, and approved the following three documents drafted by the Preparatory Committee: the Common Program of the CPPCC; the Organic Law of the CPPCC; and the Organic Law of the Central People's Government. The Common Program provides detailed instructions to be followed during the transitional period of the "People's Democratic Dictatorship." Included are provisions regarding foreign, political, military, economic, and educational policy. The Organic Law of the CPPCC outlined powers and procedures for that body to follow until such time as an election of a National People's Congress could take place. The Organic Law of the Central People's Government was a provisional constitution describing the hierarchial structure of the proposed new government and outlining the functions of the various state organs.

Before it adjourned on September 30, 1949, the CPPCC adopted a national anthem, selected a national flag, and changed the name of its new capital from Peiping to Peking. All was in readiness for the Proclamation of the People's Republic of China which followed the next day.

Pertinent Literature

Meisner, Maurice. *Mao's China: A History of the People's Republic.* New York: The Free Press, 1977.

Maurice Meisner, with his accustomed scholarship and lucidity, offers his readers this illuminating study of a period of China's recent political and intellectual history. The author of numerous works on modern Chinese history, Meisner devotes much of his latest effort to the ideas of Mao Tse-tung and his attempts to construct a socialist society for his country.

Recognizing that no political order emerges suddenly and that the Chinese Revolution of the People's Republic is the product of particular circumstances and experiences inherited and transmitted from China's past, the author begins his narration with a general inquiry into the Chinese historical environment from which Chinese Marxist revolutionaries emerged. He provides an account of the conditions they encountered and shows that the ideologies of the Communist revolution were drawn not from the millennial Chinese tradition, but from modern Western intellectual sources. He then assesses the accomplishments of what is now called the "Maoist Era," from the time Mao Tse-tung announced the birth of the new state in 1949 to the time of his death on September 9, 1976. Meisner's stated objective is to measure the Chinese Communist performance against the Marxist goals and standards they set for themselves. He succeeds impressively.

Meisner divides his book into a five-part chronology which covers not only relevant aspects of Chinese Marxist ideology, including theories of revolution, class struggle, state form, utopianism, contradictions, "the people," "democratic dictatorship," "people's democracy," and the "transition from socialism to communism," but also major Chinese domestic issues of industrialization, land reform, agricultural collectivization, and bureaucracy. In addition, he provides a systematic analysis of the erratic changes in policies and practices that characterize the Maoist regime; namely, the two Five Year Plans, the Commune Movement, the Hundred Flowers Campaign, the Great Leap Forward, and, finally, the Cultural Revolution.

The power of Mao's Chinese government, Meisner discloses, rested ultimately on the forces of violence—the army and the secret police—rather than on what some believed to be rule through ideological education or Confucian "moral suasion." According to Meisner, the secret police developed a vast oppressive security apparatus. The army, equally oppressive, was used by Mao for a variety of nonmilitary duties, including political organization, economic production, ideological education, and mobilization of the masses. Also enlisted for repressive purposes was the Red Guard, composed of teenagers, young adults, and others fanatically devoted to the Chairman; this group helped to launch the Cultural Revolution. Their aim was to uphold the "purity" of Mao's revolutionary ideology. Briefly, they caused great turmoil and ultimately were brought down by officials within the Communist Party.

It was Chou En-lai, asserts Meisner, who made the Herculean effort to persuade the repressive organizations to end their indiscriminate attacks and work for national harmony; and it is Chou En-lai and not Mao whom Meisner credits with much of the continuity and stability that the civilian state structure was to enjoy during its first, and often turbulent, twenty-five years. Seemingly, Chou En-lai, the most intelligent and subtle of the Chinese high-ranking officials, often found himself in a position of vulnerability because of policy differences between himself and Mao. As Chairman of the Republic, it was Mao who originally appointed Chou to positions of authority, and it was Mao, undoubtedly, who caused Chou's partial loss of authority in 1957. The accounts of conditions under which policy differences caused dissension between these two men and other important members of the Party comprise the most interesting segments of Meisner's book.

We learn that seven years after the founding of the People's Republic the leaders of the Chinese Communist Party believed that they had succeeded, by using prevailing Marxist-Leninist criteria, in transforming China into a basically socialist country. Meisner explains that in spite of their use of the Russian model, China remained poor and impoverished, and the transition to "socialism" resulted in bureaucratic forms of rule and control. Moreover, the general institutionalization of the postrevolutionary order, and especially the Soviet-borrowed methods of the First Five Year Plan, had given rise to the emergence of new political and economic elites, many of whom had difficulty in accepting certain tenets of

Communism. In addition, a significant number of Chinese intellectuals, critical of the evils of bureaucracy, still did not believe in Communism.

On January 14, 1956, Chou En-lai reported on the problems of the intellectuals and elites to the Central Committee of the Party. He suggested that they be granted freedom and professional autonomy so that their particular areas of specialization could best be utilized for state purposes. As a result, Mao informed the intelligentsia that their unproletarian thought would be tolerated as long as nothing untoward was said or done against the regime. This policy statement was followed by Mao's speech of May 2, 1956, launching his Hundred Flowers Campaign. Momentarily, it was believed that toleration and freedom for intellectuals would be the order of the day. However, Mao soon revised his statements and a less liberal attitude followed. Mao viewed dissidents as antiparty and antisocialist representatives of the reactionary bourgeoise line bent on reverting to capitalism. To overcome this tendency, he mounted the Great Proletarian Cultural Revolution, forcing the entire nation "to struggle against and smash those persons in authority who are taking the capitalist road . . . and to transform education, literature, art and other parts of the superstructure that do not correspond to the socialist economic base." The Cultural Revolution ended with the total reestablishment of the rule of the Leninist Party.

Meisner concludes that the legacy of Mao is an ambiguous one; for it is marred by a deep incongruity between its progressive socioeconomic accomplishments and its retrogressive political features. He maintains that even though Maoism discarded Stalinist orthodoxies and methods in forging a new pattern of economic development, it retained Stalinist methods of bureaucratic political rule. Its greatest shortcoming, according to Meisner, was its reluctance or inability to grant institutional guarantees of freedom.

Mao's China is a richly interesting book that provides readers with a thoughtful and systematic assessment of an exciting period in China's history.

Davies, John Paton, Jr. *Dragon by the Tail: American, British, Japanese, and Russian Encounters with China and One Another*. New York: W. W. Norton and Company, 1972.

During the gray period in United States history known as the McCarthy Era, a small group of dedicated foreign service officers who reported from China in the early 1940's were excoriated by Senator Joseph R. McCarthy and others for supplying misinformation concerning the relative strength of the Chinese Nationalist and Communist military forces and for having "lost China." John Paton Davies, Jr., was one of this group, as were John Service, John Carter Vincent, John K. Emerson, and Edmund Chubb. Considered a security risk for accurately predicting that Chiang Kai-shek would be defeated, Davies was subjected to a number of departmental interrogations after which he was summarily dismissed by Secretary of State John Foster Dulles for exercising "bad judgment." After many years of living in virtual exile in Peru, he was finally exonerated by a more enlightened State Department and given security clearance in 1969.

Davies' book is refreshing, stimulating reading. It is not, as one might surmise, a work of self-righteous indignation or justification; it is, rather, an exciting history and memoir by a gifted writer who provides not only a richly detailed perspective of China's development in the 1930's and 1940's but also an inside view of the bureaucratic and personal infighting among officials of the United States State Department over China policy.

Davies was born in China in 1908 of missionary parents. After receiving his initial education in China, he was graduated from Columbia University in 1932. He then served as an American diplomat during the time of the Chinese and Japanese War, was a political aide to General "Vinegar Joe" Stilwell during World War II, held long discourses with Chou En-lai and Mao Tse-tung in their stronghold at Yenan, and while on assignment to the American Embassy in Moscow at the end of the war with Japan observed the deterioration of relationships among Stalin, Chiang, and Mao.

Much of Davies' book focuses on the time he spent as Stilwell's diplomatic aide. He shows that the purpose of Stilwell's mission to China was to keep Burma from falling into Japanese hands. The encounters between Stilwell and Chiang, as Davies relates them, are intriguing. He reveals that Chiang Kai-shek was reluctant to place his troops under Stilwell's command. Seemingly, Chiang wished to divert his men, and the supplies and equipment he received from the United States, to another campaign. Consequently, when Chiang requested a billion-dollar loan from the United States, Stilwell refused, and as a result, became an object of distrust to Chiang and his family.

The visit Davies made to Yenan, where he spoke with Mao Tse-tung and Chou En-lai, is especially interesting. He reported from there on November 7, 1944 that

> . . . the Chinese Communists are backsliders. . . . The saints and prophets of Chinese Communism . . . lust after strange gods of class compromise and party coalition, rather shamefacedly worship the golden calf of foreign investments and yearn to be considered respectable by worldly standards. All this is more than scheming Communist opportunism.

It was his belief that through control of supplies and aid the United States could exert considerable influence on postwar Communist China. Mao, he believed, would cooperate with the United States for economic reasons. It was shortly after this report was delivered that Davies was fired by Dulles.

In the epilogue to his book, Davies remarks that Mao Tse-tung and Chou En-lai secretly sought an invitation to meet with the President of the United States in Washington in January, 1945. They were rebuffed. In July, 1971, however, the President secretly tried to arrange for a meeting with Mao and Chou in Peking. He was invited. One wonders what the course of Chinese, Russian, and United States history would have been if Washington's handling of Chinese affairs had not been one of pervasive confusion and ineptness as depicted so vividly by Davies. — *A.O.B.*

Additional Recommended Reading

Crozier, Brian and Eric Chou. *The Man Who Lost China: The First Full Biography of Chiang Kai-shek*. New York: Charles Scribner's Sons, 1976. A critical biography of Mao Tse-tung's arch opponent which concludes that Chiang Kai-shek was "not only a deeply flawed leader, but in the classical sense of Greek tragedies, a tragic one."

Fitzgerald, C. P. *Mao Tse-tung and China*. New York: Pelican Books, 1977. Designed for the student and general reader, this work provides an introduction to the life and thought of Mao Tse-tung and the complicated history of the Chinese Revolution.

Seymour, James D. *China: The Politics of Revolutionary Reintegration*. New York: Thomas Y. Crowell Company, 1976. Examines the various ways in which the Chinese have brought about their own political integration; appended are copies of the Constitution of the People's Republic of China and the Constitution of the Communist Party.

Shaw, Bruno, ed. *Selected Works of Mao Tse-tung*. New York: Harper & Row Publishers, 1970. In this carefully edited abstract of Mao Tse-tung's overwhelmingly wordy four-volume Selected Works, the editor attempts to provide an understanding of Mao's motivations, reasoning, and genius as a political and military strategist.

Snow, Edgar. *Red Star over China*. New York: Random House, 1938. This classic work is Snow's account of the long interviews he had with Mao Tse-tung in a Yenan cave in late 1936, following the Communist's Long March.

_____. *Red China Today: The Other Side of the River*. New York: Random House, 1962. An inquiry into all aspects of Chinese life; a well-documented book, useful to both laymen and specialists, which includes an appendix and bibliography.

Solinger, Dorothy J. *Regional Government and Political Integration in Southwest China, 1949-1954: A Case Study*. Berkeley: University of California Press, 1977. Examines the problems of a Southwestern province in China at the time of the Communist takeover and focuses on the role played by regional government officials in achieving political integration.

WILLIAM APPLEMAN WILLIAMS PIONEERS COLD WAR REVISIONIST HISTORIOGRAPHY

Type of event: Intellectual: reinterpretation of historical events and political motives
Time: The 1950's
Locale: The University of Wisconsin at Madison

Principal personages:
WILLIAM APPLEMAN WILLIAMS (1921-   ), a historian and author of *The Tragedy of American Diplomacy* (1959)
GABRIEL KOLKO (1932-   ), a historian and author of *The Politics of War* (1967)
WALTER LaFEBER (1933-   ), a historian and author of *America, Russia, and the Cold War* (1967)
ROBERT H. FERRELL (1921-   ), a diplomatic historian

Summary of Event

From time to time, historians develop interpretations of the past which are novel enough, and relevant enough, to affect the way their readers perceive the present. One such historian was Charles Beard, who published *An Economic Interpretation of the Constitution* in 1913. His insistence on the economic motivations of the Founding Fathers was widely accepted, and contributed to a disillusioning belief that the United States had been led into World War I simply for the benefit of war profiteers. In similar fashion, certain historians over the last generation have criticized and revised the conventional interpretations of American foreign policy—especially the policies of the Cold War years. The spreading influence of this group during the 1960's was significant in arousing hostility to the Vietnam War.

The first of these revisionist historians was William Appleman Williams. His first book, *American-Russian Relations, 1782-1947*, appeared in 1952, in an atmosphere of violent anti-Communist feeling; the country was fighting the Korean War, and McCarthy was denouncing leftist infiltrators. Scholars generally agreed with national leaders that the Cold War was the consequence of Russian aggression and Marxist ideology. Few questioned the need to contain Communism, and many believed that negotiation with the "Red" governments was futile. Into this environment Williams tossed a very different way of viewing the Cold War: he argued that the Soviet Union was not a willful aggressor, and that the conflict between Russia and the United States was more the result of mutual misunderstanding than deliberate evil on either side.

To arrive at this interpretation, Williams departed from two traditional assumptions about the Soviet Union. He suggested that the Russian leaders were not simply Marxist ideologues, but rational persons with attitudes and aspirations comparable to those of the Americans; and he suggested that Soviet foreign policy was not primarily determined by Communist doctrine, but by long-standing Russian goals which had existed long before the October Revolution. Through this approach, a more sympathetic portrait of Russia emerged. The nation had always feared invasion from the West, and had actually suffered it three times: from Napoleon in the nineteenth century, and from Germany in two world wars. Was it not understandable that Russia should seek a protective buffer in Eastern Europe? The Soviet regime had been attacked by thousands of British, French, and American troops in its early days after World War I, and had barely defeated them. Was it surprising then that the Soviets distrusted their British and American allies in World War II? While the United States had lost three hundred thousand men in defeating Hitler, the Russians had suffered as many as twenty million deaths. Could they be expected to be as optimistic as the Americans in the hour of victory?

Williams argued that this perspective was completely lacking among such American leaders as President Harry S Truman and Secretary of State James Byrnes. Like other Americans, they felt triumphant and secure after the war and sought a new age of freedom in the postwar world. The United Nations would keep the peace, and the American economy would revitalize both capitalism and democracy in Europe and Asia. To such leaders, Soviet intentions to create a "sphere of influence" in Eastern Europe represented a breach of the war's purposes and a Communist threat to the rest of the world. Thus did hostility spring up between the

two superpowers, locking them in a mutual distrust that led inevitably to a divided Europe, and then a divided planet. As in a Greek tragedy, the outcome of the Cold War was wanted by no one and caused by everyone.

The immediate impact of Williams' theory was negligible. He was an unknown scholar and admitted that very little evidence on postwar diplomacy was available; consequently, few even bothered to refute his arguments. As years passed and the Communist threat receded, however, his work received increasing attention, and by 1959, when he published *The Tragedy of American Diplomacy*, Williams was a controversial figure. In this second work, he elaborated upon an American "view of the world" which affected foreign affairs. This view was dominated by the concept of the Open Door, initially used by John Hay in urging all Western Powers to compete peacefully in late nineteenth century China. Throughout the twentieth century, suggested Williams, the policies of the United States had been dominated by a desire to ensure a free market throughout the world; this would be the best means of promoting prosperity at home and democracy abroad. In this sense, there was never an "isolationist" period between the world wars, for during this period American capitalism expanded overseas to become a crucial consideration in the affairs of foreign governments. In the aftermath of World War II, the Open Door philosophy mandated a political and military course of action which accompanied economic expansion—that is, opposition to Communism. In this effort, the United States soon found itself supporting rightist dictatorships and suppressing democracy. What had originated in largely benevolent purposes evolved into a philosophy of reaction.

By the 1960's, revisionism became a distinct school. A growing number of young historians, some of them trained by Williams himself, expanded upon his criticisms of American foreign policy. The evidence in the archives that were being opened up lent strong support to many of their contentions, and the failure of American policy in Vietnam made Williams appear to be almost prophetic. Success made the revisionists even more controversial; Gabriel Kolko, in *The Politics of War* (1967), expanded the critique to American economic and political history, and Gar Alperovitz, in *Atomic Diplomacy* (1967), suggested that the dropping of the atomic bombs on Japan was chiefly a tactic to frighten the Soviet Union. More traditional diplomatic historians, among them, Robert Ferrell and Arthur Schlesinger, launched vigorous counterattacks, pointing out misused or ambiguous evidence in revisionist writing. A middle ground gradually appeared, and moderate revisionist Walter LaFeber's survey *America, Russia, and the Cold War* (1967) became almost the bible of a new orthodoxy.

Despite these later developments, the importance of Williams' work remains undiminished. Many of the revisionists have simply presented leftist interpretations of available evidence. Because of the scarcity of documentation available during Williams' early career, he was forced to develop an extensive theoretical framework for his arguments. The books which resulted are remarkably creative, and their implications have still not been fully absorbed by either conservative or radical historians in America.

Pertinent Literature

Ferrell, Robert H. "Truman Foreign Policy: A Traditional View," in *The Truman Period as a Research Field: A Reappraisal.* Edited by Richard S. Kirkendall. Columbia: University of Missouri Press, 1972, pp. 11–45.

Few things are as predictable as the course of an argument between historians. The critic of a controversial work will tend to cite his opponent's poor documentation, circular reasoning, and simplistic assumptions. The defending author may concede some minor points, but holds (and plays) the trump card: his critic has failed to grasp the essential, and invariably subtle, meaning of his work. This pattern has held with disheartening regularity in the debate between revisionist and traditional diplomatic historians (producing reviews with such titles as "A Study in Creative Writing"), and on the whole it has shed much anger and very little light.

Robert Ferrell's article on the historical controversy over the Cold War is a praiseworthy exception to the general tendency. Although Ferrell sharply attacks the revisionists and predicts their extinction as a school, his approach is analytical and his arguments reflect a careful consideration of revisionist reasoning. The vigor of his partisanship is on the surface of his writing—he confesses of the radical historians that "I may as well admit that I find it difficult to believe any of their arguments"—and manages to endow his essay with a refreshing objectivity.

A major purpose of the essay is to discuss the reasons why a revisionist school should have developed at all. Ferrell suggests that it had something to do with age: many of the most prominent revisionists were born in the late 1930's, became aware of the world in the midst of World War II, and reached maturity during the reaction against Joseph McCarthy. By being brought up at a time when Russia was an ally, and entering graduate school when extreme anti-Communism was being rejected, they could easily reject older historians as too unquestioning in their support of American foreign policy. Just as Hemingway's "lost generation" had rejected World War I, so the new generation of historians could dismiss the rationale for the Cold War. Ferrell suggests that this general disillusion fed upon itself, as the revisionists exchanged misgivings and developed their own enclave of radicalism. The argument is interesting, but overlooks the fact that the leading member of the school, William A. Williams, is the same age as Ferrell himself.

Ferrell also oversimplifies his essay by considering his opponents as a monolithic whole. Revisionists argue from a number of very different theoretical standpoints; they are united chiefly by their criticism of United States policy. Some of them view American mistakes as the errors of Truman and Dean Acheson, while others blame the underlying attitudes held by all policymakers throughout the period. Ferrell makes an effective argument for the similarity of Roosevelt's and Truman's hostility towards the Soviet Union, but he does not point out that this actually supports the contentions of some revisionists.

Despite its analytical tenor, Ferrell's essay often reveals a tinge of bitterness and represents an example of the difficulties facing any dialogue between traditional and revisionist historians. The central problem is perhaps a differing belief about the purposes of history. For most traditionalists, the task of the historian is to establish what happened in the past and to judge individuals by the standards of their contemporaries. To plumb any deeper, they suggest, forces the writer to hypothesize and guess, and this leads to distorted, manipulated history. The followers of Williams and Kolko, however, believe that the real value of history lies in this theorizing; it is then that one gets beyond mere facts and into the essential meanings and trends of the past. The two schools disagree not only on interpretations and conclusions, but on approach and method, making dialogue very difficult. Thus, it is understandable that Ferrell should accuse the revisionists of creating a "usable past"; but it is not necessarily fair.

Williams, William Appleman. *The Contours of American History*. Chicago: Quadrangle Press, 1966.

In 1961, when Williams was first achieving general recognition as an important new historian, he attempted to present an extensive overview of his theoretical framework in *The Contours of American History*. The result was disastrous: the book was denounced as unscholarly, distorted, "loaded" history, and then promptly ignored. Nonetheless, it remains perhaps the best exposition of Williams' ideas.

In an opening chapter entitled "History as a Way of Learning," Williams suggests a pair of motive forces in historical development: ideologies and economics. He uses ideology in the broadest sense of the term. To make sense out of their environment, people create their own *Weltanschauung*, or explanation of the world. Every society has a dominant view of the world, and this affects the way social problems are seen and solved. Economic development, on the other hand, operates largely independent of people. Williams agrees with a good deal of Marxist economics, and stresses the importance of class antagonism in affecting social institutions and outlooks. But despite his use of the jargon, his belief in the interaction of ideas and economic change separates him from Marx. For Williams, the essence of historical change is succession of ideological ages, each of which flourishes in a special environment, but declines and falls before another age arises to deal with a new economic and social context.

American history is composed of three such ages. The first was the Age of Mercantilism, named for a philosophy which existed both in England and the American colonies. Mercantilism stressed the importance of treating society as an economic organism, which required nourishment and order to survive. Williams argues that the American Revolution resulted from a conflicting application of the philosophy: English leaders treated the colonies as a part of the larger, English organism, and tried to keep them as an agricultural "sector." The Americans began to perceive themselves as a separate organism, and saw English rule as simple tyranny. Once the Revolution had succeeded, the philosophy of mercantilism was strong enough to bond thirteen independent states into a larger nation.

Mercantilism was eventually succeeded by "Laissez Nous Faire" in the nineteenth century, a philosophy adapted to the needs of an expanding frontier and a youthful capitalism. Its followers believed that the independence of the individual and the absence of governmental interference were the keys to a virtuous and prosperous society; the triumph of this philosophy was symbolized by the destruction of the Bank of the United States under Andrew Jackson. As the frontier slowly vanished during the century and the early "captains of industry" gave way to large corporations, the need for intervention and order in the economy became apparent.

Thus arrived the age of "Corporate

Syndicalism," a period when policy-makers were preoccupied with the need of balancing the large organizations—big business, labor, and government—which had become dominant in society. The solution was a quest for security, epitomized by the domestic policies of the New Deal: pensions for the old, legal recognition for the unions and financial guarantees to banks and business. In foreign affairs, syndicalism led to the "Open Door" policies, an effort to harmonize the rest of the world with American political and economic ideals.

The Contours of American History was intended to be less of a scholarly work than an interpretive essay, and it fulfills this purpose when Williams arrives at the present. He suggests that the United States is on the verge of yet another new age, and he reveals both his optimism and his radicalism in suggesting that we may have a hand in deciding what philosophy shall dominate our future. By understanding history, we can shape it; and by choosing democratic socialism, he suggests we may fulfill the past. — *R.H.S.*

Additional Recommended Reading

Bernstein, Barton J., ed. *Politics and Policies of the Truman Administration*. Chicago: Quadrangle Books, 1970. A selection of articles by leading revisionists on both domestic and foreign policies from 1945 to 1953.

Combs, Jerald A., ed. *Nationalist, Realist, and Radical: Three Views of American Diplomacy*. New York: Harper & Row Publishers, 1972. Combs has selected ten major periods of American foreign policy and contrasted articles by historians of the three "schools" for each case; the result is an intriguing comparison of differing historical perspectives.

Gardner, Lloyd C. *Architects of Illusion: Men and Ideas in American Foreign Policy*. Chicago: Quadrangle Books, 1970. An analysis of eleven key political actors who fashioned the American perception of Russia in the early years of the Cold War.

Patterson, Thomas G., ed. *Cold War Critics*. Chicago. Quadrangle Books, 1971. A series of essays discussing various influential voices; includes ideas of Walter Lippmann and Henry Wallace, who opposed or criticized the Cold War in the 1940's.

Theoharis, Athan. *Seeds of Repression: Harry S Truman and the Origins of Mc-Carthyism*. Chicago: Quadrangle Books, 1971. Theoharis argues that Truman's efforts to rally support behind his anti-Communism and Cold War policies were responsible for the hysteria that permitted McCarthyism to flourish.

Ulam, Adam B. *The Rivals: America and Russia Since World War II*. New York: The Viking Press, 1971. One of the most respected nonrevisionist histories of the Cold War.

THE IMPACT OF TELEVISION ON SOCIETY

Type of event: Sociological: electronic entertainment and news broadcasting
Time: 1950 to the present
Locale: All countries with television facilities

Principal personages:

E. WILLIAM HENRY, Chairman of the Federal Communications Commission (FCC), 1965

FRED W. FRIENDLY (1915-   ), a television producer

NEWTON MINOW, Chairman of the FCC, 1961

EDWARD R. MURROW (1908-1965), a television newsman

WILLIAM S. PALEY (1901-   ), Chairman of the Columbia Broadcasting System (CBS)

DAVID SARNOFF (1891-1971), Chairman of the Radio Corporation of America (RCA)

Summary of Event

Television has had greatest influence in the United States; at the same time, programs produced in the United States have often dominated the medium as it developed in other nations, at least until the 1970's, when African, European, and Latin American countries, as well as Canada, began to limit the number of imported programs.

There could have been no television without the pioneering work of dozens of nameless scientists in the laboratories of American Telephone & Telegraph (AT&T), Westinghouse, and General Electric (GE) in the 1920's and 1930's, and of such persons as Edwin H. Armstrong, who invented FM, which carries television sound. Nevertheless, the important names in the medium's growth are to be found on the payrolls of the corporations which own the networks. William S. Paley, Chairman of the Columbia Broadcasting System (CBS), and David Sarnoff, Chairman of the Radio Corporation of America

(RCA), the corporate parent of the National Broadcasting Company (NBC), provided the organizational drive needed to take the medium out of its experimental novelty stage into that of the major entertainment force in the nation. These men, of course, were not philanthropists, and their actions were guided by the profit motive. For the corporations, television is a way to make money, and that viewpoint has caused criticism and consternation, both within and without the television industry. Fred W. Friendly, news and documentary producer and Chairman of CBS News from 1964 to 1966, resigned in protest when the network chose to broadcast reruns of *I Love Lucy* and *The Dick Van Dyke Show* rather than live coverage of the Senate Vietnam hearings. Friendly and Edward R. Murrow paid for newspaper advertisements of Murrow's *See It Now* episodes devoted to Senator Joseph McCarthy when the network refused to publicize the programs. Outside the industry, Newton Minow, Chairman of the Federal Communications Commission (FCC), the bureau charged with regulating the medium, called television "a vast wasteland" in 1961; his charge apparently did not have much impact, for four years later his successor, E. William Henry, called the weekly prime time schedule "an electronic Appalachia."

When World War II ended and the consumer products boom began, television networks and television set manufacturers were ready. By 1949-1950, television had moved ahead of radio in popularity. Such popular radio programs as *The Hit Parade* and *Gunsmoke* switched to television, and new stars, such as Lucille Ball and Desi Arnaz in *I Love Lucy*, Sid Caesar and Imogene Coca in *Your Show of Shows*, and Jack Webb in *Dragnet*, became favorites. By 1956-1957, eighty percent of all homes (forty million) had their television sets turned on an average of five hours a day, while advertising revenue reached a billion dollars. Ten years later, there were sixty-five million sets in the United States, and viewing time had almost doubled to sixty hours a week per set. In fact, it is only in the late 1970's that there has been a decline in viewing time.

For many years, it was fashionable to say that television destroyed the movies, but revisionist film historians have shown recently that weekly film attendance was already declining when television began to grow; perhaps a truer reading of events is that the electronic medium simply gave patrons an excuse to stay home—one which they were already seeking. What did the millions of people see on the small screens? Hour after hour, day after day, a most fantastic mélange of entertainment (first live, then filmed, now videotaped) and news events paraded through American and foreign living rooms.

The question of violence on television has been and still is the longest continuing debate about the influence of the medium on the average viewer. Police, cowboy, and spy shows have ranged from gentle humor to violent mayhem. In 1958, there were thirty Western programs in prime time. Not all of them seemed to exploit violence for the sake of violence, but almost all of them had at least one fight or quick-draw gun showdown per episode. By 1960, one antiviolence group presented the results of a one-week, prime time tabulation: it itemized hundreds of murders and attempted murders depicted in the entertainment programs, along with dozens of robberies, jailbreaks, burglaries, and fistfights. Periodically the networks and producers present nonviolent shows with great ballyhoo, while at the same time denying that television programming can influence anyone to commit violent acts. After an ineffective attempt by the networks in 1975 to create a "family hour" early in the evening which would shield children from violence, groups of parents and educators have begun to pressure and even to boycott corporations which sponsor violent programs. Unfortunately, since advertising time is at a premium, when one sponsor withdraws another quickly is found. In 1978, a woman sued a network and a local station claiming that a program depicting sexual assault caused the rape of her daughter. The court ruled against her, and television, at least temporarily, has legal agreement that it has not created what one critic called "a climate for murder."

Not all of the prime time has been filled with violent dramas or shallow situation comedies. During the early 1950's, the medium's Golden Age, as some writers call the decade, there was another genre: the anthology program. Such shows as *Playhouse 90, Studio One*, and *Kraft Television Theatre* presented live, often original dramas, such as Paddy Chayefsky's *Marty* and Gore Vidal's *Visit to a Small Planet*. These programs were soon replaced by lighter filmed comedy series or action-oriented adventure programs, but in the 1970's aesthetically interesting, dramatically polished programs produced by the British Broadcasting Corporation (BBC) in England (which began broadcasting in the mid-1930's) began to appear on public television stations.

Regardless of the positive or negative aspects of entertainment programs, television's greatest impact upon worldwide culture is based upon its ability to show instantly live events to all parts of the world. For American audiences, the 1950's brought three major live political events: the crime committee hearings chaired by Senator Estes Kefauver in 1951, the "Checkers" speech by vice-presidential candidate Richard M. Nixon in 1952, and the confrontation between Senator Joseph McCarthy and the United States Army over the question of Communist infiltration in 1954.

Although President Harry S Truman had refused to use either radio or television for his 1948 campaign, by the 1960's television was a major factor in all politics. Some historians feel that John F. Kennedy's victory in 1960 was due partially to the poor showing Vice-President Nixon made in the first of the live television debates between the two candidates. *Telestar I* in 1962 allowed truly instantaneous worldwide transmissions through satellite technology. People in Europe and Asia were able to see the nation mourn during President Kennedy's funeral, as well as to witness the live, on-camera murder of Lee Harvey Oswald, the alleged assassin of the President. Fascinated audiences around the world watched the disclosure of wrongdoings in connection with Watergate in 1973 and 1974, capped by the resignation of the President.

On a more positive note, in July, 1969, six hundred million people in forty-nine nations watched Neil Armstrong set foot on the moon. At the other extreme from such broadcasting from outer space is the multiplicity of local programming; in Los Angeles, for example, seventeen cable channels provide intimate contact for ethnic and racial groups by broadcasting in five languages: English, Spanish, Japanese, Chinese, and Korean.

Pertinent Literature

Barnouw, Erik. *Tube of Plenty: The Evolution of American Television*. New York: Oxford University Press, 1975.

This volume is basically a restating and updating of *The Image Makers: A History of Broadcasting in the United States Since 1953*, the third and final volume of Barnouw's broadcasting history series.

As both a participant in and critic of television, Barnouw provides historical information and anecdotal insights regarding the rapid rise of television as the primary entertainment medium in the United States. The battle between the news and the entertainment divisions of the three networks provides him with the locus for his most intriguing stories. These stories are not presented in a gossipy style or as sensational exposés. Most of the information is available from other sources, but when Barnouw presents the data in a context of what might have been if the medium were not almost entirely a profit-oriented one, the implications must cause all of us to pause for a moment and to wonder. Such contemplation is best illustrated by Barnouw's discussion of television's handling of the two major sociocultural events of the 1960's and the 1970's: Vietnam and Watergate.

While some commentators cite the continual presence in American living rooms of news clips from Southeast Asia as a positive force in ending the war, Barnouw presents the opposite opinion. According to him, the networks for a long time allowed themselves to present only those facts which supported the viewpoints of Presidents Lyndon B. Johnson and Richard M. Nixon, and of the Pentagon. Johnson had three television sets side-by-side so that he could watch simultaneously all three network news programs. On more than one occasion, Walter Cronkite emerged from the broadcast studio to find a call from the White House awaiting him with criticism of a news item which the President considered inappropriate. Many network reporters in Saigon accepted daily briefings from the military command as all the news there was. It was only after the manipulation of the events surrounding the Tonkin Gulf incident became known that the networks began to allow questioning statements by their editorial commentators.

In much the same way, network news lagged far behind the print media in exposing the Watergate facts. Even today some critics claim that President Nixon was forced to resign because of pressure from television, the "nattering nabobs of negativism," as Vice-President Spiro Agnew called the newspeople before he, too, resigned. Again, in Barnouw's view, the opposite is more true. For example, CBS canceled its "instant analysis" of presidential broadcasts because the White House disapproved.

Such timidity and fear also were evident in the late 1940's and the 1950's when television was subjected to the anti-Communist pressures of the Cold War and of McCarthyism. Historically more attention has been focused upon the Hollywood Ten and movie blacklisting, but blacklisting was even more prevalent in television, and it was often a case of accusation by inference and innuendo. In 1950, the editors of *Counterattack: The Newsletter of Facts on Communism* published *Red Channels: The Report on Communist Influence in*

Radio and Television; immediately, 151 persons, whom Barnouw calls "the most talented and admired people in the industry," found themselves out of work. Networks and advertising agencies soon developed "security offices" which routinely checked out everyone. Those not hired seldom were told by whom or of what they were accused. Barnouw gives details on one such case, that of WCBS disc jockey and television talk-show panelist, John Henry Faulk, who was fired in 1956 because of sponsor pressure.

One of Faulk's strongest supporters was Edward R. Murrow. If there is a star in this book, it must be Murrow, whose *See It Now* is one of the highlights of television's "Golden Age" of the 1950's. It was Murrow who finally publicly questioned the methods and validity of the charges being made by Senator Joseph McCarthy, and it is when discussing Murrow's broadcasts and the occasional outspoken documentaries of the early 1960's, such as NBC's "White Paper on the U-2 Affair," *CBS Reports*' "Harvest of Shame," and ABC's "Yanki No!," that Barnouw's view of what television could be is most apparent. Documentaries, those programs which fall between straight news and entertainment, are his favorites; such favoritism is logical when

we realize that he wrote *Documentary: A History of the Non-Fiction Film*, that he wrote scripts for television documentaries, and that in the 1960's, all television documentaries were filmed. Back then, television, which took so many viewers out of movie houses, seemed the ideal medium to support the documentary film, which had never done well in commercial theaters.

Unfortunately, documentaries are often controversial and do not fit neatly into happy-ending formulas, while sponsors demand happy endings with as little controversy as possible. Thus, documentaries began to appear less and less, because the content tended to be realistic and without easy solutions, a configuration which did not seem appropriate for the selling of soap, toothpaste, and deodorant.

Selling, after all, is the function of commercial television, but Barnouw does not place all blame for mediocrity on sponsors; networks must bear part of the blame; viewers who allow themselves to be sold to also are responsible. The chilling result, in Barnouw's view, with millions of viewers absorbed in football games, Westerns, and situation comedies, "seemed an American equivalent of the Roman 'bread and circuses.'"

Adler, Richard and Douglass Cater, eds. *Television as a Cultural Force*. New York: Frederick A. Praeger, 1976.

This collection of nine essays from the "Workshop on Television" conducted by the Aspen Institute Program on Communication and Society covers a range of scholarship from popular to academic. On the other hand, Peter H. Wood's "Television as Dream" and Kevin Ryan's "Television as a Moral Educator" show the difficulty of applying esoteric theories, Freudian dream analysis, and Lawrence Kohlberg's "Cognitive-Developmental Approach to Moral Development," to a popular medium.

Several of the authors are concerned with television criticism. Inadvertently, they demonstrate the most difficult problem with such criticism: the ephemerality of any given program. Thus, when Wood discusses episodes of *Kung Fu* and Robert S. Alley comments upon dialogue from *Marcus Welby, M.D.* in his article on "Media Medicine and Morality," we are faced with the problem that neither program is now available in prime time. The subtlety of the entertainment programs which last for several seasons (and only one article discusses nonentertainment, news programs) as a "cultural force" is also discussed in terms of the reliance of these programs upon formula/convention and the weekly episode which builds upon all those which preceded it. A film critic or a literary reviewer can discuss a movie or book with the knowledge it will be around for a while. But of what value is a positive or a negative discussion of the escapades of Archie Bunker the night before, unless the critic writes about character development in that particular episode in relationship to all other weekly installments of *All in the Family*? Such long-term criticism may be the only answer for the situation-comedies which fill much of the weekly television schedule.

Another support for criticism based upon character development is found in Richard Adler's discussion of Raymond Williams' "flow" theory, that is, "the uninterrupted following of one thing by another," especially as it applies to television watching in the home. Although Marshall McLuhan called television the media which involves the viewer the most, few people give it undivided attention. When the phone rings or someone knocks at the door or the kids come in needing something, most people respond to these external stimuli and ignore the television set. The scriptwriters, networks, and sponsors know all these intrusions occur, and they know they should not, must not, program a narrative whose complexity demands undivided attention. At the same time, the size of the screen and its inherent visual simplicity prohibit complex design patterns.

Finally, Kenneth M. Pierce makes an interesting observation in "The Bunkers, the Critics, and the News" when he discusses Archie and Edith talking about "things about which [they] know very little." In an age when millions of viewers are exactly like Edith and Archie in that they depend upon the twenty-four minutes or so of network news each night for all they know about the world, if they talk about current events at all, it is on the basis of knowing "very little." — *J.C.C*

Additional Recommended Reading

Friendly, Fred W. *Due to Circumstances Beyond Our Control*. New York: Random House, 1967. The producer of Edward R. Murrow's *See It Now*, of *CBS Reports*, and of the famous documentary "Harvest of Shame" provides insight into the problems of news *versus* entertainment in the commercial television networks.

—————————. *The Good Guys, the Bad Guys, and the First Amendment: Free Speech Versus Fairness in Broadcasting*. New York: Random House, 1976. An attempt to shed light on the controversy over what constitutes free speech and what constitutes personal attack.

Rather, Dan. *The Camera Never Blinks: Adventures of a TV Journalist*. New York: William Morrow and Company, 1977. Comments about major news events of the 1960's and 1970's, as well as a discussion of how newspeople affect events by featuring or down-playing certain aspects of developing stories.

Whelan, Kenneth. *How the Golden Age of Television Turned My Hair to Silver*. New York: Walker and Company, 1973. A "behind-the-scenes" anecdotal collection about the "good old days," enhanced by the author's delightfully cynical sense of humor.

Wilk, Max. *The Golden Age of Television: Notes from the Survivors*. New York: Delacorte Press, 1976. A book of nostalgic stories by the author of many of the live drama shows of the late 1940's and early 1950's.

Youngblood, Gene. *Expanded Cinema: The Audio-Visual Extensions of Man*. New York: E. P. Dutton, 1970. Presents a radical new art form, "synaesthetic cinema," which can be presented through global television.

THE LANDING OF UNITED NATIONS FORCES AT INCHON

Type of event: Military: bold amphibious landing to counter a successful invasion
Time: September 15, 1950
Locale: Inchon, South Korea

Principal personages:

GENERAL DOUGLAS A. MACARTHUR (1880-1964), Commander in Chief of the United States forces in the Far East and Supreme Commander of the United Nations forces in Korea

MAJOR GENERAL OLIVER P. SMITH (1893-   ), Commander of the United States 1st Marine Division in Korea

SYNGMAN RHEE (1875-1965), President of the Republic of South Korea

GENERAL JOSEPH LAWTON COLLINS (1896-   ), United States Army Chief of Staff

ADMIRAL FORREST PERCIVAL SHERMAN (1896-   ), Commander of Naval Operations in Korea

Summary of Event

The imaginative and controversial United Nations amphibious landing at Inchon, South Korea, constitutes one of the more striking ironies of the entire Korean conflict. Conceived during the very first week of the Korean fighting in June, 1950, the Inchon concept was developed at a time when the whole of South Korea had suddenly fallen under siege from a massive onslaught of Soviet-armed North Korean forces and was on the brink of total collapse.

On instructions from President Harry S Truman during this initial week, General Douglas MacArthur left his occupational command headquarters in Japan and flew to the Seoul front to survey the extent of the crisis. Once on the peninsula, the wreckage of the South Korean military position became obvious to MacArthur. Seoul itself, the South

Korean capital, had been overrun within three days and the pro-Western government of Syngman Rhee forced to flee farther south. Some forty-four thousand Republic of Korea (ROK) troops had been lost, as well as thirty percent of their small arms weapons. In addition, it became apparent that the invaders intended to press throughout the South as far as the vital port at Pusan. Coupled with a then-likely unification and control of all Korea would be the potential threat that the Communist forces, especially aircraft, would pose to Japan, Okinawa, and Chiang Kai-shek's Nationalist Chinese remnants on Formosa.

The United Nations' reaction to this blatant overland invasion had been relatively quick and determined in support of South Korea. But time would now be required to organize an effective military relief effort among the participating nations. Time, however, was MacArthur's least available commodity, as his personal visit to the battlefront outside Seoul amply indicated. The crucial Pusan port was a mere 170 miles from the spearheads of the North Korean columns, and virtually no positioned defense remained to impede this drive.

A heralded veteran commander of the American victory in the Pacific over Japan, MacArthur had faced debacles before. In the early months of 1942, he had been driven out of the Philippines by an aggressive Japanese offensive which he lacked the resources to halt. Now, eight years later, he faced a similar dilemma in his lack of readily available units with which to maneuver. Certainly there were United States troops, ships, and aircraft in the Far Eastern areas, but their immediate presence on the battlefields of South Korea again demanded time for strategical and logistical coordination.

Yet MacArthur saw in the rapidity of the North Korean advance in the South an opportunity that appealed to his gambler's instincts and strategic expertise. The North Korean penetration had dangerously extended their ability to supply adequately their own most advanced units. If this thread could be severed by a strike deep within the enemy's rear zones, it could play havoc with their invasion and conceivably produce a North Korean withdrawal. Thus, not only would the danger to Pusan be removed, but also the entire military situation would undergo a radical transformation.

MacArthur, during that first week's observation of the front, had selected the unlikely port of Inchon for his surprise operation. Inchon was literally at Seoul's coastal doorstep and posed risks, although amphibious landings were certainly not unfamiliar to MacArthur after his years of "island hopping" warfare against the Japanese in the 1940's. It is perhaps surprising, then, that veteran Marine and Navy officers, as well as Army Chief of Staff Joseph Lawton Collins and Admiral Forrest Sherman of Naval Operations, immediately questioned the viability of an Inchon strike. They were particularly anxious about the hazardous terrain, which, together with Inchon's staggering tides, the second deepest in the world, would make any landing risky. Beyond this were more far-reaching considerations, such as the possible reaction of Chinese forces stationed across the Yalu river in Manchuria, and the problems of inadequate data on the North Korean defenses around Inchon. Furthermore, there was the worry that even a successful assault on Inchon might not produce the immediate desired effect of relieving the threatened perimeter forming around Pusan far to the southeast.

Despite these sound and logical reservations, MacArthur saw the magic of just such an endeavor. Before a wary Joint Chiefs of Staff assembly in Tokyo on August 23, MacArthur argued that his Inchon concept had merit largely because of its unorthodox nature. He drew the analogy of British General James Wolfe's amazing assault on French forces under Montcalm at Quebec in 1759, in which a seemingly impassable wall of cliffs was scaled with startling ease largely because the defenders had concluded that such an avenue of approach was militarily out of the question.

On August 29, MacArthur finally received from Washington the necessary go-ahead for his plan, and on September 15, 1950 (a date chosen because the waters off Inchon would be as navigable as conditions would ever allow), the 1st Marine Division under Major General Oliver P. Smith successfully seized the tiny Wolmi-do Island (also known as Moontip Island) inside Inchon harbor. Naval guns and Marine airpower had prepared the way for the assault with a series of bombardments, and the island hazard fell into Marine hands in less than an hour, with no United States casualties.

True to MacArthur's hopeful expectations, the port of Inchon quickly capitulated, with only marginal further resistance. Once on shore, the Marine units captured the important Kimpo Airfield, while backup support from the 7th Division (which came ashore at Inchon as a second wave but was unopposed) made it possible to seize the airstrip at Suwon, south of Seoul. Perhaps most vital of all, however, was the successful cutting of the Seoul-Pusan roadway.

Within two weeks of the Inchon landings, the bulk of the North Korean invasion effort had been decimated. Entire units had surrendered, and the roads were cluttered with hastily abandoned vehicles and weapons. In the mad retreat northward, some 130,000 North Korean troops were taken prisoner, and virtually all of the South was restored to the Syngman Rhee government, which was once again functioning in the capital of Seoul.

Of course, the MacArthur-led United Nations operation at Inchon did not end the conflict; two more years of seesaw engagements ripped across the Korean landscape both north and south of the 38th parallel dividing line. Chinese intervention, the celebrated Truman-MacArthur controversy, and the seemingly endless exchange of verbiage at the peace talks in Panmunjom were yet to come. Still, the Inchon landing stands as a watershed of the war, partly for its daring, but mainly for its impact on all subsequent events. Without the successful conclusion of this surprising maneuver, it is very possible that Korea today would be totally within the Communist sphere of influence in Asia.

Pertinent Literature

Leckie, Robert. *Conflict: The History of the Korean War, 1950-1953*. New York: G. P. Putnam's Sons, 1962.

Since the emergence of the United States as a significant military force in the world arena at about the time of the Spanish-American War of 1898, there have been numerous occasions which have put this less than century-old status to the test. Colossal confrontations such as the two world wars have been total conflicts in which the full economic and civilian resources of the United States could be called upon to unleash a technological advantage few others could match. In addition, these worldwide endeavors carried with them a sense of moral and human commitment for Americans; the purpose was clear, as were the forces to be opposed. All that remained was to get the job done and done right.

The Korean "conflict," as President Truman preferred to term it, was a radically different kind of crisis. As the first actual military combat operation of the United States during the formative period of the Cold War, the Korean fighting gave evidence that the rules were changing. An undeclared war (the Russian United Nations delegate, Jacob Malik, called it an "internal civil war") in the shadow of atomic weaponry, the Korean conflict technically involved the United States as only one component (albeit the largest one) of a United Nations task force designed to halt the aggressive efforts of North Korea. The desire to keep the fighting as limited in scope as possible so as not to alter unduly the delicate state of affairs in Europe and elsewhere necessitated the reliance upon purely conventional forces even though more coldly efficient weapons were available. Unlike World War II, for example, the Korean War was a "police" effort and was thus highly restricted in terms of geography, objectives, and options available to the powers involved. As such, despite its relatively acceptable stalemate-ceasefire arranged in 1953, the Korean War has never been a cause for

admiration or spirited speeches of praise in the United States. And, unlike the vast majority of other American war involvements, Korea has not been the subject of endless military retrospectives by authors.

Robert Leckie, a Marine veteran of the Pacific in World War II and the author of numerous books and articles on military history, is widely considered to be among the foremost in his field. His *Conflict: The History of the Korean War, 1950-1953* is considered to be not only the first full-scale history of the conflict, but also the best. While genuine attention is given to the loftier political and ideological aspects so much a part of the war, Leckie's primary focus is upon the peculiarities, frustrations, and ingenuity that dominated the combat itself.

No operation of the war is more graphically depicted in this volume than the celebrated United Nations landing at Inchon in 1950. Masterminded by General Douglas MacArthur during the earliest days of the North Korean invasion, its implementation some three months later turned the tide of the fighting in the South and salvaged what could easily have been the collapse of the Seoul government permanently. In particular, Leckie vividly outlines the seemingly impossible obstacles facing the Inchon concept which led many of the highest ranking military minds of the United States to question seriously the wisdom behind MacArthur's plan. Additionally, the author considers the problems of maintaining a necessary level of secrecy about the operation once the decision to proceed with it had been reached. Japan, where the details of the plan were formalized in the summer of 1950, was a country rife with informants, spies, and Communist sympathizers. To further prevent Communist forces from positioning themselves at the Inchon site, diversionary bombardment had been conducted elsewhere, particularly by a British task force which hammered at Chinnampo to the north, and the *U.S.S. Missouri*, which performed a similar role on the east coast of Korea near Samchok.

Complete with easily visualized map renderings of the Inchon landing zone, Leckie painstakingly walks the reader through what is literally an hourly survey of the landing, amply crediting the officers and units that took part. The tactical particulars that Leckie includes on the operations are without equal in any other retrospective on the event.

If Leckie's book can be said to have any limitations, they may stem from the understandable absence of concrete information regarding the plans, reactions, and feasible debates which occurred within the enemy camp. Unlike World War II, about which substantial writing from the point of view of former German officers has been published, the Korean War has been a difficult subject for historians to research. Leckie and other Western military historians remain victimized when writing about the Korean War because of continued Cold War suspicions and lack of access to primary sources behind the ideological barriers.

Leckie's account can be appreciated at a variety of levels, however. From the observations of heads of state to the ground-level endurance of the individual infantryman, this book illustrates an unmistakable fact: that the Inchon landing in particular, and the Korean War in general, contain all the classic elements of military combat at its most demanding.

Poats, Rutherford. *Decision in Korea*. New York: The McBride Company, 1954.

Decision in Korea was written almost immediately after the ceasefire settlement, if it can be termed that, arrived at in 1953 at Panmunjom. As such, it is a somewhat hurried attempt to look at the Korean conflict in terms of its meaning and its particulars. What liabilities may result from this situation are offset, however, by the interesting perspective given on certain events such as the Inchon landing in 1950.

It seems apparent from Poats's work that the Inchon operation was perhaps the forerunner of the flexible and highly mobile style of warfare that the United States has preferred to rely upon in subsequent years. While the numbers of United States forces involved in the Inchon operation were actually fairly limited in relation to the sizable numbers of North Koreans involved in the invasion of the South, the United States operation was blessed with a far more fluid kind of weaponry. In particular, the United States Navy provided MacArthur and the United Nations with a tremendously flexible Armed Forces which the North Koreans lacked. In one respect, it could be said that the North Korean invaders were conducting a cross-country assault in the manner of World War II in Europe, while the United States-led United Nations operation was clearly designed for combat of a more unorthodox nature.

In Poats's treatment of MacArthur, however, it does become clear that the Inchon strike was not entirely beyond the norms of military sanity. It remains an axiom of military strategy to strike at the opponent where he is the weakest and particularly to take advantage of situations in which he has overextended himself. MacArthur's own strategy at Inchon, then, is perhaps closely allied to the kind of "flexible defense" that German Field Marshal Manstein employed against the attacking Soviet divisions in the Ukraine in 1944. In MacArthur's Inchon operation, however, the objective was not only to stem the tide temporarily (as was more the case with Manstein), but to seize the initiative and begin a counteroffensive which he felt would substantially alter the complexion of the war itself.

It becomes apparent also that the United Nations' role in the Inchon plan was marginal at best. The landing itself was almost exclusively a United States planned and conducted strike, although the British did assist somewhat in the diversionary naval maneuvers further north along the coast. In truth, the Inchon operation was perhaps General Douglas MacArthur's most enlightened military action of his controversial career in that it involved a greater risk of setbacks than did his increasingly favorable position against the Japanese in the Pacific in late 1942 and afterwards.

As is typical of the books written on the Korean War, however, Poats's work only treats the Inchon landing as one segment of the overall fighting. It is viewed, realistically enough, as the beginning of the turning point in the war, yet it is handled in fairly limited terms and cannot be said to be the focal point of his book.
— *T.A.B.*

Additional Recommended Reading

Berger, Carl. *The Korea Knot: A Military-Political History*. Philadelphia: University of Pennsylvania Press, 1964. A broad look at the peculiarities of the Korean War as a whole with its political implications as well as the warfare itself.

Futrell, Robert Frank. *The United States Air Force in Korea, 1950-1953*. New York: Duell, Sloan and Pearce, 1961. Focuses on the extensive use of American air power in the war and contains some interesting comments on the air role in the Inchon landing in 1950.

Geer, Andrew. *The New Breed: The Story of the U.S. Marines in Korea*. New York: Harper & Brothers, 1952. A close look at the vital role of the United States Marines in the Inchon assault.

Higgins, Trumbull. *Korea and the Fall of MacArthur: A Precis in Limited War*. New York: Oxford University Press, 1960. Deals considerably with the ousting of MacArthur as a result of his dispute with President Truman, but also includes a focused look at the limitations MacArthur faced in fighting the war under undeclared circumstances and political repercussions.

Whitney, Courtney. *MacArthur: His Rendezvous with History*. New York: Alfred A. Knopf, 1956. A biography which deals especially with MacArthur's Korean involvement; a good study of the commander and his concepts.

Willoughby, Charles A. and John Chamberlain. *MacArthur 1941-1951*. New York: McGraw-Hill Book Company, 1954. A study of MacArthur's war years including World War II and Korea; the Inchon operation is well covered as an example of MacArthur's expertise.

EXPLOSION OF THE FIRST HYDROGEN BOMB

Type of event: Scientific: development of the fusion bomb
Time: Early 1951-March 1, 1954
Locale: Elugelab Island; Siberia; and Bikini atoll

Principal personages:

JULIUS ROBERT OPPENHEIMER (1904-1967), theoretical physicist and Director of the Los Alamos Laboratories

EDWARD TELLER (1908-   ), Hungarian-born atomic physicist and "father" of the hydrogen bomb

STANISLAW MARCIN ULAM (1909-   ), mathematician who developed idea of the lithium hydride bomb

JOHN VON NEUMANN (1903-1957), Hungarian-born mathematician and physicist who invented the MANIAC computer

HARRY S TRUMAN (1884-1972), thirty-third President of the United States, 1945-1953

BRIEN MCMAHON (1903-   ), United States Senator and Chairman of the Joint Congressional Committee on Atomic Energy

GENERAL HOYT VANDENBERG (1899-   ), United States Air Force Chief of Staff

LEWIS L. STRAUSS (1896-   ), member of the Atomic Energy Commission

LUIS WALTER ALVAREZ (1911-   ), American-born atomic physicist who helped lobby for the production of the hydrogen bomb

ERNEST ORLANDO LAWRENCE (1901-1958), American-born atomic physicist and Nobel Prize-winner for the invention of the cyclotron

Summary of Event

In the summer of 1942, J. Robert Oppenheimer, a theoretical physicist, invited several other leading American physicists to Berkeley, California, to decide how to develop atomic weapons for the war against Germany. At this meeting, Edward Teller, a Hungarian-born physicist, suggested development of a fusion, or hydrogen, bomb. The idea for the fusion bomb came from the type of thermonuclear reactions thought to exist in the interior of stars: two ions of deuterium (or "heavy" hydrogen) fused to make one atom of helium, releasing about four million volts of energy. Most of the scientists had, however, been thinking in terms of a fission bomb, using the enormous energies set free when heavy atoms are split in a nuclear reaction. Although the fusion, or hydrogen, bomb was potentially more powerful, there were many more theoretical and practical problems involved in its development. One of these "problems" was the fear that the hydrogen bomb might be capable of igniting the oceans in one vast chain reaction, thus winning the war by demolishing the earth.

The assembled scientists decided to begin work on the fission bomb and to shelve temporarily the problem of fusion. Oppenheimer became the Director of the Los Alamos Laboratories, where the first operable atomic bomb was designed and constructed. Edward Teller also went to work at Los Alamos, but never accepted the decision to concentrate on the fission bomb: he continued to nurse his fusion idea. The other Los Alamos scientists worked hard and successfully on fission: in July, 1945, the first atomic bomb was exploded in Alamogordo, New Mexico. By this time, the Germans had surrendered and the Japanese were reported to be seeking peace, but President Harry S Truman still made the decision to drop the bomb—possibly, it has been argued, perhaps unfairly, to impress the Russians. The explosions were indeed impressive: the cities of Hiroshima and Nagasaki were destroyed and a hundred thousand people were killed.

After the war, many of the scientists began an intensive lobbying effort against the use of nuclear weapons. Teller, now virtually alone in his desire to create the hydrogen, or "Super" bomb, was opposed by Albert Einstein and the Emergency Committee of Atomic Scientists. In August, 1949, however, the United States learned that the Soviet Union had exploded its first atomic weapon, "Joe 1"; and many military and government officials were shocked to discover that the United States was no longer the only nuclear power.

Teller and his colleagues, Ernest O. Lawrence, inventor of the cyclotron, and Luis Alvarez, began an intensive lobbying effort to develop the "Super," and they gained many influential friends, including Senator Brien McMahon, Chairman of the Joint Congressional Committee of Atomic Energy; General Hoyt Vandenberg, Air Force Chief of Staff; Omar Bradley, Chairman of the Joint Chiefs of Staff; and Lewis L. Strauss, the most conservative and powerful member of the Atomic Energy Commission. The nine leading scientists who were members of the General Advisory Committee of the Atomic Energy Commission, under the chairmanship of Oppenheimer, all advised against production of the "Super." The five members of the Atomic Energy Commission concurred with this decision by a vote of four to one; but this entire system for decisionmaking on the use of atomic power was negated. On January 31, 1950, a committee of three met at the White House. Louis A. Johnson, Secretary of Defense, Dean Acheson, Secretary of State, and David Lilienthal, Chairman of the Atomic Energy Commission, voted two to one in favor of the "Super," with Lilienthal opposed. That afternoon, President Truman announced his decision to proceed with the rapid development of the hydrogen bomb.

In 1950, it was not yet clear whether the hydrogen bomb would work. In principle, heavy hydrogen would fuse when ignited by the heat of an atomic blast. A mixture of deuterium and tritium (both being forms of heavy hydrogen) would ignite more readily than deuterium alone. The heavy hydrogen had to be kept in liquid form and thus required refrigeration. The first model of the "Super," therefore, was a fission bomb coated with layers of deuterium and tritium and enclosed in a huge refrigeration unit, weighing sixty-five tons. Since this thermonuclear icebox was not a practical weapon, it was called a thermonuclear "device," and was named, by some of the scientists, "The Superfluous." This device was exploded on the island of Elugelab in the South Pacific on November 1, 1952, sinking the entire island and carving a mile-long crater in the ocean floor. The American scientists did not know that the U.S.S.R. had already exploded a similar thermonuclear device in 1951; this fact, known only to President Truman and a few of his top advisers, was kept a well-guarded secret, even from Teller.

By 1951, however, Edward Teller and Stanislaw Ulam, a mathematician, had already developed a new idea for a workable bomb which would be made with lithium deuteride instead of the tritium-deuterium mixture and would need no refrigeration. Neutrons produced by the first fission explosion would turn lithium into tritium, resulting in a practical "dry" bomb. The idea was, in Oppenheimer's words, "technically sweet," but required enormously complicated mathematical calculations. The scientists agreed to work six days a week and to take night shifts in the computer section, but John von Neumann made the most important contribution: a new and much more advanced computer, which

he named the MANIAC.

On August 8, 1953, however, Georgi Malenkov, the Soviet premier, announced that the Americans no longer had a monopoly on the hydrogen bomb; several days later, radiation traces showed that the Soviet Union had exploded a "dry" lithium hydride bomb.

On March 1, 1954, the United States responded with a new twist: the three-stage fission-fusion-fission bomb, coated with uranium isotopes for maximum destructive power. This bomb, "Shoot 1," was exploded in the Bikini atoll with the power of about twenty million tons of TNT. The uranium coating guaranteed a very widely distributed radioactive fallout; a crew of Japanese fishermen on the *Lucky Dragon*, one hundred and twenty miles away, became sick and were hospitalized; one of them died.

The idea that the Russians had exploded a hydrogen bomb before the Americans added fuel to the fires of the McCarthy witch-hunts. Looking for a scapegoat, security officials accused Oppenheimer of having opposed the development of the hydrogen bomb. A three-man Personnel Security Board judged his case: Thomas A. Morgan, an industrialist, and Gordon Grey, a newspaper and broadcasting executive, voted against him, while Ward Evans, a professor of chemistry, voted in his favor. In 1954, Oppenheimer was denied security clearance and his power was broken; Edward Teller, Ernest Lawrence, and Lewis L. Strauss became the new scientific advisers for the Cold War.

Explosion of the First Hydrogen Bomb

Pertinent Literature

Blumberg, Stanley A. and Gwinn Owens. *Energy and Conflict: The Life and Times of Edward Teller*. New York: G. P. Putnam's Sons, 1976.

This is the first authoritative biography of Edward Teller, based on hundreds of hours of interviews with Teller, his family, and associates, and on Teller's own letters, papers, and memorabilia. The authors have been thorough in their research, given the fact that many aspects of their subject are still masked by official secrecy. Their thoroughness is marked by their discovery of a fact hidden even from Teller: that the Soviet Union exploded the first thermonuclear device early in 1951. The principal designer of the Soviet hydrogen bomb was Andrei D. Sakharov, more recently known as a Soviet dissident. In an apparent excess of secrecy, scientists in the United States were not told of this Soviet explosion and were left to assume that they were the world leaders in fusion bomb development.

Any good biography combines intimacy with its subject and a certain critical distance, allowing both understanding and objectivity. In this book, the authors display a cool and somewhat dispassionate interest in Edward Teller, tempered with admiration for some of his positions—particularly his opposition to scientific secrecy—and a sympathetic warmth for a difficult man facing difficult decisions. The distance one feels is in part due to Teller, who refused to talk about his family or his childhood, and is in part due to the authors' own political perspective. Blumberg and Owens are politically liberal, whereas Teller is moved by a profound and passionate anti-Communism.

Energy and Conflict tells the story of Teller's flight to the United States, his involvement with the Los Alamos laboratory, his campaign for the development of the hydrogen bomb, and his growing distress with Oppenheimer and other atomic scientists who refused to share his sense of the urgent need for thermonuclear weapons. It provides a more comprehensive account of the scientific and technical processes involved in the various stages of hydrogen bomb development than do other histories of this period, although here, again, many of the details are still classified.

The most important technical breakthrough was the lithium hydride bomb, which required no expensive tritium or clumsy refrigeration apparatus. Curiously, the basic conception of this bomb had been described in 1946 by an Austrian physicist, Hans Thirring, in a commercially published book, *The Story of the Atom Bomb*. Thirring's book, however, was not read by atomic scientists in the United States, and the idea for the first workable United States bomb is usually attributed either to Edward Teller or to Stanislaw Ulam, also working in the Los Alamos laboratory in 1951. Teller presented his plan for a lithium hydride bomb at a strategy meeting of the Atomic Energy Commission in June, 1951, and it was then accepted (the details of

Teller's design have, however, never been made public).

In 1953, the Soviets exploded the first true hydrogen bomb; in 1954, security hearings were held on Oppenheimer. Teller was the only leading scientist to testify against Oppenheimer, and as a result, he found himself painfully excluded by many of his old friends in the scientific community. He has since found himself uncomfortably identified as a warmonger for his view that nuclear weapons can be of great advantage in a limited war, and for his opposition to nuclear test ban treaties. The physicist I. I. Rabi has called him "an enemy of humanity."

However, Teller has been so outspoken in favor of nuclear weapons that he has tended to take the blame for attitudes that are quite widely shared by political leaders in the United States and, most probably, by their counterparts in the Soviet Union. Both powers seem more concerned about their chances of "winning" a nuclear war than about the immense destruction involved. Even the current levels of nuclear tests are contributing to the worldwide incidence of cancer and genetic abnormalities, although Teller is one of those who feels that fears of radiation hazards have been greatly exaggerated, and that genetic abnormalities are not necessarily harmful.

Since the 1950's, Teller has become a powerful behind-the-scenes force in federal policy; he was a member of President Nixon's Foreign Intelligence Advisory Board and of Rockefeller's Commission on Critical Choices for Americans. He has acted as consultant to at least ten defense contractors and a dozen government agencies; he advised the establishment of a multibillion-dollar Energy Trust Fund to underwrite the capital needs of private corporations in the development of synthetic fuels and nuclear power plants. With many Armed Forces officers and major industrialists, Teller belongs to the right-wing American Security Council; he has become more of a political adviser than a scientist. Blumberg and Owens provide many fascinating insights into this complex man who remains a powerful force in scientific and political circles.

Davis, Nuel Pharr. *Lawrence and Oppenheimer*. New York: Simon and Schuster, 1968.

This book gains its power from the dramatic juxtaposition of the personalities and politics of Ernest O. Lawrence and J. Robert Oppenheimer. The composite portrait of the two men is constructed from the available written records and also from the memories of men: Davis interviewed about one hundred of the scientists' colleagues, including many of this century's most distinguished atomic physicists. This carefully crafted and elegantly written account is absorbing reading; the drama is compelling and the detail convincing.

No single account of the scientific, moral, and political controversies surrounding the work of the atomic scientists can hope to be completely objective or to present every man in the image in which he would like to be viewed. Davis is, perhaps, too kind to Oppenheimer and too harsh on Lawrence, but Oppenheimer is the hero of this story. The bias, if it is such, is readily understandable as a corrective to the vilification of Oppenheimer's reputation during the McCarthy period. Lawrence emerged from the disputes over the hydrogen bomb heaped with money and honors; Oppenheimer died in 1967, officially still regarded as a security risk to the United States.

At the security hearings in 1954, Oppenheimer was asked if he was really the most influential atomic scientist in the country; he answered that Lawrence had, in many ways, more influence. Neither man was intimately involved in the theoretical development of the hydrogen bomb, but both were deeply implicated in the politics surrounding its production.

Lawrence and Oppenheimer first met as young professors in the physics department of the University of California at Berkeley: Lawrence the Midwesterner, a brash and enthusiastic experimental physicist, Oppenheimer the Easterner, a quiet and brilliant theoretician. At Berkeley, Lawrence built even bigger and more powerful cyclotrons for splitting atoms; Oppenheimer worked on the most advanced aspects of theoretical physics. Lawrence turned increasingly to the wealthy and powerful men who could finance his expensive projects; Oppenheimer turned to the campus radicals and intellectuals concerned with the struggles against Fascism in Europe. Lawrence continued to consort with millionaires, while Oppenheimer gradually, and sometimes uneasily, joined the effort to build ever bigger and more powerful weapons.

In 1949, Lawrence joined Edward Teller in lobbying for a crash program to develop the hydrogen bomb; he talked to his millionaire friends, to congressmen, and to Army and Air Force generals. Teller was to persuade the physicists, although here he was less successful than Lawrence had been. Lawrence and his friend, financier Lewis L. Strauss, must take much of the credit for persuading congressional and military men that the "Super," or hydrogen bomb, was a necessary weapon against the Soviet Union.

Oppenheimer, as Chairman of the General Advisory Committee of the Atomic Energy Commission, represented the scientists opposed to development of the hydrogen bomb. It is doubtful whether Oppenheimer ever personally persuaded, or had an interest in persuading, other scientists to share his view; the evidence suggests that many of the others held stronger moral positions on the question than he did. Indeed, the objections to the Super bomb were not simply moral ones; many opposed it on practical, theoretical, or even financial grounds, arguing that it would be cheaper and more effective to develop better atom bombs than to devote resources to a new and untested thermonuclear weapon. The main military advantage of the hydrogen bomb seemed to lie in the psychological use of terror, since it could so easily wipe out whole populations.

By leading us through the intricacies of the history of the development of nuclear and thermonuclear weapons, Davis provides a fascinating account of the politics of American science as played out at the highest scientific, governmental, and military levels. His account is not a reassuring one, but rather one that explodes the comfortable assumption that scientific policy and the ethical questions it involves can best be left to the experts. Perhaps the most disturbing discovery is that scientific specialists who tried to act as a moderating influence, urging caution in the development of horrifying new weapons systems, could be so easily overruled by a few men who, as Davis shows, were responsible only to the competitive hysteria of the nuclear arms race. — E.F.

Additional Recommended Reading

Jungk, Robert. *Brighter Than a Thousand Suns: A Personal History of the Atomic Scientists*. New York: Harcourt, Brace, 1958. A good, clear history of nuclear weapons development which concentrates especially on the moral issues involved.

Compton, Arthur Holly. *Atomic Quest: A Personal Narrative*. New York: Oxford University Press, 1956. The history of the atomic bomb by one of the leading physicists involved in the Manhattan Project.

Rabi, I. I., Robert Serber, Victor F. Weisskopf, Abraham Pais and Glenn Seaborg. *Oppenheimer*. New York: Charles Scribner's Sons, 1969. Oppenheimer's life and work as sympathetically recalled by his fellow scientists.

Curtis, Charles P. *The Oppenheimer Case: The Trial of a Security System*. New York: Simon and Schuster, 1955. A lawyer's detailed discussion of the Oppenheimer hearings, including long excerpts from the original transcripts.

Moss, Norman. *Men Who Play God: The Story of the H-Bomb and How the World Came to Live with It*. New York: Harper & Row Publishers, 1968. A British journalist's report on the thermonuclear age including vivid portraits of Edward Teller, strategic analyst Herman Kahn, and conscientious protester Pat O'Connell.

Oppenheimer, J. Robert. *The Open Mind*. New York: Simon and Schuster, 1955. The physicist's popular lectures on atomic weapons and the relationships between science and society.

Teller, Edward and Allen Brown. *The Legacy of Hiroshima*. Garden City, N.Y.: Doubleday & Company, 1962. Teller gives his account of the development of the hydrogen bomb and argues that the United States should be prepared to use nuclear weapons.

Rapoport, Roger. *The Great American Bomb Machine*. New York: E. P. Dutton, 1971. A vivid account of the manufacture and testing of nuclear weapons, attempting to warn the public of the dangers involved.

THE FOREIGN POLICY OF JOHN FOSTER DULLES

Type of event: Diplomatic: ideas and conduct of a Secretary of State
Time: January 20, 1953-May 24, 1959
Locale: The United States and the world

Principal personages:

JOHN FOSTER DULLES (1888-1959), United States Secretary
of State, 1953-1959

DWIGHT DAVID EISENHOWER (1890-1969), thirty-fourth President of the United States, 1953-1961

GAMAL ABDEL NASSER (1918-1970), President of Egypt,
1956-1970

KONRAD ADENAUER (1876-1967), Chancellor of the Federal
Republic of Germany, 1949-1963

CHIANG KAI-SHEK (1887-1975), President of the Republic of
China (Taiwan), 1950-1975

Summary of Event

President Dwight D. Eisenhower reportedly said of John Foster Dulles that he had been in training for Secretary of State since he was five (or, in some accounts, seven) years old. Like most such remarks, it has some truth. Dulles' grandfather, John W. Foster, was Secretary of State under Benjamin Harrison, and an uncle by marriage, Robert Lansing, was Woodrow Wilson's Secretary of State. Dulles himself served at the Hague Conference in 1907, while still a Princeton undergraduate, and at the Paris Peace Conference and on the Reparations Commission after the Peace Conference. During the 1920's and 1930's, he was among the country's most successful international lawyers. The preliminaries of World War II and the war itself led to his involvement in the moral and religious bases of postwar planning, and in Republican politics. After service as part of the bipartisan support for the United Nations, and as adviser to the Truman Administration, he accepted Governor Thomas E. Dewey's appointment as United States Senator from New York. Defeated in his campaign for election to that office, he returned to the advisory position with the Department of State, and to active service in negotiating the peace treaty with Japan in 1951. He supported General Eisenhower in the preconvention battle against Senator Robert A. Taft and in the election campaign of 1952.

With such a background, Dulles' appointment to the post of Secretary of State was virtually assured. Aspects of his background suggest a variety of characteristics which have been singled out to explain his policies and style.

One such explanation insists on the religious and moralistic character of Dulles' view of the world—a world divided between good and evil, with little room for ambiguity or compromise. Another explanation stresses

690

his lawyer's qualities—not so much "legalism" as the habit of adversary proceeding and skill in the use of language. The first, perhaps too crudely put, meant an obligation to do one's best for the client (as Secretary for the United States) and to let the other parties (allies as well as opponents) look out for themselves. The second, this view holds, meant a care for language that was precise, but not always unambiguous. The seemingly strong and categorical statement might, on rereading, be restricted and modified by "the fine print."

Still another explanation, seemingly at odds with the "moralistic" view, finds Dulles to be realistic and pragmatic, succeeding in the legal profession, serving Democratic administrations while maintaining his credentials as a Republican and as Secretary, concerned with relations with President, Congress, and public opinion as much as with other nations.

Such biographical and psychoanalytic fact and speculation touch only one of the influences on a foreign policy maker. For a Secretary of State, the policy is not even primarily his, but the President's; however strong the Secretary, however great the mutual trust, there is no question who is the chief. Dulles, it would seem, knew this well; he and Eisenhower developed a remarkable partnership, but in several cases, the President modified, if he did not overrule, the Secretary.

The world outside, in "objective reality" and in the view of the diplomat's countrymen, is a further influence. For Americans in the 1950's the prime fact of foreign affairs was the power and hostility of the Soviet Union, the head and center of a seemingly monolithic worldwide conspiracy. A series of events (and of what may have been nonevents, but were believed) had strengthened this conviction of Soviet imperialism abroad, tyranny at home, conspiracy within the United States, and weakness, at best, in American response. Dulles' promise of liberation, not mere containment, was in tune with this popular feeling.

World Communism, the enemy, must be met on every front. Building on the model of the North Atlantic Treaty Organization (NATO), the United States initiated or encouraged alliances in the Persian Gulf and Southeast Asia, such as the Southeast Asia Treaty Organization (SEATO). Primarily military, the alliances promised to restrain Soviet expansion. To augment the struggle against world Communism, Dulles advanced a new military-diplomatic strategy for which he is best remembered, the promise of massive retaliation.

In retrospect, it has been argued that what Dulles was trying to avoid was the prospect of United States involvement in local wars and episodes on the periphery of the Soviet Union, and keeping open the possibility that the response to Soviet aggression or infiltration might be not local, but aimed directly at Moscow. As a consequence, however, with a new United States dependence on thermonuclear weapons—"a bigger bang for a buck" according to Secretary of Defense Charles Wilson—the "massive" threat evoked reactions of fright among allies.

In Europe, the alliance system required military force to confront the Red Army, though hardly to match it. In the eyes of the United States, this required a large and integrated European force; for many Europeans, the stumbling block was the prospect of a rearmed Germany. In complicated negotiations, Dulles found rapport with Konrad Adenauer, the West German Chancellor, and difficulties with Charles de Gaulle and with the French government more generally. The threat of an "agonizing reappraisal" of United States relations with its allies was another controversial phrase on Dulles' list.

In Europe, too, the difficulties of liberation became clearer. Dulles had insisted that the liberation he spoke of would be by peaceful means, involving the destruction of the Soviet power by a moral reaction to its wickedness and tyranny. Germany remained divided; despite official pronouncements from both sides for unification, the division hardened and was accepted tacitly with the creation of the two German republics; West Berlin remained within the geographical confines of East Germany. The Soviet satellites in Eastern Europe were still satellites; any hope of fundamental change in that situation was dampened by the brutal suppression of the Hungarian revolt in October, 1956, by Soviet forces.

In Asia and Africa, there was tension for the United States, and particularly for Secretary Dulles, who was caught between the American condemnation of colonialism and the ties to the former colonial powers, notably Britain and France. One case with tragic repercussions for the fu-

ture was Indochina, and especially Vietnam, where the United States rendered aid to the losing French effort but refused to supply manpower. Dulles briefly attended the Geneva conference of 1954, which tried to settle the war and provide for elections. He refused to recognize the Chinese presence, and would not allow the United States to sanction officially the arrangement dividing Vietnam.

Never accepting the Communist victory in the Chinese Civil War, the Eisenhower Administration continued to recognize Chiang Kai-shek and his regime on Taiwan as the legitimate government of China. On the other hand, despite talk of "unleashing" Chiang, there was no effort made on his part to recover the mainland, nor did he receive any real encouragement from the United States government.

Fear of Communism in the Middle East may have been the motive in first negotiating and then refusing to help finance Egyptian President Gamal Abdel Nasser's proposed Aswan High Dam on the Nile. When Nasser closed the Suez Canal, and Great Britain, France, and (separately but simultaneously) Israel attacked Egypt, Dulles put the United States in opposition to its allies and on the same side (in United Nations vote) as the Soviet Union.

Some modern students see a continuity of policy, or at least of attitude, from the Truman-Acheson direction of foreign affairs to that of John F. Kennedy, Lyndon Johnson, and Dean Rusk. Whatever the long-term continuities, John Foster Dulles put a mark of his own on the United

States and the world of his day.

Pertinent Literature

Hoopes, Townsend. *The Devil and John Foster Dulles*. Boston: Little, Brown and Company, 1973.

A full biography of its subject, Hoopes's book concentrates on Dulles' years in the State Department, and with justice—these are what make him an important figure in twentieth century history. As the title more than implies, it is written with wit and irony, though not without sympathy.

Writing seriously about recent history and the life and work of living or recently dead personages has not only the difficulty of bias and perspective, but also of material. On the one hand, there is a truly enormous amount of information, much of which is trivial or inaccurate; on the other hand, vital facts and explanations are in papers or tapes that are not yet available.

It is for these reasons that Hoopes's work, though as near to definitive as can reasonably be expected at this stage, is still in some ways tentative. He has worked with the Dulles Papers at Princeton University, especially the transcripts of Oral History interviews included with them. He also makes use of memoirs, newspaper and magazine accounts (not all listed in his bibliography), and a selection from the mass of secondary writings: not quite the professional historian's model, but soundly based. Hoopes's own experience in government, though not in the Eisenhower-Dulles years, adds insight.

For Hoopes, as for most other Dulles scholars, the two notable fea-tures of Dulles' background are the diplomatic precedents—grandfather, uncle, and his own early experience—and the religious character of his upbringing. Notable, too, is the evidence of an unusual intelligence and of a kind of intellectual arrogance which may have been its price. Success as a lawyer may have strengthened those qualities; it brought Dulles, both by way of his work on reparations and his legal connections with international business and finance, into continuing concern for and knowledge of world affairs.

Hoopes analyzes Dulles' first book, *War, Peace, and Change*, published in 1939, and its contrast to some later attitudes. The book, he argues, is a cool, nonmoralizing, abstract, and legal effort to find causes and preventions of war. Human nature in this account is selfish, and there is a strong tendency in all groups, including nation-states, to strengthen unity by means of external threat, to make the enemy not merely dangerous but wicked. Hoopes is less interested in Dulles' legal and almost Wilsonian proposal for countervailing pressure against the group selfishness of the nation-state, than in the change in attitude which followed. Indeed, it was almost at the same time, as he reads the story, that Dulles became interested in religion and in religious answers to the problems of war and peace. Hoopes suggests there may have been personal motivations; he several times suggests that Dulles in the 1920's and 1930's was not much interested in religion. This attitude changed, however, with the approach and outbreak of World War II.

The point is not only that Dulles' first real prominence on the national scene was that of a leader in Protestant Church thinking and planning for the peace after the war. More significant was the moral and religious tone of his thinking through the following years: the fundamental argument that Communism was evil, democracy of the American kind good, and the conflict between the two irreducible.

Hoopes traces this attitude through the important years from 1945 to Dulles' death in 1959. He notes as well, however, Dulles' ability to serve the Democratic administration while keeping his Republican connections, and to maintain relations in 1952 with both the Taft and Eisenhower camps within his party.

Hoopes proceeds with the story of Dulles' role and character as Secretary of State. Among the major episodes which the author discusses are Dulles' involvement in the fateful crisis over Suez, and the possibly more fateful beginnings of involvement in Vietnam; his continuing confrontation with the Soviet Union; and his continuing nonacknowledgement of Communist China. Realistically,

though Dulles is the center of the story, Hoopes does not make him the only mover and shaker. Eisenhower's personal touch on policy, the author believes, may have restrained Dulles.

Hoopes is aware, too, that circumstances and what Marxists call objective conditions put limits on human possibility. In fact, he suggests that, though Dulles in speech seemed to leave little room for maneuver or accommodation, he was aware of the possibilities and the limits. It is Hoopes's implication that different approaches *might* have thawed the Cold War—somewhat, if not all the way to *détente* in the 1950's.

Hoopes, in summarizing the character and career of Dulles, believes that other qualities besides his moralism, limited his vision and his ultimate success. His lawyer's habit of advocacy, of dealing with problems as subject to the adversary process, is one; related is Hoopes's judgment that he was in diplomacy a tactician, not a strategist, who was too often concerned with the immediate issue and its too often temporary settlement. Yet, for Hoopes, the fundamental root of Dulles' policy and of its failure lay in his belief not only in the wickedness but also in the weakness of Communism. It was, as Hoopes says, a belief which Dulles shared with most Americans.

Gerson, Louis L. *The American Secretaries of State and Their Diplomacy*. Vol. XVII: *John Foster Dulles*. New York: Cooper Square Publishers, 1967.

The original series of biographies, of varying lengths, of the Secretaries of State of the United States appeared in the 1920's. This volume is part of a continuation of that series up to 1961. Most or all the volumes share certain characteristics; attention is concentrated on the subject as

Secretary, with only a minimum of his career before and after that office; the treatment is factual, though not unsympathetic; the only illustration, perhaps symbolically, is the frontispiece—from the portrait of the subject in the collection of the Department of State.

Gerson's account of John Foster Dulles fits the pattern. Arranged by topic rather than chronology, it is still a lucid and orderly presentation, resting on manuscript sources and interviews. The problem-by-problem approach does help clarity, though interrelationships are not always made explicit. The style is sober, a shade formal, the manner factual, sympathetic in most cases, but critical.

The very solidity of the details conveys better than rhetoric could have the burden of Dulles' task and the diversity of problems which beset the State Department, and the United States, in the 1950's. Gerson's book in sum, provides a compendium of brief accounts of the episodes, issues, and limitations of policy in Dulles' time in office. — *G.J.F.*

Additional Recommended Reading

Beal, John Robinson. *John Foster Dulles*. New York: Harper & Row Publishers, 1957. The earliest full-scale biography, written while Dulles was alive and based in part on interviews with him.

Goold-Adams, Richard. *John Foster Dulles: A Reappraisal*. New York: Appleton Century Crofts, 1962. A sympathetic British view.

Guhin, Michael A. *John Foster Dulles: A Statesman and His Times*. New York: Columbia University Press, 1972. Stresses the realism of Dulles' thought and policy.

Mosley, Leonard. *Dulles: A Biography of Eleanor, Allen, and John Foster Dulles and Their Family Network*. New York: The Dial Press/James Wade, 1978. A group biography of the Dulles family.

Dulles, John Foster. *War or Peace*. New York: The Macmillan Company, 1950. Contains Dulles' views before he became Secretary of State.

Finer, Herman. *Dulles over Suez*. Chicago: Quadrangle Books, 1964. A critical view of Dulles' policy regarding the Suez Crisis.

THE ESTABLISHMENT OF THE DEMOCRATIC REPUBLIC OF VIETNAM

Type of event: Political: Nationalist movement and Communist revolution in Vietnam
Time: 1954
Locale: Vietnam

Principal personages:
HO CHI MINH (1890-1969), Communist leader of Viet Minh who set up the Democratic Republic of Vietnam at Hanoi
PHAN BOI CHAU (1867-1940), an early twentieth century Vietnamese revolutionary who sought an Asian alliance against the West
BAO DAI (1911-   ), Vietnamese Emperor at Hué, backed by the French to lead a non-Communist government in South Vietnam; abdicated August 26, 1945
VO NGUYEN GIAP (1912-   ), Vietnamese general trained by Chinese Communists
PIERRE MENDÈS-FRANCE (1907-   ), French Premier at the time Vietnam was divided at the seventeenth parallel
NGÔ DINH DIEM (1901-1963), leader of non-Communist Republic of Vietnam in south, 1955

Summary of Event

The emergence of the Communist government in North Vietnam in 1954 under the leadership of Ho Chi Minh had its roots in an evolving Nationalist movement against French colonial rule that dated from the mid-nineteenth century. Resistance to the French first took form in 1888 when an imperial regent sought to restore the Nguyen Dynasty. After 1900, however, reformist leaders were influenced by Western ideas on modernization, education, democracy, and economic and social change. This process was escalated to revolutionary activity by Phan Boi Chau, who attempted to organize an Asian alliance against Western imperialism and conferred in Japan with China's Nationalist leader, Sun Yat-sen. Vietnamese Nationalism thus received inspiration from both European ideas and the Asian experience in revolutionary change.

By 1927 the Nationalist Party of Vietnam (Quoc-Dan Dang) was created in the northern region of Tongking. Patterned after the Nationalist Party in China and fiercely anti-French, it sponsored a political assassination in 1929 and a military uprising at Yen Bay near the Chinese border in February, 1930. Although these efforts were ruthlessly crushed by the French, declining exports because of the worldwide depression and increasing crop failures and famine created a serious economic malaise that fostered popular sentiment against the French and consequent sympathy for the budding Nationalist cause.

A more radical wing of Vietnam's Nationalist movement, which eventually gave it leadership and direction, was led by the Communists. Most prominent among them was Ho Chi Minh, born in 1890 and named Nguyen Van Tranh. His youth was spent traveling and living in the West, where he supported himself in various trades and learned Western languages. It was in London and Paris during World War I that he began to accept anticolonial and socialist concepts. While in Paris in 1917, he contributed articles to *Le Populaire* and other leftist journals. Reflecting his Nationalist feelings at that time, he took the name Nguyen Ai-Quoc (Nguyen the Patriot). His liberal inclination had not yet turned to Marxism, as his interests for Vietnam centered on self-rule and equal rights. By 1920, however, Nguyen became a member of the French Socialist Party; and his journalistic work soon included contributions to *L'Humanité*, a Communist paper in Paris.

During the early 1920's, before the Nationalist Party was organized, Nguyen's political thought had progressed more rapidly from anticolonialism to liberalism to socialism and finally to Communism. He helped to organize the Communist Party of Vietnam in 1930, but it had to go underground in 1933 following some abortive urban strikes and peasant uprisings in Tongking. During this period, Nguyen was imprisoned as a revolutionary after escaping to Hong Kong; but he was released for lack of evidence.

After 1937, Nguyen and his fledgling Communist Party cooperated with anti-Fascist groups and began to work with Vietnamese Nationalist groups, particularly those exiled in China. After World War II reached Southeast Asia in 1941, Nguyen became the leader of these groups, as Secretary General of the "League for the Independence of Vietnam," and he took the name Ho Chi Minh. In the final stages of the war, the Chinese Nationalists and the Americans helped Ho get into Tongking with military equipment. When the Japanese withdrew from the border areas in the spring of 1945, Ho gained control of seven northern provinces. Ho was now a leader of the Vietnamese Nationalist movement (the Viet Minh League) with a hard-core Communist following. Nevertheless, Ho had an uneasy relationship with another Chinese-sponsored Vietnamese Nationalist Party (Dong Minh Hoi), and he had competition from a Communist Trotskyite faction in Cochin-China in the south as well as religious groups such as the Catholic Cao Dai and Buddhist Hoa-hao.

By late summer, 1945, Ho Chi Minh had become the strongest political-military force in Vietnam. The weak Emperor Bao Dai at Hué abdicated, on August 26, in favor of Ho's "Democratic Republic of Vietnam," and the guerrilla forces of Vo Nguyen Giap, who was himself trained by the Chinese Communists, held a strong base in Tongking. On September 2, 1945, Ho Chi Minh felt confident enough to proclaim his government's independence at Hanoi. To minimize Communist leadership in Ho's united front, however, the Communist Party was overtly dissolved in November, and more non-Communists were recruited for the government.

The immediate postwar scene in Vietnam was complicated by the surrender of Japanese troops to the Allies. Chinese forces occupied the area north of the 16th parallel and British forces south of it. With the British came Free French forces that retook control of Saigon. The Nationalist Chinese in the north, meanwhile, allowed the Viet Minh to continue at Hanoi. When the Nationalists withdrew in the spring of 1946, the Viet Minh were solely in control. By this time, two movements, anticolonialism and domestic revolution, were merging together.

In the following year, Ho Chi Minh's relations with the French went from cooperation to civil war. On March 6, 1946, France recognized the "Democratic Republic of Vietnam" as a "free state within the Indochinese Federation and the French Union." French troops were allowed in Hanoi, and Cochin-China was separated from Vietnam and placed under a puppet regime. This tenuous arrangement fell apart when the French bombarded Haiphong on November 23, 1946, and the Vietnamese attacked the French in Hanoi on December 19. These actions began an embittered civil war that lasted nearly eight years. As the Communist leadership of the Viet Minh became more evident, the French attempted to reestablish former Emperor Bao Dai in a rival non-Communist, Nationalist

regime at Saigon in June, 1949. The French, however, failed to attract anti-Communist Nationalists to the Saigon government.

The conflict in Vietnam soon entered the Cold War. The Soviet Union and the newly established People's Republic of China recognized Ho Chi Minh's government, while the United States and Great Britain recognized Bao Dai. American arms went to the French, and Chinese economic and military support went to the Viet Minh, who became increasingly Communist in content and style.

When the Pathet Lao ("Free Laotian") movement invaded Laos with Viet Minh support, the French planned to disrupt the operation by building a defensive position at Dien Bien Phu in northwestern Vietnam. Surrounded by the artillery of Vo Nguyen Giap, the French surrendered this last stronghold in the north on May 7, 1954. At this time, an international conference on Asian problems had already convened in Geneva. Through the efforts of Pierre Mendès-France, the French Parliament approved a settlement whereby Ho Chi Minh's Communistic Democratic Republic of Vietnam would govern north of the seventeenth parallel, and Bao Dai's Republic of Vietnam, with Ngô Dinh Diem as Premier, would govern the south. Late in 1955, however, Diem replaced Bao Dai through elections and became head of state.

Pertinent Literature

Lacouture, Jean. *Ho Chi Minh: A Political Biography.* Translated by Peter Wiles. New York: Random House, 1968.

The personal acquaintance which the author, Jean Lacouture, had with Ho Chi Minh and the movement he led adds a perceptive dimension to the Western understanding of one of the more dynamic leaders in the Communist world. Taking the reader through Ho's evolution from anticolonial Nationalist to Communist revolutionary, the author explains both the forces that pressured Ho and their effect upon his character and leadership qualities.

Like most Western-educated Asian intellectuals, Ho Chi Minh learned liberal and socialist ideas from the colonials themselves. While in London and Paris as a youth, eking out a living performing menial tasks such as dishwashing and shoveling snow, Ho found time to read political books and talk at length with European leftists and Asian expatriates who shared his anticolonial feelings. Especially enlightening to Ho was the sympathy he found among French workers for socialism. He learned that not all Frenchmen were colonial oppressors and that the circumstances of an exploited native of a colony was similar to that of a European worker. This realization and the knowledge Ho gained about labor organizations and political parties were to serve him well later. Lacouture contends that had Ho remained in Vietnam, he might never have evolved beyond being a strong Nationalist concerned only with discarding the French.

By 1920-1923, Ho Chi Minh had joined the socialist movement, and he became an active contributor to leftist journals such as *Le Paria (The Outcast)*, which he founded and edited. Before he left Paris, Ho had joined the ninth cell of the French Communist Party. Ho's Nationalist consciousness, Lacouture points out, was still evident in his expressed concern that European Communists were not doing enough for colonial countries and were ignoring the plight of the oppressed Asians. Another difference from the urban-industrial proletariat of Europe was his belief, expressed in an article in *L'Humanité*, that a peasant revolt in Vietnam was feasible and necessary. He believed, like Mao Tse-tung, that the Asian peasant would revolt if given the proper organization and leadership, and he sought the assistance of the Communist International. Ho's peasant origin always remained strong despite his years of wandering by sea and residing in the urban-industrial society of Europe.

The milestone of Ho Chi Minh's socialist education came with his participation in the Fifth Congress of the Communist International (1923-1924). At the end of his Russian visit, Ho was a revolutionary. He spent much of the next twenty years in China, in part organizing exiled revolutionaries in Canton and writing tracts that show the application of Marxist-Leninist doctrine to the struggle for Vietnamese independence, such as his *Chemin de la révolution (The Road to Revolution)*. Once the Vietnamese Communist Party (Vietnam Cong San Dang) was organized in 1930 (changed soon to Indochinese Communist Party), Ho Chi Minh's revolutionary movement became overt. Nevertheless, the predominance of Nationalism remained and was strengthened with the Viet Minh organization in 1941. Lacouture explains that Ho was patient and saw the Nationalist movement and revolutionary change in Vietnam coming in successive stages.

Ho's character is given considerable attention by the author, who sees him as a mild-mannered but determined man who knew how to handle people and win their confidence and loyalty. Lacouture regards Ho as a skilled negotiator who could turn setbacks into advantages and whose revolutionary strategy was inspired by Lenin. He was adept, for example, in determining the "favorable moment" for taking action, and he always focused his efforts on the "main adversary" and avoided diversionary efforts against lesser enemies. Political organization and strategy, rather than theories or doctrine, were Ho's most important traits. Lacouture also views Ho as somewhat compromising and less militant than some of his followers. Ho, for example, was willing to surrender some gains for strategic reasons, such as his acceptance of an association with the French Union in March, 1946, and the division of Vietnam in July, 1954, despite the victory in the north and growing support in the south. Lacouture believes that the four decades of relentless fighting convinced Ho that one does not win altogether or lose altogether. In addition, Lacouture notes that, despite the fanatical zeal for his cause, Ho preferred persuasion to compulsion in order to win acceptance, and that he personally disliked violence. Finally, Ho Chi Minh is seen as a man who earned the affection of his people, who knew him as "uncle" Ho.

Hammer, Ellen Joy. *The Struggle for Indochina*. Stanford, Calif.: Stanford University Press, 1954.

In contrast to Jean Lacouture's study of Ho Chi Minh and the Nationalist-Communist movement in Vietnam, Ellen Joy Hammer sees the upheaval as a "world problem" having strong repercussions on the international scene. In her detailed narrative of the Franco-Vietnamese War, Hammer concentrates on the years 1949 to early 1954 before the conclusion of the Geneva Conference that led to a divided Vietnam. It was during this period that the Communist leadership of the Nationalist movement became more obvious and was internationalized by competing interests in a political bipolar world. In this context, the turning point had been the Communist victory in China and the placement of Communist forces on the borders of Vietnam. This development and the outbreak of war in Korea led to a reassessment of policies in Asia and consequent stiffening of resistance by the non-Communist nations.

The positions of nations were sharply drawn. The People's Republic of China, the Soviet Union, and other Communist countries recognized the Viet Minh government, while the United States, Great Britain, Cambodia, and Laos recognized the French-sponsored government in Vietnam, led by Emperor Bao Dai. Military and economic aid were given to each side in the dispute by sympathetic supporters. Asian countries such as India, Burma, and Indonesia saw the war in Nationalist terms, as a struggle of the Asian people to end Western imperialism. Communist leadership was not considered important, and Hammer believes that the Vietnamese people agreed. The shrill cry for independence was strong, and several Asian nations, such as India, Pakistan, Burma, Indonesia, and the Philippines, had already achieved their independence.

For the French, internationalization of the war allowed them to claim that their fight was not a colonial conflict but a resistance against Communism. Inherent in the ideological foundations of both sides in the conflict, however, is a series of dilemmas. First, the French wanted total control over events and over their influence in Vietnam, and they sought to limit foreign involvement on their side. While accepting American financial assistance, for example, the French were concerned about American opposition to the restoration of French rule after World War II and the growing American pressure to give the Indochinese greater independence. Moreover, the French feared the potential of growing American economic and political power in the region. The French clearly wanted American support but not American predominance. A second dilemma emerged in the French support of Bao Dai. The Vietnamese who fought on the side of Ho Chi Minh and also those under Bao Dai wanted independence. Because it was popularly known that the French patronized Bao Dai, the latter lost support and found it increasingly difficult to attract non-Communist Nationalists to

join his government.

The drive for independence, Hammer believes, was a crucial factor in determining the outcome of the conflict. Time and events, such as the Chinese Communist victory, worked against France and her supporters; thus, it became increasingly difficult for the non-Communist Nationalists to seize the initiative from the Communists. Sympathy from France's European friends, members of the North Atlantic Treaty Organization, was insufficient; even their aid was limited because of their concern over draining European defenses. It was only toward the approach of the Geneva Conference that more substantial American aid was sent, and that was done to deter last-minute gains by the Viet Minh rather than for a victory drive.

The persistence of the war for nearly eight years, Hammer further contends, was due to blunders on both sides. The French ignored the fact that they were in the midst of a popular Nationalist movement, and they refused to deal with it. The Vietnamese, on their part, allowed the leadership of the Nationalist movement to be taken over by the Communists, and consequently it lost potential friends and support around the world. As the war continued, the anti-French, Communist-led, Nationalist movement gained strength; and in contrast, the people of France, both from the Left and the Right, wanted the war to end. It had become too costly at one billion dollars annually and was seriously weakening the French economy. Moreover, each side grew concerned that foreign military forces might be added to the other side (Chinese supporting the Viet Minh and Americans supporting the French) and that a wider conflict would result.

This excellent study, one of a series sponsored by the Institute of Pacific Relations, ends before the Geneva Conference had concluded its business, but it provides a broad view of how the powers got there.

—L.H.D.G.

Additional Recommended Reading

Fall, Bernard B. *Street Without Joy*. New York: Frederick A. Praeger, 1964. A history of selected episodes from the insurgency in Vietnam through the battle of Dien Bien Phu, with a briefer account to 1964.

──────. *The Viet-Minh Regime: Government and Administration in the Democratic Republic of Vietnam*. New York: Institute of Pacific Relations, 1956. Describes and evaluates the Viet Minh state, focusing on political, military, and economic problems from 1941 to 1954.

Halberstam, David. *Ho*. New York: Random House, 1971. A brief biography of Ho Chi Minh and the revolution he fostered.

Lancaster, Donald. *The Emancipation of French Indochina*. London: Oxford University Press, 1961. An excellent account of the Vietnam conflict to the Geneva Conference and independence in 1954; the Nationalist movement in the twentieth century is given full attention.

McAlister, John T., Jr. *Viet Nam: The Origins of Revolution*. New York: Alfred A. Knopf, 1969. A monograph for the Center of International Studies (Princeton). Evaluates the background of the Vietnam revolution from 1940 to the end of 1946.

O'Ballance, Edgar. *The Indo-China War, 1945-54: A Study in Guerrilla Warfare*. London: Faber and Faber, 1964. A history of the war explaining its stages of development.

Tanham, George K. *Communist Revolutionary Warfare: From the Vietminh to the Viet Cong*. New York: Frederick A. Praeger, 1967. Discusses the Viet Minh military strategy and tactics, 1946-1954; includes chapters on the Viet Cong and American military participation.

Turner, Robert F. *Vietnamese Communism, its Origins and Development*. Stanford, Calif.: Hoover Institution Press, 1975. Considers how the Communists gained control of the anti-French colonial movement and how they kept control since 1954; also considers the relationship of the Vietnamese Communist movement to the international Communist movement.

ESTABLISHMENT OF THE SOUTHEAST ASIA TREATY ORGANIZATION (SEATO)

Type of event: Diplomatic: treaty establishing mutual security organization for the Southeast Asian region
Time: September 8, 1954-February 19, 1955
Locale: Manila, Philippine Islands; Southeast Asia

Principal personages:

DWIGHT DAVID EISENHOWER (1890-1969), thirty-fourth President of the United States, 1953-1961

JOHN FOSTER DULLES (1888-1959), United States Secretary of State, 1953-1959

H. ALEXANDER SMITH (1880-   ), United States Senator from New Jersey

MICHAEL JOSEPH (MIKE) MANSFIELD (1903-   ), United States Senator from Montana

HO CHI MINH (1890-1969), leader of North Vietnam

Summary of Event

Southeast Asia is a term of geographic convenience which has imprecise cultural and political meaning. Within the region as usually defined is a diversity of island, peninsular, and mainland territories whose peoples differ in language, religion, and culture. In almost all the areas of Southeast Asia (except the highlands), tropical and subtropical climates determine the environment; many of the people engage in the growing of rice. Politically, the entire area, with the exception of Thailand (Siam), experienced European or American rule in the late nineteenth and early twentieth centuries.

Throughout the region, World War II brought enormous change. Japanese conquests not only removed the colonial rulers, but drastically damaged Western prestige. Nationalist movements grew, directed first against the Japanese, and later, after the Japanese surrender, against restoration of the old colonial hegemonies. Communists, whether local, Moscow-trained, or Chinese-inspired, played a part in these movements, the importance of the various interventions varying with the situation. The United States, which had pledged the independence of the Philippines, fulfilled that promise in 1946; generally unsympathetic to colonialism, America was bound by alliances in World War II and the Cold War to the colonial powers, Britain, France, and the Netherlands.

In parts of Southeast Asia, the end of colonial rule came with little contest. Other lands, however, such as Indonesia (the former Dutch East Indies) and French Indochina, had to fight for their independence. In Vietnam, a former French colony, the Viet Minh, centered in Hanoi and the North and led by Ho Chi Minh (a

Communist-nationalist), defeated the French forces. At Geneva in July of 1954, the French and other powers agreed to French withdrawal and a temporary division of Vietnam.

President Dwight D. Eisenhower, Secretary of State John Foster Dulles, and many other Americans saw in the events in Vietnam the threat of Communist expansion through Southeast Asia. The United States government, to counter the threat, proposed a regional defense treaty. The precedent was the North Atlantic Treaty Organization (NATO) in which the twelve signatories in 1949 (with later additions) set up a permanent regional defensive alliance.

The Treaty for the collective defense of Southeast Asia was drafted at Manila and signed on September 8, 1954, by representatives of eight nations. In most cases, the delegates were the foreign ministers of their states. The United States delegation was composed of Secretary of State Dulles and two United States Senators, H. Alexander Smith, a Republican, and Mike Mansfield, a Democrat. The Asian nations joining the Southeast Asia Treaty Organization (SEATO) were Pakistan, the Philippine Republic, and Thailand. Australia, New Zealand, Britain, France, and the United States also signed. India held aloof because of its policy of neutrality, and possibly because of the participation of Pakistan. Both Indonesia, under Sukarno's leadership, and Burma were neutral or antagonistic. Singapore and Malaya did not join because they were still members of the British Commonwealth. The states of Indochina, according to the Geneva Convention, had to remain neutral.

According to the treaty as finally signed, the parties acknowledged their obligations under the Charter of the United Nations; they pledged to settle disputes by peaceful means and to refrain from force, in accord with the Charter and purposes of the United Nations. They promised self-help and cooperation in developing their capacity to resist aggression and to prevent internal subversion directed from outside the region. Each pledged to foster free institutions and to cooperate in economic development.

Article IV, the core of the Treaty, recognized aggression against one member as an attack on all; each promised to resist aggression on the other members by measures in accord with its constitutional processes. In the event that a signatory reported a threat to its security (but not outright aggression), all members would consult together on appropriate measures to be taken. Further articles provided for the establishment of a council; made explicit that the obligations of the Treaty did not supersede or conflict with either the obligations of membership in the United Nations or any other treaty to which a signer might be a party; and provided for the admission of other states to membership.

The Treaty defined the area to which it applied as "the general area of the Southeast Asia," including the territories of the Asian members, and "the general area of the Southwest Pacific, not including the Pacific area north of 21 degrees 30 minutes north latitude." This definition excluded Formosa, the Pescadores, and Hong Kong. The Treaty was to go into effect as soon as a majority of those signing deposited ratifications with the government of the Philippines.

The United States appended an "understanding" to the Treaty that it was Communist aggression against which it was taking a stand; the usual explanation of this step is that it was intended to safeguard the United States from any conflict between India and Pakistan. By a separate Protocol the treaty signers extended its guarantee to the states of Laos, Cambodia, and "free Vietnam," though they were not members.

On the occasion of the Manila Conference in September, 1954, the parties also issued a Pacific Charter, obviously modeled in name after the Atlantic Charter issued on August 14, 1941, by President Franklin D. Roosevelt of the United States and Prime Minister Winston Churchill of the United Kingdom. In the Pacific Charter the delegates promised to adhere to the principles of equal rights and self-determination, to promote conditions favorable to those principles by peaceful means, and to cooperate in working toward higher living standards, economic progress, and social well-being.

The requisite ratifications were deposited at Manila by February 19, 1955; because of the site of the signing, the Treaty is frequently known as the Manila Pact, but its headquarters were established at Bangkok, Thailand. A secretariat and permanent staff was appointed, while the governing Council was composed of the foreign ministers or their representatives. A body of military advisers was organized, but, unlike NATO, SEATO had no unified command.

In the subsequent troubles in Laos and in the conflict in Vietnam, the United States rather than SEATO took action. The Treaty required unanimity, which proved impossible to obtain in the critical instances, so Secretary Dulles and other United States spokesmen based American actions in Vietnam and elsewhere in Southeast Asia on obligations and instruments other than the Treaty. Critics therefore found the Treaty and the organization of little real value, except for some of its gestures toward economic and cultural cooperation. Supporters regarded SEATO as an integral part of the American effort to contain Communist aggression and subversion in Southeast Asia. In particular, supporters point to the fact that SEATO members Australia, New Zealand, Thailand, and the Philippines supplied troops to the unsuccessful United States effort to combat Communist aggression against South Vietnam.

Pertinent Literature

Crozier, Brian. *South-East Asia in Turmoil.* Harmonsworth, England: Penguin Books, 1966.

Brian Crozier, a British journalist and lecturer, writes from a considerable experience in the Far East and Southeast Asia, including his acquaintance and interviews with a number of the leaders in the region.

He himself remarks on the difficulty of obtaining accurate information on such a troubled area; one man remembers the same episode or estimates a situation quite differently from another. Crozier's effort is only in part factual; much of his brief book is an attempt to understand the unique forces at work in Southeast Asia.

Central among these forces is nationalism. Crozier points out that nationalism among the peoples of Southeast Asia has too frequently been ignored or misunderstood by Westerners. Part of the misunderstanding arises from the fact that Southeast Asia is not a historical and cultural unit, so that general statements about the area are likely to be misinterpretations. Even within a present "nation," linguistic, religious, and cultural diversities and even antagonisms are common, and cut across the pattern of national aspirations.

Modern nationalism, Crozier insists, has its roots in resentment of colonial rule before World War II, and possibly even in ancient traditions, but its real surge came with the Japanese conquests. The sight of Asians driving out the Europeans was a blow from which colonial rule never recovered; and the behavior of the Japanese as conquerors roused many peoples in Southeast Asia to resistance. Crozier notes, however, that in many cases there were ties between Japanese puppets and resistance groups, so that cooperation after the war was easy.

Civil war in China and the victory of Mao Tse-tung and the Communists raised other possibilities relevant to SEATO and its position. For Asians, the movement in China may have seemed as much national as Communist. There was inspiration in the sight of the greatest Asian power successfully freeing itself of European concessions and special privileges. Also, the fact that China promised to end the rule of landlords and money lenders cannot have displeased Southeast Asian peasants, who responded to the promise, whatever the reality. Thus, the movements in Southeast Asia, Crozier argues, however essentially national, were often led or influenced by Communists, many of them nationals, but often trained and directed from Moscow or later Peking. It was this fact, that led Secretary Dulles and other Americans, especially the military, to want to take steps to limit the expansion of Communist power in Asia. To limit or contain that power, the United States relied primarily, in Crozier's view, on its naval and air power. To legitimatize and strengthen its actions, the United States needed the cooperation of the Asian states; hence its support for the creation of SEATO.

It is a virtue of Crozier's approach that without losing sight of the importance of Asian nationalism and antiimperialism, he still sees the reality and the danger of Communist subversive and paramilitary activity. He knows something about the leaders, even their disguises and "cover names." This sharpens his verdict in 1965-1966 that the history of SEATO "has not been a success story."

Establishment of the SEATO

Clubb, Oliver Edmund, Jr. *The United States and the Sino-Soviet Bloc in Southeast Asia.* Washington, D.C.: Brookings Institution, 1962.

Clubb, a fellow of the Brookings Institution at the time of publication, prepared this analysis originally as the basis for a seminar. The book raises issues, asks important questions, and presents alternatives; it reflects the author's experience both as a student and as a research analyst.

The sharpest conflict, as Clubb sees it, is between the Soviet bloc and the United States, which must achieve its objectives while paying heed to a variety of differing and sometimes conflicting parties and movements. The Eisenhower Administration, he points out, had much the same view of the unity and military character of the Communist threat as its predecessor, the Truman-Acheson Administration. Clubb traces briefly the policies of the Soviet Union and Communist China—the "Sino-Soviet bloc"—in various countries of Southeast Asia. The Soviet Union, according to his analysis, was moving at the same period toward a policy of at least accommodation with local nationalist movements, and toward the use of political rather than military and revolutionary methods.

It is in the light of this analysis that Clubb views SEATO. With the French defeat at Dien Bien Phu and the subsequent Geneva Conference in 1954, United States efforts to bring united Western power to the aid of France against what United States officials saw as a Communist thrust southward came to naught. Dulles' idea of SEATO, then, was as a means of saving as much of Southeast Asia as possible. In Clubb's view, the hope was doomed by the unwillingness of the other powers—Britain and France—to support strong measures. The SEATO Council rule that all decisions must be unanimous proved to be a major weakness of the organization.

Considering continued support of SEATO as one of several possible policies for the United States, Clubb discusses what he regards as the organization's advantages and defects. One principal advantage is that it offers a legal framework for American policy. The disadvantages, as he sees them, are many. SEATO separates its Asian members from the rest of Southeast Asia and alienates the non-aligned Asian countries. It does not really guarantee against political and ideological Communist "aggression," and, as the Laotian and other experiences suggest, it leaves the response to military aggression ultimately to the United States. — *G.J.F.*

Additional Recommended Reading

Vandenbosch, Amry and Richard Butwell. *The Changing Face of Southeast Asia.* Lexington: University of Kentucky Press, 1966. An account of the situation and politics of the region, with particular attention to United States policy.

Eisenhower, Dwight D. *Mandate for Change, 1953-1956.* Garden City, N.Y.: Doubleday & Company, 1963. A reminiscent account by one of the principals involved.

Buss, Claude A. *Southeast Asia and the World Today*. Princeton, N.J.: D. Van Nostrand Company, 1958. A brief account of the region and its problems, with documentary appendixes.

Cottrell, Alvin J. "The Eisenhower Era in Asia," in *Current History*. LVII (August, 1959), pp. 84-87 and 117-118. A summary of United States foreign policy in the light of the overall Asian situation.

CONGRESS PASSES THE FORMOSA RESOLUTION

Type of event: Political: passage of a joint resolution affirming presidential power to defend Taiwan and offshore islands
Time: January 24-29, 1955
Locale: Washington, D.C., Taiwan, Quemoy, and Matsu

Principal personages:

DWIGHT DAVID EISENHOWER (1890-1969), thirty-fourth President of the United States, 1953-1961

JOHN FOSTER DULLES (1888-1959), United States Secretary of State, 1953-1959

CHIANG KAI-SHEK (1887-1975), President of the Republic of (Nationalist) China, 1950-1975

CHOU EN-LAI (1898-1976), Premier of the People's Republic of (Communist) China, 1949-1976

WALTER F. GEORGE (1878-1957), United States Senator from Georgia

JAMES P. RICHARDS (1894-   ), United States Representative from South Carolina

WILLIAM F. KNOWLAND (1908-   ), United States Senator from California

Summary of Event

In 1949, as the Communists took over mainland China at the end of the Chinese civil war, Generalissimo Chiang Kai-shek, President of the Republic of (Nationalist) China, withdrew with part of his government and army to the island of Formosa (Taiwan in Chinese) and the nearby Pescadores Islands. Formosa and the Pescadores had been held by the Japanese from 1895 until their return to China in 1945, at the end of World War II. Chiang claimed that his was still the legitimate government of China and announced his intention to return to the mainland and to power. His troops also held other islands off the China coast, notably Quemoy, a short distance from the port of Amoy; Matsu, off Foochow; and also the Tachens, located about two hundred miles to the north of Matsu.

Both Chiang and the Chinese Communists held that Taiwan was a province of China and Quemoy and Matsu were part of the mainland province of Fukien. Though Quemoy and Matsu were small, both sides saw them as stepping-stones. In Chiang's view, they were strategic for a return to the mainland; to the Communists, they were a step toward the inclusion of Taiwan in their regime. The islands were staging-points for occasional raids on the mainland and came under air attack from the Communists.

The United States had supported Chiang in the civil war, and recognized his regime as the legitimate government for all China. The Korean War (1950-1953) and the Chinese

709

Communist role in it strengthened American antipathy toward the Communists. Military and economic aid went to Taiwan, and the Seventh Fleet patrolled the Formosa Strait to prevent invasion. Chiang increased the armament and garrisons on Quemoy and Matsu against the advice of many individuals in the American military establishment. The mainland regime placed even larger forces on the shore facing the islands. In August and September, 1954, the Communists began a bombardment of the islands, killing two United States military advisers.

Throughout the autumn, debate over policy continued, both within the United States and between the United States and its allies. Some individuals on the Joint Chiefs of Staff and some members of Congress (such as Senator William F. Knowland of California) were willing to encourage Chiang in a return to the mainland and to give United States support to his forces on Quemoy and Matsu. Others saw in such steps either continued defeat for Chiang, or involvement in a major Asian war ("World War III" in some predictions), or both. Secretary of State John Foster Dulles viewed the Formosa and offshore islands question within the context of the Cold War, then at its height. To him, the maintenance of a strong Chinese Nationalist presence off the coast of mainland China would keep the Chinese Communist regime off balance, while offering some hope to those who wanted it overthrown.

As a result of these debates within the government, a somewhat more definite policy toward Nationalist China began to emerge. On December 2, 1954, the United States and Nationalist China concluded a mutual defense treaty. No specific mention, however, was made in the treaty about the offshore islands. Consequently, a month later, the Chinese Communists launched bombardment and air attacks on these islands. Hence, on January 24, 1955, as the attacks continued, President Dwight D. Eisenhower sent a special message to Congress in which he asked for authority to use the Armed Forces of the United States to protect Formosa, the Pescadores, and what he vaguely referred to as certain "closely related localities." This authority, like the mutual defense treaty, would not commit the United States in advance to the defense of the offshore islands, nor would it limit United States action in advance.

President Eisenhower pointed out that the measure was not a constitutional necessity; he already had the requisite authority both as Commander in Chief and under the terms of the mutual security treaty already signed but not as yet ratified by the Senate. He wanted a demonstration of the unity of the United States and its resolve, while making thoroughly clear the authority of the President. In Communist China, Premier Chou En-lai called the message a "war message."

The message went to the new Eighty-fourth Congress, which had a Democratic majority in both houses. In response, the Chairmen of the respective committees, Democrats Walter George in the Senate and James P. Richards in the House, introduced the joint resolution which became known as the Formosa Resolution.

The resolution took as its premise the vital interest of the United States in peace in the western Pacific, and the danger to peace from Communist attacks in the area. It took note of the statement of mutual interest in the treaty submitted to the Senate. It therefore resolved

> That the President of the United States . . . is authorized to employ the Armed Forces of the United States as he deems necessary for the specific purpose of securing and protecting Formosa and the Pescadores against armed attack, this authority to include the securing and protection of such related positions and territories of that area now in friendly hands and the taking of such other measures as he judges to be required or appropriate in assuring the defense of Formosa and the Pescadores.

The House passed the resolution on January 25, 1955, by a vote of 410 to 3. In the Senate committee, an amendment to turn Formosa and the Pescadores over to the authority of the United Nations, and giving authorization to the President only until the United Nations acted, was defeated. Another amendment to limit the authority to Formosa and the Pescadores also lost. A similar amendment to draw a line back of Quemoy and Matsu, limiting the President's authority to Formosa and the Pescadores, was introduced on the Senate floor by Senator Herbert Lehman of New York. It was defeated 74 to 13. The Senate passed the resolution 85 to 3, on January 28, 1955, and President Eisenhower signed it the next day.

The mutual security treaty with Nationalist China was ratified in February. Efforts to persuade Chiang Kai-shek to reduce his forces on Quemoy and Matsu and make them mere outposts failed. That same month, however, Chiang did evacuate the Taschen Islands, which the Communists promptly occupied. Communist Premier Chou En-lai, in an attempt to strike a conciliatory note, told the Afro-Asian Conference meeting in Bandung, Indonesia, in April that his country did not want war with the United States. He further expressed his willingness to negotiate on Far Eastern issues, including that of Formosa. As a result, by May, without formal statement or agreement, there was an effective ceasefire in the Formosa Straits.

In the wake of the passage of the Formosa Resolution and the ratification of the mutual defense treaty with Nationalist China, President Eisenhower addressed a letter to British Prime Minister Winston Churchill on February 19, 1955, in which he set forth his ideas on the importance of defending Formosa and the offshore islands. The United States depended on an island (Formosa) and a peninsula (Korea) as its defense line in Southeast Asia. The loss of Formosa would be a serious break in that line. The weakening of Chiang Kai-shek's forces could mean the loss of Formosa. The denial of their expectation to return to mainland China would be destructive of their morale. Therefore it was important to the United States not only to aid in the defense of Formosa, but also not to accept, or seem to accept, the loss of the offshore islands, which were of strategic importance in launching a return to

711

the mainland. These ideas helped set the posture of United States policy in the Far East for some time to come.

Judgments of the Formosa Resolution at the time of its passage and in historical perspective must depend in large part on attitudes toward the larger question of policy toward China. First of all, the overwhelming vote in Congress in favor of the Formosa Resolution may be taken as clear evidence of opinion there, and presumably of opinion throughout the country that Communist expansion must be resisted, but the United States ought not be involved in further war. From another, though related, per-spective, the Formosa Resolution was a reflection of the Cold War mentality which saw no possibility for diplomatic recognition of the Communist regime on the Chinese mainland. Later, in the aftermath of the Tonkin Gulf Resolution of 1964, granting the President wide powers during the Vietnam War, the Formosa Resolution was criticized in retrospect as setting a dangerous precedent. Opponents of the Vietnam War viewed both resolutions as abdications of Congressional responsibility, while those who supported either or both regarded them as expressions of national unity.

Pertinent Literature

Bueler, William M. *U.S. China Policy and the Problem of Taiwan.* Boulder: Colorado Associated University Press, 1971.

Bueler's effort is an analysis of United States policy—future as well as past—toward Taiwan. Such policy, he proposes, has to be based on the national interest and is, of course, part of the larger policy toward China. It is important to note that Bueler wrote before the Nixon Administration took public steps to forge new relationships with Communist China, though Bueler did foresee some such change.

The book breaks logically into two—a brief summary of past policy, administration by administration; and an analysis of policy assumptions and realities. Bueler puts special stress on the Taiwanese people, as distinct from the "mainlanders" who came with Chiang Kai-shek.

This concern, his account makes clear, was not the chief, or even an important, item in the thinking of those who made policy for the United States. In his discussion of the Eisenhower Administration, he focuses first on Secretary of State John Foster Dulles. Though Dulles had earlier indicated some acceptance of the *fact* of Communist power in mainland China and, as Secretary, had even suggested that nonrecognition need not be eternal, his opposition to international Communism was plain and deep. Support for Chiang's government on Taiwan kept open an alternative, which would worry the Communist regime, and offer some hope to those who wanted it overthrown.

Eisenhower's thinking, Bueler contends, was more simply strategic.

The island line of defense was important to the United States, and Formosa was a link in that chain. Chiang's army was therefore essential, and the hope of recovery of the mainland essential to the army's morale; that the hope might be unrealistic does not seem important in this calculation.

Bueler's account strongly suggests that Eisenhower himself was convinced neither of the possibility of an early recovery of the mainland, nor of the importance of the offshore islands; his only concern was for morale. He was disturbed over Chiang's commitments to the islands, but unable to press him far without upsetting "morale."

Bueler suggests that the Formosa Resolution itself repeated what everybody knew—that the United States was committed to the defense of Formosa and the Pescadores—and left open the question that everybody was asking: what about Quemoy and Matsu? He notes that Eisenhower's account in his memoirs seems to omit the status of the offshore islands. "This omission might be the result of careless writing rather than unclear thinking," but it indicates "something less than precision" in Eisenhower's mind. The unwritten alternative is that the imprecision and ambiguity, at least in the resolution, were calculated. Similarly, Bueler notes that the resolution and general policy deterred a Communist attack on Formosa and avoided a decision; however, he says, the underlying problem remained unsettled. A fairly obvious conclusion is that Eisenhower may have regarded any "settlement" as more risky than continued ambiguity.

Bueler's estimate is that Eisenhower, except for his strategic doctrine, was probably less firm, perhaps less concerned at the beginning, about Communist China than many of those around him. The strength of their opposition to Communist China, however, along with Chiang's ability to resist pressures, helped fix the policy. Republican Senators and Representatives, State Department advisers, and the military for the most part, were all committed to "Free China" and to treating the People's Republic as an outlaw. So, according to Bueler, was the great majority of the American public. This helped fix not only the resolution of 1955, but also policy toward China and Taiwan through the succeeding years.

Rovere, Richard H. "Letter from Washington," in *The New Yorker*. XXXI (February 26, 1955), pp. 90-100.

Richard H. Rovere's is a contemporary view from the vantage point of Washington politics, written in the sophisticated style of the magazine—wry, sometimes witty, sometimes cynical.

He takes as his starting point a confusing speech of John Foster Dulles. He suggests, however, that a simple, candid statement about policy toward the offshore islands would have been even more confusing—possibly to the Secretary himself.

Eisenhower, Rovere thinks, seemed against war—but he might have been in a minority in his Administration. He also seemed to be winning. He had to deal with opposition from the military; Rovere suggests that here his own enormous military prestige gave him an advantage another president might not have had.

It was most unusual, in Rovere's opinion, that the general beat the politician. Senator Knowland, according to Rovere, had reason to oppose those portions of the resolution and the mutual defense treaty which "re-leashed" Chiang Kai-shek. (The agreement committed Chiang not to act without consent of the United States.) Moreover, the resolution's expression of hope for a ceasefire was not exactly what Knowland and those like him wanted. Yet, says Rovere, they really had no choice but to go along.

Interestingly, Rovere claims that Congress did not really want to take the responsibility which the resolution imposes; they were afraid of it; they would much rather leave it to the President. This is, of course, a contention it would be hard to prove; but in the light of other and later congressional actions, it is a stimulating observation. — *G.J.F.*

Additional Recommended Reading

Eisenhower, Dwight D. *Mandate for Change, 1953-1956.* Garden City, N.Y.: Doubleday & Company, 1963. The President's own account of his first term, with a chapter recounting his Taiwan policy.

Rankin, Karl Lott. *China Assignment.* Seattle: University of Washington Press, 1964. The United States representative to Chiang's government offers reminiscenses strongly supportive of that regime.

Dean, Arthur H. "United States Foreign Policy and Formosa," in *Foreign Affairs.* XXXIII (April, 1955), pp. 360-375. An explanation of United States policy by an adviser and frequent negotiator for the Eisenhower Administration.

Vital Speeches. XXI (February 15, 1955), pp. 1026–1040. Contains texts of Eisenhower's message asking for the Formosa Resolution, Senator George's speech for it, and Senator Wayne Morse's against it.

SIGNING OF THE WARSAW PACT

Type of event: Diplomatic: formalization of Soviet policy toward Europe
Time: May 14, 1955
Locale: Warsaw, Poland

Principal personages:

NIKITA SERGEEVICH KHRUSHCHEV (1894-1971), First Secretary of the Communist Party of the Soviet Union, 1953-1964; and Chairman of the Council of Ministers (Premier) of the Soviet Union, 1958-1964

NIKOLAI ALEKSANDROVICH BULGANIN (1895-1975), Chairman of the Council of Ministers (Premier) of the Soviet Union, 1955-1958

VYACHESLAV MIKHAILOVICH MOLOTOV (SKRYABIN) (1890-), Foreign Minister of the Soviet Union, 1953-1956

MARSHAL IVAN STEPANOVICH KONEV (1897-1973), Commander in Chief of Warsaw Pact armed forces

Summary of Event

The Warsaw Pact— or, more formally, the Treaty of Friendship, Cooperation and Mutual Assistance Between the People's Republic of Albania, the People's Republic of Bulgaria, the Hungarian People's Republic, the German Democratic Republic, the Polish People's Republic, the Rumanian People's Republic, the Union of Soviet Socialist Republics, and the Czechoslovak Republic—was signed on May 14, 1955. To a large extent this multilateral alliance must be seen as an outgrowth of Soviet concerns over the rearming of the Federal Republic of Germany. The Soviet Union formally protested the Western arrangements providing for the creation of West German armed forces and the entry of West Germany into the North Atlantic Treaty Organization (NATO). The Soviets served notice in November, 1954, that the remilitarization of West Germany would lead to new security measures in Eastern Europe. The actual signing of the Warsaw Pact was preceded by the Moscow Conference of the future members in November-December, 1954. At this time Soviet Foreign Minister V. M. Molotov presented a rather blunt statement regarding the revival of German militarism and the need for "special vigilance" and "practical measures."

Molotov's militant anti-Western stance was not entirely maintained by the subsequent Warsaw Conference. The new Soviet leaders, Nikita Khrushchev and Nikolai Bulganin, had only recently asserted themselves in a power struggle with Georgii Malenkov, who led a faction in the Soviet Politburo associated with the commitment to *détente*. The Khrushchev-Bulganin leadership, however, was similarly inclined to adopt a somewhat softer foreign policy posture than the one advocated by Molotov. Thus, the language and terms of the

715

Warsaw Pact, reflected the new Soviet priorities in international affairs.

It is certainly appropriate to view the Warsaw Pact as the Soviet counterpart to NATO. Indeed, the Warsaw Pact's role as a military alliance opposing NATO has increased over the years. The Soviet Union has been maintaining sizable combat-equipped forces in a forward deployment in the Warsaw Pact area, supported by tactical air and missile elements, and reinforceable from the Soviet Union. Nevertheless, concern over the developments in NATO were not the sole reason for the Warsaw Pact. The period following Stalin's death in 1953 had seen considerable diversity and agitation for increased independence on the part of the Eastern European satellite states, a phenomenon known as polycentrism. The changing political environment in Eastern Europe required new approaches and methods in the continuing efforts to sustain Soviet control over the area. The creation of a formal treaty organization, together with invigoration of the Council for Mutual Economic Assistance (COMECON), established under Russian auspices in 1949, appeared to be an excellent response to Soviet needs.

The eleven articles of the Warsaw pact provided for consultation on all issues of common interest, the peaceful settlement of conflicts, and joint defense. The military convention is the most important part of the treaty; it allowed for the disposition of troops under the joint command for purposes of mutual defense. Soviet Marshal I. S. Konev was appointed Commander in Chief, and the ministers of defense of the other member states became his deputies. Each of these deputy commanders was put in charge of the troops contributed by his own state. The headquarters, with a permanent staff of the joint armed forces and certain auxiliary bodies, were located in Moscow. For purposes of policy coordination, a political consultative committee was established.

Subsequent military integration efforts by the Soviet Union included the standardization of equipment and the development of a common infrastructure. Moreover, considerable effort was made to indoctrinate officers and men in loyalty to the "socialist camp." Key positions in the satellite armies were awarded, as a matter of course, to Soviet-trained officers. The German Democratic Republic was initially excluded from participation in the joint command; it was given equal status at the first meeting of the political consultative committee in Prague, in January, 1956. As a deliberate counter to the developments in NATO, the East German National People's Army was created and integrated into the joint command.

In retrospect, it is important to note that at the time of its inception the Warsaw Pact was primarily designed to strengthen the Soviet position at the Geneva Summit Conference, held in July, 1955. The Soviets envisioned a European collective security treaty, which, when achieved, would provide for the simultaneous termination of NATO, the supplementary Paris agreements, and the Warsaw Pact. As an alternative to this maximum goal, the Soviets proposed a nonaggression treaty between the members of each alliance. However, no steps were taken on either proposal at that time.

In its initial stages, then, the Warsaw Pact served the Soviet Union essentially as a Cold War political device. Indeed, during the first years of the treaty's existence, the Soviet Union was not very intent on developing its potential as an integrated military alliance. The existing bilateral agreements with individual Eastern European states were sufficient with regard to the deployment of Soviet troops to counter American influence in Europe. However, certain features of the pact, such as its "legitimizing" the presence of Soviet troops on East European soil, gradually appreciated in value for the Soviet Union. The latter came to regard the Warsaw Pact as a highly useful instrument in East-West relations and in furthering its hegemonal interests in Eastern Europe. The pact could be effectively utilized as a coordinating mechanism for foreign policy and the achievement of a uniform external posture. More importantly, it facilitated the achievement of general conformity to Moscow's policy line for the area itself. Moscow was able to promote what it called "fraternal bloc solidarity," and any member straying too far from the line could be subjected to disciplinary action behind the collective façade of the Warsaw Pact.

The provisions of the treaty were reinterpreted to allow for "legitimate" intervention in the affairs of member states, including the use of force, under the doctrine of "proletarian internationalism." Such disciplinary and policing functions became a significant part of Soviet policy and practice over the years. The most extreme instances have been the interventions in Hungary in 1956 and in Czechoslovakia in 1968. The resort to military force to bring these countries to heel, did not, of course, depend on the Warsaw Pact. However, it was politically and ideologically most expedient to give these operations a multilateral appearance.

Pertinent Literature

Remington, Robin Alison. *The Warsaw Pact: Case Studies in Communist Conflict Resolution*. Cambridge, Mass.: MIT Press, 1971.

Robin Remington's study of the functioning of the Warsaw Pact is certainly among the best available on the subject. The major portion of the book deals with the resolution of various conflicts between the Soviet Union and other member states. Remington attempts to use behavior in conflict situations as an index of attitude change regarding the Warsaw Pact. Appropriately, the book begins by tracing the origin of the pact. The reader is informed about the power struggle within the Communist Party of the Soviet Union, the clash of views between Molotov, who saw the pact as an instrument of military preparedness and socialist consolidation, and Khrushchev, who viewed it as a Cold War political device.

Remington argues that each Soviet response to intra-Communist conflict in Eastern Europe imposed its own future limitations. The Warsaw Treaty Organization had barely begun to take root when Khrushchev started his systematic campaign to demolish the myth of Stalin. The de-Stalinization process, a critical move on the part of Khrushchev in the innerparty struggle of the CPSU, had massive repercussions in Eastern Europe as a whole; various elements interpreted it as a rejection of Stalinist methods and as the advent of liberalization and national independence. Riots and massive public demonstrations flared up in Poland and Hungary in the fall of 1956. The respective regimes attempted to respond to some of the demands and expectations, defying directives to the contrary from Moscow. Clearly, Soviet control over political developments in Eastern Europe was slipping. In October, 1956, the Soviets decided to intervene directly in Poland and Hungary. In the case of Poland, a Soviet delegation went to Warsaw and, backed by alerted Soviet troops stationed in the vicinity, was able to bring matters back under control. In the case of Hungary, as is only too well-remembered, the great popular uprising ultimately led to the massive use of Soviet military force to crush the rebellion and to reestablish a regime subservient to Moscow. The Soviet use of armed might was justified under the Warsaw Pact terms, although these terms refer only to aiding a member state threatened by aggression and do not state what to do in case of civil war. The Soviet action was presented as a response to "the sacred duty" to protect the "achievements of socialism." Reviewing the events in Hungary, Remington notes that there was no consultation within the context of the Warsaw Pact. The political consultative committee did not meet at all during this time of crisis.

Despite the initial impotence, however, Remington skillfully demonstrates that the events of 1956 increased the importance of the Warsaw Pact to the Soviet Union. It was extended by way of increased military integration and additional bilateral treaties covering the stationing of Soviet troops on Eastern European territory. The new stronger emphasis on the Warsaw Pact as a safeguard for the internal construction of socialism constituted, in effect, a further significant extension. Nevertheless, in the emerging Soviet-Albanian conflict, the Soviet Union found itself unable to intervene. Meanwhile, the Sino-Soviet rift had allowed China to become an alternative source of support within the socialist camp, which the Albanians deftly utilized. By 1961, the relations between Albania and the Soviet Union had deteriorated to a point of no return, and the leaders violently denounced each other. Still, the Soviets did not use force. The developments merely led to the *de facto* exclusion of Albania from the Warsaw Pact. Its membership was simply ignored until 1968, when the multilateral invasion of Czechoslovakia precipitated Albania's formal withdrawal from the Warsaw Pact.

Remington's analyses of the Soviet-Rumanian and the Soviet-Czechoslovak conflicts project in a particularly effective manner the changing conceptions and uses of the pact. The tensions between the Soviet Union and Rumania resulted from the latter's active resistance to the policies of increased economic integration within COMECON. In general, the Soviets seemed to go out of their way to demonstrate good will and refrained from overt hostile actions. The Rumanians bargained successfully with the Soviets to scale down the plans for specialization and integration within COMECON and the "perfecting" of the Warsaw Pact. In short, Rumania was able to maintain its independent posture in the face of rising Soviet pressure to strengthen the military capacity of the pact. In this instance, Moscow's methods of coping with a direct challenge to its authority differed remarkably from those employed at other times.

Certainly, the Rumanian case stands in stark contrast to the Czechoslovak case which followed. The Soviet leadership responded to the Czechoslovak developments by opting at first for negotiation and diplomatic pressure. As these were to no avail, a full-fledged military invasion was carried out in August, 1968. The action was referred to as multilateral, for five other Warsaw Pact members (only Rumania avoided any participation) had been dragged in as accomplices. However, the subsequent Soviet theoretical justification, known as the "Brezhnev Doctrine," did not even mention the treaty. It talked about the limited sovereignty within the socialist community, where international law must be subordinated to the laws of the class struggle. Remington, incidentally, draws a poignant comparison between the Soviet intervention in Czechoslovakia and that which the United States resorted to in the Dominican Republic in 1965. Both are, in a sense, manifestations of "crisis management" practiced by the two superpowers. Despite the divisive effects of the invasion of Czechoslovakia, the military activities of the Warsaw Pact were intensified. Moscow is, apparently, even more intent on its further "perfection."

Wolfe, Thomas W. *Role of the Warsaw Pact in Soviet Policy*. Santa Monica, Calif.: The Rand Corporation, 1973.

In this brief study, Thomas W. Wolfe, a well-known authority on Soviet affairs, attempts to assess the impact of the so-called *détente* atmosphere in Europe on the Warsaw Pact. Several important East-West agreements were achieved in the early 1970's, entailing the potential for an eventual transformation of the existing two-bloc security system. Wolfe does not think that fundamental changes, such as the replacement of NATO and the Warsaw Pact by an all-European security system, are in the offing; nevertheless, significant changes in the role of the Warsaw Pact in Soviet policy can be expected. One reasonable assumption is that the pact will gain in importance to the Soviet Union in a time of flux and relaxation of tensions in world politics. Soviet official statements, in fact, reiterate the importance of Warsaw Pact cohesion in all negotiations with the West. The uses of the treaty organization for purposes of policy coordination among the partners, although not essential, are sufficiently important to warrant its continuation and further expansion.

Wolfe argues that if military advantage were the only criteria to be weighed, the role of the Warsaw Pact would have to be considered relatively minor. The Soviet need for a regional military coalition has been declining. Basically, Soviet military strategy has always stipulated that its security requirements in Europe would be met by its own forces. The forward deployment of combat forces, which are in strength well beyond what might be required for internal policing, suggests that the Soviet Union expects to carry the brunt of any military conflict. This military posture indicates the presence of some doubt regarding the reliability of the alliance members as well.

Clearly, factors other than purely military must be considered, in order to explain the Warsaw Pact's importance to the Soviet Union. These factors are primarily political and ideological in nature. In essence, the Warsaw Pact enables the Soviet Union to advance its will through political means; it gives its hegemony in Eastern Europe a collective façade. Therein lies its chief value for the Soviet Union. However, in the final analysis, there remains the traditional backstop of Soviet armed might. — *M.G.*

Additional Recommended Reading

Brown, James F. *The New Eastern Europe: The Khrushchev Era and After*. New York: Frederick A. Praeger, 1966. A country-by-country survey of the important political, economic, and cultural developments that signaled a turning point in the history of Communism.

Brzezinski, Zbigniew K. *The Soviet Bloc: Unity and Conflict*. New York: Frederick A. Praeger, 1961. Early and highly acclaimed systematic study of the relations among the Communist states, containing useful background information on the Warsaw Pact.

Ionescu, Ghita. *The Break-Up of the Soviet Empire in Eastern Europe*. Baltimore, Md.: Penguin Books, 1965. Slightly tinged by wishful thinking, this book is nevertheless a good analysis of East European aspirations toward more independence and the resultant Soviet problems of maintaining dominance.

London, Kurt, ed. *Eastern Europe in Transition*. Baltimore, Md.: The Johns Hopkins University Press, 1966. A general treatment of East European affairs which places the Warsaw Pact in a broader perspective.

—————. *The Soviet Union: A Half-Century of Communism*. Baltimore, Md.: The Johns Hopkins University Press, 1968. Chapter 6 on Soviet relations with Eastern Europe is specifically helpful.

Wolfe, Thomas W. *Soviet Power and Europe, 1945-1970*. Baltimore, Md.: The Johns Hopkins University Press, 1970. An excellent general work on Soviet policy toward Europe.

THE GENEVA SUMMIT CONFERENCE

Type of event: Diplomatic: meeting of leaders of four major Cold War powers to discuss issues of mutual concern
Time: July 18-23, 1955
Locale: Geneva, Switzerland

Principal personages:

DWIGHT DAVID EISENHOWER (1890-1969), thirty-fourth President of the United States, 1953-1961

NIKOLAI ALEKSANDROVICH BULGANIN (1895-1975), Premier of the Soviet Union, 1955-1958

NIKITA SERGEEVICH KHRUSHCHEV (1894-1971), First Secretary of the Communist Party of the Soviet Union, 1953-1964

ROBERT ANTHONY EDEN (1897-1977), Prime Minister of Great Britain, 1955-1957

EDGAR FAURE (1908-   ), President of France

Summary of Event

The year 1953 witnessed several developments which proved to be extremely significant for the atmosphere and character of the Cold War: in January Republican Dwight D. Eisenhower became President of the United States, ending twenty years of Democratic administrations; in the Soviet Union the death of Joseph Stalin in March was followed by what appeared to be an inauguration of collective leadership; and in July the conflict in Korea came to a halt with surprisingly little change from the pre-1950 situation there. As a result of these events, hopes emerged in various quarters that the rigid Cold War postures which the Soviet Union and the United States and its Western allies had assumed since 1946 might be moderated and that solutions to some of the issues separating them might be found. Indeed, in the next few years the climate in which East-West relations were conducted im-

proved to such a degree that some observers, drawing on the title of Soviet writer Ilya Ehrenberg's novel, began to speak of "The Thaw" in the Cold War.

Only a month after Stalin's death, Winston Churchill, speaking again as Britain's Prime Minister, suggested that the time for improving East-West relations had arrived. He called for a meeting of the principal Cold War powers in order to resolve some of the major issues dividing them. Two months later in the House of Commons he reissued his call. The response from Washington was cautious; the Department of State, now under the leadership of John Foster Dulles, indicated that the Eisenhower Administration would not consider holding any direct talks with Soviet leaders until they had demonstrated their good faith in some tangible fashion. On the other side of the Iron Curtain, the Soviet government reacted favorably to Churchill's invitation but refused to consider any preconditions for such a meeting. Thus, for the time being at least, it appeared that the two superpowers remained intransigent in their respective Cold War attitudes.

By the fall of 1954, however, there were indications that the Eisenhower Administration was beginning to soften its stance. The President implied in November that a summit meeting might be possible, but not until after the Paris Accords had been ratified. The Paris agreements, signed in October, 1954, provided for the complete independence of West Germany, with membership in the North Atlantic Treaty Organization (NATO), a move the Soviets had vociferously condemned and hoped the French would prevent. When it became clear, however, that the Paris Accords would be ratified, the Soviet stance also began to shift. On the initiative of the Soviet Government, negotiations for a peace treaty with Austria were resumed. Previously, the Soviets had maintained that the final Austrian peace treaty would have to await a disposition of the German unification problem. Ultimately, on May 15, 1955, the foreign ministers of France, Great Britain, the United States, and the Soviet Union met in Vienna and signed a treaty with the Austrian government putting an end to Allied occupation and guaranteeing its neutrality and complete independence. By this treaty the Soviets not only secured Austria's neutrality, a condition they would later propose for Germany, but also demonstrated the good faith for which the American government had asked. The ma-

chinery was put in motion for a meeting of the leaders of the four major Cold War powers.

On March 20, partly in response to the Austrian treaty negotiations in progress, Walter F. George, Chairman of the Senate Foreign Relations Committee, announced his support for a four-power conference later that year. Three days later President Eisenhower told reporters he would go anywhere to serve the cause of peace, and very shortly afterwards Edgar Faure, President of France, expressed similar views, while Churchill's successor, Anthony Eden, agreed that the time was right for such a meeting. Thus, on May 10, a joint note from the three Western powers invited the Soviet Union to join "in an effort to remove the sources of conflict between us." On May 26, the Soviet Government accepted the invitation to a summit meeting to begin in Geneva, Switzerland, on July 18. The final diplomatic preparations for the Geneva Summit Conference were made by the four foreign ministers on June 20, on the occasion of a United Nations General Assembly meeting in San Francisco.

Just prior to departing for Geneva, President Eisenhower appeared before the nation on television to express his hope that the coming meeting would "change the spirit that has characterized the intergovernmental relationships of the world during the past ten years," and that the new spirit would constitute a major step toward peace. Many observers, however, agreed that neither Eisenhower nor any of the other major participants privately expected any really positive results. Probably the most each side hoped to achieve was propaganda favorable to its point of view. Indeed, the conditions were right for making propaganda points; nearly twelve hundred representatives of the press gathered in Geneva to cover the talks, and the advance publicity portrayed the meeting as perhaps the most important gathering of leaders since the end of World War II. It was, indeed, the first summit conference held since the Potsdam Conference in the summer of 1945.

The first plenary session of the conference opened on July 18 in the Palais des Nations, an old League of Nations building. It was obvious from the outset that this would not be a meeting of leaders on an informal, personal level, as Churchill had proposed. Forty men sat down around four tables arranged in a square, with rows of additional assistants and observers stretching out behind them. According to arrangements made in San Francisco, President Eisenhower, the only chief of state present, was the first chairman and the first to address the group. He declared that the issues which should receive priority consideration were those concerning German unification under a freely elected government, disarmament with supervision and inspection, and improved East-West communications. French President Edgar Faure followed, emphasizing the need for a peace treaty with Germany and disarmament through some kind of international organization. Anthony Eden also stressed German unification and proposed a five-power security pact to include Germany, with the possible creation of a demilitarized zone in Europe between East

and West. The last of the four leaders to speak was Soviet Premier Nikolai Bulganin. Bulganin advocated an end to the arms race and a ban on nuclear weapons; a system of collective security including all European states and the United States; an end to NATO, the Paris Accords, and the Warsaw Pact; and the reunification of Germany—but not as a member of NATO. He rejected any discussion of the governments of Eastern Europe and ended his comments with a plea for strengthened economic ties and increased contacts in culture and science.

On the basis of the four opening statements, the four foreign ministers drafted an agenda of topics for discussion. Included were most of the issues mentioned above: German unification, European security, disarmament, East-West contacts, neutrality, and, at Soviet insistence, Far Eastern problems. When the sessions resumed the next day, President Eisenhower agreed not to raise the issue of Eastern European governments, while rejecting the inclusion of the Taiwan situation (the Communist Chinese claims to that and other islands held by the Chinese Nationalists) in the discussions. From this point discussions proceeded, with each of the four leaders participating and expressing views on the various issues on the agenda. Unfortunately, a spirit of compromise did not characterize the talks; rather, each side appeared intransigent, extolling the merits of its own proposals and criticizing those of the others. One fact emerged clearly in the discussions: the Soviets were going to make no concessions to the Western point of view, especially on the matter of Germany's future. The principal Soviet delegates, Bulganin and Nikita Khrushchev, did not rule out Germany's eventual reunification, but the necessary preconditions had the effect of pushing a final German settlement far into the future.

Since the four-power leaders could not agree on how to move the discussion beyond mere statements of position, and the four foreign ministers were unable to offer positive recommendations on how to proceed, the Soviet delegation, on July 20, presented a specific proposal for a treaty of European collective security. Failing to gain support for this project, they came back the next day with a proposal for a nonagression pact between the NATO and Warsaw Pact nations until a collective security agreement could be concluded. The Soviet leaders also presented a draft disarmament agreement calling for reductions in the sizes of armed forces and including an agreement not to use nuclear weapons, pending an absolute ban. The Soviet disarmament proposal opened the door for Eisenhower to attempt a master propaganda stroke.

Eisenhower had brought with him a so-called "open skies" proposal, which only awaited a propitious moment for presentation. In direct response to the Soviet disarmament proposal, Eisenhower again emphasized the great importance of effective inspection and supervision. As a demonstration of America's good will and good faith, he proposed that the powers exchange "a complete blueprint of our military establishments, from beginning to end, from one end of our countries to the other." Facilities for aerial photography would also be provided for further verification. It was a startling proposal. Bulganin initially responded that "it seemed to have real merit," justifying Soviet study of the project; but this favorable Soviet reaction was short-lived, for, immediately upon breaking for recess, Khrushchev approached Eisenhower to declare his disagreement with Bulganin's assessment. In Khrushchev's view, "the idea was nothing more than a bald espionage plot against the U.S.S.R."

During the final two days of the talks no new specific proposals emerged. The delegates restricted themselves to generalities about the need for better methods of communication, travel, and study between the two sides. The final day, July 23, consisted essentially of platitudinous closing statements reiterating the positions taken earlier by the respective delegations, with some debate about directives to the four foreign ministers who were to continue the discussions.

In the final analysis, little of a positive, tangible nature was achieved at the Geneva Summit Conference. The informal, intimate conversations which Churchill had proposed never developed. Eisenhower had no private talks with Khrushchev, now obviously the most important man in the Soviet Union. The dramatic Open Skies project had little chance of acceptance, and on August 4, Bulganin officially rejected it in a speech before the Supreme Soviet. He nevertheless termed the Geneva Talks a success in that they had reduced the tensions between East and West. Eisenhower subsequently expressed optimism for future East-West relations because of the "Spirit of Geneva." Probably the most important result of the Geneva Summit was that both sides were talking and communicating again and making clear their respective positions on vital issues. That tension was somewhat reduced was evidenced by the fact that very soon, exchange visits between American and Soviet scientists, scholars, and artists, as well as some highly placed political figures, began taking place.

Pertinent Literature

Eubank, Keith, *The Summit Conferences, 1919-1960*. Norman: University of Oklahoma Press, 1966.

Professor Keith Eubank's widely known monograph on the 1938 Munich Conference undoubtedly provided some of the inspiration for this broader, more generalized study of that twentieth century diplomatic practice known as the summit conference. Such conferences have involved face-to-face meetings by high-ranking government leaders to undertake what previously had been left primarily in the hands of the professional diplomats. Eubank summarizes the origins, courses, and results of seven summit conferences from World War I to the 1960's: the Paris Peace Conference; the Munich Conference; the World War II conferences at Teheran, Yalta, and Potsdam; the 1955 Geneva Conference; and the 1960 Paris Conference. The book is organized chronologically with some chapters describing the backgrounds or origins of the various conferences and others devoted to the meetings themselves. A final chapter contains a number of the author's conclusions concerning the costs, risks, and benefits of summit conferences as a method of conducting foreign policy. The 1955 Geneva Conference is thus treated in the historical context of twentieth century summit diplomacy.

Eubank maintains that in the post-World War II years a high-level summit conference involving the major powers was not possible before the middle 1950's because of the Cold War attitudes which dominated East-West relations. However, the events of 1953, especially the death of Joseph Stalin, seemed to herald a new era, and several prominent statesmen, most notably Winston Churchill, began to advocate a summit meeting involving the leaders of the great powers as a means of resolving some of the major issues dividing them. Continuing mutual suspicions plus the fact that several important diplomatic negotiations were in the crucial stages of development delayed such a meeting until the summer of 1955. By 1955 a more favorable atmosphere existed since the former Allies had finally reached agreement and signed a peace treaty with Austria.

Thus, in July, 1955, leaders from the United States, the Soviet Union, France, and Great Britain met in

Geneva to suggest possible solutions to various problems of mutual concern and to appeal through propaganda to world public opinion for support for their respective proposals. Eubank suggests that it is unlikely that any of the leaders attending the conference expected to achieve any concrete results, and for that reason as well as some others no serious effort was made to negotiate a resolution to their differences. However, the appearance of effort was important because world public opinion expected it; Eubank noted that on the eve of the conference evangelist Billy Graham concluded a crusade in Geneva with the statement: "Never before have so many looked to so few for so much."

Unfortunately, several factors precluded a successful outcome for the conference. While the powers might agree upon the principal issues deserving their attention, they could not agree on possible solutions. Even the Western Powers differed in their approaches to the question of Germany's future, for example. Anthony Eden had proposed preliminary discussions between the Western Allies before the Geneva meeting but Eisenhower had rejected the idea. This sign of disunity encouraged the Soviet leaders to take intransigent positions concerning such matters as European security, disarmament, and German unification. Also, the Western statesmen were not able to negotiate freely on the German question because of promises made to Chancellor Konrad Adenauer about Germany's future. Consequently, as the author points out, "the four leaders never seriously tried to negotiate

by putting forward proposals which they thought had any chance of agreement. The quartet dealt only in generalities and propaganda, each trying to outpoint the other in publicity." Little wonder then that the Geneva Conference produced so few tangible results. According to Eubank, nothing really changed as a result of that meeting; the powers merely understood a little better where the other side stood and how far it would go to secure its goals. One thing seemed clear: neither side "would risk upsetting the balance of power" for the sake of its goals in Central Europe. On the other hand, the East and West were at least talking to each other once again.

Based on the records of the Geneva Summit Conference of 1955 and on the other conferences discussed, Eubank reaches several conclusions about the values of such meetings for achieving the goals of foreign policy or solving international crises. For example, heads of state or prime ministers seldom accomplish their primary objectives, and probably more could be achieved more efficiently by experienced professional diplomats. Such conferences rarely "bridge the differences between the power blocs" and frequently only serve "as vehicles for propaganda." Time and timing are almost always factors in determining the outcome of such meetings. Heads of government usually cannot be away from their capitals for long periods of time, and consequently inadequate attention is given to the problems for which the conference has been convened; because of time shortage, bad decisions are often made under pressure to achieve at least a semblance of agreement. As for timing, Eubank points out that the Geneva conference, for example, "came too late to bring the Soviet leaders to agreement; a meeting in 1953 soon after Stalin's death might have produced a more solid agreement."

Another drawback of summit meetings is the attention which they attract and the public scrutiny to which their deliberations are subjected. As Eubank noted, "the Geneva meeting, with gigantic staffs and monster news conferences, wherein each side tried to score points, did not facilitate a quiet atmosphere conducive to thoughtful negotiation." The personalities of the participants have also been influencing factors in the various conferences. Contrary to the expectations of the American people, Eisenhower's charm was not sufficient to win acceptance of the American proposals by Soviet leaders. Khrushchev comes across as another hard-nosed Soviet negotiator who used the "Geneva Conference to find out how far the Western powers would let him go in Central Europe, and his diagnosis paid off when he destroyed Hungary in 1956."

On the basis of these and other conclusions, Eubank maintains that "no summit conferences should be undertaken without serious consideration of all the consequences," and that "in the future, calling a summit conference amid a world crisis should be undertaken only as a last, desperate resort."

Fontaine, André. *History of the Cold War: From the Korean War to the Present.* Translated by Renaud Bruce. New York: Pantheon Books, 1969.

This is the second volume of a magnificently written diplomatic history of the world during the half century which followed the 1917 Bolshevik Revolution in Russia. This volume covers the fifteen years from the outbreak of the Korean War to the mid-1960's, that period during which it seemed the Cold War was the most intense. André Fontaine thus treats the 1955 Geneva Summit Conference in the context of the long-standing struggle for power between Soviet Communism and its opponents. He does not confine his study to Europe or even to the Western world; the entire globe has provided the arena for the Cold War and therefore provides the setting for his book.

In a single chapter entitled "The Spirit of Geneva," Fontaine presents the Geneva Conference as simply one of a series of events which suggested a developing *détente* between East and West. He begins the chapter with a discussion of the threatening Far Eastern situation involving the offshore Chinese islands of Quemoy and Matsu, and the United States Government's decision to assist Chiang Kai-shek in holding them against Mao Tse-tung's government on the Chinese mainland. The tough line taken by the United States provoked reactions even among her allies but appeared to have the desired impact in the Far East. On April 23, 1955, at the Bandung Conference of Asian and African nations, Chou En-lai announced China's willingness to "negotiate . . . a *détente* in the Far East and particularly in the region of Formosa." A month later the Chinese Communists halted their activities in the Formosa Strait and at the end of May, China, in an apparent gesture of good will, released four Americans from its prisons. Fontaine explains this new conciliatory Chinese attitude as follows: "'The peace offensive' which was to result in the 'summit' at Geneva was on its way, and it was important that nothing arose in Asia to put it in jeopardy." The implication is fairly obvious; pressure was put on Mao's government from various quarters, including probably the Soviet Union, to moderate its policies in the Far East, at least for the time being.

Fontain next shifts attention to European developments and discusses the diplomatic maneuvers which led to the signing in October, 1954, of the Paris Accords granting sovereignty, independence, and eventual membership in the North Atlantic Treaty Organization to the Federal Republic of West Germany. The author pays particular attention to the vain attempts by the Soviet Union to generate opposition to the Accords, especially in France. Once the Paris Accords had been signed and ratification by the concerned nations appeared assured, the Soviet government initiated a shift in policy. Whereas before it had been extremely obstinate in negotiations for an Austrian peace treaty, it now became quite the opposite, with the result that on May 15, the Austrian State Treaty was signed in Vienna by representatives of the Austrian, American, British, French, and So-

viet governments. The signing of this treaty opened the door to preparations for a summit meeting of the Big Four powers, for the Soviet government successfully persuaded its former allies that the treaty was a symbol of Soviet good will. Fontaine comments with insight on the possible motives behind this Soviet move. It appears that a concern about the future of Germany was a major factor and that the Soviet government was thinking of a Germany which, like Austria, would be committed to complete neutrality. For the time being, however, a continued division of Germany suited Soviet interests more.

Thus, at Geneva, when Soviet leaders Bulganin and Khrushchev met with Prime Minister Eden, President Faure, and President Eisenhower, Germany's future was often the subject of discussion, with the Soviets consistently refusing to consider any solution except their own. At best, Eisenhower was able to get the Russians to agree to a statement which tied eventual German reunification to free elections and both the United States and the Soviet Union to the issue of general European security. What that amounted to in reality, however, was a maintenance of the *status quo* in Central Europe.

According to Fontaine, the failure of the Geneva summit was signaled by Khrushchev's rejection of Eisenhower's "Open Skies" proposal. Failure was reaffirmed later in the year in October when a Big Four Foreign Ministers' conference in Geneva, "convened to implement the resolutions of the July 'summit,'" adjourned after three weeks without accomplishing a thing. Fontaine maintains, however, that the failure of the Geneva Conference did not mean a complete collapse of the emerging *détente* as evidenced by, among other things, "Russia's return of the naval base at Porkkala to Finland; the reduction of the Red Army by 600,000 men; the exchange of agricultural delegations between the U.S.S.R. and the United States," as well as Soviet participation at an international conference to discuss peaceful uses of atomic energy.

André Fontaine has written an absorbing account of the Cold War which any student of the period will find instructive and provocative. The notes at the end of each chapter provide helpful suggestions for additional reading, while the chronology of events and the thumbnail sketches of significant personalities are also extremely useful aids. — *T.D.*

Additional Recommended Reading

Barraclough, Geoffrey. *Survey of International Affairs, 1955-1956.* London: Oxford University Press, 1960. This volume of a periodically issued series covers the major events and developments during the designated time period in all parts of the world in a readable, straightforward, noninterpretive style.

Eisenhower, Dwight D. *Mandate for Change, 1953-1956.* Garden City, N.Y.: Doubleday & Company, 1963. Eisenhower's memoirs of his first term in office include a fairly lengthy chapter on the Geneva Conference which treats not only the formal discussions but also the informal and social sidelights.

Khrushchev, Nikita S. *Khrushchev Remembers.* 2 vols. Translated and edited by Strobe Talbott. Boston: Little, Brown and Company, 1970. This memoir contains a chapter on the Geneva Conference but says little about the substance of the discussions and, interestingly, makes no mention of Eisenhower's "Open Skies" proposal.

LaFeber, Walter. *America, Russia, and the Cold War, 1945-1975.* New York: John Wiley and Sons, 1975. Suggests that the Geneva Conference had no chance of succeeding because each side formulated proposals which it knew beforehand would be unacceptable to the other.

Plischke, Elmer. *Summit Diplomacy: Personal Diplomacy of the President of the United States.* College Park: Bureau of Governmental Research, College of Business and Political Administration, University of Maryland, 1958. Analytical rather than historical study of the processes, methods, goals, limitations, and so on, of presidential diplomacy.

Ulam, Adam B. *The Rivals: America and Russia Since World War II.* New York: The Viking Press, 1971. Attempts to demonstrate that policies pursued by the United States and Russia were frequently based upon false assumptions and ungrounded fears and thus caused various opportunities to promote peace to be missed.

MERGER OF THE AFL AND THE CIO

Type of event: Economic: merger of two federations of American labor unions
Time: December 5, 1955
Locale: New York City

Principal personages:

GEORGE MEANY (1894-1980), President of the American
Federation of Labor (AFL)

WALTER PHILIP REUTHER (1907-1970), President of the Congress of Industrial Organizations (CIO)

ARTHUR JOSEPH GOLDBERG (1908-   ), General Counsel
to the CIO and the United Steelworkers

JOSEPH ALBERT WOLL (1904-   ), Counsel to the AFL

DAVID JOHN MCDONALD (1902-   ), President of the
United Steelworkers

WILLIAM F. SCHNITZLER (1904-   ), Secretary-Treasurer of
the AFL

JAMES BARRON CAREY (1911-   ), Secretary-Treasurer of
the CIO

Summary of Event

From late in the nineteenth century until the 1930's, the American Federation of Labor (AFL) was the principal, though never the only, body of organized American labor. In structure it was a federation of national and international unions, with the individual unions maintaining a great deal of autonomy. Most of the affiliated unions were composed of skilled laborers organized by their crafts or skills. The 1920's, and even more so the early Depression years (1929-1932), hurt Federation membership and prestige. This downward trend, however, was abruptly halted in 1933 with the inauguration of President Franklin D. Roosevelt and his New Deal program. New Deal legislation, such as section 7A of the National Industrial Recovery Act (1933) and the later National Labor Relations Act, or Wagner Act (1934), encour-

aged formation of unions by the legal guarantee of free collective bargaining.

This encouragement, along with other events and conditions, led to new organizing drives. Several groups within the Federation, in particular, the United Mine Workers led by John L. Lewis, argued that the drives could not be successful unless they followed the principle of industrial unionism, organizing workers by the industry in which they worked rather than by craft—for example, auto workers, not machinists. This principle was opposed by many of the leaders of the older craft unions. Personal allegiances and antagonisms, ideology and partisanship, all embittered the argument.

In 1935, insisting that the AFL was not reaching the mass production industries, John L. Lewis of the United

730

Mine Workers, together with the leaders of other unions, formed the Committee on Industrial Organization, still within the Federation. After violent debate, the AFL revoked the charters of the several unions representing the Committee on Industrial Organization, which in 1938 were organized as an independent federation and renamed the Congress of Industrial Organizations (CIO).

Over the succeeding years, the CIO built a number of industrial unions, notably in automobile manufacturing and steel, and took a more active part in general politics and social change than had been the AFL tradition. Antagonism between the movements continued, but circumstances frequently led to parallel, if not common, action, and sometimes to cooperation. This was especially the case during World War II, when both organizations were represented as labor's spokesmen. Likewise, after the war, their common opposition to what they regarded as hostile legislation led to common positions on a number of issues of mutual interest.

The division remained, however, for even the efforts of President Franklin D. Roosevelt to bring about unity had been of no avail. By 1952, time and personnel change seemed to alter the situation. Both William Green, longtime President of the AFL, and Philip Murray, President of the CIO, had died; John L. Lewis, who had withdrawn the United Mine Workers from the CIO, was still a presence, but not part of the necessary negotiations.

The new leaders, George Meany of the AFL and Walter Reuther of the CIO, began talks early in 1953.

Later that year, committees formally instituted by the boards of the two organizations met and appointed a subcommittee of three members from each federation to frame a plan of unity. The subcommittees included, respectively, the two chief officers of each—Meany and Secretary-Treasurer William F. Schnitzler for the AFL, Reuther and Secretary-Treasurer James B. Carey for the CIO, with, first, Matthew Woll of the Photo-Engravers, and then Harry Bates of the Bricklayers for the AFL, and David McDonald of the United Steelworkers for the CIO. As a necessary preliminary, the subcommittees worked out and won approval for a "no raiding" agreement, by which unions of the two organizations agreed not to recruit members from unions of the other.

Though it did not please all the union leaders, the agreement went into effect. The next step, in February, 1955, was the drafting of a merger agreement by the subcommittees, with the assistance of their lawyers, Arthur Goldberg for the CIO and Joseph Albert Woll (son of Matthew Woll) for the AFL. The draft, rapidly drawn up, went to the full committees, which also approved it.

The proposed agreement took what George Meany called "the short route"—admission of all affiliated unions of both federations. The independence of the constituent unions was to be respected; jurisdictional disputes—a major practical worry— were to be settled by negotiation. Craft and industrial unions were to have equal status. The agreement was approved by the governing boards, and the two counsels were instructed to draft a constitution for the new body. This in turn was revised and approved in May, 1955, by subcommittees, committees, and the two boards. Arrangements were made for separate, simultaneous conventions in New York City, on December 1, and the convention of the united body, on December 5, 1955, which met in the same city under the combined name of AFL-CIO. The question of a name, which might have provoked recriminations, was settled by the combination of the two preexisting names.

The two conventions adopted the constitution; the new body met without serious complications. On Reuther's nomination, Meany was unanimously elected President of the AFL-CIO and, on Carey's nomination, Schnitzler became Secretary-Treasurer. By prearrangement, vice-presidencies and seats on the Executive Council and smaller Executive Committee were apportioned among the leaders of the AFL and CIO.

The constitution made the convention, regularly meeting every two years, the governing body, with in-terim powers assigned to bodies with progressively smaller numbers, more frequent meetings, and more day-to-day power: the General Board, the Executive Council, and the Executive Committee. The constitution denounced Communism and other totalitarian systems, and provided for the expulsion of unions dominated by Communists. It also condemned corrupt and racketeering influence in the affiliated unions and gave the council power to investigate and recommend action. The united federation had, in some constitutional terms, powers that the old federations had not had.

On December 5, 1955, the convention ended nearly twenty years of division; while some unions remained outside the AFL-CIO, notably the United Mine Workers, the new federation represented most of organized American labor. Union membership statistics are, for various reasons, imprecise, but the usual figure of fifteen million members in the new federation made it the largest single body in American labor history, and, quite probably, in the free world.

Pertinent Literature

Goldberg, Arthur J. *AFL-CIO: Labor United*. New York: McGraw-Hill Book Company, 1956.

As a labor lawyer and as General Counsel for the CIO, Arthur Goldberg was a participant and draftsman in the meetings and negotiations leading to the reunion of the labor federations. His account, however, is not an autobiographical or "inside" view; in fact, he notes in his introduction that he has refrained from revealing details which he learned in his confidential capacity as a lawyer. This book is, in fact, very much a lawyer's account—it is precise, largely unemotional, and concerned with carefully recorded detail. Nevertheless, Goldberg's account is not merely that of an "objective" observer. In his introduction he explicitly states his belief in unions, which he sees as integral to American democratic society. He does not, however, defend, excuse, or ignore, union abuses; he denounces Communism, corruption, and undemocratic and discriminatory practices.

While Goldberg praises the diversity of American unions in the "shop-centered" or limited tradition which sees the union's job as that of securing better wages, hours, and working conditions for its members, his sympathies are more strongly with those unions and leaders whose concerns are broader and reach the whole society. This sympathy provides the tone of the book. Basically, however, the account is a "play-by-play," or meeting-by-meeting report of the steps toward unity. The necessary background of union history and the formation of the CIO are presented; also included is a discussion of negotiations for the new AFL-CIO, and a lawyer's examination both of the new constitution and of particular issues, such as corruption, Communism, and discrimination.

The report includes arguments and opponents of the merger, but only when they were public. What backroom deals there were, if any, what personal ambitions and animosities, do not appear. Even more innocuous anecdotal and personal touches are rare—George Meany going to the grand piano in the meeting-room to celebrate the "agreement," or Walter Reuther unhappy about meeting in Miami Beach, and about luxurious surroundings in general.

Very usefully for the student, Goldberg includes some eighty pages of appendixes containing not only the agreement and the constitution, but lists of officers and of constituent unions of the two federations, and other documentation, adding to the informative character of the account. If the facts are the principal contribution of the volume, however, it may be Goldberg's faith in American labor unions that persists longest in a reader's mind.

Goulden, Joseph C. *Meany: A Biography of the Unchallenged Strong Man of American Labor*. New York: Atheneum Publishers, 1972.

Because George Meany was one of the chief architects of labor unity, his biography is of importance for that chapter in his career; even more important, however, is the fact that his career and character lend insight into the labor movement and its history.

Born in Harlem and reared in the Bronx, a child of second- or third-generation Irish, he was the son of a plumber and leader of the plumbers' union local. He followed his father into both careers, becoming a busi-

ness agent and rising in the union bureaucracy. He moved to the head of the New York Federation of Labor, and then to the Secretary-Treasurer's post in the American Federation of Labor. In those years, Meany learned not only the workings of organized labor on the state and national levels, but also the mechanics of lobbying, and service and cooperation in a variety of functions. He also developed, in the years of the Cold War, a considerable interest in labor on the international scene.

Goulden's portrait is of a largely self-educated, tough organizer with little in the way of intellectual interests beyond the union movement. It is also the portrait of an active leader, frustrated in some ways during the years as second in command, but demonstrably taking charge once he moved, without election, into the presidency of the AFL.

If, on the one hand, the deaths of earlier leaders removed the personal obstacles to unity, there remained, as Goulden details, many other difficulties. Within both organizations there were forces blocking the way to unity, among them a struggle for leadership in the CIO and the reluctance of powerful AFL unions to have their jurisdiction, or their opportunity for expansion, limited. The shadow, or presence, of John L. Lewis, promoting unity on his own terms and in his own way, fell across the preliminary negotiations.

The two organizations had cooperated in various undertakings during the Korean War, which gave hope for unity until one of the important committees, the United Labor Policy Committee, was dissolved by the withdrawal of the AFL in 1951. Goulden traces this to a feeling on the part of the AFL that the CIO had broken unity in voting in the International Federation of Free Trade Unions. Behind that immediate charge lay the long-standing suspicion on the part of Meany and many others of Communist influence in the CIO. For its part, the CIO raised the accusation of corruption in some AFL unions, an accusation supported by congressional hearings and official and journalistic investigations.

The answer of the AFL and Meany to the latter charge was that the national and international unions were autonomous, and that the Federation had no constitutional power over them. Meany and the AFL Executive Council did finally attack the much-publicized problem of corruption in the Longshoremen's Union, convincing the skeptical at least of their good intentions. Reuther's clear avowal that he did not want the presidency of the united body removed another block. Goulden suggests that, besides his desire for unity, Reuther's reluctance to give up his base in the Auto Workers did not pose a threat to the projected unity of the AFL and CIO.

In any case, Meany moved through the obstacles on his side, and, whatever his feelings about the CIO leaders, he kept the doors of communication open. Goulden again suggests that besides a real and consistent desire for unity, Meany felt that the need for unity was urgent because of the atmosphere of the Eisenhower Administration (in Meany's terms, the "Business" Administration). Labor could not afford division in such times. It was Meany who suggested and worked for the "short road"— unity first followed by the solution of such problems as jurisdiction afterwards; taking the "long road" might have delayed the process indefinitely. — *G.J.F.*

Additional Recommended Reading

Cormier, Frank and William J. Eaton. *Reuther*. Englewood Cliffs, N.J.: Prentice-Hall, 1970. A biography of the CIO leader who brought his organization into the merger.

Taft, Philip A. *Organized Labor in American History*. New York: Harper & Row Publishers, 1964. A leading study by one of the respected labor historians.

Ruskin, A. H. "AFL-CIO: A Confederation or, Federation? Which Road for the Future?," in *Annals of the American Academy of Political and Social Sciences*: *The Crisis in the American Trade Union Movement*. CCCL (November, 1963), pp. 36-45. Deals with the problems of the merged organizations.

"All Together," in *The New Yorker*. XXXI (December 17, 1955), pp. 28-29. A light but revealing account of the merger convention.

KHRUSHCHEV DENOUNCES STALIN

Type of event: Political: speech condemning the policies of a past head of state
Time: February 24-25, 1956
Locale: Moscow

Principal personages:

NIKITA SERGEEVICH KHRUSHCHEV (1894-1971), First Party Secretary of the Communist Party of the U.S.S.R., 1953-1964

JOSEPH STALIN (IOSIF VISSARIONOVICH DZHUGASHVILI), (1879-1953), Dictator of the U.S.S.R., 1924-1953

LAVRENTI PAVLOVICH BERIA (1899-1953), head of the security forces, including the Secret Police under Stalin

ANASTAS IVANOVICH MIKOYAN (1905-1970), First Deputy Premier of the Presidium of the Communist Party of the U.S.S.R.

VLADIMIR ILICH LENIN (ULYANOV), (1870-1924), founder and head of Communist Russia, 1918-1924

Summary of Event

The Twentieth Congress of the Communist Party of the Union of Soviet Socialist Republics convened in February, 1956, approximately six months before its originally scheduled date. This was the first meeting of delegates from the Communist Party throughout the Soviet Union since the death of Joseph Stalin, the Soviet Dictator, in March, 1953. In the wake of his death, a struggle for power had ensued which resulted in Nikita S. Khrushchev's becoming First Secretary of the Party. This choice occurred in an atmosphere which ostensibly promoted greater emphasis on the principles of "collective leadership" at the highest echelons of Soviet power. In Soviet-dominated Eastern Europe a number of uprisings, protests, and strikes followed soon after Stalin's death, but by the end of 1953 they had been suppressed. In the Soviet Union itself the first reaction to Stalin's passing had been sorrow and grief which spread throughout much of the populace. Increasingly, however, discontent and criticism of Stalinism began to appear. Within the Party leadership itself what might be called a "de-Stalinization" faction emerged centered on the person of First Deputy Premier Anastas Mikoyan. Khrushchev was not yet identified with this faction, and as late as the fall of 1955 he was still seeking, or at least not shunning, public identification of himself with Stalin.

As the time approached for the Party Congress, it became increasingly apparent to the leadership, de-Stalinizers and others as well, that something needed to be done about the lingering ghost of Stalin. The Congress, which convened on February 14, was, as usual devoted to tedious party business, economic re-

736

ports, repetitive speeches laden with Marxist homilies, and other such matters. On February 16, however, Mikoyan addressed the assembly, criticizing Stalin's leadership and referring to it as having been based on the "cult of personality." He also alluded critically to the manner in which Soviet history had been written during the period of Stalin's regime. Less strident remarks along the same lines were included in speeches by Deputy Premier Georgi M. Malenkov and Premier Nikolai Bulganin on February 17 and 21, respectively. In retrospect, it can be said that these speeches set the stage for Khrushchev's lengthy and dramatic speech of February 24-25. Some observers have suggested that the de-Stalinizers, with Mikoyan taking the lead, had forced Khrushchev's hand by their pronouncements of the previous days. Considering the text of the Khrushchev speech itself, however, and noting the enormity of the task involved in undertaking such a denunciation, it is unlikely that Khrushchev decided on the speech during the days of the Congress itself. It is likely that the speech, which covers nearly one hundred typescript pages, had been prepared weeks, if not months, before the Party Congress began.

A speech of such length and complexity, of course, included many details, allusions, and emendations. Along with Stalin, the single figure who bore the greatest brunt of Khrushchev's attack was Lavrenti Beria. Beria himself had been restored from disfavor to Chief of the Security Forces in early 1953, just before Stalin's death, but was arrested at the end of June and executed in December of that year. Khrushchev used the opportune occasion of the speech to emphasize Beria's participation and collaboration in Stalin's crimes and to justify his execution.

The speech began with Khrushchev's citing of praise for the fact that under Vladimir Lenin, the founder of Communist Russia, the Central Committee of the Party had existed as "a real expression of collective leadership." Throughout this first section of the speech, and at numerous other places in it, Khrushchev repeated praise for Lenin's enlightened leadership, and simultaneously picked away at Stalin's "deviations" from Leninism. In particular, he quoted copiously from Lenin's "Last Testament," transcribed shortly before his death in January, 1924, with ample allusions to his fears about Stalin and warnings about his personal foibles and desires for self-aggrandizement. To add weight to these points in the speech, copies of the "Last Testament" were distributed to all delegates in attendance. The general tone of these accusations formed the basis for Khrushchev's accusation that Stalin created in the Soviet leadership over the thirty years of his rule a grandiose "cult of personality."

Khrushchev then turned to the most moving and spectacular part of his speech—the recounting of the reign of terror that had been carried out through repression and mass purges in the mid- and late-1930's. This section of the speech, volatile in content, often has a dispassionate and matter-of-fact tone about it. Khrushchev was careful to maintain that by the time the purges began, Trotskyites, Zionovievites, and other dangerous deviationist elements in the Soviet Union and in the Party had already been defeated. Hence, he implied that the real enemies of Soviet Communism were no longer a threat, meaning that the purges and persecutions which followed were unnecessary. By filtering the term "enemy of the people" through the prism of his own megalomania, Stalin came to destroy "many honest Communists." Stalin's purge of "old Communists" of the Civil War period received special attention.

In shifting to the next section of the speech, which focused on Stalin's ineptitude as a wartime leader, Khrushchev dealt very critically with the purges of the military high command. Throughout this section of the speech culpability for this "massacre of the innocents" is repeatedly ascribed to Stalin individually or to Beria and "his gang." Khrushchev's account does name others who were involved, but these allusions do not combine into an indictment of the mechanisms of the purges since this might have resulted in assignment of responsibility to many others who were implicated or involved in the undertaking, including Khrushchev himself.

Among the most "grievous consequences" of the purges, in Khrushchev's eyes, was the annihilation of military commanders and political workers whose usefulness for preparing the Soviet Union for the German military attack in 1941 would have been great. This occasioned a lengthy denunciation of Stalin's misunderstanding of Hitler and the entire question of preparing for the defense of the nation against German attack.

In this section, Khrushchev touched on many personal anecdotes serving to illustrate instances of Stalin's incompetencies and misguided leadership, especially in the first months of the war. Again, Stalin's personal megalomania is made to appear as the primary source of Soviet military weakness in the struggle.

Returning to the theme that Mikoyan had touched on in an earlier speech to the Congress, Khrushchev then criticized in detail the ways in which Stalin had been glorified in Soviet historical accounts and in the media in general. Finally, Khrushchev was especially critical of Stalin's leadership in agriculture (a field in which Khrushchev claimed expertise), and then ended the speech by reverting to the theme of Stalin's destruction of Leninist principles as having immobilized and debilitated the Party leadership throughout his years as First Secretary.

The speech was made to a closed meeting, but a number of the texts of it that have subsequently appeared indicate points of agitation or expressions of agreement among the assemblage. It is reported that at one point, when he was denouncing the purges, an anonymous note was sent to the rostrum to Khrushchev. It asked why he had said nothing when all of this was going on. Khrushchev read the note, asked for the writer to stand, and, after a time, when no one stood, said "there's your answer."

Response to the speech from outside the Soviet Union was slow in coming. Within weeks the various Communist Parties of the Soviet-bloc States in Eastern Europe had endorsed Khrushchev's denunciation of

Stalin. During the next few months, however, Communist Parties elsewhere expressed criticism of the document. In Western Europe the leadership of the Italian Communist Party was especially articulate in pointing out the "co-responsibility on the part of those who denounce Stalinism." In China, news of the speech was received with dismay and condemnation by the Communist leadership of that country.

Pertinent Literature

Cranshaw, Edward. *Khrushchev: A Career.* New York: The Viking Press, 1966.

Cranshaw's biography of Khrushchev's political career places the 1956 speech in which Stalin was denounced in a unique and meaningful perspective. The book does not deal at length or in detail with the speech itself; rather, it offers a number of highly interpretive perspectives on it.

The interpretation places heavy emphasis on the fact that the anti-Stalin speech occurred in concert with another speech to the Twentieth Party Congress which contained "epoch-making modifications to Leninist canon." While the latter speech created the basis for an entirely new era in Soviet foreign policy—renouncing the notion of inevitable war, preaching "revolution without violence," and recognizing "different paths to socialism" for different peoples—the former potentially created the basis for an entirely new era in Soviet domestic policy. The Western world, however, did not recognize the significance of the reality of change in the official Soviet line, possibly because reports of the "Denunciation of Stalin" speech were more spectacular to Western observers.

Cranshaw strongly debunks the legend that Khrushchev was persuaded at the last minute to make the speech denouncing Stalin. Khrushchev, the author argues, had already attacked Stalin's crimes as early as June, 1955, in a speech at Sofia, Bulgaria. The contention is advanced that Khrushchev was setting the pace in the growing hostility toward Stalin, emerging at the upper echelons of party leadership in 1955-1956. Cranshaw acknowledges, however, that the key phrase in the denunciation of Stalin, accusing the deceased leader of having developed a "personality cult," may likely have been suggested by other party leaders. This, Cranshaw surmises, might have occurred as their way of setting up a groundwork to make it more difficult for Khrushchev to establish a "personality cult" of his own.

Cranshaw's interpretation has Khrushchev already firmly in control of the Party prior to the Twentieth Party Congress, and, moreover, argues that the immediate outcome of the Congress was "all in Khrushchev's favor." The author carefully delineates the theme of Khrushchev's anti-Stalin speech: Khrushchev denounced Stalin as the "Enemy of the Party," not as the "Enemy of the People." Khrushchev attacked Stalin's torture and murder of good, honest Communists, but not, for example, Stalin's actions against Trotskyites,

Bukharinites, and other deviationist elements. Nonetheless, Cranshaw maintains that Khrushchev's message might have been interpreted by the Soviet people legitimately as beckoning the dawn of a new era. In all, Cranshaw views the 1956 Party Congress as marking a commitment on the part of the Party to break with Leninism, which meant breaking with Stalinism as well. That Khrushchev and those in power besides him would, nonetheless, have to evoke the legend of Lenin to legitimate their hold on power was to produce many of the difficulties and contradictions in Soviet politics for the next decade. While an official Soviet version of the speech was not published, the U.S. State Department issued a version which was never contradicted by Soviet authorities. At all odds, news of the speech spread quickly, both inside and outside the Communist world. Cranshaw's account indicates widespread popular discussion of its contents, at least at Party meetings throughout the Soviet Union. This produced signs of change, which were greeted in a variety of ways—elation, enthusiasm, confusion, increased criticism, and even desolation. Such reactions are sketched anecdotally by Cranshaw. Here, too, Cranshaw finds signs of Khrushchev's strength, for he not only took on and carried through the task of denouncing Stalin, but

also rode the waves of tumult and confusion that ensued from the denunciation.

Thus, Cranshaw concludes that in February, 1956, Khrushchev was at the summit of his career. The two "secret" speeches at the Party Congress reflected and accentuated his command of power. This interpretation is in contradiction to most views of Khrushchev's grasp on power, and the motivation for and significance of the speeches. While acknowledging that his view would not be endorsed by the majority of experts on Soviet affairs, Cranshaw nonetheless adheres to it without reservation.

The "Denunciation of Stalin" speech is seen, then, as a document reflecting Khrushchev's attainment of leadership. It betokens his rejection of the legend that had come before him, and as a political device was an instrument of Khrushchev's making, through which he asserted that very power to which he had attained. Nonetheless, while the directions indicated in the speeches were clear, the means of later attaining them were not. This, Cranshaw believes, is a primary problem in interpreting the "Denunciation of Stalin" speech which he implies is understandable in the broadest sense only in its relationship to the accompanying "Revision of Leninism" speech of February, 1956.

Wolfe, Bertram D. *Khrushchev and Stalin's Ghost*. New York: Frederick A. Praeger, 1957.

This book is a well-organized analysis of the Khrushchev denunciation, and is surprisingly rich in placing the speech in its historical context. Although Wolfe's analysis appeared within a year and a half after the event itself, it demonstrates a thoroughgoing attempt to interpret the

Khrushchev speech in a broad context. The author, a scholar of Marxism in its various forms, proclaims Khrushchev's 1956 address to be the most important document in all of modern Communism. While it might be argued that this is a exaggeration, Wolfe proceeds to demonstrate convincingly that the speech is, indeed, significant in what it reflects about Communist thinking.

Wolfe begins his account with background information leading to the speech and furnishes commentary and speculation about Stalin's death. He does not discredit entirely the possibility that the leader's end was hastened by his immediate cohorts at the pinnacle of power. Wolfe points out that with Stalin's death the problems of succession faced the Soviet leadership. In general, Wolfe argues that the problem of succession is always difficult in any totalitarian state, and the Soviet Union, at this juncture in 1953, was no exception. The leadership had to improvise the transition to a new leader who wound up being Khrushchev. In doing so, the new leadership demonstrated that its policies in many ways deviated not one iota from Stalinism. The book touches briefly on Stalinism in industry, agriculture, and nearly every aspect of Soviet public life. Even the arrest and execution of Beria by the new leadership was clearly in the Stalinist tradition. Moreover, it had taken Stalin nearly a decade to launch purges of his enemies, whereas Khrushchev and the new leaders took less than one year to rid themselves of Beria and "his gang."

Wolfe views Khrushchev's denunciation speech as a point of departure, not for the revocation of Stalinism, but rather as establishing Khrushchev's own dictatorial power within the Soviet system. It is Wolfe's interpretation that totalitarianism is endemic to the Soviet Communist system, and deeply rooted in it. Therefore, the Khrushchev speech is considered to be a subtle and convoluted reassertion of the Soviet totalitarian tradition passing over into new hands. The author weaves an argument which points to the hollowness and shallowness of the Khrushchev speech as a critique of Stalinism. The real significance of the speech is discovered in its reflection of a totalitarian mentality.

Wolfe is thus asserting that the speech itself, especially Khrushchev's denunciation of the "cult of the personality" of Stalin, can actually be decoded as Khrushchev's assertion of his own "personality cult." The emerging personal dictatorship of Khrushchev seems to differ in kind from Stalin's dictatorship only because personalities differ. It does not differ, however, in its basic nature.

The book explores the tradition of totalitarianism dating from Lenin. The implication is that Khrushchev's speech is, in fact, most accurately analyzed as an extension of an elaboration on that tradition. In the words of the aphorism sometimes applied to so-called revolutionary events, "the more things change, the more they stay the same"; this is at the base of Wolfe's analysis and interpretation. The author roots Khrushchev's politics and public temperament in the very same political tradition that produced Stalinism. Thus, the "event of the denunciation speech" pales against the broader background of its setting—the developmental background of totalitarianism in the Soviet Union.

In summary, Wolfe's analysis of the instance in which Stalin was denounced is harsh. The interpretation and analysis here avoids much of the detailed discussion of the political machinations that led to the speech's being presented. Rather, the interpretation cuts through the immediate precipitating elements behind the speech which is a topic for many authors. Instead, we come to view it as an element of "change without substance" in Soviet politics. While the speech might be said to be an attempt to remove the ghost of Stalin, the spirit of him remains present in the speech itself. That spirit must, however, be understood as fundamental to the Soviet system, and not to Stalin's personality. — *P.M.*

Additional Recommended Reading

Brumberg, Abraham, ed. *Russia Under Khrushchev: An Anthology from Problems of Communism*. New York: Frederick A. Praeger, 1962. Contains articles on nearly every aspect of Khrushchev's regime with emphasis on foreign affairs; several articles on the Twentieth Party Congress are informative.

Alliuyeva, Sveltana. *Twenty Letters to a Friend*. New York: Harper & Row Publishers, 1967. Stalin's daughter clarifies some aspects of her father's career with interesting sidelights on the attacks against him.

Khrushchev, Nikita S. *Khrushchev Remembers*. 2 vols. Translated and edited by Strobe Talbott. Boston: Little, Brown and Company, 1970. These memoirs, aside from the immediate sensationalist response to their appearance, provide the reader with insights into both a mind (Khrushchev's) and a mentality (that of Soviet Communism).

Shapiro, Leonard. *The Communist Party of the Soviet Union*. New York: Random House, 1965. A detailed, thorough study of the Party; the circumstances surrounding the "Denunciation of Stalin Speech" and the results thereof are treated with insight.

Tibor, Méray. *Thirteen Days That Shook the Kremlin*. London: Thames & Hudson, 1959. This account of the Hungarian revolt gives ample background on the problems of an apparent departure from Stalinism in Soviet policy.

CASTRO SEIZES POWER IN CUBA

Type of event: Military: fall of dictator leads to profound change in political system
Time: December 2, 1956-January 1, 1959
Locale: Cuba

Principal personages:

FIDEL CASTRO (1927-   ), leader of the guerrilla forces and key figure in the post-revolutionary government

FULGENCIO BATISTA Y ZALDIVAR (1901-1973), Dictator of Cuba whose repressive regime was overthrown by Castro's forces

GERARDO MACHADO Y MORALES (1871-1939), American-backed Dictator overthrown by the Cuban Revolution of 1933

RAMÓN GRAU SAN MARTÍN (1887-1969), reformist leader who was twice president of Cuba

SUMNER WELLES (1892-1961), the United States Ambassador to Cuba who persuaded Batista to overthrow Grau

Summary of Event

Although there have been many revolutions in Cuban history, "The Cuban Revolution" of 1959, which ousted Dictator Fulgencio Batista and replaced him with Fidel Castro, is "*the* Revolution" in the same sense that the revolution of 1917 is "*the* Russian Revolution." The 1959 Revolution led to a profound transformation of the social, economic, and political systems. Furthermore, like other cataclysmic revolutions, its causes are not readily distinguishable if the only events examined are those immediately preceding it. Since the revolution climaxed a long historical struggle, it can best be understood within the broader historical context which produced it.

Cuba was one of the first Latin American nations to be colonized by the Spanish, and it was the last to achieve formal political independence. While most of the other Latin American nations gained their independence in the 1820's, Cuba did not shake off the Spanish yoke until 1898, for a variety of reasons. Given its strategic location in the Caribbean, it was viewed by the Spanish as a vital staging area for any attempt to regain control of the mainland. It was also easier for the Spanish fleet to control. Nor was the Cuban elite as anxious to attain independence as were the dominant classes elsewhere. The chilling example of the slave revolt that brought Haiti both independence and a tyrannical black government in 1804, led Cuba's sugar planters to fear that independence for their nation would also precipitate an unpleasant social revolution. Finally, the United States actively discouraged Mexican and Colombian attempts to promote the Cuban cause. Although the United States might have found annexation of Cuba an acceptable alternative, it was not then feasible, and continued control of Cuba by a weak Spain was thought to be a better alternative than a feeble independent Cuba which might easily be swallowed up by a European nation far more powerful than Spain. Already a combination of strategic concerns and developing economic interests had made the United States the enemy of Cuban autonomy.

Ironically, periodic Cuban independence struggles brought final freedom from Spain only after the United States intervened in 1898. The Cubans fought for three bloody years before the United States, with a minimal loss of American lives, acquired both Puerto Rico and the Philippines, and, almost incidentally, occupied Cuba. In a sense, the Cubans were robbed of what they considered an almost certain victory by our last-minute intervention. Then they discovered that the price for the withdrawal of American troops was the incorporation into their new constitution in 1901 of the infamous Platt Amendment, which gave the United States a legal right to act as the ultimate arbiter of their political affairs—a right exercised to the full on numerous occasions.

During the next third of a century, the American ambassador, and at times American military forces, dictated political outcomes in Cuba. Not coincidentally, American banks dominated the economy and American interests bought up the largest plantations and mills in the rapidly expanding sugar producing sector of the economy, the prosperity of which now became critical to the health of the entire Cuban economy. The United States was the most important customer for Cuban exports, the source of most Cuban imports, and the leading source of support for Cuba's extraordinarily dependent economic and political leadership. Consequently, discontent with Cuba's leaders was always automatically associated with bitter anti-American outbursts.

By the time the Cuban revolution of 1933 displaced the American-backed Dictator Gerardo Machado, all of the opposition forces were attacking what they called *plattistas* and *entreguistas*, people who supported the Platt Amendment and sold out or surrendered the country's economy to others. If the revolution of 1895 had failed to produce true independence because of American intervention in 1898, then this broadly popular uprising was aimed at rectifying that failure. Once again, however, the Cubans were robbed of an unequivocal victory by last-minute American intervention. Before the revolution could get completely out of hand, the American ambassador persuaded Machado to resign. The reformist forces behind the revolution were briefly able to place Ramón Grau San Martín in the presidency with the help of a Sergeant's Revolt led by Fulgencio Batista. However, the United States withheld recognition of the Grau government, and Sumner Welles, the United States Ambassador, soon persuaded Batista to overthrow Grau. In return, the United States finally abrogated the Platt Amendment in 1934. What could have been a great symbolic victory for Cuban nationalism was reduced in meaning when it was obtained for

Cuba as part of a maneuver to preserve United States interests.

In the next twenty years, the sugar economy stagnated; United States investment in the rest of the island's economy doubled; tourism, gambling, prostitution, and organized crime were added to the other United States contributions; and a series of Batista-dominated governments were followed by two reformist-oriented governments whose inefficiency and corruption completely discredited the original leadership of the Revolution of 1933. Another military *coup* returned Batista to power in 1952, this time as a full-fledged repressive dictator, and set the stage for Fidel Castro to lead the revolutionary struggle by picturing himself as the inheritor of the cause of José Martí, the martyr-hero of the original independence struggle.

On July 26, 1953, Castro led an attack on the Moncada Army barracks in Santiago de Cuba, the second largest army barracks in the country. Although the attack was a miserable failure and led to Castro's imprisonment, it was the first armed action against the dictatorship; it made Castro the focal point of subsequent anti-Batista activity, and it provided a name for his revolutionary organization—the 26th of July Movement.

After spending time in jail, getting out as part of a general political amnesty, and spending a brief period in normal political activity, Castro left for Mexico to prepare another violent assault on the Batista government. When he landed on December 2, 1956, government troops were waiting for him. Only twenty or thirty of his small band of followers survived

to struggle with him to the Sierra Maestra mountains from which he was to direct a successful guerrilla struggle. On December 31, 1958, Fulgencio Batista fled the island. The details of the third-rate military struggle against Batista are not important because there were no major battles and no impressive victories. The guerrilla effort did not directly defeat Batista; at the end, Batista's army still had Castro's forces hopelessly outgunned and outmanned, and could still have prevailed, if they had had the will to fight. What robbed them of the will to fight was the complete delegitimization of the Batista government they were defending in the eyes of every important sector of Cuba's society. The extremely repressive fashion in which Batista responded to opposition produced revulsion even among those who were his natural allies. Batista's final legacy to Cuba was the weakening and discrediting of all the institutions which could have limited the Castro regime to the reformist goals of the guerrilla struggle. But Castro operated within a power and legitimacy vacuum that permitted him to move toward a more fundamental restructuring of Cuban society during the first two years of his rule. This, then, is the significance and meaning of the Cuban Revolution which culminated in Castro's triumphal arrival in Havana in January of 1959. The underlying causes of its success combined with the immediate circumstances of the Revolution to make possible one of the few twentieth century cases of fundamental system change and transformation.

Pertinent Literature

Ruiz, Ramón Eduardo. *Cuba: The Making of a Revolution.* New York: W. W. Norton and Company, 1968.

For those who are interested in understanding the forces which produced a successful revolution in Cuba in 1959, this is an ideal book. In developing his interpretation of the Cuban Revolution, Ramón Eduardo Ruiz places the events of 1959 in the context of Cuban history and also reviews the major interpretations an informed student of the subject would want to explore, accepting and rejecting their arguments as his view of the evidence dictates. Only his discursive and essayistic writing style limits the didactic value of the work, though only moderately. That limitation is overcome by a final chapter, which truly serves as a summary and ties the earlier analytic wanderings together.

Ruiz begins by addressing what he calls "The Cuban Paradox": ". . . it was Cuba and not its poverty-burdened neighbors that had a social revolution." The paradox was created by the peculiar love-hate relationship the Cubans had with the United States. Cuba had benefited economically from its relationship with the United States. In 1956, per capita income in Cuba was the second highest in Latin America. On the other hand, the profitable relationship with the United States was based on a dependent and vulnerable sugar economy. The Cuban upper strata had little coherence as a class, having emerged largely in the twentieth century, and being totally dependent on foreign interests. They preferred American products, sent their children to American schools, and imitated American customs. On the other hand, every Cuban intellectual, and most of the politicians, blamed the United States for Cuba's problems, and pictured the North Americans' materialism in the uncomplimentary words of the widely read *Ariel* by the Uruguayan José Enrique Rodó, and in the equally uncomplimentary words of their own writer-hero of the independence struggle, José Martí.

Nor is the paradox a true paradox to scholars who specialize in studying revolution. Although government officials and the common man are constantly surprised when revolutions occur in places that are not mired in the lowest depths of poverty and degradation, Ruiz is able to cite such varied authorities as Crane Brinton, Chalmers Johnson, and Leon Trotsky as sources for the widely accepted observation that revolutions take place where some improvement has made optimism possible, but further advance seems to be blocked by unexpected obstacles. A quotation from Crane Brinton helps make the point:

> These revolutionists are not worms turning, not children of despair. These revolutions are born of hope, and their philosophies are formally optimistic.

In the Cuban case, it was because they had experienced economic development that they could conceive of further progress and be ready to act on the frustrations produced by the declining purchasing power of the Cuban peso after World War II. The inherent weakness of Cuban society, and Batista's mistakes, also contributed to the creation of a situation in which a relatively weak guerrilla movement could make a successful revolution.

Ruiz is far more satisfactory in explaining why the Cuban Revolution took place than he is in dealing with the Revolution's turn toward Communism and the Soviet Union. For example, Ruiz maintains that Theodore Draper was essentially correct when he said that ". . . Castro turned to the Communist bloc without either having requested or having been refused aid by the United States." This is altogether too simple a statement to reflect accurately a fairly complicated sequence of events. Castro certainly needed to maintain his legitimacy by engaging in antiimperalist rhetoric in the early stages of his regime, but there were signals that might have been intended as hints that the United States should make the first explicit public overtures. Castro decided to speak in mid-April, 1959, to the American Society of Newspaper Editors in Washington. As he was about to leave for Washington, he indicated that his top three economic advisers would also be making the trip. They would be along because they would be engaged in negotiations in the United States and Canada to obtain loans and improve trade relations. Felipe Pazos, who was then the President of the National Bank of Cuba, reports that officials of the State Department and the International Monetary Fund were almost forcing loans on him. Castro, however, had already shifted direction and had publicly claimed that Cuba was not interested in any loans. Whether he did this for tactical reasons related to domestic opposition to being *entreguistas* like earlier Cuban leadership groups, or to strengthen his bargaining position with the United States, the mere fact that he was the first to raise the loan issue, and did indeed bring the three top economists with him, suggests that Castro was searching for a way to obtain and accept American aid without undermining his regime. There were other such hints, such as his proposal at an OAS meeting that the United States fund a multilateral aid program to *all* of Latin America, but the earlier American interest had disappeared. Ruiz does not, however, convey the nuances of this critical period, nor satisfactorily explain Castro's embrace of the Soviet Union.

Whatever its limitations as an explanation of the radicalization of the Cuban Revolution, Ruiz's book is a fine source for the pre-1959 developments that help explain the original coming to power of the revolutionary regime.

Gonzalez, Edward. *Cuba Under Castro: The Limits of Charisma*. Boston: Houghton Mifflin Company, 1974.

Although this book is primarily concerned with examining and explaining contemporary Cuba, five of its ten chapters deal with the pre-1959 events and conditions that account for the revolution's occurrence and the shape it took. Edward Gonzalez believes that ". . . the past placed few restraints on Cuba's 'runaway revolution,' while providing much of its radical impulse." He therefore looks to the past to explain much of the present.

However, in Gonzalez's view, we cannot locate the causes of the Cuban Revolution in the kinds of economic and social factors that help account for the major revolutions that transformed Mexico, Russia, and China. Cuba did not suffer from social divisions, socioeconomic deprivations, or underdevelopment, to nearly the same degree. Divisions did exist, of course, but he argues they had little causative significance in the first stage of the Revolution. Only later, when Castro radicalized the Revolution, did they take on significance. The radicalization process deprived the revolutionary government of much of its earlier support. It was able to develop a mass base as an alternative source of support by politically exploiting the urban-rural division which existed, appealing to the black and mulatto population which had suffered discrimination in the past, and adopting an agrarian policy addressing Cuba's socioeconomic inequities which were, however, less acute than those in most other Latin American countries. Though Castro, *ex post facto*, justified the Revolution by pointing to policies rectifying past wrongs in these areas, Gonzalez maintains that the past wrongs in the socioeconomic realm were not the cause of the Revolution.

Gonzalez argues instead that a rev-olutionary situation developed primarily because of political factors. Furthermore, those same political factors are thought to have been the source of the Revolution's radical thrust once in power. Of course, the social and economic conditions are not without significance in this interpretation—but theirs is, however, a directly political significance. The old order was discredited by the chronic unemployment, rural poverty, socioeconomic inequities, and semideveloped and dependent economy.

Not only were dictators like Machado and Batista discredited by these continuing problems, but so were the reformists who had earlier led the opposition against them. Even if the reformists were not as arbitrary and repressive when in power as the dictators had been, they were equally, if not more, opportunistic and corrupt. As a result, Gonzalez is able to make a very convincing argument for the *generational* nature of Castro's Revolution. The failures of the governments of Ramón Grau San Martín and Carlos Prío Socarrás discredited the entire "generation of 1930," as it was known in Cuba, that had provided the leadership in the abortive 1933 Revolution.

Thus, the Cuban Revolution was a *generational* phenomenon. By launching the attack on the Moncada barracks on July 26, 1953, Fidel provided himself and the entire "generation of 1953" with a legitimizing myth. Their courageous and foolhardy action was in stark contrast to the older generation's less machoistic approach to dealing with the Batista government. It was the "generation of 1953" that continued to play a dynamic role as guerrilla warriors in the Sierra Maestra campaign. Their age group also supported the new regime in much higher proportions than the older generations and supplied much of the new regime's personnel. Even those of the earlier generations who supported the regime and held high leadership positions found themselves isolated, suspect, and ineffectual when the regime became more radical. "As a result, neither the old political class nor its institutions could break the tempo of the Revolution, much less effectively challenge the young *fidelista* leadership." Thus, the Castro regime was free to abandon the old order without encountering meaningful resistance.

Although the discrediting of earlier institutions and leadership explains why it was so easy for Castro's regime to move in a radical direction, other factors are needed to explain why that route was chosen. Gonzalez suggests that the heritage of Cuba's frustrated nationalism and the mental set encouraged by the relatively brief armed struggle together provide an explanation for the radical choice made.

Nationalism was important because Cuban liberationist aspirations had been thwarted by the United States interventions in Cuba until the moment Castro came to power. Defiance of the United States was the natural idiom in which to express nationalist sentiment. Furthermore, political freedom required a turn away from the economic system that symbolized American ways and also seemed to encourage continued Cuban economic subordination to the United States.

The mentality fostered by the armed struggle was important because it led to an insistence on maximal goals, a willingness to demand sacrifices, an insistence that will and desire could overcome the greatest obstacles, and a belief that a determined vanguard was more to be trusted than the unreliable masses. Together, the heritage of frustrated nationalism and a spectacularly successful guerrilla campaign provided the attitudes and outlooks that make Castro's switch from his pre-1959 position understandable.

In sum, Gonzalez has provided a most convincing set of explanations for the radicalization of the Cuban Revolution. The reader may perhaps be left with reservations about the validity of Gonzalez's deprecation of the socioeconomic factors as an explanation for the occurrence of the Revolution, but he will undoubtedly find much of value in his stress on political factors as an explanation of the character that the new regime assumed. — *B.F.*

Additional Recommended Reading

Del Rio, Eduardo (RIUS). *Cuba for Beginners: An Illustrated Guide for Americans*. New York: Pathfinder Press, 1970. A satirical Latin American view of Cuba's development in the shadow of the United States by the Mexican caricaturist RIUS.

Thomas, Hugh. *Cuba: The Pursuit of Freedom*, 1762-1969. New York: Harper & Row Publishers, 1971. A massive book indispensable for the study of the Castro revolution.

Matthews, Herbert L. *Fidel Castro*. New York: Simon and Schuster, 1969. One of the best available biographies of Castro written by the journalist who first interviewed him in the Sierra Maestra for the *New York Times*.

Draper, Theodore. *Castro's Revolution: Myths and Realities*. New York: Frederick A. Praeger, 1962. An early, influential, and critical study, containing many interpretations scholars now reject.

Taber, Robert. *M-26, The Biography of a Revolution*. New York: Lyle Stuart, 1961. Still the best general study of the Castro movement in the 1950's.

Guevara, Ernesto Che. *Episodes of the Revolutionary War*. New York: International Publishers, 1969. An eyewitness account of the guerrilla campaign by one of Castro's chief lieutenants.

COMMUNICATIONS AND METEOROLOGICAL SATELLITES

Type of event: Technological: satellites and their benefits to mankind
Time: 1957 to the present
Locale: The United States and Europe

Principal personages:

KONSTANTIN EDUARDOVITCH ZIOLKOVSKY (1857-1935), Soviet scientist who laid the theoretical foundation for modern rocket development

ROBERT HUTCHINGS GODDARD (1882-1945), American scientist who launched the first liquid fueled rocket

HERMANN OBERTH (1894-   ), Rumanian-born mathematician who founded the German "Society for Space Travel" and authored books on space exploration

WERNHER VON BRAUN (1912-1976), German-born scientist who helped develop German World War II rockets and after the war assisted with the United States space program

ARTHUR C. CLARKE (1917-   ), an English author of science fiction and science fact

Summary of Event

There can be little doubt that the artificial earth satellite has proven the wisest investment of the space age. Since the launch of the Soviet *Sputnik I* on October 4, 1957, these unmanned orbiting instrument platforms have opened entirely new vistas for science, permitting the collection of vital data otherwise unobtainable by observers who remain shielded by the shifting filter of the atmosphere. Nor have the benefits of satellite technology been limited to pure science. From their unique vantage point in space, satellites have made possible revolutionary advances that affect the lives of every citizen. In areas ranging from forestry and agriculture to city planning and ecological problem-solving, the earth satellite has been a major contributing factor in the success of attempts to improve the quality of life on earth. The fields of meteorology and communications provide the clearest evidence of the extent to which the high technology of spaceflight has been turned to the direct benefit of all mankind.

The possibility of an unmanned earth satellite was not seriously considered until the end of World War II. In order to understand the background of the achievement it is necessary to return to the early years of the twentieth century, however.

Spaceflight is an age-old dream, the origins of which are to be found in our ancestors' wonder at the awesome array of the moon, planets, and stars in the night sky. The first steps toward realization of the dream were taken by three great pioneers of astronautics, working between 1900 and 1940. The Soviet scientist Konstantin Ziolkovsky, Robert H. Goddard of the United States, and the Rumanian-born German mathematician Hermann Oberth, working independently, established the theoretical basis for spaceflight. Taken collectively, the work of these three men demonstrated the mathematical possibility of flight beyond the atmosphere.

Robert H. Goddard took an additional step when he built the world's first liquid propellant rocket, flown at Auburn, Massachusetts on March 16, 1926. Throughout the 1930's, small bands of amateur enthusiasts continued to advance the state of rocketry, and the work of German experimenters during the years between the wars was particularly noteworthy. Working under the technical leadership of Wernher von Braun and the sponsorship of the German Army, a team of German technicians succeeded in creating the *A-4*, better known under the designation *V-2*, the world's first large liquid-propellant rocket capable of reaching extreme altitudes. Designed and originally employed as a weapon, captured *A-2*'s were shipped to the United States and the U.S.S.R. in 1945, where they were used to carry the first scientific payloads into the upper atmosphere. Other "sounding rockets," or high-altitude research vehicles, followed in the wake of the *A-2*.

The earth satellite was first conceived as a "long playing rocket," returning the same sort of information as the earlier vehicles, but remaining at higher altitudes for extended periods.

The possibility of a manned platform orbiting in space had been suggested many years earlier by the three pioneers of astronautics, but the postwar revolutions in electronics and miniaturization opened the way for automated satellites. The first generation of unmanned spacecraft, launched by the U.S.S.R. and the United States as part of the International Geophysical Year (1957-1958), performed purely scientific missions. It was apparent, however, that a vehicle in orbit above the earth could be put to more practical uses.

As early as 1945, Arthur C. Clarke, the British writer of science fact and science fiction, had provided a detailed suggestion for the use of a radio relay satellite in synchronous orbit 22,300 miles above the surface of the earth. At this altitude a satellite would be able to view almost an entire hemisphere and would appear to hover over one spot on the earth's surface. Eric Burgess, another pioneer British student of spaceflight, suggested a similar vehicle to be used as a navigation satellite. The possibility of an earth observation satellite capable of returning photographs of the earth's cloud cover had been suggested by the American meteorologist Harry Wexler in the 1950's. Two years of successful experience with scientific satellites prepared the way for the realization of each of these three suggestions by 1960.

Communications satellites can be grouped roughly into three categories. The earliest United States communications satellite, *Echo I* (1960), was a passive reflector from which radio signals could be bounced from one point on earth to another. The active satellites which followed accepted a ground signal, then amplified and rebroadcast it. *Telestar I* (1962), the brain child of Bell Laboratories' John R. Pierce, provided the first convincing demonstration of the potential of such a craft by opening experimental transatlantic television service. The foundation of INTELSAT, the international communications satellite consortium (1964) and COMSAT, the United States member organization, made possible the widespread utilization of communications satellite technology. Beginning with the INTELSAT I satellite (1965), INTELSAT has flown five series of spacecraft, the most recent being INTELSAT 4-A. Each of these vehicles has operated at synchronous altitude, forming an increasingly effective communications network that included more than ninety of the world's nations operating a total of ninety-two ground stations in 1975.

The third type of communications satellite is capable of accepting, storing, and rebroadcasting programs on demand. The first such direct broadcast satellite, ATS-6, was launched by the National Aeronautics and Space Administration (NASA) in 1975. Unlike most communications satellites, which require large, powerful, and complex ground stations so that the equipment in space can be as simple as possible, the ATS-6 program involved the use of powerful transmitters and antennae in space. Inexpensive ground equipment could thus be employed to provide communications services for isolated areas. The unique capabilities of the satellite were demonstrated in experimental programs ranging from medical relays, linking Alaskan clinics to specialists in the United States, to a series of television broadcasts that brought special programming to Appalachian schools and introduced millions of residents of small Indian villages to new farming methods and birth control techniques.

A new generation of domestic communication satellites has made its appearance since the launch of *Westar* in 1974. Designed to provide improved communications service for restricted national or geographic areas, the continuation of domestic satellite systems, with the international INTELSAT network, has brought the advantages of space-based information exchange to the most remote areas of the globe.

The U.S.S.R. has operated its own system of satellite communication since 1965. Known as *Molniya*, the first generation of Soviet communications satellites traveled in eccentric orbits carefully chosen to link the far flung corners of the U.S.S.R. *Intersputnik*, a cooperative organization of eight Eastern Bloc nations, was established in 1971 but enjoyed little success in its attempts to rival INTELSAT.

The second major area in which the applications satellite has been put to effective use is in meteorology. Like the communications satellite, the meteorological satellite has undergone extensive growth. *Tiros I* (Television Infrared Observation Satellite), the world's first satellite to provide cloud cover photographs of the earth's surface, was launched in 1960. By 1966 ten of these vehicles had been orbited.

The experience gained with the TIROS series was embodied in the nine TOS (Tiros Operational Satellite) satellites launched between 1966 and 1979. TOS vehicles operated in pairs, each of which carried different imaging systems. The second group of operational meteorological satellites, ITOS (Improved Tiros Operational Satellite) was placed in service in 1970 and continued in use through 1978. Much more sophisticated than their predecessors, the ITOS vehicles not only provided improved imagery, but gathered a variety of other data useful to meteorologists. The TIROS N satellites, the first of which was launched on October 13, 1978, are designed not only to return higher resolution images but also to collect data from automated ground and ocean stations for rebroadcast to central collection points.

In addition to the operational weather satellites mentioned above, several experimental series, including NIMBUS and ATS (Applications Technology Satellites) have tested new imaging and data collection equipment.

The launch of GOES (Geostationary Operational Environmental Satellite) in 1975 opened a new phase in the study of the earth's weather from space. Unlike the earlier TIROS, TOS and ITOS vehicles, which were placed in polar orbits, GOES operates at synchronous altitudes. The GOES program is supplemented by similar synchronous satellites to be operated by the Japanese government and the European Space Agency. The resulting international network will enable scientists to view the pattern of weather over the entire earth simultaneously. Current plans call for a cooperative Global Atmosphere Research Program (GARP), a concerted international effort to understand the operation of the world's weather.

The National Oceanic and Atmospheric Administration (NOAA), an agency of the United States Department of Commerce, is responsible for operating the United States meteorological program and for utilizing the information provided by the satellites in the preparation of reliable weather forecasts.

As in the case of the communications satellite, the U.S.S.R. operates an independent system of meteorological spacecraft. The initial operational series, *Meteor*, was a success. Beginning in 1966 the United States and the U.S.S.R. began an exchange of meteorological data that demonstrated the potential for East/West cooperation in space.

Pertinent Literature

Clarke, Arthur C. *The Promise of Space*. New York: Harper & Row Publishers, 1968.

The Promise of Space is the best one-volume introduction to astronautics available. The author, Arthur C. Clarke, is himself something of a spaceflight pioneer. One of the small band of enthusiasts who made the British Interplanetary Society a center for trustworthy information and well informed speculation on astronautics during the 1930's, Clarke has retained his position as one of the most reliable and readable authorities in the field for more than three decades. Perhaps the most widely read science fiction author of his generation, he is also a distinguished writer of science fact.

The present volume is the latest in a series of Clarke books designed to serve as a primer for the space age. The opening section of the book traces the history of mankind's interest in the heavens and the means by which the dream was realized. In addition, Clarke provides the clearest possible discussion of the physical principles underlying spaceflight. The general reader is introduced to the mysteries of velocity, orbital mechanics, and the operation of a rocket in a painless and thoroughly enjoyable manner.

As one might expect, the man who has earned the title "father of the communications satellite" is at his best when describing the birth and development of the unmanned spacecraft. The general principles that underlie all satellite operations are emphasized. Clarke makes use of well-chosen analogies and clear, concise explanations that lead the reader step-by-step through the intricacies of space flight while avoiding the dangers of oversimplification that have marred less successful accounts of the subject. In short, Clarke's discussion of the physics of orbital flight is the classic against which all others should be measured.

Having laid a basic foundation, the author provides an excellent discussion of the way in which the applications satellite has assisted in the solution of earth-bound problems. While his treatment of the individual satellite series is now a bit dated, it serves as a good introduction to the first decade of achievement in the field.

Since Clarke's account is intended as a general treatment of the entire field of astronautics, lunar and planetary probes and manned spaceflight are considered in detail. Clarke charts the milestones of both United States and U.S.S.R. programs and offers his thoughts on the future.

As one of the most successful prophets of the space age, the author's speculations deserve special attention. He outlines the possibilities for advanced lunar bases and manned expeditions to the planets. The author's vision of mankind's future in space is enormously exciting, but remains firmly based in reality. Like his "extraterrestrial relay" communications satellite proposal of 1945, Clarke's suggestions for the utilization of space can be realized; the limits are solely political, social, and economic, not technological.

Paul, Günter. *The Satellite Spin-Off: The Achievements of Space Flight.* Washington, D.C.: Robert B. Luce, 1975.

In view of the almost unlimited potential of the applications satellite in a wide variety of fields affecting the lives of all citizens, the number of books on the market dealing with the subject in nontechnical terms is surprisingly small. There is, for example, no general survey of earth satellites for the lay reader. Most of the books dealing with unmanned applications spacecraft that have appeared over the past decade have become so quickly outdated as to be of little value to those seeking to remain current in a rapidly advancing field.

Günter Paul's *The Satellite Spin-Off* is an exception. Paul, a physicist with the Institute for Extraterrestrial Research of the University of Bonn and a member of the German Society for Air and Space Flight, is a knowledgeable author with a gift for presenting difficult material in understandable terms. He has wisely chosen to approach his subject from the viewpoint of the information user rather than that of the engineer or technician. The volume touches but lightly on the difficult questions of satellite technology, concentrating instead on the way in which the unique capabilities of unmanned spacecraft have contributed to the solution of human problems.

Paul presents a comprehensive survey of the major areas in which applications satellites have been employed. The strongest sections of the volume, however, are those dealing with communications and meteorological satellites.

Several fine chapters trace the evolution of INTELSAT and COMSAT, detailing the manner in which these organizations have spearheaded a revolution in the communications industry. The growth of interest in both regional and direct broadcast satellites is also detailed. The author compares the Soviet satellite communications system unfavorably to the smoothly functioning INTELSAT network.

Paul also includes a solid account of satellite meteorology. A description of the operation of our earth's weather system prefaces a discussion of the new possibilities for improved forecasting offered by the earth satellite. He shows how observations of changing weather patterns from orbit enable meteorologists to spot evolving weather patterns at the earliest possible moment and thus follow the growth and development of potential problems. Paul cites specific cases, such as that of Hurricane Camille, in which satellite observations have saved thousands of lives.

The author also covers other practical applications of the earth satellite. He explains how the Earth Resources Technology Satellites have demonstrated their value in areas ranging from agriculture, forestry, city planning, and pollution control. Similarly, he shows how the military reconnaissance satellites have become a major element in the strategic planning of both the United States and the U.S.S.R. In sum, Paul provides a clear analysis of the way in which the unique orbital vantage point of the unmanned satellite has been turned to mankind's benefit.
— *T.D.C.*

Additional Recommended Reading

Ley, Willy. *Rockets, Missiles and Men in Space*. New York: The Viking Press, 1968.
   Informative study on rocketry and the launching of various types of satellites.
Braun, Wernher von and Frederick I. Ordway. *A History of Rocketry and Space*

Exploration. New York: Thomas Y. Crowell Company, 1975. A valuable work on rocketry by a pioneer in the field.

Clarke, Arthur C. *Voices from the Sky: Previews of the Coming Space Age*. New York: Harper & Row Publishers, 1965. A brilliant British science fiction novelist provides a perceptive study of space exploration.

Widger, William N. *Meteorological Satellites*. New York: Holt, Rinehart and Winston, 1966. Provides the reader with much background information on the launching of meteorological satellites.

Mueller, George E. and Eugene R. Spangler. *Communication Satellites*. New York: John Wiley and Sons, 1964. An comprehensive look at the expanding use of communications satellites.

THE EISENHOWER DOCTRINE
ON THE MIDDLE EAST ENUNCIATED

Type of event: Diplomatic: announcement of United States policy in the Middle East,
and operation in Lebanon
Time: January 5-March 9, 1957; July-October, 1958
Locale: Washington, D.C., and Lebanon

Principal personages:

DWIGHT DAVID EISENHOWER (1890-1969), thirty-fourth President of the United States, 1953-1961

CAMILLE CHAMOUN (1900-   ), President of Lebanon, 1952-1958

GAMAL ABDEL NASSER (1918-1970), President of Egypt, 1956-1970

GENERAL FUAD SHEHAB (1902-1973), Commander of the Lebanese Army, later President of Lebanon

ROBERT MCCLINTOCK (1909-   ), United States Ambassador to Lebanon

ROBERT DANIEL MURPHY (1894-   ), United States Deputy Under Secretary of State

Summary of Event

In the aftermath of the Suez crisis of October, 1956, the United States government reconsidered its position and policies in the Middle East. Acting through the United Nations, and for once in agreement with the Soviet Union, the United States had brought about the withdrawal of British and French forces from Egypt. The entire episode seemed not only to have weakened Western unity, but also to have strengthened the position of the Soviet Union in the Arab countries, and that of Gamal Abdel Nasser, the Egyptian President, as the leading spokesman of Arab nationalist feeling.

The Eisenhower Administration saw a vacuum in the Middle East which it feared would be filled by Soviet influence. President Eisenhower, therefore, offered a statement of policy which became known as the Eisenhower Doctrine.

Issued as a message to Congress on January 5, 1957, after consultation with congressional leaders and with Dag Hammarskjöld, the Secretary-General of the United Nations, it proposed that the United States fill the vacuum with economic and military aid. Eisenhower asked the new Eighty-fifth Congress to appropriate $400,000,000 for two years for economic and military assistance to the nations of the Middle East, and to authorize the use of United States forces on the request of any nation in the region threatened by Communist aggression.

Besides the provision of assistance, one purpose of the presidential request to Congress was to give the Soviet Union warning of American in-

758

tentions to prevent any Soviet expansion in the Middle East, and to make clear and public the national support for those intentions.

In some respects, the Eisenhower Doctrine followed the precedents of the Truman Doctrine of 1947 and the Formosa Resolution passed by Congress in 1955. It differed, however, from the Truman Doctrine in its application to a particular area; the Truman Doctrine, though occasioned by problems of Greece and Turkey, was a promise of United States support for any people resisting aggression. Moreover, neither earlier proposal carried the proviso that armed forces be sent only on the request of the other nation.

The House resolution on behalf of the President's request, introduced the same day, was approved by the Foreign Affairs Committee by a vote of twenty-four to two on January 24, and by the entire House on January 31 by a vote of 355 to 61. Senate action was slower. In debates in early March, Senator Richard Russell, of Georgia, proposed an amendment which would have deleted the military and economic assistance, but the amendment lost. A proposal by Senator J. William Fulbright of Arkansas for a white paper from the State Department detailing United States relations with the region also failed. Finally the Senate passed the resolution, with some limiting changes, on March 5, by a vote of 72 to 19; the House accepted the Senate version on March 7, by 350 to 60; the President signed it on March 9, 1957.

The announcement of the Doctrine met mixed reactions. The votes in the Congress were probably indicative of general support; they are notable because of the fact that the Democratic party had majorities in both houses. The public trust in President Eisenhower, so recently reelected, was one factor; the general mood of the Cold War was another.

Reactions abroad were less favorable; the denunciations from Moscow and Peking were expected; Prime Minister Jawarharlal Nehru of India thought the dangers of aggression exaggerated and felt that the interests of peace were not forwarded by the American action. The reactions of the Arab lands, led by Egypt, were also unfavorable. A mission led by former Representative James P. Richards in the spring of 1957 did not even visit Egypt or Jordan and found only Lebanon ready to accept the Eisenhower Doctrine.

Lebanon's history and situation explain both that acceptance and the later application of the Doctrine to that country. Alone among the Arab countries, which were overwhelmingly Muslim, Lebanon had a large Christian population; in the absence of accurate statistics, estimates place it near a majority. The ties to Rome of the majority of these, Maronites and other Catholics of non-Latin rites; the American Protestant missionary and educational effort since the early nineteenth century; and the experience of French rule or mandate, all gave Lebanon a view of the West and a relation to it different from the other Arab nations.

Independent Lebanon had developed political and social traditions of its own to deal with religious differences. The most notable example was the tradition that the President be a

Christian, the Prime Minister a Muslim. Under the surface, however, religious and regional hostilities were often bitter.

These internal strains were increased and intensified by Arab feeling inflamed against Israel and by "Nasserism"—the extreme Arab movement toward unity and belligerence intimately associated with Egypt's leader.

The immediate occasion of trouble in Lebanon was the possibility that President Camille Chamoun intended to have his term extended contrary to the Lebanon constitution. Opposition forces organized against this move, some religious, some political opponents of Chamoun, some supported by Syrian and Egyptian interests. Civil strife on this issue broke out in May, 1958.

Just as this turmoil in Lebanon seemed to be subsiding, an unexpected crisis erupted in Iraq. On July 14, 1958, a bloody revolution overthrew the pro-Western Iraqi government. President Chamoun appealed to the United States out of fear that the *coup* in Iraq was the result of a Soviet-Nasserite plot that would soon be reenacted in Lebanon. Accordingly, on July 15, on the orders of President Eisenhower, units of the Sixth Fleet landed United States Marines in Lebanon to preserve order.

With the aid of Robert McClintock, the United States Ambassador, the American troops were kept in positions where they did not affect the local political situation. Robert Murphy, United States Deputy Under Secretary of State and an experienced diplomat, worked with the differing Lebanese forces to achieve settlement.

Whatever ambition he had entertained, Chamoun now gave up any intention of another term. With some difficulty, the negotiators persuaded General Fuad Shehab to accept the Lebanese presidency, to which he was elected by parliament on July 31. As Commander of the Army, Shehab had tried to maintain an impartial position, and he was one of the few people acceptable to almost all factions.

The exercise of the Eisenhower Doctrine thus resulted in accommodation. The Marines were finally withdrawn on October 25, 1958.

Pertinent Literature

Qubain, Fahim I. *Crisis in Lebanon*. Washington, D.C.: The Middle East Institute, 1961.

Qubain's is a detailed account of the troubles of Lebanon which peaked in the crisis of 1958. The background of the history, geography, and the religious and regional divisions of the country is sketched. Westerners (except Middle East experts) will find this introduction useful, because so little of it is part of the information of even generally informed persons.

Even less familiar and less understandable is the detailing of personal, factional, and traditional feuds and antipathies. Realistically, these aspects are often determinants in the quarrels and confrontations of a country such as Lebanon. To outsiders looking for deep motivations, these disputes are likely to seem petty.

Qubain, however, takes into account not only such antagonisms, making the point that many Lebanese are still governed by old clan traditions; he also takes notice of tensions between peasants in a traditional society and the modernizing entrepreneurs of Beirut. His account of the crisis in Lebanon, therefore, is heavy with detail. Still, he sees large forces at work: Communist infiltration; the charges of corruption and nepotism against the Chamoun government, with additional weight from religious feeling; the pressures from across the border, including, or perhaps especially, Cairo Radio, with its tremendous influence on the Arab populace.

Qubain does not really argue the virtues or vices of the Eisenhower Doctrine as doctrine. He does see the American intervention as salutary. He considers the Marine landing and presence in Lebanon unique in that it disturbed the local life as little as possible; it was truly impartial and nonpartisan.

Probably the chief difference between the Eisenhower Doctrine as applied and other measures and doctrines of intervention is only implied in Qubain's account, but it is of primary importance: the Marines *were* withdrawn. This was not an effort to take power permanently in the area or even to bolster a "friendly" government, but to prevent domestic disruption from opening the country to forces hostile to the United States.

As Qubain is detailed about the personalities involved in bringing on the crisis, so is he also specific about the negotiations which brought it to an end. He pays tribute to the patience and skill of Ambassador McClintock. General Shehab, according to the author, wanted above all to keep the army out of politics, and was himself reluctant to take the presidency. Qubain sees him, however, as finally convinced that no one else would be acceptable to the major parties and groups at odds—a situation Qubain himself believes to have been genuine.

A considerable portion of the book is devoted to important and interesting documentation, little of it from the United States, such as the statements of Lebanon's case before the United Nations and excerpts from the Egyptian press attacks on the Lebanese government.

Graber, Doris A. "The Truman and Eisenhower Doctrines in the Light of the Doctrine of Non-Intervention," in *Political Science Quarterly*. LXXIII (September, 1958), pp. 321-334.

Graber's concern is with the doctrines, rather than their application. Both the Eisenhower and Truman Doctrines are statements of a policy of intervention, though Eisenhower's is a more limited policy. It is restricted in geographical area, confined to *armed* aggression, and requires the request of the country on whose behalf the United States intervenes.

Graber's question is how these

doctrines can be consistent with the doctrine of nonintervention. Rather quickly, she disposes of one form of the question: nonintervention is not a principle of traditional international law; rather, the question is raised by an *American* doctrine or tradition. In the thinking of most Americans, this has been a basic principle of their country in foreign affairs from the earliest days of the republic, and is sanctified by the names of Washington, Jefferson, and Monroe.

Graber subjects that view to historical analysis. The doctrine was promulgated in the first years of the United States, the late eighteenth and early nineteenth centuries. Intervention was then commonly accepted in European thought and practice. The United States was a new nation, relatively weak among the powers, and nonintervention, was then a matter of national advantage rather than law and morality. This was especially the case when the American promise not to intervene in Europe could be linked to a demand that European powers not intervene in the Americas.

The United States, of course, did not adhere to the doctrine uniformly and absolutely. Graber lists some of the instances, particularly the surge of imperialism at the turn of the nineteenth century. Viewed as a policy of national advantage, the doctrine need not be absolute; in fact, in that view, it *ought* not to be regarded as unbreakable.

But, says Graber, the American public would have had difficulty with such a pragmatic and flexible policy. For purposes of American thought the doctrine was put in moral and absolute terms. Graber implies that this may have been conscious on the part of policymakers. In fact, she suggests that one advantage of the doctrine of nonintervention for the policymakers and for United States foreign policy in the nineteenth century was that it could be used to dampen the fervor of ethnic groups desiring the support of the United States for their homeland or national group.

The rise of the totalitarian regimes in Europe and Asia made nonintervention in the absolute sense a less and less usable doctrine. The Truman Doctrine, in Graber's view, was the response to the new circumstance. The United States, however, did not have the power to intervene against Communist aggression of any kind anywhere and everywhere, which was what Truman's statement promised, or seemed to promise. Therefore, as Graber sees it, the more selective Eisenhower approach limited itself in area, type of aggression, and the consent of the other country.

Even this doctrine, in view of intervention and nonintervention as methods of national policy, may still go too far. Graber raises two questions, not of doctrine but of practice and United States national interest. Under the Eisenhower Doctrine, must the response be automatic upon the request of another government? Can the intervention be limited to instances of serious harm, or threat of harm, to the United States? Such questions cloud the future application of the doctrine. — *G.J.F.*

Additional Recommended Reading

Eisenhower, Dwight D. *The White House Years: Waging Peace, 1956-1961*. Garden City, N.Y.: Doubleday & Company, 1965. Contains Eisenhower's own account of the Eisenhower Doctrine.

Atyeo, Henry C. "The United States in the Middle East," in *Current History*. XXXII (March, 1957), pp. 160-164. A contemporary account of the Doctrine and congressional action.

Hitti, Philip K. *Lebanon in History, from the Earliest Times to the Present*. London: Macmillan and Company, 1962. Traces the history of Lebanon from earliest times.

Howard, Harry N. "The Regional Pacts and the Eisenhower Doctrine," in *Annals of the American Academy of Political and Social Science*. CCCCI (May, 1972), pp. 85-95. Sees the Doctrine as an outline of a policy, rather than a policy itself.

Rondot, Pierre. *The Changing Patterns of the Middle East*. New York: Frederick A. Praeger, 1961. Places the American action in a Middle Eastern context.

THE INTERNATIONAL GEOPHYSICAL YEAR

Type of event: Scientific: international cooperation to study the planet earth
Time: July 1, 1957-December 31, 1958
Locale: Worldwide

Principal personages:
SYDNEY CHAPMAN (1888-1970), President of the international committee which planned the International Geophysical Year
LLOYD VIEL BERKNER (1905-1967), officer of the IGY's Bureau of Directors
JAMES ALFRED VAN ALLEN (1914-   ), discoverer of the radiation belts girding the earth which bear his name

Summary of Event

The International Polar Years of 1882-1883 and 1932-1933 set precedents for international cooperation in scientific activities. In 1950 a former participant of the second polar year, American geophysicist Lloyd Berkner, proposed a third polar year. The International Council of Scientific Unions agreed to sponsor it. Since the scope of the proposal gradually expanded from polar to global research, the International Council in 1953 established a special committee for an international geophysical year (Comité Special de l'Année Geophysique Internationale). This committee, known as the CSAGI, represented a variety of scientific disciplines and international unions. Its purpose was to plan and coordinate the International Geophysical Year (IGY), which was scheduled for 1957-1958, to coincide with the twenty-fifth anniversary of the second International Polar Year and with an eighteen-month period of high solar activity. In the forefront of the activities of the CSAGI was Sydney Chapman, the noted British geophysicist who was its president.

By definition, the IGY focused on geophysical problems. Its thirteen scientific programs included studies of the earth, air, and space, and emphasized the earth in the relations of its parts and in relation to space. Subjects of major interest dealt with phenomena that would show significant change during an eighteen-month period, such as atmospheric and oceanic currents and solar activity. The CSAGI planned that most of the scientific stations would be established in the polar regions, the equatorial zone, and along three lines joining pole to pole. In addition, the committee scheduled world "days," alerts, and intervals for simultaneous observations of phenomena by observers stationed throughout the world.

Data exchange proved to be a critical factor in the IGY plan. The exchange system had two goals: the free circulation of all data obtained, and the protection of data from loss or destruction. To accomplish these goals, the CSAGI created three World Data Centers to house complete sets of IGY data; one was in Washington, one in Moscow, and one divided among several participating nations. The CSAGI also established a journal, the *Annals of the IGY*, in which to publish results of scientific observations.

Without implying diplomatic recognition of any government, the CSAGI invited scientists of all nations to participate in the IGY. Political considerations of the two Chinas, however, posed an unsolvable problem. In 1955 the Communist, or Mainland, Chinese began to attend IGY conferences and to plan their country's projects; but they agreed to participate only if the Nationalist Chinese of Taiwan did not. When the latter belatedly joined the IGY in 1957, the Mainland Chinese formally withdrew from the international effort.

More than sixty nations and more than five thousand scientists participated in the IGY. The CSAGI provided international coordination and uniform instructions for otherwise independent national activities. Scientists in each participating country selected, planned, and implemented their respective national projects. The scientists considered the cooperative and worldwide collection of data necessary for the progress of the geophysical sciences, and they welcomed the opportunity to use research techniques involving recently developed instruments such as cosmic ray recorders and electronic computers. Governments supported the international venture by funding national IGY programs and by providing logistic support for the projects.

The most sensational IGY activity was the use of artificial earth satellites to gather scientific information about the earth. The satellite program dramatically demonstrated the emergence of the Soviet Union as a scientific and technological leader, and it initiated space exploration just as other IGY projects were completing geographical exploration of the earth. Both the United States and the Soviet Union had announced plans to launch satellites as one part of their respective IGY programs, yet *Sputnik I* in October of 1957 surprised the world. By the end of 1958, Soviet achievements included not only the first successful launch, but also better launching vehicles and larger satellites. The Americans launched more satellites, placed superior instruments in them, and used more efficient methods of tracking and recovering them.

The only major dispute regarding data exchange arose from the satellite program. The Soviets used military rockets for their launchings and thus refused to exchange information about the rockets. The United States, in contrast, employed mostly nonmilitary technology and freely released its information. Although the two countries never agreed on what specific data were to be exchanged, Americans severely criticized the Soviet refusal to release rocket information. Both nations exchanged all scientific data gathered by the satellites.

Interdisciplinary teams were located in Antarctica, which was previously almost inaccessible for scientific observation. Seven nations agreed to lay aside territorial claims and to accept "internationalization" for the scientific purposes of the IGY. Eleven nations established a total of forty-eight stations in Antarctica. The results were impressive. Particularly significant were the confirmation that Antarctica is a continent rather than a series of ice-covered islands, and the discovery in the atmosphere of a jet stream encircling the continent.

Masses of scientific information and valuable discoveries resulted from the IGY activities. For example, it was confirmed that the earth is slightly pear-shaped because of the irregular distribution of its mass; that there are currents deep in the oceans and in the ocean trenches; that the ice content of the earth is 4.5 million cubic miles, forty percent more than previously estimated; that auroras result from solar activity that disturbs a magnetic line in the upper atmosphere; and that ultraviolet light, gamma radiation, and X-rays come from the sun and solar activity. It was further confirmed that Allen radiation belts (named for their discoverer, James Alfred Van Allen) are in space at the outer edge of the earth's magnetic field; that nuclear explosions in the atmosphere can create artificial radiation belts; and that the upper atmosphere is an active place with no definite border between it and space.

The IGY did not end abruptly in December of 1958; activities continued on a reduced scale throughout 1959, which was designated the year of International space, oceans, and Antarctica. The IGY's influence extended beyond its scientific programs and discoveries. The "year" marked the emergence of the Soviet Union as a scientific leader, the peaceful disposition of Antarctica as a continent reserved for scientific activity, the initiation of space exploration, and the unprecedented rise in government appropriations for science. Perhaps most important, the IGY stimulated a dramatic increase in the role of science in international affairs.

Pertinent Literature

Sullivan, Walter. *Assault on the Unknown: The International Geophysical Year.* New York: McGraw-Hill Book Company, 1961.

Walter Sullivan was the reporter assigned to full-time coverage of the IGY by the *New York Times*. He reported on the IGY from its inception to its close, and for his work he received the George Polk Memorial Award in journalism. In writing this book, Sullivan draws upon his dispatches to the newspaper, providing a chronological report of the newsworthy events, scientific and diplomatic, of the IGY. His perspective is that of an American observer on a scientific adventure.

Sullivan claims that the most significant aspect of the IGY was its rocket and satellite program. His brief opening chapter deals with this program, as do several later chapters that detail the Soviet and American projects, particularly the well-publicized American program with its delays, difficulties, and final successes. Despite previous announcements of

Soviet and American plans to launch satellites and despite American uneasiness about the Soviet achievement of placing the first satellite in space, the satellites awed the public; they captured imaginations. According to Sullivan, "in 1957 man opened the door to the solar system, and perhaps beyond." Without a doubt, satellites became the foremost news story of the IGY.

The book repeatedly draws attention to situations in which political and military considerations influenced the IGY, most notably the crisis of the two Chinas and the Soviet secrecy about rocket technology. No event, however, spoiled the international spirit of cooperation. The last-minute entrance of the Nationalist Chinese effectively excluded the Mainland representatives from formal participation, but Mainland scientists completed many projects originally planned for the IGY. The Soviets withheld information on rocket technology, but they released all scientific data gathered during the spaceflights. Territorial claims in Antarctica, seismographic studies to detect underground bomb blasts, and the Soviet proposal to extend the IGY (to help maintain their position at home) also involved political or military considerations.

One case of American secrecy was the Argus project to explode atomic bombs in the atmosphere. The object was to observe global effects of the resulting radiation, which was successfully done. Argus was not an IGY project, but an American satellite that detected its effects was part of an IGY project. All data obtained by the satellite thus were to be made public. When Sullivan uncovered information about the project, the United States government asked him to withhold publishing it because public disclosure might upset the Geneva talks then under way; the talks were on suspension of nuclear weapons tests. The United States was also reluctant because the data had military implications. After holding the story for months, Sullivan published his information; and his book contains an excellent account of the sensitive situation.

Reports of Sullivan's travels contain glimpses into the daily operations of IGY stations. Particularly interesting are the accounts of the South Pole stations in Antarctica and the Arctic ice-floe stations near the North Pole. Occasional anecdotes add a personal element to the scientific projects.

Descriptions of the major IGY programs, on the other hand, tend to read like lists of technical information. This dryness is appparent partly because the book presents the scientific discoveries and results of the IGY rather than the scientific questions that prompted the particular studies, and partly because the thirteen scientific programs are, of necessity, discussed one by one. Individual programs and projects are part of the whole, but the whole is something more than all the parts. At numerous stations throughout the world, for example, scientists observed solar and atmospheric phenomena—electric winds, sun flares, auroras, eclipses, clouds of solar gas, cosmic rays, ionized gases—in attempts to unravel the mysteries of the earth as a planet in an ocean of air and in space. In contrast to the achievements of the individual projects and participants, the achievement of the IGY was that phenomena were recorded on a global scale. As the book repeatedly states, scientists from many nations cooperated to make observations, and they did so during the Cold War.

Wilson, John Tuzo. *I.G.Y., the Year of the New Moons*. New York: Alfred A. Knopf, 1961.

The author of this highly readable account was President of the International Union of Geodesy and Geophysics, a member union of the International Council of Scientific Unions, during the IGY. A Canadian geophysicist, Wilson traveled to many IGY projects and meetings. This book contains the story of his travels and of the scientific activities, explains the scientific basis for each major subject of IGY observation, and discusses IGY contributions to these studies with emphasis on new questions raised rather than on discoveries made. The book is about "the excitement of the scientists."

Written for nonscientists, the book contains excellent discussions of the organization and scientific content of the IGY. A chapter on the 1957 meeting of the International Union of Geodesy and Geophysics, for example, discusses the nature of international unions and their relations to the International Council of Scientific Unions and to the IGY. Each union is a supportive agency which promotes (rather than engaging in) scientific activities by maintaining services for data collection and publication, by sponsoring worldwide ventures, and by hosting meetings as forums for international exchange. Union members represent national scientific societies and academies. There are international unions for a variety of scientific disciplines and specialties. Each union belongs to the parent International Council of Scientific Unions, which in turn includes representatives from the unions on its committees. The International Council and its CSAGI coordinated the interdisciplinary and international program of the IGY. Other chapters of Wilson's book focus on scientific organization at the national and project levels.

In addition to major projects discussed in the book, the IGY program included subjects of lesser interest, such as the earth's gravity. Since gravity does not vary with time, IGY participants could not measure its change. In this and other cases, the IGY gave scientists the opportunity to visit out-of-the-way places and take extensive measurements. Similarly, participants improved longitude and latitude measurements by using observations made at stations throughout the world and even made aboard satellites in space. For all IGY subjects, more observation stations and instruments were placed in service.

The book compares the geophysical programs of both Chinas, praising the Mainland program. Even though the Mainland scientists did not participate formally in the IGY, they welcomed a visit by Wilson and showed off their various geophysical projects. Regarding rocket technology, the book pointedly states that the two countries involved failed to reach an agreement on the release of data. In any event, according to scientist Wilson, "the remarkable thing is not that there is an exchange, but that anyone in view of the difficulties involved recovers any data worth exchanging."

Wilson does not allow satellites and space exploration to overshadow the focus of the IGY on earth: the satellites were merely tools used to gather data. Nevertheless, acknowledging the romantic aspect of the satellite program and the public awareness of satellites, the book is subtitled "the year of the new moons."

Concluding that the IGY increased international cooperation in science, the book argues that the IGY is an example of how to conduct international relations not only in science but also in other fields. Similar claims appear in most literature on the IGY. As a scientist, Wilson observed a change in the nature of geophysics during the IGY. Because of the IGY, the earth sciences received increased financial support, aroused greater public interest, and built many more scientific stations. Isolated workers became linked into cooperative networks. The IGY helped to diversify earth science and to transform it into planetary science. To understand the physics of the earth, geophysics, one needs to study the earth in its place in the universe. The IGY made this obvious. — *A.M.*

Additional Recommended Reading

Chapman, Sydney. *I.G.Y.: Year of Discovery*. Ann Arbor: University of Michigan Press, 1959. A short account by British geophysicist Chapman, chairman of the executive bureau of the CSAGI.

Ross, Frank, Jr. *Partners in Space: A Study of the International Geophysical Year*. New York: Lothrop, Leet and Shepard Company, 1961. An excellently illustrated popular account of the IGY.

Eklund, Carl D. and Joan Beckman. *Antarctica, Polar Research, and Discovery During the International Geophysical Year*. New York: Holt, Rinehart and Winston, 1963. An excellent and well-illustrated account by the scientific leader of an American station in Antarctica during the IGY.

Czechoslovak Academy of Sciences, Mathematico-physical Section. *International Geophysical Year and Cooperation in Czechoslovakia 1957-1959*. Praha, Czech.: Nakladatelství Československé akademie věd, 1960. A summary of the results of Czechoslovakia's investigations during its participation in the IGY program.

Fraser, Sir Ronald. *Once Round the Sun*. New York: The Macmillan Company, 1957. Published during the IGY, this book discusses the IGY program in the context of existing boundaries of geophysical knowledge.

Marshack, Alexander. *The World in Space*. New York: Thomas Nelson and Sons, 1958. A well-illustrated elementary text of geophysics which treats the IGY as a huge scientific expedition.

Hyde, Margaret O. *Exploring Earth and Space*. New York: Whittlesey House, McGraw-Hill Book Company, 1957. A book for young readers which has gone through several editions.

THE LITTLE ROCK SCHOOL DESEGREGATION CRISIS

Type of event: Sociological: attempted public school desegregation following Supreme
   Court decision
Time: September, 1957
Locale: Little Rock, Arkansas

Principal personages:
   ORVAL E. FAUBUS (1910-   ), Governor of Arkansas
   DWIGHT DAVID EISENHOWER (1890-1969), thirty-fourth Pres-
      ident of the United States, 1953-1961
   ELIZABETH ECKFORD, one of the first black students to be
      turned away from Little Rock Central High School in Sep-
      tember, 1957
   VIRGIL T. BLOSSOM, Superintendent of Schools of Little
      Rock
   DAISY BATES (1920-   ), President of the Arkansas Na-
      tional Association for the Advancement of Colored People
      (NAACP)
   BROOKS HAYS, United States Congressman from Arkansas
      who attempted to mediate between President Eisenhower
      and Governor Faubus

Summary of Event

The United States Supreme Court, in the case of *Oliver Brown et al.* v. *Board of Education of Topeka et al.*, 1954, declared racial segregation in tax-supported schools to be unconstitutional. It further ordered that the process of desegregation proceed with "all deliberate speed," under the supervision of the federal courts. In response, the school board of Little Rock prepared, and in May, 1955, adopted, a plan of desegregation. Little Rock had the reputation of being a progressive city in which racial relations were untroubled; the board's proposal was moderate, even minimal. Dr. Virgil Bloom, Superintendent of Little Rock schools, supported the board's plan. Integration was to be gradual, beginning in 1957 at the senior high school level. The

expectation was that one high school would remain all or nearly all white, and one all or nearly all black, while a few blacks would attend Central High School.

Public opposition to and support of the plan grew in intensity; legal moves to prevent its operation were defeated in the United States District Court in the summer of 1957. Preparations were made for the enrollment of a small number of black students (ultimately nine). On September 2, the day before the opening of school, Governor Orval E. Faubus, declaring that he had knowledge of "imminent danger of riot, tumult and breach of the peace," ordered units of the Arkansas National Guard to Little Rock. On September 3, when Elizabeth Eckford attempted to enter

Central High School, the Guard blocked her while a crowd verbally attacked her.

A school board request for delay was refused by the federal judge, who said he was asking the Department of Justice to investigate the obstruction by state authorities. Exchanges between Governor Faubus and President Dwight D. Eisenhower argued the respective legal positions, while the Guard remained at Central High School. On September 14, the Governor met with the President at Newport, Rhode Island, where Eisenhower was vacationing. Each issued a statement of understanding and support for the law, and, under court order, Faubus removed the National Guard on September 20. On Monday, September 23, the black students managed to enter the school. The crowd outside was restrained by city police, but grew in numbers; there were also increasing numbers of threats, with several beatings and incidents of violence. School authorities and police agreed on the withdrawal of the students at noon.

On September 24, President Eisenhower ordered units of the 101st Airborne Division to Little Rock after his proclamation ordering the mob to "cease and desist" was ignored. Under protection of the troopers, the black students returned to school on September 25.

The paratroopers remained, and the students continued to attend for the school year 1957-1958. Crowds still gathered in protest, and incidents of shoving, tripping, and name-calling occurred within the school. One of the black girls was suspended and then expelled for displays of anger.

Fearing the threats of armed whites riding by in cars, blacks barricaded and armed themselves, notably Mr. and Mrs. Lucius Christopher Bates. Mr. Bates was a newspaper publisher; Mrs. Bates was President of the Arkansas National Association for the Advancement of Colored People (NAACP), leader of the struggle for desegregation, mentor to the black students, and a favorite target of the segregationists' abuse.

The troops withdrew at the end of the school year. One black student was graduated; the rest were promoted. Over the summer of 1958, new legal processes were attempted. The school board asked to have integration steps postponed for two and a half years. The district court approved, but first the Circuit of Appeals and then the Supreme Court reversed the decision.

In August, the Arkansas legislature passed a group of laws providing for the closing of schools threatened by integration and for local referenda on integration or segregation; for state funds to go to private schools in places where public schools were closed to prevent integration; for a requirement that teachers list organizations to which they belonged; and for various other measures designed to hamper the work and legal activity of the NAACP.

Governor Faubus signed the bills—most of them after the Supreme Court refused to permit postponement of desegregation—and in September ordered the closing of Little Rock senior high schools. For the school year 1958-1959, the high schools remained closed. Proposals to lease the public high school buildings to the

771

newly formed private school association were enjoined by the courts, but private high schools operated nonetheless, and in this and in other ways most Little Rock high school students obtained some schooling. Public elementary and junior high schools remained open and segregated.

During 1958, Governor Faubus was elected to a third term as governor, and Congressman Brooks Hays, a self-styled "moderate" who had attempted to bring Governor Faubus and President Eisenhower to agreement in their 1957 negotiations, was defeated for reelection by Dale Alford, a segregationist. Increasing support for reopening of the schools, however, led to a recall election for the Little Rock school board, in which three segregationists were removed.

The reconstituted school board provided for the reopening of Little Rock high schools in August, 1959, after federal court decisions had declared the closing unconstitutional but had upheld a new Arkansas pupil placement law. Under that law, the school board assigned six black students to two of the high schools, leaving one all white and one all black.

Events in Little Rock, especially the confrontations of September, 1957, attracted national and international attention. Reporters, photographers, and television cameras focused on the Arkansas city. Integrationists and segregationists in the United States, as well as friendly and unfriendly observers abroad, made the situation in Little Rock a test case, not only of educational policy, but of racial ideals and practice generally.

Pertinent Literature

Bates, Daisy. *The Long Shadow of Little Rock: A Memoir.* New York: David McKay Company, 1962.

As President of the Arkansas branch of the NAACP, Daisy (Mrs. Lucius Christopher) Bates was bound to be involved in the struggle to desegregate Little Rock schools; her husband's position as editor of a black newspaper further put the family in the center of the storm. Segregationist attacks usually treated her as the ringleader of their opponents. They may have been right; certainly she was both planner and spokeswoman.

Daisy Bates's memoir of the Little Rock crisis, therefore, can hardly be expected to be impartial or coldly factual. Years after the event, she is still convinced of the rightness of her cause and still belligerent toward its enemies. If there are disadvantages to such a personal account, there are enormous benefits as well—not only in the kind of information that only a participant and leader can convey, but in the sense of struggle and the intensity of feeling. The NAACP's court battles involved Mrs. Bates not as attorney or petitioner, but as an organizer and supporter who found the appropriate petitioners to make the court case. She also acted as spokeswoman before the school board and other bodies. Some of the suppressed impatience, frustration, and sheer anger these processes roused comes through in this account.

Though Mrs. Bates and her friends and supporters thought the original school board plan of desegregation inadequate, they planned to put it into effect. The author was a prime mover in selecting the black students to register at Central High School and in preparing them and their parents for their ordeal. Her insistence that they maintain their dignity and not respond to insult or provocation was almost totally fulfilled. Obviously, this type of behavior was good "public relations"; but it is also obvious that neither Mrs. Bates nor the students saw it as that alone.

It was at the Bates home that the children were instructed, from the Bates home that they went to Central High School, to the Bates home that they returned; it was their headquarters for support and mutual protection. But Mrs. Bates's genuine affection and admiration for the students is part of the story, too; a less personal, less involved account could not capture for readers the experiences of those black students. Mrs. Bates calmed their fears and heard out their anger. She was counselor and supporter for their parents as well, upon whom the strain was also severe.

If this part of the story has heartening notes despite the stress described, other parts are more unrelieved. The experiences of the students at school were ugly enough. For the parents of the black students, there was harassment and in some cases loss of jobs or the threat of loss. The Bates family newspaper suffered low subscriptions and falling advertising until it was forced to cease publication. Nor is physical violence absent from the account. Bomb threats, gunfire in the street, and smashed windows, led some of the parents, especially the Bateses, to post armed guards. The author's tone is not antiwhite, though the segregationists are the enemy. She has praise and sympathy for those whites who supported the cause, or at least took a stand against violence, but she notes that several of them did not stay in Little Rock, and one committed suicide.

There is not much theorizing in the author's memoir, either about the moral and legal bases of the struggle for school desegregation, or about tactics; she is too convinced of the justice of the cause to argue it. She simply fights with the methods at hand, which are militant but nonviolent. There is a feeling of bitterness in the narrative, but not of regret for the battle. The author leaves the question unanswered of whether the battle will ever be won.

Blossom, Virgil T. *It Has Happened Here*. New York: Harper & Brothers, 1959.

Virgil Blossom was superintendent of schools in Little Rock during the years of the desegregation crisis, and therefore bore responsibility for the administration of the official school board plan. It is easy to picture him as an educational administrator, wary of divisive issues and of "politics," caught in one of the most emotional and divisive of issues, and one inescapably political. This is how he pictures himself: as a man between two fires, as much bewildered as alarmed. He stresses his Southern background and sympathy, and his reputation in Little Rock—he was "Man of the Year" just before the crisis. One can read between the lines, that school desegregation was not his will or desire. Both officially and privately, however, he saw no alternative but to follow the Supreme Court's order to prepare a desegregation plan for Little Rock schools. Blossom's position, whatever else may be said of it, was not calculated to please either segregationists or integrationists, since it was too moderate to satisfy either camp.

According to the author, no one expected the vigorous legal contests before the opening of school. Blossom and the school board were enjoined from integrating by the county court on August 29, 1957, but successfully sought reversal from the United States District Court the next day, with school opening set for September 2. Neither the Board nor city officials, according to Blossom, expected violence, nor did they anticipate the depth of feeling of the segregationists. The factor they did not consider at all, the real stumbling-block in Blossom's account, was Governor Orval Faubus. What the author found particularly upsetting was the Governor's unpredictability and unavailability for comment. Faubus either could not be reached, or refused to answer questions about his plans, or answered evasively.

The title of the book is a play on the title of Sinclair Lewis's novel *It Can't Happen Here*, about Fascism in the United States in the 1930's. The title implies that the target of Blossom's anger is not so much ideology or racism, as demagoguery and the mob passions upon which it plays. Blossom sees Little Rock's experience as an example of that kind of demagogue/mob rule which could take over anywhere that citizens and officials do not insist on following reason and law. A second target is the indecisiveness of the Eisenhower Administration, which made possible the growth of demagoguery and mob violence.

Blossom's account of the Little Rock crisis, with its details of negotiations, meetings with irate mothers, emergency phone calls to and from the police, and so forth, is indispensable. Most important, however, is the picture it paints of the state of mind of the community and of the author himself. — *G.J.F.*

Additional Recommended Reading

Record, Wilson and Jane Cassels Record, eds. *Little Rock, U.S.A.* San Francisco: Chandler Publishing Company, 1960. A collection of documents, newspaper accounts and editorials, and other materials.

Sherrill, Robert. *Gothic Politics in the Deep South: Stars of the New Confederacy.* New York: Grossman Publishers, 1968. Contains a chapter on Faubus, much of it ironic; the book as a whole suggests the context of Southern demagoguery.

Wilhoit, Francis M. *The Politics of Massive Resistance.* New York: George Braziller,

1973. More of a "scientific" approach to the Southern reaction to school desegregation.

Campbell, Ernest Q. and Thomas F. Pettigrew. *Christians in Racial Crisis: A Study of Little Rock's Ministry*. Washington, D.C.: Public Affairs Press, 1959. Analyzes the roles and activities of the Protestant clergy.

Hays, Brooks. *A Southern Moderate Speaks*. Chapel Hill: University of North Carolina Press, 1959. An account by the Congressman from the Little Rock district who attempted to mediate between partisans.

Ashmore, Harry S. *Arkansas: A Bicentennial History*. New York: W. W. Norton and Company, with the Association for State and Local History, Nashville, Tennessee, 1978. A history of Arkansas with an account of the "Faubus" era.

THE SOVIET UNION LAUNCHES *SPUTNIK*

Type of event: Technological: first launching of an artificial satellite into orbit
Time: October 4, 1957
Locale: The Soviet Union

Principal personages:
DWIGHT DAVID EISENHOWER (1890-1969), thirty-fourth President of the United States, 1953-1961
NIKITA SERGEEVICH KHRUSHCHEV (1894-1971), First Secretary of the Communist Party of the Soviet Union, 1953-1964; and Chairman of the Council of Ministers of the Soviet Union, 1958-1964
KONSTANTIN EDUARDOVITCH ZIOLKOVSKY (1857-1935), Russian aeronautic theoretician
WERNHER VON BRAUN (1912-1976), Director of the German, and then the American rocketry programs
SERGEI PAVLOVICH KOROLOV, Director of the Soviet rocketry program

Summary of Event

On October 4, 1957, the Soviet Union ushered in the Space Age by placing a 184-pound artificial satellite into orbit around the earth. *Sputnik I* (the Russian word means both "companion" and "moon") soon became not only a symbol of the technological achievement of the human race, but also a part of the rivalry between the world's two superpowers known as the Cold War. It raised important issues of prestige and military security for the United States and contributed to international competition in space flight and arms production.

The year 1957 was the second of President Dwight D. Eisenhower's second term. Despite the interracial violence in Little Rock, Arkansas, the United States was generally a complacent nation. The postwar decade had been one of unparalleled American prosperity, prestige, and self-confidence. In the Soviet Union, Nikita Sergeevich Khrushchev had just decisively won the muted power struggle that had begun at the death of Joseph Stalin four years before. One of Khrushchev's schemes was to reduce the military budget by relying more on nuclear deterrents than on conventional forces. He was consequently a firm patron of the U.S.S.R.'s missile program.

The year was also the last twelve months of an eighteen-month international research period known as the International Geophysical Year. As part of the program, scientists in both the United States and the U.S.S.R. had pledged to launch artificial satellites to orbit the earth and gather scientific data about the upper atmosphere. The American plan was announced on July 29, 1955; the Soviets followed suit three days later.

The Soviets, however, were no

latecomers to the field of space exploration. One of the most important theorists of rocketry, astronautics, and interplanetary travel was Konstantin Eduardovitch Ziolkovsky, a Russian schoolteacher. Ziolkovsky's pioneer work in liquid fuel rocketry, largely neglected before the Revolution of 1917, received significant attention from the new Soviet regime. Ziolkovsky himself was elected to the Soviet Academy of Sciences in 1919.

Despite these early theoretical beginnings and subsequent practical experiments both in the U.S.S.R. and the United States, it was Germany which took the lead in ballistic rocket development in the years before World War II. In 1936, the Nazi Government built a rocket-development center at Peenemunde on the Baltic coast. It was there that a German research team headed by Wernher von Braun, under pressure from Hitler to find a "wonder weapon" that would compensate for the Allies' advantages in resources and manpower, developed first the V-1 "buzz-bomb," and finally the V-2. The latter weapon was a major advance on all previous ballistic rockets, and was to provide the base from which both American and Russian efforts would develop in the postwar years.

It was not the Russians, however, but the Americans, who reaped the major benefit from the German research and experience. At the end of the war, the German Rocket team surrendered *en masse* to the Americans. The scientists were given a five-year contract and sent, with their documents and a number of V-2's, to the United States.

The Soviets' share of the scientific booty was significantly smaller. The Peenemunde center was largely destroyed by the Germans before it fell into Soviet hands. The Soviets did capture two of Germany's three V-2 production plants, but only a few of the all-important scientific personnel ended the war in Russian hands.

What the Soviets got, however, they put to work immediately, while the Americans wasted their advantage in dalliance, corporate competition, and interservice bickering. Only in the early 1950's were scientists put to work on the Army's Redstone rocket. The first small ballistic missile was launched in 1953. Work on larger missiles, the intermediate range (IRBM) Thor and Jupiter, was divided between the Douglas and Chrysler corporations. The Thor was an Air Force Project, while the Jupiter belonged to the Army. The yet larger Intercontinental Ballistic Missiles (ICBM) were given highest priority in 1954, but neither the Titan nor the Atlas had been successfully launched by 1957. Meanwhile, the earth satellite program, Project Vanguard, was separated from the military missile program, and eventually ended up under Navy jurisdiction; it suffered from relative neglect. The Army team, under Braun, also hoped to orbit a satellite, but as late as 1956 the Defense Department refused to give them the go-ahead.

The Russian program started from a more advanced and organized scientific base and moved faster. The efforts of Ziolkovsky's followers were organized by the Soviet government as early as 1933, and for several years their efforts were competitive with those of the Germans. Following the war, this already established group of scientists, under the leadership of Sergei Pavlovich Korolov, began to work on the V-2's they had captured. They adapted and improved the V-2's and used them for the basis of their own experiments. Within several years they had improved the V-2 design significantly; and by 1949 they had even fired a two-stage rocket to a height of 390 kilometers.

This information, together with other detailed data on the Soviet missile program in the 1950's, has become available only comparatively recently. To contemporaries, the Soviet program was shrouded in secrecy. Western observers, however, seem to have ignored even the information the Soviets were permitting to appear. On November 27, 1953, A. N. Nesmeyanov, President of the Soviet Academy of Sciences, stated that artificial earth satellites were now feasible. In April, 1955, the formation of a team of scientists to develop such a satellite was announced; in August, 1955, the Soviets indicated the approximate orbit and launch date; and on August 27, 1957, they announced the launching of their first ICBM. On October 1, 1957, the bandwidths for the satellite's transmissions were announced. Throughout all this time, especially during the summer of 1957, Soviet press articles about rocketry and satellites were growing more frequent and explicit.

Nonetheless, the actual launching of the satellite, on October 4, stunned and alarmed the United States. The consternation was compounded twenty-nine days later when *Sputnik II*, carrying a laboratory dog, was suc-cessfully orbited by the Soviets. Two conclusions leaped at once to American minds. American science and technology, whose preeminence had been undoubted throughout the postwar era, had been surpassed by a nation considered to be second-rate. The blow to national pride and self-confidence was staggering. Some feared that Third World nations would now find Soviet-style Communism, which had brought Russia from peasant backwardness to technological triumph in forty years, an attractive alternative to capitalism. Moreover, the military implications triggered genuine fear. A missile powerful and accurate enough to place a 184-pound satellite in orbit was capable of reaching any target in the United States. The Soviet Union had developed thermonuclear capability in 1953. To many, the specter of the ultimate weapon had come to life in the hands of the enemy.

In retrospect, we know that the Soviet lead in ICBM's was less impressive than it looked. Soviet ICBM strength was actually only 3.5 percent of American estimates. For the next few years, Khrushchev was forced to play a game of bluff, a game that some analysts think led to the Cuban Missile Crisis of 1962. At the time, however, the so-called "missile gap" played a large role in American technological development and became an important issue in the 1960 presidential election. While it would be inaccurate to consider this the beginning of the Soviet-American arms race, it is certain that from this date the stockpiling of nuclear weapons and the development and construction of missiles took on a greater urgency and began to consume larger amounts of both countries' budgets.

Another result of the Soviet launching of *Sputnik I* was the rapid development of the American space program. Following an embarrassing failure in December, 1957, the budget of the Vanguard program was increased. This project did succeed in orbiting a three-pound satellite on March 17, 1958. The honor of the first successful American orbital flight, however, had gone to von Braun's Army team, which was pressed into a crash satellite program following the launch of *Sputnik*. On January 31, 1958, a modified Redstone rocket with extra fuel tanks and three upper stages had placed the thirty-one-pound *Explorer I* satellite into an earth orbit. Defeated in the satellite race, many Americans hoped that their nation would regain its prestige by placing a man on the moon.

Pertinent Literature

Shelton, William. *Soviet Space Exploration: The First Decade*. New York: Washington Square Press, 1968.

This companion volume to Shelton's *American Space Exploration: The First Decade* traces the history of the Soviet space program from its theoretical beginnings under Ziolkovsky to the tragic death of Soviet Cosmonaut V. M. Komarov in the 1967 *Soiuz I* flight. The first five chapters, which carry the account through the launch of *Sputnik*, also place Russian developments in the context of events occurring in American and German rocketry and astronautics. While the geopolitical implications of events are not ignored, the focus is on the technological aspects. Shelton's background as a scientific reporter attached to the American space program is evident from his deft treatment of technical material.

Important aspects of the history of the Soviet space program are treated in depth; in addition, there are concise, interesting biographical sketches of the main figures. Shelton devotes a significant part of the first section of the book to examining the controversial question of how much the Russians benefited from the fruits of the German program. His conclusions are summed up in the words of one of the Germans: "The U.S. got the brains; the Russians got the mechanics." Moreover, these German engineers were used only to assemble and test-fire the first V-2's that the Russians had captured. As Wernher von Braun testified before Congress: "German scientists . . . did not, to any appreciable extent, actively participate in the hardware phase of the rocket and missile program in the Soviet Union." The Soviet program was run by Russians, and to them belongs the honor of its achievements.

Shelton also examines, although in somewhat less detail, the record of the American satellite program and some of the reasons for the delays. According to one German scientist, whom he quotes, the Peenemunde team was given virtually nothing to do during its first five-year contract:

"We taught each other English," he stated, "played chess . . . von Braun wrote a book on a space trip to Mars. All of us were frustrated." He also shows convincingly that the Americans had no reason to be surprised by *Sputnik*. The Soviets, he believes, gave ample indication of the advanced state of their rocketry and of their preparations for a launch. The American reaction to the launch is not treated in depth.

The later chapters of the book follow the history of the Soviet program until 1967 and discuss in detail Soviet achievements with automatic earth satellites and lunar and planetary probes. One chapter is devoted to the problem of potential military applications.

Shelton seems to be making one important statement throughout the whole book. Do not misjudge the Russians, he is saying. Do not consider their flights as primarily propaganda-oriented, do not underestimate their expertise, and do not believe calumnies about their carelessness with human life. Such distortions are not only insulting, but harmful as well; and they are likely to lead to surprises and alarms like those that followed *Sputnik*. The Soviet program, like the American, is staffed by dedicated, competent men and women who are inspired by motives of scientific curiosity and patriotism. They have been responsible for impressive and valuable scientific achievements.

Caidin, Martin. *Red Star in Space*. New York: Crowell-Collier Press, 1963.

Martin Caidin's book was written five years before Shelton's and is consequently much more detailed in its treatment of the first years of the Soviet space program; it is also more inspired by the Cold War mentality itself. Caidin writes from a competitive perspective. The United States is in a race with the Russians, and is losing. Some of the reasons he sees for the American disadvantage are ignorance, misinformation, and self-delusion about the Soviet program, as well as hypocrisy about our own motives. The book is meant to set the record straight.

This intention, together with its detailed information, makes the book valuable for readers today, even though its ideological perspective has become somewhat outdated. In debunking the myths which he feels

hampered American understanding of the situation, the author presents a wealth of data on the history of the Soviet space program. There is a detailed examination of the Soviet program before the war, with a long biography of Ziolkovsky. Caidin examines the question of German participation in the Soviet space program through the records of Congressional committees, Allied intelligence reports, and interviews with German scientists. He concludes that the Germans played only an insignificant part in the Soviet program. Moreover, he traces the origin of the notion that German participation had made a difference to an unguarded remark made by President Eisenhower at a press conference on October 9, 1957.

Caidin also enumerates the long

list of announcements, journal articles, and statements from Soviet sources that should have warned Americans that the Russians were capable of orbiting a satellite and were indeed planning to do so. In his chapter entitled "Timetable," the author lists thirty-six pieces of evidence that appeared between Nesmeyanov's statement in 1953 and the launch of *Sputnik* in 1957. These statements, Caidin says, give a clear picture of the goals and abilities of the Soviet space program; and they are only a sample of the material published in the Soviet press. He also shows how the number of statements increased as the launch date approached. The extensive use of translations from Russian-language documents enriches the book.

The remaining chapters are concerned with the successful lunar probes launched by the Soviet Union in 1959, as well as the orbital flights of Cosmonauts Y. Gagarin and H. S. Titov in 1961. In each of these cases the United States had numerous forewarnings: thus the hollowness of attempts by American commentators to explain away Soviet accomplishments.

The book is written in a vivid, journalistic style and contains a great amount of detail, both personal and technological. Throughout the book, Caidin emphasizes the precision and expertise of the Soviet space effort, together with the scientific importance of Soviet accomplishments. His book is an attempt to awaken Americans to the fact that they are in a race with a very talented rival, and to arouse them to a more realistic appraisal and a more comprehensive effort. — *P.A.*

Additional Recommended Reading

Daniloff, Nicholas. *The Kremlin and the Cosmos*. New York: Alfred A. Knopf, 1972. Devotes considerable space to *Sputnik*; although the book shows a lack of technological expertise, the author's knowledge of Russian is an advantage.

LaFeber, Walter. *America, Russia, and the Cold War, 1945-1975*. 2 vols. Translated and edited by Strobe Talbott. London: John Wiley and Sons, 1975. An analysis and critique of American foreign policy which shows the importance of domestic political factors in determining the foreign policy of nations.

Shelton, William. *American Space Exploration: The First Decade*. Boston: Little, Brown and Company, 1967. An informed layman's account of the development of American rocketry and astronautics.

Witkin, Richard. *The Challenge of the Sputniks*. Garden City, N.Y.: Doubleday & Company, 1958. A fascinating collection of articles and speeches documenting the American reaction to *Sputnik* and constituting a valuable source for understanding the mood and concerns of the nation.

Goldsen, Joseph M., ed. *Outer Space in World Politics*. New York: Frederick A. Praeger, 1963. A collection of Rand-inspired articles on various political implications of the space race, written by noted Western political scientists and economists; while some of the pieces are flawed by chauvinistic rhetoric, others remain valuable.

Wukelic, George E., ed. *Handbook of Soviet Space Science Research*. New York:

The Soviet Union Launches Sputnik

Gordon and Breach, Science Publishers, 1968. A highly technical, comprehensive guide to the first ten years of the Soviet space program which contains references to translated Soviet studies and covers Soviet rockets, satellites, and space probes; the results of Soviet physical and biomedical experiments; Soviet applications of artificial satellites; and Soviet views on extraterrestrial life.

OPENING OF THE ST. LAWRENCE SEAWAY

Type of event: Technological: opening of a major trade route from the Great Lakes to the Atlantic Ocean
Time: 1959
Locale: Upper Midwestern and Northeastern United States and Southeastern Canada (Ontario and Quebec provinces)

Principal personages:

HARRY S TRUMAN (1884-1972), thirty-third President of the United States, 1945-1953

DWIGHT DAVID EISENHOWER (1890-1969), thirty-fourth President of the United States, 1953-1961

DOLLIER DE CASSON, a Superior of the Sulpician Order whose dream led him to make the first crude attempts at beginning a Seaway in the late seventeenth century

WILLIAM HAMILTON MERRITT (1793-1862), a visionary from Southern Canada whose interest in the idea of a Seaway led him and friends to dig the Welland Canal in the early nineteenth century

LIONEL CHEVRIER, a historian, Member of the Canadian Parliament, and one of Canada's most ardent and influential advocates of the Seaway in this century

Summary of Event

The opening of the St. Lawrence Seaway in 1959 celebrated an engineering triumph readily comparable with the building of the Suez Canal or the Panama Canal; and its long-range effects on the North American "heartland" region can be compared with those of the Suez Canal on the interior of Egypt. For the first time, the heretofore isolated, land-locked towns and cities of the American and Canadian interiors—Chicago, Duluth, Cleveland, Toledo, Toronto, Fort William, and Port Arthur—became deep water ports capable of competing favorably with established ocean ports such as Montreal, New York, and Baltimore in the transportation of crude commodities such as grain and iron ore. In fact, the shipping distance between certain Northern European ports (for example, Hamburg and Bremerhaven) and such an inland American city as Cleveland was actually shorter than it was between those ports and New York City.

Valuable as the St. Lawrence Seaway has demonstrated itself to be to the upper tier of American Northeastern states, it may seem strange that it was not constructed much earlier than it was; however, various disagreements, fueled by such matters as Canadian and American nationalism, and the smouldering antipathy existing between American states bordering the pre-Seaway lakes and rivers, conspired to delay construction until 1954, when the first large-scale building began. But it was not only feuds that hurt the Seaway's prospects: everything from the Great Depression to World Wars I and II dampened enthusiasm for the project.

The story of the St. Lawrence Seaway goes as far back as the time of Jacques Cartier, the discoverer of the Grand Banks fishing grounds. In 1536 Cartier, who was in the employ of Britain, is credited with having had a grandiose vision of sailing ships going far into the North American interior by means of a deep water passage. At that time, of course, the necessary technology was not available; so Cartier's recurring dream was laid to rest—for the time being. Later, another visionary, Superior Dollier de Casson of the Sulpician Order, hoped to see the day when French ships would sail up the St. Lawrence river to the Great Lakes basin by using a grand canal which he would construct; but his idea came to little. Lionel Chevrier, a historian and Member of the Canadian Parliament, notes that "As the explorers were followed by commerce, it became supremely frustrating that it was not possible to load grain at Duluth and sail it to Amsterdam; or load textiles at Liverpool and unload them at Chicago."

Seaway visionaries and advocates such as William Hamilton Merritt, whose friends joined him in the initial dragging and digging of the Welland Canal in the early nineteenth century, kept alive the hope that one day the ocean and lakes would be joined, just as the Welland Canal had joined Lake Ontario and Lake Erie. Perhaps the single most impressive case for a Seaway was presented by the example of the successful Erie Canal (built in the early nineteenth century by American-Irish laborers), connecting New York City with the towns and cities of Upstate New York. The Erie Canal—at least until railroads came upon the American scene—was the most efficient purveyor of goods from one place to another. Its operational costs were the lowest to be found, and from the day it opened the Erie made money, so jammed was it by barge traffic.

The St. Lawrence river had been a useful avenue of trade for centuries, supplying Montreal and the smaller Canadian cities along its banks with durable and crude goods, and foodstuffs. Many felt that trade could be enormously expanded by the addition of locks and canals linking the river to the Great Lakes beyond. Aware of the pressing need for more electrical power, both Americans and Canadians found that a Seaway link with the St. Lawrence river made sense. In 1930, the St. Lawrence Power Development Commission formed the Power Authority of New York State, a precursor of later power authorities; in 1932, a Great Lakes Treaty was brought before the United States Senate, but was not ratified; and in 1941 an agreement between the United States and Canada was signed. Because of World War II, however, nothing came of this Great Lakes/St. Lawrence Basin agreement.

After the war, President Harry Truman wanted a Seaway, but Congress refused to enact appropriate legislation, in part because of the intense lobbying efforts of East Coast shippers and others who felt that the creation of a Seaway would not serve their interests. Yet, all of the lobbying notwithstanding, great numbers of Americans had by that time come to the conclusion that a Seaway would be in the best interest of the United States, if only because of the vast amount of electricity that would be generated by Seaway power stations. By 1950, Ontario and New York agreed on a plan for the creation of one enormous power station and two large dams on the St. Lawrence river.

With public funds available for the immense task, President Truman, not wanting the Canadians to build a Seaway without American participation, was in favor of beginning the project at once. Advocates of the Seaway argued that it would not damage the coastal economies, as Eastern Congressmen feared. They also argued that the project would be self-supporting and thus a genuine boon for the hard-pressed taxpayer. Nevertheless, the first attempt to garner congressional support failed in a vote on June 18, 1952, and the Seaway proposal was sent back to committee. Canadians, dismayed but still determined, went ahead with their own plans to create a Seaway, realizing that one thousand miles of it would be within Canada, and that Americans would ultimately cooperate, since sizable portions of the Seaway would be located in the Northern New York State area. President Dwight D. Eisenhower, recently inaugurated, was at first deeply skeptical about the proposed water route; later, he came to support it, in part because of the persuasive powers of Lionel Chevrier and other prominent Canadian leaders.

In 1953, support for the Seaway increased rather dramatically. Not surprisingly, much of that support came from congressmen representing the Midwestern states in the Great Lakes region. More surprising was the enthusiasm of Senator John F. Kennedy of Massachusetts, who argued against the congressional tendency to vote regionally rather than keeping the interests of the nation at large in mind. After many floor battles and behind-the-scenes intrigues, Congress approved the creation of a Seaway on May 6, 1954.

From 1954 to 1959, massive public works—on a scale heretofore unknown even in Suez and Panama— were undertaken by American and Canadian construction teams. The creation of enormous locks, the deepening of the Welland Canal, and the dredging of channels proceeded without serious difficulties, and in June, 1959, the dream of Cartier and Casson became a reality when Queen Elizabeth II presided over the formal opening of the St. Lawrence Seaway.

How successful the Seaway has been is a matter of opinion, but one thing is generally agreed upon: it has not been the revenue producer that its supporters had hoped it would be. That is not to say, however, that the Seaway has been a financial white elephant. The number of ships traveling the 2,400 miles of the Seaway has been on the increase since 1959, with the latest (1978) government figures showing that an average of fifty million tons of cargo pass through the Seaway system each year. The $416,000,000 spent between 1954 and 1959 has not been repaid because the shipping rates set in the 1950's have not even been paying the interest on the capital costs involved in the operation. Nevertheless, the Seaway has created jobs and opened an awe-inspiring avenue of foreign trade for the interiors of America and Canada.

Pertinent Literature

Willoughby, William R. *The St. Lawrence Waterway: A Study in Politics and Diplomacy*. Madison: University of Wisconsin Press, 1961.

William Willoughby's *The St. Lawrence Waterway* is the most complete account available of the "plans and proposals that have been brought forward . . . and in some cases acted upon—for improving the Great Lakes and St. Lawrence river for navigational purposes." However, the "plans and proposals" are not his sole subject; to do justice to his narrower subject, Willoughby discusses engineering and economic matters relating to the development of the St. Lawrence Seaway. He astutely charts the many rivalries—state *versus* state, region *versus* region, national governmental agency *versus* agency—that held back the completion of the long-sought water route to the sea. All of the various political intrigues given here form, in the author's words, "an intricate but exceedingly interesting pattern."

Willoughby has researched his subjects with considerable care and perseverance, having obtained information from such quarters as the University of Toronto, Harvard University, Princeton University, the United States Federal Power Commission, the Power Authority of the State of New York, and the Ontario Hydro-Electric Power Commission, as well as from various Canadian and American officials from departments of state and interior. His study, funded in part by St. Lawrence University, The Social Science Research Council, and the American Philosophical Society, is a social history, beginning with the first Canadian proposals for a Seaway and ending with the Seaway's first year of operation.

From Willoughby, one learns why the idea of an inland passage connecting the Canadian and American cities of the Great Lakes basin with the sea remained an elusive, though provocative, dream from the time of Dollier de Casson (the late eighteenth century) to the early twentieth century. Rapids such as the Cascades and the Coteau above and immediately below Montreal, the Long Sault near Barnhart Island, the fierce rapids of the treacherous Niagara river, and the highfalls of the St. Mary's river presented would-be canal builders with formidable barriers. Another problem was that these rivers tended to ice over during the coldest part of the winter, blocking Great Lakes area traffic and forcing it to go overland to the Atlantic seaboard cities. Competition from the Mississippi river, the main Midwestern commercial artery of water trade, as well as the Hudson river to the east, helped stop the building of the Seaway.

Fears of a revival of war with Britain and the apathy of people living in parts of the United States and Canada which had no contact with the St. Lawrence river or its tributaries, kept the Seaway issue moot during the nineteenth century. Yet, so many persons in lower Canada and the upper Northeastern United States stood to gain so much from the opening of such a commercial trading route that the Seaway idea stayed alive. Also, as American and Canadian interests became more intertwined and as the threat of a British invasion of the United States decreased, influential persons in the governments of Canada and America took note of a water route's possibilities. Moreover, the arrival of the steamboat, the invention of the canal lock, and other technical innovations made a St. Lawrence link more and more plausible.

The decline of regional frictions on both sides of the St. Lawrence helped improve the chances for the construction of the Seaway. American regional disputes, fired by East Coast shippers' fear of overly intensive competition from Midwestern shipping companies, dock workers' fear of losing their jobs, and warehouse owners' fear of going bankrupt, gradually lost their severity as the twentieth century progressed. Simultaneously, a temporary respite in the tensions between the French-speaking Canadians and their English-speaking brothers was also encouraging. In general, the French Canadians did not seem overly interested in a Seaway, while their English counterparts were very interested.

These political, regional, and ethnic squabbles did not, of course, entirely fall by the wayside; local and international jealousies continued to plague those who met together to discuss the need for constructing a Seaway. Nevertheless, the St. Lawrence project eventually became a reality.

Chevrier, Lionel. *The St. Lawrence Seaway*. New York: St. Martin's Press, 1959.

This book by a member of the Canadian Parliament and an intermediary on the Seaway project presents the story from an insider's point of view. Despite occasional bursts of nationalistic rhetoric and sometimes overly subjective assessment of events, Chevrier tells the Canadian side of the story in a manner that is at once scholarly and highly personal. So many statistics about dollars, square cubic feet of concrete poured, dimensions of rivers, lakes, and locks are given, that the reader is left with a vivid impression of just how big an undertaking the St. Lawrence Seaway was. For example, one small area near the Beauharnois power station required that 750,000 cubic yards of concrete be poured and that a four-lane highway tunnel be blasted from solid rock.

As early as 1928, Chevrier became fascinated by and dedicated to the idea of a Seaway joining the Great Lakes and the ocean, and he was convinced that such a plan could be carried out in the not-too-distant future. As a Member of Parliament from Stormont, he was able to speak for the Seaway on numerous occasions; moreover, as Minister of Transport (1945-1954) and President of the Seaway (1954-1957), he came to know all facets of the route. Drawing upon this expertise as well as upon recollections of his conversations with persons influential in approving construction of the waterway, Chevrier offers readers a substantial grounding in behind-the-scenes developments. His account is an adequate introduction to early visionaries and canal planners such as Casson, who was among the first to dream of a Lakes to ocean passage, and William Hamilton Merritt, the man who began linking the rivers together, creating the Welland Canal.

Among his better discussions is that of the Erie Canal's impact on the people living along or near the St. Lawrence river and other streams. Chevrier argues that the Erie Canal, often neglected in Seaway scholarship, proved conclusively that large-scale planning could lead to highly profitable results. Also impressive is Chevrier's discussion of how the hydroelectric power issue eventually led to the creation of the Seaway. Set back by such calamities as a depression and two world wars, the Seaway idea was given increasing attention in the post-World War II years by both President Truman and President Eisenhower. What really produced results, though, was the Canadians' initiative in creating a viable string of electric power plants along the St. Lawrence and other rivers touching Canadian soil. With the utmost reluctance, the United States Congress, spurred on by Canadian impatience over the hydroelectric issue and by its fear that Canada might undertake the entire project independently, finally agreed to the concept of a joint power authority operated by the United States and Canada.

President Truman, although he favored development of the Seaway, was out of office before anything substantial could be done; but his successor, President Eisenhower, enfranchised the Power Authority of the State of New York to "develop the U.S. Share of the power on the St. Lawrence," an act which angered private utility companies who lost huge contracts to this state bureau. After some disappointment in Canada's Parliament over the American "intrusion" into the Seaway project, Canadians were eager for American participation to begin. After some heated battles between Canadian and American officials about the limits to be applied to America's role in building the Seaway, and after heated debate in Congress, the final directive to begin was given in 1954, and the digging started.

The construction of the canal route progressed remarkably smoothly, unlike the proceedings of the Tolls Commission, which were plagued with arguments for some time.

At last the Seaway opened to ship traffic in 1959, nearly three hundred years after Cartier had voiced his hope that an inland passage could be cut, linking the vast interior of North America to the European trade routes on the coast. Chevrier knows probably better than anyone all of the work and hope that went into its creation. — *J.D.R.*

Additional Recommended Reading

Mabee, Carleton. *The Seaway Story*. New York: The Macmillan Company, 1961. One of the most complete accounts of the Seaway, tracing its beginnings and building, and discussing its future.

Hartley, Joseph R. *The Effect of the St. Lawrence Seaway on Grain Movements*. Bloomington: Indiana University School of Business, 1957. Although somewhat dated, this early study of Seaway grain shipping offers a discussion of the economic importance of the Seaway.

The Billion Dollar Story: The International St. Lawrence Seaway and Power Development. Massena, N.Y.: St. Lawrence Valley Souvenir Company, 1970. Because of the dearth of literature dealing with the Seaway project, this illustrated guide with maps and pictures of construction is one of the best sources to consult.

The Seaway in Canada's Transportation: An Economic Analysis. Ottawa: D. William Carr and Associates, 1970. Canadian perspective on the Seaway's past economic performance and its potential.

Marine Traffic Control: St. Lawrence River. Ottawa: Queen's Press, 1968. One of the few books to be found dealing with the Seaway giving insights into the massive job of supervising barge traffic on the St. Lawrence river section of the Seaway.

ADMISSION OF ALASKA AND HAWAII INTO THE UNION

Type of event: Legal: statehood granted to former United States territories
Time: January 3 (Alaska admitted), and August 21, 1959 (Hawaii admitted)
Locale: Alaska and Hawaii

Principal personages:

KAMEHAMEHA I (1758?-1819), the first Hawaiian monarch to extend reign to all seven islands, 1795-1819

KAMEHAMEHA II (1797-1824), monarch at the time momentous alterations in religious and social fabric of the Islands took place, 1819-1824

LYDIA LILIUOKALANI (1838-1917), last reigning Hawaiian monarch, 1891-1894

SANFORD DOLE (1844-1926), first Governor of Hawaii and one of the Islands' principal planters

ERNEST HENRY GRUENING (1887-   ), staunch advocate of Alaskan statehood and a Territorial Governor

THEODORE ROOSEVELT (1858-1919), twenty-sixth President of the United States (1901-1909), who opposed the incursions of Eastern industrialists in Alaskan Territory

DWIGHT DAVID EISENHOWER (1890-1969), thirty-fourth President of the United States, 1953-1961

ALEKSANDR BARANOV (1747-1819), head of the Russian-American Company in Alaska in late eighteenth to early nineteenth century

Summary of Event

The admission of Alaska and Hawaii into the Union in 1959 vastly extended the physical boundaries of the United States, adding considerably to American influence in the Northern and Southern Pacific. U.S. possession of Alaska, with its 586,000 square miles of tundra, mountains, and lakes situated in both Eastern and Western Hemispheres, and of the Hawaiian Islands, with their tiny area but unmatched tropical beauties, brought American civilization to the gates of Siberia in the north and to those of Japan and the Philippines in the south. The inclusion of Alaska and Hawaii into the Union came only after intense debates in the United States House and Senate in which some congressmen voiced xenophobic concerns for the "racial impurity" that they feared would result from granting citizenship to Aleuts, Tlingits, Eskimos of Alaska, and (especially) to the Japanese, Chinese, and Filipinos of Hawaii.

By admitting these territories to statehood, Americans reaffirmed their belief in manifest destiny: the expansion of their own unique sort of civilization. In doing so, they also realized the important implications of an

790

American state (that is, Alaska) being but a stone's throw from Russia, and the strategic importance of islands serving as a valuable staging ground in the South Pacific in the event that Russia one day might choke off crucial sea lanes in that region.

What went relatively unnoticed were the sociological implications of Hawaiian statehood, for here was a state in which the majority of the population was non-Caucasian. In Hawaii, ever since Captain James Cook opened the islands to the West in 1778, Occidentals and Orientals had intermarried, forming a fascinating society unlike that anywhere else in the world. Hawaii provided—and continues to provide—a rare glimpse into a nearly utopian society, proving that people of various racial and ethnic backgrounds can live harmoniously together.

Although the State of Alaska did not promise to be a place where Indians, Eskimos, and whites intermarried to nearly the extent that the various races did in Hawaii, it was of real importance to big businessmen and environmentalists alike because of its mineral and timber resources found in a virtually unimaginable stretch of wilderness from the Pacific to the Arctic. Here, in fact, was the final American frontier: one last enormously rich and as yet unexplored stronghold of riches and serenity.

To trappers and soldiers of fortune, Alaska—at least since the Gold Rush of 1899—has offered freedom from the constraints of civilization as well as a chance for instant wealth. Environmentalist groups such as the California-based Sierra Club have sought to block industrial development and other forms of what they term "exploitation" that would, in their estimation, lay waste America's only great wilderness by destroying the incredibly vulnerable tundra ecology. Industrialists, on the other hand, maintain that industry and nature can peacefully coexist. They feel that by carefully monitoring timber cutting, mining, and drilling for oil and natural gas, the environment can be saved at the same time that more people can find employment.

Like Alaska's admission to the Union, Hawaii's admission raised the question of whether the Islands would be exploited to death by mainland tourism and industrialization. Prior to statehood, Hawaiian environmentalists argued that the delicate balance of nature of the islands could be irrevocably upset by industry and hordes of tourists; today, some of their worst fears have been realized. A geometrically expanding tourism rate has had a real impact on Hawaiian flora and fauna; rarer species of plants and animals have all but disappeared.

Both Alaska and Hawaii have also had their share of conflicts through the centuries, most of which in modern times have stemmed from their territorial status—an ambiguous one at best. In the Islands there once existed a hereditary monarchy having autocratic powers. The first Hawaiian king to be visited by Westerners, Kamehameha I (1795-1819), was truly lord of all he surveyed and a leader having power over life and death. Until the time of Kamehameha I, ritual wars and human sacrifice were practiced; but during his reign the white men from England and, later,

America, forever transformed Hawaiian society, bringing Western ideas and aspirations. First came the contact between English sailors and the sexually liberated Hawaiian *wahines*, whose favors were easily purchased. Unfortunately, this first mixing of Polynesians and whites brought Western diseases to the Islands; syphilis, gonorrhea, cholera, and "black plague" killed thousands. Also, Western ways were fatal to many Hawaiian religious and social customs. Under Kamehameha II (1819-1824), Hawaiian culture, unable to withstand the new inducements of mercantilism and New England Congregationalism, slowly degenerated, creating what one writer calls a "lotus-eater's culture." Islanders fell into a pattern of life which was neither Hawaiian nor fully Western—an uneasy amalgam of East and West.

The coming of the whaling ships further insured that Hawaii would become a source of conflict between British and American interests, for each nation saw in these islands a natural trading base for that part of the world. The ever-increasing China trade made rich men out of Hawaiian chiefs who sold the sandalwood produced on the islands; but it made the Western traders who did the actual shipping of the substance even richer. Slowly, these traders were out-maneuvering the native aristocrats who continued to exert control over the land of the Islands. Eventually, the native authorities would be toppled by the white men who bought the land and used it for growing sugar and pineapples.

The arrival of missionaries from New England also increased the power of Western ideas and weakened the hold of traditional beliefs in Hawaii. In the early nineteenth century, these emissaries, believing that Hawaiians were almost beyond heavenly help, worked hard and long to educate their charges in the ways of God and Western man. So thoroughgoing was their success that by the mid-nineteenth century very little remained of the Hawaiians' belief in local gods. By introducing Western education and Western medical practices, the missionaries actually bettered the Hawaiian standard of living in a lasting and significant way. From the ranks of missionaries' sons and daughters came the Doles and Cookes who would create the "Big Five" family corporations that still control much of Hawaii's land.

A landmark year in Hawaiian history was 1848, when Orientals began to enter the Islands in large numbers. So many came that by 1899, seventy-five percent of all Hawaiians were of Oriental ancestry. They came to work the mammoth plantations, where they were paid little and worked unmercifully. Strikes occurring in the early twentieth century ended in bloodshed but obtained for the workers a reasonable wage.

A second landmark year for Hawaii was 1893, when planters under the leadership of Sanford Dole forced Queen Lydia Liliuokalani to step down from the throne. Dole became President of the Republic of Hawaii proclaimed in 1894. Four years later the planter-proclaimed republic was annexed by the United States and made a territory with Dole as the first governor. Hawaii remained a territory until 1959, although for many

Hawaiians statehood had been desired ever since the annexation in 1898. When statehood did come in August, 1959, it was because the majority of Hawaiians wanted it, and because sufficient numbers of "mainlanders" had been persuaded that Hawaii would be a welcome addition to the United States. The new State of Hawaii, with its unique geographical location and phenomenal success as a melting pot, gave America a showcase in the South Pacific.

Alaska, like its sister state, Hawaii, has been a staging ground for nations. First came the Russian fur traders under the direction of the explorer Vitus Bering, many of whom died during the journey to the Aleutian Islands. However, many fortunes in fur were made. Vigorous leadership was given by Grigori Shelekhov, founder of the first permanent base of trading operations in Alaska, and his successor, Aleksandr Baranov, a man of fierce ambition who created Sitka as his capital in 1799.

Russian interest in Alaska waned in the nineteenth century, so that by 1867, William Seward, the American Secretary of State, was able to buy the enormous parcel of Alaskan land for a mere $7,000,200. Unexplored and largely ignored, Alaska languished as a United States Army-controlled possession; finally, in 1880, the discovery of gold in the Klondike triggered a burst of interest in Alaska which lasted until around 1900, when the rush played out. As a frontier region, Alaska was as rough-and-ready a place as the American "Wild West" had been. Few women attempted the trip north; the men who went to Alaska lived an often undisciplined

bachelor existence made tolerable by drink and card playing. Certainly, the poems of Robert Service and the novels of Jack London accentuated the Alaskan male's rugged image, making it the stuff of legend.

After 1900, Alaskans grew increasingly resentful over the neglect which they suffered at the hands of the federal government. Thus, in 1906, Congress permitted Alaska to send a representative to Washington, but only as a nonvoting observer. Six years later, Congress granted Alaska territorial status under a governor appointed by the president. The bicameral legislature that was established did not have the authority to pass laws dealing with excise, game, or fur; Congress, moreover, reserved the right to veto Alaskan legislation. Such abuse angered many Alaskans to such an extent that they became avowed supporters of statehood. One of the staunchest proponents of statehood was Ernest Gruening, the last territorial and first state governor. However upset the Alaskans were about governmental neglect, their protests went virtually unacknowledged by Congress and most presidents (although Theodore Roosevelt, Franklin Delano Roosevelt, Harry Truman, and Dwight Eisenhower showed themselves sympathetic to the idea of statehood).

The potency of the statehood argument grew after World War II; for, during the war, Alaskans noted, the Territory had proved to be nearly as valuable an Army and Navy base of operations as Hawaii had been. As Russian influence grew in the postwar era, Alaskan statehood became increasingly desirable, since the Territory formed a natural barrier against Siberia and, by extension, Soviet aggression. Then, too, Americans living in the "lower forty eight" came to realize how rich in resources Alaska was. In addition, people noted how greatly Alaska would add to the physical dimensions of the United States if it were admitted to the Union.

In 1959, Alaska came into the Union operating under a state constitution created in 1956. Alaskans were delighted by the ending of territorial status, yet were made uneasy by the threat of continuing control of Alaskan land (three-fourths of which is federal property) by the United States government

Problems persist in both Alaska and Hawaii. Unlike Hawaii, Alaska has a problem with racism. Aleuts, Tlingits, and Eskimos alike are wary of white Americans who have deceived them in the past. In particular, they worry about their ancient ways of life being destroyed by the advance of Western technology. Whites, for their part, distrust Indians and Eskimos, partly because of racist feelings and partly because they fear that these peoples will hold back development of the Alaskan interior by

their protests over "white incursions into native lands." Unemployment, which is extremely high most of the time, and the serious depressions often engendered by the long winters of short days, are also problems for Alaskans.

In Hawaii, one of the major concerns has to do with tourism and the rapid expansion of cities—especially Honolulu. Tourists, although they bring large amounts of money with them, may be overrunning the tiny Islands, destroying animal habitats and rare plants. Commercialism in its most blatant form has been introduced, and that worries Islanders who fear that what remains of their culture may be entirely destroyed by Mainland habits. As Honolulu expands, Hawaiians worry about the quality of life there falling off, and about the city's crime rate rising as its celebrated *ambience* vanishes.

Yet, for the most part, Alaskans and Hawaiians appear pleased with their entry into the United States. Both groups of people have added much to America's perception of itself as a varied nation of many peoples bound together by a common destiny.

Pertinent Literature

Davis, Gavan. *Shoal of Time: A History of the Hawaiian Islands*. New York: The Macmillan Company, 1968.

No more up-to-date and authoritative history of the Hawaiian Islands can be found than Gavan Davis' *Shoal of Time: A History of the Hawaiian Islands*, a book at once readable and scholarly in its attention to detail. Beginning with the first en-

counter between the Westerner (that is, Captain James Cook) and the Polynesian (1778), Davis tells the story of a paradise, if not lost, at least transformed. As in most meetings between Europeans and natives, the Europeans seized upon the initial good will of the natives and took advantage of their less advanced state of civilization. But it was venereal disease rather than bloodshed that took its toll of the Hawaiian population.

However, although they brought disease to the Islands, the British sailors were far from an unwelcome presence on Hawaii. The Hawaiian people—especially the willing women who rowed out to meet the sailors—were very taken by Westerners and their ways. Cook's successors—the captains, the planters, the missionaries—brought Hawaii not unwillingly into the modern world of the nineteenth century.

Even before white men landed in Hawaii, the Islanders, cut off from all contact with other civilizations for centuries (though they had been among the most courageous sailors of ancient times), had settled down into a rather monotonous—if pleasant—existence, devoid of real challenges to their considerable ingenuity. From the West came a whole new world of possibilities—not to mention the wonders of scissors, knives, mirrors, and nails.

Hard workers, the Hawaiians impressed the foreigners, who saw in them good plantation workers. Also, they were needed as sandalwood harvesters. During the reign of King Kamehameha I, American traders connived to corner the China sandalwood trade, outdoing the British and setting the stage for the eventual American dominance of Hawaiian trade. After 1819, the year of the very influential King Kamehameha I's death, the social and religious customs of native Hawaiians began to be eroded by the inexorable pressure of Western culture. Shortly after Kamehameha's death, the *Kapu* social and religious order of the Islands was destroyed forever. It would not be long before the monarchy itself would be dismantled by power-seeking Americans (1894). Under Queen Liliuokalani, a woman unaccustomed to her queenly duties, the Islands became a republic under the control of planters like Sanford Dole.

Employing tactics both ethical and otherwise, Hawaiian aristocrats were replaced by Yankee traders-turned-plantation-owners such as Dole and W. G. Irwin, the latter a man who as much as anyone managed to monopolize the Hawaiian sugar crop in the 1880's. Such huge plantations required the massive importation of workers from the not-so-distant Orient: from China, Japan, and the Philippines. From this mixture of peoples would emerge the representative twentieth century Hawaiian, an amalgam of many people from many backgrounds. In the twentieth century, the nonwhite populace of Hawaii, increasingly well-educated and informed, has risen above the second-class status assigned by the white islanders.

Gruening, Ernest. *The Battle for Alaska Statehood.* College: The University of Alaska Press, 1967.

Ernest Gruening, noted author, former Territorial Governor of Alaska (1939-1953), and, more recently, United States Senator from Alaska, has written a most detailed and personal account of the in-fighting, compromises, and triumphs of the struggle for Alaskan statehood, lasting throughout the first fifty-nine years of this century. This history, written to celebrate the hundredth anniversary of the American purchase of Alaska from Russia (in 1867), is a quintessential insider's story, told by a man who learned to love the Alaska of countless lakes, endless forests, and endless possibilities, after having been named Territorial Governor by President Franklin D. Roosevelt.

Though at times marred by irrelevant detail and trivial comment, *The Battle for Alaska Statehood* carefully traces the statehood movement from the mid-1940's to Alaska's admittance into the Union in 1959.

So detailed is Gruening's book that one is continually being told about such things as who voted for whom in such-and-such a town. We learn how really few Alaskans there are, and what a large percentage of this comparatively small group care deeply about Alaska's problems with Washington, D.C., and their future as a state. Highly individualistic, Gruening's Alaskans constantly express their contempt for those bureaucrats so far from "the country" who would tell them where they can fish and hunt, prospect for gold, or build a home. What they want is to be left alone to find their own destiny amid the wilderness. That is why most Alaskans came north from the "lower forty-eight" in the first place—to escape from the rules and regulations of an increasingly middle-aged society. One

senses from Gruening's descriptions of his state that it is a country of the untrammeled spirit, a place far different from others, a world away from the world.

The fight for statehood was long and for the most part tediously inconclusive. Congressional debates in the 1950's were long on talk and short on substantive action. Gruening, one of Alaska's most eloquent partisans, made persons with little or no conception of its problems conscious of Alaska's need for statehood. Joining him were other statehood advocates: Henry Jackson of Washington State and President Harry Truman, to name but two. Gruening tells of the harried write-in campaigns, the entreaties addressed to congressmen who had not made up their minds, the desperate telephone calls to save crucial votes. He even includes such intriguing stories as that of the Texas delegation's refusal to support statehood in the House, apparently because they were worried about Texas being outstripped by a larger state.

Returning again and again to his main theme, Gruening recounts the past abuses of Alaska's citizenry by the "despotic" federal government (some Alaskan Territorial residents were so angry that they were actually ready to start fighting a second American Revolution at one point). It was no easy task for people in "the country" to persuade fellow Americans to listen to their case. Only through the dedicated lobbying efforts of stump speakers like Gruening did the statehood effort come to flower. —*J.D.R.*

Additional Recommended Reading

Smith, Richard Austin, *et al. The Frontier States: Alaska and Hawaii.* New York: Time-Life Books, 1968. Splendid pictorial essays and informative text introducing the reader to the history, customs, and outlook of the inhabitants of the nation's newest states.

Simpich, Frederick. *Anatomy of Hawaii.* Toronto: Coward, McCann, and Geoghegan, 1971. A Hawaiian resident's personal view of Hawaii's colorful past and present.

Gruening, Ernest. *The State of Alaska.* New York: Random House, 1954. One of several accounts by the ex-Territorial Governor; discusses the "neglect and discrimination" Alaskans suffered prior to achieving full citizenship in 1959.

Rogers, George, ed. *Change in Alaska: People, Petroleum, and Politics.* College: The University of Alaska Press, 1970. A fairly detailed rendering of Alaskan growing pains in the years immediately following the conferral of statehood.

Horwitz, Robert H. and Norman Meller. *Land and Politics in Hawaii.* Honolulu: University of Hawaii Press, 1966. A brief but helpful study dealing with the writing of Hawaii's crucial land laws which replaced the public land laws previously enacted.

Lind, Andrew W. *Hawaii's People.* Honolulu: University of Hawaii Press, 1955. A Hawaiian sociologist's examination of the unique state of racial relations in Hawaii.

SIGNING OF THE ANTARCTIC TREATY

Type of event: Diplomatic: attempt to establish peaceful international cooperation in
  Antarctica
Time: December 1, 1959
Locale: Washington, D.C.

Principal personages:

DWIGHT DAVID EISENHOWER (1890-1969), thirty-fourth President of the United States, 1953-1961

HERMAN PHLEGER (1890-   ), head of the United States delegation to the Antarctic Conference and chairman of the Conference

PAUL CLEMENT DANIELS (1903-   ), United States diplomat and principal preconference negotiator

VASILI KUZNETSOV (1901-   ), head of the Soviet Union delegation to the Antarctic Conference

Summary of Event

The Antarctic Treaty is notable as one of the few instances of East-West diplomatic accord during the era of the Cold War. The Treaty came about as an outgrowth of the International Geophysical Year (IGY): July, 1957, to December, 1958. For those eighteen months, physical scientists of many nations participated in a multitude of cooperative research programs and mutually shared the data they gathered about the earth, the atmosphere, and outer space.

One of the earth regions intensively studied during the IGY was Antarctica. Teams of scientists from twelve countries—some seven hundred men in all—went to the bottom of the world to investigate geology, weather, glaciers, and other physical phenomena of the frigid continent. More than sixty scientific research stations were established at different locations on the Antarctic continent: Great Britain had sixteen stations, the United States seven, and the Soviet Union three or four. In

accordance with the IGY theme of mutual cooperation, and necessitated by the extremely hostile environment, the scientists at those stations put aside national self-interest and prestige and worked together in relative harmony.

The spirit of concord, unfortunately, did not extend to the home governments of the Antarctic scientists. The southernmost continent became, even before the IGY ended, a locus of controversy among rival nations, as several issues emerged to create international friction. One concerned the use of the Antarctic for earth satellite launching bases. Scientists had found that the South Polar area would be an excellent site for earth-orbiting satellite bases. Satellites launched from either the South or North Pole areas could provide unequaled surveys of almost the entire earth. However, that fact also had military implications: satellites equipped with nuclear devices could, it appeared, give important military

798

advantages to any nation that built such bases in the Antarctic.

A related issue concerned the possible introduction of nuclear energy facilities into Antarctica. Some IGY scientists spoke of the desirability of building nuclear reactors to provide heat and power for permanent settlements on the frozen continent. There was also talk of utilizing the enormous empty spaces of the Antarctic for testing nuclear bombs. But the thought of endangering the Antarctic environment by radioactive pollution from such activities, and by the possible firing of nuclear intercontinental ballistic missiles, caused considerable apprehension among scientists and the general publics of several nations.

Still another issue had to do with possible natural resources of Antarctica. Geologists determined that large coal deposits lay beneath the Antarctic ice, and they assumed the existence of many other minerals there also; also, the abundant marine life in the seas around the Antarctic continent might be a rich source of food for any nation that controlled those waters. A universal assumption in the mid-1950's that the constantly rising world population probably would soon deplete the existing resources of the earth, particularly of food, led to increased nationalistic interest in the Antarctic.

Underlying all other issues, however, was the matter of territorial claims in the Antarctic continent. Beginning with Great Britain in 1908, seven nations had laid claim to Antarctic lands before the IGY: Argentina, Australia, Chile, France, New Zealand, Norway, and Great Britain. These claims were based on the rights of discovery of certain parts of the continent and, in some cases, on actual physical occupation of some locations. Several nations had established weather stations, post offices, and other physical manifestations of their claims. Significantly, neither the United States nor the Soviet Union had ever laid formal claim to Antarctic territories. However, as the potential military, economic, and prestige value of Antarctic holdings emerged during the IGY, both of the superpowers began to assert that earlier discoveries and explorations by their nationals gave them rights which must be recognized. On several occasions in the 1940's and later, jurisdictional disputes between nations claiming Antarctic territory had broken out; on one occasion in 1948 there had nearly been war between Great Britain and Argentina. These disputes prompted repeated calls for a general settlement of Antarctic claims, either through the United Nations or through multilateral agreements.

Now, in the 1950's, the harmony shown by the Antarctic IGY scientists inspired a renewed interest in the possible settlement of the Antarctic issues. In early 1958, both Prime Minister Harold Macmillan of Great Britain and President Dwight Eisenhower of the United States recommended that positive diplomatic steps be taken. The twelve nations that had Antarctic claims, or which had participated in the IGY programs there, were invited by Eisenhower to send representatives to meet in the United States for preliminary talks. Some fifty private confidential negotiating sessions were held in 1958 and 1959, attended by representatives from the United States, Great Britain, the Soviet Union, Australia, Argentina, Belgium, Norway, Chile, France, Japan, New Zealand, and South Africa. By May, 1959, it was announced that the private sessions had attained resolution of the major Antarctic issues, and that a final conference to promulgate an Antarctic treaty would convene in Washington, D.C., in October.

President Eisenhower chose Herman Phleger of California to lead the United States delegation at the Washington conference. Assisting Phleger as alternate would be Paul C. Daniels, a veteran American diplomat, who had been the chief spokesman for the United States in the preceding private session. The Soviet Union sent a six-man delegation led by Vasili Kuznetsov, First Deputy Foreign Minister. Other delegates included Ambassador Esler Dening of Great Britain; Walter Nash, Prime Minister of New Zealand; Richard Casey, Australian Minister of External Affairs; Ambassador Koichiro Asakai of Japan; and Eric Louw, Foreign Minister of South Africa.

The first session of the Washington Antarctic Conference opened on October 15, 1959, in the auditorium of the Department of the Interior. Christian Herter, the American Secretary of State, welcomed the delegates, and responses from each delegation followed. Richard Casey asserted that "substantial agreement had been reached in all important fields." Kuznetsov said that the conferees agreed that "a regime for Antarctica should be established on an international basis." At that,

Adolpho Scilingo, delegate from Argentina, protested. Argentina had long vehemently insisted on retention of its national claims to Antarctic lands, and Scilingo declared that the conference had not been convened "to institute regimes or create structures." "It is not the mission of the conference to alter or to change anything," he explained—meaning that Argentina did not intend to surrender its claim to any international organization. Obviously the important questions had not been settled in the private sessions, as Casey had asserted. Further negotiations would be necessary before a treaty could be written.

The conference delegates, therefore, divided into two committees: Committee I would work on scientific matters, and Committee II would try to resolve the thornier legal and political questions. Reports that leaked from the closed meetings of Committee II indicated that the principal areas of dispute were the persistent demands by Argentina and Chile that their territorial claims be recognized and guaranteed, as well as the insistence by the Soviet Union that nuclear testing in the Antarctic be absolutely prohibited. Many days of further bargaining and compromises followed, until, after nearly six weeks of discussion, the Washington conferees produced the multilateral Antarctic Treaty on December 1, 1959, and signed it in the names of their respective governments.

The Treaty is a seven-page document consisting of a short introduction followed by thirteen rather brief articles of agreement. The principal articles provide that Antarctica shall be used for peaceful purposes only; that all measures of a military nature are to be prohibited, as well as the testing of any type of weapon (Article I). The second Article permits freedom of scientific investigation, while Article III urges that the international scientific cooperation which existed during the IGY be continued. In Article IV, the principle of "freezing" all Antarctic territorial claims is asserted: no renunciation or diminution of existing land claims is required, but no new land claims or enlargement of present claims will be accepted. The matter of an international regime for the administration of Antarctica is not mentioned. However, in Article VI the Treaty exempts any claims which nations may have to the seas around Antarctica from the "frozen" status; this was apparently done to satisfy the Latin Americans. Article V firmly prohibits any nuclear explosions or the disposal of radioactive waste in the Antarctic. To promote the objective of the Treaty and adherence to its provisions, Article VI permits any of the contracting nations to send observers to inspect any and all Antarctic stations, installations, and equipment of any other nation, with complete freedom of access to be given to the observers.

The remaining Articles provide for subsequent periodic conferences by the contracting nations to formulate and consider "measures for the furtherance of the principles and objectives of the Treaty," and for amendment or modification of the Treaty by a majority of the contracting parties. Any disputes under the Treaty are to be settled by voluntarily agreed-upon mediation or arbitration, or taken to the International Court of Justice. Finally, there is a provision whereby any nation which is a member of the United Nations may accede to the Treaty and participate in its terms, if that nation so requests.

No precise time limit of the Treaty is given. However, after thirty years from its adoption, any of the contracting parties may call another conference to review the operation of the Treaty and presumably substantially modify or discontinue it.

The governments of most of the signatories promptly approved the Treaty. In the United States, President Eisenhower waited until February, 1960, before sending the Treaty to the Senate for ratification; this was apparently done so that the approval would coincide with an international economic conference being held in Geneva. Opposition to the Antarctic Treaty in the United States then surfaced, coming principally from conservative legislators and patriotic organizations. The opponents made little more than token resistance to ratification, however, and the debates on the Senate floor were desultory. On August 10, 1960, the United States Senate approved the Treaty by a vote of sixty-six to twenty-one, and it was signed by Eisenhower one week later.

Still, the Treaty did not come into force until June 23, 1961, primarily because of delayed ratification by the legislatures of Argentina and Chile, where opposition had been intense. In proclaiming the Treaty to be in force, President John F. Kennedy said with approval that "first and foremost, this Treaty provides that the vast Antarctic continent shall be used for peaceful purposes." Or, in the words of one of the conference delegates, "If the olive branch of peace has to be carried into the world from the barren wastes of Antarctica, then paradoxical as it may seem, it is as good a starting place as any."

In the years since ratification, there have been several conferences of the signatory nations at which minor matters were resolved, such as banning the introduction of alien fauna and flora into Antarctica and forbidding injury to indigenous plants and animals. As provided for in Article VII of the Treaty, sporadic inspections of scientific stations and other installations have been carried out, most often by American observers. Scientific research continues on the frozen continent, but all territorial claims have stood in abeyance, and none of the other issues which so disturbed the nations in the mid-1950's has reappeared to cause trouble.

The Antarctic has, since 1961, attracted very little attention from the rest of the world and is seemingly no longer a point of contention, a condition which can in part be credited to the wisdom of the makers of the Antarctic Treaty of 1959.

Pertinent Literature

Taubenfeld, Howard J. *A Treaty for Antarctica.* Washington, D.C.: The Carnegie Endowment for International Peace, 1961.

Howard Taubenfeld is an American law professor with a particular interest in diplomacy and international law who was himself actively involved in promoting ratification of the Antarctic Treaty. He published this study after the Treaty was approved to explain its background and provisions.

Taubenfeld begins by tracing the several Antarctic territorial claims from their origins in the nineteenth and twentieth centuries, and appends a map of the continent to illustrate the different-sized pie-shaped sections into which the Antarctic continent is nominally divided by the claimant nations. Those territorial claims were founded either upon the premise of original discovery of a certain part of the continent, or upon the argument that men from a particular nation had been first to explore some portion of Antarctica. The difficulty here is that the nations which made the first sightings were not always the same nations that made explorations, causing a conflict over primacy of claims.

Two principles also entered to complicate the Antarctic claims. One is the principle of "contiguity," which holds that if Antarctic lands lie closely contiguous to the territory of a nearby nation, then that nation may lay rightful claim to those lands; the South American nations favor this principle because parts of Antarctica are close to their coasts. The second is the principle of "continuity," which holds that the nation which first discovered or explored a portion of the Antarctic coast has a right to adjoining land inward from the coast continuously all the way to the South Pole. It is the continuity principle which has resulted in the pie-shaped sectors shown on Antarctic maps.

Over the years there have been efforts to resolve the claims by arbitration, judicial mediation, or even by force; and attempts have been made to apply legal precedents reached in other parts of the world to the Antarctic. In 1933, for example, the Permanent Court of International Justice decided in the *Eastern Greenland Case* that while the nation of Denmark occupied and settled only a small portion of eastern Greenland, the Danes could nevertheless exercise sovereignty over all the remaining uninhabited regions of Greenland. That decision might, it appeared, be applied to Antarctica on the continuity principle. But the International Court in the Greenland case also specified that Danish sovereignty might be exercised only "in the absence of competition" from other nations. Since competition already existed in Antarctica, the applicability of the Greenland decision there was dubious. All such decisions under international law were found either inapplicable or unacceptable to the Antarctic claimants.

Both the United States and the Soviet Union took ambivalent positions regarding their own Antarctic claims in the 1940's and 1950's, neither completely relinquishing their rights nor forcefully asserting them. There were, from time to time, recommendations that the whole Antarctic continent be placed under United Nations trusteeship and a system of mandates similar to that which had been used after World War I be set up. But for several reasons the United Nations trusteeship idea was dropped, and instead the interested nations wrote the multilateral Treaty of 1959 in which the two superpowers forced the suspension of all Antarctic land claims, including their own.

The Treaty is, of necessity, a collection of compromises—as most negotiated settlements are—and is therefore imperfect. It does not provide for any general government or administration of the Antarctic continent; there are no formal arrangements for joint or cooperative scientific or developmental ventures; and the provisions for observation and inspection of bases and installations are inadequate. Nevertheless, the negotiators at Washington produced what Taubenfeld calls a "modest, limited and relatively costless attempt at international controls." It was only a small step toward international peace, but it was a good beginning.

The Antarctic Treaty. Hearings Before the Committee on Foreign Relations. United States Senate. Eighty-sixth Congress, Second Session. Washington, D.C.: U.S. Government Printing Office, 1960.

In June, 1960, open hearings were held by the Senate Foreign Relations Committee in which supporters and opponents were invited to present their views regarding the Antarctic Treaty. Speaking in opposition to ratification on the first day of the hearings were Senators Clair Engle of

California and Ernest Gruening of Alaska, and Representative John Pillion of New York. Senator Engle opened by comparing the valid claims that the United States had in the Antarctic with the very sketchy Russian rights there. He stressed what he regarded as the vital military importance of Antarctica, as well as the vast economic potential of the continent. He also argued that the Antarctic would be a better location for nuclear testing than other sites because residual radioactivity would be a negligible threat there. Summing up, Engle was opposed to the Treaty because it would reduce the preeminent rights of the United States and grant the Soviet Union a position of equality. When asked whether it was not contrary to United States policy to seek additional territory, Engle replied that such a policy should not apply where the only population consists of a few penguins.

Senator Gruening expressed the opinion of many Americans when he said he did not trust the Russians to abide by any treaty arrangements; the Soviets had broken too many treaties in the past. Gruening wanted all Antarctic claims to be stated and clarified and then negotiated before any treaty was ratified. A century hence, Gruening argued, there might well be new inventions which could be used to support a substantial population in the Antarctic; he urged us not to take any hasty action now by which the United States could lose its Antarctic claims in the future when there might be opportunity to exploit them.

Representative Pillion's criticisms of the Treaty were most harsh; he spoke of the Soviet Union as an interloper in the Antarctic, and of the Treaty as a sign of weakness and appeasement by the United States. He suggested ominously that "persons" in the United States State Department and at the National Science Foundation had used the IGY as a "cloak" for penetration and eventual domination of the Antarctic by the Soviet Union. Rather than agreeing to this Treaty, Pillion wanted the United States to extend the Truman Doctrine to Antarctica, advise the Soviets that they were in unlawful trespass there, and insist that they get out entirely.

On the second day of hearings, proponents of the Treaty spoke. Herman Phleger recapitulated the principal points of the Treaty which he had helped to write, emphasizing the right of inspection by which United States representatives could go freely anywhere on the continent. He compared this to the "open skies" proposal for nuclear sites inspection recently advanced by President Eisenhower. Phleger also argued that even if the Treaty terms were violated in the future, the United States would have lost nothing; new arrangements could then be made. Other Treaty proponents who spoke included Dr. Laurence Gould, chairman of the Committee on Polar Research of the National Academy of Sciences, and Admiral David Tyree, Antarctic Projects Officer of the United States Navy. Both said, in effect, that the Treaty was the best possible technique for preserving the cooperation which had characterized the International Geophysical Year, and urged its ratification.

Further opposition was voiced by representatives of several organizations, the Daughters of the American Revolution and the Sons of the American Revolution, among others; but the Senate Foreign Relations Committee decided, after the two days of hearings, to recommend ratification. The committee voted unanimously to make that recommendation to the full Senate, and the committee chairman, Senator J. William Fulbright, then led the debates on the Senate floor for approval.
— *J.W.P.*

Additional Recommended Reading

United States Department of State. *The Conference on Antarctica: Washington, October 15–December 1, 1959*. Department of State Publication #7060. Washington, D.C.: U.S. Government Printing Office, 1960. Contains the welcoming address by Secretary of State Herter and the statements of the several delegations; also includes the membership of all the delegations.

United States Department of State. "The Multilateral Antarctic Treaty," in *United States Treaties and Other International Agreements*. Vol. 12, part I. Washington, D.C.: U.S. Government Printing Office, 1961. Gives the full and official text of the treaty.

Hayton, Robert D. *National Interests in Antarctica*. Washington, D.C.: U.S. Government Printing Office, 1959. An annotated bibliography of works on the origins and problems of the Antarctic land claims.

Shackleton, Edward. "Antarctica, the Case of Permanent International Controls," in *World Affairs*. CXXI (May, 1958). Advances the arguments in support of United Nations jurisdiction over Antarctica.

THE CIVIL RIGHTS ACTS OF THE 1960'S

Type of event: Legal: correcting racial discrimination through legislation
Time: The 1960's
Locale: Washington, D.C.

Principal personages:
JOHN FITZGERALD KENNEDY (1917-1963), thirty-fifth President of the United States, 1961-1963
LYNDON BAINES JOHNSON (1908-1973), thirty-sixth President of the United States, 1963-1969
MARTIN LUTHER KING, JR. (1929-1968), first President of the Southern Christian Leadership Conference
HUBERT HORATIO HUMPHREY (1911-1978), United States Senator and later Vice-President of the United States
EVERETT MCKINLEY DIRKSEN (1896-1969), Minority Leader in the United States Senate

Summary of Event

The Civil Rights Acts of the 1960's were passed primarily to protect the constitutional and legal status of blacks, although other minorities have also benefited from them. Blacks have unique problems in their bid for acceptance on an equal basis into society because of the long history of slavery, their high visibility, and their large numbers.

Just as the denial of equal status has a long history, so also do the efforts to end discrimination. The first major step was the abolition of slavery and the adoption of the Thirteenth Amendment after the Civil War. The Fourteenth Amendment was adopted in 1868, giving citizenship to blacks and prohibiting states from denying persons equal protection of the law or the taking of life, liberty, or property without due process of law. To complete the guarantees of citizenship to blacks, the Fifteenth Amendment, ratified in 1870, prohibited states from denying the right to vote to anyone because of race, color, or previous condition of servitude. However, the usefulness of the Fourteenth Amendment to stop discrimination was largely nullified by the Supreme Court in 1896. The case of *Plessy* v. *Ferguson* upheld state laws that required racial segregation in public conveyances and decided that "separate but equal" did not deny equal protection. The pattern of segregating blacks in public and private facilities which were commonly unequal to those provided for whites continued until 1954 when the Supreme Court in *Oliver Brown et al.* v. *Board of Education of Topeka et al.* held that facilities separated by race, in this specific case, public education, could not be equal.

There was general resistance to this decision, and in the face of the unwillingness to comply with court-ordered equality, blacks in the mid-1950's turned to boycotts in their drive to achieve equal access to public

806

accommodations. In addition to equal access to public accommodations, the movement concentrated upon securing the right of blacks to register and vote in places where they had systematically been refused this right since the end of Reconstruction.

Partly in response to these demands, the Congress in 1957 passed the first civil rights bill since Reconstruction. This Act created a commission on civil rights to investigate charges by citizens that they had been deprived of their right to vote because of race and gave the Attorney General authority to institute civil suits. Only a few cases were brought in the next three years, and there were a number of adverse court decisions which further weakened the Act. In 1960 Congress passed another Act permitting the Justice Department to bring voting suits against a state and requiring local officials to retain voting records and produce them for the federal government. The 1960 Act was only a little more satisfactory than the 1957 Act, and pressure to end discrimination continued to mount.

The movement reached a crescendo in 1963. Martin Luther King, Jr., one of the foremost leaders of the movement, began a drive against discrimination in Birmingham, Alabama, in April. It began with sit-ins, but soon turned into a confrontation, which by early May took a serious turn. By mid-May clashes spread across the South. President John F. Kennedy made a speech to the nation and called upon the people to resolve the issue. On June 19, he submitted a comprehensive civil rights bill to Congress, but it was still stalemated

there at the time of his assassination. President Lyndon B. Johnson adopted the bill as a major goal and asked the Congress to enact it as a memorial to President Kennedy. After a difficult struggle the bill passed the House only to face a filibuster in the Senate. Ending the filibuster was crucial to passage of the bill in the Senate. Senator Hubert H. Humphrey, coordinator for the civil rights forces in the Senate, knew that the support of Senator Everett M. Dirksen, the Republican leader of the Senate, was necessary to end the filibuster. Humphrey and others therefore negotiated with Senator Dirksen, and in return for some changes in the language of the public accommodation and fair employment practices sections of the bill, Senator Dirksen worked to end the filibuster. The bill was passed July 2, 1964.

The law has eleven titles, the most important of which prohibit racial discrimination in public accommodations, employment, and education. Significantly, the Act provided that federal funds could be withheld if there were racial discrimination in their use. Consequently, some federal aid to schools was withheld because of discriminatory practices of school officials.

Although the 1964 Act was extremely important in advancing the civil rights of minorities, blacks were still denied the right to vote in parts of the South. The legislation of 1957 and 1960 had not been successful in removing these abuses, but the Voting Rights Act of 1965 has proved to be an ingenious and effective protection of the right to vote. In general, the law provided for the suspension of literacy or other voting tests and gave the Attorney General the authority to appoint federal examiners to supervise registration in states or political subdivisions if fifty percent or less of the voting-age population was not registered and did not vote in the 1964 election. The day after the signing of the bill, the Justice Department announced the voting areas affected by the bill, and federal voting examiners were promptly sent. Within one year the number of blacks registered to vote in the six Southern states affected was estimated at 1,289,000.

Thus, progress was made in removing discrimination in voting, but other problem areas remained. For example, there were a number of instances in which civil rights activists were harmed and in a few cases murdered. Yet little effort was made to bring the guilty to trial, or if trials were held, they were often a farce. It was the quality of justice being meted out to those committing serious crimes against civil rights activists that led President Johnson to propose the Civil Rights Act of 1966. Even though it passed the House, it did not become law but was reintroduced in 1968 and ultimately became part of the Civil Rights Act of 1968. This bill was intended to protect a person's free exercise of civil rights. It made it a federal offense to interfere with a person's right to vote, attend public schools, obtain employment, and enjoy the facilities of hotels, restaurants, and other public accommodations. The bill also protected activists who might be urging the exercise of civil rights.

The Civil Rights Act of 1968 has perhaps become known for its fair housing provisions, which were added in the Senate as an amendment. The greatest controversy centered around the fair housing requirement for the single-family home. A compromise was reached which would bar discrimination immediately in federally owned housing and multiunit dwellings with federally insured or underwritten mortgages and would bar discrimination in multiunit housing with the exception of owner-occupied dwellings of four or fewer units beginning December 31, 1968. Not until January 1, 1970, was discrimination prohibited in single-family houses sold or rented through brokers. This was the last of the civil rights acts of the 1960's, and it is perhaps noteworthy that the vote in the House came the day of the funeral of Martin Luther King, Jr.

Pertinent Literature

Muse, Benjamin. *The American Negro Revolution from Nonviolence to Black Power*. Bloomington: Indiana University Press, 1968.

Benjamin Muse, a Fellow of the Potomac Institute, has written broadly about the problem of integration. His other books include *Ten Years of Prelude: The Story of Integration Since* *the Supreme Court's 1954 Decision* and *Virginia's Massive Resistance*. In *The American Negro Revolution* he gives a careful, detailed, and sympathetic account of the black revolution of the 1960's. The main theme of the book is the transformation of a peaceful, nonviolent, national movement shared by blacks and whites into the violence of the riots in the cities and the assassination of Martin Luther King, Jr., in the last part of the decade.

Muse thinks the impetus for the demands for equality after one hundred years of discrimination was the discovery by blacks during the bus boycott in Montgomery, Alabama, in 1956 that protest could be made successfully without the bloody retaliation of earlier times. Soon, however, the bloody retaliation did come; on September 15, 1963, a black Baptist church in Birmingham was bombed, and four little girls were killed. This was followed shortly by the use of police dogs, electric prods, and jets of water from firehoses against women and children in racial confrontations. These events were widely covered by the national press and television, and they seared the conscience of the nation to stimulate widespread support for the blacks' effort. Thus, a true national movement emerged. Although the first demands for ending discrimination came in the South and were directed against the overt system of racial segregation and denial of voting rights, demands were made in the North to end discrimination in employment and to improve the quality of housing available to blacks.

There were many features about the racial conflict of the 1960's which set it apart from earlier racial strife. At least in the early part of the 1960's, nonviolence was the predominant philosophy, in large measure because of the important leadership role of King, who was President of the Southern Christian Leadership Conference. Also, in the 1960's a wide spectrum of the black population was involved, including the traditional middle class and the educated and somewhat more militant youth. In addition to the cohesive philosophy of nonviolence and the diversity of black support, the racial encounters of the 1960's contrasted with earlier racial conflicts because they were initiated by blacks. Formerly, racial strife was precipitated by white attacks upon blacks for some perceived improper conduct by a black. Another important difference was the support of a large number of whites which is well illustrated by the march on Washington on August 28, 1963, which Muse sees as the apogee of the nonviolent first half of the decade. The large crowd of 200,000 white and black people captured the attention of the nation, and many themes of the movement were set by the speeches and songs of the march.

The movement in the 1960's gained general support because its objectives were consistent with democratic philosophy. For example, prominent demands were for the right to vote and be treated equitably. As late as 1964, blacks found voting difficult or impossible in one hundred counties in the South. Also, blacks were unable to use restaurants and other public accommodations, and Americans had been made vividly aware of this by the sit-in demonstrations. By 1963, the pressure to remove these inequities had mounted, and President Kennedy asked Congress to pass a law which would remove discrimination in education, public accommodations, and employment. There was strong opposition in Congress led by powerful Southern Senators and Congressmen who held key committee positions. Muse describes in detail the bargaining and negotiating in 1963 which contributed to the eventual passage of the bill even though it was not passed until after the assassination of President Kennedy. Muse gives much credit to President Johnson, Senator Everett Dirksen, and the clergy for the passage of the Act in 1964.

The enactment of the 1964 Civil Rights Act did not immediately solve racial problems or end discrimination against blacks. A series of boycotts was directed against the schools to protest the failure to stop *de facto* segregation. The first major school boycott was in New York City, but many cities in the North experienced such boycotts in 1964. These were countered by organized activity of whites to preserve the neighborhood school. Before the year was over, a number of cities had some rioting and looting, which usually grew from some real or alleged brutality of the police. This rioting, however, was minor compared to that which occurred in 1967 and 1968.

Just as the 1964 Civil Rights Act did not resolve the issue of racial segregation in schools in the North, it did not substantially improve the opportunity for blacks to register and vote in the South. In 1963 the Voter Education Project had added many blacks to the rolls in some areas of the South, but it had not met with any success in Alabama and Mississippi. Because of the continued disenfranchisement of blacks in those

two states, King and his organization, assisted by the Student Nonviolent Coordinating Committee, launched a major registration drive in Mississippi in early 1965. The main purpose of the drive was to encourage blacks to demand their rights and to bring their grievances to the attention of the nation. As a part of this overall effort, a march was begun to Montgomery from Selma in the spring of 1965. State troopers, acting upon orders of the Governor, stopped the marchers. When the marchers refused to turn back, the troopers charged them with tear gas bombs and night sticks. The indignation of the nation created the political climate that made possible the passage of the 1965 Voting Rights Act.

Momentous as the civil rights legislation of 1964 and 1965 was, the explosive riot in the Watts section of Los Angeles in 1965 showed that racial problems had not ended. The Johnson Administration adopted the stance that black violence was a product of deprivation and offered a series of proposals to improve the economic position and quality of life for blacks. A number of these proposals became law and together they made up the so-called war on poverty. In spite of these programs, urban violence continued with riots in Newark, Chicago, Detroit, and other cities. The public reaction to these riots was diverse: some people were still sympathetic to blacks, but others were angry and frightened. Muse has no explanation for the change from the hope and good will of the March on Washington to the riots in the cities except to acknowledge a "stubborn aversion of whites to personal association to Negroes."

Levitan, Sar A., William B. Johnston and Robert Taggart. *Still a Dream*. Cambridge, Mass.: Harvard University Press, 1975.

In *Still a Dream*, Sar A. Levitan, professor of economics at the George Washington University; Robert Taggart, Executive Director of the National Manpower Policy Task Force; and William Johnston, Research Associate at the Center for Manpower Policy Studies, assess the progress blacks have made toward the goal of equality since 1960. They rely upon data of the United States Bureau of the Census to chart the massive changes which have occurred in black income, employment, education, and housing. They analyze the impact of the Civil Rights Acts of the 1960's because the public policy established in these Acts was the end of discrimination in education, employment, public accommodations, and housing.

The task of determining whether discrimination has diminished is difficult for a number of reasons. It is hard to know whether the change in participation by blacks results from changes in discriminatory practices or some other reason. Moreover, there is an interrelationship among employment, education, and housing opportunities. Thus, the difficulty of determining diminishing discrimination in one area is complicated by the influence of discrimination in another area. For example, discrimination in housing may reduce the opportunity for equal education and employment. The analysis is further complicated because a number of programs were enacted in the 1960's to aid the poor,

and blacks benefited proportionately more from these programs because a disproportionately large number of them were poor.

The difficulty of separating the improvement which comes from reduced discrimination from other factors is illustrated by the change in the economic position of blacks during the 1960's. The median income for black families was fifty-six percent of white median family income in 1960 but increased to sixty-two percent in 1972. Although this shows improvement for blacks, their movement into better-paying and higher status jobs may be a better indicator of more equal employment opportunities. The present distribution of blacks on the occupational scale shows improvement over the 1960 picture. The clustering of blacks at the lower range of the employment ladder may have been due in part to lower educational levels, but "equalizing" education and occupation would suggest that the remaining difference in income between blacks and whites is explained in part by discrimination. Despite gains, changes in discriminatory labor market practices have not been noteworthy.

The change in discrimination in housing is more difficult to assess than in employment. More blacks owned their own homes in 1970 than in 1960—up to forty-two percent from thirty-eight percent—but their homes were worth only sixty percent as much as whites'. Also, fewer nonwhites lived in substandard units in 1970 than in 1960. But if the degree of segregation is the measure of discrimination, there was no improvement, because segregation was greater in 1970 than in 1960. Even though the Civil Rights Act of 1968 included a fair housing provision, the single-family house was not affected until 1970; therefore, the impact of the federal law could not be expected to be great during the 1960's.

Thus, serious efforts to end discrimination in housing came only after 1968, but efforts to desegregate schools began much earlier. One of the more effective enforcement tools was the authorization in the 1964 Civil Rights Act to cut off federal funds to any program practicing racial discrimination. The following year Congress authorized the expenditure of $1 billion to schools with disadvantaged children. Together, these acts set the stage for an effective attack upon school segregation, and by June, 1967, funds to 129 school districts had been cut off. Sixty of these decided to comply with nondiscrimination requirements in order to receive the federal funds. Most of these efforts were directed toward school districts in the South because the 1964 Act prohibited attempts to correct racial imbalance resulting from housing patterns. Progress toward desegregation was great in the South, with eighty-eight percent of blacks in desegregated schools by 1972 in the Southern states and the District of Columbia. The change may not have been as great as these figures indicate because there was some indication of separation of students by race once they got inside the school. The pic-

ture, however, was quite different in the central cities of the North, where segregation increased. By the end of the decade, in thirteen of the fourteen Northern cities with the largest number of black children, ninety percent or more of the black children were in majority black schools. If measures other than desegregation are used, there was improvement in the education of blacks. More blacks were going to school, graduating from high school, and attending college. But even here the picture of progress was clouded; the achievement of black children was lower than others whether measured by standardized achievement tests or as a percentage of children enrolled at grade levels below their age group. Thus, black educational advancement in the 1960's showed considerable progress although not optimum advancement.

Along with advancement in education and income, the political power of blacks increased, in part because of the Voting Rights Act of 1965. The gain in voter registration was in the South where the proportion of registered voting-age nonwhites climbed from twenty-nine percent in 1960 to sixty-two percent in 1971. Nevertheless, the larger proportion of blacks with low income and education still depressed voter participation.

The progress blacks have made in income, employment, education, and political participation paradoxically has been accompanied by an increase in divorce, separation, illegitimacy, and welfare rates. Blacks are overrepresented among welfare recipients even when their higher incidence of poverty is considered. The authors look at a number of possible explanations for this. For example, rapid technological change has reduced employment opportunities for the uneducated and unskilled, and this affects blacks more than whites. Government aid programs funneled through women and children make men more dependent and may weaken family ties. In addition, racial segregation has facilitated the development of a pervasive set of non-middle-class values. For these and other reasons, the authors conclude that continued government effort to eliminate discrimination is important. But even if its efforts are not immediately successful, they feel the process has created a momentum that will continue. — *D.F.P.*

Additional Recommended Reading

Coombs, Norman. *The Black Experience in America*. New York: Twayne Publishers, 1972. A sympathetic social-cultural treatment of blacks and their contributions and unique problems in the United States down to the present time.

Friedman, Leon, ed. *The Civil Rights Reader*. New York: Walker and Company, 1967. A collection of major documents of the civil rights movement together with important speeches.

Report of the National Advisory Commission on Civil Disorders. New York: E. P. Dutton, 1968. An analysis of the causes of the riots that occurred in the cities in the summer of 1967 and recommendations for remedies.

Humphrey, Hubert. *Beyond Civil Rights*. New York: Random House, 1968. The floor leader in the Senate for the 1964 Civil Rights Act gives his personal account of the political history of the civil rights bills of the 1960's.

Dorsen, Norman. *Discrimination and Civil Rights*. Boston: Little, Brown and Company, 1969. A legal scholar presents and comments upon the constitutional development and landmark civil rights cases.

EMERGENCE OF THE DRUG CULTURE

Type of event: Sociological: increase in drug usage among various groupings of society
Time: The 1960's
Locale: Worldwide but major focus in North America

Summary of Event

In the early 1960's, law enforcement officials in the United States and Canada believed they had the problem of illegal drugs solved. Except for a slight rise following World War II, the number of heroin addicts in the United States had been declining steadily since 1920. In all of Canada there were only twenty marijuana arrests in 1962, only slightly more in the United States. Then, suddenly, the use of drugs, particularly marijuana, mushroomed. In Canada, marijuana arrests had risen to 4,215 in 1969 and to 12,000 in 1970. In the United States, marijuana arrests by state authorities rose to 18,815 in 1965, 61,834 in 1967, and 188,682 in 1970. A Gallup poll found that in 1967 less than one percent of college students had ever used hallucinogens; by 1969 the number had quadrupled; by 1970 it had risen to fourteen percent, and by 1971, to eighteen percent. A poll in 1976 found that among eighteen- to twenty-five-year-olds, fifty-three percent had tried marijuana, twenty-nine percent had experimented with hallucinogens, and four percent had tried heroin. This increase in drug usage was accompanied by drug lyrics in popular songs, drug logos on T-shirts, at least one large circulation magazine devoted to the practice of drug-taking, and the proliferation of "head shops" marketing all varieties of drug paraphernalia. Shocked parents, journalists, and educators concluded that a drug culture had emerged.

Did a drug culture emerge in the 1960's? A closer look indicates that, in a sense, the United States has always been a drug culture. Alcohol and tobacco (which pharmacologically are drugs) have been used to excess by Americans literally since the arrival of the first colonists. Since World War II, misuse of prescription drugs such as amphetamines and barbiturates has become a problem for millions of Americans. However, there are major differences between this "traditional" drug culture and that which emerged in the 1960's. Alcohol, tobacco, and prescription drugs are legal and are used mainly by adults. The increase in drug use in the 1960's involved illegal drugs used mainly by young people.

What emerged in the 1960's was not exactly a drug culture, but rather a youth culture in which drugs played an important part. With the exception of a small number of "beats" represented by the poet Allen Ginsberg and the author Jack Kerouac, American youth in the 1950's tended to conform to the norms and values passed down to them by their parents. These norms and values were based on the Protestant ethic, a belief that hard work, virtue, and conformity were highly valued personal attributes. For a number of reasons not central to this essay, belief in the Protestant ethic began to be challenged among youth in the 1960's by what sociologists Jerry Simmons and Berry Winogard have termed the "hang-loose ethic." As they describe it,

> One of the fundamental characteristics of the hang-loose ethic is that it is irreverent. It repudiates, or at least questions, such cornerstones of conventional society as Christianity, "my country right or wrong," the sanctity of marriage and premarital chastity . . . the accumulation of wealth, the right and even competence of parents, the schools and the government . . . to make decisions for everyone . . . in sum, the establishment.

Other observers of the social scene in the 1960's noted the same phenomena but gave it different labels, some positive, some negative. A fairly typical and influential positive view came from psychologist Charles Reich in his book *The Greening of America* (1970). Reich envisioned youth of the 1960's as having entered "consciousness III," a state of mind that repudiated the materialistic base of Western society and substituted a belief in total liberation.

Along with rejecting their parents' beliefs regarding work, education, marriage, and the like, many youths in the 1960's also rejected their parent's values regarding drug usage. Influenced by persons such as the novelist Ken Kesey, who would drive into areas such as Haight-Ashbury in a psychedelic painted bus and distribute Kool-Aid spiked with LSD, and Harvard Professor Timothy Leary,

who actively promoted LSD, young people began using drugs in ever-increasing numbers. As the statistics cited earlier indicate, the real explosion occurred in usage of marijuana and hallucinogens, mainly LSD, with a much smaller increase in the usage of hard drugs such as heroin.

American society was profoundly disturbed by the youth culture in the 1960's because of the unconventional behavior and irreverent ideas that characterized it. Because one of the most visible features of the youth movement was drugs, the natural tendency was to blame all of the movement's disturbing features on drug usage. Parents felt that "my children are using drugs; my children are rejecting my values and life style; therefore, drugs are the cause of my children's strange behavior." As appealing as this view is, it is not supported by most social scientists who have studied the youth culture. They assert drugs were a symptom, rather than a cause, of changes among youth and society in the 1960's. The two reports of the prestigious National Commission on Marihuana and Drug Abuse support this position.

By the end of the 1970's, the major features of the youth culture, including its attitude toward drugs, had been integrated into the fabric of American society. Acceptance of the use of marijuana has increased to the point that marijuana laws have been referred to as "the new prohibition," indicating that harsh, repressive laws are no longer legitimized by a large proportion of the population. Statistics indicate that use of the more bizarre and dangerous drugs that became popular during the 1960's, such as LSD and "speed," has declined. However, new and sometimes more dangerous drugs, such as cocaine and PCP, or "angel dust," have appeared to take their place. Drug usage is a part of American culture and will remain so for the foreseeable future.

Pertinent Literature

Ray, Oakley S. *Drugs, Society and Human Behavior*. St. Louis, Mo.: Mosby Press, 1978.

In this well-written, nicely organized book, Oakley Ray attempts to provide an inclusive explanation of drug usage in contemporary American society. Ray, a professor of both psychology and pharmacology, utilizes material from psychology, sociology, physiology, pharmacy, and history in his analysis of drug use in America. Major sections of his book are devoted to the contemporary drug scene in America, laws pertaining to drug use, personal and social problems caused by drugs, the pharmacological and physiological action of drugs, and an in-depth analysis of each major category of drug.

Ray contends that the key to understanding drug usage in our society is the understanding that drug-taking is behavior and, as such, shares common principles with any other type of behavior. Basically, according to Ray, people engage in drug-taking behavior because it maximizes pleasure and minimizes pain. Extending this principle to the societal level, Ray argues that for a psychoactive drug to be widely used in a society, it must be integrated into and fill some need in that society. In other words, if our society were satisfactorily filling the needs of all its members, it would not be necessary for some people to take drugs to increase pleasure or decrease pain.

Ray's analysis of drugs and drug usage leads to a conclusion in which he attempts to explain the increase in drug usage that occurred during the 1960's. The increase is attributed to the complex interaction of a number of technological and social variables. Paramount among the technological variables is the faith that twentieth century Americans have developed in the ability of technology to solve all of our problems. With the rapid development of a number of "wonder drugs" during World War II, Americans began to believe that drug technology would solve a whole new range of problems. The attitude developed that if you are unable to sleep, unable to wake up, unable to lose weight, depressed, all you have to do is take a pill and the problem will be solved. Since the 1940's, Americans have relied more and more on an ever-increasing number of drugs to solve an ever-widening range of problems.

Combined with the increased availability of, and faith in, drugs, several social factors contributed to the drug explosion in the 1960's. Of major importance was the erosion that began, following World War II, of traditional standards and arbiters of behavior. Accepted patterns of behavior have been rapidly shifting, leaving fewer black and white guidelines. The traditional institutions of church, family, and school have not been able to slow this process nor have they been successful in establishing new guidelines for behavior. Closely related to this erosion of traditional behavior guidelines has been the acceptance of increased personal freedom and rights that has accompanied the civil rights and women's liberation movements. This emphasis on personal freedom has had a marked effect on what is considered moral, legal, and acceptable in the areas of sex and censorship. This emphasis on increased personal responsibility for behaviors that do not harm others, combined with the erosion of traditional behavioral guidelines, has created a social situation with few barriers to experimentation with drugs.

These technological and social factors combined in the 1960's to create an environment in which experimenting with drugs was not taboo. As more and more people began to use drugs, some of the old prejudices regarding drug use began to erode. When the common conception of the drug user was of a lower class person, a foreigner, or a derelict, it was easy to view drug use as bad, immoral, or sinful and to compartmentalize the drug, the user and the seller and condemn all three. Now that drugs are being used by white, middle-class college students, who have traditionally been thought of as good, it is not so easy to label drug-taking as sinful. This changing conception of the drug user has further eroded people's resistance to experimenting with drugs.

Ray concludes the book with a proposal for what he feels would be a rational approach to drug abuse. He suggests that we analyze the problem along two dimensions, one being whether the drug is legal or illegal, and the other being whether the drug is simply used, misused, or abused. He suggests that we not concern ourselves too much with persons who use or even slightly misuse a drug even if the drug is illegal, but rather with those persons who abuse a drug, whether legal or illegal, because these are the individuals whose life style is disruptive and expensive to society. Ray suggests that among individuals with a satisfactory relationship to society, there is a low incidence of drug abuse. Extensive drug abuse occurs only when drugs fulfill individual needs that are not being met by the society. Thus, the answer to reducing drug abuse, or at least to preventing any increase, is to modify society in ways that will provide for individuals' needs to the extent that they do not need to rely on drugs. Thus, according to Ray,

. . . the basic question in the area of drug use is one of social philosophy: what kind of society do we aspire to, how can we increase the opportunities and specify realistic, socially integrative goals for our citizens to reach out for. . . . Before any actions are taken in prevention, law enforcement, or treatment, we must answer the philosophical questions about our social goals that the drug scene has posed for us.

Unfortunately, Ray does not suggest what these answers might be.

Rublowsky, John. *The Stoned Age—A History of Drugs in America*. New York: G. P. Putnam's Sons, 1974.

This highly readable book is an attempt to explain the current drug scene in America by putting it into historical context. The major theme of the book is that the drug problem in America is more a creation of misinformation and irrational fears than of the effects of drugs upon users, or of users upon society. In order to support this argument, a succinct history of each of the major types of drugs currently used in America is given, with a careful analysis made of the actual dangers of each drug. This information is compared to the amount of effort devoted to controlling each drug's use and the severity of penalties for illegally using each drug. Rublowsky's main argument is that United States drug policy is highly irrational—some of the most socially damaging drugs—alcohol and tobacco, for example—are the least regulated, while the least damaging drugs, such as marijuana, are the most heavily regulated.

Rublowsky begins with a fairly objective description of the current drug situation in America and the society's reaction to it. What statistics are available indicate that fifty-five million Americans smoke tobacco, forty to fifty million use sedatives, stimulants, and tranquilizers, fifteen million have a drinking problem, ten to fifteen million are regular users of marijuana, one million regularly use hallucinogens, and approximately 300,000 use narcotics. In an attempt to deal with this problem, six hundred million dollars are spent annually on federal, state, and local drug programs. As indicated by the above statistics, there is no doubt that a massive drug problem exists in America today. However, according to Rublowsky, the principal problem does not stem from the effects of the drugs, but rather from the fact that they are illegal. The actual effect of drugs upon users, it is argued, is not nearly as damaging as the effects of the criminalization of drug users. The fact that drugs are illegal forces the prices to such high levels that users often must turn to crime to support their habits. Also, there is no way to control the quality of illegal drugs. This results in many deaths because of the impossibility of a user's knowing exactly what he is taking.

The author devotes a considerable portion of the book to a discussion of individual drugs from their introduction into America until the present time. Included in this discussion is a fascinating account of the ritualistic use of mild hallucinogens by native Americans before Columbus, and of how the introduction of a much more powerful drug, alcohol, totally destroyed their culture in a relatively short period of time. Chapters are also devoted to alcohol, tobacco, marijuana, opium and its derivatives, hallucinogens, and synthetic drugs such as amphetamines and barbiturates. Each chapter contains a description of the drug, its effects on the user and society, its legal status, and trends in use of each drug into the 1970's. Special attention is paid to the massive increase in drug use occurring during the 1960's.

Rublowsky concludes the book with an attempt to explain why the counterculture that emerged during the 1960's was so susceptible to drugs. Most of the blame is attributed to the trend that emerged after World War II in America of looking to drugs to solve many problems, ranging from sleeplessness to depression to obesity. Rublowsky feels that this attitude, promoted by mass media advertising of drugs, combined with the postwar baby boom, inevitably resulted in the drug explosion of the 1960's.

Rublowsky's analysis of drug use in America has one major shortcoming. The author is so determined to make the point that drug policy in America is irrational that he slants his analysis. In his discussion of the legal drugs Rublowsky overemphasizes the amount of danger from the drugs and the extensiveness of their use. When discussing the illegal drugs, he downplays their danger and use. This attitude results in a biased report that mars an otherwise fine book. — *P.R.P.*

Additional Recommended Reading

Cortina, Frank Michael. *Stroke a Slain Warrior*. New York: Columbia University Press, 1970. A sensitive journalistic description of seventeen drug addicts whom the author feels represent common "types" of drug abusers.

Coombs, Robert H., *et al.*, eds. *Socialization in Drug Abuse*. Cambridge, Mass.: Schenkman Publishing Company, 1976. A compilation of twenty-three articles that collectively analyze drug use as learned behavior that reflects the norms and life styles of a significant subculture of our society.

National Commission on Marihuana and Drug Abuse. *Marihuana: A Signal of Misunderstanding*. Washington, D.C.: U.S. Government Printing Office, 1972. A well-written, concise report, with two massive appendices, which presents the most comprehensive and thorough analysis of marijuana use available.

Grinspoon, Lester and Peter Hedblom. *The Speed Culture—Amphetamine Use and Abuse in America*. Cambridge, Mass.: Harvard University Press, 1975. A thorough, although occasionally technical, analysis of amphetamine abuse in the United States.

Johnson, Bruce D. *Marihuana Users and Drug Subcultures*. New York: John Wiley and Sons, 1973. This somewhat technical book applies sociological subculture theory in an attempt to explain patterns of drug use among American youth.

National Commission on Marihuana and Drug Abuse. *Drug Use in America: Problem in Perspective*. Washington, D.C.: U.S. Government Printing Office, 1973. A more than four thousand-page report which defines "drug abuse," analyzes underlying causes of drug use and abuse, examines how we are responding to drugs both publicly and privately, and makes a number of recommendations as to how our nation can come to grips with the drug issue.

GROWTH OF THE
SEPARATIST MOVEMENT IN QUEBEC

Type of event: Political: efforts to obtain independence through the electoral process
Time: 1960-1976
Locale: Province of Quebec, Canada

Principal personages:
RENÉ LÉVESQUE (1922-   ), Prime Minister of Quebec and
separatist spokesman
PIERRE ELLIOTT TRUDEAU (1919-   ), Prime Minister of
Canada, 1968-1979
CLAUDE MORIN (1929-   ), a political strategist for the sep-
aratists
JACQUES PARIZEAU, an economist and financial adviser
PIERRE BOURGAULT, an early separatist leader

Summary of Event

The question of Quebec's independence, which has become a major issue in Canadian politics, has its roots
in the last century. Although the
modern movement toward an independent Quebec began in the late
1950's, the earliest stirrings of separatist activities may be traced to 1837,
when Louis-Joseph Papineau, a
French-Canadian political leader, led
an abortive revolt against the British-
controlled government. The insurrec-
tion was rapidly quelled, but the
memory of the nineteenth century
rebels often served to inspire those
who envisioned an independent Quebec.

The first of the modern separatist
groups was founded in 1957 by Raymond Barbeau. Known as the Lau-
rentian Alliance, it was a politically
conservative group. A more important organization, the *Rassemblement
pour l'Indépendance nationale* (RIN),
appeared in 1960, and Pierre Bourgault emerged as its leader. Other

smaller separatist groups were also
founded; but RIN became the most
significant.

In June, 1960, the Quebec Liberal
party won the provincial elections
and launched what was later called
the "Quiet Revolution," a time of
profound change in the structure of
Quebec society. In 1963, René
Lévesque, the Minister of Natural
Resources in the provincial cabinet,
directed the nationalization of the
hydroelectric industry in Quebec.
This economic reform was followed
in 1964 by a massive reorganization
of the educational system. The entire
period of the "Quiet Revolution" was
also marked by French-speaking
Quebeckers' renewed pride in their
linguistic and cultural heritage. In
spite of the provincial government's
efforts to improve the quality of life
in Quebec, a number of Quebeckers
felt that the pace of reform was too
slow and that only independence
from the rest of Canada could pro-

vide the proper climate for change. In addition to the legitimate separatist groups already mentioned, a small band of terrorists known as the *Front de Libération du Québec* (FLQ) sought to achieve independence through violence. As early as 1963, the FLQ set off bombs in Montreal, causing political tensions to rise throughout the province. The terrorists, who did not believe in the electoral process, were condemned by all the political parties in Quebec.

This period of unrest continued, and in the fall of 1967, René Lévesque, the former Liberal Minister, declared to party members in his Montreal district that Canadian federalism as then constituted threatened the survival of French-speaking Quebec. Accordingly, he proposed that Quebec seek independence from Canada, with political separation to be followed by some type of economic union. His arguments were ultimately rejected by the Liberal Party, which favored maintaining its link with the federal government in Ottawa. Lévesque subsequently resigned from the Liberal Party and in November met in Montreal with a group interested in his proposals for an independent Quebec. Those attending formed the Sovereignty-Association Movement, which quickly absorbed RIN and other separatist organizations in Quebec. Lévesque, a former television commentator and a brilliant orator, soon emerged as the most prominent spokesman for independence.

In 1968 the Sovereignty-Association Movement became an official political party whose goals were clearly enunciated: the creation of a French-language sovereign state, the establishment of a democracy that would be not only electoral but also economic and cultural, and the negotiation of an economic treaty with Canada. In October, the separatist movement became an even more cohesive political force as the Parti Québécois was founded at a convention in Quebec City. The new party, replacing the Sovereignty-Association Movement, brought together persons from all social classes who sought a separate status for Quebec.

The year was pivotal not only for proponents of independence but also for those who favored the federalist option. Pierre Elliott Trudeau, a native of Montreal, was elected leader of the federal Liberal Party on April 1, 1968. In June, when his party won the support of the electorate, Trudeau became Prime Minister of Canada. Although he was a champion of French-Canadian language and culture, Trudeau sharply condemned political nationalism in Quebec. Accordingly, with Trudeau's victory, the battle lines were drawn for future struggles between the federalist and separatist groups.

During the next two years, FLQ terrorists continued to disrupt the normal political process in the province. On October 5, 1970, the FLQ first kidnapped James Cross, a British diplomat, and later, Pierre Laporte, a member of the provincial cabinet. Canadian Prime Minister Trudeau invoked the War Measures Act and sent federal troops into Quebec. This decision was hailed by most Canadians, but many Quebeckers believed that federal intervention was unnecessary. Lévesque, while condemning the terrorism of the FLQ, vehemently criticized Trudeau for his use of the army. Lévesque favored a negotiated settlement. The "October Crisis," as it was called, was a traumatic experience for Quebec. Pierre Laporte was eventually murdered, and the whole country mourned his death. After the crisis ended, much bitterness remained over the way the federal government had handled the problem. The separatists were sharply critical of the Prime Minister.

During the early 1970's, the Parti Québécois continued to seek reform by democratic means. In the provincial elections of 1973, the PQ won only six seats of 110 in the National Assembly, but party members were encouraged because they had won thirty percent of the popular vote. In 1973 Claude Morin, a former Liberal minister, joined the PQ and proposed separation in stages, with the question of independence to be decided in a referendum. The PQ was further strengthened when Jacques Parizeau, a highly respected economist, became the party's financial adviser. Lévesque, working with his advisers, continued to plan for the next provincial elections.

In the fall of 1976, the PQ adopted Claude Morin's strategy of calling for a referendum prior to political separation from Canada. Lévesque's earlier concept of an economic union was also accepted by the PQ. On November 15, 1976, the elections were held and the Parti Québécois scored a dramatic victory, capturing 71 of 110 seats. The PQ also won forty-one percent of the popular vote, an increase of eleven percent in three years. As a result of his party's triumph, Lévesque became Prime Minister of Quebec.

The referendum on the independence of Quebec will be held before the end of the decade. Although no one can predict the outcome, it is safe to say that Quebec will evolve in new directions. All political parties in the province now agree that Quebec's status must change, either through constitutional reform or separation. The question of which route to follow will be determined by the voters of Quebec.

Pertinent Literature

Saywell, John. *The Rise of the Parti Québécois 1967-1976*. Toronto: University of Toronto Press, 1977.

This useful account, prepared by one of Canada's leading historians, is collected from political surveys first published in the *Canadian Annual Review* from 1967 to 1975. Saywell has added a prologue and a final chapter on the victory of the Parti Québécois in November of 1976. The author carefully traces the rapid growth of the separatist movement in Quebec, relying frequently on quotations from journalists who relate the events as they happened.

In the introduction, Saywell provides the historical background for the narrative. Quebec had never fit easily into the Canadian confederation, and political independence from

Canada appeared to be a desirable option to many French-speaking natives of Quebec. The dream of separation remained merely a remote possibility until the 1960's, when the political climate in Quebec changed rapidly. Revolutionary terrorists, mostly members of the FLQ, attracted worldwide attention with their violent acts. In the long run, however, the revolutionaries were less a threat to Canadian unity than was the evolution of voter opinion. Gradually Quebeckers began to favor some form of political independence for themselves. Although many hoped to effect changes within the framework of the federal system, others saw separation as the only viable choice.

Before 1967, the separatist movement lacked a political leader who could unite diverse elements to form an effective party. When René Lévesque, the son of a Gaspé lawyer, decided to bring together those favoring an independent Quebec, the situation quickly evolved. Lévesque proved to be the catalyst that had been lacking, and the stage was set for the rise of the new party. After the prologue, the author devotes each subsequent chapter to a review of the important political events of each year, from 1967 to 1976, in Quebec. During the first two years of this period, the most significant development was the birth of the Parti Québécois and its development under the leadership of Lévesque. After resigning from the Liberal Party in the fall of 1967, Lévesque founded the Sovereignty-Association Movement, which was reborn a year later as the Parti Québécois. Early in 1968, he published a political book, *Option*

Québec, which immediately became a best seller. Although a public opinion poll in October indicated that only eleven percent of Quebeckers favored separatism, Saywell notes that the PQ already had an estimated twenty-five thousand members throughout the province. The new party continued to organize and to improve its public image in 1969.

In the chapter covering 1970, the author stresses two significant events: the provincial elections and the terrorist kidnapping of two public figures. In April the Parti Québécois faced its first electoral test as provincial voters chose members of the legislative assembly. The established Liberal party responded to the separatist challenge and won easily, gaining 72 of 108 seats. In spite of winning only seven seats, the PQ was encouraged by the fact that it had received twenty-three percent of the popular vote in its first attempt. The federalists were elated, but Saywell suggests that their optimism was premature since the seeds of political and social antagonism remained in Quebec.

In October, Quebec was faced with a grave situation when terrorists kidnapped a provincial cabinet minister and a British diplomat. Lévesque drafted a statement urging the government to negotiate with the abductors in order to free the victims. The document was signed by a group of prominent Quebeckers: businessmen, union leaders, journalists, teachers, and politicians. However, the government preferred to utilize federal troops against the terrorists. The author sees the crisis as a turning point for Quebec, and quotes Quebec journalist Claude Ryan, who wrote that the crisis "forced a basic re-examination of Quebec society and its relations with Ottawa."

In 1971, the PQ declined because the terrorists' violence of the previous autumn had been associated by some with separatist politics. In spite of this temporary setback, the PQ continued to seek independence through the electoral process. Although the party managed only modest gains in the 1973 elections, Lévesque and other PQ strategists optimistically pursued the goal of a separate status for Quebec. In the fall of 1976, their efforts were rewarded by the voters, who elected a PQ majority to the Quebec legislature.

Even when describing the often turbulent events of this period, Saywell maintains his objectivity. His judiciously balanced account provides a detailed history of this critical period in Quebec's development, and is a useful resource for scholars of North American politics.

Provencher, Jean. *René Lévesque: Portrait of a Québécois*. Toronto: Gage Publishing Limited, 1975.

This informative biography of René Lévesque provides useful insights into the man who has become the most prominent spokesman for the separatist movement in Quebec. The author uses numerous documentary sources, including several long interviews with Lévesque himself. The book, originally published in French, has been effectively translated into English by David Ellis.

The author traces the significant events in Lévesque's life from the 1920's to the early 1970's. René Lévesque was born on August 24, 1922, in New Carlisle, a small town in the Gaspé section of Quebec. His father, Dominique, was a lawyer whose passion was reading; he had a large personal library and taught René to read at an early age. At five years old, the son announced that he wanted to become a writer—a precocious intellectual development which seemed to foreshadow his later interest in journalism.

Young René grew up in a bilingual environment and was equally comfortable speaking English or French. As he matured, he observed that the large commercial fishing enterprises frequently treated the Gaspé fishermen in a high-handed manner. This arbitrary attitude left a lasting impression on the young man and led to his enduring interest in social justice.

In 1933, at the age of nine, René entered a Catholic seminary school in the town of Gaspé, where he began his French classical studies. He remained in this school until 1937, when his father died suddenly. That year René had a summer job at radio station CHNC in New Carlisle, where he served as a news editor and announcer. This experience was to prove significant when in later years he went on to a career in radio and television journalism.

After the death of Dominique Lévesque, the family moved to Quebec City, where René enrolled at Garnier College in 1938. There he gained his first experience in print journalism, writing for the school newspaper. Lévesque subsequently left Garnier and entered the Quebec City Seminary. In 1941, he enrolled in the Law School at Laval University, but left the University in 1943 before receiving his degree.

The author notes that the next phase of Lévesque's life was closely tied to the American military effort in World War II. In preparation for the impending invasion of Europe, the United States Office of War Information (OWI) was seeking a bilingual support staff; Lévesque reported to the OWI branch in Montreal for an interview, easily met the linguistic requirements, and left for London in May of 1944. He was attached to the French-language section of the American Broadcasting Station in Europe, where he edited news items and read broadcasts to the French population. In 1945, he covered the activities of American and French troops in France and Germany. Lévesque's experiences during the war provided the background for his later distinguished journalistic career.

In 1946, Lévesque returned to Québec and became a newsman for the Canadian Broadcasting Corporation. In June, 1951, Lévesque was sent as a war correspondent to cover the conflict in Korea. The event marked a turning point in his career, since his high-quality broadcast reports established his reputation as a top journalist. In 1955, he was invited to accompany Lester B. Pearson,

Canada's Minister of External Affairs, on a trip to the Soviet Union, where he became the first Western journalist to interview Nikita Khrushchev.

Lévesque later developed a television program devoted exclusively to current affairs. The program was extremely popular in French Canada and its high journalistic standards added to his outstanding reputation. The author also notes that after Lévesque interviewed French Vice-Premier Guy Mollet, the visiting statesman called Lévesque the most intelligent journalist he had ever met.

In 1960, after establishing himself as Quebec's best-known and most respected commentator, Lévesque decided to enter politics. The program of the provincial Liberal Party, which was committed to social justice, strongly impressed him, and he ran as a Liberal candidate in an urban district of Montreal. On June 22, 1960, he won a close victory and went on to serve in the provincial cabinet. In the late 1960's, he resigned from the Liberal Party and founded the Parti Québécois, subsequently becoming the leading advocate of political independence for Quebec.

René Lévesque has become the living symbol of the separatist movement. In order to grasp the complex political situation in French Canada, it is essential to have some understanding of this dynamic political leader—an understanding which Provencher's biography competently provides. — *J.J.H.*

Additional Recommended Reading

Wade, Mason. *The French Canadians 1760-1967*. New York: St. Martin's Press, 1968. A scholarly, two-volume history which provides a detailed account of Quebec's development from its origins to the "Quiet Revolution."

Dumont, Fernand. *The Vigil of Quebec*. Toronto: University of Toronto Press, 1974. A collection of humanistic essays, written by a renowned Quebec sociologist, which contains an opening section addressed to English-speaking readers who wish to understand Quebec's culture.

Rioux, Marcel. *Quebec in Question*. Toronto: James, Lewis & Samuel, 1971. The author, a separatist scholar from Montreal, defines Quebec as a colony and defends the independence movement.

Milner, Henry. *Politics in the New Quebec*. Toronto: McClelland and Stewart Limited, 1978. A slightly biased analysis of the political system in contemporary Quebec which emphasizes the significance of social and economic factors in French Canada.

Lévesque, René. *An Option for Quebec*. Toronto: McClelland and Stewart Limited, 1968. A provocative political essay containing Lévesque's arguments for a separate Quebec as well as his program for independence.

Hughes, Everett C. *French Canada in Transition*. Chicago: University of Chicago Press, 1943. A well-documented sociological study which examines the effects of industrialization on Quebec's traditional society and provides useful background for understanding the contemporary political situation.

ATTEMPTS TO CONTACT
INTELLIGENT BEINGS IN SPACE

Type of event: Scientific: efforts made to communicate with extraterrestrial life
Time: 1960 to the present
Locale: Worldwide

Principal personages:

FRANK DONALD DRAKE (1930-   ), Cornell University astronomer who pioneered the first radio telescope search with Project Ozma

ROBERT DIXON, Ohio State University astronomer who advocates searching the 21 cm. wave length for an alien beacon

VSEVOLOD TROITSKY, Soviet radio astronomer who searched for alien electromagnetic signal leakage

BENJAMIN MICHAEL ZUCKERMAN (1943-   ) and

PATRICK EDWARD PALMER (1940-   ), Green Bank radio telescope investigators who conducted a more extensive Drake-type search, Ozma II

CARL SAGAN (1934-   ), Cornell University astronomer and colleague of Drake who is famous for his SETI (Search for Extra-Terrestrial Intelligence) investigations

PHILIP MORRISON (1938-   ), Cornell University physicist responsible for much SETI investigation

GERRIT L. VERSCHUUR (1937-   ), University of Chicago astronomer who searched for alien signals on the 21 cm. wave length

Summary of Event

Are human beings the only intelligent life in the universe? This intriguing question has been philosophically explored from classical times but only seriously investigated during the last two decades. The twentieth century development of radio astronomy and scientific discoveries on planetary formation argue against the uniqueness of earth and in favor of extraterrestrial intelligence. Not until 1959, however, when two physicists at Cornell University, Giuseppe Cocconi and Philip Morrison, published a seminal article in *Nature* (a British journal) on contacting alien intelligence, did modern investigations with improved radio telescopes (parabolic dish antennae) seriously begin. Since then, about ten major searches have been publicized.

The first pioneering effort, Project Ozma, was a modest search conducted by astronomer Frank Drake in the spring of 1960 at the National Radio Astronomy Observatory in Green Bank, West Virginia. Two nearby stars, Tau Ceti and Epsilon Eridani, were monitored on the 21 cm. region of the radio spectrum, the hydrogen line. Three months of observations yielded negative results.

Though Drake's effort was tentative, since he observed only two stars on a single frequency, he concluded that there is no detectable transmitting civilization within twelve light years of earth. His conclusion, although debatable, further discouraged the many skeptics in the scientific community. At the same time, his investigation encouraged a few enthusiasts, since Drake demonstrated that existing equipment with limited data processing instrumentation could be utilized to detect artificial beamed signals of reasonable strength from space.

Eight years later at Gorky State University in the U.S.S.R., astronomer Vsevolod Troitsky and his associates observed eleven stars, including Tau Ceti and Epsilon Eridani, and scanned the Andromeda galaxy. Operating their 15 mm. wide radio dish at both 21 and 30 cm., they studied each star twice and particularly examined the 30 cm. band width, a hydrogen, water-based frequency. All the stars in our galaxy that were checked were less than sixty-two light years away and were monitored ten minutes at a time. No emissions were recorded. The Troitsky search, though wider in parameters, was similar to Drake's in targeting observations and band width restrictions, and it indicated a need for a wider scan of the celestial neighborhood.

In 1970, Soviet researchers extended their observations to a total of one hundred stars and embarked on a different observational approach. Using dipole antennae and a reflector, Troitsky and his colleagues searched omnidirectionally at three frequencies in the decimeter band for sporadic electromagnetic radiation (unintentioned leakage) which could result from extraterrestrial engineering activity. Simultaneous observations took place at two, then four, receiving stations 1,500 km. in latitude and 8,000 km. in longitude apart, in order to distinguish signals of space origin from those of earth origin. Many coincident, mainly daylight, emissions were recorded that were attributed to an interaction between solar radiation and earth's magnetosphere. None were from other stars. Assuming that an alien technology would continue to leak electromagnetic signals much as earth does via radio and television carrier waves and radar, the Troitsky group continued their search and sought ways to improve reception.

In 1973, Nikolai Kardashev, a prominent member of the group, announced that he had received an alien signal using a spiral antenna wound into the shape of a cone one meter high. The signal was later identified as terrestrial. Unabashed, Kardashev has continued his study. Overcoming or filtering out earth's noise is a most difficult task facing Kardashev and other investigators. Their listening for alien beacons and radio leakage is limited for the most part to the hydrogen- and water-based frequencies because these are low in terrestrial and cosmic noise interference.

Echoing the belief of many astronomers that communicative aliens would choose to broadcast on a low noise frequency, in 1972 Gerrit Verschuur, Professor of Astronomy at the University of Chicago, used the most sensitive 21 cm. receiving equipment available. He achieved sensitivity estimates a thousand times better than Troitsky's. At the Green Bank, West Virginia, site of Drake's study, he monitored ten stars, including Tau Ceti and Epsilon Eridani (by now standard targets) and Barnard's star. Selections were based on the stars' proximity to earth and their similarity to our sun. Verschuur used two radio telescopes with dishes 140 feet and 300 feet in diameter, respectively, which were equipped to detect a beacon with energy as low as 500 kw. Five minutes of observing time equaled four days of observation with the original Ozma equipment. However, no transmissions were detected. Hypothesizing on his failure, Verschuur conjectured that the 21 cm. wave length may not be an ideal alien broadcasting channel. It may even be kept radio-quiet, as on earth.

Later in 1972, Benjamin Zuckerman and Patrick Palmer initiated a more extensive search, Ozma II, at Green Bank, using the same antennae. Observing six hundred nearby stars with possible planetary systems like ours, perhaps all of the likely candidates within eighty light years of our sun, Zuckerman and Palmer have so far not been successful. The discouraging results may indicate that no alien civilization in our stellar neighborhood cares to contact us, or that interstellar contact does not occur on the 21 cm. wave length. As a signaling frequency, it may be too weak or too primitive.

Another study begun in 1972 by S. Bowyer and colleagues at the University of California at Berkeley makes use of a one-hundred-channel system installed on the eighty-five-foot Hat Creek radio telescope. Operating on a shoestring budget, Bowyer's search is a secondary or parasitic study that takes place in conjunction with other types of astronomical observation. In this way, the particular sky locations and listening frequencies are determined on the basis of the primary observations. While this strategy makes follow-up and scanning promising target areas very difficult, it does extend the scope of the observations.

In 1973, Robert Dixon and D. M. Cole at Ohio State University initiated a more ambitious, wider-scope survey—an all-sky search. Using the University's 100×31 m. radio telescope to search the entire 21 cm. hydrogen line for signals from a broad sweep of stars, the astronomers are still hopeful for positive results. They reason that an alien civilization desiring contact with other intelligent life will transmit signals in all directions on a wave length comparatively free from noise, or the 21 cm. wave length. Until an alien beacon is discovered, their speculation is at least as valid as Zuckerman and Palmer's contrary opinion.

Expanding listening attempts even further, Canadian researchers Alan Bridle and Paul Feldman in 1974 started monitoring the water line frequency at 1.35 cm., the wave length emitted by actual water molecules in space. Based at Canada's Algonquin Radio Observatory, they are using a 150-foot radio telescope to observe five hundred stars similar to our sun. Despite negative results, Bridle and Feldman did make a secondary discovery: they verified detection of the heaviest interstellar molecule, cyanodiacetylene (HC_5N), one of the basic components of living systems on earth.

Their discovery was particularly exciting because it renewed faith in the belief that other life forms exist because their constituents are not peculiarly terrestrial.

The most recent search, begun by Drake and astronomer Carl Sagan in 1974-1975, involved the transmission of a three-minute message consisting of 1,679 binary pulses represented by zeros and ones at a rate of ten a second to the 300,000 stars in the cluster Messier 13. The message, which was also transmitted in an all-sky sweep at Arecibo, Puerto Rico, breaks down into a pictogram of basic facts about earth. It was not a major attempt at interstellar communication, however, since it was short, targeted, and sent on a 24,000-light-year trip, a distance too great for a speedy reply.

Most of the work at Arecibo, however, involves listening for signals from nearby stars and those in the galaxies Messier 33, Messier 49, Leo I, and Leo II, on three-four frequencies, including the 21 cm. band width. This conforms to the consensus opinion that a search for extraterrestrial life (dubbed SETI) is best directed toward listening in or eavesdropping on the cosmos since human attempts at actual interstellar contact are still too feeble, inconclusive, and rudimentary to be otherwise effective.

In the face of two decades of failures, astronomers continue to envision other ground-based SETI projects. Prevailing Russian and American opinion favors the construction of at least a hundred radio telescopes to scan the skies in an approximate 16 km. cluster. To defray the cost, the mammoth signal collecting power could also be used for more precise tracking of space probes and for more detailed mapping of planetary surfaces. Labeled "Project Cyclops" in the United States because the 16 km. cluster would resemble the eye of a fly when viewed from space, the project is completely planned, but prohibitive in cost. Without Congressional approval, the project must remain on the drawing board, and astronomers in the United States must continue to maximize the use of existing instrumentation, as in 1960. The Russians may be first to build such an array. Consideration is being given in the United States, however, to further modification of existing equipment and to the use of an orbiting space telescope. Both an orbiting telescope and/or a radio telescope array on the far side of the moon would improve reception since the terrestrial noise factor would be reduced or even eliminated.

While SETI projects have been increasingly varied and incremental, the effort expended has been relatively sporadic, specialized, and conducted in rarefied scientific isolation. Speculations as to where to search, and how and why, remain unanswered. Earthlings have only tuned in to a handful of star systems on a few frequencies out of billions of possibilities. Focusing on water-based frequencies, often called the microwave window, may be especially limiting since it presupposes that other civilizations are water-based, like our own, and most likely to transmit on a commonly shared molecular band width. Also, we may wrongly assume that a civilization comparable to or more advanced than ours would communicate via radio telescopes. Radio waves are slow message carriers over interstellar distances, and communicative aliens may transmit on something better. Perhaps there is a language of space used by member planets in a galactic club that earthlings must discover and decipher before intentional contact can occur.

An overview analysis supports modification of existing radio telescopes or construction of newer ones with greater signal collecting power. Such investment may not, however, be necessary. Earth has been broadcasting its presence for decades through inadvertent leakage from FM radios, television carrier waves and radar. We may already have been discovered by alien life forms who do not consider us advanced enough to warrant their attention. On the other hand, in the absence of evidence of contact or discovery, the initiative may be left to us. While further efforts may not lead to a handshake, they may enable humans to detect signals that can be identified as artificial and therefore the product of a technological civilization. From such signals, even from a high gradient in the signals, man could hypothesize about the inhabited planet's size, rotation, and areas of population density. Such revelations, at the very least, would answer many age-old questions about the uniqueness of creation.

Pertinent Literature

Ferris, Timothy. "Seeking an End to Cosmic Loneliness," in *New York Times*. LXV (October 23, 1977), p. 31.

Ferris' article is a qualitative overview of American efforts to contact extraterrestrials. Citing a growing acceptance among the scientific community that alien intelligence exists, he covers current popular theories. The article mainly focuses, however, on the attempts of the Morrison Committee in 1977 to convince Congress that funding of a long-term SETI project is necessary.

The Morrison Committee, chaired by Philip Morrison of Cornell University, longtime proponent of interstellar communication attempts, views man's exploratory drive as an insatiable ambition that must extend to outer space. This prime motivation coupled with recent biological, geological, and astronomical discoveries of earth's formation and evolution, convinced the membership that a long-term, full time radio telescope search of the cosmos should begin at once. The overwhelming body of physical evidence favors the evolution of alien life, since the constituents necessary for life to evolve exist in the cosmos.

Philosophically, Morrison's beliefs are exciting, but they are empirically indeterminate. All SETI search results have been negative, with debatable conclusions. Scientists frequently disagree as to where to search and on what wave length. Underlying all reservations is a fear of wasting money. Still, search attempts continue; and they may be expanded by NASA (the National Aeronautics and Space Administration). Though Congress vetoed funding in 1978 of a NASA-sponsored search based on the Morrison Committee report, the original proposal is sound and not yet entirely abandoned.

Operating on a miserly $20 million budget over a period of six years, NASA envisioned a search strategy involving two teams of researchers. One team at the Jet Propulsion Laboratory in Pasadena, California, using antennae in the Mojave desert, was to map the sky visible from that point in a wide-targeted search. The second team at the NASA/Ames Research Center in Northern California would concentrate on earth's immediate solar neighborhood, star systems no more than a hundred light years away. No immediate results were expected, but the immense search of space and the time involved promised eventually to yield a message decipherment, even if that took a hundred years. A key element in the project would be perseverance, a quality lacking in so many previous studies. Though hoping an alien-beamed message would reveal the existence of a cosmic community of various planetary civilizations, Morrison theorized that at the least, a transmission would prove that an advanced technological civilization can exist and not destroy itself.

Not all astronomers are so optimistic. Ferris quotes the fear of the British Sir Martin Ryle that we may contact belligerent aliens who will attack earth. The famous American astronomer Frank Drake refutes that argument on the basis of earth's having already announced its existence through the broadcast media. He therefore sees no reason not to be more audacious and aim for deliberate contact.

Drake's optimism, as infectious as Morrison's, resulted in his formulation of an equation that estimates the number of possible communicative civilizations in our galaxy. Proven facts and intelligent speculations yield an impressive hypothesis concerning the possibility of alien life forms. The logical reaction, then, is to reach out for contact and expect to succeed. Despite his optimism, however, Ferris does not propagandize. This is an article of large ideas about a complicated task phrased in laymen's terms; but they are ideas perhaps more exciting than those entertained by Christopher Columbus and his fellow navigators.

Ridpath, Ian. *Worlds Beyond: A Report on the Search for Life in Space*. New York: Harper & Row Publishers, 1976.

This author's treatment of the question of extraterrestrial life is traditional. Detailing the origins of our solar system and the evolution of earthly life, he describes how the particular chemical and biological processes involved here can occur anywhere, under the proper conditions. His study eventually develops into a comprehensive analysis of the whys and wherefores of SETI projects and the future of space exploration. The most salient feature to emerge is the reality of a worldwide space consciousness that is ever growing in size and commitment.

In his chapter "Communicating with the Stars," he evaluates major search strategies of the 1960's and 1970's and makes suggestions on how to optimize signal reception. He considers omnidirectional scanning as too diffuse and limiting in power, and target observation as too restrictive in scope.

Ridpath favors an international aerial cluster concept, with partially steerable antennae located in each hemisphere to sweep over the galactic plane every few minutes. The project could begin with a limited area scan that would gradually extend to the entire plane as equipment was added and technology improved. On a long-term basis, the project could eventually eavesdrop on domestic alien transmissions.

While radio telescope listening is recommended, another viable transmission medium, the optical frequency, is also considered. On this frequency, lasers are shot into space on the dark lines of the spectrum via giant infrared mirrors. The signal would not be a message carrier at first, but could be recognized as artificial and therefore of intelligent origin. The possibility exists that inhabitants on light-producing planets like Jupiter would see in infrared and be more inclined to communicate on an optical frequency. However, unlike radio waves, lasers cannot be detected at all times of the day and night and in all weather. Radio waves are also more reliable than interstellar probes that travel far too slowly to be feasible.

Although he is critical, Ridpath does not discredit any ongoing strategy; rather, he suggests improvements. Interstellar communication is too young a science and too laborious an activity to be discouraged. What is needed is greater automation, with replacement of obsolete equipment to cut fatigue. Boredom resulting from listening to one star at a time could be offset by interspersing or alternating targeted searching with conventional research. By gradually expanding the operational scope of large engineering projects like Cyclops so that the facility can provide solar power during the day, scientists can justify its cost and ensure its continued existence, even if the stargazing results are dispiriting.

Assuming that communication occurs, the author summarizes the views on what type of alien intelligence we may expect to contact. At a Soviet-American Conference on SETI held at the Byurakan Astrophysical Observatory in Soviet Armenia in 1971, representatives debated the problem of semantics. A majority opinion stressed the unlikelihood that another civilization would be similar to earth's in historical background. Messages could be fully understood only if a cosmic Rosetta stone could be transmitted. We cannot even assume that mathematics as we know it is a universal. The axiomatic bases may be different on another world. Perhaps the best interpretation earthlings can make is to recognize a signal as artificial.

Another theory involves the idea of cybernetic civilizations directed by mechanical superbrains. Purely biological societies may not otherwise be able to interact over long interstellar distances; they may be far too slow at decoding and encoding messages.

Cultural differences may also be so great that the ensuing strain of physical contact would not be beneficial. Machines would not have to contend with this factor, and that would make them better emissaries.

Who or what will transmit to earth or respond to our beacons remains a ponderable science and science fiction question. The means to this two-way reception will most likely be electronic, and the message received will probably come from an ultra-long distance. Matters would be simplified if earthlings could learn a common language (called Galactic?) whereby many societies could be contacted. We can expect any contact to cause a cultural shock on earth, though the less physical the contact, the less shocking. Our ignorance about extraterrestrial life makes space a vast frontier whose probing is inevitable as scientific interest mounts; there is nothing, including international sanctions or controls, that will stop mankind from probing. The earth has become an ordinary planet in space as a result of all the space exploration to date, and a focus outward naturally follows. Man's final destiny may truly be the stars, and he may be on the verge of discovering this truism. These are some of the all-embracing philosophical ideas expressed in Ridpath's thorough coverage. Often poetic in expression, they represent an honest, unbiased appraisal of mankind's place in the universe and his future evolution. — *A.C.R.*

Additional Recommended Reading

"Eavesdropping on the Galaxy," in *Intellect*. CVI, no. 2390 (November, 1977), pp. 190-192. The prerequisites for life to exist on other planets are engagingly described.

Eberhart, Jonathan. "Giving Ourselves Away," in *Science News*. CXIII, no. 9 (March 4, 1978), pp. 138-139. Describes significance of television carrier wave leakage into outer space.

Murray, Bruce, *et al*. "Extraterrestrial Intelligence: An Observational Approach," in *Science*. CXCIX, no. 4328 (February 3, 1978), pp. 485-492. Covers the major search attempts to contact alien intelligence, using existing radio telescope antennae.

——————— . "Six Searches for Extraterrestrial Civilizations," in *Science News*. CIX, no. 9 (February 28, 1976), pp. 132-133. Six major attempts to listen to distant hypothetical planetary civilizations are analyzed.

——————— . "Searches for Intelligence Beyond Earth Continue," in *Physics Today*. XXIX, no. 5 (May, 1976), pp. 18-19. Several prominent researchers comment on types of major SETI attempts and the conclusions reached.

Sullivan, W. T., III, *et al*. "Eavesdropping: The Radio Signature of the Earth," in *Science*. CXCIX, no. 4327 (January 27, 1978), pp. 377-388. An illustrated discussion of the types of information about earth that can be gleaned from terrestrial radio leakage into space.

Thomsen, Dietrick E. "Looking for LGM's," in *Science News*. CX, no. 21 (November 20, 1976), pp. 332-333. A discussion of radio frequencies and instrumentation suited for broadcasting and receiving interstellar signals.

"BLACK HOLE" INVESTIGATIONS

Type of event: Scientific: theoretical and observational investigations of black holes as predicted by the general theory of relativity
Time: 1960 to the present
Locale: Universities and institutes in the United States, England, and the Soviet Union

Principal personages:
  ALBERT EINSTEIN, (1879-1955), the theoretical physicist who developed the general theory of relativity in 1915
  KARL SCHWARZSCHILD, the mathematician who solved the field equations for collapsing stars in 1916
  JULIUS ROBERT OPPENHEIMER (1904-1967), the atomic physicist who provided a theoretical description of black holes in 1939
  ROY P. KERR, the mathematician who provided a more precise solution to field equations in 1963
  NIKOLAI SHAKURA and
  RASHID SUNYAEV, the Soviet astrophysicists who provided theoretical studies of black holes in binary star systems
  MARTIN JOHN REES (1942-   ), the astrophysicist who did theoretical studies on black holes
  STEPHEN WILLIAM HAWKING (1942-   ), the theoretical physicist who brought together general relativity and quantum mechanics in black hole investigations

Summary of Event

In 1905 Albert Einstein developed his special theory of relativity, providing a dramatic reinterpretation of our concepts of time and space. One part of the theory involved the idea that time and space form a four-dimensional continuum. The special theory of relativity did not, however, deal with one of the most important forces in nature: gravitational attraction. In 1915, Einstein developed the more comprehensive general theory of relativity, which showed how the nature of space-time is altered by the presence of a gravitational field. In 1916, the German astronomer Karl Schwarzschild applied the new theory to the mathematical problem of describing the curvature of space-time produced by a massive collapsing star. He found that space close to the star could become so warped that it would close in on itself completely. Nothing could escape from this space-time warp, and the result was a "black hole" in the universe.

General relativity theory was mathematically very complicated and appeared to have little direct relationship to physical reality, so for many years only mathematicians and theoretical physicists were actively concerned with it. In 1939, J. Robert Oppenheimer, the American atomic physicist, worked out theoretical descriptions of neutron stars and black holes, but at the time these entities were considered to be purely theoretical. Observational astronomers thought that real stars did not collapse beyond the "white dwarf" stage—the smallest and coolest stars detectable by visible light. When quasars and pulsars were discovered in the 1960's, however, astronomers suddenly became very interested in general relativity and in the theoretical prediction of the existence of "black holes" in space.

The solution to Einstein's field equations provided by Karl Schwarzschild in 1916 had assumed that black holes were static. However, stars and galaxies rotate, and a more realistic mathematical model of the black holes, incorporating rotation, was needed. In 1963, mathematician Roy P. Kerr published a solution to the field equations including rotation and thus laid the basis for further investigations. One consequence of this solution is the idea that rotating black holes may form "bridges" between otherwise separate universes. This mathematical conclusion is, however, highly idealized, and does not necessarily represent physical reality.

Astronomers now faced the challenge of trying to test the theory observationally. In 1964, two Russian astrophysicists, Ya. B. Zel'dovich and O. Kh. Guseynov, proposed a method for detecting black holes. A black hole on its own could not be detected, but one accompanied by a visible star in a binary system could be studied through its influence on its companion. The gravitational attraction of the unseen black hole should produce a Doppler effect, a shifting of the visible light wavelengths, in the spectrum of the visible star. The Soviet astronomers searched through catalogues of binary star systems and finally found five possible black holes; none, however, could be identified with certainty. In 1968, Virginia Trimble and Kip S. Thorne of the California Institute of Technology revised and extended the Zel'dovich-Guseynov list; but again, none of their cases was definite. All could perhaps be explained by other hypotheses.

The next method for identifying the black holes involved X-ray astronomy. Theorists suggested that turbulent gases orbiting and being gradually sucked into black holes should emit X-rays. These could not be detected from the ground because they would be absorbed by the earth's atmosphere. Rockets would be needed.

In 1970, a satellite named "Uhuru," the Swahili word for "freedom," was launched into orbit off the coast of Kenya, in celebration of the seventh anniversary of Kenyan independence. It carried two X-ray telescopes, and, as it orbited the earth, it sent back signals each time an X-ray source was detected. By 1974, over 160 separate X-ray sources had been found.

None of the new X-ray sources coincided with those that astronomers had selected from the star catalogues. At least six of the new ones, however, were binary sources. One of them, "Cygnus X-1" in the constellation of Cygnus the Swan, seemed a particularly good candidate. According to theory, a black hole must have at least three times the mass of the sun, and Cygnus X-1 qualifies in that respect at least twice over. It is invisible, but its companion star is a blue supergiant. Astronomers believe that the gases given off by the giant star emit X-rays as they fall into Cygnus X-1, a black hole. Even in this case, however, there may be other explanations for what is observed. Different astronomers hold rival theories, but the "black hole" hypothesis seems to offer the simplest explanation.

In 1971, astrophysicists began to make detailed theoretical studies of binary star systems. The first investigations using Newtonian gravitational theory were carried out by Nikolai Shakura and Rashid Sunyaev at the Institute of Applied Mathematics in Moscow, and by Martin J. Rees at the University of Cambridge in England. Later analyses in the Soviet Union and the United States were done on the basis of general relativity. All suggested similar structural models for the relationship between a supergiant star and a black hole in a binary system.

These studies suggest that the gravitational attraction of a black hole pulls gases from the giant star, and these gases then go into orbit around the black hole. Centrifugal and gravitational forces flatten the orbiting gas into a thin disc (called the "accretion disc"), like a giant version of the rings of Saturn. Friction between different layers of the gas generates temperatures greater than one million degrees Kelvin, and the hot gases then emit X-rays. The gases slowly spiral in towards the black hole and disappear into it when they reach its

edge, or "event horizon." The accretion disc of Cygnus X-1 is about two million miles in diameter, whereas the black hole itself is probably only twenty miles in diameter.

In order to make more detailed studies of black holes, astronomers will need more information about X-ray sources in the sky; they are now eagerly awaiting results from the launching of High Energy Astronomy Observatories in the 1980's. These spacecraft will be capable of very sensitive observations which may result in the discovery of numerous black holes scattered through space. Meanwhile, astrophysicists are continuing their theoretical investigations. The black holes discussed above may be termed "normal"; the existence of supermassive and miniholes has also been suggested. British astrophysicist Stephen Hawking has investigated the behavior of mini black holes, probably formed at the creation of the universe in the "big bang." Hawking's major contribution has been to bring together general relativity and quantum mechanics in the investigation of black holes. According to the laws of quantum mechanics, tiny black holes will gradually destroy themselves by emitting particles and radiation. A mini black hole in the process of dying would not be "black" at all, but a fireball powerful enough to supply all the energy needed by the earth for several decades. At the same time, it would be small enough to fit inside the nucleus of an atom. We do not know what the future investigations of black holes may bring; we know only that these invisible entities are likely to offer some of the most exciting discoveries in the scientific exploration of our universe.

Pertinent Literature

Asimov, Isaac. *The Collapsing Universe: The Story of Black Holes*. New York: Walker, 1977.

Isaac Asimov, with more than one hundred books to his credit, has well earned his reputation as our most popular and prolific science writer. This new book on black holes is probably the best starting point for the general reader. Asimov hates to leave anything unexplained; he begins at the beginning, which in this case means with an explanation of the structure of the atom and the forces within it. Concepts such as "density" and "gravitation," which are often taken for granted, are here given careful attention.

Asimov then discusses the gravity, density, and formation of the planets. Having started with relatively familiar objects, he moves on to the stars and explains the nuclear reactions generating the heat and light of the sun, which is simply our closest and therefore most familiar star. Normally, these nuclear reactions produce enough heat to balance the gravitational forces pulling inward. As a star runs out of nuclear fuel its core contracts, while the outer regions expand enormously; fusion reactions then occur at the center of the star, creating iron nuclei. As these thermonuclear reactions dwindle and fail, gravitational forces predominate, and the star will collapse into a "white dwarf" and gradually cool.

The more massive a collapsing star, the more forcibly it will shrink, and the more tightly it will compress the electronic fluid at its core. Stars more than 1.4 times the mass of our sun will collapse with such force that the electrons and protons in the electronic fluid will be smashed together. Protons and electrons will combine as neutrons; the dense, collapsed star will then be composed entirely of neutrons and be known as a "neutron star."

In a neutron star, gravitational forces are balanced only by the nuclear force which holds the neutrons apart. If the mass of the original star is sufficiently large, however, even these nuclear forces will be unable to oppose the gravitational pull, and the star will go on collapsing indefinitely. As it continues to contract, the gravitational force at its surface will continue to increase, until nothing—not even a ray of light—will be able to escape. Such a supercollapsed object would therefore be invisible and would be known as a "black hole."

Asimov describes a number of theoretically possible ways of detecting the existence of black holes. First, he mentions the effort to detect gravitational waves, as predicted by Einstein's theory. American physicist Joseph Weber claimed to have found gravitational waves in the 1960's, but others have so far been unable to confirm his results. Another possible technique involves the attempt to detect the curvature of light from a galaxy as it passes close to the intense gravitational field of a black hole; this, however, has never been observed. A third method involves detecting the X-rays which should be given off by turbulent clouds of gas and dust spiraling towards a black hole. The X-ray sources already found at the center of some globular clusters of stars may be evidence of black holes. A very compact and energetic source of X-rays has even been found at the center of our own galaxy, suggesting that a black hole is present. (Astronomers are, however, unlikely to conclude that this is the case until they have been able to rule out all other possibilities.)

Another method of detecting black holes involves the existence of binary stars—two stars that revolve around each other. If both are black holes, a double X-ray source should be observed, and several X-ray binaries are now known. If only one of the pair is a black hole, we should be able to detect one visible star and one X-ray source. Such a pair was found in 1971 by the satellite Uhuru in Cygnus X-1 and its companion, a blue supergiant star. Cygnus X-1 is invisible but too massive to be either a white dwarf or a neutron star. The evidence suggests that this invisible object is indeed a black hole.

Asimov ends with an entertaining gallop through recent cosmological speculations: the "big bang," the oscillating universe, the Cosmic Egg, the white holes, and the wormholes of imaginative theorists. He concludes with what is perhaps the strangest idea of all: that the entire universe is a black hole, and that its apparent oscillations are but "the unimaginably slow breathing cycle of a universe-sized black hole." Asimov's lively style, his sure grasp of the theoretical literature, and his determination to leave no scientific concept unexplained, make this book an admirable introduction to the subject of black holes.

Kaufmann, William J. *Relativity and Cosmology.* New York: Harper & Row Publishers, 1977.

This book gives a brilliantly simple account of Einstein's general theory of relativity—the essential background for understanding black hole concepts and their importance for modern cosmology. Popularizers of relativity theory are often tempted to present it as absurd or fantastic, with examples of astronauts getting younger inside shrinking spaceships; their readers are impressed at the cost of remaining mystified by the peculiarities of scientific theory. Kaufmann manages to avoid all this, and instead presents relativity as absolutely logical. Indeed, he successfully shows how relativity can make "common sense."

Kaufmann explains why general relativity is now the center of interest in astronomy, and is indeed required in order to explore the implications of new observations made since the 1960's. For astronomers, the concept of a four-dimensional space-time continuum is especially important. Distances, for example, are commonly measured in units of time; a "light year" is the distance traveled by light in one year. Thus, if we look at an object one light year away, we are really looking at it as it existed one year ago. Most astronomical objects are, of course, much farther away, and therefore we see them as they existed much longer ago; we see their history. Kaufmann liberally sprinkles his book with space-time diagrams, which are very helpful in learning to perceive events in a relativistic framework. He explains basic concepts of relativity, such as the idea that gravitational fields are manifested by a curvature of four-dimensional spacetime, and clearly describes the three classical observational tests of general relativity. He suggests that the beauty and simplicity of Einstein's theory are arguments for its validity.

From this point, Kaufmann goes on to describe the processes of stellar evolution and the theoretical prediction that if a star of sufficiently great mass continues to contract it will eventually become so dense that it will form a black hole. Its gravitational field becomes so strong that space-time folds in over itself, and the star thus "disappears" from the universe. Kaufmann explains in considerable detail the behavior of light rays (photons) in the highly warped spacetime surrounding a black hole. Light rays passing by the black hole will be deflected by gravitational attraction; if aimed at exactly the right angle, they will actually go into orbit around the black hole. Light rays approaching more closely will spiral into the center and disappear.

Kaufmann provides remarkably clear explanations of the implications of the Schwarzschild and Kerr solutions to Einstein's field equations. The Penrose diagrams he uses are a means of visually presenting spacetime in such a way that the reader can understand the relationship between the concepts without necessarily following the mathematics involved. Kaufmann also briefly explains the observational attempts to identify black holes, discusses the discovery of quasars, and describes the effort to detect gravitational waves. The final chapters are devoted to theories of the shape, creation, and fate of the universe. He presents the possible geometrical models of the universe very clearly and concludes that the evidence favors a "flat," or Euclidean universe. He also explains why most astronomers now accept the "big bang" theory of the origin of the universe. The "big bang," or primordial explosion, is thought to have occurred about fifteen billion years ago, and to have started the continuous expansion of the universe.

An alternate approach to cosmology is the Hoyle-Narlikar theory developed in the mid-1970's. This involves a reformulation of general relativity theory to include the idea that the masses of particles are increasing with time. This approach permits a complete reinterpretation of the structure and behavior of the universe. It implies that the universe is not expanding; the galaxies are simply growing smaller and farther apart with time. In contrast to the "big bang" theory, this has been called the "whisper cosmology." Readers who closely follow Kaufmann's explanations will gain as complete an understanding of current astrophysics as is possible without mathematical expertise. — *E.F.*

Additional Recommended Reading

Kaufmann, William J. *The Cosmic Frontiers of General Relativity*. Boston: Little, Brown and Company, 1977. A more detailed version of the text reviewed above.

Penrose, Roger. "Black Holes," in *Scientific American*. CCIII (May, 1972), pp. 38-46. A brief, clear description of the concept of black holes.

Thorne, Kip. "The Search for Black Holes," in *Scientific American*. CCV (December, 1974), pp. 32-43. Discussion of attempts to identify black hole candidates.

Hawking, Stephen. "The Quantum Mechanics for Black Holes," in *Scientific American*. CCVIII (January, 1977), pp. 34-40. A brief introduction to the quantum mechanics of mini black holes.

John, Laurie, ed. *Cosmology Now*. New York: Taplinger Publishing Company, 1976. A series of papers by theoretical astronomers, originally given as talks on the British Broadcasting Corporation (BBC).

Berry, Adrian. *The Iron Sun: Crossing the Universe Through Black Holes*. New York: E. P. Dutton, 1977. Cosmological speculation about the future possibility of using black holes for intergalactic space travel.

Taylor, John G. *Black Holes: The End of the Universe?* New York: Avon Books, 1978. A professor of mathematics explains black holes and ponders their implications for the basic questions of human existence.

Moore, Patrick and Iain Nicolson. *Black Holes in Space*. New York: W. W. Norton and Company, 1976. A clear popular account of the concept of black holes.

Golden, Frederic. *Quasars, Pulsars, and Black Holes*. New York: Charles Scribner's Sons, 1976. A lively discussion of modern astronomy, including a chapter on black hole investigations.

Friedman, Herbert. *The Amazing Universe*. Washington, D.C.: Special Publications Division National Geographic Society, 1975. Lucid text and gorgeous color photography; several sections on black holes.

Sullivan, Walter. *Black Holes: The Edge of Space and Time*. Garden City, N.Y.: Anchor Press/Doubleday, 1979. An engrossing account of one of the great mysteries of astronomical science.

CÉSAR CHÁVEZ ORGANIZES THE FARM WORKERS

Type of event: Sociological: first successful unionization of agricultural workers in
  American labor history
Time: 1960 to the present
Locale: California

Principal personages:
  CÉSAR CHÁVEZ (1927-   ), President of the United Farm
    Workers (AFL-CIO)
  DOLORES HUERTA (1930-   ), Vice-President of the United
    Farm Workers Organizing Committee
  LARRY ITLIONG, Assistant Director of the United Farm
    Workers Organizing Committee
  FATHER THOMAS MCCULLOUGH, an active supporter of farm
    worker unionization
  FATHER DONALD MCDONNELL, a priest who taught César
    Chávez methods of organizing
  FRED VAN DYKE, the first major grower to support farm
    worker organization
  FRED ROSS, head of the Community Service Organization,
    whose methods were used by César Chávez in community
    organizing

Summary of Event

One of the most remarkable developments in recent labor history has been César Chávez's successful drive to unionize agricultural workers in California. Long a bastion of resistance to unionism, California growers and their businesses have been brought increasingly under collective bargaining agreements with Chávez's United Farm Workers of America, AFL-CIO. This union organizing drive has extended far beyond economic demands alone. Chávez's movement marks the confluence of trade unionism, community organization, and ethnic consciousness.

California has long been the center of the richest, most powerful agricultural businesses in the United States. Increasingly since 1900 the family farm has come to characterize California agriculture less and less. In place of the traditional family farm, California agriculture is marked by the operation of corporate farms—operations owned by outsiders and firms with no background in farming. As a result, California agriculture has been labeled "agribusiness," and has reached a scale of operations and landholding far more extensive than farming operations in other parts of the country. This fact has presented obstacles to effective union organizing drives prior to that of Chávez. Unlike factory entrances, which are usually few in number and easily leafletted by union organizers, California agribusiness operations extend over

842

peripheries as extensive as twenty-five or thirty miles, leaving union organizers with no focal point for leafletting. Picketing can only by thinly spread surrounding a typical field. Thus the physical aspects of the "factories in the fields" have traditionally hindered the movement toward unionization of agricultural employees.

There have been significant additional barriers to unionization of California farm workers. Of key importance has been the historic ethnic and racial heterogeneity of the farm labor force. Vastly different groups have entered the farm labor market in great waves. In the days of the California Gold Rush (c. 1848), native-born Anglo-Americans entered farm work as the gold fields were played out. Simultaneously Chinese laborers moved into the fields. Following the Chinese Exclusion Act (1882) the growers looked to another Oriental group—the Japanese—for a "tractable" labor force. As the Japanese developed their own farms and businesses, the growers in this century have relied on Mexicans, Filipinos, and itinerant Americans (both black and whites) for workers. Heterogeneous labor markets are difficult for unions to penetrate.

There have been few concerted attempts to organize this polyglot labor force in this century. In the 1910's, the Industrial Workers of the World (IWW) made the first union soirees into California agriculture. But the IWW had distinct liabilities in approaching farm workers. The union was overtly radical in outlook, fanning intense employer opposition for the IWW's stand against private enterprise. In a seminal strike against the Durst Farm in 1913, IWW-inspired strikers were attacked by vigilantes, though it was the union leaders who were later imprisoned for long terms on conspiracy charges. The IWW also failed to establish permanent locals, reacting rather to crisis situations only. One final liability was that few IWW organizers were from the ranks of farm workers. California criminal syndicalism statutes, coupled with Federal surveillance of the IWW nationally during World War I to ward off sabotage, marked the effective end of the IWW attempt to unionize California's farm workers.

During the turbulent years of the 1930's, Communist trade unionists made a second attempt to organize agricultural workers. Party-run unions affiliated with the Trade Union Unity League set out to organize workers ignored by the craft unions of the American Federation of Labor. The TUUL-affiliated Cannery and Agricultural Workers Industrial Union led a series of massive and often violent strikes against California growers in 1933. These strikes generally led to increased wages. Yet the CAWIU had its own set of liabilities not dissimilar to those of the IWW. For example, Communist union leaders did not come from the rank and file of the farm labor force. The typical farm worker responded to the CAWIU for bread and butter increases in the piece rate, not to Marxism. As a result, the Communists did not succeed in building permanent locals. Workers responded to the CAWIU in crisis situations such as wage cuts, but not for the long run; and the Communists were, of course, subject to intense employer opposition.

Apart from radical unions, the regular labor movement began to turn its attention to organizing farm workers after the founding of the Committee (later Congress) of Industrial Organizations, the CIO. From 1937 through 1961, the CIO attempted through numerous organizing drives and a variety of CIO affiliates to unionize California agriculture. All of the CIO campaigns failed, though for reasons different from the IWW or CAWIU failures. When the CIO began a concerted attempt to organize in the late 1940's and early 1950's, it did so lacking the fervor and commitment that had typified earlier CIO organizing drives. By the time the CIO approached farm worker organization, its outlook was that of "Big Labor" in the postwar era. Union organizers were paid professionals, not rank and filers or amateurs. They seldom had had *any* experience with unionizing outside industrial cities. Despite massive amounts of money spent in numerous union campaigns, California farm workers could not be unionized by the labor leadership of the 1930's. A movement developing independently from the CIO would ultimately successfully unionize California agriculture. That movement would rise from the ranks of the farm workers themselves and be led by César Chávez.

Chávez was born in 1927 in Yuma, Arizona. His father was a Mexican immigrant fleeing the turmoil that characterized Mexican society after the revolution of 1910. The Yuma property belonged to Chávez's grandfather. During the 1930's, misfortune beset Chávez's family and property which it owned in Yuma was lost. Chávez joined his father as the elder Chávez became an itinerant farm worker. Itineracy forced young Chávez to change schools thirty times before he was obliged to drop out during the eighth grade. Chávez then joined his father as a field hand. He took part along with his father in several of the strikes of the 1930's and 1940's, when the "seed of unionism" was planted in his mind. Chávez was, above all else, indigenous to the rank and file farm workers—a crucial advantage in his future union work.

Beyond Chávez's union experiences, however, the genesis of what would become the United Farm Workers lies outside the AFL-CIO. Several major forces beyond unionism contributed to the ultimate success of the UFW. The first of these contributions was made by a handful of dedicated Roman Catholic priests through the 1950's and early 1960's. Most notable on behalf of the farm workers was Father Thomas McCullough, known as the *bracero* priest for his active social work among temporary Mexican immigrants brought to the California fields by the controversial *bracero* programs. Under these programs, Mexican nationals had provided the growers with a pool of low-paid nonunion workers living in squalid poverty. Another notable priest, Father Donald McDonnell, taught César Chávez the Church's teachings on social justice and the right of workers to organize, along with a crash course in labor history. Both priests broke important ground in organizing the Mexican-American community and they pioneered the use of the house meeting to organize workers away from the work place. A great contribution was also made by Fred Ross, with his Community Service Organization, who brought Chávez into his first concrete experiences in community organizing. The CSO employed the methods of Saul Alinsky (the founder in Chicago of The Back of the Yards Organization and The Woodlawn Organization) in organizing communities into agencies directed toward wide-ranging social change.

Based on such training, Chávez's first organizing work in Delano, California, was quite successful. He was both a field hand and a member of the Mexican community; he fused economic improvement, community improvement, nonviolent social change, and ethnic pride in organizing his first group, the Agricultural Workers Association, in 1960. Extending beyond this base, Chávez by 1962 had made connections with the Agricultural Workers Organizing Committee, an AFL-CIO group that had its strongest base among Filipino farm workers under the leadership of Larry Itliong. In 1965, the AWA and the AWOC merged to form the United Farm Workers Organizing Committee with the official support of the AFL-CIO.

The union scored its first victories in securing contracts with some of the largest agribusiness grape growers. It did so after a protracted strike, running from the late 1960's into the early 1970's, marked by competition from the Teamsters, who were "softer" on the growers, and a well-organized UFW-sponsored nationwide boycott of nonunion table grapes. By the early 1970's the union had successfully concluded collective bargaining agreements with most major grape growers and wineries, covering an estimated twenty-five percent of all farm workers in California. The jurisdictional dispute with the Teamsters was resolved by mutual agreement in 1974, which left the UFW with exclusive jurisdiction over the field hands employed by California growers.

The UFW continues to grow in strength and attract support. A lettuce boycott has produced some successful UFW contracts and the union plans to extend benefits of unionism to farm workers throughout the state of California and ultimately to farm workers throughout the nation. The union cause has been joined by Dolores Huerta, a remarkably effective organizer of female field hands. In many ways Chávez's crusade shares the features of earlier labor movements such as impoverished rank and file membership, charismatic leadership, and idealism—all qualities not associated with contemporary successful "Big Labor."

Pertinent Literature

London, Joan and Henry Anderson. *So Shall Ye Reap*. New York: Thomas Y. Crowell Company, 1970.

Most of the literature about the rise of the United Farm Workers is dominated by biographies of Chávez. The record consists of books primarily by journalists active in covering the UFW from the Delano Strike (1965) onward. The assessment of the UFW by labor historians will, by and large, be a development of the future. At present, London and Anderson's book is the only scholarly coverage of the UFW available. Joan London is the daughter of novelist Jack London and has been publications editor for the California Federation of Labor for many years. Henry Anderson holds advanced degrees in sociology and public health. Together, London and Anderson have produced a fine work in social history or historical sociology.

In their analysis, the rise of Chávez's union marks the culmination of what sociologists call a social movement, in this case a social movement directed at changing basic conditions for the farm workers. Chávez's success, however, has been the result of all the previous attempts to unionize agribusiness. London and Anderson trace this long history extremely well. They begin with the development of lush California agriculture through intensive irrigation techniques. They describe vividly the multicultural work force that evolved in the fields through

time and all of the abortive attempts by radicals and by the regular labor movement to organize this labor market. The authors also systematically debunk various racist myths that have been used by the growers to rationalize and justify the extreme exploitation that traditionally characterized farm work.

The authors then explain the development of Chávez's movement along with its immediate antecedents, using a generally biographical approach; the book closes with detailed chapters on key personnel in the rise of the UFW: Father McCullough, Dolores Huerta, Ernesto Galarza, Fred Van Dyke (a grower who supported Chávez), and, of course, Chávez himself. These biographical chapters are excellent and give the reader a real sense of what it was like to be there during the unionization drive.

The sole weakness of this account is its age: it misses the developments of the 1970's. Nevertheless, as a profile of the entire course of farm labor history, written by participants and observers of the movement in recent decades, *So Shall Ye Reap* is a succinct, scholarly, and informative account of the highest order.

Taylor, Ronald B. *Chávez and the Farm Workers*. Boston: Beacon, 1975.

This book typifies the many available biographies of the charismatic leader of the UFW, César Chávez; it has the advantage of a 1975 publication date, which allows it to take into account recent UFW triumphs and setbacks. The author, Ronald B. Taylor, is a journalist who works for

the Fresno *Bee*. He is the author of one prior book on farm labor problems, *Sweatshops in the Sun: Child Labor on the Farm* (1973).

Taylor's book, like so many others about Chávez, is sympathetic to the UFW. Chávez as a subject seems to evoke this support from most people who have had contact with him (except the growers). Following a discussion of Chávez's 1974 union activity, the author traces Chávez's life from his youthful involvement with the labor movement of the 1930's and 1940's. The book is constructed using the interview technique. It gives readers an intimate view of Chávez as both a public and private figure. What emerges is the career of a modest, unassuming, rank and file farm worker and his meteoric rise to leadership on the crest of a wave of social activism. What success the UFW has attained has yet to change César Chávez, unlike other union leaders in American labor history whose life styles were changed radically by their careers. Chávez remains an idealist, driven by a deep concern for social justice and by a nonviolent organizing approach in the face of intense employer violence. He is typical of the charismatic leaders who usually emerge during periods of rapid social change, such as Mohandas K. Gandhi or Martin Luther King, Jr.

This sympathetic account accurately portrays Chávez as he is. In addition, Taylor somehow gained interviews with key growers, who are given ample space in this book to express their extremely hostile views of Chávez and the UFW. The book ends with the still-current uncertainty about UFW's future. The Teamsters could still renege on their no-raiding pledge which would be to the advantage of the growers. Also unclear is the government's future policy of *bracero* programs. If reenacted, the *bracero* approach could once more flood the farm labor market with underpaid, nonunion Mexican nationals; the *bracero* movement had been extremely destructive of past farm worker unions. Facing these possible future uncertainties, César Chávez and his union remain, sustained by faith and idealism: *Nosotros venceremos!*
— *E.A.Z.*

Additional Recommended Reading

Matthiessen, Peter. *Sal Si Puedes: César Chávez and the New American Revolution*. New York: Random House, 1973. An expanded version of a two-part series in the *New Yorker*, with good background on Chávez and his union.

McWilliams, Carey. *Factories in the Field: The Story of Migratory Farm Labor in California*. Boston: Little, Brown and Company, 1939. The classic work on early California farm unionism.

Day, Mark. *Forty Acres: César Chávez and the Farm Workers*. New York: Frederick A. Praeger, 1971. A participant-observer study covering the years 1967-1970 written by a socially conscious Catholic priest.

Fodell, Beverly. *César Chávez and the United Farm Workers: A Selective Bibliography*. Detroit: Wayne State University, 1974. Extremely important compilation since so much of UFW history is covered in periodicals rather than full-length books.

THE CHANGING SOCIAL CONTRACT

Type of event: Political: shift in public perception of its relationship to government
Time: 1960 to the present
Locale: The United States

Summary of Event

social contract *n* [trans. of F *contrat social*]: an actual or hypothetical agreement among individuals forming an organized society or between the community and the ruler that defines and limits the rights and duties of each
—*Webster's New Collegiate Dictionary*

This is the definition of what originally was the catchword for Jean Jacques Rousseau's radical-democracy, but it has since come to be associated with John Locke's liberal-democracy. Rousseau held in *The Social Contract* (1762) that when "each of us puts his person and all his power in common under the supreme direction of the general will, and . . . we receive each member as an indivisible part of the whole," then this act of association by each contracting party "creates a moral and collective body composed of as many members as the assembly contains votes." There is no hint of *quid pro quo* here, simply the suggestion that the consent of each to abide by the group's determinations is justified by virtue of everyone else having consented to do the same. It is a matter of right procedure.

Locke, on the other hand, writing in 1690 was more concerned with the substance of the contract, with its guarantee that the government—conceived of as separate from society—uphold the law of nature which dictates that "no one ought to harm an-

other in his life, health, liberty, or possessions." This natural law, being *a priori*, is present even in the precivil state of nature; however, "a known and indifferent judge, with authority to determine all differences according to the established law," is absent. Thus men form a political contract in order to obtain an impartial, and thereby just, implementation of the substantive prohibitions in the law of nature. "The great and chief end of Men's uniting into Commonwealths, and putting themselves under government," wrote Locke, "is the Preservation of their Property." The Founding Fathers, of course, followed Locke's political theory to its final conclusion when they wrote in the Declaration of Independence that "whenever any Form of Government becomes destructive of these ends [Life, Liberty and the pursuit of Happiness], it is the Right of the People to alter or to abolish it, and to institute a new Government."

In the election of 1964, a full forty percent of the voters supported Barry Goldwater's individualist-conservative challenge to the mainstream's New Deal liberalism; in 1968, nearly fifteen percent turned out to vote for George Wallace's third-party populist challenge from the right (though clearly he would have drawn many more voters had he been running on a major party's ticket); in 1972, again approximately forty percent expressed their dissatisfaction with mainstream policies by supporting George McGovern's populist challenge from the left. And 1978 brought a property-tax revolt as well as an unprecedented surge of public-worker strikes. What has been happening during the last two decades to call forth such forms of protest from the public? Why are the "Nifty Fifties" merely a faint memory to be recaptured only by television's *Happy Days*, radio's oldies-but-goodies, and Hollywood's *Grease*? Why the felt need to catch Saturday Night Fever, dance Disco-Mania, experience Close Encounters, and be Born Again? Why the remake of the Depression-era diversion of King Kong, the return to The Wizard of Oz, the resurrection of Superman?

Hard times—here is perhaps the main reason. People are seeking some escape from the harsh socioeconomic realities of today. And harsh realities they are, including such facts as the following: From 1950 to 1970, the percentage of self-employed persons has been cut in half. Between 1960 and 1973, aid to families with dependent children has increased almost seven hundred percent; yet the proportion of the average annual AFDC family payment to the median family income has been declining. Median family income, adjusted for inflation, was at practically the same level in 1978 as it had been in 1967, even though the number of working wives increased from forty percent in 1970 to forty-six percent in 1977. Catastrophic illness involving as few as two weeks in a hospital could bankrupt eighty-eight million Americans who have either inadequate health insurance protection or else none at all. Only one-fourth of the families in 1976 could afford a new home at the median price of $44,200 compared with one-half who could afford the $23,400 median-priced home in 1970. Real purchasing power dropped between 1973 and 1978 by six percent. Nothing like this has happened since the Great Depression.

It is no wonder, then, that a Roper survey released by the Labor Department in September, 1978, concluded, "What is new . . . and alarming is the finding that unlike all previous measures, the public feels things are not going to get any better in the future." More people now than at any time since World War II believe that the government is failing to keep its part of the bargain, failing to protect the life, health, liberty, and possessions of the citizenry. In fact, whereas only fifteen percent of the public saw the government in 1959 as "the biggest threat to the country in the future," nearly half the public saw it so in 1967 and in 1978. Much has indeed transpired since the 1950's— so much that the state of affairs as we entered the 1970's led David Rockefeller to observe in the *Wall Street Journal* that "in view of the emerging demands for revision of the social contract, a passive response on the part of the business community could be dangerous."

The most recent political manifestation of the public's changed attitudes is the passage of the Proposition 13 referendum by a two-to-one vote in California. California's property taxes were cut on June 6 of 1978 by an average of roughly fifty-five percent; and three months later, a *Los Angeles Times* poll found that more Californians were liking Proposition 13 than earlier had (though naturally those Californians, a third, who had experienced cutbacks in services were liking it less). True, much of the support for the proposition reflected the fact that California had the fourth highest per capita property tax among the states and that lost local property-tax revenues could be regained from the state's substantial budgetary surplus. Nevertheless, support for a cut in local property taxes has been found to exist nationwide, and by the same overwhelming margin as on the West Coast. One *caveat* is in order, however. A CBS-*New York Times* poll reveals that fully half of those favoring property tax cuts do so in the belief that "fat could be trimmed but public services wouldn't have to be." And an ABC-Lou Harris poll found that most would *oppose* such cuts if it meant reducing spending by thirty-five percent on *any* of several public services. The responses ranged from over fifty-five percent opposed to the cuts if it

so affected "the number of teachers in public schools" to over seventy percent if it similarly affected "aid to the elderly, disabled and poor." Thus the tax revolt represents more than simply a rejection of New Deal liberalism. It is an expression of frustration with government's will or ability to deliver the goods it promises—goods that the people regard as their due as taxpaying members of the American political system.

Hence we see the dramatic doubling of the forty percent who in 1958 thought "the government wastes a lot of the money paid in taxes" to the eighty percent two decades later. Whether "waste" is the main reason that so much tax money is spent in ways that fail to provide the public services desired is, of course, open to question. But there is no doubt that the strains on the "social contract" in the 1960's and 1970's have made many people declare that they are completely disillusioned with the way government is handling fiscal problems. Demands for improvement will probably continue to grow.

Pertinent Literature

O'Connor, James. *The Fiscal Crisis of the State*. New York: St. Martin's Press, 1973.

Our modern "warfare-welfare" state, says O'Connor, is undergoing a fiscal crisis that neither taxing nor borrowing can substantially alleviate. Government expenditures are outrunning revenues at greater and greater rates, and this fiscal crisis is rooted in our present political economy. The expansion of the state sector is the counterpart of the growth

of the "monopoly sector"—that portion of the economy composed of firms whose scale of production is the largest and whose control over their markets is the greatest. Both sectors have grown at the expense of the competitive sector. But the state has benefited little if any from its own expansion.

The government's expenditures are

described by the author as essentially serving the interests of the monopoly sector. Giant corporations, relying primarily on advanced technology for production, create surplus labor and surplus capacity. In other words, they are able to produce more than consumers can afford to consume. True, owing to the presence of strong unions and the corporation's ability to translate increased wage-costs into higher prices, monopoly-sector wages are the highest; but this simply means that competitive-sector workers are caught between low incomes and high prices. Thus, the monopoly-sector's products cannot be bought as fast as they can be made and consequently capacity utilization rates go down, profits suffer, and stagnation begins. Enter the government. By socializing many of the costs of physical and human investment—such as highways, utilities, office buildings, education, and research—the government contributes to the maintenance of profits. Profits are also sustained by the government's military expenditures. But these items represent only the more visible part of the monopoly-sector's pressure on government to spend. There are indirect pressures as well.

The competitive sector, for example, with its labor-intensive production and comparatively low profit rates, has had to turn for help to the very government that has contributed so much to the ever-encroaching growth of the monopoly sector. Competitive businesses, small businessmen, and farmers seek protective legislation (for example, fair-trade laws and right-to-work laws) and also financial aid (loan guarantees and farm subsidies) in their losing struggle against both big labor and big business. Yet the most notable recent surge in public spending has been in another area of "social expenses of production." O'Connor points out that the surplus labor created by the capital-intensive monopoly sector, namely, technological unemployment, is transferred to the competitive sector, where capital productivity (hence profits) is increased mainly by the cutting of labor costs. This influx of technologically unemployed then further depresses the position of competitive-sector workers, who already earn relatively little, often not enough to put them above the poverty line, or else work only intermittently, if at all. Competitive-sector workers thus increasingly turn to the state for economic assistance. And so—aside from the aged, the widowed, and the disabled—the rise in the welfare budget is actually another example of state spending rooted in the growth of the monopoly sector. Aid to families with dependent children would be largely eliminated if there were enough decent-paying jobs available to keep potential breadwinners from having to abandon their families in order to qualify for this aid. The state, then, is called upon to spend for not only the growth of the monopoly sector, but the disruptions this sector causes in the competitive sector as well.

The main problem with having the state undertake these expenditures is, continues the author, that it costs more per unit done than in the monopoly sector. For while the state (like the monopoly) sector is relatively insulated from market forces, it is so as a result not of control over the market but instead by its ability to tax and borrow at will. Thus the state finds itself paying for nearly everything it uses at rates effectively determined elsewhere. Defense contracts are the best-known illustration. But certainly no less important is the cost of public labor. Wages in the state sector are, for a variety of reasons, driven toward the high wage levels existing in the monopoly sector. The monopoly-sector wages, however, are artificially high; for unions in that sector have implicitly accepted the introduction of labor-saving innovations (even if this yields long-run technological unemployment) in return for wages pegged to productivity and the cost of living—the latter being especially important since increased wage costs are passed along to the consumer in the form of inflation. State wages tend to lag behind monopoly wages precisely because they are rising in order to approach the artificially high rates found in the more efficient sector. But the state (postal service excluded) cannot increase its prices to get additional revenue. It must borrow more or tax more.

O'Connor's analysis is therefore useful in providing a perspective by which to assess the recent surge of public-worker strikes. At the end of the summer of 1978, some thirty-five

thousand teachers were on strike, involving almost a million schoolchildren—four times as many teachers and children as were affected at the same time the year before. When firemen struck in Memphis, they were joined by police, who ignored a court order to go back to work; the mayor called in the National Guard. About fifty-five percent of the nation's half-million police department employees are represented by unions or similar organizations. "In the old days," says the head of the largest organization of police officers, "they didn't want to have anything to do with labor unions for their security. But with Proposition 13 out on the West Coast, they know . . . they are in trouble." Opposition to public-employee strikes has increased; about sixty-five percent are now against allowing policemen or firemen to strike, up by more than ten percentage points from 1975. As taxpayers, most of the people want nothing that will add to their tax burden. Yet for many of the millions who work in the service-oriented state sector, striking for higher pay to help offset the inflation issuing from the monopoly sector is—in the face of the present fiscal crisis—the only way left for them to try to make ends meet.

Miller, Arthur H. "Political Issues and Trust in Government: 1964-1970," ("Comment" by Jack Citrin, "Rejoinder" by Miller) in *American Political Science Review.* LXVIII (September, 1974), pp. 951-1001.

In the article covering 1964 to 1970, Miller concludes that "support" for the federal government has decreased substantially—as indicated by sharply declining trust in government by both whites and blacks, but especially the latter—and that the decreased trust is partially related to changes in attitudes toward two salient issues, namely, racial integration and the Vietnam war. He also concludes that those favoring "centrist" policies are less cynical politically than those preferring noncentrist policy alternatives, and that the relatively high level of cynicism among noncentrists is explained by their dissatisfaction with the policies of *both* parties. Furthermore, data trends suggest that the continuation of centrist policies will cause trust to continue its decline, making it more difficult to carry on centrist politics and thus raising the probability of "radical" political change.

Citrin accepts Miller's view that policy-related discontent is a source of political cynicism, but he questions the *validity* of the trust-in-government scale, the *impact* of cynical attitudes on behavior, and the *conclusion* that a continuation of so-called centrist policies will inhibit the restoration of public confidence in the American political system. Miller's index of trust consists of five items that ask about how much the government can be trusted to do what is right; how crooked, how wasteful, and how smart are the people in government; and whether the government is "pretty much run by a few big interests looking out for themselves" or else is it "run for the benefit of all the people." Crosstabulating this index, as Citrin does, with attitudes toward our form of government shows that only a fourth of those with the lowest level of trust in government "can't find much about our form of government to be proud of" or think that "change in our whole form of government is needed to solve the problems facing our country." Citrin thus concludes that the trust index seems to be measuring mere disapproval of incumbent political leaders rather than alienation from the political regime—a conclusion buttressed by crosstabulations showing relatively high correlations between political trust and attitudes toward candidates and incumbents.

But regardless of whether the trust scale is really measuring attitudinal support at the level of regime or of the authorities, there is the question of whether the *behavior* of politically cynical persons is much different from those more trusting. Citrin's contention here is that mistrust in government, as operationalized by Miller, produces neither political activism nor political apathy, which he believes "reinforces the argument that many cynical responses merely record opposition to incumbent officeholders or largely ritualistic expressions of fashionable clichés." And if this is the case, the basis of his third and final quarrel with Miller's article has of course been firmly established. For if the position is accepted that expressions of discontent are either behaviorally meaningless and/or systemically irrelevant, it then follows that a continuation of centrist policies will in no way interfere with the possibility of the public's trust in government being restored. Quite the contrary; all that may be needed, as Citrin says, is "a modest 'winning streak' and perhaps some new names in the lineup." Furthermore, using 1972 data, he holds that it can no longer be said that those who feel that *neither* party offers viable policies are among the most distrustful citizens.

Miller's "Rejoinder" naturally seeks to refute Citrin's points by offering evidence that declining trust in government *does* signify a lessening of confidence in the political system itself, that political disaffection *does* influence behavior, and that political cynicism *does* result from dissatisfaction with centrist policies. The institutional rather than simply incumbent focus of the evaluation represented by the trust index is shown in two ways: cynics are much more likely than others to believe that elections (or parties) do not make the government "a good deal" responsive; and, cynics are substantially more likely to believe that "change in our whole form of government is needed." The behavioral impact of trust in government is demonstrated in several ways: the simplest involve turnout, direction of the vote, and voter images of the candidates in the 1972 election. The most striking way, however, involves the finding that in 1972, not only are the cynical social-change advocates more likely than the trusting ones to approve of various forms of political protest, but the cynical social-control advocates dissatisfied with policies are also considerably more likely to approve of protest than their trusting counterparts.

Finally, the inability of centrist policies to restore political trust is suggested by the fact that even though President Richard Nixon was a popular incumbent, from 1970 to 1972 the association between dissatisfaction with Republican—or Nixon's—policies and political cynicism stayed the same for Republicans. Obviously, then, to use Miller's words, "much more than a friendly face in the Oval office is necessary for government to be judged responsive and trustworthy." And no doubt President Jimmy Carter is now learning that this is all too true. — *E.G.D.*

Additional Recommended Reading

Gallup, George H. *The Gallup Poll: Public Opinion 1972-1977.* 2 vols. Wilmington, Del.: Scholarly Resources, 1978. A complete compilation of the surveys conducted by the American Institute of Public Opinion, 1972-1977.

Harris, Louis. *Confidence and Concern: Citizens View American Government.* Washington, D.C.: U.S. Government Printing Office, 1973. Report of a Harris survey which measured confidence in various institutions, issues of concern, public involvement with government, the perceived operation of government, and what the public wants the government to do.

Institute for Social Research, University of Michigan. "Political Trust Stays Low as Economic Attitudes Worsen," in *ISR Newsletter.* II, no. 3 (1974). Notes that as of autumn, 1974, even those persons who still have high political trust are becoming increasingly cynical about how the government is handling worsening economic problems such as inflation and unemployment.

——————— . "Watergate Crisis Had Indirect Impact on Deteriorating Trust in Government," in *ISR Newsletter.* III, no. 3 (1975). Examines trust in the Presidency, Congress, and Supreme Court, 1972-1974.

Kolko, Gabriel. "Working Wives," in *Science and Society*. XLII (Fall, 1978), pp. 257-277. Statistically based, historical-oriented analysis of the effects of working wives on the structure of the working class, which effectively challenges a number of commonly held beliefs regarding socioeconomic trends in America.

Mosley, Hugh. "Is There A Fiscal Crisis of the State?," in *Monthly Review*. XXIX (May, 1978), pp. 34-45. Takes issue with several of O'Connor's "fiscal crisis" theses, arguing that his competitive *versus* monopoly sector distinction is unrealistic, his political analysis flawed, and his view of the structural limits of state expenditures inaccurate.

Pechman, Joseph and Benjamin Okner. *Who Bears the Tax Burden?* Washington, D.C.: The Brookings Institution, 1974. Short, figure-filled study that explores the actual distribution of taxation at the federal, state, and local levels, using a number of alternative calculations based on various assumptions concerning tax incidence.

Stern, Philip. *The Rape of the Taxpayer*. New York: Random House, 1973. Explains the operation and results of the federal income tax "loopholes" in terms the average reader can understand, often through hypothetical examples that supplement the actual figures generously supplied.

EMERGENCE OF CONSUMER AWARENESS

Type of event: Sociological: movement to gain consumer protection through legislation
Time: 1960 to the present
Locale: The United States

Principal personages:

RALPH NADER (1934-   ), author of *Unsafe at Any Speed* (1965), and consumer advocate

ABRAHAM A. RIBICOFF (1910-   ), Chairman of Senate Subcommittee on Executive Reorganization

ESTES KEFAUVER (1903-1963), United States Senator, and coauthor of Kefauver-Harris Drug Amendments

JOHN FITZGERALD KENNEDY (1917-1963), thirty-fifth President of the United States, 1961-1963

LYNDON BAINES JOHNSON (1908-1973), thirty-sixth President of the United States, 1963-1969

Summary of Event

The consumer awareness movement of the 1960's and 1970's has been variously depicted as a unique event on the American scene, as the third phase of a movement which began almost one hundred years ago, and as a logical culmination of a movement which began with the Mail Fraud Act of 1872. Each view has merit. The movement reached new and unprecedented heights in the Ninety-first and Ninety-second Congresses, in each of which more than one hundred consumer-oriented bills were introduced in comparison to the twenty-five consumer laws passed in the previous ten years. Yet, the consumer movement is traceable to the late 1880's. However, because of apathy, only eleven pieces of legislation favorable to consumerism were passed in the years from 1872 to 1959.

There are many theories to account for the intense change witnessed in this sphere, from the overall social climate, to the economic changes wrought by a change from an agrarian economy to a postindustrial society, to a political change from a pro-industry government to one which takes on more responsibilities toward individual citizens' rights. Some analysts posit the necessity of dramatic events to bring unsavory conditions to the public's attention and/or muckrakers to focus the public's eye on these conditions, while others feel individual heroes are needed to lead public opinion. All of these factors are evident throughout the movement.

The first consumer legislation passed in the United States was the Mail Fraud Act of 1872, which made it a federal crime for anyone to use the United States mail to defraud others. As is the case in most legislation, the act was the result of a demonstrated need. The problem always has been to demonstrate such need strongly enough to withstand the powerful lobbying forces of major groups with vested interests. The passage of the 1906 Pure Food and Drug Act and the Meat Inspection Act was motivated not by the unsanitary conditions of food handling and processing and the marketing of dangerous and unproven patent medicines, but by a combination of the hard work of Dr. Harvey W. Wiley of the Department of Agriculture and the exposé of Upton Sinclair's book *The Jungle*, in which the horrendous conditions of the meat-packing industry were so graphically detailed. Again, the 1938 Federal Food, Drug, and Cosmetic Act was given impetus by two shocking events: the 1933 publication, *100,000,000 Guinea Pigs*, a detailed account of the dangerous products of many major companies as well as the obviously fraudulent companies; and the Elixir Sulfanilamide scandal in 1937, in which more than one hundred people died after taking the elixir which had not been pretested before being put on the market. But these cases were short-lived ones which ended with watered down legislation giving the public a false sense of security.

The only hero who stands out as a persistent consumer advocate in the past is Dr. Harvey W. Wiley, the head of the chemistry division of the Department of Agriculture in the last decades of the nineteenth century. More than any other individual, he was responsible for the passage of the Pure Food and Drug Act through his incessant research into the adulterations being introduced into foods and patent medicines and his never-ceasing publicizing of his findings.

More illustrative of the persistence of the consumer movement are the consumer groups which have survived to the present day. The first consumer organization was the National Consumers League organized in 1899 to press for food and drug legislation and child labor protection. Consumer Research, organized in 1928, and Consumers Union of 1936, are still in existence today and publishing their respective bulletins.

World War II slowed the consumers movement which had been gaining some momentum under Franklin D. Roosevelt's New Deal, and the period immediately after the war was devoted to catching up materially. It was an era of rapid technological change and increasing prosperity accompanied by a politically conservative mood. President Eisenhower's Administration, staffed largely by business executives, yielded few advances for consumerism. Proposed Truth in Lending legislation was feared by the business community and was consequently staved off. Ironically, one advance achieved during this era was in medicine. Rather than force large segments of the public into the embarrassment of declaring poverty, it was decided to make the Salk polio vaccine free, thus letting "socialized medicine [in by] the back door," according to the Secretary of Health, Education, and Welfare, Oveta Culp Hobby.

With John F. Kennedy's election to the presidency in 1960, things began to change. Part of the reason was that the time was right. The movement had been stalled for many years during which the greatest technological advances (especially in television with its all-pervasive advertising) had occurred to clutter the marketplace with an unprecedented array of competing products for a more affluent public. Consumerism was reviving all over the world. In 1960, Consumers Union of the United States joined consumer organizations of London, Australia, The Hague, and Brussels as charter members of the newly formed International Organization of Consumer Unions (IOCU) to foster the interchange of techniques and test results.

Although President Kennedy personally did not accomplish much in tangible results, he gave a precedent-setting message to Congress calling for four basic consumer rights: "the right to safety, the right to choose, the right to be informed, and the right to be heard."

Other public officials were leading the fight for consumer legislation, such as Senator Estes Kefauver, who fought the Pharmaceutical Manufacturers Association and the entire drug industry for four years for passage of the 1962 Kefauver-Harris Drug Amendments requiring pretesting of new drugs, generic labeling, and the filing of new drugs with the Pure Food and Drug Administration. He was aided in his efforts by the then-developing thalidomide scandal in Europe, where human fetuses had developed phocomelia—short stubs like flippers instead of arms and legs—after their mothers had taken thalidomide. A similar tragedy was averted in the United States because the Pure Food and Drug Administration had refused to approve the drug.

Another involved legislator was Senator Abraham Ribicoff, who helped bring Ralph Nader to promi-

nence by calling him as a witness before his committee's automobile safety hearings. Senators Philip Hart, Gaylord Nelson, Walter Mondale, and Warren Magnussen were also involved in advancing the cause of the consumer.

Probably the most important catalyst for the consumer movement of the 1960's, however, was Ralph Nader. Nader's book *Unsafe at Any Speed*, published in 1965, arraigned the automobile industry for its lack of concern for automobile safety. In the course of the investigation, it was learned that General Motors, whose Corvair came under the most severe attack in Nader's book, had hired a detective agency to investigate Nader's private life in efforts to discredit him. This revelation, possibly more than Nader's actual testimony, solidified public opinion and led to the passage in 1966 of the National Traffic and Motor Vehicle Safety Act which, for the first time, gave the government the authority to dictate safety standards for new and used cars and tires.

Subsequent to the hearings, Nader has taken up other consumer causes and organized his "Nader's Raiders," who investigated the Federal Trade Commission and issued a report in 1968. In the same year, he set up the Center for the Study of Responsive Law, in Washington. D. C. In 1970, his Raiders investigated the Interstate Commerce Commission, the Federal Food and Drug Administration, and various areas of concern such as air pollution, airline safety, nursing homes, and the medical profession. With the proceeds from his successful law suit against General

Motors, he established the Public Interest Research Group (PIRG), which has subsequently spread to several college campuses throughout the country, so that by the mid-1970's the individual groups in twenty-six states numbered fifty-eight with a membership of 500,000 students on 135 college campuses.

President Lyndon B. Johnson also took up the cause of consumerism and exhorted Congress to pass an unprecedented amount of legislation in his State of the Union message of 1968; and he let industry know he intended to continue pushing hard for such legislation. His Great Society program was a return to New Deal-type consumer interests.

In addition to the popular successes of Nader and other consumer activists, the time was now propitious for consumerism. The public was more educated, more affluent, and had more leisure time. Products had become much more sophisticated and complex, while quality control of the mass production process failed to keep pace. Finally, inflation led to increased quality expectations which were not realized, resulting in more consumer frustration.

By the late 1970's, governmental regulatory agencies had proliferated so that there now exist a Consumer Product Safety Commission, an Environmental Protection Agency, an Occupational Safety and Health Administration, a National Transportation Safety Board, as well as numerous agencies in the various state and local levels and in the private sector. There are laws to regulate prescription drugs, medical devices, and over-the-counter medicines; a new law regulates the building and safety of mobile homes; federal laws establish standards for the safety of automobiles and for the recall of those found to be unsafe; another law clarifies warranty coverage; and the Truth-in-Lending Act requires full disclosure of annual interest rates. Many voluntary advances have also been achieved: many corporations have established consumer relation departments, and are more responsive to consumer complaints; some insurance companies are writing their policies in clear, unambiguous language; and the American Bar Association House of Delegates voted to allow advertising for legal services if such advertisements are "presented in a dignified manner."

So far has the consumer movement advanced that some of its efforts have been counterproductive. Federal bureaucracy has burgeoned so that the Food and Drug Administration's 1977 budget was $245 million for a staff of 7,600. Besides complaints of the cost which must be borne by higher taxes, critics claim that overregulation has set American medicine back ten years behind that of Britain, and that it is delaying medical breakthroughs. The Consumer Product Safety Commission, established in 1972, is criticized as slow and inefficient. After four years the Commission had set only three product safety standards. The Commission's action in mandating children's night wear to be fireproof led to the use of Tris, a chemical retardant later found to be carcinogenic. The Truth-in-Lending Act left loopholes which caused some lenders to increase credit charges or begin to charge interest where they had not previously. The 1974 Employee Retirement Income Security Act was so complicated that it is estimated that 10,000 companies terminated pension plans rather than comply. The 1975 Magnuson-Moss Warranty Act led to weakened warranties in some cases and the dropping of warranties in others.

Although the consumer movement has gained unprecedented advances in the 1960's and 1970's, the inefficiency and cost of the large government bureaucracies may lead to a waning of the movement. Combined with the widespread tax revolt of the late 1970's, the attitude of the public toward increased government control over too many areas of modern life may mandate a return to less protection of the consumer through governmental edict.

Pertinent Literature

Haskins, James S. *The Consumer Movement*. New York: Franklin Watts, 1975.

James Haskins puts consumerism in its overall context, tracing it back to the Middle Ages when the marketing process was much simpler than in modern technological societies. Originally, most transactions were conducted between neighbors, or at least in a person-to-person manner in which the buyer dealt directly with the purveyor of goods. In such a face-to-face dealing, the buyer had the ability to examine the merchandise, and if he later felt deceived he could deal directly with the vendor. The amount of goods was severely limited, so the buyer's choice was not as difficult as it is in the present day. It was under such circumstances, Haskins points out, that the dictum of *caveat emptor*, or "let the buyer beware," originated. From the time the consumer had to deal with middlemen, or sellers who were not neighbors or personal acquaintances, according to Haskins, the selling transaction has been loaded in favor of the seller.

The consumer movement in the United States is traced to the first consumer protection legislation passed in the 1800's, beginning with the Mail Fraud Act of 1872. Haskins recounts the major legislation of the nineteenth century, which was not very voluminous despite the fact that more than one hundred bills were introduced into Congress before the Federal Food and Drugs Act was passed in 1902. The problem was that the consumer had little power to counter the industries which effectively lobbied against government regulation. Those major bills which were passed were usually as a result of a notorious scandal or an effective muckraking exposé of conditions in an industry, such as Upton Sinclair's *The Jungle*, which led to the passage of the Meat Inspection Act of 1906.

Haskins emphasizes the importance of the advent of advertising as a large business in itself in the 1920's. Advertisements in newspapers, magazines, billboards, and the infant radio industry gave an impetus to proliferation of products and goods as well as convinced the public of their desire for such goods. In 1928, Consumer Research was organized to "compare, test and evaluate products and to publish its findings" in its magazine, *Consumer Bulletin*, a publication which continues to the present day under the name of *Consumers Research Magazine*. Though Consumer Research and its splinter group, Consumers Union, are still thriving, Haskins says their efforts were insufficient. What was needed, in his opinion, was a new consumer awareness and heroes to lead the movement.

This awareness was supplied by television and its proliferation of advertisements which, in turn, led to rising costs of products as well as greater diversity of competing products, many of which are virtually indistinguishable to the layman. For example, Haskins points out, one half of the paper products available today were not in existence fifteen years ago. In the 1960's, agitation increased for new consumer laws; new consumer groups were formed, letter writing campaigns to congressmen were organized, and newsletters informing the public of unfair selling practices were published.

The most important impetus, in Haskins' opinion, was the emergence of a hero, and that hero was Ralph Nader, who charismatically gained the public's attention when it was disclosed that General Motors had had private detectives investigate his personal life to discredit his attack against the automobile industry. Haskins credits Nader with convincing the public that government regulatory agencies not only did not serve the public, "but actually worked against, the public interest." He then recounts Nader's activities in investigating government agencies and industry.

Next, Haskins delves into the various industries of concern to the consumer movement and recounts the advances gained in each through government legislation. The areas covered are the automobile, clothing, toy, food, drug, cigarette, and credit industries. In each of these he considers the gains in the four areas of concern: "Safety, Quality, True and Fair Advertising, and Price."

In a chapter devoted to "Big Business," Haskins gives six stages that business usually follows in countering the attacks of consumers, including absolute denial, discrediting of critics, creation of public relations departments, intense lobbying, and formation of fact-finding studies, before actually responding to consumer demands. This last stage, he feels, is usually in response to court decisions and legislation.

Haskins' final chapter looks to the future and gives advice to consumers on what they can do as individuals. He lists various publications which inform the public, as well as newspapers and magazines which have consumer-oriented complaint columns. He also points out the various state and local consumer protection organizations. Although he speaks as an advocate for consumerism (most writers on this subject take involved positions for or against consumerism) and favors continuing vigilance on the part of the public, he shows some optimism in the greater education of the public, especially in specific high school and college courses which have been inaugurated as a result of the movement.

Bishop, James, Jr. and Henry W. Hubbard. *Let the Seller Beware*. Washington, D. C.: The National Press, 1969.

Bishop and Hubbard consider consumerism as a "revolutionary change in attitude of its practitioners," rather than as revolutionary economics. In their view, consumerism has gone through three distinct phases in the United States, each phase with its own characteristic hallmarks.

The first phase began as a result of a system which spawned "robber barons" who held the public in thrall because of the increasing distance between buyers and sellers. The sellers had all the power. The first legislation affecting consumers was the Sherman Antitrust Act (1890), which was instigated, according to Bishop and Hubbard, for the benefit of industry, as were all the early laws regulating industry. The Interstate Commerce Commission (1887) likewise was not to protect citizens as consumers so much as to protect the producers of manufactured goods from being manipulated by the transportation industry. In 1914, the Federal Trade Commission and the Clayton Anti-Trust Act were primarily designed to help industry and were only indirectly in the consumers' interest. Only the Pure Food and Drug Act and the Meat Inspection Act were passed with consumers primarily in mind.

The second round of consumer legislation, beginning in the 1930's, was marked by the emergence of independent consumer groups and the Sulfanilamide scandal. Because of the marketing of Elixir Sulfanilamide without previous testing by the chemical company, hundreds died after taking the lethal mixture. Congress was induced to strengthen Pure Food and Drug legislation in the ensuing publicity created by the publication *100,000,000 Guinea Pigs* by Frederick Schlink and Arthur Kallet in 1933.

The current round of consumerism began in the 1960's, but is traced to the 1950's when four thousand deaths were attributed to the London pollution in 1952. These deaths dramatically illustrated the potential dangers of environmental pollution.

In Bishop and Hubbard's analysis several factors influenced the beginning and cessation of each round of consumerism: a dramatic or catastrophic event which brought the dangers to the public's attention, and a major war which diverted attention from the problem. In addition, they point out a strong correlation between a President committed to consumer interests as opposed to one dominated by commercial interests.

A key impetus given the current consumer movement was the election of President John F. Kennedy. In 1962, Kennedy issued the first consumer message to Congress ever. In the same year, Rachel Carson's book *Silent Spring* further clarified the problems of ecological damage being done. But most significant to the cause of consumerism in 1962 was the thalidomide scandal in Europe. The United States was spared such a catastrophe because the Pure Food and Drug Administration had refused to relent under intense lobbying of the drug industry and approve the drug for the United States. Ralph Nader's

Unsafe at Any Speed, which assailed the poor safety record of the automobile industry, and the subsequent Senate hearings on automobile safety thus culminated an ever-growing public awareness of the plight of the individual consumer against unregulated big business.

After presenting such an overview of the consumer movement, the book analyzes each phase of consumerism, showing those areas they have in common and those in which they differ. The authors express a hope and belief that the current phase differs qualitatively from the two previous ones largely in the fact that the current leaders of the movement are "advocates, not reformers"; that is, the antibusiness muckrakers of the past have been replaced by concerned individuals who are not out to change the economic system but are dedicated to the idea that "enlightened selling practices are just as much in the best interests of corporations as they are of the consumers." Thus, they believe consumer advocates such as Ralph Nader will have a longer lasting effect on consumerism than advocates of the past. They point out that Nader, for example, has turned to other areas of concern, such as gas pipelines and X-ray radiation hazards. The enactment of much consumer legislation already adds to the probability that the consumer movement will endure. The author points out that as a result of stronger legislation, government and major corporations are now more responsive to consumer complaints. Three letters from private citizens eventually led to the recall of 80,000 automobiles, and five letters about defective tires led to a congressional hearing on the subject.

As is usual in such books, Bishop and Hubbard became advocates of the cause in presenting some of their ideas on where the consumer movement should direct its energies in the future. They point out that many areas are still in need of reform (at the time of printing). They are still not satisfied with the gains in automobile and tire safety. The need for more regulation of drugs and foods, especially meats, fish, and chicken, is vividly illustrated with examples of shortcomings in these industries. Other areas of benign neglect such as door-to-door salesmen, moving firms, and the lumber industry, are called to attention.

The authors call for a reevaluation of the advertising industry in its broader social context. They point out that advertising as we understand it today is still an essentially young industry which has grown from spending virtually nothing (they trace modern advertising as a distinct industry in the United States to the 1880's) to a total annual budget of $200 million in less than one hundred years. They plead that advertising has not provided consumers proper information to make a valid choice among competing products and that the industry should face the questions of what moral responsibilities it has to the public. — *R.A.G.*

Additional Recommended Reading

David, Nina. *Reference Guide for Consumers*. New York: R. R. Bowker, 1975. An annotated bibliography of all media materials dealing with the consumer movement, with cross references and separate indexes of authors, titles, and subjects covered.

Faber, Doris. *Enough! The Revolt of the American Consumer*. New York: Farrar, Straus and Giroux, 1972. A popularized account of the consumer movement stressing the personalities involved, beginning with Dr. Wiley's work in the Department of Agriculture in 1883.

Consumer Protection: Gains and Setbacks. Washington, D. C.: Congressional Quarterly, 1978. Individual reports evaluating the consumer movement's actions along with an up-to-date assessment of the status of consumerism in legal services, antitrust activities, media reform, health and smoking, job safety, and related issues; with bibliographies.

Gaedeke, Ralph M. and Warren W. Etcheson. *Consumerism: Viewpoints from Business, Government, and the Public Interest*. San Francisco: Canfield Press, 1972. Selection of essays representing viewpoints of various concerns dealing with the history of consumerism and related topics, with appendices containing major legislation.

Nadel, Mark V. *The Politics of Consumer Protection*. Indianapolis: Bobbs-Merrill, 1971. Traces the political history of the consumer movement in an attempt to prove that liberal democratic policymakers are more responsive to consumer-related interests.

McCarry, Charles. *Citizen Nader*. New York: Saturday Review Press, 1972. Covers Nader's political life and the areas of consumer movement in which he and his cohorts have been involved.

Peterson, Mary Bennett. *The Regulated Consumer*. Los Angeles: Nash Publishing, 1976. Presents the conservative side of the consumer movement; pleads for more benign regulation of what the author calls an "inherently uneconomic—and ironically, anti-consumer" regulation which she considers "a threat to a free society."

EMERGENCE OF THE AMERICAN INDIAN REFORM MOVEMENT

Type of event: Sociological: American Indian protests against government policy
Time: 1960 to the present
Locale: Alcatraz; Wounded Knee, South Dakota; and Washington, D.C.

Principal personages:
RUSSELL MEANS, a leader of the American Indian Movement (AIM)
DENNIS BANKS, a leader of AIM
WILLIAM KUNSTLER, a liberal lawyer who took part in the powwow at Wounded Knee
RALPH ABERNATHY (1926-   ), a civil rights advocate who participated in Wounded Knee talks
RICHARD WILSON, Oglala Sioux Tribal Council President
RICHARD MILHOUS NIXON (1913-   ), thirty-seventh President of the United States, 1969-1974
LA DONNA HARRIS (1931-   ), a mixed blood Comanche who is a political activist and the founder of Oklahoma for Indian Opportunity
N. SCOTT MOMADAY (1934-   ), a Kiowa-Choctaw and the author of the Pulitzer Prize-winning novel *House Made of Dawn*
VINE DELORIA, JR. (1933-   ) a Standing Rock Sioux and the author of *Custer Died for Your Sins*

Summary of Event

It is not surprising that the 1960's, a decade that supplied history books with Birmingham, Watts, Kent State, the Chicago Democratic Convention, and the assassinations of John Fitzgerald Kennedy, Martin Luther King, Jr., and Robert Francis Kennedy, also would mark the emergence of the Indian Reform Movement and Red Power. This period of history gave birth to the minority consciousness and the resultant sense of power that accompanies emerging self-awareness. Where the American Indian was concerned, this force made itself heard in Alcatraz, in Washington, D.C., in Wounded Knee, and during The Longest Walk.

The Indian cry for reform, while partially inspired by the turmoil of the era, was not an attempt by Indians to join the militant bandwagon. Four hundred years of injustice finally exploded, and native Americans, a nonviolent people, were forced to arm themselves against powers bent on destroying their culture and their identity as a people. The Indians were tired of forces who desired assimilation and Smithsonian Institutionalization. They were degraded by forces which saw the Indian as the Lone Ranger's Tonto. Indians were exhausted by poverty, alcoholism,

865

high suicide rates, and short life spans. But above all, Indians were frustrated by the future forecast that predicted a continuance of the poverty cycle and erosion of the Indian heritage.

Obviously the future of the native American is grim, and this is the force behind Red Power. Knowing what lies ahead if the cycle continues, Indians are in desperation trying to make themselves heard. Through occupation of land, marches, and protests, input into federal agencies, and literature and other media, Indians are fighting the deplorable statistics.

In one such attempt to gain recognition of their plight, a group of one hundred belligerent native Americans seized the empty federal prison at Alcatraz Island in 1969. Desiring to use the abandoned building as a cultural center, Indians offered to purchase it from the federal government for a "fair" price: glass beads and red cloth valued at twenty-four dollars. The major purpose of the occupation, however, was media exposure, which Indians received in abundance.

Nationwide exposure was achieved again in 1972 as militant Indians seized the Bureau of Indian Affairs, (BIA), the paternalistic bureaucracy that oversees Indian welfare. Led by Russell Means and Dennis Banks, the takeover soon degenerated into vandalism as the BIA structure suffered 1.4 million dollars in damages and the loss of federal records. As in the episode at Alcatraz, the goals of the occupation were vague, with media exposure the most obvious purpose.

In the late winter and spring of 1973, Indians again chose to occupy land, and again, Banks and Means were there. The site was historic Wounded Knee, South Dakota, where in 1890, federal troops murdered three hundred Sioux men, women, and children in the final massacre of America's Indian Wars. Capitalizing on the emotional charge that accompanies reference to "Wounded Knee," three hundred Sioux and members of the AIM seized eleven residents of the tiny town, holed up in a hilltop church, and insisted they would stay until their demands were met. Several prominent names from the 1960's were there to sit in as demands were discussed, most notably Ralph Abernathy, civil rights advocate, and William Kunstler, liberal lawyer for populist causes.

Many incidents precipitated Wounded Knee II. In Custer, South Dakota, a white man had been charged with manslaughter, not murder, in the death of an Indian. The American Indian Movement had retaliated with the destruction of the Custer Chamber of Commerce building. Leaders of the Oglala Sioux, the tribe inhabiting the Wounded Knee area, had denounced the AIM vandalism, but the AIM continued its protest as it marched, seized the trading post, and took hostages in Wounded Knee. At this stage of the protest, the major goal seemed to be the denunciation and harassment of the Oglala Sioux Pine Ridge leadership, especially tribal president Richard Wilson. Russell Means, an infant dropout from the Pine Ridge reservation, admittedly craved the position of Oglala Sioux president, and was anxious to denounce Wilson.

But there was more to Wounded Knee than jealousy over chieftainship and alleged financial irregularities on the Pine Ridge Reservation. Richard Nixon had raised Indian hopes with a promise in 1970 to begin intensive Indian education programs. Those programs never began. Similarly, Nixon appointed a special task force on Indian grievances and Congress assembled its own committee. Neither ever met. This is not to imply that all government in this era was deaf to Indian demands. Native Americans found friends and political allies in Walter Mondale, Edward Kennedy, Robert Kennedy, and Fred Harris, the Oklahoma Senator. It was his wife, La Donna Harris, who founded Oklahoma for Indian Opportunity. But it was the disappointment of the Nixon years that frustrated Indians and was in part responsible for Wounded Knee.

The 1973 siege of Wounded Knee accomplished several positive goals. Indians did receive a promise of an investigation of the Pine Ridge Reservation, a consideration of civil suits to protect Indians from injustice committed by federal authorities or tribal leaders, a task force to investigate the 1868 treaty between the United States government and the Sioux, and a meeting on Capitol Hill between Indians and White House spokesmen. The cost of this gain was a staggering five to seven million dollars, one hundred indictments, and two deaths.

National recognition for the native American was again achieved in 1978, although this time nonviolently, during The Longest Walk, a march that spanned the continental United States and ended in Washington, D.C., in July of that same year. Representing eight tribes from all parts of the country, Indians, many dressed in tribal garb, marched three thousand miles in five months to protest legislation aimed at stripping treaty rights and possibly abolishing reservations. Indians planned a week-long protest in the nation's capital to focus attention on their plight. It was to be a peaceable demonstration, so as to avoid the complications of the 1972 march on the BIA headquarters. The advantages of the walk were apparent. The Indians were heard, and many were spiritually energized. The Longest Walk was a step forward into a future that should not be as grim as the past.

The Longest Walk was not the only peaceable expression of native American sentiment during the Indian Reform Movement. A wealth of excellent literature, most notably N. Scott Momaday's Pulitzer Prize-winning *House Made of Dawn* (1968) and Vine Deloria, Jr.'s *Custer Died for Your Sins* (1969), expressed the same inner turmoil, alienation, frustration, and desire to be heard that were the sources of far more bloody protests.

The Indian Reform Movement is far from its conclusion; in fact, it is only beginning. The young native American is not willing to live with the squalor, degradation, and broken promises that his father's generation endured. The young Indian is a fighter, and America will hear more of his voice and see more of his blood until such a time as the Indian is satisfied once again with his lot in life.

Pertinent Literature

Locke, Raymond Friday, ed. "History, Red Power and the New Indian," in *The American Indian*. New York: Hawthorn Books, 1970.

In an attempt to explain to the white man what the Red Protest involves, Locke looks at far more than the new Indian of the 1960's and 1970's. His goal is to explain the motivating force behind the modern rebellion: the Indian's discovery that he has a rich heritage and culture that demands preservation.

The first settlers who came to this continent in search of religious freedom immediately labeled the Indian an "uncivilized savage." This stereotype continued, long after many Indians had become Christians and were no longer "savage" by the original rules of the game. Like "savage," "uncivilized," too, was a gross misnomer. Locke gives evidence that the Indians were a highly technical, skilled people who had an extremely well developed civilization. Early Indian technology included the cultivation of corn in central Mexico six thousand years ago and the building of a city in Bolivia at the time of Octavius Augustus that rivaled any building in Rome. The city Tiahuanaco, built thirteen thousand feet above sea level, was constructed with one-hundred-ton stone blocks that demanded precision fit since they were joined without mortar. The stones required transportation from the mine to the city, a journey across mountainous terrain. These same Indians adorned their city with painted pottery, one of the most significant achievements in pre-Columbian art.

Locke only briefly cites the Mayas, Toltecs, Incas, and Aztecs in evidence that Indians had an advanced civilization, at least equal to the European civilizations of the time. Locke deplores use of the "savage" label. If the Indian were ever savage, argues the author, it was only for the purpose of self-preservation once he came into contact with the European.

Locke's search for the Indian's roots leads him to a study of the origin of the Indian species. He explores several popular theories: that ten thousand years ago, Indians crossed a land bridge over the Bering Strait; that Indians are the lost people of Israel; that Indians arrived in this country by ships blown off course; that Indians are descendants of Folsom, Clovis, or Sandia man.

What Locke is certain of is that the American Indian has ancient roots on this continent and had developed skills for tracking and killing beasts ten thousand years before Christ. The Indians twelve thousand years ago in New York hunted caribou; they also inhabited southern Illinois, the Mohave Desert, and Alabama. The land is not the white man's, but rightfully belongs to the Indian.

This rediscovery by the Indian that he does have a heritage and culture of which to be proud is part of the motivating force behind Red Power. Increased pride, self-awareness, and desire for self-respect augment the Indian drive to be an Indian and not an assimilated white. This cognizance has made the Indian more aware that the government erodes his pride by treating him as a second-class citizen. Red Power is a cry for self-respect.

This cry is being heard in Alcatraz, where Indians are hoping that the United States government will present the island to them as a gift for an Indian cultural center. Red Power is the force behind the Nevada Paiutes who are rallying against white destruction of Pyramid Lake, and the New Mexico Taos who are demanding title to forty thousand acres of holy land that is rightly theirs. Red Power is part of the pride behind the founding of the American Indian Educational Publishers, a publishing house totally administered by American Indians. It is the drive behind the Navajo's founding their own college and a Navajo reservation school. Red Power and its attendant pride is the pulse behind the rewriting of the Indian history, an ongoing priority at the Navajo reservation school. It is the pride that authored *House Made of Dawn*. Red Power is the struggle to be Indian in a white world, and Locke's background study contributes much to this cause.

Shusky, Ernest. *The Right to Be Indian*. San Francisco: The Indian History Press, 1970.

A nonobjective look at the Indian plight, *The Right to Be Indian* is nevertheless worthy of consideration because it is from the Indian viewpoint, a voice that has long been ignored in the annals of history. This short monograph deals with the special problems of the Indian: his educational system, his reservation, his self-concept, and his future.

The educational outlook for the Indian is grim. While there is a higher number of Indian students entering college than ever before, eighty percent drop out. Others estimate that the average Indian completes only five and one half years of schooling, with fifty to one hundred percent dropping out. There is no single factor affecting these high rates. The multiplicity of factors include uncertainty as to availability of financial aid at the college level. Seeing a standard curriculum as irrelevant to the work he must do on a reservation, being taught by textbooks that portray him as savage, and viewing school as a place where he learns very little about his own rich cultural past, the Indian youth understandably has little motivation to stay in school. Sociologists add to Shusky's list of factors, speculating that teachers who fail to understand the Indian culture are probable factors in the high dropout statistics. The teacher who does not understand that an Indian youngster's way is to be "seen but not heard" misinterprets this attitude and considers the child "shy" or "slow." An Indian child's reluctance to answer a question when a "brother" has answered incorrectly is misinterpreted as "stupidity." The school is not a place for personal success, hence the high dropout factor. All the attendant problems of dropping out, of course, follow in turn.

People with little education are often victims of poverty, and the average dwelling on the reservation is poor by middle-class standards.

Eighty-one percent of Indian families must still haul water to their two-room homes. Occupation of these small dwellings average 5.4 people per house. Eighty-three percent of reservation homes have inadequate means of disposing of human waste. Other sociologists augment Shusky's findings with statistics that are equally sad. The life expectancy of the American Indian is forty-four years. He has health problems associated with poverty and a substandard environment: a high suicide rate and alcoholism. For the teenage Indian, suicide rates are three times as high as the national average. Alcoholism is a major problem. One source cites a Midwestern reservation of four thousand adults, sixty-five percent of whom were arrested for drunken driving at least once in a three-year span.

The future of the reservation is just as disappointing as the prognosis for the individual Indian. Reservations have dwindled to a mere fraction of their original size through treaty violations. Historical records show that in 1887, Indians occupied 138 million acres of land. Today they are left with fifty-five million acres. On a skeletal reservation, an Indian cannot live well.

On the land that is left, there is still much annual wealth, but in the area of agriculture, only twenty-five percent of that wealth returns to the Indian. In 1968, the Bureau of Indian Affairs reports show that 170 million dollars were grossed in agriculture, but the native American share was 58.6 million. In oil and minerals, Shusky estimates that while in 1967 thirty-one million dollars were earned by tribes, billions went to corpora-

tions. In the area of lumbering, a 1967 statistic proves that only twelve percent of the total lumber cut was handled by the tribal sawmills. Shusky concludes that the federal government's program of developing natural resources on the reservation for the Indian is a sham, since the majority of the money is diverted elsewhere.

Not only are their reservations not economically prospering, Indians have very little right to change the course of the reservation's future. Reservation management is largely in the hands of the BIA, a significant handicap for the Indian community. While tribes do elect tribal officers, those officers operate only in an advisory capacity to the BIA, and even then, tribal officers are not so much representatives as policemen. Hence, it is only through Congressmen that the BIA can be pressured. The BIA-reservation relationship is not unlike that of the trustee/guardian and minor.

The self-concept of the Indian is low. He is a dropout from the educational system. He cannot be trusted to run his own reservation. He is relegated continually to the position of the child. He is not even afforded the courtesy of being allowed to preserve his heritage as forces insist he assimilate into the mainstream of middle-class America as other minorities have done for years. He is not respected for his status as a special citizen, as a first American. Instead, he is a special problem requiring a bureaucracy and a staff of thousands to keep him in tow. How can the Indian retain his self-respect in circumstances such as these?

The Right to Be Indian is the plea

of the native American to be heard and to be respected. It is his request to manage his own life. The native American belief is that if allowed to run his own affairs, all else will follow in turn—self-confidence, education, and ultimately, prosperity for the Indian nation. — *C.W.T.*

Additional Recommended Reading

Andrist, Ralph K. *The Long Death.* New York: The Macmillan Company, 1964. A detailed history of the Plains Indians from 1840 through Wounded Knee in 1890 which factually presents battles and heroes from the Appalachians to the Rockies.

Brown, Dee. *Bury My Heart at Wounded Knee.* New York: Holt, Rinehart and Winston, 1970. An Indian history of the American West in the second half of the nineteenth century; a well-documented look at the coming of the white man and the subsequent breaking of the Indian nation as it existed then.

Debo, Angie. *A History of the Indians of the United States.* Norman: University of Oklahoma Press, 1970. A comprehensive history of the native American which devotes its last two chapters to the problems of the Indians of Alaska and to the renewed hope for native Americans in general.

Deloria, Vine, Jr. *Custer Died for Your Sins.* New York: The Macmillan Company, 1969. A detailed look at the turmoil the Indian experiences when dealing with white society as a whole, written by a Standing Rock Sioux and thus from the Indian perspective.

Momaday, N. Scott. *House Made of Dawn.* New York: Harper & Row Publishers, 1968. A Pulitzer Prize-winning novel by a Kiowa-Choctaw which personalizes the alienation of the native American.

"The Angry American Indian Starting Down the Protest Trail," in *Time.* LXXXXV (February 9, 1970), pp. 14-20. An excellent overview of the Indian past, the protests of the present, and the future of the American Indian.

"Indians: Return to Wounded Knee," in *Newsweek.* LXXXI (March 12, 1973), pp. 27-29. A short article which explores the origins and the first week of Wounded Knee II.

"In the Wake of the Siege at Wounded Knee," in *U.S. News & World Report.* LXXIV (May 21, 1973), pp. 112-113. A summarization of the losses and gains by the conclusion of the Wounded Knee crisis of 1973.

"The Siege of Wounded Knee," in *Newsweek.* LXXXI (March 19, 1973), pp. 22-23. A report of the second week of the Wounded Knee crisis.

ENVIRONMENTAL LEGISLATION PASSED SINCE 1960

Type of event: Legal: congressional efforts in behalf of a cleaner environment
Time: 1960 to the present
Locale: Washington, D.C.

Principal personages:
>   RICHARD MILHOUS NIXON (1913-   ), thirty-seventh President of the United States, 1969-1974
>   HENRY M. JACKSON (1912-   ), United States Senator and Chairman of the Interior Committee and NEPA's Chief Architect
>   EDMUND SIXTUS MUSKIE (1914-   ), United States Senator and Chairman of the Air and Water Subcommittee of the Senate Public Works Committee
>   JOHN DAVID DINGELL, JR. (1926-   ), United States Representative and Chairman of the Fisheries and Wildlife Conservation Subcommittee of the Merchant Marine and Fisheries Committee
>   HENRY SCHOELLKOPF REUSS (1912-   ), United States Representative and Chairman of the Subcommittee of the House Government Operations which deals with conservation and natural resources
>   JIMMY (JAMES EARL) CARTER (1924-   ), thirty-ninth President of the United States, 1977-

Summary of Event

Saving the environment became a major political issue in the United States in the late 1960's. Scientists, conservationists, and other interested persons concerned with the many forms of air and water pollution and the rate of natural resource depletion brought on by an affluent and industrialized society, all concurred that a clean environment could not be obtained without enforced collective action. Through persistent effort these groups prevailed upon Congress and the President to assume responsibility for the passage of appropriate legislation. Responding to the tide of public interest, President Richard

Nixon declared in 1969, in his first State of the Union Address, that he would propose to Congress "the most comprehensive and costly program in this field in the nation's history."

Not to be outdone by a Republican President, the Democratic Congress put forth an environmental program of its own and provided funding in excess of what the President had requested. On February 17, 1969, Representative John Dingell (a Democrat from Michigan) with the support of Representative Henry Reuss (Democrat, Wisconsin) and others introduced a bill in the House of Representatives "to provide for the establishment of a Council on Environmental Quality." In the Senate on the following day a bill with similar aims was introduced by Senator Henry Jackson (Democrat, Washington). After protracted debate, joint Senate and House conferences, and bipartisan sponsorship and support, the two bills culminated in the National Environmental Policy Act (NEPA)—one of the most far-reaching environmental laws ever passed by Congress.

NEPA requires that federal agencies take environmental factors into full account in all their planning and decision-making. Its objective is to treat the environment as a single interrelated system and to give environmental considerations national priority. It establishes a three-member Council on Environmental Quality (CEQ) in the office of the President to act as guardian of environmental affairs and to oversee and coordinate all federal and state environmental efforts, including parks and wilderness preservation, wildlife, natural resources, and land use. The Council also advises and assists the President in preparing an annual report to the Congress and the nation on the state of the environment.

One of the most controversial provisions of the Act, and one without a close statutory precedent, is the Environmental Impact Statement (EIS) requirement, mandating federal agencies to provide written accounts of all their major environmental decisions, detailing potential environmental consequences. Alternatives to proposed agency actions must also be submitted. Senators Jackson and Edmund Muskie (Democrat, Maine) succeeded in getting Congressional approval of this "action-forcing" mechanism to guarantee agency compliance with the Act's objectives. The EIS substantive mandate provides a basis for citizen challenge and judicial review of all federal administrative environmental decisions. Since 1970, thousands of such statements have been filed and numerous lawsuits have been brought under the Act—with varying results.

In December of 1970, according to a reorganization plan recommended by President Nixon, Congress created the Environmental Protection Agency (EPA) to consolidate under a single authority all federal environmental activity. Brought under unified direction and regulation, therefore, are the agencies involved with air and water pollution programs, solid waste management, noise abatement, pesticide control, pure food regulation, toxic chemical management, and the setting of radiation standards. The second major environmental agency created in 1970, again at the request of the President, is the National Oceanic and Atmospheric Administration (NOAA). Situated within the Department of Commerce, NOAA consolidates oceanographic and atmospheric monitoring and weather forecasting programs and provides for conservation.

In 1970, the Ninety-first Congress concerned itself with other environmental issues. It passed the Federal Insecticide, Fungicide, Rodenticide Act (FIFRA) requiring all pesticides shipped in interstate commerce to be registered with the EPA, and including in the Occupational Safety and Health Act (OSHA) a provision obligating employers to provide a work environment for employees that is devoid of "recognized hazards." In addition, Congress implemented some important antipollution legislation passed during President Johnson's Administration, including the Resource Recovery Act, which amended the Solid Waste Disposal Act of 1965 and promoted local planning and recycling efforts; the Water Quality Act, which amended the 1965 Water Pollution Control Act and imposed liability on those responsible for oil spills and hazardous substance discharges from on-shore and off-shore vessels and facilities; and the Clean Air Act, which amended the Air Quality Act of 1967, and set strict exhaust emission standards for the automotive industry with demands that over a four-and-a-half-year period, automobiles be made ninety percent cleaner than they were in 1970. In addition, the Clean Air Act requires states to clean up stationary sources of pollution and imposes standards on them as well. The imposition of these emission standards was delayed by Congress a number of times because the automobile industry maintained that the technology to meet the goals had not been devised, and that such standards would reduce fuel efficiency.

The 1972 session of Congress also gave serious attention to environmental matters. Among other things, it recognized noise as a serious contaminant injurious to health and welfare and passed the first comprehensive Noise Control Act. With its enactment of the Marine Mammal Act, it called attention to man's widespread abuse of marine life and sought permanent moratoriums on most kill-

ing of sea mammals. Through the Coastal Zone Management Act, it encouraged states, including those on the Great Lakes, to develop and operate coastal zone management programs. Under the Federal Environmental Pesticide Control Act, it gave authority to the EPA to identify and register all pesticides. Finally, under the Federal Water Pollution Control Act, it set goals for eliminating all pollutant discharges into United States waterways by 1985, with an interim goal of making the waters safe for fish, shellfish, wildlife, and recreation by 1983. This effort to restore and maintain the chemical, physical, and biological integrity of the nation's waters was vetoed by President Nixon because of "staggering, budget-wrecking" costs. A determined Congress, however, overrode the veto and the water bill became law.

By 1973, however, various business groups—such as the United States Chamber of Commerce, the National Association of Manufacturers, the American Petroleum Institute, the Business Roundtable, and individual trade firms—joined forces to protest the staggering cost of maintaining clean air and water. They argued that choices had to be made between environmental quality and economic development. Meanwhile, an energy shortage developed, necessitating some changes in environmental policy.

Congress responded to the crisis by passing the controversial Trans-Alaska Pipeline Authorization Act (1973), authorizing right-of-way permits and construction of a pipeline to transport crude oil from Prudhoe Bay in Alaska across seven hundred and ninety-nine miles to the ice-free port of Valdez. Environmentalist groups, such as the Wilderness Society, Friends of the Earth, and the Sierra Club, deemed the measure inimical to sound ecological and conservation practices and filed suit in the federal courts questioning the legality of the permits and seeking to enjoin the construction of the pipeline. Through litigation, they were successful in delaying the building of the trans-Alaskan line for four years. Finally, a federal district court ruled the permits in order and dissolved the injunction; the Alaska Pipeline was finally completed in 1977. The court further ruled that the nine-million-dollar, six-volume impact statement prepared by the Department of the Interior satisfied NEPA requirements, thus settling another issue raised by the environmentalist organizations. In the face of citizen concern over an ever-growing fuel shortage, Congress sought to avoid further construction delays by passing a law that effectively prevented environmentalists and the courts from interfering again with the Alaskan project. Some of the gains the environmentalists had made in previous years were seemingly thwarted by this congressional action.

During the Nation's Bicentennial Year, economic and energy considerations took precedence over environmental matters. The President for the second time in two years successfully vetoed a surface mining control bill, and Congress was unable to strengthen the Clean Air Act. In spite of these disappointing losses for the environmentalists, a few notable pieces of legislation were passed: the Toxic Substances Control Act, giving the government broad authority to regulate the production, distribution, and use of all potentially hazardous chemicals; the Resource Conservation and Recovery Act, permitting the EPA to control hazardous wastes; the Federal Land Management and Policy Act, authorizing the Secretary of the Interior to institute a wilderness and land use program under the Bureau of Land Management; and the Fishery Conservation and Management Act, seeking to bring high seas fishery under sound conservation management policy.

The long impasse over federal regulation of strip mining was broken during the first session of the Ninety-fifth Congress with passage of the Surface Mining Control and Reclamation Act; and some progress was seen in the battle against water pollution with the formulation of a program designed to clean the nation's waters by the mid-1980's. During its second session in 1978, Congress enacted the Endangered American Wilderness Act to preserve the nation's parks for recreation. Money was appropriated to expand national parks by more than a million acres, bringing the total to 15.7 million acres across the country. Congress also tightened restrictions on off-shore oil and gas drilling and provided for imposition of fines on those responsible for oil spills.

In May of 1977, President Jimmy Carter delivered a comprehensive environmental message on the state of the environment, the first given by a president in four years, outlining a wide range of proposals to improve environmental quality. He made it clear that effective control of man's impact on his environment requires concerted action at all political levels, from local to global. In 1978 he created a Regulatory Council to help reduce adverse effects of "overlapping regulations," and proposed new standards for the government's role in financing systems that will pacify both environmentalists and a Congress committed to governmental economy. Because, he said, innumerable choices must be made between environmental quality and economic development, he pledged to promote better cooperation between government and industry to solve some of the remaining serious problems. Congress also has a continuing responsibility toward that end.

Pertinent Literature

Liroff, Richard A. *A National Policy for the Environment: NEPA and Its Aftermath.* Bloomington: Indiana University Press, 1976.

In this well-documented and critical volume, Liroff traces the legislative history of the National Environmental Protection Act (NEPA) from its genesis through the fifth year of its operation. He also describes the role of the Council on Environmental Quality (CEQ), notes administrative response and congressional reaction to NEPA, focuses on how environmentalists managed to gain access to federal courtrooms, and closes with an examination of the substantive changes appearing by 1975 in agency decision-making.

Congress, we are told, did not really enact a national environmental policy when it passed the National Environmental Protection Act. Rather, it enacted only a statement of national environmental policy. According to Liroff, policy evolved from the totality of federal actions; and those actions and their impacts "were shaped by CEQ interpretation of NEPA, by the agencies own procedural guidelines, by the litigation initiated by environmental activists, and by the response of Congress to judicial decisions resulting from environmental lawsuits."

Liroff contends that the implications of NEPA were undoubtedly lost on members of Congress. Although the stated intent of the Act was to provide a statute mandating all federal agencies to consider the environmental impact of agency actions that "significantly affect" the quality of human environment, and although the Act requires environmental impact statements detailing the potential environmental consequences and alternatives to proposed actions, its broad language makes the Act's meaning uncertain. Liroff argues that the absence of clear criteria within the law by which the legal adequacy of a decision could be adjudged encourages the judiciary rather than the administrative agency to define and enforce the law's requirements, something that was not contemplated by Congress. He points out that only once during its entire deliberation over passage of the Act did Congress question judicial review of agency action. The fact that possible numerous lawsuits could be initiated because of the Act's ambiguities was not anticipated. If Congress had known what it was doing, Liroff quotes sources as stating, NEPA would not have become law.

Initial efforts by the CEQ are lauded by Liroff, who claims the Council compiled an impressive record during the early years of its existence. In spite of the nebulous position delegated it by NEPA, the CEQ was able to elevate its role from that of passivity to one of more active involvement both in defining adequate agency procedural compliance and in reviewing impact statements. In addition, the Council was instrumental in promoting international environmental cooperation; and its less successful efforts were due in part to conflicting assignments. As guardian of environmental concerns within the executive branch of government, the CEQ was obligated to advise the President confidentially concerning federal programs in progress; in addition, it had to be the public's source of information on environmental problems. If the CEQ felt compromised by this duality, it soon discovered that it could, within limits, publicly criticize agencies without impairing its effectiveness as a White House adviser. How it could accomplish its goals would depend, of course, on the President in office and the capabilities of the CEQ officers themselves.

In his comprehensive treatment of federal agencies' compliance with NEPA, Liroff is less than complimentary. He charges that although agencies had great latitude in formulating policy and devising rules,

the agencies, with few exceptions, demonstrated little imagination in interpreting and implementing the statute's mandate. This mandate is to identify and measure environmental impacts; to formulate and evaluate various alternatives; and to involve and advise the public to the greatest possible extent concerning agency actions. One factor that influenced agency behavior, the author believes, was the seeming lack of congressional concern for either procedural or substantive compliance with NEPA. (Another factor which he might have mentioned is that NEPA was a revolutionary concept, and administrators were treading uncharted ground.) Great ingenuity would be demanded of the CEQ to determine and pursue the public good.

Liroff makes us aware of the fact that the emergence of the environmental protection suit is one of the most significant legal developments of the 1970's. The willingness of the courts to allow private individuals and conservationist groups to challenge government agencies to discharge their environmental responsibilities is adequately discussed. Liroff attributes the legal cases to a general public distrust of federal agencies, a desire to clarify meaning of the vaguely worded action-forcing procedures, and the quest for a new weapon to compel federal agencies to give serious weight to environmental matters. The courts shaped NEPA, Liroff believes, in a manner unprecedented in the history of the development of federal programs.

By 1975, some substantive changes in agency decisionmaking could be detected. A large body of case law had developed providing precedents for the application of NEPA procedures to a wide array of agency actions. Federal projects had been modified, delayed, or halted, and stringent controls had been instituted all in the name of a cleaner environment. Although Congress' desire to institutionalize environmental sensitivity had not yet been fully realized, progress had been made.

Quarles, John. *Cleaning Up America.* Boston: Houghton Mifflin Company, 1976.

John Quarles, a chief administrator of the Environmental Protection Agency from its inception in 1970, provides a lively account of the Agency's first five and a half years. He begins his narration with a confession. "I am a federal bureaucrat," he states, "I am a part of the faceless, gray government machine. I am one of those government officials whom cartoonists make fun of and editorialists stick pins in. . . ." As a bureaucrat-turned-environmentalist, he provides interesting anecdotes, behind-the-scenes vignettes, and perceptive asides that focus on the autonomy and internal symmetry of a governmental body which is characterized as one of the most powerful agencies in the United States. Certainly, it is the most important regulatory agency created by Congress since the New Deal period.

The Agency, Quarles tells us, is one of the results of the protest movement that developed in the late 1960's. It has a total work force of ten thousand people, operates a variety of programs including research, technical analysis, standard-setting, and enforcement, and makes grants of approximately one hundred million dollars per year to state and local environmental agencies.

In a series of intriguing episodes, Quarles first broadly describes the creation of the EPA: how the idea of the agency emerged from the President's plan to streamline government operations; how the proposal triggered an immediate conflict in the Cabinet over who would be in control; how the Interior Secretary's criticism of the President resulted in the Secretary's loss of control; how a man with no environmental experience became Director of the EPA; and how the new Director met the challenge of his new job. Quarles then limns a personal portrait of the new Director that makes him one of the true heroes of the environmental crusade.

Quarles speaks of the relationship between the White House and the EPA and indicates that President Nixon never became a hero of the environmentalists; he explains how the dynamics of government operations arise from the interplay of politics in setting government policy and the hard realities of running government programs. He reveals that a group of subordinates who rarely if ever talked to the President hammered out an executive order that resulted in rigorous standards being placed on industrial plants discharging pollution; and he relates how an auto decision ensnarled the EPA in a conflict between public health and the public need to drive to work, a situation which pitted the Agency against the giant automobile industry.

Finally, Quarles explores, in very brief compass, a problem that he only slowly came to recognize: that government does not begin to attack a problem until that problem has become so severe that the public demands action. He deplores the fact that government always has to catch up. Although our government may be responsive, it is so only after delayed reaction. Quarles claims that the lag time between need and response is measured in years, and questions whether we shall "always be able to afford that delay?" He believes it is necessary to establish controls in advance to prevent crises from occurring.

The worth of this book lies in its descriptions of environmental policy formulation. The author is able to command and keep our attention when he provides a glimpse of life as it is lived day-to-day by the decision-makers. All is not as it seems, we soon learn. The casual observer of the Washington scene might assume that vast authority is exercised by persons holding high government positions. Not so, Quarles informs us. While their opinions can influence basic policy, this influence is limited by other political forces that impinge in ways that the decision-makers have no power to resist. He cites as examples the numerous organizations interested in conservation in the 1960's. Formerly these groups operated individually and with reference to specific issues, but when clean air and water became a significant public problem, they banded together and became a formidable political force. On April 22, 1970, they staged an effective nationwide Earth Day demonstration which was adequately noted by the press, another power force. Congress responded by quadrupling its appropriations for building municipal sewage treatment plants. At the same time, President Nixon reportedly studied a poll showing that protection of the environment had become the third most important political issue for voters, decided to be on the right side of a political cause, and called for the creation of an environmental regulatory agency. However, when support of the environment conflicted with the Administration's support of big business, and big business threatened to withhold political contributions, another change in environmental policy took place. A further policy change was caused by economic pressures brought on by an Arab oil embargo.

Cleaning Up America is stimulating reading. Quarles not only clearly demonstrates the need for continued government attention to environmental problems but also convinces us that at least one federal agency is doing an exemplary job toward that end. — *A.O.B.*

Additional Recommended Reading

Ackerman, Bruce A., Susan Rose-Ackerman, James W. Sawyer, Jr. and Dale W. Henderson. *The Uncertain Search for Environmental Quality.* New York: The Free Press, 1974. An effort in the late 1960's to clean up the Delaware river by the

Delaware River Commission is the basis for this multidisciplinary study which questions the way in which water pollution problems have been defined and resolved.

Barros, James and Douglas M. Johnston. *The International Law of Pollution*. New York: The Free Press, 1974. Contains materials on pollution in oceans, atmosphere, and international rivers and lakes; documents on international cooperation in pollution control are also included.

Baxter, William. *People or Penguins: The Case for Optimal Pollution*. New York: Columbia University Press, 1974. Argues that policymakers should emphasize economic analysis and monetary incentives to solve pollution problems.

Berry, Brian J. L., *et al. Land Use, Urban Form and Environmental Quality*. Chicago: University of Chicago Press, 1974. Originally prepared for the Environmental Protection Agency, this report covers aspects of environmental deterioration including air, water, solid waste, noise, pesticides and radiation.

Brown, F. Lee and A. O. Lebeck. *Cars, Cans and Dumps*. Baltimore, Md.: The Johns Hopkins University Press, 1976. A detailed economic assessment of solid waste disposal in rural areas of New Mexico, along with a model statute dealing with the nuisance of abandoned motor vehicles.

Enloe, Cynthia H. *The Politics of Pollution in a Comparative Perspective: Ecology and Power in Four Nations*. New York: David McKay Company, 1975. Global survival problems such as overpopulation, exhaustion of natural resources, environment destruction, and the threat of nuclear extinction are discussed in this interesting study.

Whitaker, John. *Striking a Balance: Environment and Natural Resources Policy in the Nixon-Ford Years*. Washington, D.C.: American Enterprise Institute for Public Policy Research, 1978. A White House deputy assistant evaluates the Nixon Administration's record on the environment and concludes that it was the most productive since the time of Teddy Roosevelt.

INVENTION OF THE LASER

Type of event: Technological: development of an operating laser
Time: 1960 to the present
Locale: The United States and the Soviet Union

Principal personages:

ALBERT EINSTEIN (1879-1955), physicist who was awarded the Nobel Prize for Physics in 1921

NIELS BOHR (1885-1962), physicist who was awarded the Nobel Prize for Physics in 1922

CHARLES HARD TOWNES (1915-   ),

NIKOLAI GENNADIEVICH BASOV (1922-   ), and

ALEKSANDR MIKHAYLOVICH PROKHOROV (1916-   ), physicists who shared the Nobel Prize for Physics in 1964

ARTHUR LEONARD SCHAWLOW (1921-   ),

THEODORE HAROLD MAIMAN (1927-   ),

ALI JAVAN (1926-   ),

WILLIAM RALPH BENNETT, JR. (1930-   ), and

DONALD HERRIOTT, American physicists

V. A. FABRIKANT, a Soviet physicist

GORDON GOULD (1920-   ), an American physicist and industrial researcher

Summary of Event

So many people have contributed to the development of the laser that no one person can properly be called its inventor. Understanding the operation of lasers depends upon knowledge of optics; atomic, molecular, and solid state physics; quantum physics; electrodynamics; and engineering. Assigning priorities for the creation of the laser concept is a controversial undertaking. To understand the contributions of various persons, a brief description of the ideas basic to laser operation is necessary.

Several of the most fundamental concepts were originated by Albert Einstein, who discovered the elementary particle or photon character of the electromagnetic field. Niels Bohr explained the emission and absorption of light by atoms as the transition of the atom between discrete energy states characterized by particular electron orbits in the nucleus. The energy of the photon, or light quantum, equals the difference in energy between the atomic energy states involved in a transition. The frequency of the electromagnetic wave, composed of swarms of photons, is directly proportional to the photon energy. Thus, absorption and emission are visualized as absorption and emission of individual photons, each having a specific energy, from an electromagnetic wave.

In 1916 Einstein concluded that in addition to the processes of spontaneous emission of photons and the

881

absorption of photons, a third process must be operating—the process of induced or stimulated emission, which may be regarded as the inverse of absorption. Absorption occurs when photons are removed from an electromagnetic wave by energetically upward atomic transitions taking place when electromagnetic waves of specific frequencies interact with matter. Stimulated emission occurs when photons are added to an electromagnetic wave by energetically downward atomic transitions induced by the presence of an electromagnetic wave in matter. Light amplification is possible through stimulated emission. Absorption instead of amplification usually takes place, since many atoms under equilibrium conditions require more atoms of a given energy group to be in the lower energy state; thus, more photons are absorbed by upward transitions. For amplification, sufficient numbers of atoms—more than one-half—must first be excited to a high energy state and then "induced" to a lower energy state by a wave of the correct frequency. The condition wherein an upper energy level is more densely populated than some lower energy level is called a "population inversion." The preparation of population inversions in suitable materials is one of the major keys to laser operation. The design of resonant optical cavities to support laser oscillations is also an indispensable consideration.

Since the nineteenth century, the study of the interaction of electromagnetic radiation and matter, called spectroscopy, has formed a foundation for knowledge of both light and matter. Of the many contributors to the field of spectroscopy, V. A. Fabrikant of the U.S.S.R. is notable for writing, in 1940, of the possibility of amplifying incident electromagnetic waves in a medium having an inverted population. Fabrikant and his students filed a patent with the Soviet Patent Office in 1951 entitled "A Method for the Amplification of Electromagnetic Radiation (Ultraviolet, Visible, Infrared and Radiowaves)." The patent was subsequently granted in 1959.

In retrospect one can see a pattern in inventive thought. The fundamental knowledge is widely available, and many people can act to achieve nearly the same final result. About this time (around 1950) three men, Charles H. Townes of the United States and Nikolai G. Basov and Aleksandr Prokhorov of the Soviet Union turned their attention to the problem of the laser. In 1964 all three were to share in a joint Nobel Prize in Physics "for fundamental work in the field of quantum electronics, which has led to the construction of oscillators and amplifiers based on the maser-laser principle." The term "maser" refers to Microwave Amplification by the Stimulated Emission of Radiation; "laser" refers to Light Amplification by the Stimulated Emission of Radiation. In July, 1954, Townes, H. J. Zeiger, and J. P. Gordon announced the first operation of a maser based on an inverted population of ammonia molecules as the active substance. In October, 1954, Basov and Prokhorov published a theoretical article analyzing the operation of a different type of maser from that operated by Townes. Thirty-eight years had elapsed between the original theoretical concept of stimulated emission and the experimental accomplishment of a microwave generator based on stimulated emission by Townes and his collaborators.

Townes had another very important collaborator, Arthur L. Schawlow, of the Bell Telephone Laboratories. The two men coauthored an outstanding text on microwave spectroscopy, published in 1955. Later, they worked to extend the stimulated emission principle from the microwave region toward the visible region. Schawlow and Townes published a landmark paper in *The Physical Review* (December 15, 1958) entitled "Infrared and Optical Masers," in which the conditions for laser oscillations were analyzed. There quickly followed a United States patent awarded to Townes in 1959. However, in 1959 not a single workable laser existed; no one had yet produced the necessary amplifying medium.

The final step was made when Dr. Theodore Maiman of Hughes Aircraft constructed the first operating laser. Maiman's discovery was first announced in the public press during July, 1960. His laser operated on a pulsed basis, using a ruby as the amplifying medium. Interest soon turned to the operation of lasers on a continuous basis. In 1963, Ali Javan, William Bennett, and Donald Herriott obtained a basic patent on continuously operating gas discharge lasers.

It is not to be expected that the invention of the laser be stated as a simple chronological progression of ideas and accomplishments. For example, the invention of the laser is complicated by a patent recently granted to Gordon Gould. Gould was a graduate student in 1957 at Columbia University, where Townes also held his academic position. During the time Townes was developing his ideas, Gould was implementing his own. He attempted to have his ideas patented. After almost twenty years, in 1977, Gould was granted United States Patent 4,053,845 for "optical pumping," meaning detailed schemes for obtaining a population inversion. According to *Barron's Weekly* (February 27, 1978), if all five of the Gould patent applications are allowed, the patents will cover ninety-five percent of a multibillion dollar laser market.

The issuance of a United States patent seems to provide powerful support for Gould's claim to be an inventor of the laser. Only time and litigation will finally settle the matter of how many inventors the laser really has.

Pertinent Literature

Marshall, Samuel L., ed. *Laser Technology and Applications*. New York: McGraw-Hill Book Company, 1968.

This account of lasers is recommended to the nonspecialist for two reasons. It is of interest as a historical document in a fast-moving technology and is also a readable account of the fundamental considerations of laser operation which does not require mathematical skills of a high order. The foreword by Theodore H. Maiman, although only a page long, very accurately forecasts accomplishments of the next decade. The prediction of the application of the laser to mass communication has happened so rapidly that even Maiman must be a little surprised.

The book comprises nine chapters and two appendixes; each chapter and appendix was written by a different author. The presentation is authoritative and avoids faults common to review books of this nature. The presentation is even; the differences in style between chapters are minimal. Chapter 1 is of particular interest because it contains a chronology of specific developments in lasers.

In the period following Maiman's demonstration of an operating laser, excitement among the scientific community was high. The more pragmatic observers of the laser field were not quite sure how the promise was to be turned into economic gain. Some skeptics went so far as to refer to the laser as a solution for which no problem had yet been found. This book, and others of its type, is very important in bridging the gap between scientific demonstration and full-scale operation in an economically profitable sense. Less than two decades after Maiman's demonstra-tion, the laser is the basis for a multibillion dollar industry.

Chapters 2 and 3 provide a background in solid state physics, optics, radiation theory, and the theory of the laser. These chapters are highly condensed and will be appreciated best by those persons having some background in physics. Chapters 4 through 7 comprise about one-half of the book and present details of semiconductor, glass, crystal, and gas lasers. This material is somewhat dated, but is basically sound for any nonspecialist.

The rest of the book is a survey of technical applications. The explosion of applications in the last decade makes the last portion of the book outdated if the reader is seeking the latest knowledge. Less than one page is devoted to holography; and only slightly more than one page is given over to chemical applications. The development of holography and the use of the laser for isotope separation have been very important recent developments; also, the use of lasers for surveying and building has been a very important use of the continuous wave helium-neon laser.

For the nonphysicist but technically literate reader this book is recommended. Not that matters are treated in a simple manner; on the contrary, the authors deal honestly with problems and yet do not get too technical or parochial.

O'Shea, Donald C., *et al. An Introduction to Lasers and Their Applications*. Reading, Mass.: Addison Wesley, 1977.

This volume is well suited for anyone with a background of college level physics; it is obviously intended to be used as a one-semester course in lasers and supplements those areas in optics and physics which pertain directly to the laser. More than half of the book is devoted to the physics of the laser. The basic properties of coherent light and the materials used in the various types of lasers are discussed. Techniques for the control of laser output are presented, including Q-switching, mode locking, and modulation. A thorough but qualitative introduction to solid state lasers is included.

The remainder of the book describes some of the applications of lasers to practical and scientific problems; the fields of laser fusion and lightwave communications, for example, are discussed at some length. The entire field of laser application is so broad that it may be best to use laser technology as material specific to other courses—for example, laser use in surveying, rather than provide a compendium of applications. The material is very readable and should have value for anyone seeking an understanding of laser operation.
— *G.R.M.*

Additional Recommended Reading

Schawlow, A. L. and C. H. Townes. "Infrared and Optical Masers," in *The Physical Review*. CXII, no. 6 (December 15, 1958), pp. 1940-1949. Concerns optical cavity and the conditions necessary for laser oscillation.

Lengyel, Bela A. "Evolution of Masers and Lasers," in *American Journal of Physics*. XXXIV (October, 1966), p. 903. Contains details concerning the development of masers and lasers.

Nobel Lectures, Physics, 1963-70. Amsterdam: Published for the Nobel Foundation of Elsevier Publishing Company, 1964-1972. A collection of essays delivered by Nobel Laureates at the awarding of the Nobel Prize.

Van Pelt, W. F., *et al. Laser Fundamentals and Experiments*. Washington, D.C.: U.S. Government Printing Office, 1970. (Intended primarily for high school instructors.) Includes laser fundamentals and laser safety and presents experiments on scattering, absorption, reflection, refraction, polarization, coherence, diffraction, and holography.

Charschan, S. S., ed. *Lasers in Industry*. New York: Van Nostrand Reinhold, 1973. Contains background on lasers with practical information on industrial usage.

Goldman, Leon and R. James Rockwell, Jr. *Lasers in Medicine*. New York: Gordon & Breach Science Publishers, 1971. A worthwhile book on an important subject.

Lasers and Light: Readings from Scientific American. San Francisco: W. H. Freeman and Company, 1969. Preface by Arthur L. Schawlow. Collection of articles for the average reader.

PRESSURE FOR PRISON REFORM

Type of event: Sociological: growth of a social movement advocating major changes in the correctional system
Time: 1960 to the present
Locale: The United States

Summary of Event

In the late 1960's and early 1970's, American prisons were rocked by a series of violent riots. California's Soledad Prison alone was the scene of the death of seven guards and twelve prisoners between 1966 and 1968. Nationwide, thirty-nine prison riots broke out in 1969 and fifty-nine in 1970. By far the most dramatic outbreak was the 1971 Attica Prison riot in New York in which thirty-nine persons were killed and eighty-eight injured. This violence, combined with steadily increasing crime rates, focused attention on the failure of prisons to deter potential criminals or to rehabilitate convicted ones and resulted in a demand for prison reform.

Actually, the 1960's and 1970's push for prison reform is only the latest in a series of reform efforts going back almost two hundred years. In fact, the whole idea of prisons was itself a reform effort. Prior to the American Revolution, punishment for persons convicted of crimes in the American colonies was swift and sure. The person was either executed or was dealt some form of corporal punishment such as flogging, branding, or mutilation. Jails were used only to detain persons awaiting trial or execution of their sentences.

Shortly after the Revolutionary War Quaker reformers, offended by the brutality of the criminal justice system, developed the idea of im-

prisoning people for varying lengths of time as punishment for criminal acts. The result was the establishment, in 1790, of the Walnut Street Jail in Philadelphia, the world's first modern prison. The idea behind the establishment of prisons was that people would not only be punished in a less brutal fashion, but that they would also be helped to see the error of their ways and would emerge from prison as reformed and useful citizens.

From the very beginning prisons have been criticized for failing in the rehabilitative function. People placed in prison have been observed upon release not to be reformed, but rather to be hardened and more prone to criminal behavior than they were when they went in. As a result of their apparent failure, American prisons have undergone a steady stream of reforms for the entire two hundred years of their history. New and bigger prisons have been built, educational programs and psychological counseling introduced, and the notion of early release under parole supervision adopted. In spite of reforms, current statistics indicate that prisons are still failing to rehabilitate offenders and to protect society from crime. Currently more than one billion dollars a year is spent to keep 1.3 million offenders in the five thousand local jails and the four hundred state and federal prisons in the United States. Over forty percent of these inmates are projected to be back in prison within five years of their release.

The rash of prison violence that sparked the current push for prison reform was a result of several related factors. A major factor was that the steady migration of minority group members from rural to urban areas during the 1940's and 1950's had increased the minority population of prisons and created overcrowding and an atmosphere of racial tension. This development, together with the Civil Rights movement of the 1960's, focused attention on prisoners' rights and contributed to many inmates' perception of themselves as political prisoners. Contributing to the tension was the fact that while the majority of prisoners were black and urban, the majority of guards were white and rural. The overcrowding, overrepresentation of minority groups in prisons, lack of sensitivity of prison employees, combined with the radical movement of the 1960's, created a prison atmosphere highly charged with racial and class hostilities. The result was the series of violent episodes referred to above that once again called national attention to the failure of prisons and the plight of prisoners, and created a renewed demand for reform.

Current efforts at prison reform fall into two major approaches. The first is the traditional approach which accepts the concept of imprisonment as society's answer to crime, but attempts to modify the prison system to make it more effective. Advocates of this approach point out that although 1.3 billion dollars is invested yearly in our prison system, less than five percent is spent on rehabilitative programs. They argue that inmate rehabilitation programs have never been given a fair chance and that behavioral science is developing new techniques that promise to be more effective than those previously used. One of the current rehabilitative techniques that penologists feel has great promise is the use of behavior modification. This technique is based on the belief that criminal behavior is learned through positive rewards to the criminal and, therefore, can be unlearned by giving him negative sanctions for undesirable behavior and positive rewards for desirable behavior. Patuxent Institution in Maryland is one prison that has pioneered these methods. By improved behavior, prisoners work their way up from one level of rewards to the next, receiving on the various levels such positive reinforcements as vocational training, picnics with their families, and parole.

The second approach to prison reform is much more radical. Advocates of this approach argue that prisons are failures because the basic concept of locking people up is bad. They assert that the reason all previous efforts at prison reform have failed is because it is not possible to reform people while they are locked up. Prisons, the argument goes, should be limited to those prisoners who are a clear danger to society, estimated to be fifteen to twenty percent of the total number currently locked up. The other eighty to eighty-five percent would be diverted from prison by a combination of decriminalizing crimes without victims, sentencing convicted criminals to pay back victims of their crimes, and substituting community treatment centers for prisons. In these centers convicts would be able to remain in their home community, keep their jobs, and maintain contact with their families while undergoing individualized programs of rehabilitation. Massachusetts has used this method in its juvenile corrections system and has closed most of its juvenile institutions since the early 1970's.

Cutting across both of the above approaches to prison reform is the push for recognition of civil rights of prisoners. For years the courts considered prisoners as nonpersons, individuals who had, as a result of their criminal acts, given up all civil rights. Since the 1960's, groups such as the American Civil Liberties Union have bombarded the courts with a series of suits that have eroded this concept to the point that a number of states are currently under court order to improve their facilities, programs, and general treatment of prisoners.

As we move closer to 1980, the dramatic flare-ups of prison violence have subsided and confrontations between prisoners and prison administrators have moved almost entirely into the courts. Prisons are in little danger of going out of business, as some reformers advocate, but the courts are applying increasing pressure to eliminate overcrowding, provide rehabilitation opportunities, and eliminate the exercise of arbitrary authority by prison officials. Going to prison in the United States is still not a pleasant experience, as some critics assert, but hopefully recent reforms will result in imprisonment doing more good than harm.

Pertinent Literature

McKelvey, Blake. *American Prisons: A History of Good Intentions*. Montclair, N.J.: Patterson Smith, 1977.

This book is an update of the author's 1936 work, *American Prisons: A Study in American Social History Prior to 1915*. In it, Blake McKelvey, a professional historian, traces developments in penology in the United States and relates these to trends in society and to developments in correctional theory. While objective, McKelvey's account is sympathetic to the prison reformers and administrators whose efforts he chronicles. McKelvey describes how, first relying on religion and then on science, successive generations of administrators and reformers have developed new procedures and programs for the rehabilitation of criminals, generally with the best of intentions, but often with tragic results.

McKelvey divides the history of prisons in the United States into five broad, overlapping periods. The first period began in 1786, and it was during this period that the first true prison was established in Philadelphia. The prisons of this period were called "congregate" prisons because the inmates lived in large groups. This period ended in the 1820's because of the discovery that keeping inmates in large groups contributed to their preying on one another and engaging in vicious and riotous practices. To correct these problems the congregate prisons were gradually replaced, after 1820, with more substantial penitentiaries equipped to handle hundreds of prisoners in individual cells. In these prisons inmates were expected to maintain a strict vigil of silence and solitude, the belief being that they would be reformed by contemplating the error of their ways. By the 1860's prison administrators realized that a regimen of silence and solitude was more likely to produce insanity than penitence, so a new group of reformers began gradually to introduce programs of education, constructive work, indeterminate sentences, and release under parole supervision with the hope that these methods would produce reformed individuals.

By the first decades of the twentieth century these latest reforms, like the previous efforts, were found to be having no effect on recidivism rates and on crime rates in general. Penologists, believing they were on the right track but had not gone far enough, added programs of psychological classification and treatment to the prison agenda. It was felt that by separating the reformable from the incorrigible criminal, and giving psy-

chological treatment to the former group, prisons would become effective. Unfortunately, however, measures of prison effectiveness still demonstrated that these institutions were miserable failures. During the 1960's, the fifth period of prison reform began and is still in process. Current reform efforts emphasize new treatment techniques, due process, prisoner rights and, most importantly, often question the whole idea of putting people in prison. Suggested alternatives to prison are that small community-centered programs should be established, and that many victimless deviant behaviors (such as drunkenness, drugs, and prostitution) should be decriminalized, thereby reducing the prison population.

McKelvey's presentation of the history of prison reform is very thorough and his research is painstaking. Unfortunately, he is much better at gathering and presenting facts than he is at synthesizing them. It is difficult to follow, or even to discern, his main themes and arguments. However, McKelvey's exhaustive presentation of facts makes one theme stand on its own—for all the time, money, and effort that has been expended on prison reform, nothing yet has been done that has had any effect on the problem of crime in society.

Mitford, Jessica. *Kind and Usual Punishment: The Prison Business*. New York: Alfred A. Knopf, 1975.

In this book social critic Jessica Mitford turns her attention to the penal system in the United States. The title is derived from the Eighth Amendment to the Federal Constitution which prohibits the cruel and

unusual punishment of criminals. The main point Mitford attempts to make in this book is that even though our system for the punishment of criminals is constitutionally permissive, it is neither kind nor usual. In the process of demonstrating that our penal system engages in what she feels constitutes cruel and unusual punishment, Mitford attacks a number of features of the system, including the indeterminate sentence, psychological treatment programs, medical experimentation, and work programs.

The indeterminate sentence is a concept developed by nineteenth century reformers under which a convicted criminal is not sentenced for a set number of years. Instead, he is sentenced for a period of time ranging from a minimum to a maximum number of years, the exact number being left to the discretion of prison officials. If the convicted person behaves well in prison, officials can release him after the minimum amount of time. If he does not behave well, he can be imprisoned for the maximum amount of time. The theory behind the indeterminate sentence is that it will motivate prisoners to cooperate with prison officials in their own rehabilitation so they can regain their freedom in the shortest possible time. According to Mitford, the indeterminate sentence has resulted in increasing the average length of time spent in prison, has been administered in an arbitrary manner, and in the hands of prison officials has become a potent psychological weapon for inmate manipulation and control. Instead of serving to gain inmate cooperation, the indeterminate sentence is a major cause of inmate bitterness and resentment. Among the prisoners interviewed by Mitford, the indeterminate sentence was their major grievance.

A frequent demand made by prison reformers is for an increase in the amount of money spent for psychological treatment programs in prisons. As a result, these programs have steadily increased during this century. The underlying theory of treatment is that prisoners are not "bad" but merely "maladjusted" and that the application of psychological therapy can make them well and thereby put an end to their criminal behavior. Mitford feels that in reality treatment programs in prisons are not conducted as a help to prisoners but rather serve as "a device for breaking the convict's will to resist and hounding him into compliance with institution demands." She cites numerous studies which have concluded that treatment programs have failed as demonstrated by the fact that recidivism rates have never decreased as a result of these programs.

In one of the most disturbing chapters in her book, Mitford discusses medical experimentation in prisons. It has been common practice for many years for researchers to pay prisoners to serve as subjects for medical experimentation. Mitford reveals through her interviews with prisoners how the men are willing to subject themselves to a degree of pain and danger that would be unacceptable to free people, because participating in medical experiments is one of the few ways prisoners can earn extra money and privileges. She chronicles numerous dangerous experiments that have been conducted in prisons with few administrative controls and no procedure for the protection of the human subjects.

Prison officials have long believed that the provision of employment contributes to the rehabilitation of inmates as well as relieving the monotony of prison life. It is believed that the inmate will learn good work habits and, ideally, a skill that will equip him for life following release. Mitford attacks prison employment as being a slave system where convicts are paid between two and sixteen cents an hour, making some prison industries among the most profitable businesses in the world. She criticizes prison employment as meaningless in terms of future career options for released prisoners. The classic example of this is the manufacture of license plates. Prisoners learn a skill related to making license plates, but the only place they can use the skill is in prison, because this is the only place where license plates are made.

Mitford is very skeptical of current efforts at prison reform. She reviews how people have been attempting to reform prisons for more than one hundred years, and every effort has failed. Recidivism rates have not decreased, and prisons have not become easier to run. She believes that reform efforts have consistently been turned into bigger budgets for prison administrators who have used the money for more of the same types of programs as those that have failed in the past.

Mitford claims that attempts to reform prisons by enlarging and improving programs to rehabilitate prisoners are doomed to failure because "prisons are intrinsically evil" and there is, therefore, no hope for success. She writes that "the first principle of reform should be to have as few people as possible confined, for as short a time as possible." To accomplish this she proposes that as many offenses as possible be decriminalized and that sentences (longer in the United States than in any other country) be vastly reduced. In addition, she proposes that sentences be for a definite amount of time and release be unconditional with no parole supervision required.

Mitford makes a strong case, presented very well, for the elimination, or at least drastic reduction, of prisons in our society. However, she does not deal with one fundamental point. Prisons represent an attempt, albeit a poor one, to deal with the problem of crime in our society. If prisons are a failure, and we eliminate them, we are still faced with the problem of how to deal with criminal behavior. Mitford does not suggest a solution to this problem. — *P.R.P.*

Additional Recommended Reading

Buckley, Marie. *Breaking into Prison: A Citizen Guide to Volunteer Action*. Boston: Beacon Press, 1974. A brief, well-written book which provides useful information for citizens wishing to become involved in prison work; the perspective is entirely from "within the system," and the action suggested is therefore of a very conservative nature.

Atkins, Burton M. and Henry R. Glick, eds. *Prisons, Protest & Politics*. Englewood Cliffs, N.J.: Prentice-Hall, 1972. A book of well-chosen readings that describe the current wave of prison reform.

Carter, Robert M., Daniel Glaser and Leslie T. Wilkins. *Correctional Institutions.* Philadelphia: J. B. Lippincott, 1977. A book of thirty-eight readings providing a well-rounded, although occasionally academic, view of the current state of correctional theory and practice.

Fogel, David. ". . . *We Are the Living Proof . . ." The Justice Model for Corrections.* Cincinnati, Oh.: W. H. Anderson Company, 1975. A practicing penologist advocates eliminating the "fortress prison" and employing discretion in sentencing, parole, and administration.

Goldfarb, Ronald. *Jails: The Ultimate Ghetto.* Garden City, N.Y.: Anchor Press/ Doubleday, 1975. Asserts that jails are the twentieth century's poorhouses because their inmate populations are mainly comprised of persons too poor to raise bail or to pay fines.

Sellin, Johan Thorsten and Richard D. Lambert, eds. *Prisons in Transformation.* Westport, Conn.: Greenwood Press, 1972. A view from inside the profession by two practicing correctional administrators.

PRESSURE OF MINORITIES FOR PERSONAL EQUALITY

Type of event: Sociological: rise of a new egalitarianism
Time: 1960 to the present
Locale: The United States

Principal personages:

MARTIN LUTHER KING, JR. (1929-1968), leader of the moderate, nonviolent wing of blacks demanding civil rights legislation in the 1950's and 1960's

HUBERT HORATIO HUMPHREY (1911-1978), a long-time liberal who, in the Senate and the Vice-Presidency, pushed for greater social equality in the United States

EARL WARREN (1891-1974), Chief Justice of the Supreme Court, 1953-1969; and judicial advocate of civil liberties

BETTY FRIEDAN (1921-   ), author of *The Feminine Mystique* (1963) and leader of the National Organization for Women

Summary of Event

Though America was a land that proclaimed the inherent equality of men, its people assumed for a very long time that their real lives would be very unequal. At the same time, one may detect in American politics an ongoing pressure for a more egalitarian society. Some fifty years after the Declaration of Independence, state after state buckled to the abolition of rules allowing only property owners to vote. Forty years later, slaves were freed and given weak guarantees of equality; and half a century after that, progressive taxation was introduced by the federal government. Thus have rights slowly diffused in the United States—until the last generation, when pressure groups and liberal beliefs created their own momentum for spreading equality in many areas.

The most important contributor to this pattern of change was the Civil Rights movement, an effort spear-headed by millions of blacks for the eradication of discrimination in the deep South and elsewhere. The movement was fostered and actively supported at crucial times by influential and numerous white liberals. During the first half of the twentieth century, large sections of Northern society were effectively insulated from any contact with blacks, except for extraordinary individuals such as Booker T. Washington and Marion Anderson who penetrated normal social barriers. Such groups were often shocked to learn that most blacks were effectively kept on the lowest rung of society through formal and informal restraints, and liberals encouraged the development of black colleges, less discrimination in the federal government, and larger social welfare expenditures. Such moves helped to create a group of black leaders—in the Urban League, the NAACP, and the churches—dedicated to widespread agitation for new laws against discrimination.

The movement began in earnest at the end of World War II. The war unified the nation and opened to blacks new opportunities which provided a taste of what real social equality could be like. The Cold War produced fervent belief in the freedom of America; but the treatment of blacks seemed to many people too inconsistent with the nation's ideals. These disparate influences resulted in strong support for civil rights legislation, most dramatically in the civil rights plank Hubert Humphrey succeeded in passing for the 1948 Democratic platform.

The following decade was filled with disappointments for the Civil Rights movement. The Truman Administration, committed and willing to sponsor the desired legislation, ran into repeated opposition from Southern conservatives who stifled the bills in committee. President Eisenhower was also friendly to moderate civil rights, and the needed majorities appeared on Capitol Hill; but yearly filibusters destroyed the legislation. Largely through the efforts of Majority Leader Lyndon Johnson, a bill was finally passed which spoke strong words against discrimination—the Civil Rights Act of 1957—but because it lacked enforcement provisions, it was generally ignored. The forces for integration previously had won a hollow victory in 1954, when the liberal Warren Court ruled in *Oliver Brown et al.* v. *Board of Education of Topeka et al.* that segregation in the schools was unconstitutional. Despite a few dramatic efforts at integration, the overwhelming majority of schools (especially in the South) remained separate and unequal.

By the 1960's, black resentment had swelled into large protests, independent, or even defiant, of the white liberals. Enormous nonviolent marches led by the Reverend Martin Luther King, Jr., frightened most people, and aroused Northern sympathy only because the use of police dogs and other actions of Southern police were so extreme. A growing consensus, cresting in Johnson's 1964 presidential victory over Barry Goldwater, sparked the passage of the Civil Rights Acts of 1964, 1965, and 1968, as well as assorted educational aid and antipoverty programs. This body of legislation, elaborately enforced, obliterated the legal obstacles to black equality. All that remained were the informal burdens of black ignorance and white prejudice. The battle against these began with further Supreme Court rulings which sought to promote integration of the schools (a step beyond merely outlawing segregation) through forced busing of children within school districts.

The remarkable achievements of the black movement could not go unnoticed by other social activists. With the issue of equality raised, a large number of groups claiming oppression rushed to the fore. The most dramatic of these was "the minority that is a majority": the Women's Movement. Women's protest came into notice in the mid-1960's, when such feminists as Germaine Greer, Kate Millet, and Betty Friedan, author of *The Feminine Mystique* (1963) and leader of the National Organization for Women, argued that the spirit of women was being crushed by a culture that assigned them a passive, mindless role. As women became more aware of themselves as a "class," a variety of specific legislative demands emerged: more day-care centers, "equal pay for equal work," more supportive divorce laws. Such efforts culminated in pressure for the Equal Rights Amendment, which passed Congress early in 1972 and was sent on to the states.

The Women's Movement was qualitatively very different from the black movement. Blacks sought to enter white society, not to change it fundamentally. But the new consciousness of many women seemed to some to threaten basic social institutions—most conspicuously, the family—and was undoubtedly a contributing factor to social changes which acquired a new momentum in the early 1970's, such as a larger female work force, a higher divorce rate, and a sharply lowered birth rate. There were also moral implications, stressing a deeper individualism and greater toleration for diverse mores.

In the first half of the 1970's, the national consciousness discovered a long series of groups protesting discrimination and claiming greater equality. Some groups, such as Indians, Chicanos, migrant workers, and Puerto Ricans, sought the sort of social inclusion blacks had demanded. Others, including the elderly and homosexuals, were primarily interested in bringing about more tolerance and awareness of problems. In some cases these efforts were very successful. Wheelchair ramps in many public buildings, for example, signify an unprecedented concern for the problems of the handicapped.

There has been a "majority reaction" to the continual pressure exerted by minorities. By 1970, the enthusiasm of many liberals for civil rights had cooled to a tolerant acceptance. The bulk of Americans, including many minorities, showed strong signs of resentment at the efforts of various groups to obtain special legislation. Hostility to forced busing was only the most obvious manifestation of this anger; it was also directed against Indians who claimed enormous chunks of land, homosexuals who openly declared their sexual preferences, and feminists who "threatened" the home. Many individuals were not only bothered by the piece of the pie they felt themselves losing, but by the individualistic values minority groups seemed to advocate. Blacks and women were offended in large numbers by the militance of people claiming to be their leaders. Such feelings were often mixed and muddled, but they produced a general and widespread conservatism on issues of social change.

The magnitude of this reversed feeling was surprising. After sailing through thirty state legislatures, the Equal Rights Amendment suddenly lost momentum in late 1973. Some states which had passed the measure held referendums, reversing their endorsement. Ordinances against homosexuals were revived and strengthened in many cities. The Supreme Court modified programs for affirmative action in its Bakke decision in 1978. Studies demonstrated that middle-class blacks and women were the main beneficiaries of civil rights legislation, throwing in doubt the effectiveness of any government action against these problems. The effects and duration of this new conservatism were uncertain, but at least one important change had been achieved by the minority pressures: Americans as a whole were far more aware of their divergent needs, sufferings, and goals.

Pertinent Literature

Nisbet, Robert. *Twilight of Authority*. New York: Oxford University Press, 1975.

This work by Robert Nisbet is concerned with the decline of Western culture and society: the "twilight age" of the twentieth century. Nisbet perceives a decline of art, of morals, of genius, and of social order, all tied into a broader decline in the "political community" of the democracies. His work is individual and unique, but he exemplifies many of the conservative scholars who have recently argued against the new egalitarianism in the United States.

The argument made in *Twilight of Authority* runs roughly as follows. Democracy does not happen naturally, but is a special achievement of modern society. As the Church did in the Middle Ages, it has provided an essential base around which a new and varied culture could appear and flourish. The success of the democracies is dependent upon a conception of citizenship that gives the authority and restraints which Nisbet, as a conservative, sees as necessary for social order. This citizenship is based upon an enthusiastic participation in the state, a wholesome patriotism, a respect for existing institutions, and an acceptance of only gradual change.

The long-range search for greater equality is one of the greatest enemies to proper citizenship in Nisbet's scheme. He accepts it as an almost inevitable feature of democracy (as Alexis de Tocqueville did 150 years ago in *Democracy in America*), but at the same time finds it destructive to democracy. Its immediate effects undermine man's sense of community by eroding the natural hierarchies that exist among any group. Individuals become dependent upon the distant state for their equality and for the psychic security once provided by the community. As the state becomes a caretaker of these needs, its bureaucracy grows and its regulations stiffen. Politics loses its function as a forum for determining policy, but instead is a competition for control of bureaucratic power.

This power leads to self-destruction. As the political process erodes the authority of church, family, and business, it erodes the varied and assorted ties that make people interested in the society around them and in politics. This part of Nisbet's argument sounds very much like Edmund Burke and other classic conservatives: egalitarianism leads to the abandonment of tradition, strips life of its interest, and causes unrestrained hedonism. Apathy and decay overtake politics, leaving the military to take over the state.

Such is the dire forecast offered by Robert Nisbet. The solutions he offers to get out of this predicament are seemingly banal; he suggests little more than turning the clock back to revive private enterprise, voluntary associations, local ties, stronger church, closer families, and so on. Tides of history should be far stronger than any feeble will of conservatism. Interestingly enough, however, his advice appeared at a time when millions of Americans appeared determined to take it. Regardless of what politicians might manage or fail to do, there was little doubt in the mid-1970's that most people sought many of the renewed ties Nisbet advocates. This conservative revival, ironically, brings the credibility of Nisbet's entire argument into question. If there is such a self-regulating mechanism in society, could there be any reason to fear the movements for greater equality and individualism in the preceding decades? Could society not move linearly, but in circles? The author would reply, no doubt, wait and see.

Glazer, Nathan. *Affirmative Discrimination: Ethnic Inequality and Public Policy.* New York: Basic Books, 1975.

The Supreme Court decision on *Alan Bakke* v. *Regents of the University of California*, 1978, has brought the debate over affirmative action into a new stage. By prohibiting "racial quotas," the decision prevents job and admission choices from being made for solely racial reasons; but the continuing importance of racial considerations sharply divides observers, especially those who were so united in passing the Civil Rights Acts of the 1960's. Is affirmative action a new form of discrimination, or is it a necessary remedy to past discrimination? It is the most thorny of liberal debates.

Affirmative Discrimination is one of the most convincing attacks on affirmative action. Rather than arguing from liberal or philosophical grounds, which can easily be turned to defend the opposite point of view in this debate, the book is primarily historical. It suggests that affirmative action goes against deeply ingrained and generally beneficial American tradi-tions and conceptions of what is just.

Many of those in the Civil Rights movement, as well as other minority efforts, have argued that the United States has always been a racist, oppressive society. Not only through slavery, but in American treatment of poor immigrants and Indians, the Anglo-Saxon majority has tended to dislike individuals different from themselves; hence, they have tried to maintain an exclusive society. Such an argument leads to the conclusion that affirmative action is necessary. Regardless of the laws, whites will tend to discriminate unless they are directly forced to do otherwise.

Glazer rejects this entire line of reasoning. He believes that the United States was created in a uniquely tolerant environment. Ethnic and religious differences were accepted as a matter of course—if anything, they were a source of pride. Without doubt, those who were newcomers to the United States, or who showed conspicuous cultural and superficial differences, suffered discrimination and worse. But American beliefs always had a mitigating effect upon such mistreatment. To the author, it is more significant that slavery was abolished—which required a true humanitarian spirit—than the fact that it naturally arose in the seventeenth century.

Affirmative action goes against these traditions by writing privilege into the law. A very large consensus of Americans supported civil rights legislation in the 1960's because oppression of the blacks seemed such an obvious injustice. Busing and quota hiring may have sociological justifications, but they are in direct opposition to American ideals of equality. As a result, they have given new life to racist feelings which previously showed signs of fading away. To enforce such unpopular laws, Glazer concludes, is to defeat the very purpose of the laws: it codifies racial distinctions, instead of ignoring them.
— *R.H.S.*

Additional Recommended Reading

Berman, William C. *The Politics of Civil Rights in the Truman Administration*. Columbus: Ohio State University Press, 1970. A solid historical study showing the clash of political interests which stymied civil rights legislation.

Fraenkel, Osmond K. *The Rights We Have*. New York: Thomas Y. Crowell Company, 1974. Neatly describes the various individual freedoms guaranteed by the Constitution and developed by the courts.

Lockard, Duane. *Toward Equal Opportunity*. New York: The Macmillan Company, 1968. A study of state and local government responses to the civil rights movement.

Stevens, Leonard A. *Equal!: The Case of Integration vs. Jim Crow*. New York: Coward, McCann, 1976. Recounts the history of the "separate but equal" doctrine, which legalized segregation for sixty years before the landmark case of *Oliver Brown et al.* v. *Board of Education of Topeka et al.*

Warren, Robert Penn. *Who Speaks for the Negro?* New York: Random House, 1965. An unusual and fascinating exploration of black culture and ideas in the South by perhaps the greatest living Southern author.

DISCOVERY OF QUASARS

Type of event: Scientific: identification of astronomical radio sources with unexpected physical properties
Time: 1960-1963
Locale: Observatories with large radio telescopes, especially the one located at Parkes in Australia

Principal personages:
SIR MARTIN RYLE (1918-   ), compiler of the Cambridge catalogue of radio stars
ALLAN REX SANDAGE (1926-   ), an astronomer at Palomar, California
HONG-LEE CHIU, an astronomer at the Goddard Institute for Space Studies
CYRIL HAZARD, a British astronomer working at Parkes, Australia
MAARTIN SCHMIDT (1929-   ), a Dutch-American astronomer at Palomar, California
JESSIE LEONARD GREENSTEIN (1909-   ) and
THOMAS MATTHEWS, astronomers at California Institute of Technology

Summary of Event

Radio astronomy has largely developed since World War II. Many physicists and research scientists who had been involved in the development and deployment of radar during the war later adapted these radio techniques to radio astronomy.

Usually, the radio waves they found were generated by dust clouds or galaxies and were thus more or less spread out over portions of the sky. In the 1950's, however, a number of highly compact radio sources were discovered which could not be identified with galaxies. In 1960, Sir Martin Ryle, a British astronomer, compiled the *Third Cambridge Catalogue of Radio Stars*, which listed all the strong compact radio sources then known. (This provided the location and a number identification for each source, as, for example, 3C 273.) In the same year, American astronomer Allan Sandage investigated several of the unidentified radio sources. He found that three of them were associated with strange dim blue stars, and that one of these, termed 3C 48, trailed a faint jet of matter.

In 1961, astronomers regularly observed the source 3C 48, and the resulting photometric records showed that its light output varied over time. This seemed a clear indication that the sources must be stars and not galaxies, since, on the basis of relativity theory, an object as big as a galaxy could not show such variations in brightness. However, the spectra of these sources were very peculiar and could not be properly identified with those produced by elements usually found in stars. The strange objects were thus called "quasi-stellar radio sources." In 1964, the astronomer Hong-Lee Chiu coined the term "quasar" by which they are now generally known.

The identification of the quasars required accurate measurements, using very large radio telescopes which could give their position with some precision. In 1963, a team of astronomers led by Cyril Hazard used the radio telescope at Parkes in Australia to measure the position of the radio source 3C 273. Their method, called "lunar occultation," had previously been developed by optical astronomers. When the moon passed in front of the quasar, the astronomers could accurately measure the times at which its radiation first disappeared, and then reappeared. A combination of several measurements gave a precise reading of the position of the radio source. Hazard found that the source 3C 273 actually consisted of two components. The weaker one was associated with a fairly bright blue star, and the stronger one with a fainter jet of matter trailing beside the star.

As this star was relatively bright, the Dutch-American astronomer Maartin Schmidt was able to make a detailed survey of its spectrum. At first, none of the spectral lines could be identified. Then Schmidt decided to see whether these lines could be understood if a redshift or a blueshift correction were applied. (When an object emitting light is moving at extremely high speed, its spectral lines will be slightly shifted to the blue end of the spectrum if it is moving towards the observer, and to the red end of the spectrum if it is moving away from the observer.) To Schmidt's surprise, he found that if he applied a large redshift correction, he could identify the strange lines as those of quite ordinary substances: hydrogen atoms, magnesium atoms, and ionized oxygen.

Two other American astronomers, Jesse Greenstein and Thomas Matthews, then reexamined the spectrum of 3C 48, and found that this too could be understood by applying a very large redshift correction. The results of all these observations and calculations were published in the British scientific journal *Nature* in 1963. By the end of the year, several more of the radio sources had been identified and were seen to have similarly large redshifts.

The interpretation of these initially mysterious spectra did not, however, solve the problem of the quasars. Indeed, it simply served to show how important and surprising they were. Many astronomers associated the redshifts with high velocities arising from the general expansion of the universe. If the universe is expanding, the further away an object, the faster it is receding. When the redshift of the quasars was used to measure their velocity, and hence their distance, they were shown to be more than a billion light years away. This meant that they were the most distant objects in the universe. Such enormous distances, however, also meant that the quasars were extraordinarily bright: one hundred times as luminous as the average galaxy.

The more that was known about the quasars, the stranger they seemed. In 1963, Harlan Smith and Dorrit Hoffleit examined the Harvard collection of astronomical photographs dating back to 1887. They were able to identify the quasar 3C 273, and found that it had been fluctuating in brightness with a period of about ten years. Such variations implied that the quasars must be relatively small objects (in astronomical terms) and deepened the mystery of how they generated their enormous energies.

It became evident that the quasars had broken all the usual astronomical "rules," and that they might well prove the key to understanding the fundamental evolutionary processes of the universe. It is likely that the future solution of the problem of the quasars will involve the creation of a whole new cosmology and a new conception of the nature of our universe.

One of the most fascinating of recent speculations suggests that the quasars may be "white holes," cosmic centers for the creation of matter and energy. "Black holes," in which matter and energy are destroyed, have been the subject of recent investigations in astrophysics. Some have suggested that the white holes and black holes might even be linked together by "cosmic wormholes" or "cosmic subways" in space. Matter sucked into the black holes might be leaked across to the white holes, and thrown out in the form of huge quantities of radiation. In this way one can imagine that matter and energy are continuously being recycled in the universe. Instead of a single Big Bang as the origin of the universe, as some theorists propose, the quasars might represent a continuing series of "little bangs," an ongoing process of creation.

Pertinent Literature

Bova, Ben. *In Quest of Quasars: An Introduction to Stars and Starlike Objects.* New York: New American Library, 1969.

This is a lively and popular discussion of modern astronomy, accessible to readers with little previous knowledge of physics or astrophysics. The author is also a science fiction writer, and well understands how to present his subject in an appealing manner. He uses the discovery of quasars to introduce the pleasures and excitement of cosmological speculations to the lay reader, and the book is well illustrated with simple diagrams of basic concepts, tables of observations, and photographs of many of the phenomena described.

Bova first briefly describes the series of observations which led to the recognition that quasars were peculiarly puzzling astronomical objects: according to the most widely held interpretation of the spectral redshift, very distant objects, moving away from our galaxy at speeds up to eighty percent of the speed of light. On this interpretation, the quasars must be extraordinarily brilliant, producing vast amounts of energy, in order to be both relatively small and yet still visible with optical telescopes. Bova also discusses the theory of the local origin of quasars and shows why astronomers have been divided between "distant" and "local" theories, neither group being able to account satisfactorily for all the observations.

Much of this book is devoted to an explanation of the basic physical and astronomical concepts necessary for understanding why quasars appeared so paradoxical to astronomers. Bova provides simple accounts of spectroscopy, the production of energy within stars, the parallactic shift method of measuring stellar distances, and the sequences of stellar evolution. He devotes one chapter to galaxies and radio galaxies, and another to a discussion of current cosmological theories from the Big Bang theory of the origin of the universe, to the steady-state theory and the theory of the oscillating universe.

This introduction lays the basis for a further discussion of the observational and theoretical properties of quasars. Quasars have a starlike visual appearance, but vary in both radio and light energy emission, often within surprisingly short times, and sometimes within minutes. Although first discovered by radio astronomy, many radio-quiet quasars have since been found. After discussing the problem of determining the distance of the quasars, Bova turns to the problem of explaining their vast energy production. He suggests a number of different possible mechanisms which could generate such enormous energy: gravitational forces, stellar collisions, supernova chain explosions, and the mutual annihilation of matter and antimatter.

The author provides brief but reasonably clear explanations of these ideas and the difficulties associated with each of them. His discussion will not prove satisfying for the serious reader, but is intended simply to introduce the theoretical speculations current at the time of writing. Those whose curiosity is aroused can then progress to somewhat more technical sources for further information. Bova provides just enough data to show why quasars are such a challenge to astronomers, to point out their implications for cosmology, and to inspire the reader's interest to read more about the quasars and other discoveries of modern astronomy.

Kahn, Frenz D. and Henry P. Palmer. *Quasars, Their Importance in Astronomy and Physics*. Cambridge, Mass.: Harvard University Press, 1967.

The authors of this work are, respectively, Professor of Astronomy and Senior Lecturer in Radio Astronomy at the University of Manchester in England. Their book provides much technical information about quasars, their observed properties, and the theoretical models developed to explain them. At the same time, theirs is a compact book, and one written in a much more literate style than many scientific works. It is accessible to the general reader who is willing to expend a little effort in order to gain an informed understanding of the problem of quasars.

The book begins with an explanation of the series of observations in the early 1960's which led astronomers to realize that the previously unidentified strong radio sources were puzzling new objects: the quasars. A clear description is included of the method of lunar occultation first used by Cyril Hazard and his colleagues for examining the radio source 3C 273. The authors cover the optical properties of quasars observed between 1963 and 1967, from the phenomenon of the redshift to that of the variations in brightness shown by several of the sources. They then explain the different methods used to make accurate measurements of the positions of these radio sources.

A radio telescope does not provide as precise measurements as does an optical telescope because the wavelength of the radiation it uses is a million times longer than that of light. One method of getting around this difficulty is to use two widely separated telescopes in an arrangement called a radio inferometer. Kahn and Palmer explain the principles on which radio measurements are made, provide photographs of major telescopes in England and the United States, and show diagrammatically the patterns of radio traces they produce. They note that radio observations of quasars show fluctuations similar to those found by optical measurements. These radio observations suggest that quasars are associated with very violent astronomical events.

The second part of the book describes results taken from various branches of physics which may help to explain the nature of quasars. The authors argue that although scientists studying extragalactic phenomena are often tempted to invent new theories, it is preferable to resist such speculation, and instead, to try to explain unexpected observations in terms of accepted physical laws.

First, they describe the mechanics of charged particles. Since it is certain that fast-moving charged particles are abundant in quasars, and since it is highly likely that quasars are permeated by magnetic fields, current knowledge of the dynamics of charged particles moving in magnetic fields should be very useful in understanding the physics of quasars.

Second, relativity theory is an essential tool for the discussion of quasars. The authors briefly describe special relativity and general relativity and suggest that the energy of quasars may be derived from the gravitational energy of very large masses, considerably larger than that of the sun. One of the consequences of the general theory is that gravitational energy can produce a redshift in the light emitted by large masses, but the amount of this redshift is normally too small to be observable. Gravitational energy can also be released by large masses when they contract, although the theory predicts that, at a specific degree of compactness, no radiation will be able to escape, and the object will therefore cut itself off from the rest of the universe as a "black hole."

Kahn and Palmer then provided brief discussions of cosmology and stellar evolution. They calculate the quantities of energy that could be released by a static body of great mass, and conclude that such a body would have to break up before it had produced enough energy (either gravitational or nuclear) to account for the energy production of quasars. They then suggest that this radiated energy might be increased by synchotron radiation, involving fast electrons. (Fast electrons are electrons with speeds comparable to the speed of light.)

Finally, the authors summarize the different theories developed since 1963 to account for the quasars. They state that the existence of gravitational fields sufficiently strong to produce the observed redshift in quasar spectra would prevent the emission of some of their characteristic spectral lines. They therefore conclude that the spectral redshift should be attributed to the effects of high velocities. They find that the luminosity of quasars is typically from one thousand to ten thousand times that of our own galaxy, and that the total emission of energy during the lifetime of a quasar is at least 10^{60} erg, or about one hundred million times that of the total energy radiated by the sun in its lifetime.

The "local origin" theory of the quasars suggests that they are much closer to the earth than other theories propose. If so, their high velocities can be imagined to have been produced by a vast explosion, perhaps one hundred million years ago. Since all observed quasars are moving away from us, the explosion must have occurred quite close to our galaxy. Astrophysicists do not, however, like to suppose that there is anything unique about our own galaxy, and they therefore admit that other parts of the universe must have their own quasars—perhaps another million groups of quasars. Kahn and Palmer enumerate a number of difficulties with the theory of the local origin of quasars and conclude that it is unlikely to be true. They then return to the assumption of a cosmological, or distant, origin for the quasars.

Next, they discuss the possible theoretical candidates for explaining the source of energy in quasars. One is the energy produced by the annihilation of matter and antimatter. Intergalactic gas containing matter and antimatter might condense under gravitational attraction to the extent that annihilation reactions could occur. The problem here is that one would expect the energy released to be radiation of extremely short wavelength, whereas quasars emit strongly at long wavelengths.

The authors conclude that the energy released by quasars can best be explained by a combination of gravitational and nuclear energies. They argue that as the quasar contracts, it must split up into several parts which go into orbit around one another. Radiant energy escapes into space and becomes visible as trailing luminous jets. As each part of the quasar continues to contract, it will in turn split into smaller parts, creating a hierarchy of orbiting masses. An unsteady magnetic field develops which may cause some of the electrons to accelerate into fast electrons, thus increasing the energy produced.

Kahn and Palmer cheerfully recognize that their hypothesis produces its own difficulties; they claim that it is more probable than the alternative theories, but admit that we are only at the beginning of our efforts to understand the quasars. Their book appears to be a careful and balanced account of research on these questions and should be helpful to anyone who wishes to understand these debates on a nonspecialist level. — *E.F.*

Additional Recommended Reading

Merleau-Ponty, Jacques and Bruno Morando. *The Rebirth of Cosmology*. Translated by Helen Weaver. New York: Alfred A. Knopf, 1976. A broad view of the history of cosmology, with alternate sections written by an astronomer and a philosopher.

Hey, J. S. *The Evolution of Radio Astronomy*. New York: Neale Watson Academic Publications, 1973. A history of radio astronomy up to 1970 by one of those closely involved in its development.

Lovell, Bernard. *Out of the Zenith: Jodrell Bank, 1957-1970*. New York: Harper & Row Publishers, 1973. A comprehensive and detailed history of recent research carried out in radio astronomy at Jodrell Bank, including a chapter on the discovery of quasars.

Burbidge, Geoffrey and Margaret Burbidge. *Quasi-Stellar Objects*. San Francisco: W. H. Freeman and Company, 1967. A careful summary of all the relevant technical literature about quasars up to early 1967.

Golden, Frederic. *Quasars, Pulsars, and Black Holes*. New York: Charles Scribner's Sons, 1976. A lively and informed popular account of modern astronomy, including a brief review of the history of astronomy, by the science editor of *Time* magazine.

Gribbin, John. *White Holes: Cosmic Gushes in the Universe*. New York: Delacorte Press/Eleanor Friede, 1977. The most up-to-date cosmological speculations translated into layman's language; many wild and wonderful ideas.

Asimov, Isaac. *The Collapsing Universe: The Story of Black Holes*. New York: Walker, 1977. A masterly survey of modern astronomy by the dean of all popular science writers.

THE U-2 INCIDENT AND THE COLLAPSE
OF THE PARIS SUMMIT CONFERENCE

Type of event: Diplomatic: international crisis stemming from the capture of an
American spy plane over Russian territory
Time: May, 1960
Locale: Washington, D.C., Moscow, Sverdlovsk, and Paris

Principal personages:
DWIGHT DAVID EISENHOWER (1890-1969), thirty-fourth Pres-
ident of the United States, 1953-1961
NIKITA SERGEEVICH KHRUSHCHEV (1894-1971), First Secre-
tary of the Communist Party of the Soviet Union, 1953-
1964; and Premier of the Soviet Union, 1958-1964
FRANCIS GARY POWERS (1929-   ), pilot of the captured
U-2 plane

Summary of Event

In the spring of 1960, the world was
basking in a feeling known as "the
spirit of Camp David," so called after
the presidential retreat in Camp
David, Maryland, where President
Dwight D. Eisenhower had met in
September, 1959, with Nikita Sergeevich Khrushchev, the First Secretary of the Communist Party of the
Soviet Union. For the first time since
the Potsdam Conference in 1947, the
leaders of the two most powerful nations on earth had talked face to face.
While nothing substantive was accomplished in these conversations,
they provided an optimistic ending
for Khrushchev's good-will tour of
the United States, and people began
to think that the Cold War that had
lasted for more than a decade was
coming to an end. Now all hopes were
placed on the Paris summit conference to be held on May 16, 1960, between Khrushchev, Eisenhower, the
British Foreign Minister, Harold
Macmillan, and Charles de Gaulle,
President of France.

Such a "Big Four" Summit was
long overdue. The problem of a divided Germany, and especially the
status of West Berlin, had reemerged
to plague world leaders. Germany
had been divided into four zones of
occupation, each administered by a
different member of the "Big Four."
Berlin, the capital and largest city in
Germany, lay deep within the Soviet
zone. It, too, was divided into four
administrative sectors. The original
partition had been intended as a temporary measure, a compromise between Russian fears of a united, prosperous, and armed German nation
and American concern to build a
strong bulwark against Communism
in Central Europe.

Neither Russian fears nor American plans had greatly changed in the
postwar years, so the uneasy temporary compromise had simply remained. Across the years 1947-1949,
the three Western zones began to
merge economically and politically,
and on May 8, 1949, they formed

themselves into the Federal Republic of Germany with Bonn as the capital. On October 7, 1949, the Soviet (Eastern) zone became the German Democratic Republic. The situation in Germany was a frequent point of Soviet-American friction.

In late 1958, the situation had flared up again. The continued American rearming of West Germany excited Soviet fears, especially when some of the more recent supplies included artillery and bombers capable of handling nuclear weapons. The Soviets also considered the proposed integration of West Germany into a close economic union with France, Italy, Belgium, the Netherlands, and Luxembourg (the European Economic Community, or Common Market) to be a threat to their interests. Between November 10 and 27, 1958, therefore, they made a series of proposals and demands concerning the divided city of Berlin which essentially gave a six-month deadline to the Western powers to end their occupation of Berlin. The Soviets said they would turn over administration of their sector to the German Democratic Republic; that nation would also control the access routes to Berlin. The Western powers also had to leave by that time, or turn administration over to a United Nations peacekeeping force. The Western powers, especially the United States, found these terms unacceptable, since they did not recognize the German Democratic Republic as a legal government. They would ignore or force any GDR checkpoints, they said. An attack on the GDR would be considered an attack on the Soviet Union, the U.S.S.R. replied. Later, Khrushchev removed the six-month deadline so that the subject could be discussed at Paris.

Ever since his victory over his rivals, G. M. Malenkov, N. A. Bulganin, and V. M. Molotov, in July, 1957, Khrushchev had been the unchallenged leader of the Soviet Union. As First Secretary of the Communist Party and Premier of the Soviet Union, he occupied the most powerful positions in the Party and state executive hierarchies. Since 1957, he had become one of the strongest advocates of increased consumer goods production, opposing the traditional Soviet emphasis on heavy industry and defense spending. One of the most important correlaries of this program was a policy of "peaceful coexistence" with the West; lowered tensions, he hoped, could allow for a lower defense budget.

Khrushchev's attitude was highly controversial in the Communist world, and within the Soviet Union itself. The Chinese Communists were especially concerned about the implications of the doctrine of peaceful coexistence. While the Sino-Soviet split was not to emerge into the open until 1962, the issue of *rapprochement* with the West had already soured relations between the two states. A similar point of view could be heard within the highest circles of the Russian Communist Party, from the military leaders—who did not trust the West—as well as the advocates of heavy industry, who were unenthusiastic about the whole thrust of Khrushchev's policies. Khrushchev's Camp David initiative, therefore, had been undertaken against heavy internal opposition, but his power was such that he did not have to worry about this opposition as long as his policy was showing visible results. Yet he needed a clear victory at the summit to ensure his domestic political position.

At 8:55 A.M. on May 1, 1960, however, an American U-2 high-altitude reconnaissance plane was shot down by a Soviet ground-to-air missile near Sverdlovsk, three hundred miles into Soviet territory. The pilot, Francis Gary Powers, did not succeed in destroying the plane, and both he and it fell into Soviet hands. On May 5, Khrushchev reported the incident to the U.S.S.R. Supreme Soviet, without mentioning that both the pilot and the plane had been recovered. Later that day, the United States released a "cover story" maintaining that the plane was collecting scientific data on the Turkish-Soviet border and had probably strayed across. Two days later, Khrushchev disclosed Powers' capture and confession, exploding the cover story issued by the United States. Khrushchev's statement embarrassed the United States but did not close the door to the summit, since Khrushchev added that he was willing to believe that President Eisenhower had not known of the flight. The Americans at first seemed willing to take advantage of this loophole, but later vacillated; and on May 11, President Eisenhower took responsibility for the U-2 flights, which had been going on since 1956, calling them a "distasteful . . . necessity." Although a moratorium was called on future flights, the United States would not say that they were going to cancel them altogether.

Inside the U.S.S.R., the American acknowledgment of responsibility and apparent determination to continue the overflights came as a decisive blow to Khrushchev's policy of peaceful coexistence. On May 10 or 11, Khrushchev was apparently outvoted in a meeting of the Presidium of the Central Committee of the Communist Party, and a hard-line stand at the summit was mandated. At the first meeting of the conference later that month, Khrushchev announced that the U.S.S.R. would not participate unless the United States repudiated the U-2 program and punished those responsible for instituting it. Eisenhower, of course, refused, and the much-vaunted summit never took place.

The diplomatic consequences of the collapse of the summit were less than expected. On his way back to Russia, Khrushchev withdrew his plan to turn over administration to Berlin and its approaches to East Germany. Thus, the Berlin question did not explode; but neither was it settled. Eisenhower's successor, John F. Kennedy, would find this one of the first diplomatic problems with which he had to deal.

For Khrushchev, the consequences were somewhat more severe. His reverse in the foreign policy arena strengthened his domestic critics. This opposition was expressed in a shakeup in the top leadership of the Party in which some of Khrushchev's most loyal supporters were demoted. Khrushchev's own position was never in danger, but from 1960 onward he was forced to share more and more power with the other party leaders. For some analysts, the U-2 incident marks the beginning of Khrushchev's decline, which ended in his ouster in 1964.

Pertinent Literature

Tatu, Michel. *Power in the Kremlin: From Khrushchev to Kosygin*. Translated by Helen Katel. New York: The Viking Press, 1969.

Michel Tatu is a French journalist whose specialty is "Kremlinology," which can be defined as the attempt to penetrate the monolithic façade of Soviet leadership politics by the close analysis of public indicators such as the wording of announcements and speeches, personnel changes, and the order in which leaders line up on the podium on Red Square in Moscow. This book is an excellent example of this method, showing both its strengths and its limitations. It applies these techniques to the period between 1960 and 1966, and the first part of the book is devoted to the U-2 incident and its consequences.

The U-2 affair marks a major turning point in Soviet politics for Tatu. It marked the failure of the policy of peaceful coexistence to achieve Soviet foreign policy aims, especially in Berlin. This failure was a personal defeat for Khrushchev, and "served as a catalyst for the latent opposition of his domestic critics." These critics were able to force first a change of personnel in the higher party organs and then a reversal of certain of Khrushchev's policies that they found most distasteful. This shift was a return to collective leadership, and presaged, although it did not render inevitable, Khrushchev's eventual fall.

The techniques with which Tatu supports his thesis are as interesting as the conclusions he reaches. Kremlinology is based on several assumptions, one of the most important of which is that changes in the balance of power at the top of the Soviet hierarchy will be revealed to knowledgeable people by subtle signs and nuances of emphasis in public statements. Often what is not said is as important to a Kremlinologist as what is said. For example, Tatu infers that A. I. Mikoyan, one of the advocates of a moderate foreign policy, was in disfavor following the U-2 overflight when an honorary title of his was left out in two consecutive articles in *Pravda*, and a speech was made about an incident in the Russian Revolution of 1917 in which he had been a central participant, without his name being mentioned. From evidence such as this, Tatu deduced not only that Mikoyan's position was on the decline, but also that Khrushchev's foreign policy must be coming under attack within the walls of the Presidium.

Tatu also interprets the personnel changes that followed the crisis using similar techniques. By examining the previous statements of the various actors on policy issues, the pattern of their careers, and even the warmth of their praise of Khrushchev on ceremonial occasions, he is able to guess their level of allegiance to the First Secretary. He then divides the Presidium and the Party Secretariat between Khrushchev's "clients," his "allies," and the latent opposition. Thus, when Leonid Brezhnev, who had started his career under Khrushchev's protection and had been vocal in his support for the First Secretary on a number of important issues, was "freed" of his work in the Party Secretariat, and his place taken by F. R. Kuzlov, who owed Khrushchev nothing, Tatu considers the change one of the more overt signs of the limitations being placed on Khrushchev's power following the U-2 incident.

Ulam, Adam B. *The Rivals: America and Russia Since World War II*. New York: The Viking Press, 1971.

Just as Michel Tatu interprets the U-2 incident against the background of Soviet domestic politics, Adam Ulam sets it in the context of Big Power politics. For him, Khrushchev's diplomatic maneuvers over Berlin in 1958-1960 were part of a Soviet master plan to keep both West Germany and Communist China from developing nuclear capability. The first Soviet move came on March 3, 1958, when the Soviets presented the United States with a plan that had ostensibly originated with Adam Rapacki, the Foreign Minister of Poland. The Rapacki plan proposed that Central Europe be turned into a nuclear free zone, and that no "atomic, hydrogen, or rocket weapons" be manufactured or deployed in Poland, Czechoslovakia, the German Democratic Republic, or the Federal Republic of Germany.

When the Western powers rejected this plan, according to Ulam, Khrushchev began his series of threatening moves around Berlin. His purpose was not to force the Western occupying powers out of Berlin, but merely to force a summit conference. This explains, among other things, his studied intransigence before Camp David, followed by his sudden removal of the six-month deadline on Berlin, and finally his abandonment of the whole ploy after the collapse of the summit. At the summit, Ulam argues, Khrushchev was planning to offer a trade to the West. If he received their support for a nuclear-free zone in Central Europe, he would help create a similar zone in the Pacific, including Japan and Communist China. To the West, which knew little about the Sino-Soviet difficulties, it would seem a fair exchange, but the Soviets would actually be reaping a double advantage, since they really did not want to have a nuclear neighbor on their southern border, even if it were a Communist country.

For Ulam, this subtle plan was disrupted well before the shooting down of the U-2. The Chinese saw through Khrushchev's maneuvering and announced in April, 1960, that they would not be bound by any agreement in which they did not participate formally. Since the United States had not yet recognized the Chinese Communist government, that rendered the Soviet trade unlikely. The crash of the U-2 was a blessing in disguise for Khrushchev, because it got him out of a fruitless diplomatic situation.

This insightful interpretation of the U-2 incident, of course, is only one part of Ulam's history of Russo-American relations from 1944 to 1968.

His treatment of this incident, however, is consistent with the main thrust of the book as a whole. Ulam argues that American policy in this episode was not guided by a realistic appraisal of the advantages and disadvantages various options held for America; had it been, the Americans would have adopted the Rapacki plan when it was first offered. American statesmen were blinded, during the U-2 incident and throughout the Cold War, by an overly ideological, moralistic perception of the world that rendered them incapable of seeing the national aspirations which Ulam believes underlay the Communist rhetoric. His book is an argument that a more realistic view of the U.S.S.R. and a more realistic assessment of American goals is the only way to achieve a successful foreign policy. — *P.A.*

Additional Recommended Reading

LaFeber, Walter. *America, Russia, and the Cold War, 1945-1975*. New York: John Wiley and Sons, 1975. An analysis and critique of American foreign policy in this period which show the importance of domestic political factors in determining the foreign policy of nations.

Powers, Francis Gary and Curt Gentry. *Operation Overflight: The U-2 Spy Pilot Tells His Story for the First Time*. New York: Tower Publications, 1970. Powers' personal story of the U-2 program, his flight, imprisonment, and subsequent experiences in a critical United States.

Khrushchev, Nikita S. *Khrushchev Remembers*. 2 vols. Translated and edited by Strobe Talbott. Boston: Little, Brown and Company, 1970. These authenticated and annotated memoirs provide a rich, earthy account of Khrushchev's years in power. The U-2 incident is discussed in the second volume.

Ulam, Adam B. *Expansion and Coexistence: The History of Soviet Foreign Policy, 1917-1967*. New York: Frederick A. Praeger, 1968. The most complete description and analysis of Soviet foreign policy.

Wise, David and Thomas B. Ross. *The U-2 Affair*. New York: Random House, 1962. A journalistic account of the U-2 incident that uses the experience of Powers as a framework within which to describe the events of May, 1960.

Eisenhower, Dwight D. *The White House Years: Waging Peace, 1956-1961*. Garden City, N.Y.: Doubleday & Company, 1965. This second volume of Eisenhower's memoirs contains his justification for American policy and action during the U-2 incident.

ESTABLISHMENT OF THE ORGANIZATION OF PETROLEUM EXPORTING COUNTRIES (OPEC)

Type of event: Economic: control of a fossil fuel to raise its price
Time: September 10-14, 1960
Locale: Baghdad, Iraq

Principal personages:
ABDULLAH TARIKI (1919-   ), Oil Minister of Saudi Arabia
PEREZ ALFONSO, Oil Minister of Venezuela
MOHAMMED RIZA PAHLEVI (1919-   ), the Shah of Iran
FUAD ROUHANI (1907-   ), first Secretary-General of OPEC

Summary of Event

After World War II, the main participants on the supply side of the international oil market were the traditional producing countries (for example, the United States), the seven major international oil companies (Esso, Shell, British Petroleum, Gulf Oil, Texaco, Mobil, and Chevron), and a group of newer producers composed mostly of underdeveloped countries such as Venezuela, Saudi Arabia, Iran, and Indonesia. As these newer producing nations and others like them rose to prominence in the international market, they found their economies becoming increasingly dependent on revenues earned from oil. Changes in the world price of oil could mean large increases or decreases in foreign exchange earned from exports and, in consequence, large fluctuations in the ability to pay for imports of manufactured goods, upon which these countries' plans for economic development depended.

Although the pricing system by which the "take" of the producing nations was determined went through several stages of evolution in the postwar period, the main change was a simple one. Flat royalty payments, by which producing nations received a fixed sum of money per barrel extracted by the oil companies, were abolished, and artificial "posted prices," by which receipts were tied to the profit earned from the sale of the oil, were substituted in their place. In times of low or falling petroleum prices, the royalty system helped the producing nations maintain a stable income; in times of high or rising prices the posted prices were even more advantageous. In general, world demand for petroleum has grown rapidly during the postwar period, and conditions have been conducive to rising prices, with the result that petroleum producers, unlike producers of other primary products, have felt confident about their markets and the security of their export revenues.

This was not the case, however, in the late 1950's. The world price of crude oil began to fall, in part as a result of expanded Russian sales around the world, with negative effects on oil exports from several countries. In Venezuela, for example, the total value of exports of crude

912

oil fell by more than four percent in 1958 and continued to decline until 1961. The decline of world oil prices affected other underdeveloped producing countries similarly. For the Middle Eastern countries, in fact, the situation was worse than for Venezuela. Events made these previously naïve countries subject to the vagaries of the international marketplace.

Although the decline in the price of oil was largely the result of forces beyond the control of the international oil companies, it was they who brought the bad news to the producing nations by reducing posted prices. Given the cartellike appearance of the international oil industry, the producing nations finally began to act upon their long-held feeling that a countercartel might be desirable. An Arab Petroleum Congress, including observers from Venezuela and Iran, convened in Cairo in 1959. In September, 1960, in response to another reduction in posted prices, Iraq convened a second conference at Baghdad, and invited four other countries: Saudi Arabia, Iran, Kuwait, and Venezuela. Together, these five countries were responsible for eighty percent of world oil exports.

At last conditions were such that the economic and political differences of these producers could be subordinated to the pursuit of a larger goal, namely, a world price of oil higher than that which would prevail if the traditional structure of the market were allowed to continue. Thus, at the urging of Abdullah Tariki, the Oil Minister of Saudi Arabia; Perez Alfonso, the Oil Minister of Venezuela; and, to a lesser extent, Mohammed Riza Pahlevi, the Shah of Iran, the conference participants agreed to become charter members of a new body, the Organization of Petroleum Exporting Countries (OPEC).

Since the meeting at Baghdad, eight more countries have joined OPEC, making a total of thirteen. The additional members, in order of their joining, are: Qatar (1961), Indonesia (1962), Libya (1962), Abu Dhabi (1967), Algeria (1969), Nigeria (1971), Ecuador (1973), and Gabon (1975). Several major producers, including the United States, Russia, Mexico, Canada, and recently, the United Kingdom, do not belong. Nevertheless, today more than ninety percent of the crude petroleum entering international trade is produced in OPEC countries.

OPEC was originally conceived as a defensive organization. The founding resolution stated, that "Members shall demand that Oil Companies maintain their prices steady and free from unnecessary fluctuations and that Members shall study and formulate a system to ensure the stabilization of prices by . . . the regulation of production. . . ." Although regulation of production is the means by which any cartel contrives a shortage in the market it serves, OPEC has always emphasized its self-protective aspects. Initially, at least, there was much truth in this characterization.

The reaction of the international oil companies to the founding of OPEC was one of mild annoyance; they were accustomed to postwar militancy in the underdeveloped countries and were reconciled to the possibility of making concessions to

OPEC. Indeed, led by Fuad Rouhani, its first Secretary-General, OPEC succeeded in forcing the companies to stop cutting the posted price of crude petroleum, although it failed in getting the companies to restore the posted price to previous levels. Although OPEC, like most cartels, had trouble maintaining internal cohesion after the initial fanfare, the cartel succeeded during the 1960's in raising the share of the member countries in the revenues obtained from the worldwide sale of oil. A prominent figure during these early struggles was Sheikh Zaki Yamani, who replaced Tariki as the Oil Minister of Saudi Arabia, and who has continued in office.

The reactions of world governments to OPEC varied, but in general they were not particularly hostile. Underdeveloped countries applauded OPEC's attempt to resist what they saw, rightly or wrongly, as the overwhelming power of multinational corporations and/or Western capitalism. However, underdeveloped countries must also pay the higher oil prices OPEC has succeeded in enforcing. The United States, too, was supportive, at least initially. OPEC was seen as a stabilizing factor in Middle Eastern politics and a bulwark against Russian influence in that part of the world. In many ways, American policy has continued to be supportive, although today the United States is trying to find ways to cope with OPEC's enormous economic and political power. Because of that power, official criticism of OPEC in the West has tended to be muted; occasionally, praise is bestowed when OPEC shows what is euphemistically called "restraint" in wielding its monopoly power.

In any case, OPEC has gradually acquired the power to set a world price of crude petroleum far in excess of what the free market would dictate. Furthermore, a cut in production by the OPEC nations would have the severest consequences for the world economy, promoting recession or depression throughout the world and obstructing the efforts of poor nations to achieve economic development. The huge wealth that OPEC members control is one of the biggest components of international capital movements and one of the most important determinants of the rates at which currencies are exchanged. As a result, that economic leverage has given the OPEC nations tremendous political leverage, especially in the Middle East.

Pertinent Literature

Mikdashi, Zuhayr. *The Community of Oil Exporting Countries*. Ithaca, N.Y.: Cornell University Press, 1971.

Mikdashi's book is a detailed description of OPEC's structure, history, and objectives; it also offers sophisticated explanations of its behavior and policies in terms of the economics of the international petroleum market, a feature lacking in many other books about OPEC. The discussion, however, is largely nontechnical and thus comprehensible to the educated layman. Although the book was published before OPEC's successful attempt in 1973 and 1974 to increase crude petroleum prices to unprecedented levels, the author's understanding of the organization is quite deep; nothing has happened since the book's publication that contradicts its main theses in any significant way. Naturally, the reader desiring a detailed treatment of the 1970's should consult other sources.

Chapter 1 is a concise history of the events leading up to the formation of OPEC, beginning with the year 1947. A wealth of background detail is presented on the postwar structure of the world oil market and on preliminary efforts at cooperation among the newer producing nations. Chapter 2 ventures a more detailed analysis of the nature and functioning of the world market for crude petroleum in order to set the stage for an in-depth analysis of OPEC's structure and functioning.

Chapters 3 through 6 present a meticulous account of the internal workings and politics of OPEC, including a discussion of the subgroup OAPEC (Organization of Arab Petroleum Exporting Countries) and where it fits into the overall picture. The main virtue of this section of the book is that, apart from providing valuable background information, it is a useful case study of how a cartel interacts with the larger economic environment and how it deals with the problems it faces. The reader quickly recognizes that cartels are not monoliths—appearances to the contrary notwithstanding.

In Chapter 7, the author discusses the economics of oil in further detail with special reference to the relationship of oil exports to the economies of the OPEC countries. The discussion is somewhat technical, but sets the stage for the final chapter, which deals with the future of cooperative effort among underdeveloped oil-producing nations. The general conclusion is that, while differences in economics, politics, and culture exist among OPEC countries that tend to drive them apart, the mutual harmony of their larger interests is likely to promote greater solidarity in the future. This prediction, made in 1971, has proved accurate so far.

Copp, Anthony R. *Regulating Competition in Oil*. College Station: Texas A&M University Press, 1976.

Although this book is not exclusively about OPEC, it is an extremely useful case study of how one country, the United States, has developed its oil policy during the postwar period. One long chapter, however, is devoted to OPEC; in it, the author makes clear how American policy has been affected by the rise of the organization.

In Chapter 1, Copp offers a basic description of the structure of the oil-refining industry and the government's role in it. Chapter 2 examines how public policy toward oil-refining has evolved since 1900, with special emphasis on the post-1932 period. One theme of the chapter is that public policy in the 1970's, the decade of OPEC's fullest flowering, has seen

". . . the evolution of new administrative energy planning bureaucracies and price controls on crude oil and refined products." Although previous policy was not strictly laissez-faire, recent policy has implied a quantum leap in government involvement in the oil industry. Chapter 3 is a detailed treatment of how government influences the microeconomics of the refining industry. The impact of government on supply and demand for specific refined products of crude oil is analyzed; the approach is semitechnical.

Chapter 4 is narrower in focus than the others, dealing only with a specific rationale for government action: national security. Copp points out that the domestic petroleum industry itself has backed oil import quotas and other restrictions in the name of national security. This chapter is something of an antidote to the easily held view that government always imposes regulations against the wishes of the private sector. Part of the discussion is technical. Copp uses technical material to argue that by causing a misallocation of resources, federal controls have tended to contradict the national security rationale for imposing regulations in the first place.

Chapter 5 is a detailed examination of recent federal policy toward the refining industry, while Chapter 6 traces OPEC's rise to world economic power.

Chapter 7 contains an evaluation of American energy policy, which is largely negative. Copp argues that policy has led to a misallocation of resources and resulting waste and urges further research and development to find new sources of oil and gas, and favors the deregulation of natural gas. His sentiments are echoed by many other writers on energy, although the deregulation of natural gas is a politically controversial issue in the United States.

One of the strengths of this book is its careful documentation and scrupulous marshaling of empirical evidence in support of positions. Thus, although the argument is incisive, Copp's monograph is also a useful sourcebook for those uninitiated in the subtleties and complexities of national energy policy. In the words of one reviewer, this book is ". . . unequivocally the best researched and most well-written volume on U.S. petroleum policy to appear to date." — *J.R.H.*

Additional Recommended Reading

Adelman, Morris A. *The World Petroleum Market.* Baltimore, Md.: The Johns Hopkins University Press, 1971. A superb description of the world market for oil by a leading economist.

Campbell, R. W. *The Economics of Soviet Oil and Gas.* Baltimore, Md.: The Johns Hopkins University Press, 1968. A study of oil policy in the Communist bloc.

Odell, Peter R. *Oil and World Power.* Harmondsworth, England: Penguin Books, 1974. A sober treatment of the world oil market emphasizing politics and diplomacy.

Rybczynski, T. M. *The Economics of the Oil Crisis.* London: Macmillan and Company, 1976. A collection of excellent readings about the worldwide oil crisis of 1973-1974.

Sampson, Anthony. *The Seven Sisters*. New York: The Viking Press, 1975. An inflammatory but well-researched account of the role of the major international oil companies in the postwar oil market.

Vernon, Raymond. *The Oil Crisis*. New York: W. W. Norton and Company, 1976. Another book of readings about the oil crisis of 1973-1974.

FRITZ FISCHER PUBLISHES
GERMANY'S AIMS IN THE FIRST WORLD WAR

Type of event: Intellectual: major work in twentieth century European historiography
Time: 1961
Locale: West Germany

Principal personages:
  FRITZ FISCHER (1908-   ), Professor of History at the University of Hamburg, West Germany
  GERHARD RITTER (1888-1967), Professor of History at the University of Freiburg, West Germany

Summary of Event

Following Germany's defeat in World War I and her acceptance of the punitive Treaty of Versailles, which, among other things, required her to accept the entire blame for the war, a debate opened among historians, journalists, and assorted polemists on both sides of the Atlantic as to which nation or nations had been responsible for the disastrous conflict. This debate was conducted in the aftermath of Western civilization's most bloody and ruinous struggle and in the midst of grave economic and political crises which flowed directly from that conflict; it did not take place in an atmosphere which lent itself to objective and detached judgments concerning the origins of the conflict nor of the aims of those nations that participated in it. There was bitter disagreement as to who was "guilty," but powerful arguments were brought to bear showing that Russia, Austria-Hungary, Germany, England, and France could all be assigned at least some portion of the blame. There was also considerable sympathy for Germany's position in the years preceding the conflict and

in the Sarajevo crisis of 1914 which led to the outbreak of war.

Many histories were written in the interwar period in an attempt to fix the responsibility for the conflict, notably Sidney B. Fay's revisionist *The Origins of the World War*, which sought to mitigate the harsh verdict meted out to Germany by the peacemakers and historians. All these works were superseded in the post-World War II period, in the opinion of most historians outside Germany, by the Italian Luigi Albertini's three-volume work, *The Origins of the War of 1914*, which was translated into English in 1952. Albertini's research rested on a thorough inspection of the major document collections published by various European governments since World War I, many of which had not been available to earlier researchers and scholars. He concluded that the German government was largely responsible for plunging Europe into war in 1914, and his work was sufficiently thorough to still the debate until Fritz Fischer reopened it, this time within Germany itself, with the publication in 1961 of *Griff nach der Weltmacht* (translated into English in 1967 as *Germany's Aims in the First World War*). Fischer, a Professor of History at the University of Hamburg, while adding many details to Albertini's account, essentially agreed with the latter's conclusion that Germany had to bear much of the responsibility for the outbreak of the war, laying out his case forthrightly and explicitly in something of the manner of an indictment. His research indicated that he probably exhausted official records on this subject.

It was not Fischer's intention to analyze the pre-1914 origins of World War I in any detail; this ground had been gone over repeatedly in the interwar period by those trying to fix the "war guilt," and Albertini had probably written the definitive work in this area. Nor was Fischer concerned with the war aims of the victorious Allied powers in the conflict; after Lenin seized power in Russia, the Bolshevik government published the secret treaties concluded among the Allies, and the peace treaties agreed to at the close of the conflict give considerable indication as to what their plans and expectations were. He was concerned with the aims of Germany and the German people after the conflict opened in the summer of 1914, a totally new area of research for those interested in trying to fix the responsibility for the war since most of the literature prior to Fischer stopped with the outbreak of war.

The heart of Fischer's research and findings rests upon a document dated September 9, 1914, and initialed by the Chancellor of the German Em-

pire, Theobald von Bethmann-Hollweg, which lays out in considerable detail a plan for German conquest and domination of Europe and Africa. All of Central Europe was to be conquered and administered by Germany, and satellite states were to be set up on the eastern and western borders of this *Mitteleuropa* zone; central Africa would be taken from coast to coast. Fischer contends that Bethmann-Hollweg had managed the Sarajevo crisis of 1914 so as to have a showdown with Germany's naval, military, economic, territorial, and diplomatic adversaries; she thereby hoped to break out of the "encirclement" which Russia, England, and France had managed to effect around her. Germany was to be raised to the status of a world power. Bethmann-Hollweg's policy ran the risk of war, which he fully understood; the war came, and the September program followed shortly. Fischer maintains that the subsequent history of the conflict was merely an attempt by the German ruling circles to carry out this program. When Germany did win the war against Russia on the Eastern front, the treaty of Brest-Litovsk set up a greater Germany in Eastern Europe buttressed by satellite states.

Fischer maintains that it was not a narrow clique of militarists, politicians, and diplomats that attempted to put the September program into effect, but virtually the entirety of German society including bankers, industrialists, intellectuals, and even socialists that embraced Social Darwinism and German racial superiority as justifications for their grandiose plans and programs. He is extremely harsh on Bethmann-Hollweg, who previously was viewed as a mild-man-nered administrator-intellectual caught up in a system beyond his con-trol, and he extends this harshness to an indictment of most of German so-ciety. Fischer argues that the German people became so desperate in their attempts to effect their global pro-gram that they resorted to instigating subversion in the Islamic world in an effort to destroy the British, French, and Italian empires there, and did succeed in destroying Russia from within, replacing the Tsarist regime with a Bolshevik system devoted to the destruction of every European government. Having destroyed Rus-sia in this manner, and occupying much of Eastern Europe, Germany tried in one last great offensive in the spring of 1918 to conquer France. This offensive was thwarted by the large reservoir of American troops which the Allies now had at their dis-posal. Fischer shows that the Ger-mans were prepared to go to any length and use any method to gain control of both Eastern and Western Europe.

Fischer's book was greeted in Ger-many with considerable adverse pub-lic reaction and hostility, and some circles likened the author to a traitor. Certainly the origins of the war go back decades prior to 1914 in a tangle of alliances, crises, and rivalries (mil-itary, naval, economic, and territo-rial) which are complex enough to enable generations of historians to write whole libraries on the origins and causes of the war. The whole sub-ject is sufficiently complicated to al-low the Germans an "out." Alber-tini's work was damning, but late in coming, laborious in style and trans-lation, and the work of a foreigner. Fischer, however, was a German his-torian working with German sources made fully available after Germany's defeat in 1945 and literally exhausted by the author. The result was a book that clearly and explicitly labeled Germany as the guilty party and one that could not be ignored by the Ger-man public nor by the international community of historians.

By Fischer's time German public opinion had accepted the fact that Germany under Hitler had pursued a barbaric policy of European and world conquest; in view of the naked record of the Nazi regime, there really was no alternative to conceding this point. However, Hitler and his regime were viewed as abnormalities within German history and distor-tions of basic German civilization produced by Germany's defeat in World War I, for which she was no more responsible than several other European powers. Hitler was seen as having come to power because of a set of unusual military, political, and economic circumstances flowing from World War I that would never be re-peated within German history; there-fore he could and should be forgot-ten.

Fischer's book placed this popular mind-set under considerable strain. If the entire German nation had been in accord with a plan of European and world conquest in World War I, then it seems that Hitler was not an abnormality within German history. The parallels between Germany's aims in World War I according to Fischer and Hitler's European and African conquests were too obvious to be ignored. Furthermore, Hitler's distortions of Germany's real intentions in World War I were important in enabling him to come to power in the first place. Historians and public opinion in the English-speaking world traditionally have had little difficulty with these interpretations of German history, but for Germans they represented an awful indictment of their recent history and society.

The opposition to Fischer was led by Gerhard Ritter, Professor of History at the University of Freiburg, and generally acknowledged to be the dean of German historians. Ritter charged that Fischer had selected a series of events, starting prior to World War I and running on through both World Wars, and then had woven them into an argument to suit his biased position stemming from guilt feelings concerning World War II. Fischer, according to Ritter, was bordering on an attempt at discrediting the German historical experience and hence was a threat to public order and morality. Fischer replied saying that Ritter chose to ignore an obvious thread running through recent German history because of his personal experiences in World War I. Fischer argued that it would be therapeutic for Germans to face the truth of their history. The debate between Fischer and Ritter, the former a younger man and the latter quite elderly, caused the whole dispute to appear as something of a "generation gap" problem.

Fischer's critics have generally argued that he placed too much emphasis upon the program contained in the September 9 document and that he misinterpreted it; that is, the goals stipulated in the September program were probably negotiating positions and not to be taken literally. Perhaps so, but the subsequent conduct of the war places a considerable burden on that interpretation. Fischer's book has received widespread acceptance outside Germany, and it has caused the German public to undertake a soul-searching look at their own recent history including that of the Nazi period which they had tried to sweep under the rug. The awful truth of the Nazi experience combined with Fischer's work may eventually result in thinking Germans coming to terms with what the outside world knew to be the truth long ago. Other Germans will probably never be able to accept an interpretation of German history which places dishonor on the events of a lifetime in which they were not necessarily passive participants. Still others will never be able to get beyond the excitement, drama, and sensationalism of the Nazi past, as demonstrated in the recent "Hitler Wave" raking over the popular history of the Nazi era.

Pertinent Literature

Fischer, Fritz. *World Power or Decline: The Controversy over Germany's Aims in the First World War.* Translated by Lancelot L. Farrar, Robert Kimber, and Rita Kimber. New York: W. W. Norton and Company, 1974.

The 1960's were a decade of often bitter debate within West Germany concerning the interpretations set forth by Fritz Fischer in his *Germany's Aims in the First World War*, the original German version of which was published in 1961. In 1965 Professor Fischer published a short summary of his position within that debate which was translated into English and published as *World Power or Decline* in 1974.

German textbooks have traditionally taken the position that Germany was hemmed in by hostile powers by 1914, that she was attacked in that year, and that she thus had fought World War I in an attempt at self-preservation. Since the war, German public opinion had been conditioned along these lines, the Nazis had been helped to power by such interpretations, and the events of World War II had done nothing to modify these popular conceptions. In 1961 Fischer attacked this whole national mythology head-on and accused Germany of having pursued a policy of European and even of world conquest during the conflict. He thereby opened a debate within the German historical community and generally within German society which was conducted throughout the 1960's at historical meetings and conferences, in journals and books, on the radio, and by various public media. Exchanges were heated and revealed that German history could be a very disturbing thing to many Germans. At one point an agency of the West German government withdrew financial support for an American lecture trip by the controversial Fischer; the trip was then funded by an American foundation.

In *World Power or Decline* Fischer summarizes his basic theses in the debate. He believes that German policy in the Sarajevo crisis of 1914 flowed from Germany's prewar ambitions for world power, and that her subsequent war aims also flowed from this source. These ambitions, along with a desire to overcome the growing power of socialism within Germany, caused the German government to embark on war in 1914. The precise nature of Germany's global ambitions was embodied in a September 9, 1914, document initialed by German Chancellor Bethmann-Hollweg which laid out a blueprint for conducting the war. This blueprint called for a planned commitment to European and African expansion and did not allow for improvised responses to problems and crises as they developed. Germany's aspirations were not espoused merely by a ruling elite and a few extremists but were widely shared by the mass of the German people. Military victory, however, was seen by the ruling elite to be a means of preserving the empire's conservative political system.

It is widely known that historians, economists, political scientists, and other academics are often as guilty as lesser educated members of the human race in believing what they want to believe. There is apparently no way out of this human limitation, and the debate surrounding Fischer's theses apparently never changed the minds of many with pronounced orthodox historical interpretations. Fischer, however, is convinced that his work has changed public opinion in Germany concerning World War I, and that therefore Germans are now better prepared to accept the consequences of World War II.

Fischer, Fritz. *War of Illusions: German Policies from 1911 to 1914*. Translated by Marian Jackson. New York: W. W. Norton and Company, 1975.

War of Illusions is the third and probably final book written by Fritz Fischer in the so-called Fischer Controversy debated throughout the 1960's in West Germany. The German edition appeared in 1969 as something of a grand finale to the debate and the English edition in 1975. Fischer's earlier book, *Germany's Aims in the First World War*, the theses of which were summarized and published in English as *World Power or Decline*, proclaimed Germany guilty of having started World War I and asserted that prior to and during the war Germany had plotted European and world conquest. As a result of the bitter controversy arising within West Germany following the publication of *Germany's Aims in the First World War*, Fischer felt compelled to expand on his charges that German plans for world power actually predated the outbreak of war in 1914 and that they particularly took form in the years 1911 to 1914. *War of Illusions* was his answer to the German apologists led by the prominent German historian Gerhard Ritter, who argued that Germany had no prewar expansion plans.

Fischer argues that while there were several imperialist powers in Europe prior to World War I each was unique in that each had a separate historical development; that was particularly true of Germany from the 1890's on. Hence it was not enough to say that Europe was one mass of evil prior to the outbreak of war;

some powers were perhaps more evil than others. The German Empire as forged in 1870 by Otto von Bismarck retained an obsolete feudalistic political structure superimposed on what soon became a dynamic, growing, modern industrial state. There were two built-in problems with this situation. First, the feudalistic political institutions were not permanently acceptable to the masses whose economic position was improving within the modern industrial state. Second, this state was formed late in history, and hence, by the time it entered the competition for world trade and commerce, most of the world had already been gobbled up by rival colonial powers in search of raw materials and markets.

The response of the ruling classes in Germany to this predicament was to develop a systematic plan for European and global expansion. They postulated that it was absolutely necessary that Germany have increased access to overseas markets and raw materials if her economic development were to continue. If a war were necessary in order to accomplish this end, it would also serve the purpose of diverting the restless masses from socialistic politics to an ethnic nationalism which would consolidate the position of the ruling classes. The masses were to be involved in a world crusade which would integrate them into the monarchical state.

By 1912 it was apparent that a domestic crisis was at hand in relation to retaining the absolutist political system, while the drive for an overseas empire had also largely failed by that date. Hence a general decision for war was taken as early as December 1912, if not before, in order to put through the German plan for world power. Germany's domestic situation, her military, economic, and diplomatic objectives, as well as the psychological state of the Emperor and the masses all resulted in the actual war decision in 1914. The masses did rally to the call and eagerly supported the government when the war came, including the plans for global expansion. The plan for a greater Germany retaining a conservative political system as conceived in the years preceding the world war was now to be carried out as a war policy. There was no break in policy, and the war was in no way defensive.

Fischer's books have not aroused much controversy outside Germany. His interpretations have long been present in history texts within the English-speaking world and particularly in those written by economic determinists. In Germany, Fischer was criticized for his scholarship and for his handling of the evidence, though he would appear to have consumed and digested whole archives while working on his books. The real issue in Germany was that Fischer was attempting to force through a synthesis of German history from the years preceding World War I on through the Nazi era, and this was an extremely painful process for many Germans. Fischer made his points in an aggressive, didactic fashion, offered no retreat, and in the end began the process of integrating the Nazi experience into German history—an experience with roots reaching back to the founding of the German Empire in 1870. — *J.L.C.*

Additional Recommended Reading

Albertini, Luigi. *The Origins of the War of 1914*. 3 vols. Translated and edited by Isabella M. Massey. London: Oxford University Press, 1952-1957. The definitive work on this subject which blames Germany for the outbreak of the war.

Lee, Dwight E. *Europe's Crucial Years: The Diplomatic Background of World War I, 1902-1914*. Hanover, N.H.: University Press of New England, 1974. A synopsis of old and recent literature on this subject.

Remak, Joachim. *The Origins of World War I, 1871-1914*. New York: Holt, Rinehart and Winston, 1967. A general survey of the background of the war.

Ritter, Gerhard. *The Sword and the Scepter: The Problem of Militarism in Germany*. 4 vols. Translated by Heinz Norden. Coral Gables, Fla.: University of Miami Press, 1969-1973. Written by the leader of the opposition to Fischer within the German historical community, these volumes constitute an answer to Fischer's work.

Stern, Fritz. *The Failure of Illiberalism: Essays on the Political Culture of Modern Germany*. New York: Alfred A. Knopf, 1972. Contains "German Historians and the War: Fritz Fischer and His Critics," pp. 147-158, and "Bethmann-Hollweg and the War: The Bounds of Responsibility," pp. 77-118.

Turner, Leonard Charles Frederick. *Origins of the First World War*. New York: W. W.

Norton and Company, 1970. Emphasizes military considerations.

Moses, John A. *The Politics of Illusion: The Fischer Controversy in German Historiography*. New York: Barnes & Noble, 1975. Excellent study of Fischer's neo-revisionist interpretation of Germany's role in the outbreak of World War I.

Thompson, Wayne C. "The September Program: Reflections on the Evidence," in *Central European History*. XI (December, 1978), pp. 348-364. Criticizes Fischer's evaluation of the September program.

THE BAY OF PIGS INVASION REPULSED

Type of event: Military: invasion of Cuba by a CIA trained guerrilla force
Time: April 17-19, 1961
Locale: The Bay of Pigs at Las Villas province, Cuba

Principal personages:

FIDEL CASTRO (1927-   ), Premier of Cuba, 1959-

JOHN FITZGERALD KENNEDY (1917-1963), thirty-fifth President of the United States, 1961-1963

ALLEN DULLES (1893-   ), Director of the Central Intelligence Agency

RICHARD MERVIN BISSELL (1909-   ), Central Intelligence Agency Director of Operations

ADLAI EWING STEVENSON (1900-1965), United States Ambassador to the United Nations

JOSÉ MIRÓ CARDONA (1901-1974), leader of the United Revolutionary Front

Summary of Event

In March, 1960, President Dwight Eisenhower authorized the Central Intelligence Agency (CIA), headed by Allen Dulles, to train and equip a Cuban exile guerrilla force for the purpose of infiltrating Cuba and joining the anti-Castro underground. With the cooperation of the Guatemalan government, the CIA soon established training camps in that country, and the training of Cuban exile volunteers began. By November, 1960, the CIA operation under the supervision of Richard Bissell, had changed from the training of guerrillas to the preparation of an invasion force. After that date guerrilla training ceased, and a small army was trained in conventional assault landing tactics.

Meanwhile, in the Cuban exile community in Miami, Florida, the United Revolutionary Front was formed. Headed by Dr. José Miró Cardona, who would become provisional president of Cuba upon the exiles' return, the Front in Miami managed the recruitment of soldiers for the expeditionary force, although the operation was completely directed by the CIA. Volunteers were screened for political acceptability, and leftists were discouraged or rejected. Consequently, the force in training took on a conservative character.

The CIA-directed operation ran into severe problems from the start. Numerous political conflicts which threatened to undermine the entire operation erupted among the exile volunteers. Additionally, United States involvement in the affair was supposed to remain covert; but in Miami the existence of the invasion force and the Guatemalan camps, as well as the CIA direction of the operation, were common knowledge. Increasingly, the United States press reported on the preparations in progress for an invasion of Cuba. Fidel Castro, Premier of Cuba, also knew of the exile army being trained in Guatemala.

In February, 1961, the invasion plans underwent an important change. Originally, the CIA specified the city of Trinidad as the landing point for the exile force. President John F. Kennedy decided that the invasion plans could proceed, however, only if United States support were better camouflaged. The site at Trinidad was judged too risky. In its place, the Bay of Pigs, one hundred miles to the west of Trinidad on the south-central coast of Cuba, was chosen. Trinidad was the better of the two sites for one simple reason. In the event of failure, the invasion force could have retreated into the Escambray Mountains with little difficulty. The beaches at the Bay of Pigs, on the other hand, were surrounded by the Zapata swamps. Escape to the mountains some eighty miles to the east would have been extremely difficult, if not impossible. Thus, in the event that the exiles could not establish a defensible beachhead at the Bay of Pigs, the only realistic retreat possible for them would be in the direction from which they came: to the sea.

By April, 1961, the invasion plans had taken shape. Castro's air force was to be destroyed on the ground by two scheduled air strikes against Cuban air bases. The invasion force of some fifteen hundred men would disembark under the cover of night and acquire the advantage of complete surprise. Meanwhile, paratroopers would be dropped to establish advance positions from which they could scout approaching Cuban forces and

cut off transportation routes. With the skies to themselves, the exile force would be initially resupplied at the Playa Giron airfield, close to the Bay of Pigs. Simultaneously, a diversionary landing would occur on the eastern coast of Cuba in an attempt to deceive Cuban forces about the exiles' real intentions. The main invasion force would then advance into Matanzas province with the goal of securing a defensible area of Cuban territory. This accomplished, the leaders of the United Revolutionary Front would be flown to Cuba to establish a provisional government. It was hoped that the local Cuban population might join the invaders in their fight against the Castro regime. With this possibility in mind, the supply ships accompanying the invasion force were to be stocked with arms and ammunition for four thousand men.

From the beginning, Operation Pluto, as the invasion plan was called, went badly. On April 15, 1961, eight B-26 bombers, supplied by the United States and disguised as Cuban air force planes, departed from Puerto Cabezas, Nicaragua, and attacked Cuban airfields in an attempt to destroy the Cuban air force. The bombing raid was unsuccessful. Although considerable damage was done to Cuba's small air force, the attack left unharmed two or three T-33 trainer jets, three Sea Furies, and two B-26's.

At the United Nations, Raul Roa, Cuba's Foreign Minister, charged that the attack was a prelude to invasion from the United States. Adlai Stevenson, the United States Ambassador to the United Nations, replied that the attacking planes were of Cuban origin. Because one of the planes had landed in Florida after the raid, Stevenson was able to produce photographs showing a B-26 bomber displaying the insignia of the Cuban air force. Stevenson actually believed the Cuban pilots to be defectors from Castro's own forces; he was quite unaware of the deception. The trick was soon discovered, however, when reporters pointed out certain differences in the nose cones of Cuban B-26's as compared with the one that landed in Florida. United States complicity in the air strike was apparent, and President Kennedy, at the recommendation of Dean Rusk and McGeorge Bundy, canceled the second air strike scheduled for dawn, April 17.

In the early morning hours of Monday, April 17, the invasion force (now named Brigade 2506) began to disembark at two beaches on the Bay of Pigs: Playa Giron and Playa Larga. Contrary to advance intelligence reports that the area was virtually uninhabited and that militia in the area had no communications with Havana, the invaders were spotted almost immediately, and the news of the invasion was relayed quickly to Castro's headquarters. Thus, the dangerous night landing was conducted under fire from the very start. The unloading of troops and arms progressed more slowly than planned, and at dawn there were still invasion forces on the ships. The element of surprise had not been achieved, and the force of the undestroyed Cuban planes would soon be felt. Throughout the day on Monday, events continued to go against the invaders.

Cuba's air force, particularly the jets, proved to be the decisive factor in the battle. Two of the exiles' escort ships, the Rio Escondido and the Houston, were sunk with arms, ammunition, and supplies on board. The exile air force (the Free Cuban Air Squadron), which consisted of sixteen B-26 bombers, lost half its planes. Flying from Nicaragua, the B-26's carried extra fuel and had no tail guns. Unable to maneuver quickly, they made easy targets for the T-33 jet trainers. At sea, the escort vessels which were not sunk by Cuban planes were forced to withdraw from the invasion area. On the ground, the invasion forces fought well but were hampered by wet communication equipment and a scarcity of ammunition. Only one of the paratroop drops succeeded. The other failed because the paratroopers were dropped too close to the invasion area and because their heavy equipment was dropped into the swamps, never to be found again during the remainder of the battle. With all of these problems at the Bay of Pigs, it probably made no difference in the final result that the diversionary landing on the eastern coast of Cuba never took place.

In Washington, the discouraging news from the Bay of Pigs led President Kennedy to reinstate the second air strike which earlier had been canceled. The planes of the Free Cuban Air Squadron based in Nicaragua were to strike the San Antonio de los Banos airfield at dawn on Tuesday, April 18. The following morning six B-26 bombers piloted by Cuban exile pilots were over the designated target, but unfortunately for the invading force, the bombers were forced to return to Nicaragua without dropping a single bomb because of fog and cloud cover.

On the ground, meanwhile, Castro was moving twenty thousand troops toward the Zapata swamp region as Brigade 2506 was running out of ammunition. Because the Cuban air force still commanded the skies, there was no chance to unload the remaining arms, supplies, and troops aboard the two remaining escort ships at sea.

In the early morning hours of Wednesday, April 19, President Kennedy authorized an "air-umbrella" at dawn over the invasion area. He gave permission for six unmarked jet fighters from *U.S.S. Essex* in the Caribbean to protect a B-26 attack from Nicaragua and to cover the unloading of the exile escort ships at sea. This final attempt to help the invading forces also proved to be a failure. Probably because of confusion about the difference in time zones between Cuba and Nicaragua, the B-26 bombers from Nicaragua arrived an hour early over Cuba and were shot down by the Cubans; only one escaped. The jets which were to have provided the air cover never left the *Essex*.

Later in the day on April 19, 1961, the invasion was crushed. Facing overwhelming opposition and out of ammunition, the leaders destroyed their heavy equipment and ordered a retreat into the swamps. Only a handful of exiles escaped to the sea; the remainder were rounded up by Castro's forces and imprisoned. Of 1,297 Brigade members who had come ashore, 1,180 were captured. Cuban losses are difficult to estimate. Although Castro admitted to losing less than a hundred men in battle, a more accurate estimate would be 1,250.

Pertinent Literature

Johnson, Haynes. *The Bay of Pigs: The Leaders' Story of Brigade 2506*. New York: W. W. Norton and Company, 1964.

This work is probably the most detailed account of the Bay of Pigs invasion. Johnson focuses on the scene of action from the inception of the counterrevolution against Fidel Castro's regime until the release of the prisoners who survived the ill-fated invasion. Where possible, the author has relied on first hand knowledge of the events. Most of the material for the text was culled from a mass of transcripts acquired through personal interviews with the participants in the invasion and its related events. Johnson seldom strays from his unique vantage point to speculate about the Bay of Pigs episode as it related to the constantly changing foreign policy considerations confronting United States and Soviet leaders at the time. Readers who want to know what part the Bay of Pigs invasion played in the Kennedy Administration's approach to foreign policy problems in Berlin, Laos, or the rest of Latin America, ought, perhaps to read some other work. For those who desire a superbly detailed account of the events on the beaches at the Bay of Pigs, however, this is the best book on the subject.

Johnson's work is divided into five books with an epilogue. Book One, entitled "Counter-revolution," is a description of the beginnings of the operation. Largely pieced together by first hand accounts, the three chapters in this section are told from the perspectives of the principal military leaders of the invasion forces: Manuel Artime, José Perez San Roman, and Erneido Oliva. A fascinating aspect of these first chapters concerns the subterfuge employed by CIA operatives who directed the recruitment of Cubans for guerrilla training in the mountains of Guatemala. In their dealings with the Cuban exiles, the CIA men used false names, code words, and other means to cover their true identities. According to the Cubans interviewed by Johnson, they knew they were dealing with the CIA (and hence, with the United States government), but they had no way of proving it.

Book Two, "La Brigada," chronicles the training of Brigade 2506. Johnson relates how the shift from guerrilla infiltration tactics to conventional assault landing tactics took place. Also discussed in this section is the dissension among the Cubans, the meetings in Washington between President Kennedy and his domestic and military advisers, the change in invasion targets from Trinidad to the Giron Beach on the Bay of Pigs, and the air strike on Cuban airfields. Johnson's discussion of an alternate plan in the event of failure is interesting. He suggests that Richard Bissell, the CIA director of the Bay of Pigs operation, assured President Kennedy that in the event of disaster

on the beaches, the invasion force had been instructed to move to the Escambray Mountains where it could continue fighting as a large guerrilla force. Kennedy was also assured that the Zapata swamps between the invasion point and the mountains was good guerrilla terrain. The Cubans interviewed by Johnson maintained, however, that no such plan was ever mentioned to them. Instead, they understood that United States forces would back them up if they failed.

Book Three, "The Bay of Pigs," presents an hour-by-hour account of the invasion. Johnson here renders a graphic re-creation of the military action which occurred on the 17th, 18th and 19th of April, 1961. Also included is a chapter on the futile flight through the Zapata swamps. Though the individual stories are varied, the one theme that runs throughout is defeat despite heroic effort in the midst of confusion.

Book Four, "Prison," recounts the experiences of the surviving brigade members while they were confined in Cuba. It is in this section that Johnson first comments on the reasons for the failure of the Bay of Pigs invasion. He spreads the responsibility for the failure of the operation among "all who had a hand in it." But Johnson does not allocate responsibility in equal measure. Singled out for special criticism are the military Joint Chiefs of Staff under Kennedy and the Central Intelligence Agency. He argues that the Joint Chiefs of Staff approved an invasion plan which had little chance of success. The CIA deserved even more credit for the failure. It crossed the line between intelligence gathering and policy formation with disastrous results. Its agents misled the Cuban exiles, and at times they acted contrary to United States policy.

Book Five, "Liberation," reports the efforts to secure the release of the brigade prisoners. Johnson discusses the many frustrations and ultimate success of the negotiations conducted by the Miami-based Cuban Families Committee and New York lawyer James Donovan with Fidel Castro. Much is made here of Donovan's intuitive ability to understand Castro's enigmatic personality, enabling him to bring the negotiations to a successful conclusion.

Johnson concludes that the Bay of Pigs episode taught the United States some valuable lessons. Of primary importance is the need to establish effective oversight procedures for the activities of the Central Intelligence Agency. In the light of recent investigations into CIA activities, Johnson's recommendations remain timely.

Meyer, Karl E. and Tad Szulc. *The Cuban Invasion: The Chronicle of a Disaster*. New York: Frederick A. Praeger, 1962.

Published less than two years after the defeat of the anti-Castro rebels at the Bay of Pigs, *The Cuban Invasion* analyzes what went wrong with the whole enterprise. The authors are concerned not only with the military failure of the invasion and its causes, but also with the United States posture toward Castro's Cuba and the active foreign policy role exercised by the CIA in the months preceding the invasion. Thus, a major theme of this book is that there was more wrong with the Bay of Pigs invasion than poor execution. The authors argue that it was "not only wrongly executed but wrongly conceived."

To support their critical view, Meyer and Szulc develop three subordinate themes. First, they suggest that there was an excessive poverty of imagination in United States efforts to develop an adequate foreign policy position toward the Castro regime. They argue that from early 1959 Castro desired to portray Cuba as a victim of United States imperialism. In this way he could mobilize sentiment against the United States, and be free to move his country to the extreme left. Unlike some commentators who see Castro's move to the left as the result of a series of unplanned and badly thought-out decisions occasioned by the tide of events, Meyer and Szulc assert that Castro was largely the master of those events and not a victim of circumstance. They argue that it is wrong to suggest, as some do, that the United States drove Cuba into the arms of the Soviet Union. Instead, the deterioration of United States-Cuban relations made easier the ties between Cuba and the Soviet Union. The Eisenhower Administration unwittingly abetted the achievement of Castro's objectives by allowing anti-Castro forces to operate in the United States, by strongly reacting against Castro's agrarian reform, by eliminating United States imports of Cuban sugar, and, in general, by responding to the Cuban revolution in a legalistic fashion

931

while ignoring its emotional aspects for the Cubans.

Second, the political context of the invasion was improperly understood by the Central Intelligence Agency. Even if by some miracle, the authors argue, the initial military operation had succeeded, the rebel movement would have failed in the end. Success at the Bay of Pigs would have allowed the rebels to establish a provisional government, but ultimate success would have required the support of the Cuban population. The authors argue that the CIA had failed to appreciate the popular appeal of the revolution, and consequently had recruited right-wing insurgents while rejecting the anti-Castro left wing. Moreover, the CIA depended less and less upon the Cuban underground, which was pro-revolution but anti-Castro in stance. Consequently, the invasion force and its political leadership would have been politically and logistically isolated once it was on Cuban soil.

Finally, the authors suggest that the invasion itself, its character and its objectives, were never the result of deliberate policy formation by anyone. They were, instead, the unforeseen products of a series of disconnected "reflex actions" which culminated in the existence of a trained invasion force described by Allen Dulles as a "disposal problem." By the time the Kennedy Administration seriously considered the invasion plans, the Cuban exiles were ready for action. Their existence was publicly known in the United States and in Cuba. Castro had been predicting an invasion for months, and to go forward with the CIA plans would play into his hands. To cancel the invasion would place the United States in the position of not supporting its friends. There was, according to Meyer and Szulc, no way the Kennedy Administration could easily extricate itself from the situation. The decision to proceed seemed at the time to be the least of several evils. — *C.E.C.*

Additional Recommended Reading

Alsop, Stewart. "The Lessons of the Cuban Disaster," in *Saturday Evening Post.* CCXXXIII (June 24, 1961). An excellent essay on lessons to be learned from the Bay of Pigs affair.

Bonsal, Philip W. *Cuba, Castro, and the United States.* Pittsburgh: University of Pittsburgh Press, 1971. Written by the last United States Ambassador to Cuba prior to the break in diplomatic relations in 1961, Chapter Nineteen presents the diplomatic issues at stake in the Bay of Pigs decision.

Draper, Theodore. "Cuba and U.S. Policy," *New Leader.* XXXII (June 5, 1961). A critical view of the policymaking which resulted in the Bay of Pigs disaster.

Halperin, Maurice. *The Rise and Decline of Fidel Castro: An Essay in Contemporary History.* Berkeley: University of California Press, 1972. Chapters Nine and Ten present a critical view of United States policy in the Bay of Pigs affair.

Lazo, Mario. *Dagger in the Heart: American Policy Failures in Cuba.* New York: Funk and Wagnalls, 1968. Chapters Fifteen through Seventeen of this diplomatic history present an account which suggests that the Kennedy Administration betrayed the anti-Castro movement.

Schlesinger, Arthur M., Jr. *A Thousand Days: John F. Kennedy in the White House.* Boston: Houghton Mifflin Company, 1965. Chapters Ten and Eleven present the Bay of Pigs affair from the perspective of a White House insider who opposed the invasion plans.

Sorensen, Theodore C. *Kennedy.* New York: Harper & Row Publishers, 1965. Chapter Eleven discusses the Bay of Pigs invasion in international perspective as seen by a White House insider.

Thomas, Hugh. *Cuba: The Pursuit of Freedom, 1762-1969.* New York: Harper & Row Publishers, 1971. Chapters 103 and 106 of this history of Cuba present an objective and highly detailed account of the important events before and during the Bay of Pigs invasion.

THE UNITED STATES PUTS A MAN IN SPACE

Type of event: Technological: first United States launching of a manned spaceship
Time: May 5, 1961
Locale: Cape Canaveral, Florida

Principal personages:

DWIGHT DAVID EISENHOWER (1890-1969), thirty-fourth President of the United States, 1953-1961

JOHN FITZGERALD KENNEDY (1917-1963), thirty-fifth President of the United States, 1961-1963

ALAN BARTLETT SHEPARD, JR. (1923-   ), America's first man in space

DR. WERNHER VON BRAUN (1912-1976), the leader of rocket research in Nazi Germany; subsequently America's chief missile expert and developer of the Redstone rocket

ROBERT R. GILRUTH (1913-   ), a distinguished scientist and engineer who headed the Space Task Force of Project Mercury

Summary of Event

United States Navy Commander Alan B. Shepard, Jr., became America's first man in space when he successfully piloted the *Freedom VII* space capsule on May 5, 1961. His suborbital flight, after a four-hour launching delay, lasted roughly fifteen minutes and twenty-eight seconds, attained a peak altitude of 116.6 miles and cruised about three hundred miles down the Atlantic missile range. American national pride and world prestige, badly shaken by a series of Soviet pioneering triumphs, were boosted by *Freedom VII*'s almost flawless performance. Technically, however, Shepard's ride did not equal the previous month's orbital mission of Soviet cosmonaut Yuri Gagarin. American successes had still to be assessed against a backdrop of Soviet firsts.

The United States could have probed space long before the Soviets since the principles of multistage rocketry were developed here decades earlier by an American scientist, Robert H. Goddard. The public, in its shortsightedness, ignored Goddard's theories in favor of investment in more practical enterprises such as increased consumer goods. In Nazi Germany, Goddard's ideas fired the imagination of the young German rocket scientist, Dr. Wernher von Braun, who was responsible for developing the V-1 and V-2 rockets which devastated London during World War II. After the war, Braun came to the United States where he became a leader in American rocket research. The Soviet Union, however, made greater strides in this field than did the United States after World War II. As a result, in 1957, the Soviets orbited the first earth satellite, *Sputnik I*, and followed with other spectacular shots that included

934

launching and recovering live creatures from space capsules and satellite mapping of the far side of the moon. These milestones created such alarm in the United States that space would be exploited for Soviet military advantage that the public demanded an accelerated American space program. Both President Dwight Eisenhower and President John F. Kennedy reacted to the outcry.

In 1958, President Eisenhower authorized the creation of the National Aeronautics and Space Administration (NASA) to explore space for peaceful pursuits, and he simultaneously assigned Project Mercury, America's Man in Space Program, to NASA for development. NASA immediately appointed a Space Task Group (STG), managed by Robert R. Gilruth, to recruit our first astronauts. From thousands of civilian and military volunteers, seven seasoned military test pilots were finally selected. Project Mercury received highest government priority, and planning began on six manned flights and as many unmanned flights as needed to assure the success of an orbital mission.

Project Mercury was a cautionary, intense program that focused on pilot safety. Governmental and industrial contractors were involved, as well as a work force of more than two million people. All component systems were thoroughly tested and paired with duplicate backup systems. Technicians searched meticulously for deficiencies, particularly in unsuccessful test-shot vehicles. The astronauts were trained extensively on simulators and centrifuges with all biological processes monitored. The military pro-

vided aeromedical support since no civilian counterpart existed. Expertise was culled from a variety of federal and private agencies. President Kennedy commented that no astronaut's life would be risked prematurely even if a delay benefited the Soviets. Therefore, preliminary steps such as suborbital test shots were not bypassed as they had been in the Soviet program.

The Air Force Atlas boosters, the most powerful available, were selected to launch the orbital flights and the less powerful United States Army Redstones, both developed by Braun, were designated for suborbital shots. Smaller solid propellant rockets known as "Little Joes" were also used early in the program for unmanned test shots. Each capsule had to be scaled to mate perfectly with its booster, an engineering challenge that underwent many modifications and improvements. In addition to carrying a finite payload, each capsule had to be equipped with life support and flight operations systems, a form-fitting couch, and duplicate systems which could survive firing and reentry. The Russians had already developed the necessary technology and were launching heavier payloads with larger boosters than the Atlas. As a result, American early phased testing was often demeaned by the Soviet press while followed avidly by an American public that applauded every incremental success.

The program was divided into two phases, MR for Mercury-Redstone (suborbital flights) and MA for Mercury-Atlas (orbital flights). Shepard's flight, MR3, was the first manned shot and followed the success of an unmanned shot and one carrying a small chimpanzee, Ham. The whole world viewed the event, and the world press was represented at Mission Control in Cape Canaveral. MR3 represented a Free World as well as an American initiative that would open space exploration to all nations, not only the militarily aggressive. Such openness contrasted sharply with the secrecy surrounding Soviet launchings.

Shepard arose early on the morning of his flight, dined with fellow astronauts, underwent a physical examination, and was equipped with a rectal thermometer and other biophysical measuring devices, and then assisted into his twenty-pound aluminized, tailor-made, space suit. He calmly walked to the launch pad and was strapped into the bell-shaped *Freedom VII* capsule. After four annoying holds, he was fired into space and remained in constant radio contact.

In every test, the eighty-three-foot, 66,000-pound MR3 performed beautifully. Booster cutoff occurred on schedule with immediate jettison of the escape tower above the capsule (that served to blast it free in case of launch problems). Then the clamp ring that secured the booster to the capsule was released, and three liquid propellant rockets fired to effect final separation. The Automatic Stabilization Control System corrected any wobbling and Shepard extended the periscope to view the earth below. At this point, he was weightless and after making a few performance tests, switched to manual control. In one exercise, using a control stick, he maneuvered *Freedom VII* in three separate motions—pitch, roll, and yaw—thus proving that man could function well in space in zero gravity. Since Gagarin exercised less manual control in his more extensive flightpath, Shepard achieved a small milestone for the Free World.

Minutes later, Shepard pitched the capsule to the retrofiring attitude and activated the retro sequence. This maneuver was not required to reenter a suborbital craft, but was used to test the system. After firing, the retrorocket pack was jettisoned, the periscope retracted and the capsule returned to automatic control. *Freedom VII* descended backwards with the broad heat shield to the astronaut's rear. This phase was critical since the capsule could disintegrate if the heat shield were not properly positioned to withstand scorching temperatures of more than 1000° F. As planned, the heat shield slowly burned away as the capsule gently rolled, spinning at about 10 degrees per second to distribute evenly the heat. Shepard continued to perform tasks even during peak gravity when he withstood pressures equivalent to eleven times his body weight. Around thirty thousand feet, the drogue chute, the first of three parachutes, was deployed to stop oscillation and reduce speed. The main braking parachute and recovery antennas were deployed at ten thousand feet. The last parachute, a reserve which lightened the capsule at top and checked any residual oscillation by floating upright around it, was released by Shepard at final splashdown in the Atlantic Ocean, three hundred miles south of Cape Canaveral. No leaks inhibited his exit. After opening the hatch, he crawled into a sling suspended from a hovering aircraft and was welcomed as a hero aboard the carrier *U.S.S. Lake Champlain*. He had conquered space, a hostile, unknown environment, in an unproven test spacecraft.

The MR3 success was one of the best things to happen to this country. Public confidence in the national scientific ability surged, as reflected in the significant increase in stock prices of companies associated with Project Mercury and in the decision of the Kennedy Administration to increase funding of civil and military space ventures.

Scientifically, Shepard's performance was of great value. Shepard, like Gagarin, was living proof that man could survive in space and perform many skilled tasks under varying severe stresses. His excellent postflight condition attested to the soundness of experimental ground training procedures (even though Shepard later recommended elimination and shortening of certain procedures). His use of manual override in only one minor instance when a panel light failed to flash green, demonstrated vehicle engineering competence. Since he could rely on primary systems, especially to autopilot *Freedom VII*, he was free to assess more fully the functioning of telemetry, monitoring, and ballistic trajectory systems, which were then confidently used in subsequent missions. In a sense, Shepard helped qualify Project Mercury as a sound national investment.

The pressures of publicity now called for more spectacular shots which were eventually undertaken in the Mercury-Atlas flights.

Pertinent Literature

Bell, Joseph. *Seven into Space*. Chicago: Popular Mechanics Company, 1960.

Expanding upon an article he wrote for *Popular Mechanics* magazine, the author, an ex-Navy pilot, covers the Project Mercury story from its inception to 1960. He focuses on the background and personalities of the seven military test pilots (Malcolm Carpenter, Leroy Cooper, John Glenn, Virgil Grissom, Walter Schirra, Alan Shepard, and Donald Slayton) who became America's first astronauts. Much attention is devoted to the difficult tasks of astronaut selection and training. Information was supplied by the astronauts themselves in interviews with Bell.

Bell describes how the American space program developed concurrently with astronaut training and how large a part the astronauts had in designing and modifying their own space hardware to ninety-nine percent reliability. Since no precedents existed to guide NASA in devising an adequate program, the astronauts were needed to work out engineering and tactical problems. The work load involved was tremendous and broke down into different technical areas with each astronaut specializing in one area; for example, Schirra specialized in the atmospheric life support system. To keep abreast of developments, they worked closely with major contractors and manufacturers of equipment within their assigned areas, and briefed the group on details. In this way, every phase of the program was monitored by the men who would soon risk their lives in test spacecraft.

All seven men survived highly complicated and torturous testing to qualify as astronaut trainees, a prerequisite for more rigorous physical and psychological demands. Consequently, they were not considered typical test pilots even though, according to Bell, they worked inconspicuously and did not court the press—which nevertheless courted them.

Bell breaks down the astronauts' preflight training into six basic categories: education in the basic sciences, familiarization with the conditions of spaceflight, aviation flight training, participation in the vehicle development program, physical training, and training in the operation of the Mercury vehicle. Completion of this program was the equivalent of being awarded several Master's degrees, and each astronaut had to complete it on an accelerated two-year schedule. Such intensive study enabled them to be completely familiar with the space vehicle in which they would ride, the liquid propellant fuel that would fire them into space, and the maze of scientific and mechanical equipment on board. It also conditioned them to the peculiarities of spaceflight, such as the fact that minute navigational errors could throw their vehicles miles off course. They became aware of even the most elementary procedures. These preparations substituted for a realistic simulation of an orbital flight which, at this point, could only be imagined.

Bell's coverage of Project Mercury hardware is reliable. He competently describes the dimensions of the various rocket stages, their components, and their anticipated performance capability. Capsule design and control systems are analyzed in the light of pilot safety and revealed in illustrations. Pilot functioning inside the capsule is accurately forecast. Capsule and escape tower disengagement and reentry procedures (a particularly difficult phase) later met the performance expectations outlined here.

High on the list of innovations was the perfection of a spacesuit that would maintain a life sustaining environment for the astronaut. Designed in two layers, the outer fabric of reinforced rubber was a pressure suit that could isolate the astronaut if cabin pressure failed. The inner garment provided space for ventilation and served to keep the orbit temperatures within the seventies. On Shepard's flight, undertaken about a year after this book's publication, spacesuit temperatures never climbed beyond this range, which is another tribute to program competence.

Bell concludes with a hypothetical enactment of a first trip into space, a dramatization conceived by Mercury astronauts. Play-by-play, the reactions of ground control personnel, the chosen astronaut, and technicians in various world tracking stations are created in convincing dialogue. Such true-to-life projection clearly demonstrates how seriously Project Mercury participants regarded space exploration.

A final chapter, "After Mercury,"

speculates on space travel after the project concludes. The reader is told to expect a manned orbit of and a soft landing on the moon, the building of space stations, and probes to Mars and Venus. Bell urges the public to offer increasing support of these endeavors lest the Soviets surpass us in a technology that could eventually subjugate the world. We lagged behind the Soviets for years in space achievement and woke up late to the realization that the battle between Communism and democracy would be fought to a great extent in scientific accomplishment. According to the author, our tardiness might mean another Soviet *coup*, their launching of a man into orbit first (another accurate prediction), but we still had time to match their efforts and win the space race.

An accurate and detailed inside story, *Seven into Space* is of value historically for its wealth of digestible information about America's Man into Space Program.

Gatland, Kenneth. *Manned Spacecraft.* New York: The Macmillan Company, 1976.

Kenneth Gatland, British authority on spaceflight and editor of *Spaceflight* magazine, impartially chronicles the history of Soviet and American aerospace achievements from *Sputnik I* to *Skylab*. This publication, an updated version of an earlier exposé describing and contrasting the design of various space vehicles and their operations, includes many charts, graphs, and colored illustrations as well as the wealth of technical information furnished by such aerospace contractors as McDonnell Douglas (Projects Mercury and Gemini), Rockwell International (Space Shuttle, *Apollo* command, service and adapter), and Grumman Engineering Corporation (*Apollo* lunar module). Authoritative details on Soviet engineering were harder to obtain, but are covered in depth.

Beginning with a description of Soviet space ventures, Gatland explains how the Cold War between the United States and the Soviet Union sparked Soviet investment in rocketry. In post-World War II Russia, Soviet dictator Stalin believed that in the event of an actual war with the United States, his country would need weaponry capable of target destruction on the American continent. Sophisticated ballistic missiles were soon developed and equipped with nuclear warheads based in key launching sites within the Soviet Union. Later, the technology used to develop these missiles was applied to other areas of space research, especially to satellite and vehicular design. Reacting to what was termed the "Red peril," the United States focused on Intercontinental Ballistic Missile (ICBM) weaponry development, but lagged far behind in nonmilitary objectives until the Soviets fired *Sputnik I*, earth's first successful artificial satellite.

The United States also relied on ballistic missile technology as a solid base on which to build its satellite and space probe programs. However, at the onset of the space race, President Eisenhower made clear that American efforts in manned and unmanned spaceflight would be for peaceful motives. Project Mercury, America's first man-in-space program was subsequently tagged a government-supported "civilian" enterprise.

Gatland views Project Mercury in historical perspective as an ambitious and modestly successful program, yet one that still left the Russians two years ahead in technology. Shepard's almost flawless flight was little more than a practice ride that paved the way for more complex missions. American leaps ahead did not occur until Project Gemini, Mercury's successor, that developed space vehicles capable of fulfilling the practical requirements of a manned lunar expedition, America's long-range goal.

Frequent comparisons are made between Soviet and American vehicular design. The *Vostok* capsule flown by Gagarin and six fellow cosmonauts in the first Soviet man-in-space program was spherical in shape and fitted with an all-enveloping heat shield rather than one covering only the blunt end. In place of an escape tower, an ejection seat jettisoned the cosmonaut during reentry (in all but Gagarin's test shot) as well as during any launching mishap. American astronauts continued to splash-down in their capsules until Project Gemini, when ejection seats were installed for emergencies. Both escape systems were subjected to many tests under vertical velocity. American *Mercury* designers felt they could dispense with an ejection seat because gas jets stabilized the capsules during reentry and therefore reduced the rate of sinking. The *Vostoks* lacked this modification.

The conclusion of Project Mercury still left the Americans badly trailing in hours logged in space. The first woman in space, Valentina Tereshkova, as observes Gatland, remained there seventeen hours longer than all the American astronauts put together. Also, of the six American manned missions, only four were orbital flights, even though each mission was unique and incremental in pilot control.

In Project Gemini, pilot vehicular control was further refined to encompass docking maneuvers important in orbital rendezvous. Named Gemini because two men occupied each spacecraft, the program proved that men could walk in space on tethers, operate on-board computer and radar equipment with minimal assistance from earth, and join two spacecrafts that could be made to rotate around a common center of mass to simulate gravity. Such strides made space station assembly and shuttle transportation tangible possibilities. While Soviet *Voskhod* flights duplicated many *Gemini* feats, the *Voskhod* program was not as brilliantly executed.

After Project Gemini, the Soviets and Americans more seriously considered the need for joint missions culminating in 1975 with the docking of the Soviet *Soyuz* and American *Apollo* spacecrafts. After crew exchanges and joint experiments, the crews separated to make individual tests and then returned to earth. Space cooperation rather than space war had been initiated. This first historic meeting also marked the end of an era of early space exploration begun by Yuri Gagarin and Alan B. Shepard. The greater cost and complexity of future manned flights to the planets and the construction of space station colonies will require international, not mere individual nation, support. Perhaps a final truism inferred from Gatland's test is that space exploration will save the planet earth from destruction since national rivalries can be thrust off center stage. — *A.C.R.*

Additional Recommended Reading

Emme, Eugene M. *A History of Space Flight*. New York: Holt, Rinehart and Winston, 1965. A philosophical overview of space exploration which traces the development of space technology from rough ideas to actuality; Project Mercury is examined in historical perspective.

Hotz, Robert. "MR3 in Perspective," in *Aviation Week*. LXXXIII (May 15, 1961), p. 21. The impact of Shepard's flight on the United States and the rest of the world is summarized in this editorial.

Kolcum, Edward. "Atlas Tests Key to Manned Orbital Flight," in *Aviation Week*. LXXXIII (May 15, 1961), pp. 29-33. This play-by-play account of the MR3 flight also includes launch vehicle description, analysis of data and pilot performance, and commentary on public response.

_____. "Mercury-Redstone Procedures Simplified," in *Aviation Week*. LXXXIII (June 12, 1961), pp. 31-32. The performance and monitoring tasks of Shepard's MR3 mission are detailed.

Ley, Willy. *Events in Space*. New York: Van Rees Press, 1969. A popularly written book that covers the main events in the history of manned and unmanned spaceflight.

Olney, Ross R. *Americans in Space: A History of Manned Space Travel*. New York: Thomas Nelson, 1970. Basic facts about the individual Project Mercury missions are well explained in simple layman's terms and made more comprehensible in a glossary of frequently used space terms.

RACHEL CARSON PUBLISHES *SILENT SPRING*

Type of event: Scientific: raised public recognition of the dangers inherent in the use of pesticides and herbicides
Time: 1962
Locale: The United States

Principal personages:

RACHEL LOUISE CARSON (1907-1964), an eminent writer and marine biologist

E. W. SCHWARTZE, a chemist and reformer who warned Americans about the dangers of ingesting even small amounts of arsenic

GEORGE J. WALLACE (1906-   ), an educator and reformer from Michigan State University who warned about unrestrained use of pesticides

UPTON BEALL SINCLAIR (1878-1968), a muckraking novelist who helped bring the American public to the realization that foodstuffs may be contaminated

WILLIAM HILLS, a Harvard Chemistry Professor who warned the consuming public about poisons in their food supply

Summary of Event

Rachel Louise Carson (1907-1964), born in Springdale, Pennsylvania, and educated at The Johns Hopkins University, has written four timely, provocative books dealing with the beauties of nature and the thoughtlessness of man-in-nature: *Under the Sea Wind* (1941), *The Sea Around Us* (1951), *The Edge of the Sea* (1954), and *Silent Spring* (1962).

As a marine biologist, Carson demonstrated her knowledge of the undersea life in her first three books, but in her last, *Silent Spring*, she turned to an examination of how unlimited, reckless reliance on pesticides and herbicides is ruining the earth by poisoning the soil and waters. Although ecological groundbreakers such as chemist E. W. Schwartze and Professors George J. Wallace of Michigan State University and Wil-

liam Hills of Harvard University had written warnings about pesticides' dangers, *Silent Spring* was the first account of the pesticides problem to reach a mass audience and the first to be so carefully discussed and, more importantly, heeded. Perhaps the one quality which accounts for the book's popularity is Carson's style of writing: that poetic way she has of describing the terrible effects of pesticides. Like Upton Sinclair's *The Jungle*, a turn-of-the-century novel about Chicago slaughterhouse conditions, *Silent Spring* created a firestorm of controversy which resulted in Congress' passing laws protecting the public against hazardous substances.

The segment of the American population that reacted most markedly to *Silent Spring* was the pesticides industry, a mammoth enterprise making billions of dollars a year on products that Rachel Carson said were toxic and potentially disastrous for the human race. United by her attacks on their industry, representatives of pesticides manufacturers banded together to denounce the book as a "hoax" and "fraud." Despite their denunciations, however, the Congress of the United States, supported by large numbers of voters, took what Carson said seriously enough to pass legislation banning the use of DDT.

To be sure, from the time of "Paris Green" and other early pesticides to that of DDT and chlordane, substances which deterred the spread of insects and other plant destroyers were well thought of by farmers who stood to gain much from increasing yields of crops. In fact, as Carson tells it, the public-at-large has been told for well over a century to "dust" plants to prevent the appearance of pests—and the public has believed the message. As Carson would be the first to acknowledge, however, advances in the use of pesticides brought about increases in the quality and quantity of almost every fruit, grain, and vegetable grown; in a world where famine always lurks around one corner or another, pesticide use has made sense to almost everyone. While not denying the advances brought about by the use of DDT and other substances, Carson vehemently argued for the monitoring of potentially deadly poisonous substances by local, state, and national agencies and for the complete removal of the worst offender: DDT. She knew full well that her arguments against the

mindless overapplication of potentially deadly things would be met with impassioned resistance from the makers of pesticides.

Her enemies succeeded only in making 1962 a watershed year for what has since become known as the ecology movement; hers was the book that made people "environmentally conscious." Not only did she highlight the possibility of man suffering from pesticides, but the whole idea that all life on earth was being grievously affected by chemicals that concentrate themselves in the livers and other internal organs of creatures. One creature eats another, absorbs the poisons in his victim, then is in turn eaten. Actually, those creatures that are at the very top of the food chain (for example, man, the grizzly bear, the lion, and so forth) will suffer the most damage, according to Carson's theory, for they will absorb all of the chemicals passed on from creature to creature. Those chemicals will lodge in the organs of these higher animals, shortening life expectancy as they do. So, no one is safe from the kind of ecological attack fostered by poisoned soils. As Carson put it, our "spring of life" was being tampered with—perhaps fatally.

Carson points out that it took people who were faced with the most dramatic, obvious sort of evidence that pesticides kill a very long time to conclude that they themselves were in danger of being poisoned. Unless pets died or children sickened, it seems, few people in the past thought twice about the spraying of nearby fields or orchards. On the other hand, farmers and orchard keepers either did not know about the serious side-effects of heavy spraying or did know and sprayed anyway. As Carson intimates, their record is not a good one; in fact, she places almost as much blame on farmers and orchard owners as on pesticides manufacturers in assessing blame for the ruination of our environment. In case after case, farmers and orchard keepers have refused to admit that overzealous spraying caused immediate and serious problems for livestock and small field animals like pheasants, snakes, and mice.

For their part, large chemical companies routinely refused—at least for the most part—to issue any warnings about the possible ill effects emanating from the use of their pesticides or herbicides. Moreover, state and national regulatory commissions that had the power to stop the widespread use of DDT and other known hazardous chemicals, did not choose to do so (at least until Carson's book came out).

What is particularly shocking about Carson's revelations is the extent of the chemical abuse that was—and to a certain, though more limited extent, still is—being practiced. She mentions that farmers, in their haste to eradicate this or that pest, will often kill every single living creature in a given field by dumping enormous amounts of substances on their field. What happens is that over a not-so-lengthy period of time, the poisons can add up to several pounds per square yard of soil.

Such haphazard dumping of harmful pesticides on fields can destroy the entire natural balance of life in the area affected, since the insects which are helpful to man are killed along with the insects that are pests. As was previously indicated, livestock have been poisoned to the extent that they have died in many cases. So what begins as an effort to be rid of one particular pest ends up being a draconian purge of all animal life with residual effects that will last into the future. Those pesticides whose reason for existence is to make human life better, in fact make it worse: and there is Carson's paradox.

Carson's book, of course, ended up as one of those extremely rare sorts of publishing events, being at once a bestseller and a historical landmark. *Silent Spring* worked its magic overnight: it was not long after its introduction in 1962 that the public-at-large began to complain to their legislators that not enough safeguards against pesticide poisoning were in effect. Lawmakers, both local and national, began to create the sort of legislation that would end pesticide abuse. DDT was taken off the market under a newly passed federal law, and limits on the use of other chemicals were put into effect. More importantly, perhaps, the public's attitude toward chemical spraying underwent a profound change—a change that time has shown to be irreversible.

Pertinent Literature

Whorton, James. *Before* Silent Spring: *Pesticides and Public Health in Pre-DDT America*. Princeton, N.J.: Princeton University Press, 1975.

In *Before* Silent Spring, James Whorton, eminent historian of chemistry, gives a detailed historical analysis of the unthinking overuse of pesticides in the United States by farmers and others who, in many cases, willingly create a public health hazard in exchange for greater crop yields. In particular, his is a welcome addition to literature about the use of DDT, that most deadly of sprayed chemicals, for he gives all the necessary facts from which to draw conclusions. His conclusion is emphatically stated: Rachel Carson was absolutely right about what she said in *Silent Spring*. Whorton's account makes compelling reading, for although the book is science history, it proceeds almost like a good detective novel.

As Whorton says of his exposé in his preface, ". . . if the lessons it contains are familiar, they are also worth repeating, if only to place in historical perspective our present dilemma of seemingly having to poison our food in order to protect it." Admitting the limitations of his book, Whorton observes that it will not in any fashion quell the controversy concerning Carson's *Silent Spring*. Rather, it will further enrage those in the pesticide industry and those who side with that industry's conclusions and see no harm in farmers using inorganic compounds as insecticides and herbicides. Since such substances as DDT do not, as a rule, create immediately discernible problems, they have proven difficult—if not impossible—to ban. However, Whorton's casebook is filled with accounts of similar substances such as the notorious "Paris green" of the past century whose effects were as deadly and horrible as they were slow to show up.

What the author does not do is to point at particular villains; instead, he demonstrates how a profound ignorance of harmful substances such as lead arsenate and nicotine (both heavily used on plants at one time) led to mass suffering and—in many cases—death. In fact, he demonstrates how governmental agencies such as the New York City Hall or the Ohio State Health Department often were either ineffectual in stopping the use of contaminants on fruits and vegetables or uninterested in the whole subject until events forced them to take action. Even the Pure Food and Drug Act (1906) failed to spell out adequately dangers inherent in pesticide contamination and the ways in which pesticide use could be controlled. Ambiguity again and again foiled the best efforts of lawmakers to do something about the evils of pesticide abuse.

Particularly good is James Whorton's account of the naïve boosterism surrounding the promotion of pesticides in the mid-to-late nineteenth century, a time when homemade and wagon-sold concoctions were quickly snapped up along with the latest snake oil and skunk grease cure-alls. In such an atmosphere of hucksterism, reformers such as Michigan's Robert Clark Kedzie and William Hills, Harvard chemistry professor, had a rough time convincing the public that pesticides could do great harm. A number of unsung heroes such as E. W. Schwartze, who showed that arsenic could poison one very slowly with fatal accuracy, emerge from an era when the doctrine of laissez-faire influenced all things—in-

945

cluding plant spraying.

So it went throughout the early to mid-twentieth century as well. Public outcries, however, did become more common because of the influence of such men as Schwartze, Kedzie, and Hills. Muckraking novelists such as Upton Sinclair terrorized the reading public with lurid exposés of meat-packing plants that allowed all sorts of poisons to fall into food, increasing the pressure on the United States government to do something about the abuses. The 1906 Pure Food and Drug Act was a direct result of such alarms. Inherent in it were some provisions protecting the public against heavily sprayed produce.

In the 1930's, a replacement for the obsolete Pure Food and Drug Act was found which "allowed for the establishment of legal definitions and standards for foods and for the setting of official tolerance levels for poisons unavoidably included in food prod-ucts." With this bill pending action, a great and furious debate occurred in Congress in which cosmetic and drug manufacturers protested vehemently against further "meddling." Whorton notes how this bill had to be weakened considerably before it could be passed—a sorry state of affairs.

Insecticide use, rather than being curtailed, was actually increased in the 1940's—especially after World War II when DDT became king. However, Whorton also discusses the dawning awareness of pesticides' hazards; without such an awareness, that single book, *Silent Spring* by Rachel Carson would not have had the considerable impact it did.

A serious reader could not hope for a better, more readable and interesting book about ecological disasters past and future than *Before Silent Spring*.

Rudd, Robert L. *Pesticides and the Living Landscape*. Madison: University of Wisconsin Press, 1964.

Robert Rudd's *Pesticides and the Living Landscape*, the product of Conservation Foundation funded research, attempts to answer the question, "How can we control the many thousands of plant and animal species that compete with us for food, fiber, and timber or in some way threaten our health and comfort and at the same time recognize, preserve, and enhance the productive, cultural and spiritual values that the living environment gives to us?"

The book centers on five subjects: how man exploits the living environment; how he challenges the organ-isms that interfere with his exploitation; how successful he is in controlling these competing organisms; the methods he uses to control them; and the price he pays for the methods in practice.

Written in the same year that Rachel Carson published *Silent Spring*, Rudd's book offers a more in-depth study of pesticide use and abuse than does Carson's. *Silent Spring* addresses a mass audience above all else, while *Pesticides and the Living Landscape* is more of a scientist's account (though it can be deciphered by an attentive general reader).

In his book, Rudd offers a wealth of data about the attempts to destroy insect pests, attempts which more often than not disturbed or even destroyed the ecological balance of nature in American farmlands. This is not to imply that Rudd advocates doing away entirely with pesticides. Recognizing that there exist certain pests such as the potato beetle and grasshopper that can destroy whole plantings of crops in large areas of the country, he would allow a restricted use of certain pesticides (some, like the infamous DDT, should be entirely done away with, he believes). However, the invidious practice of dumping pesticides is the worst thing one can do to a crop, for dumping contaminates the soil and creates disasters for creatures like robins that eat pesticide-laden earthworms. He would also stop all use of stable substances such as dieldrin, aldrin, and heptachlor whose effects are long-lasting (except in the rarest of instances when a "catastrophe is imminent and obvious"); encourage "cultural and faunal diversification programs that ensure more complex faunas and less stability of pest populations"; begin a "user-education program" in which the many hazards of dangerous chemicals are explained; and finally, require that the public be informed of the justification behind tax-supported pest control programs.

It would seem that Rudd is more of an optimist than was Rachel Carson. He believes that the public-at-large is capable of learning about the many perils of pesticides, provided that governmental agencies provide them with appropriate information.

Arms of the United States Government such as the National Research Council, and the Committee on Pest Control, can, he claims, do much to right past wrongs and once more allow nature to be free from human meddling.

What one comes away with after reading the book is the idea that man seems not to look before leaping; that is to say, he frequently takes the easiest path rather than think about the implications involved in what he is doing. The fire ant campaign in the Southern states serves as well as any example in *Pesticides and the Living Landscape* to illustrate this point. In the fire ant campaign, undertaken in the 1950's, a South American ant of vivid red coloration was thought to be a threat to American crops. The answer to the problem was not long in coming: heptachlor.

In fact, as much as 1.5 to two pounds of heptachlor per acre was applied in some locales, a concentration which badly contaminated the drinking water of livestock and caused the destruction of valuable reptiles such as snakes and turtles. These creatures' disappearance upset the balance of life in the swampy areas adjacent to the farmers' fields. Their obliteration, in turn, meant that the animals that fed upon them (birds of all sorts and small mammals) would die. In addition to the damage done to animal life is the slow-to-detect harm done to human beings by their own spraying. It is, in fact, creatures highest on the food chain that receive the highest dosage of chemicals.

Rudd's lesson for humanity echoes that of Carson: stop dumping or allowing the dumping of harmful chemicals on our nation's soils. If the poisoning does not stop, human life will—as well as the lives of countless other animals. There is no alternative. Either we become conscious of the grave harm we do to our environment by using dangerous pesticides or we perish. — *J.D.R.*

Additional Recommended Reading

Pesticides: Actions Needed to Protect the Consumer from Defective Products. Washington, D.C.: United States General Accounting Office, May 23, 1974. Report issued to notify Congress about the shortcomings of the Environmental Protection Agency's fight to protect people from pesticide contamination.

Environmental Protection Agency Efforts to Remove Hazardous Pesticides from the Channels of Trade. Washington, D.C.: United States General Accounting Office, April 26, 1973. Report highlighting the EPA's campaign to eradicate poisonous substances used as pesticides, published as a direct result of the public uproar over pesticides caused by *Silent Spring.*

Effects of Pesticides in Water: A Report to the States. Washington, D.C.: United States Environmental Protection Agency, 1972. Reveals government surveys proving that pesticides can be dangerous to fish and other aquatic life.

Mellanby, Kenneth. *Pesticides and Pollution.* London: Collins, 1970. A scholarly and well-documented account of how pesticides have added to the worldwide problem of pollution in recent times.

Pryde, Lucy T. *Pesticides, Food, and Drugs.* Menlo Park, Calif.: Cummings Publishing Company, 1973. Very thorough discussion of the effects of chemicals used in pesticides on people's "interior environments."

THE UNITED STATES SUPREME COURT RULES AGAINST BIBLE READING IN PUBLIC SCHOOLS

Type of event: Legal: judicial landmark regarding Bible reading in public schools
Time: June 17, 1963
Locale: Washington, D.C.

Principal personages:

EARL WARREN (1891-1974), Chief Justice of the Supreme Court, 1953-1969; and former governor of California, 1943-1953

THOMAS CAMPBELL CLARK (1899-   ), Associate Justice of the Supreme Court, 1949-1967; and the author of majority opinion in *Schempp* v. *Abington Township*

POTTER STEWART (1915-   ), Associate Justice of the Supreme Court, 1958-   ; and the author of minority opinion

EDWARD AND SIDNEY SCHEMPP, plaintiffs in the case and residents of Abington Township, Pennsylvania

Summary of Event

Like the Progressive era and the New Deal, the 1960's in the United States have assumed the stature of an important, almost classic age of reform and liberalism. Civil rights legislation, the "Greater Society" programs, and antiwar protests were all symptomatic of a general quest for greater justice. Unlike earlier episodes of reform, however, the changes of the 1960's were often introduced almost in defiance of most Americans. Although liberal measures often resulted from, and received the support of, vocal and active groups, they did not tend to reflect the goals of the "average" citizen; nor was there the kind of massive endorsement of reform that Franklin Roosevelt enjoyed in 1936. One of the prime examples of these unpopular reforms is the Supreme Court ruling, in 1963, against prayer and Bible reading in

the public schools: the case of *Schempp* v. *Abington Township*.

Although the Court's decision (by a majority of eight to one) provoked widespread disappointment and anger, it was not unexpected. For nearly twenty years, a series of eight rulings by the Supreme Court had gradually removed the practice of religious activities from state-supported schools. After World War II, a growing number of freethinkers, Jews, and liberal Protestants resisted the assumption of most local and school authorities that society was, or should be, based on the teachings of the New Testament. Most states permitted or encouraged a variety of religious exercises in the schools, ranging from Bible classes to the recitation of prayers. Increasingly, these practices were challenged in the courts. In the New Jersey case of *Everson* v. *Board of*

Education (1947), the Supreme Court defended the use of state funds to bus children to parochial schools, but warned that "a wall of separation between church and state" must be maintained. A year later, in *McCollum* v. *Board of Education*, the Court banned a program of religious instruction from the schools of Champaign, Illinois. The judges' chief objection to the Champaign system was that religious teachers were actually brought into the school, thus involving the state too heavily in religion, and pressuring dissenting students into conformity with the majority. In 1953, the Supreme Court approved a "released-time" program, in which students could apply to leave school early, in order to attend religion classes at their churches.

While the Supreme Court's opposition to classroom instruction in religion enjoyed widespread support and sympathy, even among churches, the question of school prayers and Bible reading was more delicate. Most people agreed with Justice William O. Douglas' observation that Americans were a "religious people"; it seemed entirely right and natural that the school day should begin with some recognition of the general belief in God. To prohibit *any* sort of observance in schools was tantamount, many argued, to state opposition to religion. Nonetheless, the Supreme Court ruled in *Engel* v. *Vitale* (1962) that the state-composed prayer recited in New York classrooms was unconstitutional; official prayers, the majority of Justices agreed, came dangerously close to an official religion. Widespread protest followed: Senator Herman Talmadge, for ex-

ample, called the ruling an "outrageous edict which has numbed the conscience and shocked the highest sensibilities of the nation." But a year later, in June of 1963, the Court went even further in the Schempp decision.

The case of *Schempp* v. *Abington Township* had a long history beginning in 1958. The morning classes in that district began with a reading, by class and teacher, of ten verses from the Bible and the recitation of the Lord's Prayer. A junior at the high school named Ellory Schempp was from a Unitarian family, and he objected to the Bible reading. In symbolic protest, he read the Koran to himself one morning, and was subsequently excused from the reading period for the rest of the school year. During his senior year, he was told to remain in the class and participate in the reading and recitation, and he complied. His father and uncle then took the case to court, protesting that the morning practices were unconstitutional.

The Federal Courts, on both the district and appellate level, agreed with the Schempps and ruled the Pennsylvania law that required Bible reading unconstitutional. Before the case could reach the Supreme Court, the Pennsylvania legislature amended the law to make the reading and prayer noncompulsory; thus, in October, 1960, the case was returned to the district court to be retried under the new law. Again the lower courts held the statute unconstitutional, and after five years of litigation the Supreme Court agreed.

The majority opinion of the Court, written by Tom Clark, held that Bible reading and prayer in the classroom violated two restrictions imposed by the First Amendment. The prohibition against "an establishment of religion," Clark argued, does not simply prevent the government from giving support to one religion at the expense of others; it also implies that the government should not bring its resources into efforts to perpetuate religion in general. The other prohibition of the First Amendment, that the "free exercise" of religious belief should not be restricted, was violated by the circumstances of the Bible reading. Even if a student could be excused from the exercise, he would feel pressured to remain. By standing outside in the hallway during a part of school, a student would, in effect, be ostracized because of his beliefs. While suggesting that the Bible should be studied in schools as a historical and literary work, the Court concluded that any religious use would bring the state too close to indoctrination.

The general reaction to the Supreme Court's decision in the Schempp case was hostile. Most people tended to agree with dissenting Justice Potter Stewart, who wrote that he could not see "how an official religion is established by letting those who want to say a prayer say it." At the same time, most religious and educational leaders expressed relief that the Court had finally laid down clear limitations for the schools to follow and had placed responsibility for religion firmly in the hands of families and churches. The ruling had an immediate and widespread effect upon American education.

The Schempp decision also fit neatly into the broader trends of the Warren Court and that entire era of liberalism. Although it superficially limited the power of the state, it effectively set down federal guidelines for the conduct of local education. It reasserted the Court's right to revoke state legislation. Most importantly, the ruling championed the rights of a minority in the face of an angry majority, and encouraged the independence of the individual.

Pertinent Literature

Boles, Donald E. *The Bible, Religion, and the Public Schools*. Ames: Iowa State University Press, 1965.

Both the popular imagination and some respectable scholars tend to portray crucial decisions of the Supreme Court as the work of a handful of isolated, intellectual minds. The nine men of the Court, it is charged, are able to shape the course of history with only scanty reference to the outside world. As in political history, there is a strong temptation to emphasize the role of individuals to the neglect of broader social trends. *The Bible, Religion, and the Public Schools* presents the opposite line of argument. In covering a wide array of material on the historical, legal, and cultural background of the Schempp decision, the book is fashioned around the theme that Supreme Court decisions are closely connected to the environment in which they are made.

Boles begins by tracing the history

of religious teaching in the public schools. Because the public school movement did not begin until the 1830's, it is not possible to know how the framers of the Constitution and Bill of Rights felt about the issue. Boles suggests that they would have been deeply divided: New Englanders based almost all education on religion, while Thomas Jefferson did not even permit a chaplain at the University of Virginia. As public schools began to appear, they generally did include studies of religion in their curriculum. Most communities were centered around one or two Protestant sects, and there was usually a consensus on how religion should be taught in a particular school. After the middle of the nineteenth century, however, as large numbers of Roman Catholics arrived in American schools, the issue of religious freedom was suddenly very relevant. To make the schools attractive to immigrant families, they were kept rigidly secular; religious education was increasingly taken over by the churches. By the end of the nineteenth century, there existed a widespread consensus on the importance of secular schooling. A Constitutional Amendment proposed in 1876, which would have expressly prohibited any religious teaching in public schools, failed chiefly because it was considered unnecessary.

This trend changed abruptly after World War I. The Fundamentalist movement of the 1920's attacked the "atheism" of Eastern culture. Darwinism, the Fundamentalists argued, was supplanting God in the classroom. Their agitation tied into a very widespread feeling that society was losing its traditional values and that it was becoming too "secularized." The result was a series of state laws, passed throughout the country, which permitted or required religious instruction and worship in the public schools. These provisions almost always took account of religious diversity, and thus secured a broad base of support among Protestants, Catholics, and Jews.

After World War II, these laws were increasingly challenged in the courts, and Boles carefully traces the litigation in state courts as a means of understanding the underlying issues in the Schempp case. Although most of the state decisions (by a majority of fourteen to seven) upheld existing laws for Bible reading and prayer, the range of opinion steadily narrowed down to a few basic issues: was the Bible sectarian, or could it be considered simply a general expression of any religious belief? Did Bible reading invade the rights of dissenters? Did the religious exercises constitute state support of religion? Once the issues had been stated in this way, the author implies, it was almost inevitable that the Supreme Court should rule against religion in the schools. By the 1960's, then, the pendulum had swung back; as before World War I, public education in America was secular.

Ball, William E. "Religion and Public Education: The Post-Schempp Years," in *Religion and Public Education*. Edited by Theodore R. Sizer. New York: Houghton Mifflin Company, 1967, pp. 144–163.

In this brief but intensely analytical essay, William Ball discussed the impact of the Schempp decision upon American education. He insists that although the Supreme Court ruling clarified the conduct of religious exercises in schools, it did not solve the question of what role religion should play in education. The Court did not adequately acknowledge that "the education of children is a very special thing and that religion is a very special thing"; inevitably, according to Ball, the two must overlap.

The essay lists three ways that a government may involve itself in religion: by establishing religious bodies, by providing religious instruction, and by encouraging religious worship. The federal government of the eighteenth century prohibited the first activity, but was too small to need to worry about the second and third. As government grew and public education spread, consensus emerged that religious instruction, too, should be avoided by the state. Religious worship, however, was condoned by the government: ministers were employed by the army to attend to the spiritual needs of soldiers, and Congress opened each day with a prayer.

Ball agrees with the Supreme Court that worship in the public schools is quite different. In the army or in Congress, it is assumed that those who participate in the worship do so as mature and independent adults. In the schools, however, any hint of an official position on religion would inevitably assume some of the substance of indoctrination. The state is not merely offering people a chance to exercise their religious beliefs, but taking a hand in forming those beliefs. Therefore, such activity is not proper.

But religion, as Ball defines it, is more than particular theological doctrines—it is also a code of moral and ethical principles, an awareness of deep spiritual needs, and an admission of man's imperfections. While such codes and awarenesses are naturally most expressly embodied in the various sectarian religions, in America they are also part, in a loose but very important way, of national culture and traditions. How is religion in this most general sense to be taught in school without the aid of the Bible and prayers?

The essay considers a number of possibilities. Ball rejects the idea of classes on morality, because this would be little different from classes in religion: who is to say what principles are true? A variety of "inspirational" stories and poems are used in some schools; but these are either bad literature, in which case they should be studied *as* literature. Likewise, religion can be legally studied in the schools as culture, art, literature, or music; but none of these studies, according to Ball, will really increase the spiritual awareness of the student.

Ball does not offer a definitive solution to the problem he raises. Indeed, part of the value of the essay is his genuine perplexity. But he does isolate a key point of his concern. He fears that the private parochial schools and the public secular schools will produce citizens with very different outlooks on the same basic problems. It is necessary for each type of school to have an awareness of the other's

953

concerns. A sort of philosophical humanism, an awareness of the connections between the spiritual and the mundane, is needed to link the two types of education. If this sort of understanding actually develops, Ball seems to suggest, the Schempp ruling will eventually become irrelevant. — *R.H.S.*

Additional Recommended Reading

Duker, Sam. *The Public Schools and Religion: The Legal Context.* New York: Harper & Row Publishers, 1966. An informative discussion of the major court rulings concerning religion in the schools, providing lengthy excerpts from court opinions.

Hudgins, H. C., Jr. *The Warren Court and the Public Schools.* Danville, Ill.: Interstate Printers, 1970. A concise analysis of several educational issues, ranging from academic freedom to flag saluting, and how they have been affected by Supreme Court rulings from 1953 to 1969.

Kelly, Alfred H. and Winfred A. Harbison. *The American Constitution: Its Origins and Development.* New York: W. W. Norton and Company, 1970. An excellent constitutional history, focusing on significant Supreme Court decisions and carefully tracing the interpretation of the First Amendment.

Lytle, Clifford M. *The Warren Court and Its Critics.* Tucson: University of Arizona Press, 1968. Lytle traces the reactions of Congress, interest groups, and the general public to the major rulings of the Warren Court, and tries to explain the lasting hostility to the Court.

Religion in the Public Schools. Washington, D.C.: American Association of School Administrators, 1964. This sixty-page document was one of the most important responses to the Schempp decision; it formulated new policies for schools to follow, and was generally supportive of the ruling.

Sizer, Theodore R., ed. *Religion and Public Education.* Boston: Houghton Mifflin Company, 1967. Aside from the Ball article reviewed here, this collection contains a wide assortment of provocative essays: some are partisan, while others are purely analytical.

THE NUCLEAR TEST BAN TREATY

Type of event: Diplomatic: multilateral treaty banning the testing of nuclear weapons
in the atmosphere, in outer space, and under water
Time: September 24, 1963
Locale: Washington, D.C., Geneva, and Moscow

Principal personages:

JOHN FITZGERALD KENNEDY (1917-1963), thirty-fifth President of the United States, 1961-1963

NIKITA SERGEEVICH KHRUSHCHEV (1894-1971), Premier of the Soviet Union, 1958-1964; and First Secretary of the Communist Party of the Soviet Union, 1953-1964

HAROLD MACMILLAN (1894-   ), Prime Minister of Great Britain, 1957-1963

DEAN RUSK (1909-   ), United States Secretary of State, 1961-1969

ANDREI A. GROMYKO (1909-   ), Foreign Minister of the Soviet Union

SIR ALEC DOUGLAS-HOME (1903-   ), Foreign Secretary of Great Britain

WILLIAM AVERELL HARRIMAN (1891-   ), principal American negotiator of the treaty

LORD HAILSHAM, principal British negotiator of the treaty

Summary of Event

The story of the 1963 nuclear test ban treaty has its origins in the last year of World War II. On July 16, 1945, the United States for the first time exploded an atomic bomb, at Alamagordo, New Mexico. Later, on August 6 and 9, the United States dropped the only atomic bombs ever used in wartime—on the Japanese cities of Hiroshima and Nagasaki. The end of the war came very shortly thereafter, but so also did the realization that the United States had developed the most dreadful weapon ever devised by man. Thus, from the very end of World War II, men and governments began to seek a way to outlaw or control this newly developed power. Contributing greatly to the urgency of these efforts was the development of a so-called Cold War, an ideological struggle for power and influence which aligned the Soviet Union against its former wartime allies in the West, led by the United States. While the Cold War was not a physical conflict, as World War II had been, it was nevertheless dangerous because the tension, hostility, suspicion, and fears which it generated might easily, many believed, evolve into a shooting war. If that occurred and nuclear weapons were used, it would, some contended, destroy civilization. But despite strenuous efforts, particularly by the United States government and its allies, nothing in the area of nuclear arms control was achieved for several years. During that period nuclear weapons were further developed, becoming more sophisticated and destructive. The need for controls became more and more urgent.

The initial proposals for controlling nuclear energy came from the United States, Canada, and Great Britain. On November 15, 1945, a Three-Power Declaration called on the United Nations to establish a commission to deal with issues of atomic energy. The following month a meeting of foreign ministers in Moscow from the United States, Great Britain, and the Soviet Union endorsed the creation of a United Nations Atomic Energy Commission.

On June 14, 1946, the United States delegation presented to the first meeting of the United Nations Atomic Energy Commission the Baruch Plan, named after its drafter, Bernard Baruch. The Baruch Plan called for the creation of an International Atomic Development Authority which would supervise all atomic development and see to it that the manufacture of all atomic weapons would cease and that all existing bombs would be disposed of. Soviet rejection of this proposal became clear a few days later when Deputy Foreign Minister Andrei Gromyko offered an alternative proposal which called for a voluntary commitment to destroy existing bombs and not produce any others. The Soviet proposal called for control to come after disarmament, while the Americans proposed that controls be established first. This fundamental difference would complicate all subsequent negotiations for disarmament and arms control.

For several years thereafter, discussions continued in various United Nations committees and subcommittees but without any agreement being recorded. A deadlock between the American and Soviet positions constantly blocked progress. In the meantime, the Soviet Union joined the United States as a nuclear power by successfully exploding an atomic bomb in September, 1949. Following this, there were no significant new proposals in the area of nuclear arms control to emerge for several years. Instead, each side reacted to the other's advances in nuclear technology. In October, 1952, the British exploded their first bomb; in November of the same year the United States successfully tested its first hydrogen bomb; and in August, 1953, the Soviet Union exploded its first H-bomb. Work proceeded on the peaceful uses of atomic energy, but at the same time the United States and the Soviet Union embarked on a nuclear arms race which continued thereafter virtually without interruption, even after the two superpowers had achieved a capacity for overkill.

Efforts to find some means of controlling, limiting, or even eliminating nuclear weapons continued; but fundamental differences between the two sides plagued the negotiations, and no agreements emerged. Nevertheless, the pressure of world opinion to find some way to reduce the threat of nuclear conflict mounted. On March 1, 1954, an American nuclear test conducted in Bikini Atoll in the Pacific Ocean produced worldwide reaction because of the extent of the radioactive fallout. Protests came from the Japanese government and others. On April 2, Indian Prime Minister Nehru proposed a halt to further nuclear testing. Later, Burma, in the United Nations General Assembly, called for an end to all further testing. A year later in the General Assembly both India and the Soviet Union proposed a test ban without supervision or inspection on the grounds that no significant testing could go on undetected anyway. The Western powers balked, arguing against any proposal which did not entail effective inspection and verification; still no agreements were concluded.

The year 1955, however, brought some relaxation in the relations between the United States and the Soviet Union, partly because of the so-called "Spirit of Geneva" which emerged from the Geneva Summit Conference in July of that year. This "spirit" did not produce any immediate progress in disarmament or arms control but did improve the atmosphere in which negotiations could proceed. In April, 1958, Soviet Premier Nikita Khrushchev wrote to President Dwight D. Eisenhower that the Soviet Union had decided unilaterally to halt its testing, and he called on the Western powers to do the same. Testing continued by both sides until October, but in the meantime the U.S.S.R., the United States, and Great Britain agreed to begin a new round of meetings in Geneva on October 31, 1958, aimed at a nuclear test ban treaty. Testing would be suspended for the next year. This voluntary moratorium on testing went into effect on November 3, 1958, and lasted until broken by the Soviet Union in September, 1961. In the meantime, France had joined the nuclear circle by exploding a bomb on February 13, 1960.

The Geneva meetings, properly called the Conference on the Discontinuance of Nuclear Weapon Tests, began on schedule at the end of October, 1958, and lasted for several years. In March, 1962, the work of the conference was transferred to a subcommittee of the Eighteen Nation Disarmament Conference. At first, there was some real progress, and agreement on a number of articles of a draft treaty was achieved. Then, in May, 1960, following the much publicized U-2 incident, the proposed Paris Summit Conference collapsed, and East-West tensions mounted again. The Soviet position hardened; insistence that a test ban be considered as part of a larger treaty for general and complete disarmament was now the Soviet line. That relations had deteriorated drastically was evidenced by the Soviet announcement on August 30, 1961, that the U.S.S.R. intended to resume nuclear testing which it did two days later. The United States and Great Britain responded on September 3 with a proposal for a ban on all atmospheric testing without international supervision, but when no positive reply came from the U.S.S.R., the United States resumed underground tests. On October 30, the Soviet Union exploded the largest bomb ever tested. Immediately there were new outcries in the United Nations demanding an end to nuclear testing. The General Assembly adopted two resolutions to this effect, including one submitted by the United States and Great Britain.

The next major push for a test ban came from the Eighteen Nation Disarmament Conference when it met in March, 1962. At that time a joint resolution from the eight nonaligned nations attending proposed a test ban agreement to be supervised by an international committee of experts which could conduct on-site investigations of unusual seismic disturbances at the invitation of the nation on whose territory the event occurred. The Soviet Union accepted the resolution as a basis for further discussion, while the Western powers accepted it as only one of the bases of discussion. The resolution was, in the Western view, too vague as to whether the on-site inspections would be mandatory or optional. The issue of international inspection and verification still stood in the way of Soviet-American agreement. However, efforts to find a common ground did not cease. In August, the United States and Great Britain submitted jointly two proposals to the Test Ban Sub-Committee of the Eighteen Nation Disarmament Conference. One provided for a comprehensive test ban with an unspecified quota of on-site inspections; the other provided for a partial test ban with underground testing not included and with no international control or verification required. The Soviet delegation, while informally expressing interest, officially rejected both proposals. The potential for continued negotiations lifted hopes for an eventual agreement, but such hopes were apparently shattered by the Cuban Missile Crisis in October.

Actually, the Cuban Crisis marked another turning point in Soviet-American relations. For the first time the prospect of a nuclear confrontation became very real and frightening. As a result, talks between American and Soviet negotiators resumed while the leaders in both the Soviet Union and the United States, Premier Nikita Khrushchev and President John F. Kennedy, became increasingly involved in the formulation of policies and strategy. Kennedy was especially anxious to convince the Soviets of America's sincere desire to reach some kind of agreement which would both ease the tensions and curtail the dangers from radioactive contamination of the environment. Discussion through the winter months of 1962-1963 indicated clearly that the principal obstacle to agreement was the issue of on-site inspection of unexplained seismic disturbances. Parts of the Soviet Union experience numerous earthquakes each year which produce seismic effects similar to those of low-yield underground nuclear tests. The United States, therefore, insisted that a comprehensive test ban treaty must permit at least eight to ten on-site inspections to verify the causes of such occurrences. The most that Premier Khrushchev could get the Soviet Council of Ministers to agree to was three inspections per year. By the spring of 1963, it appeared that another impasse had been reached.

President Kennedy was determined, however, not to miss any opportunity for agreement, and there were indications that Khrushchev was not averse to some kind of compromise. Consequently, on April 24, 1963, Kennedy and British Prime Minister Macmillan issued a public appeal to Khrushchev to resume negotiations for a test ban treaty, to be conducted in Moscow by high-level representatives of the three powers. By June 9, Khrushchev had sent word to Washington and London of his willingness to host the resumed talks in the Soviet capital. The following day, when Kennedy delivered the commencement address at American University, he not only announced the resumption of talks in Moscow but also declared that the United States had decided, as a sign of its sincere concern for peace, to bring to a halt its nuclear testing in the atmosphere. Such tests, he declared, would never be resumed unless other powers continued their own testing.

Kennedy's speech had the desired effect on Khrushchev, who was apparently moved by Kennedy's sincerity and determination. On July 2, in a speech delivered in East Berlin, Khrushchev responded to Kennedy's appeal by announcing that the Soviet Union was ready to agree to a limited or partial test ban treaty. Thus, on July 15, 1963, an American delegation led by Averell Harriman, a British delegation led by Lord Hailsham, and a Soviet delegation led by Foreign Minister Gromyko sat down in Moscow and in the next ten days hammered out the final treaty, which they initialed on July 25. On August 5, the "Treaty Banning Nuclear Weapon Tests in the Atmosphere, in Outer Space, and Under Water," was formally signed in Moscow by Dean Rusk, Douglas Home, and Andrei Gromyko, and on September 24, by a vote of eighty to nineteen, it was ratified by the United States Senate.

The treaty as finally signed was concise and clearly stated and consisted of only five articles. The first contained the statement of intent; namely, that the signatories agreed to cease all nuclear testing in the atmosphere, in outer space, and under water, and also underground, in the event that such tests caused radioactive debris to fall outside the territory of the testing nation. The second article concerned the procedure for amending the treaty; the third invited the adherence of other nations; the fourth defined the treaty's duration as unlimited; and the fifth pertained to the depositing of the treaty in both English and Russian with the governments concerned.

President Kennedy and Premier Khrushchev each considered this treaty a significant achievement which could pave the way for other agreements as well as contribute to a reduction in international tension. It was hoped that the Western powers could persuade France to sign the treaty, while the Soviet Union urged the Chinese Communists to adhere as well. Unfortunately, such hopes went unfulfilled: the French were determined to develop their nuclear capacity independently, and the Chinese were soon to become the fifth nuclear power by exploding an atomic bomb in October, 1964. On the other hand, more than a hundred other nations subsequently added their pledges to those of the United States, Great Britain, and the Soviet Union. A major first step had been taken toward creating a more peaceful world, as the Partial Test Ban Treaty demonstrated that confrontation need not be the prevailing characteristic of East-West relations.

Pertinent Literature

Dean, Arthur H. *Test Ban and Disarmament: The Path of Negotiation*. New York: Harper & Row Publishers, 1966.

This rather brief volume is another in the Policy Book series published by the Council on Foreign Relations. The purpose of this series, according to its editor, is twofold: "first, to provide readers in the country and elsewhere with essays and analytical studies of the highest quality on problems of world significance; and second, to contribute to constructive thinking on American policies of the future." The author of this volume is especially qualified for his task, since he was often personally and directly involved in American-Soviet disarmament and arms control negotiations.

Dean declares at the outset that one of his principal goals in writing this book is "to put this subject in a realistic light." He attempts to convey the complexity of the problems involved in disarmament and arms control, problems which cannot, he argues, be solved "by unilateral gestures and declarations on the part of the United States." He therefore not only analyzes the negotiations which finally led to the Partial Test Ban Treaty in 1963 and the other disarmament talks before and after that treaty was concluded, but he attempts also to explain the methods and problems peculiar to disarmament diplomacy, the difficulties involved in negotiating with the Soviets, the reasons for certain features of America's disarmament policies such as the insistence on inspection and verification, and the prospects for future arms control agreements.

An especially interesting chapter is entitled simply, "Disarmament Diplomacy." Here the author notes the various criticisms leveled against disarmament negotiations which go on and on interminably without producing tangible results. He defends such negotiations not in terms of the agreements or treaties concluded but rather in terms of the dreadful alternative of no negotiations at all. Dean also discusses throughout the chapter the Soviet style and tactics of negotiating. In this regard, he declares, two features are notable: "a dogmatic expectation of hostility from the outside world and an iron determination to carry out a program previously determined in Moscow and not subject to change by the diplomat in the field." Because of these attitudes, Dean notes, negotiating with the Soviets is always "a difficult and tedious process under any circumstances"; but this is especially true when the subject is disarmament. Other characteristics of the Soviet style include a tendency to deal in broad generalizations which have good propaganda value; to avoid discussion of specifics; to use patience-trying delaying tactics; and deliberately to misinterpret conversations to fit particular Soviet policy objectives. Dean insists that American negotiators must recognize such tactics and be willing to resist them, even though negotiations are prolonged and unproductive as a result. The Soviets believe that time and history are on their side and are thus very patient negotiators. Dean's discussion of these and other Soviet tactics and style is both informative and instructive.

Dean devotes an entire chapter to the issue of "Verification and Inspection." He notes that "reliable verification is, from our point of view, the cornerstone on which any structure of disarmament or arms control must rest." The Soviets, however, have consistently resisted proposals which provide for such measures. Dean discusses the possible reasons for the Soviet resistance and the best possible approaches for American negotiators to take to overcome that resistance. He also suggests some directions in which future disarmament talks might move and the kinds of agreements which might conceivably emerge. But he cautions against undue optimism and against impatience when agreements are not quickly forthcoming.

With respect to the negotiations which produced the Partial Test Ban Treaty in 1963, Dean writes from the experience of direct involvement. As chairman of the American delegation to the Eighteen Nation Disarmament Commission meeting in Geneva in 1962 and to the Nuclear Test Ban Subcommittee, he shared directly in

preparing the draft proposal which in 1963 provided the basis of the treaty which was concluded. Dean considers that treaty notable in two principal respects. First, it represents the first agreement to emerge after nearly eighteen years of hard negotiating which provides some form of control of nuclear weapons development. Second, the agreement "rests on a fairly fine balance between political advantage and risk." Those who negotiated the treaty recognized that risks were involved—a violation of the treaty might pass unnoticed, for example—but they believed the advantages outweighed the risks. The advantages included, among others, an easing of tensions, a check on the arms race, a halt to radioactive fallout from the atmosphere, and possibly a brake on the proliferation of nuclear weapons. Such advantages are real and significant, and thus offer hope that further negotiations may produce new agreements aimed at creating a peaceful world. Herein lies the principal message of Dean's book: namely, that patience and caution, perseverance and firmness, will eventually pay dividends in America's struggle to resolve its differences with the Soviet Union and to remove the threat of a nuclear holocaust.

Roberts, Chalmers M. *The Nuclear Years: The Arms Race and Arms Control, 1945-1970*. New York: Frederick A. Praeger, 1970.

Chalmers Roberts, for many years a diplomatic reporter for the *Washington Post*, has attempted in this brief volume to provide an interpretive account of the nuclear era from the end of World War II to the eve of the 1970 SALT talks in Vienna. As

a professional journalist he had occasion to attend "numerous international conferences, including all the Soviet-American summit meetings of national leaders, at which nuclear weapons more and more were at issue." Roberts' book is based, therefore, on his own personal experiences and observations as well as on research in both primary and secondary source materials. The result is a very readable, concise, and balanced survey of twenty-five years of nuclear weapons development and competition, from 1945 to 1970.

Roberts divides this period into four phases. The first, from 1945 to 1952, he calls the Baruch Plan era, during which the United States possessed a virtual monopoly on nuclear weapons until the Soviet Union began developing its own nuclear capacity. The period 1953 to 1960 marked the period of "assessment by the post-Stalin leadership in the Soviet Union and by the Eisenhower Administration in the United States." During this period, each nation pushed to increase its nuclear strength until each eventually achieved a capacity for overkill. The years from 1961 to 1967 comprised an era of "limited agreement" during which the superpowers, after the scare of the Cuban Missile Crisis in 1962, sought to place limits on the testing of nuclear weapons and a halt to their proliferation. The final phase, 1968-1970, witnessed the establishment of "rough nuclear parity" between the Soviet Union and the United States, and their decision finally to negotiate some real disarmament and arms control in the realm of strategic nuclear weapons.

The author sees two principal factors influencing the nuclear policies of the two superpowers during the period in question. One of them is what he calls the "action-reaction phenomenon," borrowing the phrase from President Kennedy's Secretary of Defense, Robert McNamara. What is implied by this term is that each side in the Cold War tends to react to the actions of the other, and in the arms race this means that whenever one nation achieves a technological breakthrough or an increase in its nuclear arsenal, the other feels obliged to catch up with or outdo its opponent, and in so doing, provokes another reaction. The second factor affecting policies involves the internal conflicts within the governments of the two superpowers. This is to say, for example, that within each presidential administration in the United States there have been sharply contrasting views regarding what America's defense posture should be and thus what its disarmament and arms control policies should be. The author contends that the same kind of debate has characterized policymaking in the Kremlin. Examples of these two influences are evident through Roberts' account.

Another factor which definitely influenced the course of American-Soviet arms control discussions throughout the period was the importance and timing of international inspection and verification of any disarmament and arms controls measures. The United States has been consistent in insisting that an effective system of inspection and verification must precede implementation of any disarmament or arms control proposals. The Soviets, on the other hand, have been equally consistent in contending that disarmament should come first. This difference of opinion became apparent as early as the discussions of the Baruch Plan in 1946. This plan, submitted by the United States to the

United Nations Disarmament Commission, proposed the establishment of an International Atomic Development Authority which would be given exclusive control of all nuclear materials, weapons, and scientific data, and thereby would be able to rid the world of the danger of nuclear warfare. This agency would also have full powers to inspect and punish violators. Soviet leaders saw this plan as a thinly veiled scheme by which the United States could maintain its monopoly in nuclear weapons. They therefore countered with alternative proposals which entailed no supervision or inspection, and only a voluntary commitment of nations not to use or produce any atomic weapons, and to destroy any already on hand. Roberts correctly defined the issue as: "which came first, the commitments to disarmament or the measures to ensure the observance of commitments?"

It was this difference of priority which probably did the most to prevent the United States and the Soviet Union from concluding a comprehensive test ban treaty in the later 1950's or the early 1960's. Despite a number of tension-producing events in the early years of President Kennedy's Administration—the Bay of Pigs incident, the erection of the Berlin Wall, the resumption of nuclear testing in the atmosphere after a three-year moratorium, and the Cuban Missile Crisis—discussions proceeded in Geneva aimed at drafting a test ban treaty. What hampered agreement was the American insistence on an adequate number of on-site inspections in cases of unexplainable seismic disturbances. The fewest the United States ever agreed to was seven, while the Soviets would agree to no more than three, arguing that any more would amount to espionage. The Cuban Missile Crisis was followed by a softening of the Soviet attitude, however, and in the summer of 1963, Kennedy sent a special delegation to Moscow in an effort to end the impasse in the test ban talks. What emerged from the July talks was the "Treaty Banning Nuclear Weapon Tests in the Atmosphere, in Outer Space, and Under Water." What made this treaty acceptable to the Soviets was that underground testing was not included and thus the treaty did not require on-site supervision and inspection to verify its fulfillment. What prompted the Soviets to accept a partial test ban treaty in 1963 when they had rejected the idea before the Cuban Missile Crisis was probably, according to the author, the deteriorating relations between the Soviet Union and the People's Republic of China.

Although Chalmers Roberts' book is brief, it is nevertheless informative, interesting, and fair. The inclusion of several political cartoons by Herblock adds an entertaining element to the account. Readers will also find the Appendixes useful as they contain the texts of various proposals and treaties including that of the 1963 Partial Test Ban Treaty. — *T.D.*

Additional Recommended Reading

Burns, E. L. M. *A Seat at the Table: The Struggle for Disarmament.* Toronto: Clarke,

Irwin & Company, 1972. An account of the disarmament and arms control negotiations from the end of World War II to the first SALT talks, written by a Canadian participant in many of the proceedings.

Epstein, William. *The Last Chance: Nuclear Proliferation and Arms Control.* New York: The Free Press, 1976. A fairly in-depth study of the diplomacy surrounding the efforts to control the build-up and spread of nuclear weapons which focuses primarily on the Non-Proliferation Treaty and its significance, but treats the 1963 test ban treaty as an important building block on the road to nuclear arms control.

Bloomfield, Lincoln P., W. C. Clemens, Jr. and Franklyn Griffiths. *Khrushchev and the Arms Race: Soviet Interests in Arms Control and Disarmament, 1954-1964.* Cambridge, Mass.: MIT Press, 1966. A very scholarly examination of the formulation and implementation of Soviet arms control and disarmament policies during the Khrushchev years which concludes that, in contrast to the policies of the Lenin and Stalin eras, Khrushchev's policies aimed at achieving real, if only limited, agreements with the West.

McBride, James Hubert. *The Test Ban Treaty: Military, Technological, and Political Implications.* Chicago: Henry Regnery Company, 1967. Analyzes the text of the Test Ban Treaty, the hearings of Senate committees, and the comments of various prominent personalities both in and out of the United States Government, and concludes that the Partial Test Ban Treaty was a mistake which has jeopardized the security of the United States.

Cousins, Norman. *The Improbable Triumvirate: John F. Kennedy, Pope John, Nikita Khrushchev.* New York: W. W. Norton and Company, 1972. The former editor of *Saturday Review* discusses his personal contacts with Kennedy, Pope John, and Khrushchev during 1962 and 1963 and his efforts on behalf of the Vatican to promote better relations between the United States and the Soviet Union, including conclusion of a treaty banning nuclear testing.

Schlesinger, Arthur M., Jr. *A Thousand Days: John F. Kennedy in the White House.* Boston: Houghton Mifflin Company, 1965. This personal memoir of the Kennedy presidential years by a Kennedy adviser and professional historian recounts in some detail President Kennedy's efforts, in the face of significant opposition within the United States, to reach an agreement with the Soviet Union banning nuclear testing.

Sorensen, Theodore C. *Kennedy.* New York: Harper & Row Publishers, 1965. The final chapter of this penetrating and moving biography of Kennedy as President covers his determined efforts to conclude even a limited test ban agreement with the Soviet Union and Great Britain.

THE CIVIL RIGHTS ACT OF 1964

Type of event: Legal: law to prevent racial discrimination
Time: July 2, 1964
Locale: Washington, D.C.

Principal personages:

JOHN FITZGERALD KENNEDY (1917-1963), thirty-fifth President of the United States, 1961-1963

LYNDON BAINES JOHNSON (1908-1973), thirty-sixth President of the United States, 1963-1969

MARTIN LUTHER KING, JR. (1929-1968), first President of the Southern Christian Leadership Conference

EVERETT MCKINLEY DIRKSEN (1896-1969), Minority Leader in the United States Senate

HUBERT HORATIO HUMPHREY (1911-1978), United States Senator and later Vice-President of the United States

Summary of Event

The 1964 Civil Rights Act, the most far-reaching civil rights act passed by Congress since Reconstruction, became effective in July, 1964. It was passed only after a vote of cloture ended a Southern filibuster; this marked the first time cloture had been invoked against a civil rights measure.

The road to the passage of the act had been long and tortuous. In June, 1963, President Kennedy addressed the nation and appealed to the conscience of the American people to cooperate to meet the growing moral crisis in race relations. On June 19, in a special message he urged the Congress to enact an omnibus bill to meet the demands of the black minority for equality. The bill he proposed included titles dealing with public accommodations, employment, federally assisted programs, and education.

The bill was reported by the House committee in November just two days before the assassination of President Kennedy in Dallas. As the stunned nation recovered, there was an outpouring of emotion for the dead President. President Johnson addressed the Congress and urged it to honor President Kennedy's memory with the passage of the omnibus civil rights bill. Johnson, who had been viewed as a part of the conservative establishment opposed to civil rights when he was Senate Majority Leader, now became its most vigorous champion. Whether this transformation came from a change of conscience, a change in position, or a desire to be seen as a national leader cannot be known, but he made a firm commitment to civil rights in his State of the Union Address. He challenged the Congress to become known as the one that had done more for civil rights than any in one hundred years. Martin Luther King, Jr., who had been at the forefront of a decade of struggle by blacks for equality,

965

gave his full support to President Johnson at this critical time. However, he announced plans to resume demonstrations, which had been suspended since the assassination of President Kennedy, to make it clear to Congress and the country that the time to pass a civil rights bill had come. This, together with the lobbying of civil rights groups in cooperation with labor and church leaders, forced the passage of the bill in the House. Despite the favorable action in the House, success in the Senate was difficult because of a filibuster. Senator Hubert H. Humphrey, who was the coordinator for the civil rights effort in the Senate, worked to gain the cooperation of Senator Everett M. Dirksen, the Senate minority leader. After compromise language was worked out with Senator Dirksen, a bipartisan vote ended the filibuster, and the Civil Rights Act of 1964 was passed on July 2.

The act contained provisions designed to eliminate discrimination in voting, public accommodations, employment, federally funded programs, and education. Although there had been Acts in 1957 and 1960 to eliminate voting discrimination, unfairly administered literacy tests continued to discriminate against blacks. The 1964 Act prohibited local officials from applying different standards to blacks and whites when administering literacy tests in federal elections. Also, completion of the sixth grade in an English language school created a presumption of literacy.

Voting was viewed as a local issue, and there was general concern by those who opposed the Civil Rights Act that it would permit undue intervention of the federal government into local affairs. This argument was significant in determining the authority of the Attorney General to bring suits concerning voting discrimination. The issue was resolved by providing that the Attorney General could bring action if he found that a "pattern of discrimination" existed to prevent citizens from voting. This limited the possible intervention in local affairs by the Attorney General since he could not bring a suit growing out of an isolated instance of discrimination against one citizen. The Act did provide for a three-judge federal district court to hear cases of voter discrimination, which then could be appealed directly to the Supreme Court. One of the problems of the 1957 and 1960 Acts was the great length of time required to bring suit and process an appeal. The voting provisions of the 1964 Act did not bring about a great deal of change, and a major voting rights bill was passed the following year.

The results of the public accommodations provisions of the 1964 Act were more impressive. Hotels, restaurants, service stations, places of amusement, and government-owned public facilities were forbidden to discriminate or refuse service because of race, color, religion, or national origin. Even though the Attorney General could intervene only in cases of general public importance, discriminatory practices in public accommodations changed dramatically, and in a short time the rigid separation of the races in places of public accommodation was over.

Ending discrimination in public accommodations proved to be much easier than desegregating schools. The strong stand by Congress against discrimination in schools was important because heretofore the courts had borne the entire burden of school desegregation, and they were vulnerable to the charge of usurping the power of Congress to make law. In cases of school discrimination, the Attorney General was given greater latitude in bringing suits than in other civil rights areas. He had only to determine that a complaint was valid and the individual was unable to maintain a suit before initiating court action. Although the Attorney General's power was more extensive, the Congress made clear that the goal was desegregation, and the 1964 Act does not give any official or court the power to order racial balance.

Guidelines issued by the Office of Education were important in reducing segregation in schools, but it is doubtful they would have been so successful had the act not also provided that there could be no discrimination in programs funded by the federal government. Since the federal government funds a great variety of programs, such as housing and urban renewal, its potential as a weapon against discrimination was great.

Along with desegregation of schools, forbidding discrimination in employment was a major portion of the Civil Rights Act. Employers were forbidden to discriminate on the basis of race, color, religion, national origin, and unlike the other parts of the 1964 Act, the section dealing with employment practices covers discrimination based upon sex. The Act covers employers' practices in hiring, paying, promoting, and dismissing employees; referral by employment agencies; and trade unions' admission of members. Ultimately, employers with twenty-five employees were to be covered, but this figure was reached gradually over three years. Employers can be required to keep records, and these records have been useful in determining practices of discrimination. An Equal Employment Opportunity Commission was established, but until a 1972 amendment it did not have power to bring suit against an employer. Before that the commission could only persuade the employer, or if that failed, refer the case to the Attorney General with recommendation that a suit be instituted. The Attorney General had the power to bring suit not only upon the recommendation of the Equal Employment Opportunity Commission, but also if there was a pattern or practice of discrimination. If a suit were brought and there was a finding of discrimination, the court was given a wide range of remedies; it could enjoin the employer from further discriminatory practice or order reinstatement of an employee together with back pay or the hiring of an employee. However, the Act specifically states that an employer is not required to grant preferential treatment because of an imbalance in the race of employees.

The 1964 Civil Rights Act is a major part of the series of civil rights acts passed in the 1960's. Although it did not immediately end discrimination against blacks, it is a significant milestone.

Pertinent Literature

Orfield, Gary. *The Reconstruction of Southern Education*. New York: Wiley-Interscience, 1969.

Gary Orfield is Assistant Professor in the Department of Government and Foreign Affairs at the University of Virginia. In *The Reconstruction of Southern Education*, Orfield describes the political institutions and forces which shaped the federal government's effort to desegregate Southern schools from 1964 to 1968. He believes our federal system gives enormous power to localities to control local institutions such as schools. Consequently, national efforts to change fundamentally the educational system can be achieved only in extraordinary instances when great national public support exists for a national policy. The courts acting alone on a case-by-case basis could not bring about far-reaching change in the racial practices in Southern schools; further intervention by the national government was needed for this.

In 1964, a series of events inflamed public opinion and generated the environment that made it possible for Congress to pass the 1964 Civil Rights Act. Title VI of the Act allowed the withholding of federal financial assistance from any program guilty of racial discrimination. Although considerable controversy surrounded the inclusion of Title VI, it was not generally expected that it would prove to be a powerful tool against racial discrimination because at the time of the debates in Congress, there was not a great amount of federal aid to education. There was some feeling, perhaps shared by the Administration, that the power of the Attorney General to bring action against discrimination included in Title VI was the more important enforcement tool. Orfield concentrates his attention on Title VI, although the combination of these powers is significant since schools which did not receive a substantial amount of aid had the option of submitting a plan to the Office of Education in the Department of Health, Education, and Welfare and getting some federal aid or not submitting a plan and being sued under Title IV and placed under a court order to integrate.

Orfield believes the Office of Education working in tandem with the Justice Department and the courts brought about a social revolution in the South. For a variety of reasons, the Office of Education was not well equipped to enforce Title VI, and the unprepared, understaffed office working against strong local political forces encountered many difficulties. Most of the officials of the Office of Education believed in local control of public schools and preferred a cooperative relationship. They did not have the aggressive attitude required for enforcement. In addition, the people were devoted to their own programs and did not want them encumbered with the controversial desegregation orders.

Further adding to the complexities, the Office of Education was not free to make all decisions, and within the

Department of Health, Education, and Welfare, there were various views about the best approach to enforcement. For example, an Assistant Secretary opposed issuing regulations, preferring to bargain with the school districts one by one because he felt regulation would encourage school districts to do the minimal amount to comply. Others felt regulations were needed to give guidance to school people as they dealt with local pressures. At first, the bargaining approach was used, but with the limited staff such confusion and uncertainty resulted that the local school people, who normally opposed federal intervention, demanded regulations because they needed help. In a few months the regulations brought about more desegregation than the courts had been able to achieve in ten years. This success was due in part to the 1965 Aid to Elementary and Secondary Education Act which made one billion dollars available to schools.

However, the compliance of the first year was largely on paper. Most of the plans that had been submitted and approved provided for freedom of choice of schools by students. When enforcement was initiated, it became clear that many tactics were employed to discourage black students from choosing to attend white schools. Orfield recounts the struggle to make new guidelines that would protect free choice and also aid in dismantling the dual school system. Another controversy surrounding the new guidelines involved the legal authority of the Office of Education to require integration of faculty, a particularly sensitive issue in the South. Integrating the faculty would signifi-

cantly aid in breaking the dual school system because it would be less easy to identify a school as black or white, and black students would more readily choose a school if it had some black teachers. The new guidelines of 1966 accelerated the process of integration substantially, bringing to sixteen percent the proportion of black students in integrated schools in the eleven Southern states, compared to one percent in 1964.

These achievements were restricted to the South. The first attempt to enforce Title VI against a Northern school district was in Chicago in the fall of 1965 and ended in a disaster for the Office of Education. Orfield feels that the selection of Chicago as the first city in the North showed a lack of political savvy, but there were also unresolved legal questions about Title VI and time pressures which contributed to the fiasco. This episode removed any hope that Title VI would be an effective tool against *de facto* segregation in Northern cities and encouraged Southerners to use political influence to avoid Office of Education regulations.

Although Title VI had brought considerable progress toward integration, the Office of Education had relied heavily upon threats and was reluctant to withhold funds because black students were often hurt. By 1966, public support for desegregation had waned, and Southern Congressmen took advantage of this to wage an attack on the Office of Education and its Commissioner. Attempts were made to restrict guidelines to freedom of choice plans regardless of whether they produced integration. The Office of Education emerged from this battle with no significant legal restraints on its enforcement power but an unwillingness to increase the desegregation requirements. The climate of Congress in 1967 remained unfavorable, and in an effort to deflect the attack, enforcement of Title VI was moved from the Office of Education to a central office for civil rights in the Department of Health, Education, and Welfare. This allowed the Office of Education to return to its former cooperative role with state departments of education and made the enforcement effort less vulnerable to the charge that the federal government was taking over the local school systems. A true social revolution had occurred in the South, but the public support needed for a federal bureaucracy to see it through until the dual school system disappeared was gone by 1968.

Glazer, Nathan. *Affirmative Discrimination: Ethnic Inequality and Public Policy.* New York: Basic Books, 1975.

Nathan Glazer is a sociologist and is the coauthor of *The Lonely Crowd* and *Beyond the Melting Pot.*

Although there was a brief time in the mid-1960's when a majority coalition produced the Civil Rights Act, controversy was intense over its enforcement. In *Affirmative Discrimination* Glazer argues the viewpoint of those who feel that federal policy since 1970 has been unwise and unconstitutional. Throughout our history there have been contradictory views toward people who are different because of race, national origin, or cultural patterns. Sometimes those who were different were welcomed; at other times there were efforts to exclude them from at least part of national life. Although acknowledging the enslavement of blacks, the near extermination of American Indians, and the holding of blacks in a position of subordination for one hundred years after the Civil War, Glazer considers it an error to say that racism defines our history or that exclusion has been the dominant theme. Overall, he thinks that a widely shared democratic philosophy and a commitment to individual freedom have prevailed and produced a willingness to allow those who are different to follow their own practices as long as they do not attempt to set up an independent polity in the United States. He believes, however, that since 1970 there has been a new policy that violates individual freedom because it separates groups and gives some groups special treatment. This leads only to bitterness among groups and turns away from our traditional emphasis on individual liberties.

Glazer thinks federal guidelines violate the 1964 Civil Rights Act's provision that an employer is not required to grant preferential treatment to any individual because of race. Prior to 1970, if an employer informed everyone of job opportunities and sought out those who might not otherwise apply, affirmative action requirements were met. Employers now are required by the guidelines to indicate the race and ethnic origins of employees in various job categories as is specifically authorized in the 1964 Act. These statistics are then used to determine whether discrimination exists. If it does, employers can be required by the court to hire specific members of minorities. Glazer disapproves of this procedure and contends it confuses imbalance with discrimination. Guidelines relating to testing also go beyond the 1964 Act, according to Glazer. Section 703(h) allows the use of professionally developed tests; yet the 1970 guidelines tell employers that they cannot use tests which distinguish or produce different outcomes for different groups unless the tests have been validated and suitable alternative procedures for hiring or promotion are not available. The Supreme Court upheld this position in 1971 even though it is difficult to find a test other than a typing test that will meet the validation standards. The Equal Employment Opportunity Commission's guidelines state that any automatic dismissal for a serious crime is discrimination unless the crime is related to the employee's ability to perform the job. The upshot of this is that the easy way out for employers is to be sure they do not have any imbalance in the employment of minorities.

Glazer attributes the shift in the interpretation of the employment section of the Civil Rights Act to require preferential treatment for minorities to the influence of the history of the stubborn resistance in the South to school desegregation. This resistance led the Supreme Court in 1969 to a decision that no further delays in desegregating schools would be allowed in Mississippi. Likewise, the Supreme Court decision in *Swann* v. *Charlotte-Mecklenburg County*

Board of Education (1971) represented a change in the character of busing, which heretofore had been used for desegregation. Since the entire county comprised the school district and had a dual system, that is, one set of schools for whites and another set for blacks, the court ordered busing so that each school would be roughly 71-29 white-black. Glazer considers this busing for racial balance rather than for desegregation and suggested the case might become a precedent for court-ordered busing between the central city and suburbs in Northern cities. However, in *Keyes* v. *School District No. I* in Denver in 1973, the court did recognize the difference between *de facto* and *de jure* segregation since intent to segregate must be shown before the court would order busing. The threat is not so easily removed, however, because Glazer thinks it takes very little to show intent in Northern cities. He gives several examples of lame duck boards voting a desegregation plan which was retracted by a newly elected conservative board, generating a lawsuit in which intent to segregate was found. He believes the word "concentration" is more appropriate than segregation to describe racial distribution in Northern cities. He therefore questions the constitutionality of court-ordered busing in Northern cities since 1973, believing it is for racial balance rather than desegregation. He suggests the proper goal is to assure that no one is penalized for belonging to a racial or ethnic group. He doubts that busing necessarily increases educational achievement. In fact, it may interfere with bilingual educational programs because it disperses the non-English speaking students.

Glazer is fearful that the pattern established by the courts in education cases will be transferred to the housing field as well. Title VI of the 1964 Act, which is used to encourage integration in schools, allows the cutoff of funds for federal housing programs. Although the Department of Housing and Urban Development has been more inclined to negotiate than to cut off funds, Glazer fears a form of affirmative action will develop, and the requirement to advertise available housing could be the opening wedge to a procedure demonstrating discrimination if a low number of minority persons purchase. He sees the possibility of affirmative action becoming goals and targets and goals and targets becoming quotas.

Glazer analyzes the political process that has allowed this new statistical and quota procedure. He considers the federal courts, which are largely immune from public opinion, to be the leader. He explores a number of reasons for the Congress and President to allow the federal bureaucracy to follow the courts and concludes that one of the strongest reasons is the general feeling that what the courts are doing is morally right. To Glazer, other reasons counteract and override the morality argument. Foremost is that this kind of enforcement is not needed, and he charts the advancement made by blacks prior to 1970. Furthermore, he sees this practice as damaging to our commitment to individual liberty since it substitutes group rights for individual rights. Another result will be greater animosity among groups.

— *D.F.P.*

Additional Recommended Reading

Harvey, James C. *Black Civil Rights During the Johnson Administration*. Jackson: University and College Press of Mississippi, 1973. An analysis of the political influences and compromises at the birth of the civil rights laws of the Johnson Administration is presented in this well written book.

Kovarsky, Irving and William Albrecht. *Black Employment*. Ames: The Iowa State University Press, 1970. In this brief, controversial study of the impact of religion, economic theory, and politics on black employment, the authors conclude enough has not been done to help blacks achieve equal employment.

Schwartz, Bernard, ed. *Civil Rights*. Vol. II: *Statutory History of the United States*. New York: Chelsea House Publishers, 1970. A valuable resource book containing the actual texts of the Acts together with debates and commentaries.

Carter, Robert L., Dorothy Kenyon, Peter Marcuse and Loren Miller. *Equality*. New York: Pantheon Books, 1965. A collection of essays written by a professor, two judges, a lawyer, and a writer who explore the problem of achieving equality and discuss the complicated issue of quotas.

McCord, William. *Mississippi: The Long Hot Summer*. New York: W. W. Norton and Company, 1965. Although the author is a social scientist, he writes from the viewpoint of a participant as he tells the story of thousands of Northerners and Southerners, white and black, who struggled in Mississippi in the summer of 1964 to end the oppression of blacks.

Zinn, Howard. *SNCC: The New Abolitionists*. Boston: Beacon Press, 1964. This is not a history of an organization but a description of many of the people and events of the early 1960's as efforts were made to end the rigid segregation of blacks.

THE FALL OF KHRUSHCHEV

Type of event: Political: peaceful *coup* of a Soviet First Secretary
Time: October 13-14, 1964
Locale: Moscow

Principal personages:

NIKITA SERGEEVICH KHRUSHCHEV (1894-1971), First Secretary of the Communist Party of the Soviet Union, 1953-1964; and Chairman of the Council of Ministers (Premier) of the Soviet Union, 1958-1964

MIKHAIL ANDREEVICH SUSLOV (1902-   ), a member of the Presidium of the Communist Party of the Soviet Union and a leading planner of the plot against Khrushchev

LEONID ILICH BREZHNEV (1906-   ), a member of the Presidium and new First Secretary of the Communist Party of the Soviet Union

ALEKSEI NIKOLAEVICH KOSYGIN (1904-   ), a member of the Presidium of the Communist Party of the Soviet Union and new Chairman of the Council of Ministers (Premier) of the Soviet Union

Summary of Event

In 1953, when Joseph Stalin, First Secretary of the Communist Party, Chairman of the Council of Ministers, and Dictator of the Soviet Union, died, Nikita Sergeevich Khrushchev was a member of the top leadership group in the Communist Party. Four years later, he had emerged triumphant from a three-way power struggle with his rivals, Georgi M. Malenkov and Vyacheslav M. Molotov, to assume the leadership of the Party and the State. While he held the posts of First Secretary of the Communist Party and Prime Minister, however, Khrushchev never wielded Stalin's dictatorial power over his fellow leaders. The memory of Stalin's bloody purges was too vivid and the desire for collective leadership too great for Khrushchev to become more than "first among equals" within the Pre-

sidium of the Communist Party of the U.S.S.R., that nation's highest decisionmaking body.

Nonetheless, Khrushchev left his distinctive mark on government policy following his victory in July, 1957. Domestically, he tried to reverse the traditional economic priorities and spend more on consumer goods production and less on heavy industry and defense. He felt that the people who set output goals for Soviet industry were too unfamiliar with the problems of production, and therefore he implemented policies to decentralize government economic planning. To insure that decentralization did not lead to reduced Party control over the economy, he divided the Party structure in half so that each region would contain two parallel Party committees—one to oversee

974

agriculture, another to oversee industry. In the fall of 1964, Khrushchev unveiled his newest agricultural plan, a massive decentralized reorganization that would involve a separate directorate to supervise each major crop.

Khrushchev was outspoken in his denunciation of Stalin's terror, and while sometimes inconsistent and opportunistic in his exposure of the evils of the past, he was instrumental in the rehabilitation of many of Stalin's victims, and in the publication of Alexander Solzhenitsyn's short novel about the Stalinist prison camps, *One Day in the Life of Ivan Denisovich*. Khrushchev's foreign policy was equally bold and unprecedented. One of the corollaries of his drive to lower defense spending was his policy of "peaceful coexistence" with the West. He advocated a policy of *rapprochement* and lowered tensions between the Communist and capitalist world, with emphasis on peaceful economic competition in place of the armed confrontations that had marked the era of the Cold War.

All of Khrushchev's policies and reforms, however, had the air of spontaneous improvisations. More original than they were organized, they characteristically were bolder in action than clearly thought out—a series of *ad hoc* measures to rectify pressing problems rather than methodical, carefully articulated solutions. To most observers, it seemed that Khrushchev pursued his goals by a series of zig-zags, and his critics complained that more often than not, the goals were never reached.

These critics comprised a sizable segment of the Communist Party leadership, since Khrushchev's innovative policies had run roughshod over many vested interests. Military leaders and those involved in heavy industry looked askance at his new emphasis on consumer goods; the central planners were dubious about his new provincial planning institutions; and the regional administrators felt threatened by the shakeup of the Party organization. Many leaders felt that Khrushchev's foreign policy put too much faith in the goodwill of the capitalist West. At the Presidium level, Khrushchev's program of "de-Stalinization" caused both criticism and some trepidation. None of the top Soviet leadership in the 1960's, including Khrushchev himself, was completely innocent of the deeds of the Stalin era, and it seemed to many that Khrushchev's denunciations were a little too vehement and were used to settle present-day political scores.

Moreover, the record of the Khrushchev regime was studded with embarrassing and costly failures, the most obvious stemming from his foreign policy. The U-2 incident and subsequent collapse of the Paris Summit Conference in 1960 had raised serious questions within the Soviet Union and the Communist world about the viability of Khrushchev's policy of *détente* with the West. Then, in 1962, Khrushchev's gamble of placing nuclear missiles in Cuba ended in a humiliating defeat for the Russians, leaving many echoing the Chinese charges that Khrushchev had erred doubly—first by adventurism, and second by capitulation. Indeed, some Soviet leaders felt that the long-simmering split between the Soviet leaders and the Chinese Communists which surfaced in 1963 was largely Khrushchev's fault.

Finally, there had been no sign that Khrushchev's policies were leading to a solution of the divided Berlin problem that Soviet leaders could accept. In fact, the autumn of 1964 had seen signs of a *rapprochement* with West Germany, signs that more militant leaders would regard as unacceptable. Domestically, some of Khrushchev's favorite agricultural schemes had ended in failure; when the 1963 harvest proved so inadequate that grain had to be bought in the West, many attributed the disaster to his heavy-handed interference and inconsistent programs in the agricultural sector.

Thus, when Khrushchev left Moscow for a holiday on September 30, 1964, he left behind him the makings of a powerful opposition coalition. Although the composition of this coalition and the timing of the *coup* they planned are not yet clear, observers are reasonably certain that the two major figures, both members of the Presidium, were Mikhail Andreevich Suslov, the Party's ideological expert, and Leonid Ilich Brezhnev, the second-ranking Party leader and "heir apparent" to Khrushchev. Aleksei Nikolaevich Kosygin, another major figure in the Presidium and a specialist in economic planning, was probably also involved in the plot from its inception. The leaders of the plot presumably sensed that the level of discontent in the Presidium was high enough to bring about a change of leaders. They quietly recruited other key figures and insured the neutrality of the military and the secret police. On October 12, 1964, with Khrushchev still in the Crimea, they broached the subject at a meeting of the Presidium and apparently received the assent even of those most inclined to support Khrushchev.

Thus, when Khrushchev was preemptorily summoned back to Moscow on October 13, he was faced with a united opposition. At a meeting of the Presidium on October 13, and again at a plenary meeting of the three-hundred-member Central Committee of the Communist Party, Suslov led the attack on the outgoing leader, enumerating his errors and criticizing his arbitrary, hasty behavior. On October 15, the Soviet press and radio stated that Khrushchev had resigned "in view of his advanced age and deteriorating health." His jobs were divided between two members of the Presidium, with Brezhnev becoming First Secretary of the Party, and A. N. Kosygin becoming Chairman of the Council of Ministers.

The only policies that the new leadership changed immediately were Khrushchev's division of the Party into industrial and agricultural committees and the decentralization of planning. Stalin also underwent a quiet but definite rehabilitation. Recent events have shown that two major threads of Khrushchev's policies—increased consumer goods production and *détente* with the West—were continued by his successors, albeit with some modifications.

An article in the October 17, 1964, edition of the Communist Party newspaper, *Pravda*, indicated that the leaders had been after a return to collective leadership and an end to ". . . harebrained scheming, immature conclusions and hasty decisions and actions divorced from reality."

Pertinent Literature

Tatu, Michel. *Power in the Kremlin: From Khrushchev to Kosygin.* Translated by Helen Katel. New York: The Viking Press, 1969.

The demise of Khrushchev is the climactic event in Michel Tatu's study of Soviet leadership politics from 1960 to 1966. In a way, the book is meant to explain this event and its significance, although the details of the *coup* of October 13-14 only occupy three chapters of it. Tatu begins his analysis in 1960 because that is the year in which he believes Khrushchev's decline began. He focuses on the details of the U-2 affair and the Cuban missile crisis to show how they contributed to the First Secretary's loss of prestige and power, and he charts the development of discontent with Khrushchev's domestic policies. The last section, which relates the events of 1964 to 1966, is written with the Khrushchev era as a frame of reference; Tatu wants to assess the changes in policy and politics since the fall.

Tatu presents facts which indicate that the conditions for Khrushchev's ouster had been building from at least 1960 onward. He shows how Khrushchev's policies had unimpressive economic results, and politically succeeded only in alienating key segments of the Party leadership, especially those connected with defense, planning, heavy industry, and regional administration. The dissatisfaction with his domestic and foreign policies was catalyzed, Tatu implies, by the fear inspired within the Presidium by Khrushchev's program of

"de-Stalinization." The Party leaders saw de-Stalinization (and Tatu effectively demonstrates that their view was correct) as a policy adopted for Khrushchev's own political ends. Since almost everyone in the high Soviet leadership was implicated in Stalin's actions, it was not hard for Khrushchev to use de-Stalinization as a device to discredit his political enemies and rivals. Nor was it hard for all the remaining members of the Presidium to feel threatened as long as this "singularly dangerous weapon" was in the hands of the unpredictable Khrushchev.

Tatu next isolates Khrushchev's final provocation involving both Soviet foreign policy and Party politics. In September and October of 1964, Khrushchev seemed about to grant major concessions to West Germany, despite the protests of East Germany and other East European Communist countries. He had even sent his son-in-law, A. I. Adzhubey, on a private fact-finding mission to West Germany—an action that circumvented Party channels and was widely seen as nepotism. Furthermore, Khrushchev's radical agricultural reorganization plan would have involved a major administrative shake-up at the top. Members of the Presidium would have had to involve themselves directly in agricultural affairs, and would have had presumably less time to devote to political decisionmaking. This situation would have left such decisions more in Khrushchev's hands. Tatu argues that, given the volatile and precarious conditions of 1964, this threat to the position of the top leadership sealed Khrushchev's fate.

According to Tatu's detailed reconstruction, the plot to depose the Soviet leader was conceived by Suslov in the early days of October. Brezhnev may have been sounded out then, but perhaps not until his return from a good-will trip to East Germany on October 11. Tatu believes that Anastei Ivanovich Mikoyan, the senior member of the Presidium, was a central figure in the plot, and was sent on October 3 to keep watch on Khrushchev at his vacation house. The details of the plot were worked out between October 8 and 10, and revealed to the Presidium on October 12.

Tatu also demonstrates that Khrushchev's fall had significant precursors; the Cuban missile crisis, for example, resulted in a major decline in the leader's prestige and power.

The spring of 1963 saw significant reversals of his policies of decentralization of planning and de-Stalinization. Several of his important protégés were demoted, and public attacks mounted against the writers Alexander Solzhenitsyn and Yevgeny Yevtushenko, who had been under his protection. Tatu shows that this activity signaled the rise in the political fortunes of the second highest leader in the Party, Frol R. Kozlov, and concludes that if he had not been crippled by a heart attack in April, "events would have taken a different turn in 1963. Khrushchev's reign would in all possibility have ended earlier."

Tatu has reconstructed a very readable story from his meticulous examination of the evidence of promotions, demotions, photographs, unexplained absences, and minute changes in the wording of speeches. As he himself states, such indirect evidence can only lead to tentative conclusions, but one has to give him credit for doing the best with what sources were available.

Hyland, William and Richard Wallace Shryock. *The Fall of Khrushchev*. New York: Funk and Wagnalls, 1968.

This in-depth study of the period between 1962 and 1964 takes advantage of both the scholarly secondary literature as well as the primary texts of Soviet newspapers and journals. The authors begin their study with the Cuban missile crisis of 1962, because they believe this to have been the beginning of a high-level opposition to the U-2 incident in 1960. They end the book at the Central Committee meeting of October 14, 1964.

According to the authors, opposition to Khrushchev resulted from a number of factors. The leadership's concern with Khrushchev's policies was mingled with their personal ambitions, their contempt for his leadership style, and fear that he was attempting to set up a self-glorifying "cult of personality" which would facilitate the consolidation of his personal power. While de-Stalinization is mentioned frequently, the authors treat it less centrally than does Michel

Tatu. Until 1964, Khrushchev's saving grace was that the opposition was divided amongst itself, and its size and composition would vary from issue to issue. By the fall of 1964, however, Khrushchev had alienated so many segments of the Party leadership that he could no longer play one group of the opposition against the other. The top leaders of the plot may have had different motivations and different ambitions, but they were united in the feeling that Khrushchev had to be deposed.

Like Tatu, the authors see Khrushchev's massive agricultural reorganization scheme as the "last straw." They interpret it, however, as just another example of Khrushchev's "harebrained scheming" and do not see the sinister political implications for the Presidium leadership that Tatu indicates. While they note Khrushchev's many foreign policy failures and build their analysis around the Cuban missile crisis of 1962, the authors conclude that these failures were not a "primary cause of his undoing."

The authors see the events of October unfolding significantly later than does Tatu. Arguing that Brezhnev would not have committed himself to a plot before leaving Moscow for six days, they believe that the plot began on his return from East Germany on October 11. In this version, Mikoyan is not the plotters' ally, and his presence at Khrushchev's vacation house is a sign that he will be found on Khrushchev's side in any major showdown.

These differences of detail and emphasis aside, Hyland, Shryock, and Tatu all agree in their general outline of the situation and their assumptions about the nature of Soviet politics. The image of monolithic unity is a façade, they argue, behind which a small group of oligarchs struggle over policies and power. Nikita Sergeevich Khrushchev was the leading figure of this oligarchy from 1957 to 1964, but his erratic policies and ambitious maneuvers created an overwhelming coalition which swept him out of power. — *P.A.*

Additional Recommended Reading

Brumberg, Abraham, ed. *Russia Under Khrushchev: An Anthology from Problems of Communism*. New York: Frederick A. Praeger, 1962. A collection of articles by major scholars of Soviet affairs, taken from the journal *Problems of Communism*, which attempts to give a picture of Soviet society and politics in the Khrushchev era.

Conquest, Robert. *Power and Policy in the U.S.S.R.: The Struggle for Stalin's Succession 1945-1960*. New York: Harper & Row Publishers, 1967. An informed and exhaustive study of Khrushchev's rise to power.

Deadline Data on World Affairs. *Soviet Union: Khrushchev's Fall*. New York: Keynote Publications, 1965. An issue of a series called *On Record* which provides a chronology of events taken from, and interspersed with quotations from, contemporary news reports.

Khrushchev, Nikita. *Khrushchev Remembers*. 2 vols. Translated and edited by Strobe

Talbott. Boston: Little, Brown and Company, 1970-1974. While the subject of his ouster was too politically sensitive for Khrushchev to treat in these memoirs, they remain an invaluable and highly entertaining source for an understanding of the era.

Linden, Carl A. *Khrushchev and the Soviet Leadership, 1957-1964.* Baltimore, Md.: The Johns Hopkins University Press, 1966. A scholarly analysis of the Khrushchev era that uses sophisticated Kremlinological techniques to show the shifting balance of forces in Soviet leadership politics.

Page, Martin. *The Day Khrushchev Fell.* New York: Hawthorne Books, 1965. This highly journalistic account relies heavily on rumors and anecdotes to produce a readable and plausible, yet ultimately unprovable description of the *coup*.

BLACK INSURGENCY MOVEMENTS IN ZIMBABWE/RHODESIA

Type of event: Sociological: militant response to white minority rule after political channels failed
Time: 1965 to the present
Locale: Zimbabwe/Rhodesia

> *Principal personages:*
> CECIL JOHN RHODES (1853-1902), English colonial business-man and administrator after whom the colony was named
> GARFIELD REGINALD STEPHEN TODD (1908-   ), liberal white Prime Minister of Rhodesia, 1953-1958
> JOSHUA NKOMO (1917-   ), leader of the African National Congress (ANC) after 1957 and of the Zimbabwe African Peoples' Union (ZAPU) after 1961
> REVEREND NDABANINGI SITHOLE (1920-   ), leader of the Zimbabwe African National Union (ZANU) after 1963, later becoming more moderate
> IAN DOUGLAS SMITH (1919-   ), Prime Minister of Rhodesia since the victory of the conservative Rhodesia Front Party in 1964
> ABEL TENDEKAYI MUZOREWA (1925-   ), founder of the United African National Council (UANC) in 1971
> ROBERT GABRIEL MUGABE (1925-   ), rival to Sithole for leadership and eventually leader of the Zimbabwe African National Union (ZANU) after Sithole's exile (1975-1977) from Zimbabwe/Rhodesia

Summary of Event

For centuries before Europeans arrived in Africa, the Shona-speaking kingdom of Monomotopa controlled parts of what is today called Zimbabwe/Rhodesia and Mozambique. Civil conflict and Portuguese power ended Shona control by the early 1800's and Ndebele-speaking Zulu peoples expanded northward from South Africa to control the southern part of today's Zimbabwe/Rhodesia. By the 1890's, whites from South Africa, Great Britain, and North America had entered from the south under the leadership of Cecil Rhodes, militarily defeating the Shona and Ndebele. Periodic revolts were suppressed by British and South African troops. In 1923, Great Britain established the area as a self-governing colony, retaining the right to intervene to protect the interests of the black majority who were not included in the governmental process.

African workers organized as early as 1927 and the Southern Rhodesia Bantu Congress was formed in 1934. Petitioning the white settlers for justice, the movement was initially ineffective; but the influx of white settlers after World War II revived the movement under a new name—the

African National Congress (ANC). Although a five-year period (1953-1958) under liberal Prime Minister Garfield Todd allowed limited multiracial partnership in government, the ANC, under Joshua Nkomo's leadership after 1957, urged Africans to work for nationalism rather than struggling for more privileges within a white system based on discriminatory laws. When the conservatives defeated Todd in 1958, the following of the ANC grew rapidly, alarming the government enough to ban it in 1959 and to arrest its leaders. New political attempts at change were also banned. By the time that the Zimbabwe African Peoples' Union (ZAPU) was formed in 1961 under Nkomo's leadership, violence was accepted as the only means of true reform. ZAPU militants were sent for military training to Ghana, Algeria, Czechoslovakia, and China.

In 1962, discontent within ZAPU led to a split, and ZAPU's former chairman, the Reverend Ndabaningi Sithole, was elected president of the splinter group, the Zimbabwe African National Union (ZANU) in 1963. ZANU called for "one man, one vote" for a Zimbabwe nation to whose people collectively all the land would belong. At that time, an estimated four million blacks owned half the land and 200,000 whites owned the most productive half.

The most conservative white party, the Rhodesian Front, won the election of 1964, and Ian Smith, the new Prime Minister, declared Rhodesia's independence from Great Britain on November 11, 1965, after a landslide referendum. Great Britain declared the constitutional *coup d'état* illegal, the United Nations condemned the unilateral action, and both ZAPU and ZANU declared open guerrilla war. South Africa declared its support for the white minority government.

The United Nations Security Council passed a resolution (No. 253) in 1968 imposing a total embargo on Rhodesian goods by all UN members. In 1971, Methodist Bishop Abel Muzorewa formed the United African National Council with hopes of working within the Rhodesian constitutional system. But guerrilla activities increased as Zambia and Mozambique aided the black nationalist struggle of their common neighbors. By now, white Rhodesian farmers customarily carried weapons and barricaded their homes; by 1973 many were leaving.

The Rhodesian Army constructed dozens of "protected villages," forcing hundreds of thousands of blacks into strategically guarded areas—an attempt to isolate the guerrilla forces from their support. Ian Smith began talks with liberation leaders offering equal representation of blacks in Parliament within forty to sixty years. By 1974, serious conversations and *détente* suggested hope for a settlement. Nkomo and Sithole were released from detention to attend the Lusaka Conference in December, where black leaders agreed to discuss a peaceful settlement once Smith agreed to the principle of majority rule. But the Prime Minister was unable to accept such a principle, thus justifying the philosophy of the more radical black leaders.

The guerrilla war intensified, and, in 1976, ZANU (now under Robert Mugabe with Sithole in exile) and

ZAPU (still under Nkomo) merged into the Patriotic Front which was unified in leadership although ZANU units were based in Mozambique and ZAPU's in Zambia. Diplomatic initiatives by Great Britain and the United States were rejected by the black leaders, who argued that the initiatives essentially preserved white privilege. Sithole returned from exile in July, 1977, to form a moderate splinter group of the African National Council, and Smith's government further encouraged the organization of moderate black groups.

On March 3, 1978, Ian Smith concluded an "internal settlement" with Sithole, Muzorewa (African National Council), and other moderate black leaders. Universal adult suffrage and independence was promised by December 31, 1978. The Patriotic Front denounced the settlement because political, military, and judiciary power would remain in the hands of the whites. By 1978, the black population of Zimbabwe/Rhodesia was about 6.4 million, or ninety-five percent of the total, while the whites numbered approximately 265,000 (four percent) but were on the decline because of emigration.

By the summer of 1978, morale was higher among the ZANU and ZAPU forces, who felt that their struggle was entering a decisive phase. On the contrary, white control was crumbling except in the larger urban areas. Ian Smith, even with the help of black moderates, was unable to win diplomatic victories with important allies such as the United States and Great Britain. As casualties mounted on both sides, so did resistance to any solution that did not appear to make the outcome worth the cost of the prolonged struggle. By the fall of 1978, the "internal settlement" appeared to be a failure.

The elections held in April, 1979, established black majority rule, with the black political groups electing seventy-two members of the new one-hundred-member parliament. Among the contending black parties, Bishop Muzorewa's United African National Council won the largest number of votes. Muzorewa, therefore, was called upon to form a new government, to take office in June, 1979. Nevertheless, the military, judiciary, and administrative bureaucracy remained under white control. The Patriotic Front condemned the April elections as a sham, the new state of Zimbabwe/Rhodesia was undoubtedly due to experience continued civil strife.

Although the Smith/Muzorewa government hoped to convince the world that black majority rule had won the day, they proved to be unsuccessful. With no peaceful solution in sight, the London conference was convened in the fall of 1979 under the chairmanship of Lord Carrington. After three months of tense bargaining, the British plan for a transition period was accepted by all parties including the Patriotic Front. The Union Jack was raised over Zimbabwe/Rhodesia on December 12, 1979, for the first time since the Unilateral Declaration of Independence in 1965. Elections under international supervision and a Commonwealth monitoring force will determine Zimbabwe's future. The major unknown factor is how many of the eighty seats reserved for blacks out of the one-hundred-seat National Assembly will represent the aspirations of the Patriotic Front whose long armed struggle brought the country virtually back to colony status in hopes that fairer elections would bring more representative majority rule. Many of the details of the plan of settlement are still to be ironed out.

Pertinent Literature

O'Meara, Patrick. *Rhodesia: Racial Conflict or Coexistence?* Ithaca, N.Y.: Cornell University Press, 1975.

No book has yet been written on the militant black nationalist movements in Zimbabwe/Rhodesia. The groups are still struggling in what may be the final chapter of their prolonged armed conflict. In this volume, an Africanist examines the contemporary black-white cleavage that is at the base of the racial conflict.

The opening chapter summarizes the history of racial attitudes after 1890 and closes with the details surrounding the constitutional *coup d'état* by the white minority on November 11, 1965. The remainder of this important volume explains how the black majority opposed white domination in three basic ways: working for change within the system; attempting to transform or destroy the system from within; and working for change, usually violently, outside the system.

O'Meara outlines the formative period and the activities of the many African political groups. To understand the black insurgency groups and the positions they have taken in recent years, one must read the entire volume; but chapters Five through Eleven deal specifically with varied black responses. The author begins with the traditional role of chiefs and then moves into African attempts to achieve constitutional reform, especially during the major years of conflict after 1961. He views the emergence of the United African National Council in 1971 as a temporary return to constitutional politics by some leaders, primarily from ZANU, who feared that Great Britain and the Rhodesian Front (the white party in power) might come to a settlement inimical to black majority interests. As O'Meara points out, any opposition believing that it has a reasonable chance to assume government responsibility will probably work within the constitutional framework and even support the prevailing system.

Since constitutional provisions for Africans have been minimal in Rhodesia, the likelihood of the black majority opting for the third type of response (working outside the system) was great, and it increased with time and with white indecisiveness. The whites seemed unable to differentiate between extreme militancy on the part of some blacks and the genuine hope on the part of others for legitimate political involvement. Furthermore, affirmation of the prevailing system through cooperation within the body politic has been threatened from within the white establishment since the Unilateral Declaration of

Independence in November, 1965.

O'Meara provides a good background for understanding the aspirations and grievances of the black insurgency movements. Although any book written on Zimbabwe/Rhodesia before 1975 is already outdated, recent splits within the black groups can be better understood after reading this volume. The author's primary purpose is to create a framework for the analysis of Rhodesian politics. In his closing chapter, he voices the reasoning behind the formation of the Patriotic Front (ZANU plus ZAPU) in 1976, well after the book was published:

> A constitutional settlement aimed at reconciling African and white interests is by its very nature a contradiction, even with some African acceptance of the terms. Such a settlement would merely legitimize the Unilateral Declaration of Independence, continue white control, and place in white hands the manipulation of the pace of African advancement.

The value of recent (1974) guerrilla activity, O'Meara states, lies not so much in the fact that scattered groups of guerrillas have the ability to take immediate control of Zimbabwe/Rhodesia, as in that they have created tension within the society. This tension, he explains, has adversely affected the economic climate, creating fear and tension among the whites not unlike that in Kenya prior to independence. White immigration to Rhodesia was already on the decline and emigration was increasing. All this, O'Meara concludes, indicates qualified guerrilla success. The author's concluding questions remain, on the whole, unanswered as yet. Will a conservative African government come into power, or will the nature of Zimbabwean society be changed? Because of the intensity of the struggle, African nationalists have been so preoccupied with the question of liberation that they have not given full consideration to the reordering of society after that has been achieved. How would the new African majority government respond to the white minority, and, by extension, to the government of South Africa? What about the ethnic rivalry between the Shona and Ndebele peoples?

O'Meara closes on an optimistic note. No matter what type of African government eventually rules Zimbabwe, it is clear that the country has great potential. A settlement will no doubt be followed by economic development and vitality. Aided by labor from Malawi, mineral wealth from Zambia, and the skills of the Zimbabweans, the old Central African Federation may once again be established, although this time on African terms.

Decolonization. V (July, 1975) and VIII (July, 1977). United Nations Department of Political Affairs, Trusteeship and Decolonization.

The 1975 issue of *Decolonization* covers the political evolution of Southern Rhodesia and the role of the United Nations therein. (When Northern Rhodesia became Zambia in 1964, Southern Rhodesia came to be called Rhodesia.) A brief history of the territory is followed by a summary of events prior to Ian Smith's Unilateral Declaration of Independence on November 11, 1965, and of developments following this turning point in white-black relations. The last section documents the UN sanctions imposed on Rhodesia and the violations of those sanctions, including the Byrd Amendment (1971) allowing the importation of copper from Rhodesia by the United States. Pressure from the UN was partly responsible for the repeal of the Byrd Amendment by Congress. The last forty pages provide tables of land distribution, average earnings of blacks and whites, exports, imports, and numerous documents, such as UN resolutions and franchise agreements under the 1961 Constitution.

While the 1975 issue of *Decolonization* provides historical background with extensive footnotes and documentation, the 1977 issue reports on the International Conference in Support of the People of Zimbabwe (and Namibia), held at Maputo, the capital of Mozambique, between May 16 and 21, 1977. Opening speeches by the UN Secretary-General and the Administrative Secretary-General of the Organization of African Unity provide some idea of the wide support given to the black insurgency movements in Zimbabwe/Rhodesia; but most important are the statements by Robert Mugabe, coleader of the Patriotic Front, and by Aaron Mutiti, representing the ANC. Mugabe, speaking on behalf of both ZANU and ZAPU, denounces the countries that violated the UN sanctions, citing in particular South Af-

rica, Great Britain, France and the United States. He notes with irony that the same countries that openly advocate a peaceful settlement "fail to employ effectively those peaceful methods that would bring down [Smith's] illegal regime." Indeed, he emphasizes that these very countries cooperated in the recruitment of mercenaries for the white minority government.

Mugabe explains why "only through war is any peace possible," and calls the Anglo-American initiative of 1976 an "Anglo-American conspiracy to legalize treason and sanction a perpetuation of colonial domination." He calls for an unqualified transfer of power to the people of Zimbabwe who have "not shed their precious blood for the last decade in order to achieve a false type of independence." He denies claims that the Patriotic Front represents extremism and recalls the patient, nonviolent political struggle that was misconstrued over the years as weakness on the part of the blacks. Mugabe claims that ZANU/ZAPU forces operate in two-thirds of the country. He describes the results of Smith's policy of herding rural populations into strategic villages, as well as the murder of black civilians and whites (including missionaries sympathetic to the Patriotic Front) by the elite Selous Scouts. Most of the murdered whites are named; and Mugabe adds:

> The struggle in Zimbabwe and indeed in southern Africa as a whole has never been against the white man *per se*. It is not a struggle for exclusive African rights. On the contrary our struggle is against an unjust system—a system of

exploitation, oppression and racial discrimination. It is a struggle for human equality and dignity.

While Mugabe's speech eloquently outlines the policy of the Patriotic Front, Aaron Mutiti's presentation represents the position of the African National Council which (thirteen months later) would be one of the parties in the "internal settlement" denounced by the Patriotic Front. Mutiti's speech is briefer than Mugabe's and somewhat more moderate in tone. But the message is the same: "The armed struggle will continue until Zimbabweans are in control of their country."

This issue of *Decolonization* concludes with texts and resolutions adopted by the conference, including a declaration on the liberation of Zimbabwe and a list of measures that the conference calls on all governments to take in support of the Zimbabwean liberation movements. The appendix contains a list of all participants. — *H.H.B.*

Additional Recommended Reading

Area Handbook for Southern Rhodesia. Washington, D.C.: Foreign Area Studies Division, United States Department of the Army, 1975. A Pentagon study with an excellent bibliography.

Good, Robert C. *U.D.I. The International Politics of the Rhodesian Rebellion.* Princeton, N.J.: Princeton University Press, 1973. Liberation movements are assessed within the larger context.

Bowman, Larry W. *Politics in Rhodesia: White Power in an African State.* Cambridge, Mass.: Harvard University Press, 1973. Analyzes the white government's relations with Great Britain, black liberation movements, and dissident whites.

Barber, James. *Rhodesia: The Road to Rebellion.* London: Oxford University Press, 1967. Furnishes excellent background to the Unilateral Declaration of Independence in 1965 and the beginnings of black rebellion.

Loney, Martin. *White Rhodesia and Imperial Response.* New York: Penguin Books, 1975. Evaluates the evolution of attitudes and positions of the three major groups: white Rhodesians, black Zimbabweans, and the British.

Arrighi, G. *The Political Economy of Rhodesia.* The Hague: Mouton, 1967. A Marxist analysis of the economic and political factors in the Rhodesian crisis.

Southern Africa Literature List. New York: The Africa Fund, 1978. Provides a list of the most recent literature on Zimbabwe/Rhodesia.

DISSENT AMONG SOVIET INTELLECTUALS

Type of event: Political: conflict between dissident intellectuals and a totalitarian
  regime
Time: 1966 to the present
Locale: The Soviet Union

Principal personages:
NIKITA SERGEEVICH KHRUSHCHEV (1894-1971), First Secre-
  tary of the Communist Party of the U.S.S.R., 1953-1964;
  and Premier of the U.S.S.R., 1958-1964
LEONID ILICH BREZHNEV (1906-   ), First Secretary of the
  Communist Party of the U.S.S.R., and *de facto* leader of
  the U.S.S.R. since October, 1964
ALEXANDER ISAYEVICH SOLZHENITSYN (1918-   ), world-
  famous Russian novelist
ROY MEDVEDEV, Russian historian, and
ANDREI DIMITRIEVICH SAKHAROV (1921-   ), Russian
  physicist, leading figures in the dissident movement
RICHARD MILHOUS NIXON (1913-   ), thirty-seventh Pres-
  ident of the United States, 1969-1974
JIMMY (JAMES EARL) CARTER (1924-   ), thirty-ninth Pres-
  ident of the United States, 1977-
YEVGENY YEVTUSHENKO (1933-   ), a popular poet in the
  Soviet Union

Summary of Event

In the late 1960's and early 1970's, Americans accustomed to thinking of Russia as a rigid totalitarian state began to hear strange reports from that distant, baffling land. Brave individuals were expressing views different from, and opposed to, the official line of the Communist Party. This new phenomenon was truly difficult to understand.

In order to understand the phenomenon of dissent among Soviet intellectuals, one must first define what the Soviet intelligentsia is. In the Soviet Union, the intelligentsia includes all of those who possess a university education. Within this intelligentsia, the major division lies between the literary intelligentsia (writers, poets, filmmakers) on the one hand, and the scientific intelligentsia on the other.

In the United States, a very large proportion of the population has a college education. In the Soviet Union, however, higher education is doled out by the State as a privilege for the fortunate few. The highly educated have far more material privileges than the average Russian worker. The highly educated have a chance of obtaining political power and influence, however, only if they are members of the Communist Party.

It is within this relatively privileged group, the Soviet intelligentsia, that dissent of various types against Soviet government policies has been most vocal. There are good historical reasons for this fact.

Throughout her history, Russia has lacked those traditions of constitutionalism and individual liberty which are found in England and the United States. During the long era of autocratic Tsarism, the government had played a predominant role in Russian economic development, and freedom of intellectual expression had been subjected to severe limitations by an official censorship. Russia never developed an independent and outspoken middle class of lawyers, businessmen, and public-spirited landowners. Such a class was beginning to come into being during the last years of the Tsarist regime, but the Bolshevik Revolution of 1917 put an end to that.

In present-day Soviet Russia, private ownership of businesses is against the law; only small, private peasant plots are exempt from this rule. Lawyers are mere servants of the State, as are factory managers. There is no free press, either, since the State and the Party control all means of public information. No independent interest group associations are permitted outside the ruling oligarchy.

It is only among writers, scholars, and scientists that the spirit of independent thinking has had any chance to grow. If educated members of the intelligentsia do not express dissenting views, nobody else will. Even the dissent among minority nationalities, such as the Ukrainians and the Jews, has been voiced chiefly by the members of the intelligentsia among them.

There had been, before 1917, a long tradition of dissent among Russian intellectuals. It had been among the Russian intelligentsia that the spirit of revolution had first taken root. The coming to power of the Communist Party, with its claim to a monopoly on the truth, made the problem of dissent potentially even greater.

Yet, in the first few years after 1921, when the Communists (then known as Bolsheviks) had finally defeated their rivals, there was a brief period of relaxation of Party controls over intellectual life. Even within the Party itself, there was controversy over the proper path for Russia to follow, especially after the death of Nikolai Lenin (the founder of the Communist regime in Russia) in 1924.

After Joseph Stalin came to power in 1929, however, all dissent was stamped out. In the 1930's, Stalin launched a reign of terror against all those whom he suspected of disloyalty. Soviet writers were forced to adhere strictly to every twist of Stalin's interpretation of Party doctrine. Innumerable lesser ranking Party members and private citizens were sent to slave labor camps, where thousands perished of cold, hunger, and maltreatment.

On March 5, 1953, Joseph Stalin died. For a while, a form of collective leadership was practiced; but this did not last for long. Soon, the struggle for power began in earnest. The leading contender in this struggle for power was Nikita Sergeevich Khrushchev, who had first risen to prominence as Stalin's lieutenant in the Ukraine. In September, 1953, Khrushchev became First Secretary of the Communist Party. In March, 1958, after bitter competition with his many rivals, he finally achieved the rank of Prime Minister as well.

Despite this achievement, Khrushchev was unable to establish dictatorial control over either the Party or the government. In order to be able to fight more effectively against his political enemies, he had decided, as early as 1956, to initiate a "De-Stalinization" campaign.

At the twentieth Congress of the Communist Party, held in February, 1956, Khrushchev had secretly denounced Stalin as a mass-murderer and a psychopath. At the twenty-second Party Congress, held in October, 1961, Khrushchev renewed his denunciation of the crimes of Stalin, this time in public. He also accused his foes within the Party of complicity in the worst excesses of the Stalin era. The foundations of unthinking intellectual conformity had been severely shaken.

Because of Khrushchev's emphasis on "De-Stalinization," the Soviet intelligentsia was now able to enjoy greater freedom than it had had before or would have in the future. On October 21, 1962, Yevgeny Yevtushenko, a popular young poet, was permitted to read publicly a poem, "Stalin's Heirs," warning of the persistence of neo-Stalinism in Party and government circles. Yevtushenko became the idol of the young and the symbol of the new liberalism.

In November of 1962, an even greater step was taken towards destroying the reputation of Stalin and Stalinism. Alexander Solzhenitsyn, who had been an inmate of Stalin's slave-labor camps from 1945 to 1953, was permitted by Khrushchev to offer for official publication a novel based on his experiences in one of the camps. Nothing had ever been published about the slave-labor camps before. The publication of Solzhenitsyn's novel, *One Day in the Life of Ivan Denisovitch*, was the high-water mark of intellectual liberty in post-Stalin Russia.

In October of 1964, Khrushchev was suddenly overthrown by a conspiracy of the members of the Communist Party Central Executive Committee. Among the triumvirate which subsequently took power, Leonid Brezhnev, the new Party First Secretary, gradually became first among equals. Khrushchev had been overthrown partly because of his blunders in foreign policy and in agricultural policy, but also because it had been feared that too much "De-Stalinization" would be dangerous to the Communist Party monopoly of power. The stage was now set, therefore, for a return to a more repressive policy towards independent-minded intellectuals.

The first signal of the return of repression was the arrest and trial, in late 1965 and early 1966, of Andrei Sinyavsky and Yuli Daniel. These two men were convicted of anti-Soviet activities for having tried to get their fictional satires on Soviet society published abroad. Soon after this trial, two events occurred which confirmed the Soviet leaders' resolve no longer to tolerate dissent among writers and other intellectuals.

The first of these events was the defeat of Egypt and other Arab states by Israel in the Six-Day War of June, 1967. Because the Soviet Union had supported the Arab states on the diplomatic front, the Israeli victory represented a severe setback for Soviet policy in the Middle East. The war awakened strong Zionist feelings among the Soviet Jews, a group heavily represented among the educated intelligentsia. There was a revival of self-conscious Jewishness among them, and many even requested to be permitted to emigrate to Israel. Not only were such people seeking to use this privilege which most Russians did not have; they were seeking to use this privilege in a way that would strengthen a country which Soviet foreign policy treated as an enemy state.

The second crucial event was the so-called "Prague Spring," the triumph of liberalism among the Communist Party leadership in the small neighboring state of Czechoslovakia, in January, 1968. The victory of the Czechoslovak reformists, led by Alexander Dubček, had been aided by the incessant criticism by Czechoslovak intellectuals of Dubček's predecessor, Antonín Novotný. In August of 1968, Brezhnev sent Soviet tanks into Czechoslovakia to crush the liberalization movement in that country. The lesson of Prague seemed to be clear: any tolerance of liberalism or dissent would be fatal to the Communist Party's monopoly of power.

Shortly after the Soviet invasion of Czechoslovakia, an underground "democratic movement" began to get organized. This movement gained support not only from Solzhenitsyn (who was no longer permitted to publish his novels), but also from the world-renowned Russian physicist, Andrei Sakharov.

Sakharov, "the Father of the Soviet H-Bomb," had played an important role in the development of modern Soviet weaponry during the late 1940's and early 1950's. By the late 1960's, however, he was becoming worried about the dangers to world peace posed by the arms race. In a memorandum to the Soviet government, written in June, 1968, Sakharov predicted the "convergence" of the American and Soviet systems, and urged vigorous action to root out the lingering heritage of Stalinism. He also called for greater freedom for the Soviet intelligentsia and an end to political trials. As late as March, 1970, Sakharov still believed that writing a memorandum to the Soviet leadership might be able to bring about an end to repression. The refusal of the Soviet government to listen to any of his ideas gradually pushed Sakharov into the camp of the dissidents.

The intellectuals involved in the "democratic movement" strongly supported the demands voiced among Soviet Jews for the right to emigrate to Israel. The dissidents' support of this demand was part of their broader emphasis on the need for a new respect for individual rights, justice, and legality in Russian life.

Though justice and legality were what they demanded, the dissenters knew that the Soviet government did not even recognize their right to publish such demands. The dissenters were forced, therefore, to resort to "self-publishing," or *samizdat.* Any article or book written by a dissenting intellectual was passed from one trusted person to another, with each person making a copy of the book or article. An entire journal, the *Chron-*

icle of Current Events (which reported on the progress of the dissident movement) was published, after April, 1968, by *samizdat.*

The Soviet dissident intellectuals were a tiny minority, with little support among the Soviet working class and peasantry. To overcome this weakness, they tried to appeal to a Western audience as well as to a Soviet one. *Samizdat* articles and books, including such classics as Solzhenitsyn's *Cancer Ward*, were smuggled abroad for publication. Such leading dissidents as Sakharov and Solzhenitsyn held interviews with American and Western European newspaper correspondents in Moscow. The newsmen's reports on what the dissenters had said would later be broadcast back to the Russian people through British and American Russian-language radio broadcasts. Some dissidents, especially those who still considered themselves to be Marxist-Leninists, even appealed to Western European Communist Parties for support against repression.

After 1968, being a dissident intellectual in Russia involved great personal risk. Dissidents were often deprived of the right to work at their professions and then sentenced to long prison terms on the grounds of "parasitism" (that is, of failure to have a job). In addition, quite a few dissidents were committed to State mental institutions by the State-employed psychiatrists on the grounds that their vocal dissent was obvious evidence of lunacy. It was probably the fear of such possible consequences of dissent that kept Yevgeny Yevtushenko, the brave young rebel poet of the early 1960's, from asso-

ciating himself with the "democratic movement" after its inception in 1968.

The relaxation of tensions between the Soviet Union and the United States, which occurred after Richard Nixon became President, did little to improve the lot of the dissidents. Instead, *détente* abroad only seemed to make Brezhnev feel free to intensify his persecution at home.

In November, 1969, Solzhenitsyn was expelled from the Soviet Writers' Union. In February, 1970, Alexander Tvardovsky, a liberal sympathetic to Solzhenitsyn, was forced to resign as editor of the influential Soviet literary magazine *Novy Mir.* In the year 1973, the Soviet press and radio began a campaign of defamation against both Solzhenitsyn and Sakharov. At the same time, a wave of arrests struck at the lesser-known members of the dissident movement. In February, 1974, Solzhenitsyn was suddenly ordered by the Soviet government to emigrate abroad. He was now free to speak his mind openly, but he could no longer be active within his beloved Russia.

In Western countries, Solzhenitsyn had often been seen as the very embodiment of the spirit of Soviet dissent. Yet he and the other dissidents did not, by any means, agree on all issues. By the time of his exile, Solzhenitsyn had come to believe that the only salvation for his country lay in a return to the old Christian values of pre-1917 Orthodox Russia. Sakharov, on the other hand, urged Russia to adopt the liberal, scientific values of the West. The difference of opinion between the two men was reminiscent of the distinction, found among nineteenth century Russian thinkers, between "Slavophiles" and "Westernizers."

The views of the historian Roy Medvedev, who had been expelled from the Communist Party in 1969, were different from those of either Solzhenitsyn or Sakharov. In his works *Let History Judge* (a history of Stalinism) and *On Socialist Democracy*, Medvedev, while severely criticizing the flaws of the Soviet system, insisted that he was a loyal Marxist-Leninist, and that a reformed Communist Party was the necessary vehicle for liberalization. Medvedev believed in a "Communism with a human face," similar to that which the unfortunate Dubček had tried to bring about in Czechoslovakia.

In 1975, Leonid Brezhnev himself unwittingly provided a new rallying cry around which all the different opinions of the dissident movement could unite. In the summer of that year Brezhnev signed the Helsinki Agreements. The United States promised to respect the existing boundaries in Eastern Europe, while the Soviet government agreed to respect the basic human rights of its own people. To Brezhnev, this appears to have been a mere paper promise. Within Russia, however, the dissidents of all stripes joined together to form "Helsinki Watch Groups" to monitor their own government's adherence to the human-rights provisions of the Agreement.

By the late 1970's the problem of Soviet dissent had become an international issue. The Congress of the United States had, from the beginning of the decade, continually pressured the Soviet regime to allow Soviet Jews to emigrate. In 1973, the Kremlin did let more Jews leave, but after that year it went back to a more restrictive policy. In November, 1976, Jimmy Carter, who pledged himself to try to secure respect for human rights throughout the world, was elected President. By 1977, both the President and the Congress of the United States joined together in denouncing Soviet repression of dissidents.

American pressure did not change Kremlin policy. In the summer of 1978, the Soviet government brought charges of espionage and treason against the young Russian-Jewish computer technician, Anatoly Shcharansky. Shcharansky had belonged to both the Jewish protest movement and the "Helsinki Watch Group." After Shcharansky had been sentenced to a twelve-year term in a "strict regime labor camp," the United States government lodged a vigorous protest against the verdict. It seemed unlikely, however, that purely verbal threats could ever induce the Soviet regime to alter its policy of repressing dissent.

If the Soviet dissident movement did not succeed in changing the policy of the regime, it certainly succeeded in tarnishing the public image of that regime throughout the Western world. In 1976, the once-docile Communist Parties of France and Italy both protested against the Soviet repression of dissent. They had to; being tarred with the brush of Soviet tyranny would have cost them too many votes. Intellectuals in Western Europe and the United States likewise protested against the Soviet record on human rights.

In the 1920's and the 1930's, Bolshevik Russia had been the mecca for discontented idealists of all countries. In the late 1970's this was no longer the case, at least not in the West. There, even left-wing intellectuals tended to regard the Soviet Union as simply a strongly militarized superpower, with a reactionary, tyrannical government.

Pertinent Literature

Rothberg, Abraham. *The Heirs of Stalin: Dissidence and the Soviet Regime, 1953-1970*. Ithaca, N.Y.: Cornell University Press, 1972.

Abraham Rothberg is an American authority on recent Russian literature. His book is a historical account of the relations between the Soviet government and dissident intellectuals from the death of Stalin to the Brezhnev era.

In Part I, "The Broken Icon: De-Stalinization," Rothberg shows how dissidence first began to flower during the years 1953 to 1964. According to Rothberg, Nikita Khrushchev, unable to dominate completely either the Communist Party or the government, was willing to use de-Stalini-zation as a club with which to beat his political enemies. To do so, he had to give Soviet intellectuals a freer rein, allowing them to begin to deal frankly with the Stalinist past. The early careers of two intellectuals who tried to confront Stalinism, Yevgeny Yevtushenko and Alexander Sol-zhenitsyn, are discussed in depth in this section of the book.

In Part II, "Artistic Dissidence," Rothberg tells the story of how Khrushchev's successors slowly but surely reversed Khrushchev's relatively liberal politics towards the literary community, replacing these policies with a renewed insistence on conformity and orthodoxy. Rothberg also shows how this new policy of repression en-couraged the growth of the first active Soviet dissident movement.

In Part III, "Political Dissidence," the author shows how the dissident movement among artists changed, after 1968, into a more general demand, among intellectuals, for a greater respect by the government for individual rights. He also shows how the Brezhnev regime stepped up the tempo of persecution after it had suppressed the liberal experiment in Czechoslovakia.

In Part IV, "Scientific Dissidence," Rothberg traces the roads to dissidence traveled by two Soviet men of learning: the geneticist Zhores Medvedev and the physicist Andrei Sakharov.

In Part V, "The Iron Heel," the author presents his conclusion. To Rothberg, the present ruling group in Moscow are "the Heirs of Stalin." "De-Stalinization," if pursued to its logical conclusion, would rock the Soviet State to its very foundations. There are few members of the present top leadership group who were not implicated in some way in Stalin's crimes. Thus, to talk frankly about the Stalinist past is to question the right of Leonid Brezhnev and the other members of the Politburo to rule Russia.

Rothberg does not think that dissent can be stamped out completely. The Soviet regime, with its goal of modernization, cannot do without the scientific intelligentsia. It is among this scientific intelligentsia, however, that the seeds of independent thought naturally ripen into the fruit of dissent.

If the Party leadership cannot completely eliminate dissent, neither can the dissenters eliminate the present system. The dissenters, Rothberg explains, are alienated from the Russian masses, who tend to be chauvinistic and antiintellectual. The dissenters, furthermore, represent only a tiny section of the Soviet educated class. They have few sympathizers in either the Soviet bureaucracy or the Soviet Army.

Though Rothberg's work is one of the most complete accounts ever published concerning the dissident movement in the Soviet Union, it is not entirely without flaws. Rothberg more or less completely ignores the Jewish emigration movement and its connections with the mainstream dissident movement.

The author makes use of many official and unofficial Soviet sources, and also of published Western sources. There are reference notes for each chapter at the back of the book, and there is also a bibliography. There are no photographs of any of the dissidents.

Barghoorn, Frederick C. *Détente and the Democratic Movement in the U.S.S.R.* New York: The Free Press, 1976.

Frederick Barghoorn, an American political scientist and a longtime expert on the Soviet Union, has written a book which is a work of advocacy as well as a work of scholarship. Barghoorn believes that, in the long run, it is impossible for a government which severely represses all dissent at home to be a genuine partner of the United States in the quest for peace.

Barghoorn's book consists of four chapters, each of which deals with a separate theme. In each of them, the author compares the views expressed by the Soviet dissidents with those expressed by the official representatives of the Soviet regime and finds the former to be much more humane and liberal, and closer to the philosophy of Western democracy, than the latter.

In the first chapter, Barghoorn gives a brief sketch of the "Conflict between the Regime and the Dissenters." He compares the repressiveness of Brezhnev with what he views as the relatively tolerant attitudes of Khrushchev.

In the second chapter, "Dissenters and Foreign Relations," Barghoorn discusses the views expressed by various dissident intellectuals concerning Soviet foreign policy. The differences of opinion among the various dissidents are carefully examined. Barghoorn tends to sympathize somewhat with the dissidents' criticism of *détente* for being too one-sided.

In Chapter Three, "Individual and Group Rights and Foreign Affairs," the author thoroughly examines the links between the general dissident movement on the one hand, and the national minority dissent of the Jews and the Ukrainians on the other. He points out that, while there is an overlap in aims between the Jewish emigration movement and the "democratic movement," there are also some differences. The latter seeks reform of the Soviet system; the former seeks escape from it. The majority of the Russian dissidents, Barghoorn makes clear, staunchly support the right of Soviet Jews to emigrate.

In the fourth and final chapter, "Suppression of Dissent and the Clash Regarding Soviet Foreign Relations," the author presents his conclusion. He believes that something must be done by the United States to encourage the Russian dissidents, although he realizes that any overt government action directed at this goal might well be counterproductive. He urges Americans as individuals to do all they can to help both the dissidents in Russia itself and those who have emigrated from Russia to the United States in search of freedom.

Barghoorn's sources are newspaper reports, other secondary works, and the published writings of the dissidents themselves. There is no bibliography, but there are excellent reference notes for each chapter to assist the reader who wants to delve more deeply into the subject. Unfortunately, all these chapter reference notes are placed at the back of the book, making it difficult for the reader to consult them. There are no photographs of any of the dissidents.
— *P.D.M.*

Additional Recommended Reading

Burg, David and George Feiffer. *Solzhenitsyn*. New York: Stein and Day, 1972. A good biography of the Russian writer and dissident.

Bloch, Sidney and Peter Reddaway. *Psychiatric Terror: How Soviet Psychiatry Is Used to Suppress Dissent*. New York: Basic Books, 1977. A revealing exposé of the forced commitment of dissidents, written by a British political scientist and a British psychiatrist, and containing rare photographs of major and minor figures in the dissident movement.

Churchward, L. G. *The Soviet Intelligentsia: An Essay on the Structure and Roles of the Soviet Intellectuals During the 1960's*. London: Routledge and Kegan Paul, 1973. An Australian political scientist argues that the Soviet dissidents, while vocal and important, really represent only a small percentage of the Soviet educated class.

Smith, Hedrick. *The Russians*. New York: New York Times Book Company, 1976. A former *New York Times* Moscow correspondent gives an in-depth report on the state of the dissident movement from 1971 until 1974.

Kaiser, Robert G. *Russia: The People and the Power*. New York: Atheneum Publishers, 1976. Contains an analysis of the relationship of the dissident intellectuals to the Russian educated class as a whole.

Schroeter, Leonard. *The Last Exodus*. New York: Universe Books, 1974. Making use of interviews with Soviet Jewish emigrants in Israel, the author gives an account of the development of the Jewish dissident movement since the Six-Day War of

1967 and describes the relationship of this movement to the more general current of dissidence in Russia.

Tökes, Rudolf L., ed. *Dissent in the U.S.S.R.: Politics, Ideology and People*. Baltimore, Md.: The John Hopkins University Press, 1975. A collection of essays, written by various American scholars, concerning the subject of political dissent in the present-day Soviet Union.

FOUNDING OF THE
NATIONAL ORGANIZATION FOR WOMEN

Type of event: Sociological: formalized advocating of equal rights for women
Time: June, 1966
Locale: Washington, D.C.

Principal personages:
BETTY FRIEDAN (1921-   ), author of *The Feminine Mystique*
KATHRYN CLARENBACH (1920-   ), head of the Wisconsin Commission on the Status of Women

Summary of Event

The National Organization for Women (NOW) was founded in June, 1966, by a group of twenty-eight women attending the Third National Conference of Commissions on the Status of Women in Washington, D.C. A few of the participants had come to the conclusion, as they attended this third conference, that the status of women in the United States would not be improved by continuing to meet in this conventional, conservative series of conferences, but rather by dramatic and direct action. Such action, they felt, would be best effected through a separate civil rights organization dedicated to achieving the full equality for women that they had hoped would come about with the passage of the Civil Rights Act of 1964, which included a ban on discrimination on the basis of sex.

Kathryn Clarenbach, head of the Wisconsin Commission on the Status of Women, was chosen as the first coordinator of NOW, and Betty Friedan, author of *The Feminine Mystique*, was elected president of the organization. Their stated purpose was "To take action to bring women into full participation in the mainstream of American society *now*, assuming all the privileges and responsibilities thereof in fully equal partnership with men."

NOW's first separate conference, held in Washington in late October, 1966, confirmed Betty Friedan as president, and went on to elect Richard Graham, former Equal Employment Opportunity Commissioner as vice president, and Caroline Davis of the United Auto Workers as secretary-treasurer. Men who are interested in furthering women's rights have been welcome from the beginning to belong to NOW, since it is the National Organization *for* Women rather than *of* women.

Task forces were set up to address the problems of women in such areas as employment, education, religion, poverty, law, politics, and the image of women in the media. Internal committees to handle such questions as public relations and membership were also formed. The membership quickly rose to many thousand in several hundred local chapters.

In the early part of the twentieth

century women had come out of the kitchen and into the political arena to fight for two causes: the right to vote and prohibition of alcoholic beverages. The suffragettes were militant and vocal and saw the cause for which they fought come to fruition. Prohibition likewise was effected although the post-World War I social revolution that was concurrent with it made more lasting changes in the lives of women.

Many women had played an active role during World War I, and even more of them did so during World War II. They were an important element in the Armed Forces and were vital in the industrial production work at home. Many women handled even the heavier labor jobs with aplomb, and when the crisis was over could congratulate themselves on jobs well done as they went back to their kitchens.

Again during the 1960's, women took up the political causes of civil rights and peace. Many women were active leaders in these movements, but a few in particular felt that if it was time to guarantee full equality of all persons regardless of race, it was also time to guarantee full equality of all persons regardless of sex. Women had fought long and hard for many good causes. Now they were fighting for themselves. Many of the earlier women's rights advocates were extreme in their views, which occasioned much publicity for them but also made many people wary of their cause. "Consciousness raising," or making their listeners aware of discriminatory practices against women, now became a primary goal. "Ms" became the form of address preferred

by many women instead of "Miss" or "Mrs." to emphasize that knowledge of a person's marital status need not be a precondition for conversation.

The founders of the National Organization for Women realized that mere rhetoric may attract news coverage, but rarely did it bring substantial change. Their goal became to address specific real problems and to seek legal and political solutions to them, largely in the tradition of supporting good causes through which women had worked together during previous decades. Many of the more politically extreme members of the New Left broke away from NOW not long after its inception because they felt that this legal/political approach was not sufficiently radical to bring about the required change they felt must be made in the total fabric of society.

NOW has pressed for such legal reforms as Title IX of the Education Amendments of 1972, and has campaigned actively in this regard for the removal of sex bias in school textbooks. They have filed petitions with the Federal Communications Commission challenging the license renewal of television stations which they feel have distorted women's news coverage and have perpetuated condescending daytime programming and commercials. They have worked ardently for the adoption of the proposed Equal Rights Amendment to the Constitution of the United States, swaying some elections through their hard work to help elect to office advocates of women's rights.

Some of these legal battles have been more successful than others in reaching the stated goal, but each has brought to the fore some aspect of   society that should be examined.

Pertinent Literature

Women: Their Changing Roles. New York: The *New York Times* and Arno Press, 1973.

This book is a compendium of newspaper articles from the *New York Times* concerning women. The articles have been gathered and reproduced as they were published originally, allowing the reader to experience the attitudes of the day which envelop the events actually being reported. Although the approach is basically chronological, starting in 1901, there are topical divisions within the larger categories.

The first section is entitled "Social Feminism" (c. 1900-1920) and reproduces a few articles that give evidence of a change in the role of women that is just being observed by the press. The initial articles are not serious in their analysis of the trend, but rather note its indicators. Those representing the years during World War I begin to echo an amazement, however, over women's previously unrecognized capabilities as they are cited for their war work. Toward the end of this section, the clippings reflect the successful battle of the suffragettes to be granted the right to vote.

The second section concerns the decade of the 1920's. The articles are an interesting combination of reports on concrete achievements by individual women, such as the first woman to serve as governor of a state, mixed with highly emotional essays on such topics as hair bobbing and the use by married women of their maiden names.

By contrast, the next section, which covers the 1930's, begins to indicate an acceptance of women in the work force. Moreover, the individual women whose accomplishments are chronicled are Frances Perkins, who served as Secretary of Labor under Franklin D. Roosevelt, and Dr. Margaret Mead, the anthropologist noted for her expedition to New Guinea.

World War II is covered in a separate section and there are a number of areas of concern evidenced in it. While previous sections have dealt with the question of working women, the new concern is for the burgeoning number of mothers forced to work because their husbands were away with the Armed Forces, and the child care problems thus created. Again there is a spate of laudatory articles about women's work freeing men for military service, and coverage of the creation of the women's branches of the Armed Forces.

"The Postwar Period" actually extends to include the early 1960's. As was evidenced after World War I, social change is the preoccupation of many of the writers, but the emphasis of this change has shifted. While the change in the 1920's seemed greatest for the single young adult, the emphasis here is on the change in family life. The evolving role of women is considered as a cause less frequently than is the evolution of the suburban life style. Nonetheless there is considerable evidence gathered here that many women were no longer merely looking for work, they were involved in careers.

Next appears a section on "Women in the Arts" which draws from the entire time span for its capsule biographies and leads to the "Sexual Emancipation" group, which also reports the changing attitudes on birth control.

The National Organization for Women, along with many other women's groups, is treated in the chapter on "Radical Feminism,"

which, combined with the section on recent changes, constitutes a large portion of the work. The latter section is a fairly diverse collection of topics from the 1970's.

The volume ends with a very short bibliography of significant titles and a subject index which would lead the reader particularly interested in NOW to appropriate areas. The strength of the work, however, is that the National Organization for Women can be considered in its historical as well as contemporary social context through the selections offered.

National Organization for Women. *NOW Origins: A Summary Description of How 28 Women Changed the World by Reviving a Revolution Everyone Thought Was Dead!* Washington, D.C.: National NOW Action Center, [n.d.].

This brief pamphlet presents the official account of the formation of the National Organization for Women. Although the same basic information can be ferreted out from other sources, this summary is both authoritative and concise.

The narrative first explains the background against which the first movement toward the organization of NOW began, at the Third National Conference of Commissions on the Status of Women in Washington, D.C., in 1966; otherwise, little history of the women's movement previous to that moment is covered. There is an enumeration of the twenty-eight founders of the organization as well as the statement of purpose which they drafted.

There follows a brief account of NOW's first organizing conference, which was held in October of the same year, again at Washington, D.C.,

and the first members of the National Board are listed in addition to the first officers.

The major concerns of the organization from its incorporation in 1967 until 1972 are briefly touched upon and indicate directions in which readers interested in more specific information can inquire. Mentioned also are the sites of the first five national conferences along with the names of the succeeding leaders. In addition, there is an explanation of the origins in 1972 of the National Women's Political Caucus and its early relationship to the National Organization for Women. The narrative ends with the 1972 election campaign.

The NOW Action Center undoubtedly will continue to publish this and other pamphlets on more specific aspects of their interests and accomplishments. — *M.S.S.*

Additional Recommended Reading

Murphy, Irene Lyons. *Public Policy on the Status of Women: Agenda and Strategy for the 70's*. Lexington, Mass.: Lexington Books, 1973. An impartial overview of the women's movement which addresses many of the issues and describes many of the organizations concerned with women; NOW is not covered in great depth.

Morgan, Robin, ed. *Sisterhood Is Powerful: An Anthology of Writings from the Women's Liberation Movement*. New York: Random House, 1970. An enlightening mixture of viewpoints from both the more and the less radical elements in the women's movement, including a seventeen-page bibliography.

Wagner, Susan. "NOW Campaigns for Law to Bar Sex Bias in Texts," in *Publishers Weekly*. CCVI (October 28, 1974), pp. 17-18. An account of one of NOW's specific concerns: the implications of Title IX as it might apply in elementary school text-books.

"State of Emergency Declared!," in *Ms*. VI (June, 1978), p. 24. A summary of the progress made toward ratification of the Equal Rights Amendment as well as a description of the actions needed to be taken to effect ratification during the allotted time.

"Women vs. ABC," in *Newsweek*. LXXIX (May 15, 1972), p. 57. A brief account of NOW's first petition to the FCC challenging a station's license renewal because of sex discrimination.

THE NIGERIAN CIVIL WAR

Type of event: Military: civil conflict springing from tribal differences
Time: 1967-1970
Locale: Nigeria

Principal personages:

SIR ABUBAKAR TAFAWA BALEWA, Nigerian Prime Minister whose assassination in January, 1966, touched off the Nigerian Civil War

GENERAL JOHNSON AGUIYI IRONSI (1924-1966), Nigerian commander who crushed the first *coup* in January, 1966, but was murdered in July, 1966

LIEUTENANT COLONEL YAKUBU GOWON (1934-   ), Nigerian Chief of State after Ironsi's death

LIEUTENANT COLONEL CHUKWUEMEKA ODUMEGWU OJUKWU (1933-   ), Military Governor of the Eastern region who became Biafra's head of state

CHARLES ANDRÉ JOSEPH MARIE DE GAULLE (1890-1970), French President who leaned in favor of Biafra though he never accorded it diplomatic recognition

Summary of Event

The Nigerian Civil War from 1967 to 1970 produced the most severe fighting independent black Africa has known. Between five hundred thousand and one million people lost their lives, and for many months, the world feared the toll would rise higher as the media portrayed the near-starvation conditions which existed in secessionist Biafra. Massive international relief provided the necessary food, however, and Federal restraint, once victory was achieved, prevented any major reprisals from being carried out against the Ibo people. The germs of this bitter civil war go back one hundred years to the beginning of the colonial period.

In the nineteenth century, the British claimed several spots along the Nigerian coastline, and when the scramble for Africa began in the 1870's, they extended these claims far inland to a line running even with Lake Chad. As a result, Nigeria is an artificial creation consisting of separate geographical regions and completely different people. The south is a low-lying, hot and humid rain forest area, inhabited by two principal tribes, the Yoruba in the West and the Ibo in the East. One hundred or more miles inland, the terrain climbs and forms a drier plateau distinctly separate from the South. Less densely populated, but with a number of large cities, the North was influenced by Arab traders who successfully introduced Islam in the sixteenth century. Foreign influence, then, accentuated natural differences, for the South was largely Christianized during the nineteenth and twentieth centuries. The Arab structures enabled the North to resist British domination better than the South, but the implantation of Christian missions meant that the Southerners, and especially the Ibo, received the most modern education. During the colonial period and the first years of independence, Ibos dominated Nigeria's administrative and commercial positions, even in the Islamic North.

The British recognized Nigeria's diversity, and as they began to give it constitutional form, they took these differences into account. Three regions, each with a good deal of autonomy, were created; the North, the West, which was the southwestern part of the country and mainly peopled by the Yoruba, and the East, really the southeast, controlled by the Ibo. The weak central government was run by a parliament in which half the seats went to the Northern region and the other half to the Western and Eastern regions. After independence, a fourth region, the Mid-West, was carved out of the East and the West to accommodate minority tribes unhappy at Yoruba and Ibo domination. The struggle for independence united these different groups, but after it was achieved in 1960 tensions rose. The Southerners were fearful that the North would use its power in parliament to overrule everyone else, while the North saw Ibos taking over positions of authority without integrating themselves. The Federation was tenuous at best.

In January, 1966, a group of young army officers murdered Nigeria's Prime Minister as well as the Premiers of the West and North, basically with an eye to ending electoral corruption which favored the North.

They did not succeed in taking over the government, however; a loyal general, Johnson Aguiyi Ironsi, an Ibo, was able to stop them. Ironsi himself did form a military government, however, and in May he made the mistake of declaring that Nigeria would become centralized, with education being the only criteria for getting a government job. This decree favored the Ibos and infuriated the North, instigating a group of Northern officers to stage a second *coup* in July, during which they murdered Ironsi. They chose Lieutenant Colonel Yakubu Gowon as their leader, but the military governor of the East, Lieutenant Colonel Odumegwu Ojukwu refused to recognize his authority. This separation was further poisoned when anti-Ibo riots broke out in the North in September, killing approximately ten thousand people. Most of the one million Ibos who lived in the North fled back to the Eastern region, and another half a million refugees flowed in from the rest of Nigeria. It became extremely difficult for the Eastern region to participate in the Federation along the pre-*coup* lines, but equally difficult for the rest of Nigeria to do without the East. For one thing, significant deposits of oil had recently been discovered there, but also important were the facts that the North's outlet to the sea passed through Iboland, and that the country relied on Ibo skills to function. Furthermore, it was feared that one secession would lead to others.

One attempt at conciliation was made in January, 1967, when Gowon and Ojukwu met in Ghana. There they agreed to a confederal structure, but Gowon backtracked later on. In turn, he reformed the four regions by creating twelve states, reducing the power of the North and taking the oil regions out of the hands of the Ibos. This move helped strengthen Gowon's position in the West and among minorities in the North, isolating the Ibos. On May 30, 1967, Ojukwu responded to Gowon's move by declaring the independence of the Republic of Biafra.

The war itself was a drawn-out affair, partly because of the difficult climatic conditions and partly because neither side had a large trained army. Biafra took the initiative in the summer of 1967 by attacking the Mid-West region, and its troops came within 135 miles of the capital, Lagos, but could go no further. The Federal government then set up an effective blockade of the secessionist state and slowly began to close in on the Ibo heartland. By the summer of 1968, the Biafrans were on the verge of mass starvation and had exhausted their military supplies. At this point, intervention on the part of numerous church organizations and the International Red Cross provided food and medicine for the beleaguered rebels, while French President Charles de Gaulle began to supply them with arms on a modest scale. As a result, the determined Ibos were able to keep on fighting, defending an area the size of South Carolina for another eighteen months. No further diplomatic breakthroughs were forthcoming, however, and eventually the more populous and better-equipped Nigerians wore down the Ibo resistance. In January, 1970, they captured Biafra's lifeline, the famous Uli airstrip, the night after Ojukwu had flown out, and Biafra surrendered.

Pertinent Literature

De St. Jorre, John. *The Brothers' War; Biafra & Nigeria.* Boston: Houghton Mifflin Company, 1972.

De St. Jorre, an English journalist for the *Observer*, has written a skillful, exciting, and comprehensive account of the war from the January, 1966, *coup* to the final days of Biafra. Although basically a supporter of the Federal cause, De St. Jorre is not insensitive to the Biafran case, and he remains evenhanded throughout. The rights and wrongs of the affair concern the author, and he is careful to point out that the January, 1966, *coup* was not an Ibo plot, and that the September massacres were a traumatic event. He does not feel, though, that the East was justified in seceding, because he favors a unified Nigeria capable of acting as a major force in world politics.

Although the author does not go into the important colonial background information, he discusses the events leading to the secession in considerable detail. He then proceeds to recount the various aspects of the war. The military situation, of course, was the most crucial. The Nigerian Army had only eight thousand men in 1967, so both sides had to construct armies from scratch. Inside the Ibo heartland, the road system was good, but the approaches to it from the rest of the country were not, so supplying an army which grew to more than 100,000 troops was a serious problem for the Nigerians. Second, communications on the Biafran side were far superior, since during the final eighteen months of the war, Ojukwu was never more than about fifty miles from his front lines. On the federal side, communications networks left a good deal to be desired, and each of the three federal divisions basically acted independently. The six-month rainy season was a major deterrent to activity, and morale was much higher on the part of the Biafrans, defending their homeland and worried about possible genocide. For these reasons, it took the Lagos government two and a half years to crush the rebellion.

The Nigerians did have the major advantages, however. By virtue of their position as the legitimate government, they had the support of the other African nations, and both Great Britain and the Soviet Union supplied them with arms throughout the war. Since the loyal part of Nigeria outnumbered Biafra three to one, victory seemed inevitable if no outside power intervened, and if they had the will to win.

Faced with an impossible situation, the Biafrans looked abroad for help. The old colonial power, Great Britain, was determined to maintain the integrity of the Federation, for a strong Nigeria gave it more leverage in Africa. The United States, bogged down in Vietnam and grateful for British diplomatic support there, stood on the sidelines, while the Russians actively aided the federal government in the hopes of winning an influential friend. Only the French were left, and though they were sympathetic, they were unwilling to go it alone on the side of Biafra. As a result, the Biafrans were stuck with such strange bedfellows as the South Africans and the Rhodesians, interested in weakening Nigeria, and the Portuguese, acting from the same motives.

Help came from an unexpected quarter. Three-quarters of the Biafrans were Christians, and hundreds of missionaries, both Catholic and Protestant, remained inside the new state. When the million and a half refugees and the blockade began to create a serious food shortage, the sympathy of church groups all over the world was aroused. On their own, and with only halfhearted support from the federal government, these organizations began the largest private airlift in history in order to feed the starving Ibos. This windfall and the foreign currency which went along with it gave the Biafrans a second chance and the opportunity to buy more arms. With the help of an American public relations firm based in Geneva, the story of Biafra also began to reach an ever greater audience, so that by the end of 1968, European and American public opinion was generally favorable to their position. The Labour government of Harold Wilson held firm in its support of the federal government, though, and while the French agreed to send a few million dollars worth of arms, they withheld diplomatic recognition and the kind of weaponry which could have genuinely turned the tide. The Biafrans defended their redoubt through 1969, but could hold out no longer and were defeated in January, 1970. De St. Jorre's account is readable, clear, and objective, a good general history of the war.

Stremlau, John J. *The International Politics of the Nigerian Civil War, 1967-1970.* Princeton, N.J.: Princeton University Press, 1977.

The international alignment in the Nigerian Civil War was extremely important to both sides. Outnumbered and outgunned, the Biafrans could only hope to win if they gathered enough foreign support to force the federal government to concede. Conversely, the Nigerians had to make sure that the rebels could not muster this kind of pressure. John Stremlau, a young scholar who spent two years in Lagos during the fighting, has written a fascinating book describing the jockeying which took place.

With their achievement of independence during the 1950's and 1960's, the African nations assumed an international legitimacy and prestige they had never before enjoyed. From the very beginning of this conflict, their opinion was of the highest importance. It was rightly perceived that if they took a decisive stand one way or another on the issue, it would be very difficult for a non-African power to counter them. As it happens, the ethnic and geographical mix which lay behind the Civil War in Nigeria exists in many African states, causing their governments for the most part to side with the Lagos regime of Yakubu Gowon. Were a secession to succeed in Nigeria, it could be imitated elsewhere, and in the recent past, Zaïre, Chad, the Sudan, and Ethiopia have all been faced with this type of problem. Consequently, when the Organization of African Unity (OAU) met in Kinshasa soon after the outbreak of fighting, it passed a resolution calling for a settlement based on the territorial integrity of Nigeria. From the beginning, the Nigerians received the massive support of the African continent, but all the same, a bitter war was a terrible embarrassment to Africans sensitive about their ability to conduct their own affairs, and pressures mounted to reach a compromise.

The war was also an embarrassment to Great Britain, who supported the federal government but had to confront a powerful pro-Biafra lobby among the church and humanitarian organizations at home. As a result, the British, through the Commonwealth Secretariat, began to prod both sides to open negotiations. For reasons of diplomacy, each party agreed, but in reality neither was flexible. In Lagos, Gowon felt he had to concur in order to maintain British friendship, but he was unwilling to accept any solution other than Biafra's reintegration into Nigeria on the basis of the twelve-state constitution he had decreed in May, 1967. Ojukwu, for his part, accepted the British offer in order to get a chance to present Biafra's case in an international forum, but he would go no further than suggesting Biafra and Nigeria form a customs union. Thus, the talks which took place in Kampala, Uganda, in May, 1968, produced no results.

In the meantime, four African nations had broken ranks and recognized Biafra. The decision by Tanzania, Zambia, the Ivory Coast, and Gabon, combined with the increasingly strident world outcry, now stirred the OAU to action. A Consultative Committee under the chairmanship of Emperor Haile Selassie of Ethiopia succeeded in convincing both sides to meet again, this time in Addis Ababa, in August, 1968. As both Gowon and Ojukwu agreed to lead their delegations personally, there were high hopes that an agreement could be achieved. Ojukwu in particular felt that through personal diplomacy he could outmaneuver Gowon and bring the war to an end. Gowon, who felt that he had been bested in an earlier meeting, decided at the last minute not to go; Ojukwu himself left Ethiopia after twenty-four hours. This rebuff doomed the proceedings, and after a month of diligent attempts by Selassie to find common ground, the talks were adjourned.

When the OAU meeting in Algiers in September, 1968, gave the Nigerian government a resounding mandate to carry on the war, the Biafran cause was dealt a serious blow. The lukewarm French support and the humanitarian airlift enabled Biafra to continue fighting, but the major breakthrough it hoped for did not materialize. For a moment, Ojukwu believed the election of Richard Nixon would lead to a change in American policy, but after an official review, Nixon decided to maintain a neutral posture. A final round of talks in Monrovia, Liberia, in April, 1969, found both sides still intransigent. Eight months later the war was over. From the beginning, Stremlau makes it clear that the cards were stacked against Biafra. Too many African nations faced similar problems to wish it success; Great Britain and the Soviet Union were supporting Nigeria for their own policy reasons, and the United States was enmeshed in Vietnam. As a result, Biafra was simply too risky a proposition for a sympathetic country such as France to put its full weight into the balance and help the rebels achieve their goals. — *S. V. D.*

Additional Recommended Reading

Akpan, N. V. *The Struggle for Secession, 1966-1970*. London: Frank Cass, 1971. A personal account of the war from the pen of a prominent Biafran civil servant.

Cronjé, Suzanne. *The World and Nigeria*. London: Sidgewick & Jackson, 1972. Primarily a discussion of Britain's policy by a pro-Biafran English journalist.

Hilton, Bruce. *Highly Irregular*. London: Macmillan and Company, 1969. The story of two British pilots who volunteered to fly food into beleaguered Biafra.

Nwanko, Arthur and Samuel Ifejika. *Biafra, the Making of a Nation*. New York: Frederick A. Praeger, 1970. Two young Biafrans have written their version of the events which led to the secession in 1967.

Niven, Sir Rex. *The War of Nigerian Unity, 1967-1970*. Totowa, N.J.: Rowman & Littlefield, 1970. A long-time British civil servant who worked extensively in Nigeria has written a history from the federal viewpoint.

Ojukwu, C. Odumegwu. *Biafra*. New York: Harper & Row Publishers, 1969. Includes speeches on a variety of subjects as well as a diary by the Biafran leader.

DISCOVERY OF PULSARS

Type of event: Scientific: astronomical identification of rapidly pulsating radio sources
Time: August, 1967-February, 1968
Locale: Mullard Radio Astronomy Observatory, Cambridge University, England

Principal personages:
ANTHONY HEWISH, Professor of Radio Astronomy at Cambridge University who received the Nobel Prize for his work on pulsars
JOCELYN BELL (NOW JOCELYN BURNELL), a graduate student at Cambridge in 1967 who first found pulsar traces
FRITZ ZWICKY, a Swiss-American astronomer who predicted existence of neutron stars in 1934
WILHELM HEINRICH WALTER BAADE (1893-1960), a German-American astronomer who predicted the existence of neutron stars along with Zwicky
JULIUS ROBERT OPPENHEIMER (1904-1967), an American physicist who worked out the theory of neutron stars
THOMAS GOLD (1920-   ), a Cornell astronomer who developed the theory of pulsars

Summary of Event

The trail that led to the discovery of pulsars began with investigations into the phenomenon of interplanetary scintillation, or more simply, the "twinkling" of radio stars. In 1952, Cambridge astronomer Anthony Hewish showed that radio stars twinkled because of the diffraction effects of clouds in the earth's ionosphere. In 1962, Margaret Clarke, a graduate student at Cambridge, noticed that three of the radio sources she was studying showed very rapid variations in intensity, and she suggested that these might be caused by irregularities in interplanetary matter. Hewish and others then observed several newly discovered quasars (quasistellar radio sources) and found similar effects. The amount of observed "twinkling" seemed to provide a good method of measuring the variations in density of interplanetary matter.

Radio telescopes were not normally built to be sensitive to rapid fluctuations, since astronomers assumed that the sources they observed emitted steady radiation. Hewish quickly drew up plans for a new type of radio telescope, especially designed to measure accurately changes in the intensity of radio signals to a fraction of a second. His new telescope consisted mainly of wires—2,047 dipole antennas—strung across a large field. Jocelyn Bell, a graduate student from Northern Ireland, was put in charge of monitoring the recordings begun in July, 1967. Each week, the telescope spun out four hundred feet of chart recordings.

By August, Bell noticed a new kind of scintillating source which appeared on the charts near midnight, just when the interplanetary scintillation became very small. At first she and Hewish assumed that it must be the effect of some kind of terrestrial interference from electrical equipment or automobile ignitions. Other possible causes of the phenomena were deep space probes or flare stars. Yet Bell noticed that the trace always appeared on the same portion of the sky.

On November 28, 1967, new strong recordings of the signals were obtained; Bell and Hewish were startled to find that these appeared as a series of radio pulses recurring exactly every 1.3373 seconds. This radio "clock" was accurate to better than one part in ten million. Such rapid and regular signals had never before been detected from extraterrestrial sources.

Measurements of the distance of the new "pulsar" showed that it lay outside the solar system, but within our galaxy. The shortness of the pulse showed that its source had to be quite small: about the size of a planet. The scientists called the new discovery LGM, short for "Little Green Men," and did not announce their findings to the press for fear of encouraging public speculation that intelligent beings on other planets were trying to communicate with earth. Afterwards, however, many American astronomers were annoyed that the English astronomers had behaved so secretively.

Anthony Hewish later said that the weeks of December, 1967, were the most exciting in his life. Right before Christmas, Jocelyn Bell found a new source of rapid pulsations which, she explained, "removed the worry about little green men, since there wouldn't be two lots signaling to us at different frequencies."

By January, the Cambridge group had found two more pulsars, and in February, 1968, their results were announced in *Nature*. In the weeks following the announcement, radio telescopes all over the world were tuned to the first pulsars, and new information flooded in. Within six months, over fifty articles on the pulsars had been published in *Nature*. Once scientists knew what to look for, they rapidly made discoveries: pulsars were found by groups of astronomers working at Harvard, at the National Radio Observatory in Green Bank, West Virginia, at Arecibo in Puerto Rico, and at Parkes and Molonglo in Australia. Pulsars were, however, very difficult to detect by routine spans of the sky, and by the end of 1971, despite intense concentration, only fifty-five had been discovered. Although the most advanced observatories were using computers to analyze the records of their radio telescopes, about three-quarters of the pulsars were discovered by the old-fashioned method of one person wading through yards of paper chart recordings. (Jocelyn Bell, for example, had analyzed several miles of these charts at Cambridge.) By the end of 1972, new search techniques had led to the more rapid discovery of pulsars, and by 1975, more than one hundred and fifty pulsars were known.

As soon as the first discovery of pulsars had been announced, theorists began to suggest ways of explaining these very rapid and incredibly precise pulsations. Perhaps one astronomical body was revolving around another, or rotating about its own axis, at intervals rapid enough to produce the pulses. Such fast pulses meant an enormously high rate of rotation, and thus an immensely strong gravitational field. Immediately, astronomers thought of white dwarfs: the small dense bodies formed when stars, having used up much of their nuclear fuel, explode and begin to die. (The Indian astrophysicist, Subrahmanyan Chandrasekhar, had shown in 1931 that all stars less than 1.4 times the mass of the sun must end their lives as white dwarfs.) Yet even the white dwarfs were not small or dense enough to be able to pulse in periods of less than four seconds.

In 1968, Thomas Gold of Cornell University suggested that only a neutron star could rotate rapidly enough to produce the pulses. If a beam of radiation were emitted at some point on the star, this could produce a lighthouse effect as it flashed across earth at each rotation. The existence of neutron stars had been predicted in 1934 by the Swiss-American astronomer Fritz Zwicky and the German-American astronomer Walter Baade. The theory had then been developed in detail by J. Robert Oppenheimer, the atomic physicist, and his graduate students at Berkeley. Neutron stars had been predicted but none had ever been observed: by definition, the

stars were too small, too dark, and too far away to be identified by optical telescopes. They were, however, just small enough to produce the kinds of radio wave pulsations that had now been recorded. Thomas Gold predicted that if the pulsars really were neutron stars, their pulse repetition rates should very slowly decrease. At the same time, Cornell astronomers working at Arecibo in Puerto Rico announced that the pulsar they had been studying in the Crab Nebula slowed by 15 millionths of a second each year. Similar slowing effects were then observed for other pulsars, and Gold's theory—that the pulsars were neutron stars—came to be generally accepted.

In 1969, a rocket was launched to search for X-rays from the Crab pulsar. It recorded X-ray pulses coincident with the radio pulses, but ten thousand times as powerful. The energy released by the X-rays was exactly that predicted by Gold's model, and showed that pulsars were indeed spinning neutron stars left behind after violent supernova explosions. The Crab pulsar, for example, is the remains of a supernova explosion which was observed by the Chinese court astronomer, Yang Wei-Te, in 1054, and was recorded in Indian rock drawings of the same period in northern Arizona.

Pertinent Literature

Lovell, Bernard. *Out of the Zenith: Jodrell Bank 1957-1970.* New York: Harper & Row Publishers, 1973.

Sir Bernard Lovell, statesman of British science, was leader of the team of radio astronomers who worked with the huge Mark I telescope at Jodrell Bank Observatory when both quasars and pulsars were discovered. This book provides a careful and detailed account of the research carried out at Jodrell Bank during thirteen years of the most exciting and important developments in radio astronomy.

While technical in parts, this record is especially appealing because Lovell has given us a personal history. We are given glimpses of the relationships between individual astronomers and told about their interests and concerns from the difficulties of getting adequate funds to the excitement of discovery. The author is not shy about expressing his own opinions on scientific and professional matters and does so with an air of authority.

He admits that, for him, "the universe is centered on Jodrell Bank," and his account emphasizes the contributions of his own colleagues and students. He tells the story of scientific research as it occurred in the social context of one observatory, and the result is a more real and realistic history than if he had tried to be completely objective and disinterested. We are reminded that science is a social process and not simply a matter of the logical progression of abstract ideas.

Here we will be concerned with the three chapters of Lovell's book that are specifically devoted to the discovery of pulsars. The account begins with a meeting of the British Science Research Council on February 21, 1968, when Fred Hoyle—best known as the originator of the concept of the steady-state universe—whispered to Lovell news of the discovery of radio sources that pulsed at intervals of about a second. Lovell's immediate reaction was that such a thing was impossible. On the way home, he could think of little but this "fantastic news," and he wondered why his colleagues at Jodrell had not told him about it. In fact, they had known nothing. The Cambridge scientists who had discovered the pulsars had managed to keep them a complete secret for several months.

Lovell had been Chairman of the astronomy subcommittee of the Department of Scientific and Industrial Research which, after some delay, had originally granted Anthony Hewish the money he needed to build his aerial equipment—but the committee members had not yet heard the startling results. The Cambridge group later said they had kept the discovery secret until they were sure that the signals had a natural, physical origin: they did not want to generate a torrent of public concern about strange signals coming from an extraterrestrial civilization. Lovell approved this secrecy as demonstrating "exemplary scientific discipline," but, like other astronomers, he was upset when Hewish refused to publish the celestial coordinates of three other pulsars discovered at Cambridge. (Other astronomers could not "tune in" on the pulsars until they knew where to find them.) It looked as though the Cambridge astronomers wanted to keep their discovery to themselves—an understandable reaction, but one in conflict with the principle of the free sharing of scientific knowledge. After a short delay, however, Hewish did agree to release all his information.

After his meeting in London, Bernard Lovell had hurried back to Jodrell Bank to begin investigating the pulsars. The radio telescope was in great demand for different research projects, and the graduate students working at the observatory did not want to be distracted from the observations they were completing for their doctoral degrees. Graham Smith, a professor of astronomy, had, however, "taken fire" at the pulsar idea, and graduate students A. G. Lyne and B. J. Rickett were persuaded to leave aside their thesis work. Within weeks, new information flooded in as the astronomers shared in the enthusiasm and excitement of the discoveries. For a year, everyone concentrated on the pulsars, and by 1971, Jodrell Bank could claim the credit for the discovery of nine new pulsars.

Lovell's account of the discovery of pulsars blends personal anecdote with scientific and technical detail about the new observations and the theories developed to explain them. In the former category, he notes his annoyance at finding that the student who first detected the pulsars, Jocelyn Bell, had originally applied to study at Jodrell Bank Observatory but had not been accepted because her application had been lost. In the latter category, he discusses, in considerable detail, the techniques used in locating pulsars and the attempts made to explain the fluctuations in the strength of their pulses.

By the fall of 1968, it had become clear that all of the pulsars were slowing down. In the spring of 1969, Australian scientists at Parkes Observatory, and American scientists at the Goldstone Tracking Station, found that one pulsar, called PSR 0833-45, had suddenly speeded up at some time between February 23 and March 2, 1969; it had then resumed its normal rate of slowing. This odd behavior was difficult to explain by any known theory; it is now thought that these sudden jumps in the rate of rotation are produced by "starquakes."

Lovell discusses the measurement of the pulse shapes and their polarization, the distance of the pulsars, the optical identification of the Crab Nebula pulsar with the remnants of a supernova explosion, and the discovery of pulsed X-rays, gamma rays, and visible light rays coincident with the pulsed radio waves first detected. He concludes the account with a brief description of Thomas Gold's theoretical pulsar model. Parts of these sections are very specialized, but Lovell's record will be appreciated by historians as an unusually honest, detailed, and sometimes humorous account of the process of scientific discovery.

Friedman, Herbert. *The Amazing Universe*. Washington, D.C.: Special Publications Division National Geographic Society, 1975.

This must be one of the most beautiful books on astronomy ever produced. It can be read for pure pleasure: the hundreds of magnificent color photographs are in the best tradition of the National Geographic Society. The photographs, paintings, and diagrams are not, however, simply for visual delight, but allow complex astronomical concepts to be more readily grasped. The sequences of stellar evolution, for example, provide an essential context for understanding neutron stars and pulsars, and are presented in a very clear and interesting manner.

Although the color plates provide the most immediate appeal of this book, the text is also excellent: intelligent and lucid, while not unnecessarily technical. The author, Herbert Friedman, is an X-ray astronomer on the staff of the U.S. Naval Research Laboratory and chief scientist of their Center for Space Research. In 1969, he led the astronomical team which discovered that the Crab Nebula pulsar emitted very powerful X-rays, thus providing confirmation of the neutron-star theory of pulsars.

Friedman tells us how he first detected X-ray emissions from the Crab Nebula in 1963, and suggested to J. Robert Oppenheimer that these might be coming from a neutron star. Encouraged by Soviet astronomer Josef Shklovsky, Friedman and his colleagues sent up a rocket in July, 1964, in an attempt to pinpoint more closely the source of the X-rays. However, their X-ray detectors were not built to detect very rapid X-ray pulsation (since such intermittent pulsations were not then known to exist), and they thus "failed" to discover the pulsars. This incident well illustrates the fact that scientific instruments can only detect the types of phenomena for which they are designed.

Friedman then tells the story of the actual discovery of pulsars in 1967, and his account is enlivened by direct quotations from the scientists involved, as well as by photographs of Jocelyn Bell surrounded by computer cards and of Anthony Hewish in a tangled array of antennas. Bell ex-

plains how she first became aware of an odd trace on her charts: a "bit of scruff" on one half-inch section of a four-hundred-foot chart. Later, she saw it again: "when it clicked that I had seen it before," Bell says, "I did a double click; I remembered I had seen it in the same part of the sky before. This bit of scruff was something I didn't completely understand (but) my brain just hung on to it. . . ." This apparently trivial observation was, of course, the beginning of an important discovery.

In 1968, the fastest pulsar of all was discovered in the Crab Nebula. It pulsed thirty times per second, which meant it was so small it had to be coming from a neutron star. Friedman provides a very clear account of the theoretical model of the pulsars developed by Thomas Gold. He explains that a neutron star, like the earth, has a solid crust and a liquid interior; unlike the earth, however, it has a surface temperature of more than one million degrees and a density of billions of tons per cubic inch.

Once the Crab Nebula pulsar had been discovered by radio astronomers, optical astronomers were able to detect visible light pulsations coming from the same source. In 1969, Friedman again searched for X-rays from the Crab Nebula, and this time, he found X-ray pulsations ten thousand times as powerful as the radio pulses. Thomas Gold had calculated the amount of energy that should be released by a neutron star as it was slowing down: the result was exactly equal to the sum of light, radio, and X-ray radiation found to exist. Astronomers concluded that they were watching a star which had died in a violent collapse and explosion and been reborn as a pulsar.

Herbert Friedman is clearly in total command of the scientific aspects of his subject, but he also writes as a man enthralled by the beauty and romance of astronomy. The words he quotes from his friend Jesse Greenstein sound as though they could also be his own: "the observing process is an irresistible adventure . . . even after 30 years. I am a telescope addict, in love with a 500-ton steel and glass monster." — *E.F.*

Additional Recommended Reading

Ostriker, Jeremiah. "The Nature of Pulsars," in *Scientific American*. CCXXIV (January, 1971), pp. 48-60. An excellent short account of the discovery and theory of pulsars.

Hewish, Anthony and Jocelyn Bell, *et al*. "Observation of a Rapidly Pulsating Radio Source," in *Nature*. CCXVII (February 24, 1968), pp. 709-713. The original announcement of the discovery of pulsars by Anthony Hewish, Jocelyn Bell, and their colleagues at Cambridge.

Hewish, Anthony. "Pulsars and High Density Physics," in *Science*. CLXXXVIII (June 13, 1975), pp. 1079-1083. The lecture delivered by Anthony Hewish in Stockholm on December 12, 1974, when he received the Nobel Prize in Physics for his work on pulsars.

Manchester, Richard and Joseph Taylor. *Pulsars*. San Francisco: W. H. Freeman and Company, 1977. A comprehensive and up-to-date review of research on pulsars, aimed at advanced undergraduate and graduate students in astronomy and astrophysics.

Lenchek, Allen, ed. *The Physics of Pulsars*. New York: Gordon and Breach Science Publishers, 1972. An edited series of lectures given at University of Maryland in 1969 by astrophysicists involved in early work on pulsars.

Smith, Francis Graham. *Pulsars*. Cambridge: Cambridge University Press, 1977. A sophisticated review of scientific work done on pulsars between 1967 and 1975.

Golden, Frederic. *Quasars, Pulsars, and Black Holes*. New York: Charles Scribner's Sons, 1976. A lively and well-written popular account of modern astronomy, including a chapter on the discovery of pulsars.

Hey, J. S. *The Evolution of Radio Astronomy*. New York: Neale Watson Academic Publications, 1973. An account of the history of radio astronomy to 1970 by an astronomer closely involved in its development.

THE FIRST HEART TRANSPLANT OPERATION

Type of event: Scientific: organ transplant
Time: December 3, 1967
Locale: Cape Town, South Africa

Principal personages:
DR. CHRISTIAN NEETHLING BARNARD (1922-   ), head surgeon
LOUIS WASHKANSKY, patient who would receive heart
DENISE DARVALL, accident victim whose heart was donated
EDWARD DARVALL, father of Denise Darvall
DR. NORMAN EDWARD SHUMWAY (1923-   ), developer of surgical procedures

Summary of Event

Hardly a day passes in our lives that we are not reminded by the media, be it the newspapers, radio, or television, that heart disease is the number one killer. Every year an ever-increasing number of people, estimated to be over one-half million people in the United States alone, are the victims of coronary thrombosis, or heart attack. An equally large number of people each year are afflicted by the myriad of other diseases and disorders that affect the heart.

For some of these victims, a simple alteration of their present lifestyle is all that will be required to assure them a relatively normal existence. For others, drugs will be prescribed, or surgery may be needed to repair a malfunctioning valve or blocked artery. But for still others, the disease may have progressed to a point where there is little or no hope given for recovery and survival.

Until December 3, 1967, such was the case. There was little or no help available for the person with a diseased heart that would not respond to drugs, or that could not be repaired using conventional surgical techniques. On that day, however, Dr. Christian Neethling Barnard made medical history by attempting and successfully completing the first human heart transplant at Groote Schuur Hospital in Cape Town, South Africa. The patient was Louis Washkansky, whose own diseased heart had been damaged beyond any possibility of repair. Prior to this operation, Washkansky had been given only a few weeks to live if surgery were not performed.

In anticipation of conducting such an operation, Dr. Barnard had assembled a surgical team of more than thirty doctors, technicians, and nurses, to study special surgical techniques and supportive services developed by Dr. Norman Shumway at the Stanford University Hospital. Doctors Barnard and Shumway were old friends, having first met while they were both in residency at the University of Minnesota, where both were pursuing advanced medical degrees. All was in a state of readiness for the operation, as far as the surgical team was concerned. What remained to be accomplished was locating a suitable donor.

The location of a potential heart donor presented a more formidable problem to the team. The ideal donor would have to be someone who had a normal, healthy heart, yet was dying from a disease or accident that had not itself damaged the heart. In addition, the donor would have to have the same blood type as the recipient, and tissue sample would also have to indicate a similar genetic structure. The matching of tissue samples was necessary in order to minimize the chance of the recipient's body rejecting the foreign organ. Aside from identical twins who share an identical genetic heritage, the risk of rejection of the newly implanted organ was high in all other patients. If the donor and the recipient of the organ had similar tissue samples (based on a genetic comparison), the risk of rejection was greatly minimized.

As far as surgical preparations were concerned, everything was ready, save the location of the donor organ. On the afternoon of December 3, Mr. and Mrs. Edward Darvall, along with their daughter Denise, had set out to visit with friends in Cape Town. En route, Mrs. Darvall and Denise stopped at a local store. As they exited the automobile and were crossing the street, both were struck by a passing car, killing Mrs. Darvall instantly and critically injuring Denise. She was taken to Groote Schuur Hospital, where emergency room attendants prepared her for examination and possible treatment. The examining physicians agreed that because of the extent of the injuries received in the accident, that there was no hope for recovery. They immediately contacted Dr. Barnard, who ordered preliminary tests to be made as to blood type and the like. It was Dr. Barnard who explained to Edward Darvall the extent and seriousness of his daughter's injuries, and sought his permission to use Denise's heart for the transplant operation so vital to the survival of Louis Washkansky. Darvall agreed to the use of his daughter's heart, and the needed donor had been found.

The one question that remained was, at what point was Denise Darvall to be considered dead? Dr. Barnard's teams had decided to use three criteria to certify death: first that resuscitation had ceased; second, that the heart had ceased to beat; and third, that there was no electrical activity in the brain as shown by means of an electroencephalogram. Once the three criteria had been satisfied, the operation could take place.

Once it had been determined that Denise Darvall was dead, the surgical team was split into two units. Each team would operate independently and simultaneously. One team would remove the healthy heart from the donor, taking care to prevent any degeneration of the heart muscle prior to its implantation in the recipient. This was accomplished by attaching the organ to a heart-lung machine which assured that a supply of oxygenated blood was circulated through the heart. The second surgical team was charged with preparing Louis Washkansky to receive his new heart. Throughout the operation Washkansky was also assisted by a heart-lung machine; he was hooked to the machine at a point above his heart, assuring that a steady supply of oxygenated blood was being circulated to his brain and other vital organs to prevent their deterioration during the surgical procedures to connect the new heart. It was Dr. Barnard who attached the heart of Miss Darvall to the aorta, arteries, and veins of Louis Washkansky. Within a period of five hours from the start of the operations, the final sutures were made, and Washkansky's new heart was in place. A small electrical shock was administered and the heart began to pump. At this Dr. Barnard exclaimed, "Jesus, dit goan werk—Jesus, it's going to work." It was now the heart of Denise Darvall that was supplying Louis Washkansky's body with the vital supply of blood his own organ had been unable to provide.

Once the doctors were sure that the heart was functioning properly, there remained only one more obstacle to overcome: to somehow prevent the natural tendency of the body to reject foreign objects from running its normal course, since it would be a perfectly natural phenomenon for the body's natural defense mechanisms to reject the newly implanted heart. To counteract such a rejection, large doses of immunosuppressive drugs were prescribed, to be accompanied by X-ray treatments. It was hoped that these drugs and X-ray treatments would work to suppress the body's defense mechanisms, thus allowing the body to adjust to the new organ.

Louis Washkansky responded well to the operation. He regained consciousness shortly after the operation, and within two days following surgery, was eating regular meals from the normal hospital menu. There were periods during which the white blood cell count would rise, an indication that the body's natural defense mechanisms were working to reject the newly transplanted heart. But each time this had happened, new drugs or larger doses of drugs and increased X-ray treatments were able to thwart the rejection process.

All went smoothly, and it seemed that Louis Washkansky's body had made the transition without difficulty, until, on the thirteenth day following his surgery, the patient complained to Dr. Barnard that he was having chest pains. Upon diagnosis it was discovered that Washkansky had contracted pneumonia; his system, weakened by the large dosages of immunosuppressive drugs, had lost its primary defense mechanisms, allowing him to contract the respiratory disorder. Massive doses of penicillin were given, but to no avail; Washkansky died on December 21, 1967, eighteen days following the successful operation. It should be noted that up until the time of his death, the transplanted organ continued to function without incident.

Within days of the original transplant attempt in Cape Town, a similar operation was attempted in the United States. Dr. Adrian Kantrowitz attempted to transplant the organ of a baby into an infant barely three weeks old. Once again the surgical teams accomplished their task, but in this case the recipient remained alive for less than six hours following the surgery before the heart ceased to function.

In the three months that followed the successful heart transplant of Louis Washkansky, a number of similar operations were attempted. The most successful of these subsequent operations was also performed by Dr. Barnard, who operated on Dr. Philip Blaiberg, a retired dentist. Dr. Blaiberg's transplant was so successful that he returned to near-normal activities following the operation, surviving for nearly two years beyond the time expected had he not received the new heart.

While a great deal of controversy has surrounded this surgical procedure, it nevertheless is a technique that has given new hope to many cardiac patients who were unable to hold any hope for the future based on conventional treatment and/or surgical techniques.

Pertinent Literature

Barnard, Christian N. "Transplants: Will Future Vindicate the Failures?," in *Chicago Sun Times*. October 18, 1970 (copyrighted 1970, Public Affairs International).

In this excellent article, Dr. Christian Barnard, the surgeon who completed the world's first successful human heart transplant, discusses the reasons for undertaking the operations, and the encouraging yet disappointing results that followed.

He cites the fact that between December of 1967 and mid-1970, one hundred and fifty-nine such operations were attempted by more than fifty different surgical teams in twenty countries. The majority of the operations were performed in 1968, with a steady decline to only six transplant operations taking place in the first half of 1970. Most of the patients succumbed within the first three months following surgery, with only one percent surviving past eighteen months.

As Dr. Barnard states, ". . . the underlying cause of both sharp rise and sharp decline is the lack of understanding of what at our present state of knowledge, heart transplantation has to offer dying patients; not a new and healthy life, but only a prolongation of life and alleviation of suffering."

Barnard also points out that none of the patients on whom he had performed the surgery died of complications arising from the surgical techniques. Rather, all succumbed to postoperative complications, due either to the rejection of the transplanted organ by the body's natural defense mechanisms, or to the adverse reaction to the drugs used to suppress the rejection process.

The author also devotes some of the article to the ethical questions that have surrounded this operation, especially to questions regarding the donor. He spends a great deal of time speaking of the criteria used to verify that death has in fact taken place, and the management of the donor prior to the certification of death. As to the ethics of the operation, he responds, "There is no ethical principle which establishes this act as unacceptable, or immoral. On the contrary, one can only conclude that it is unethical to allow such organs to putrefy with the cadaver, thus denying a potential recipient an extension of life."

Barnard also discusses the procedures used in the attempt to assure the lowest possible risk of rejection of the transplanted organ. Through the clinical comparison of blood and tissue samples from both the donor and recipient, the compatibility of the recipient and donor can be assured. The risk of rejection is by far the most delicate aspect of the entire procedure. Such a risk is present in all transplant operations, but more so in the case of the heart transplant, because unlike other organ transplant procedures (that is, kidney), there is no backup procedure available to sustain life.

The doctor sums up his feelings regarding the necessity of continuing this surgical procedure. He says, "To curb transplantation at this stage would be to strangle one of the most promising and exciting fronts of medical endeavor." He continues, ". . . only through further experience will vital organ replacement become a routine and life-saving procedure."

Barnard, Christian N. *Heart Attack: You Don't Have to Die*. New York: Delacorte Press, 1971.

In writing this book, Dr. Barnard has directed his efforts into two areas, the first dealing with the prevention of heart disease and the second with the management and care of the patient who has suffered a heart attack.

Chapter Seven is devoted to general coronary surgery, but Dr. Barnard also speaks of the heart transplant operation. It is in this chapter that one can find a clue as to the reason Barnard attempted the heart transplant operation, knowing full well the obvious risks involved. He relates the story of a case he was handling at Groote Schuur Hospital, where a young police officer had died. In speaking to his superior he related all that he had done to save the victim, to no avail. He summed up by saying, "Sorry sir, I did my best." His superior responded, ". . . let us not be too pious. Let us rather recognize that your best was simply not good enough." It was at this time that Barnard says he realized that since his best would not always provide the adequate solution, he would have to do better. When existing treatments proved inadequate, he would have to find a better way to help the patient—if the heart could not be repaired, "I could try putting in a new one."

In this chapter, Barnard gives a detailed account of the procedures used in the surgery transferring the heart from the donor to recipient. He also discusses the criteria used to determine death in the donor and describes how the heart and other vital organs will remain alive, dying in the biochemical sense only after four or more hours following the death of the brain. He also describes the procedures that can be used in the modern hospital to keep this organ "alive" for longer periods of time through the use of heart-lung machines to oxygenate the blood. The author also presents an interesting account of the workings of the body's defense mechanisms regarding the rejection of foreign objects, and how that most difficult obstacle is being overcome. His description of the rejection mechanism is most easily understood by the layman.

The ultimate success of the heart transplant seems to rest upon two facets. First, there must be continued research into the successful suppression of the body's rejection mecha-nisms. Second, we must develop a system whereby people will see the value of donating their own organs for such transplants and then making the appropriate provisions before their deaths. — *W.S.*

Additional Recommended Reading

Castelnuovo-Tedesco, Pietro. *Psychiatric Aspects of Organ Transplantation*. New York: Grune and Stratton, 1971. A collection of articles reprinted from the journal *Seminars in Psychiatry*, this book contains six excellent articles relating to the care of cardiac patients, including articles on the selection of transplant recipients and resultant psychological adjustments made by the patient and his family.

"First Human Hearts Transplanted," in *Science News*. LXXVI (December 16, 1967) Vol. 92, p. 58. This magazine article contains a description of the actual transplant operations that took place in South Africa and the United States.

"Surgery: Fascination and Lessons," in *Time*. LXXXIII (January 19, 1968), p. 50. This edition of *Time* carries the stories of the five heart transplant operations that followed in the days immediately after Washkansky's successful operation.

"Too Many Too Soon?," in *Time*. LXXXIII (January 19, 1968), p. 51. In this article the editors of the magazine attempted to gather opinion from around the world regarding the transplant operations, including not only scientific reactions, but ethical reactions taking place in regard to the coincidence of the operations.

"The Ultimate Operation," in *Time*. LXXXII (December 15, 1967), p. 64. This edition of *Time* carries a detailed description of the events of the operations and contains an excellent graphic presentation of the surgical procedures used to join the donor's heart with the recipient's own circulatory system.

Warshofsky, Fred. *The Control of Life in the 21st Century*. New York: The Viking Press, 1969. Chapter Six of this book discusses the human heart and its operation, with a small portion of the chapter devoted to the first transplant operations, and a brief discussion of the circumstances under which the operations take place.

BUILDING OF THE ALASKA PIPELINE

Type of event: Economic: proposal and construction of the pipeline
Time: 1968-1977
Locale: Alaska

Principal personages:
R. G. DULANEY, Chairman of the Trans-Alaska Pipeline System
CHARLIE EDWARDSEN, Executive Director of the Arctic Slope Native Association
WILLIAM Allen EGAN (1914-   ), Governor of Alaska
WALTER J. HICKEL (1919-   ), United States Secretary of the Interior, 1969-1970
THOMAS E. KELLY (1931-   ), Natural Resources Commissioner of Alaska

Summary of Event

In July, 1957, oil was discovered on the Kenai Peninsula of Alaska by the Richfield Company. The news initiated a rush on leases for land in the area in a fashion to which the Alaskan frontier is accustomed. Eleven years later Thomas E. Kelly, Natural Resources Commissioner of Alaska, reclassified over two million acres of North Slope land for competitive oil and gas leasing, whereupon the newly formed Atlantic-Richfield Company confirmed its findings of significant oil deposits on the North Slope. Even the most conservative estimates indicated that the oil in the North Slope was a major deposit, amounting to at least 9.6 billion barrels. Speculators poured into the state; approximately fourteen hundred corporations registered in Alaska to engage in the rush. Alaska experienced a boom not unlike the late 1800's gold rush, with all the accompanying excitement. This discovery was the advent of what was to be a significant landmark in the battle between environmental protection of natural resources and private interests.

A joint venture of Atlantic-Richfield, British Petroleum, and Humble Oil, simply called the Trans-Alaska Pipeline System (TAPS), applied for permission in 1969 to build a hot oil pipeline across the state from the North Slope to the port at Valdez. The proposal was met by organized opposition from conservationists posing questions that were not only environmental, but also technical and economic. On the basis of a cursory investigation, TAPS opted for a conventional pipeline over a seemingly efficient route, discarding proposed alternatives, such as connecting with existing Canadian pipelines.

R. G. Dulaney, the Chairman of the Trans-Alaska Pipeline System, impatiently pushed for the approval and immediate completion of the pipeline over the route to the port at Valdez. Investigations and surveys were immediately approved and under way when orders for the special forty-eight-inch pipe were placed with three Japanese companies. Meanwhile, the United States Department of the Interior set up a task force to oversee North Slope oil development; this task force was modified by President Richard Nixon to include conservation and other interests. All this took place before an application was filed for permission to build a pipeline.

Meanwhile, apparent alliances were being formed for an anticipated confrontation. One issue, the technical feasibility of a buried pipeline over the proposed route, raised several problems which the task force was unable to solve satisfactorily: the impact of an underground pipeline on the permafrost; the incidence of earthquakes in this seismologically active area; the pollution which would result both from handling the oil and from increasing human activity in a wilderness region; and native land claims.

The ensuing political confrontations at both state and national levels developed into a classic confrontation of conflicting interests. Alaska was concerned for its future; and the lure of industrial prosperity was tempered by the problems industry would bring to the environment. At the national level, Congress adopted the National Environmental Policy Act in 1969, which was to be the major tool of conservationists in influencing public policy. The law required that information be made public on adverse environmental effects, and alternatives considered, for any federally supported project.

In the late summer of 1969, the Twentieth Science Conference met in Fairbanks to discuss the future of Alaska. From that conference, it was apparent that the final solution to the question of an Alaskan pipeline was not imminent. Dissident elements were organized and were not to be regarded as powerless. The political battles that were to follow focused on the two fundamental issues of environment and native land claims. Walter J. Hickel, Secretary of the Interior and former Governor of Alaska, was thrust into a central role in these two conflicts.

On December 18, 1971, President Nixon signed into law a native land claims settlement. The bill provided Alaskan natives with full title to their land and first option on forty million acres of disputed territory. The same act provided the state of Alaska with rights to some of the land it selected and partial remuneration from the federal government for other land claims. William Egan, the Governor of Alaska, who favored construction of the pipeline, was instrumental in the passage of this legislation. Charlie Edwardsen, principal spokesman of the Arctic Slope Native Association, was very critical of the Act because it allowed the native Eskimos only surface rights to their oil-rich lands.

Once this roadblock was cleared, the focus shifted to technical and environmental issues regarding the pipeline. The challenges, delays, and legal battles continued. Finally, in November, 1973, nearly five years after the initial TAPS proposal, President Nixon signed the Trans-Alaska Pipeline Authorization Act, and construction began in 1974 on the pipeline. The pipeline was built by Alyeska Pipeline Service, a consortium of major oil companies including, among others, Atlantic-Richfield and British Petroleum.

Many problems remained. The tiny town of Valdez, swelled by the influx of pipeline workers and others rushing to a promising job market, simply had no facilities to deal with the large number of people. The struggle for land continued. The Alaskan natives sought to exercise options on the North Slope, while conservationists sought to enlarge the federal domain with parks, refuges, and national forests. The federal government was cautiously deliberate in overseeing this activity and was reluctant to re-

lease rights-of-way for construction, trying to temper decisions affecting industrial expansion with care for the environment. Overcoming such problems slowed the completion of the pipeline. Finally, on June 20, 1977, oil began to flow through the nearly eight-hundred-mile-long pipeline, stretching from Prudhoe Bay on the North Slope to the port of Valdez on the Pacific Ocean. Over about half of its length, the pipeline is elevated to protect the permafrost. The special forty-eight-inch pipeline cost $7.7 billion, with an additional $3.6 billion for equipment, drilling, and facilities.

Pertinent Literature

Berry, Mary Clay. *The Alaska Pipeline: The Politics of Oil and Native Land Claims*. Bloomington: Indiana University Press, 1975.

In a detailed account of events, the author provides an insight into the activities and happenings, the political pressures and issues, and the eventual compromise and outcome of an episode in American history that asserted public interests for environment and dramatically changed the direction of development of Alaska. Mary Clay Berry focuses on a sequence of public events in order to develop an understanding of the pressures and the struggle for approval to build the Alaska oil pipeline.

It had long been suspected that oil would be found in Alaska. Small oil fields had been discovered and production was under way as early as 1920. The United States Geological Survey in the 1950's reported attractive sedimentary basins but did not locate significant oil or gas deposits.

The large oil companies undertook searches, as the high cost prohibited many small companies from participating. But it was the small Richfield Company that found oil at the Swanson river on the Kenai Peninsula in 1957 and started a struggle that would finally be resolved in 1973 when the Trans-Alaska Pipeline Authorization Act became law.

The author focuses on two major groups that were informally allied against private interests. One was the environmentalists who were anxious to put the new National Environmental Policy Act to the test. The other group consisted of the native Alaskans who defended their land claims against the federal government. Approximately ninety-nine percent of Alaska was under federal control, and both groups sought protection of their particular interests when private interests approached the federal government to release some of these lands for exploration and oil extraction.

An interpretive historical background of Alaska's development provides an important understanding of the developments which precipitated the issue of native land claims in the 1970's. Berry points out that this issue was unresolved in 1958 when Congress approved statehood for Alaska, and she traces the developments through the 1960's from official government transcripts and publications and from the perspective of native organizations and attempts to resolve the claims.

The author documents in detail the episodes from the discovery of oil in Alaska through the formal approval to build the Trans-Alaska Pipeline System. In particular, she emphasizes the political activity in the statehouse and the Department of the Interior, headed by Secretary Walter J. Hickel. In the process, she identifies and interprets the pressures influencing the Department of the Interior and the state government of Alaska, and indicates some of the finer points regarding the decisions and actions taken apparently for the purpose of expediency. For example, Berry regards as presumptuous and hurried a series of decisions to select an arbitrary route for the pipeline, contract for a feasibility study, and contract with Japanese steel firms for a forty-eight-inch pipeline before permission was obtained to build the pipeline. Such decisions, Berry implies, eventually worked against the objectives of the oil interests. Similar episodes in the political arena are interspersed, contributing to a better understanding of the entire situation. Berry's work is not entirely objective, however, largely because it ignores the motivations and activities of the oil interests.

Berry reflects on the consequences of the pipeline construction to Alaska and the necessary adjustments that Alaska was unprepared to make. The small town of Valdez suffered from the onslaughts of rapid expansion, while the community of Fairbanks had to adjust to the environmental problems of industrialized America. The wilderness was forced to adjust to human presence. The struggle for the land continued. The environmental concerns of the public clashed with private interests and the result was a delicate compromise. But large scale industrial activity came to the last wilderness frontier of America and the era of frontier settlement and homesteading as an alternative to industrial society had come to an abrupt end.

Cicchetti, Charles J. *Alaskan Oil: Alternative Routes and Markets*. Baltimore, Md.: The Johns Hopkins University Press, 1972.

This study was supported and published by Resources for the Future, a nonprofit corporation for research and education in the development, conservation, and use of natural resources, as well as the improvement of the environment. Charles Cicchetti was a research associate with Resources for the Future at the time the study was made. He analyzes the proposed Trans-Alaska pipeline from an economic perspective, identifying anticipated costs as well as benefits. His discussion also includes a treatment of the effects of a major spillover on the environment.

Shortly after the announcement of a major oil strike on the North Slope of Alaska in 1968, a major effort to plan and develop the means to extract the oil got under way. Amid the excitement and optimistic expectations, plans for immediate construction of a Trans-Alaska pipeline to carry crude oil overland from the North Slope to the ice-free port of Valdez were hurriedly developed; but these plans met with bitter opposition from environmentalists defending a revived national conservation consciousness and from native interests defending claims to the land. Both groups criticized oil interests for the seemingly arbitrary selection of a pipeline route and for understating the technological difficulties in designing and constructing the pipeline. Oil interests had been accused of not considering alternate technologies and routes for the pipeline. In their haste to begin construction, they apparently underestimated the importance of the environmental and native claims issues and the impact that the groups representing these issues would have on the federal government and on the oil pipeline project.

Charles Cicchetti approaches the environmental issue analytically to defend the hypothesis that the environmental hazards of the proposed Trans-Alaska pipeline and the proposed transportation of the oil by boat to the West Coast would exceed the net value of the resource itself. Recognizing the highly speculative nature of assessing the future risks of a project which had no precedent and the difficulties of measuring the impact and cost of environmental damage, the author addresses another question which is of more contemporary interest. Does the proposed plan for transporting the oil by means of a hot oil pipeline across permafrost, through a region of seismic disturbances to the port of Valdez and down the coast to Puget Sound, minimize the environmental hazards?

Cicchetti's work is a scholarly analysis examining alternative routes and technologies. The author identifies characteristics of oil demand, conversion costs, and policy peculiarities that result in different values for oil in different markets. He analyzes the economic feasibility of alternatives and reaches the conclusion that the alternate pipeline route from Prudhoe Bay in the north, to Fairbanks, and then to Edmonton, Canada, along the Alcan highway would be better.

On the strength of this conclusion, the author questions the motivation of and pressures upon presumably profit-seeking entrepreneurs that led to the selection of the route over which the pipeline was finally built. He examines institutional factors as well as market factors in various regions and concludes that the Trans-Alaska pipeline alternative offered potentially higher profit from overseas markets, avoided international tangles, and provided transportation advantages by using foreign vessels.
— *J.M.F.*

Building of the Alaska Pipeline

Additional Recommended Reading

Adelman, Morris A., Paul G. Bradley and Charles A. Norman. *Alaskan Oil Costs and Supplies*. New York: Frederick A. Praeger, 1971. A series of articles analyzing supply and costs of extracting oil in Alaska.

Allen, Lawrence. *The Trans-Alaska Pipeline South to Valdez*. Seattle, Wash.: Scribe Publishing Company, 1976. A detailed description of the plans and problems of constructing the pipeline.

Roscow, James P. *800 Miles to Valdez: The Building of the Alaska Pipeline*. Englewood Cliffs, N.J.: Prentice-Hall, 1977. A detailed account of the events leading to the completion of the pipeline.

Tussing, Arlon R., G. W. Rogers and V. Fischer. *Alaska Pipeline Report*. Fairbanks, Al.: Institute of Social, Economic and Government Research, 1971. A technical report focusing on the impact of the proposed pipeline on the Alaskan economy.

POLITICAL TERRORISM

Type of event: Political: impact of terrorism in the non-Communist world
Time: 1968 to the present
Locale: The non-Communist world

Principal personages:

GEORGE HABASH (1925-   ), the leader of the Popular Front for the Liberation of Palestine (PFLP), a Palestinian terrorist group

LEILA KHALED (1945-   ), young woman terrorist and skyjacker who belongs to the PFLP

YASIR ARAFAT (MOHAMMED ABED AR'OUF ARAFAT) (1929-   ), the leader of the Palestine Liberation Organization (PLO) which is the umbrella organization of Palestinian terrorists

ANDREAS BAADER (1943-1977), West German terrorist, one of the so-called "Baader-Meinhof Gang"

ULRIKE MEINHOF (1934-1976), West German woman terrorist, a member of the "Baader-Meinhof Gang"

RENATO CURCIO, one of the leaders of Italy's "Red Brigades" terrorist group

ILITCH RAMIREZ SANCHEZ ("CARLOS") (1949-   ), Venezuelan terrorist, linked to both New Left terrorists in West Europe and to Palestinian terrorists

ALDO MORO (1916-1978), Italian politician murdered by Red Brigades in 1978

Summary of Event

In the late 1960's the average citizen of the developed world was faced with a new and frightening threat: international political terrorism.

Political terrorism, as defined here, is the commission of criminal acts involving violence or the threat of violence by private individuals and nongovernmental groups acting for the sake of political ends. The presence of a political goal or ideology, no matter how murky it may be, is crucial to this definition. The terrorist is distinguished from the guerrilla by his preference for an urban base rather than a rural one.

The terrorists of the 1960's and the 1970's could be divided into two major groups. These were the separatist-nationalist terrorists on the one hand, and left-wing ideological terrorists on the other. The Irish, Palestinian, and Croatian *émigré* terrorists, seeking to liberate their homelands by bomb and bullet, exemplify the first. The "Red Brigades" of Italy are examples of the latter.

The separatist-nationalist terrorist did, at least, have a clearly defined goal, however unattainable it might sometimes have seemed. The left-wing ideological terrorist, however, often seemed to have no concrete goal besides that of simply trying to destroy the existing order, which he believed to be corrupt and wicked.

The two types of terrorists sometimes worked in concert. On May 30, 1972, terrorists of the left-wing Japanese Red Army, acting on behalf of the Popular Front for the Liberation of Palestine (PFLP), carried out the indiscriminate slaughter of passengers at Lod Airport in Israel. When Israeli commandos killed seven PFLP hijackers at Entebbe, Uganda, on July 4, 1976, they found two West Germans among them. The mysterious young Venezuelan left-wing terrorist, Ilitch Ramirez Sanchez ("Carlos"), was also thought to have close connections with the Palestinian terrorists.

Neither type of terrorism is a completely new phenomenon. The Narodniks of nineteenth century Russia tried to use violence and assassination to overthrow the government of the Tsar. In the 1890's, the Anarchists, believing that any and all government was wicked, assassinated a President of France, a President of the United States, and a King of Italy. In the Empire of the Ottoman Turks, Armenian and Macedonian terrorists also used assassination and terrorist acts in their struggle against Turkish rule.

For most of the twenty-three-year period after World War II, however, the average citizen in the developed countries was not aware of terrorism as a threat to his way of life. In the years 1954-1962, Algerian rebels, seeking independence for their country, practiced terror against the soldiers of France. In Vietnam, in the years 1961-1973, Vietnamese Communist guerrillas used terror tactics against the Army of the United States, which was aiding the anti-Communist government of South Vietnam. These, however, were guerrilla wars, taking place in lands of the underdeveloped world.

In the late 1960's, however, terrorism became much more of an obvious danger than it had been in the past. The year 1968, when the American Ambassador, John G. Mein, was kidnaped and killed by Guatemalan leftists, marked the beginning of a worldwide wave of terrorism. Bombs began to explode, not merely in Vietnamese rice paddies, but also in the modern cities and airports of advanced Western countries. There are several possible explanations for the new wave of terrorism.

The so-called "baby boom," the sharp rise in the birth rate which had occurred in all advanced countries after World War II, had swollen the ranks of the restless young adult age groups. In the advanced countries, an unprecedented number of this generation were, by the late 1960's attending universities. Sometimes university attendance meant not merely advanced training in a specific skill, but also an exposure to new ideologies. Students embraced such ideologies as Marxism, which they understood only vaguely, with a fervor possible only for those not tied down by family or career. Coming from middle- to upper-middle-class backgrounds, they were shocked by the existence of world poverty and the continuing bloodshed of the Vietnam War. Marxism seemed to offer an explanation.

It is this absorption of left-wing ideology in the student environment which explains the rise of the "New Left" terrorist groups in Western Europe and America. Most of the members of the "Baader-Meinhof Gang" had attended West German universities. Renato Curcio, one of the best known of the leaders of the Italian "Red Brigades," had studied Sociology at the University of Trent.

The example of the Vietnam War, which turned so many Western European university students towards the terrorist left, also gave new inspiration to separatist-nationalist terrorists. After the Six-Day War of 1967, in which Israel had defeated the Arab states, many Palestinian Arab refugees became convinced that the use of "Vietnamese" tactics against Israel could reverse the verdict of the battlefield.

The very technological achievements which modern industrial society had produced in the years 1945 to 1965 helped, after 1968, to promote the growth of terrorism directed against it. The jet airplane, for example, perfected only by the late 1950's, had put rapid transportation across wide distances within the reach of the average man for the first time in history. It also made possible one of the most vicious tactics of the new terrorism: "skyjacking." In skyjacking, terrorists, having boarded a jet airplane as seemingly innocent passengers, would take control of the plane in midflight, threatening the passengers with death until governments met their demands. This type of terrorist act was first perfected by the Palestinian terrorists, who used it frequently against planes bound for

Israel. Leila Khaled, the most notorious of the skyjackers, belonged to the Popular Front for the Liberation of Palestine (PFLP), a Marxist-oriented group led by the American-trained physician, Dr. George Habash.

Television, which had become a consumer item of common use in the early 1950's, brought instant news, entertainment, and enlightenment to the masses of the Western developed countries. It also made it possible for millions of people to witness acts of terrorism. The terrorists could now subject whole populations to blackmail, compelling them to listen to their strident voices. Television magnified the impact of the terrorists' criminal deeds, which were performed at least partly for the sake of obtaining media coverage.

Publicity for the terrorists did not necessarily gain them popular support. By the end of the 1960's, there was, in advanced countries, a widespread popular revulsion against the methods used by the new terrorists. One of the most revolting of their methods was the kidnaping and murder of innocent people.

As early as 1968, Latin American terrorists had been kidnaping, and sometimes killing, American Ambassadors and other diplomatic personnel. In March of 1973, Palestinian terrorists of the so-called "Black September" group, which owed allegiance to Yasir Arafat, leader of the Palestine Liberation Organization (PLO), burst into the Saudi Arabian Embassy in Khartoum, Sudan, kidnaping the United States Ambassador to Saudi Arabia, Cleo Noel, and the United States Chargé d'Affaires,

George Moore. When the terrorists' demands were not met, the two American hostages were killed. Their crime had been their service to a government which the terrorists saw as too friendly to Israel. In October, 1977, "New Left" terrorists kidnaped and murdered West German industrialist Martin Schleyer, whose crime lay in having been a successful "capitalist." In the spring of 1978, terrorists of the Red Brigades kidnaped and killed Aldo Moro, whose crime lay in having been a prominent politician of the dominant Christian Democratic Party. The murder of Aldo Moro so sickened Italians that even the Italian Communist Party felt compelled to denounce this terrorist act.

By the late 1970's, there was, therefore, a widespread demand that something be done to end the plague of terrorism. However, there was no simple answer to the problem. Trying to satisfy the terrorists' deep-seated grievances was certainly no answer. Most of the aims of the various terrorist groups were either impossible of achievement, or undesirable. The New Left terrorists often did not even know what they really wanted, except to destroy the existing government. The demands of the Palestinians could be met only by the destruction of the State of Israel. The South Moluccan terrorists, in May of 1977, kidnaped Dutch schoolchildren to make their demands heard. Yet, the Netherlands was completely powerless to free the South Moluccan's island homeland from Indonesian rule.

It was impossible, therefore, to eliminate the "root causes" of terrorism. What was necessary was strict enforcement of the law and the co-operation of all governments of the world against the terrorist threat. In practice, both of these goals were quite difficult to accomplish.

Every government stated publicly that it would not negotiate with terrorists. In practice, however, democratic governments, faced with the cry that lives be saved whatever the cost, were often tempted to yield to the immediate demands of terrorists in order to avoid bloodshed. Yet, giving in to terrorism was certainly humiliating, and it could lead to anarchy.

The State of Israel, viewing the Palestinian terrorist movement as a threat to the existence of the Israeli nation, set up a counterterrorist organization to hunt down and assassinate Palestinian terrorist leaders. Most democratic governments, however, were unwilling to take such drastic measures against the terrorist threat. Drastic measures against terrorism inevitably reduced somewhat the liberty of the individual, and increased somewhat the arbitrary powers of the State. Liberal-minded men did not want to destroy democracy in order to save it.

It was, likewise, easier to call for the international control of terrorism than to do anything to implement it. By 1978, the Western European states were, it is true, cooperating in the fight against the ideological terrorism of such left-wing groups as the Italian Red Brigades. Russia and the Arab states, however, still condoned acts of terrorism directed against the "Zionist-imperialist" State of Israel. General Muammar Khaddafi, the dictator of the North African State of Libya, had been particularly flagrant in providing a haven from justice for anti-Israeli terrorists.

Perhaps some day, however, the Communist governments might change their minds. By the middle of the 1970's, Croatian *émigrés* were using terror tactics against the government of Yugoslavia, a nonaligned Communist state which had always smiled benevolently on Arab terror-ism against Israel. The Croatians wanted to liberate Croatia from Yugoslavia by force, just as the Palestinians wanted to liberate Palestine from "Zionist domination" by force. If all governments finally come to see themselves as potential targets of terrorism, then, and only then, will all be willing to cooperate in the fight against it.

Pertinent Literature

Bell, J. Bowyer. *A Time of Terror: How Democratic Societies Cope with Terrorism.* New York: Basic Books, 1978.

Bell is an academic who has for a long time specialized in the study of terrorism and other forms of political violence. There is, however, nothing pedantic about Bell's writing style; it is brisk and lively. His is one of the few really good books written about the subject of political terrorism in the 1960's and 1970's. The author is interested not in the terrorists themselves, nor in their psychological or political motives, but in the response of democratic governments to the threat to society which these terrorists pose.

In the first chapter, Bell deals at length with one particular example of terrorism, one which, in his opinion, sheds light on the entire problem. This is the case of the Croatian *émigré* terrorists who, brandishing home-made pot-bombs, seized control of a TWA passenger airplane in September, 1976. These terrorists compelled the pilot to drop leaflets urging freedom for Croatia from Yugoslav rule. They forced the plane to fly to Paris, where the French authorities had the tires shot out. Forced to surrender, the Croatians were returned to the United States, where they received stiff prison sentences.

Having narrated this sequence of events with his usual dramatic flair, Bell states, at the end of the chapter, the main contention of the book. There is, Bell asserts, no absolutely foolproof means of preventing terrorist incidents. In the two years prior to the Croatians' skyjacking attempt, the airlines had introduced every method they could think of to prevent such things from happening; yet, the Croatians still managed to get through the net.

In the second chapter, Bell tries to distinguish between political terrorism and mere criminal violence. He points out that many criminals and psychopaths, with no serious political goals, have often used the rhetoric of revolutionary politics. He cites Charles Manson and his tribe of murderers as an example of this phenomenon in the United States.

In the third chapter, the author traces the new terrorism back to its beginnings in 1968. Bell sees this new terrorism as clearly different from the guerrilla wars, assassinations, and other forms of political violence found in previous eras. To Bell, what is distinctive about the new political terrorism is the role of television in creating a mass audience for the terrorists' deeds and in securing publicity for their cause. He speaks repeatedly of "transnational television terrorists" and "terrorist spectaculars."

In Chapters Four through Nine, Bell discusses, with appropriate examples, the different responses of democratic societies to the various terrorist threats. During what he calls the "first round" of responses, from 1970 to 1973, the democracies gradually came to realize that terrorism was not merely a local problem, but a worldwide one. During the "second round" of responses, from 1973 to 1977, various methods of dealing with the problem were tried. Governments tried, without complete success, to secure international cooperation against terrorism. When terrorist incidents did occur, governments tried to use reason and persuasion rather than "shooting first and asking questions later." At airports, authorities tried to devise means of screening out potential skyjackers. None of these methods of dealing with the problem was completely ineffective, but none was completely successful either.

One of the threatened states, Israel, set up a counterterrorist organization to hunt down Palestinian terrorists. Bell believes that trying to fight terrorism with its own weapons, as Israel has done, is of dubious morality. Nor does Bell think that draconian penalties, designed merely to gratify the public desire for vengeance, are the proper answer. The law, he argues, must be made synonymous with justice, not merely with order.

In Chapters Ten and Eleven, Bell presents two opposing poles in the effectiveness of governmental reaction to terrorism. The Republic of Ireland, with its strong democratic tradition, has been unusually successful in minimizing the danger posed by the Irish Republican Army, a terrorist group which has enjoyed a broad measure of popular support ever since the founding of the Irish Free State in 1922. In Italy, by contrast, wrangling politicians, operating in a country with deep ideological schisms and a fragile democratic tradition, have been unable to suppress the threat posed by the Red Brigades. Yet, the Red Brigades had not even come into existence until 1967.

In the conclusion, Bell expresses his personal beliefs on the subject of terrorism. He thinks that terrorism is a threat to the safety and peace of democratic societies, yet he also thinks that people will simply have to live with it: "Beware of those offering solutions to terrorism. There are no solutions in open societies." The greatest danger posed by terrorists, according to Bell, lies not in what they themselves do, but in what they can provoke others into doing: "The terrorists cannot bomb down an open society, but an act of parliament can close one."

The value of Bell's study is enhanced by an excellent critical bibliography on the subject of terrorism.

Laqueur, Walter Ze'ev. *Terrorism*. Boston: Little, Brown and Company, 1977.

Walter Laqueur is a prolific historian who has written chiefly about the history of ideas. Thus, he does not try to excite the reader with stirring narratives of different terrorist incidents. Instead, he tries to view the whole phenomenon of terrorism cooly and calmly, in a broad historical perspective. He does not try to deal in depth with the responses of governments to the terrorist threat. Instead, he discusses five subjects: the doctrine of systematic terrorism, the sociology of terrorist groups, current interpretations of terrorism, its common patterns, and the efficacy of terrorism.

The first chapter, "The Origins," traces the origins of modern terrorism back to the assassinations and guerrilla wars of past years, while the second chapter, "The Philosophy of the Bomb," concentrates on attitudes towards individual violence among the Anarchists and Marxists of nineteenth century Russia. In the third chapter, "The Sociology of Terrorism," Laqueur treats the sources of support, organizational structure, sources of weapons, organization, and tactics of terrorist groups; he also discusses briefly the counterterrorist tactics used by governments. In the fourth chapter, "Interpretations of Terrorism," the author compares the interpretations of terrorism provided by political science with those provided by fictional literature, and finds the former far inferior to the latter.

He points out that political science, no matter how sophisticated its methods, cannot provide a basis for predicting which countries will suffer from terrorism and which ones will not. Since Laqueur does not believe that modern terrorism is either unique or unprecedented, he does not devote a whole book to it; it is only in the fifth chapter, "Terrorism Today," that he turns his attention to the postwar wave of urban terrorism which began in the late 1960's.

Laqueur distinguishes three different varieties of the new urban terrorism. These are the "trendsetter" terrorism of Latin America, the traditional home of political violence; the "separatist-nationalist" terrorism of the Palestinians and the Irish Republican Army; and the "New Left terrorism" of Western Europe and the United States.

Laqueur attempts in the conclusion of his study to judge both the morality and effectiveness of terrorism. He believes terrorism to be unjustifiable even if the grievances of the terrorists are genuine. Many grievances, he points out, simply cannot be resolved without creating new injustices. Terrorism is effective only against democracies or weak dictatorships. The state that is willing to use tyrannical means to fight terror with terror can easily suppress any terrorist threat: "If the power of democratic societies shrinks, so does the sphere in which terrorism can operate." — *P.D.M.*

Additional Recommended Reading

Clutterbuck, Richard. *Living with Terrorism*. London: Faber & Faber, 1975. This book, written by a veteran of thirty-five years in the British Army, is a guide to the average citizen on how to protect himself against terrorism.

Burton, Anthony. *Urban Terrorism: Theory, Practice and Response*. New York: The Free Press, 1976. An examination of the new political terrorism, written by a former British Army officer.

Dobson, Christopher and Ronald Payne. *The Carlos Complex: A Study in Terror*. New York: G. P. Putnam's Sons, 1977. A study, by two veteran British journalists, of the mysterious young Venezuelan terrorist and his connections with terrorist groups throughout the world.

Hyams, Edward. *Terrorists and Terrorism*. New York: St. Martin's Press, 1975. Hyams, a professional novelist writing a work of nonfiction, argues that terrorism has, throughout history, often been an essential element of beneficial political change.

Becker, Jillian. *Hitler's Children: The Story of the Baader-Meinhof Gang*. New York: J. B. Lippincott Company, 1977. This work, written by an Englishwoman, vigorously attacks the notion that these young West German terrorists were in any sense "idealists."

Cooley, John K. *Green March, Black September: The Story of the Palestinian Arabs*. London: Frank Cass and Company, 1973. A good general account of the Palestinian Arab terrorist movement, written by the Middle East correspondent for the *Christian Science Monitor*.

Alexander, Yonah, ed. *International Terrorism: National, Regional, and Global Perspectives*. New York: Frederick A. Praeger, 1976. A collection of scholarly essays on the problem of political terrorism, all written by American political scientists.

"The Blood-Hungry Red Brigades," in *Time*. XCIII (March 27, 1978), p. 43. This is one of the few articles written on the Red Brigades.

VIET CONG TET OFFENSIVE

Type of event: Military: influence of military attack on foreign policy objectives
Time: January 31-March 31, 1968
Locale: Vietnam

Principal personages:

LYNDON BAINES JOHNSON (1908-1973), thirty-sixth President
of the United States, 1963-1969

GENERAL WILLIAM CHILDS WESTMORELAND (1914-   ),
Commander of Military Assistance Command in Vietnam

GENERAL EARLE GILMORE WHEELER (1908-   ), Chief of
the Joint Chiefs of Staff

CLARK MCADAMS CLIFFORD (1906-   ), United States Secretary of Defense, 1968-1969

DEAN RUSK (1909-   ), United States Secretary of State,
1961-1969

Summary of Event

On the night of January 30, 1968, Viet Cong and North Vietnamese military units began a surprise offensive throughout Vietnam. They attacked thirty-nine of South Vietnam's forty-four provincial capitals, five of its six autonomous cities, and at least seventy-one of the 245 district towns. A Viet Cong unit even penetrated the grounds of the United States Embassy in Saigon before being killed in a furious gun fight. All over Vietnam, cities which had previously been immune from the war were attacked, occupied, and in some cases heavily destroyed as American and Vietnamese troops moved in to liberate them. The war had been going on since 1946, but it had never seen fighting like this. Two months later, on March 31, 1968, President Lyndon Johnson addressed the American people on television to announce that in the pursuit of peace, he was ordering a partial bombing halt of North Vietnam and that he would neither seek

nor accept the Democratic presidential nomination. That was Tet, two months in 1968, that changed the course of American involvement in Vietnam.

The United States had been supporting the Saigon government of South Vietnam since Vietnam was divided in 1954. The military situation had been steadily deteriorating during those years, and in July, 1965, President Johnson made a fateful decision. Henceforth American troops would not only be used in a defensive capacity of protecting American airfields but would go on the offensive. American military units would carry the fight to the enemy in what became known as search-and-destroy missions. The new policy, strongly backed by Secretary of State Dean Rusk and General Earle Wheeler, Chief of the Joint Chiefs of Staff, was to defeat the enemy. This aggressive policy required more American troops. In June, 1965, there were less than sixty

1036

thousand American troops in Vietnam. By the year's end that number had grown to 184,300. A year later it had moved to 385,300 and by the end of 1967 nearly a half million American troops were stationed in Vietnam. The war had been Americanized.

This strategy led to increased American casualties, but it did not lead to an end of the war. As Americans continued to die and peace was not in sight, public support for the war began to decline. To stop this trend, President Johnson orchestrated a series of optimistic statements by key civilian and military leaders late in 1967. The American people were assured that progress was being made or, in the language of the day, there was "light at the end of the tunnel."

Meanwhile the United States continued its strategy of making the price of war so high that the North Vietnamese would give up. Search-and-destroy missions and American bombing of North Vietnam continued. However, there was a limit to the military effort the United States would make in Vietnam: bombing of North Vietnam would stop short of provoking a confrontation with China or Russia. American troops would be limited to a number which would not require total mobilization of the American economy, something the American people would not tolerate. Though a limited war, this was not a small military effort. A half million troops had been sent; 400,000 air attack sorties per year had dropped 1.2 million tons of bombs. The enemy had lost 200,000 killed and the United States 20,000 of its own. That was the

situation when Vietnam prepared to celebrate the lunar new year of Tet.

Tet was the most important holiday in Vietnam, a time for rejoicing and traveling to see friends and relatives. It was not a time for war but a time for truce. Yet in Saigon, General Westmoreland, Commander of American forces in Vietnam, knew something was going to happen. The enemy had been building up its forces, and captured documents indicated an offensive of some kind. That the offensive came on Tet was a surprise. That it was so large and well coordinated was a shock.

Precisely what the North Vietnamese sought to gain from the Tet offensive is not clear. The captured documents indicated that they thought large areas could be seized through popular uprisings against the South Vietnamese government and the defection of whole units of the South Vietnamese army. In addition to these military goals there were psychological victories to be won. A forceful attack would discourage the United States and show the people of South Vietnam that neither their own government nor the Americans could protect them.

Militarily, the North Vietnamese lost. Though they were able to capture several cities and to hold out in the old imperial city of Hue for more than three weeks, in the end they held no city and there was no popular uprising or large-scale defection. In fact, the South Vietnamese rallied to the defense of their country to a far greater extent than they yielded to the enemy forces. Psychologically, however, Tet was a North Vietnamese victory. They had demonstrated that there was no light at the end of the tunnel. All the American bombing and search-and-destroy missions had not prevented North Vietnam from attacking virtually any place in South Vietnam. It was not important whether Hanoi had won any military victories in the battles that were fought during the Tet offensive. What was important to American officials and the American people was that little had been accomplished during two and a half years of major American fighting, and too much remained to be accomplished before peace would be at hand.

Tet reinforced the American public's dissatisfaction with the war. Perpetuation of the American policy would result in more American deaths, greater economic sacrifice at home, destruction of countless South Vietnamese towns, and the extension of human suffering over ever larger areas of Vietnam. Even then there was no assurance of victory. North Vietnam had promised a long war and the Tet offensive showed that the price would be high. The American people gradually concluded they did not want to pay that price.

Within official Washington, the Tet offensive sparked a major debate. Military leaders concluded that Hanoi had been defeated and urged the President to take advantage of this victory and expand the war. Within the Defense Department, however, was a growing number of civilian officials, among them, Secretary of Defense Clark Clifford, who doubted the wisdom of escalation or even continuation of the way the war was being fought. Their analyses showed that no progress had been made since the summer of 1965. They advised the President that the policy of confronting the enemy on the field of battle had failed. It was time to pull back and provide a shield behind which the South Vietnamese army would rebuild with American arms. Thus rebuilt, South Vietnam would fight its own war. The policy was Vietnamization. Lyndon Johnson rejected escalation and reluctantly accepted Vietnamization. Peace was still a long way off, but the course of American withdrawal had been charted.

Pertinent Literature

Schandler, Herbert. *The Unmaking of a President: Lyndon Johnson and Vietnam.* Princeton, N.J.: Princeton University Press, 1977.

Less than ten years after the Tet offensive we have the first scholarly, well-researched study of the impact of that event on United States foreign policy. Basing his research on memoirs, declassified documents, and the "Pentagon Papers," Herbert Schandler has put together a fascinating story of the bureaucratic struggle within the Lyndon Johnson Administration, a struggle which resulted in the policy of Vietnamization.

Schandler's story has four main characters: President Johnson, General Earle Wheeler, Secretary of State Dean Rusk, and Secretary of Defense Clark Clifford. President Johnson is depicted as a man unwilling to abandon his goals in Vietnam, a man who would have escalated the war except that he knew the American people would not tolerate such action. Rusk believed that military punishment would convince Hanoi that it could not win. Yet Rusk also recognized that it was necessary to persuade the American people that the Johnson Administration was being reasonable. General Wheeler, Chief of the Joint Chiefs of Staff, viewed Vietnam in purely military terms. Even in the midst of public dismay over the Tet offensive, Wheeler urged escalation, seemingly untouched by the necessity of maintaining public support. Clark Clifford is presented as a thoughtful, sensitive, rich lawyer who had supported Johnson's Vietnam policy before he became Secretary of Defense, which was scarcely a month after the Tet offensive began. As Secretary of Defense, Clifford went through a reappraisal of his position and emerged the champion of a moderate, realistic policy. Clifford is both the hero and the central character of Schandler's study.

It is Schandler's thesis that the crisis in Washington came not over the military events of Tet but because the army tried to capitalize on the Tet fighting. In Saigon, General William Westmoreland believed he had beaten back the enemy and did not need any significant number of reinforcements. But over the years the build-up in Vietnam had taken place at the expense of American strategic reserves stationed elsewhere in the world. The army had been depleted and General Wheeler was intent upon rebuilding army troop strength. To do so, Wheeler persuaded Westmoreland to

ask for 206,000 additional troops. While most of these troops would never be used in Vietnam, Westmoreland implied that he needed them.

The Westmoreland/Wheeler proposal was reviewed by Johnson's staff to see how it could be implemented. It soon became apparent that the consequences of implementation were unacceptable. An additional 206,000 troops would require a call-up of the reserves, cost an additional ten billion dollars, sacrifice domestic programs, strain the dollar internationally, and lead to massive public protests. While the President pondered his options, Clifford worked to change the policy. "I was convinced," Schandler quotes Clifford as recalling, "that the military course we were pursuing was not only endless, but hopeless."

Rather than listening to Clifford, the President heeded the words of Rusk, who favored continued pressure on North Vietnam but recognized that the public demanded some show of conciliation on Washington's part. What emerged was the presidential address of March 31, in which Johnson said he would not run for reelection and that he would institute a partial bombing halt in North Vietnam. Schandler maintains that the speech did not represent a change in administration policy. Rusk had convinced the President, Schandler argues, that the North Vietnamese would not respond to this demonstration of American moderation by agreeing to enter into peace talks. Thus, Rusk reasoned, full-scale bombing could be resumed and justified on the basis of Hanoi's intransigence. Schandler contends that Rusk and Johnson both assumed the war would continue just as it had.

At this point, Clark Clifford brought about a fundamental change in policy, not by challenging the President but simply by interpreting him to the public. Schandler argues that when a high government official says something often enough without presidential contradiction, what he says becomes policy. Clifford "launched a deliberate public campaign . . . to interpret the president's decisions in the way he felt they should be interpreted." He emphasized in public statements that the policy of the Johnson Administration was Vietnamization of the war or turning over the fighting to the Vietnamese. It was the message the American people wanted to hear and it became policy.

Schandler shows that had it not been for Clark Clifford, Vietnamization and the American withdrawal from Vietnam probably would not have been established at that time. However, Schandler overlooks one aspect of Clifford's attitude toward Vietnam. Though Clifford was the leading dove within the Johnson Administration, he did not favor withdrawal from Vietnam but victory in Vietnam through Vietnamization and negotiation. As events were to prove, defeat of Hanoi was just as illusory through Vietnamization of the war as it was through Americanization.

Braestrup, Peter. *Big Story: How the American Press and Television Reported and Interpreted the Crisis of Tet 1968 in Vietnam and Washington.* Boulder, Colo.: Westview Press, 1977.

Failure of the American effort in Indochina has naturally resulted in people asking what went wrong and who is to blame. One target of post-Vietnam criticism has been the news media whose reports helped to mold a public opinion which was against the war. The Tet offensive is a good case study of news media coverage because of its limited scope and its importance as a turning point in the war.

The author, Peter Braestrup, was himself a veteran Vietnam reporter who took pains to interview his colleagues rather than merely write about them. The book, in fact, is dedicated to the foreign journalists who were lost in Vietnam between 1961 and 1975. What emerges, then, is a thoughtful though highly critical account of crisis journalism. In a stinging conclusion, Braestrup asserts that only rarely has crisis reporting veered as widely from reality as during the Tet offensive. As a result, the picture given to the American people was far darker than the events called for, at least the picture portrayed by those news organizations with which Braestrup deals: the *New York Times*, the *Washington Post, Time, Newsweek,* the Associated Press, the United Press International, and the three television networks, ABC, NBC, and CBS.

Braestrup's major complaint is that American journalists focused on and reported the most dramatic and destructive aspects of the enemy offensive and thus failed to give a balanced picture. Hanoi suffered a military defeat during Tet, but American reporters spoke of an American defeat. Psychologically, Braestrup concludes, Hanoi also suffered a defeat but American reporters jumped to the conclusion that the opposite was true. Similarly, the reporters concentrated on the areas of greatest destruction. If five percent of Saigon was in flames then that was the only portion covered, not the ninety-five percent that was left unmolested. When the delta city of Ben Tre was destroyed by American fire power the story was covered extensively, but when mass graves of Vietnamese executed by Viet Cong were uncovered at Hue, there was little American press coverage. As a result of this biased reporting, a thick black fog of disaster hung over press and television accounts of the Tet fighting.

Braestrup blames this bad reporting on reporters' hostility toward the Johnson Administration, their inability to analyze or synthesize, and the mass media dictum of "keep it simple." The journalists' hostility was not ideological, Braestrup contends, but simply the result of reporters believing that they were being manipulated when they reported administration assurances that progress was being made in Vietnam and the war was being won. The Tet offensive seemed to prove that the generals had been deceiving them and that the situation was as bad as they had suspected. As a result, reporters saw in Tet what they wanted to see, an American defeat, and they reported what they saw.

Braestrup's more fundamental criticism strikes at the nature of the news business. American news organizations had staffed their Vietnam bureaus with young, adventurous people who had been trained to report simple, dramatic spot news. Yet Tet was a complicated battle in a complicated war. It required the synthesis and analysis which could come only from the type of skilled journalist who was not sent to Vietnam. The mass media provided the masses with dramatic pictures and words but not a clear understanding of what was happening.

These criticisms are thoughtful and reasonable. But many of Braestrup's criticisms stem not from journalistic standards but from his different perspective. Braestrup's focus is military while most of the reporters were concerned with political matters. Militarily, Tet was a defeat for Hanoi. But politically the Tet offensive showed that the war would last for a long time, and that fact was a political victory for Hanoi. When Walter Cronkite concluded that Tet was an American defeat he was wrong only from Braestrup's military perspective; Cronkite was right when he said that Tet demonstrated that the United States was "mired in stalemate."

Similarly, Braestrup's experience as a combat soldier in Korea has hardened him to the "waste and destruction" of war. He is correct when he states that Tet brought many reporters face to face with the horrors of war, and this experience colored their reports. But perhaps Braestrup misses the point. The big story coming out of Tet may not have been military victory or defeat but that modern technological war had become more barbarous, more destructive, more debased in all its aspects until, in the words of an army major at Ben Tre, "it became necessary to destroy the town to save it." — *J.G.U.*

Additional Recommended Reading

Herr, Michael. *Dispatches*. New York: Alfred A. Knopf, 1977. The author's personal account of the Vietnam War, which he covered for *Esquire* magazine during 1967 and 1968.

Hoopes, Townsend. *The Limits of Intervention*. New York: David McKay Company, 1969. The account of a former Assistant Secretary of the Air Force who became disenchanted with America's involvement in Vietnam.

Mueller, John E. *War, Presidents and Public Opinion*. New York: John Wiley and Sons, 1973. Examines the public reaction to the Korean and Vietnamese wars with considerable emphasis upon plotting the data coming from public opinion polls.

Oberdorfer, Don. *Tet!* Garden City, N.Y.: Doubleday & Company, 1971. A journalist's account of the Tet offensive.

Shaplen, Robert. *The Road from War: Vietnam, 1965-1970*. New York: Harper & Row Publishers, 1970. Reprint of twenty-two Vietnam dispatches with a postscript.

Westmoreland, William C. *A Soldier Reports*. Garden City, N.Y.: Doubleday & Company, 1976. The memoirs of the Commander of United States troops in Vietnam.

DEATH OF FRANCO AND THE RESTORATION OF THE MONARCHY

Type of event: Political: dictator names King as his successor and the King holds free elections
Time: July 12, 1968-June 15, 1977
Locale: Spain

Principal personages:

FRANCISCO FRANCO (1892-1975), Dictator of Spain, 1939-1975

DON JUAN, son of King Alfonso XIII, Count of Barcelona and the heir apparent to the Spanish throne

JUAN CARLOS (1938-   ), the son of Don Juan who was selected by Franco to be King instead of his father

MUÑOZ GRANDES, Vice-President of the Government until 1967 and Franco's most likely successor if the monarchy were not restored

LUIS CARRERO BLANCO, a Franco confidant who replaced Franco himself as Prime Minister in 1973

CARLOS ARIAS NAVARRO, appointed Prime Minister after Carrero Blanco's assassination

ADOLFO SUÁREZ GONZÁLEZ (1932-   ), first democratically selected Prime Minister of the post-Franco period

FELIPE GONZÁLEZ, leader of the Socialist Workers Party (PSOE) which finished a surprisingly strong second in the 1977 election

Summary of Event

After the chaos of the Spanish Civil War, Spain found itself in 1939 under the domination of a repressive, Fascist regime led by General Francisco Franco. Despite continual challenges, Franco died still in power on November 20, 1975. In retrospect, we can see that the years immediately before his death prepared the way for King Juan Carlos' attempt to guide Spain toward parliamentary democracy.

As a matter of fact, as early as 1947, Franco had officially turned Spain into a monarchy again, but he neglected to name a king. In the late 1960's, when he experimented with a policy of liberalization, he found that he had unleashed the forces which the economic development of the previous decade had created, and he felt compelled to withdraw concessions and revert to harsh repressive measures. It was in this context that Franco, who was already seventy-six years old in 1968, began to deal seriously with the need to name a successor and to prepare Spain for his own inevitable departure.

The obvious claimant to the throne was Don Juan, Count of Barcelona, whose father, King Alfonso XIII, had

1043

abdicated in 1931. Franco never seriously considered Don Juan for the throne because of his liberal political views and the contacts between his political circle and the opponents of the regime. Franco's Constitution, restoring the monarchy in 1947, had required that whoever was nominated to be the future king must be at least 30 years old. Don Juan's son, Don Juan Carlos, celebrated his thirtieth birthday on January 5, 1968. He had been educated in the state's military academies and seemed far more likely to preside over the desired "Francoism without Franco."

Franco first indicated his choice in a most indirect fashion. On July 12, 1968, a decree proclaimed that the heir to the throne would be second only to the head of state at all official ceremonies. Also in July, Don Juan Carlos was at Franco's side during a naval week ceremony at Santander. On July 21, 1969, Franco announced to his cabinet that he was about to nominate Juan Carlos as his successor, which he did on the following day.

By this time, the Spanish Cortes, or parliament, was the most democratic it had been under Franco. In 1967, for the first time, 108 out of the nearly 600 members of the Cortes were directly elected by the Spanish people. More exactly, they were safely elected by the properly conservative elements, "family heads and married women." In 1967 also, a so-called Organic Law (*Ley Organica*) was passed containing many provisions designed to come into operation with the death of Franco and guide Spain at the start of the post-Franco era.

These actions were the first modest steps from a frankly totalitarian regime to a modern parliamentary one. Juan Carlos has since attempted to take further steps in that direction, including the convocation, in October of 1976 under a Law of Reform, of a directly elected Cortes which has been given the duty of acting as a new constituent assembly as well.

Franco attempted to provide for the future in another way. On July 28, 1967, he removed his long-time loyal follower Captain-General Muñoz Grandes from the position of Vice-President of the Government. The Vice-President was the automatic stand-in for the head of government, Franco, in times of incapacity and was widely viewed as his likely successor. Since he would probably not, therefore, be happy with the decision to name a successor to the throne and thereby make concrete the likely restoration of the monarchy, Franco replaced him as Vice-President with long-time companion and Minister Secretary to the Presidency, Admiral Luis Carrero Blanco. In June, 1973, he went one step further. Admiral Carrero Blanco replaced Franco himself as Prime Minister. This further attempt to provide for a smooth transition to the post-Franco era was foiled when Basque terrorists killed Carrero in December of 1973.

After Carrero's death, Carlos Arias Navarro became Prime Minister. Despite Arias' earlier reputation, he presided over a period of liberalization for Franco and, after Franco's death in November, 1975, for King Juan Carlos. In July of 1976, however, Juan Carlos asserted himself by asking for the resignation of Arias and by appointing Adolfo Suárez

González as his prime minister.

In September of 1976, the right-wing General Fernández de Santiago was forced to resign his position as Vice-President of government for national security. His replacement was a liberal, Lieutenant General Gutiérrez Mellado.

In October of 1976, Spain adopted a Law for the Reform of the Cortes that provided for a directly elected democratic Assembly and Senate, whose only nondemocratic feature was that about eighteen percent of the Senators were to be chosen by the King. In preparation for parliamentary elections, the last of the major political parties, the Spanish Communist Party (PCE), was legalized in April of 1977. Elections were held June 15, 1977; they were the first free Spanish elections in more than forty years. The elections resulted in a democratic mandate for Suárez to continue as Prime Minister at the head of a new political party, the Union of the Democratic Center (UDC).

The big surprise, however, was the Socialist Workers Party (PSOE) of Felipe González, which finished a very strong second. If the Socialist Workers make further electoral advances before parliamentarianism is well established, the remarkable transition, begun in the period before Franco's death and accelerated since, may be brought to an abrupt halt by military intervention. Subsequently, the successful adoption of a new constitution in December, 1976, and the Socialist Workers' failure to gain in the second free election held in March of 1979, have served to dispel some of these fears. The new institutions are fragile and beset by many problems, ranging from the continued importance of Franco's military and *Guardia Nacional*, to the continued terrorist activity of Basque separatists, to the recent economic problems associated with stagflation and a decline of tourism. It is too soon to say for certain what the final legacy of this period will be, but developments in the last years before Franco's death and the first years after the restoration of the monarchy have ensured that there will be no return to the Fascist forms of early Francoism.

Pertinent Literature

Gallo, Max. *Spain Under Franco: A History*. Translated by Jean Stewart. New York: E. P. Dutton, 1974.

One of the great difficulties in understanding the significance of Franco's death is that so little in the way of comprehensive in-depth study of the Franco regime is available. By contrast, the Spanish Civil War which spawned the Franco regime has been studied in exhaustive detail. With the survivors of the Civil War in exile around the world, it was far easier to study that period than to analyze an existing authoritarian regime which did not wish to be studied objectively. As a result, whatever its limitations, we have reason to be grateful for the existence of Max Gallo's *Spain Under Franco: A History*. Since it is in fact a thorough, comprehensive, well-researched effort, we have reason to be doubly grateful.

Gallo's credentials for undertaking a study of this kind are excellent. For one thing, he has taught at the Institute of Political Studies in Paris. Also, he has been a regular contributor of articles on contemporary political affairs to the newspaper *L'Express*. Finally, his own Doctor of Letters degree was awarded for studies of Italian Fascism and other totalitarian regimes.

Perhaps the strongest message of Gallo's book is that an enormous gap exists between the Spain which Franco took over in 1939 and the Spain which he handed over to Juan Carlos. Spain had been as backward as Turkey and Greece and as much an underdeveloped country as most of its former colonies in the Americas. Its socioeconomic structure seemed the proper counterpart to a fairly old-fashioned authoritarian regime. By 1966, however, yearly income per capita had surpassed the five-hundred-dollar threshold into the "take-off" stage to modernity. The Spanish gross national product had more than doubled since the advent of the Franco regime. Spain's problems were no longer so much like those of the underdeveloped Third World, but more like those of most other European countries. Gallo's analysis of the Franco era enables the reader to understand why Juan Carlos had to attempt to preserve his crown by launching on the perilous path of liberalization, constitutional monarchy, and parliamentary democracy. Gallo himself, however, does not anticipate this development. Instead, he greatly overestimates the durability of Franco's apparatus and anticipates its continued entrenchment after his death.

Gallo focuses on the very successful *desarrollo*, or development plan, instituted by the Franco regime in the mid-1960's. The Franco regime's propaganda machinery saw to it that the *Caudillo* received credit for all aspects of improved economic well-being. Although the new prosperity was unevenly distributed, Gallo views the middle-class families in the under-forty generation as basically satisfied with the Franco regime and with their own lives. However, it was that very prosperity which created more modern political expectations among the middle class. It drew the conservative peasantry, long a source of support for the regime, out of the countryside and into the cities, where they became more susceptible to the appeals of the urban-based working-class parties. Increased international trade led the middle class into contacts with other countries where Spanish political institutions were not admired. Finally, the unprecedented influx of tourists accelerated the processes of social and economic change and the rate at which Spaniards encountered modern political values.

Indeed, the Franco regime itself recognized the new expectations. It was no longer a completely rigid political anachronism. The thorough censorship of the past was somewhat modified. The writings of Karl Marx and Fidel Castro began to be available in Spain. After having rigidly suppressed the regional languages for decades, the Franco regime suddenly proclaimed that it felt unthreatened by provincial idioms. In response, everything from James Bond to Jean-Paul Sartre appeared in Catalan translation.

While Gallo recounts these developments, he is misled by the periodic reinvigoration of repression and by the regime's ability to survive all past opposition movements into believing that the same essential forces would continue to dominate Spain after Franco's death. Nevertheless, his book remains a thorough and reliable account of a basically underrecorded yet extremely important period in Spanish history.

Meisler, Stanley. "Spain's New Democracy," in *Foreign Affairs*. LVI (1977), pp. 190-208.

In the absence of any book-length treatments of the post-Franco era, this long article in *Foreign Affairs* is the best available sustained treatment of the experiment with constitutional monarchy and parliamentary democracy being presided over by King Juan Carlos. The article was written by Stanley Meisler, who has been stationed for some time in Spain as a foreign correspondent for the *Los Angeles Times*.

In Meisler's view, the post-Franco era can be treated as a two-stage process of democratic reform. In the first stage, already successfully completed, a return to an open electoral process was engineered by King Juan Carlos and Premier Adolfo Suárez. With the immediate procedural problems largely resolved, Spain must face the substantive problems left as an unresolved legacy from Franco.

The first stage does not truly begin with Franco's death on November 20, 1975. Rather, it begins with a speech King Juan Carlos made to the United States Congress on June 2, 1976. In that speech Juan Carlos promised that "the monarchy will ensure, under the principles of democracy . . . the orderly access to power of distinct political alternatives, in accordance with the freely expressed will of the people."

The first step in implementing that promise was the replacement of Franco's last premier with King Juan Carlos' own choice. In July of 1976, the King appointed as his premier Adolfo Suárez, a fairly obscure technocrat who had been a minor but loyal Francoist.

Just as Franco had preferred Juan Carlos to his father for the crown because Juan Carlos was not a threatening symbol of the opposition to the old-fashioned, hard-line Francoists, so too did Juan Carlos prefer Suárez to other better-known but more threatening figures. It was a curious situation. Neither man had shown any interest in reform while Franco was still alive. Both were fastidiously loyal. Yet neither was associated with the struggles that shaped the dictatorial, inflexible figures on which Franco based his regime in its early years. They were, on the other hand, reliable enough in the eyes of conservatives. They were not expected to let things get out of hand. Suárez had actually been the minister in charge of Franco's National Movement, the party which officially represented the popular or mass arm of the regime.

Nevertheless, it was these two who presided over an extraordinary process in the next eleven months. They started by persuading Franco's hand-picked Cortes to pass a Political Reform Act which literally replaced itself. The Act provided for elections to a new bicameral Cortes. All 350 members of the lower house were to be elected by a system of proportional representation. In the upper house, 207 members would be elected by a plurality system, and an additional forty-one would be appointed by the King. The new Cortes was given the power also to act as a constituent assembly and write a new constitution.

The Political Reform Act was just one of several major changes. Franco's National Movement was actually abolished. All of the other forbidden political parties were legalized. On April 9, 1977, Suárez took the final step when he legalized the Communist party.

Juan Carlos and Suárez should not get all the credit for engineering a successful transition, however. The leftist parties also deserve credit for accepting an electoral law that Suárez promulgated by decree which favored rural conservative areas and was also biased strongly against the smaller parties. The Spanish people also deserve much credit for giving so little support to the Popular Alliance which wished to preserve the essence of the Franco regime. Free elections were held in June, 1977. When the election results were in, Suárez had led a Union of the Democratic Center, dedicated to having the Cortes write a democratic constitution, to a ma-jority of seats in the Senate and a near majority in the Congress of Deputies. Much to the surprise of most observers, the runner-up party was not supplied by the political right but by the political left. The Socialist Workers Party of Felipe González had won a third of the seats in the Congress of Deputies. Fortunately for Spain and the fragile democracy the King was nurturing, the Socialist Workers Party did no better. Neither the King nor the military was yet ready to accept a victory for any party on the left.

The election, at least, marked the successful completion of the first stage of the democratic reform—"the tearing down of the most obvious Fascist institutions bequeathed by the *Caudillo*." The second stage will be more difficult. Spain must become democratic enough to permit the continuance of representative institutions after the victory of *any* political party.

If that day is to come, the King must somehow persuade the military to take on a modern defense mission and abandon its Franco-mandated role as the ultimate repository of political sovereignty and responsibility for order and stability. The Suárez government will also need to gain control over the police, trained under Franco and still likely to treat the populace like unruly subjects rather than dignified citizens exercising their legitimate political rights. Finally, the government must somehow deal with regional demands for autonomy. Thus far the Suárez government has shown great insensitivity toward the national aspirations of the Basques and Catalans.

Meisler seems to feel that a Spain which handles all of these problems successfully can hope to become and remain fully democratic. Unfortunately, more recent problems, like the quadrupling of the price of oil, the decline in tourism, rising unemployment, and galloping inflation, pose greater threats for a fledgling democracy than for the more established democracies of Europe that are being sorely tested by them. Meisler's cautious assessment of the future prognosis for Spanish democracy may yet turn out to have been too optimistic. — *B.F.*

Additional Recommended Reading

Salisbury, William T. and James D. Theberge, eds. *Spain in the 1970's: Economics, Social Structure, Foreign Policy*. New York: Frederick A. Praeger, 1976. A useful collection of essays written before Franco's death.

Preston, Paul, ed. *Spain in Crisis: The Evolution and Decline of the Franco Regime*. New York: Barnes and Noble, 1976. Another set of attempts to anticipate the future, also written before Franco's death.

Trythall, J. W. D. *El Caudillo: A Political Biography of Franco*. New York: McGraw-Hill Book Company, 1976. The best available biography of Franco.

Thomas, Hugh. *The Spanish Civil War*. New York: Harper & Row Publishers, 1977. A thorough account of the tragic conflict.

Payne, Stanley G. *Falange: A History of Spanish Fascism*. Stanford, Calif.: Stanford University Press, 1961. A detailed history of Franco's political movement, from the Civil War through the early years of the Franco regime.

Amodia, J. *Franco's Political Legacy: From Dictatorship to Facade Democracy*. Totowa, N.J.: Rowman and Littlefield, 1977. A critical account of the changes in the later years of the Franco period.

DÉTENTE WITH THE SOVIET UNION

Type of event: Diplomatic: attempted changes in United States policy towards the Soviet Union
Time: 1969 to the present
Locale: The United States, Vietnam, the People's Republic of China, and the Soviet Union

Principal personages:
HENRY ALFRED KISSINGER (1923-   ), Special Assistant for National Security Affairs, 1969-1973; United States Secretary of State, 1973-1977
RICHARD MILHOUS NIXON (1913-   ), thirty-seventh President of the United States, 1969-1974
LEONID ILICH BREZHNEV (1906-   ), First Secretary of the Communist Party of the U.S.S.R., 1964-
MAO TSE-TUNG (1893-1976), Chairman of the Chinese Communist Party, 1949-1976
JIMMY (JAMES EARL) CARTER (1924-   ), thirty-ninth President of the United States, 1977-

Summary of Event

The world of diplomacy has undergone fundamental changes during the twentieth century, including a steady and dramatic reduction in the number of true world powers. In the year 1900, the power bases in world politics were multipolar; Germany, Austria-Hungary, Tsarist Russia, Great Britain, France, and the United States were all engaged in empire-building. Similarly, between the two world wars, Nazi Germany, Japan, Great Britain, and the temporarily isolationist United States occupied prominent positions as world powers. World War II, however, narrowed the field effectively to two major world powers—the United States and the Soviet Union—thus marking the advent of a bipolar world after 1945.

Bipolarism dominated the diplomacy of the Cold War years following World War II. Though the Soviet Union under Joseph Stalin's regime had been allied with the United States and Britain during the war, it was clear to most contemporaries of the war years that the alliance was a "marriage of convenience." At war's end, the world split into two basic camps, one allied with the Soviet Union, one with the United States. Tension increased markedly as the Communist bloc expanded by force in Eastern Europe and China. By the 1950's, the Cold War had erupted into a real conflict in Korea (1951-1953) and in the alignment of the North Atlantic Treaty Alliance (NATO) and the Warsaw Pact military alliances. Both sides ultimately were backed by the awesome power of nuclear weapons.

The Cold War with its periodic military outbursts (The Bay of Pigs, Laos, Vietnam) has been characterized by massive military expenditures on both sides of the conflict throughout the 1950's and 1960's. This arms race has been the most massive in all of human history. The Soviet Union has given top social and economic priorities to military spending through these decades, at the obvious expense of civilian, consumer-oriented production. At the same time, the United States has given its own top priority to defense expenditures, at the consistent expense of pressing social needs. This has led to recent attempts by both Soviet and American leaders to affect a *rapprochement—détente—* since the late 1960's. The primary aim of this policy has been to reduce the arms race and military tension in the world between the United States and the U.S.S.R. The *détente* policy, however, has shown limited success up to the present. The fundamental assumptions of the Cold War, founded on basic mistrust, prevail to this day. Any concessions by one side or the other have been viewed from the framework of national rather than mutual interest. Herein lies the greatest weakness of *détente* so far.

The first active application of the *détente* policy originated during the presidency of Richard M. Nixon. Though Nixon clearly initiated the policy, detailed negotiations were the work of Henry A. Kissinger, the key diplomatic figure of the Nixon presidency. Kissinger came to the Administration from an academic background. A German-Jewish refugee from Nazi Germany, Kissinger had fully assimilated himself through the United States Army and as a student and faculty member at Harvard. While at Harvard, Kissinger gradually de-

veloped into an activist scholar who would seek to influence foreign policy with his theory. He came to the public limelight through a friendship with Nelson Rockefeller. Based on his loyalty to Richard Nixon once he entered Nixon's Administration, Kissinger clearly came to dominate the foreign policy of the Nixon years, both as National Security Adviser and as Secretary of State.

A crucial point in approaching *détente* was that Nixon and Kissinger both had excellent "credentials" of a sort in redirecting American policy towards the U.S.S.R. Both were definitive conservatives and archfoes of Communism. If a liberal Democratic administration had proposed *détente* in earlier decades, they surely would have faced a massive Cold War onslaught in public opinion. Liberals, in effect, could not push for Soviet-American agreements without suffering in the wake. Conservatives such as Nixon, on the other hand, could strike up negotiations with the Russians without fanning domestic fears that he was "soft on Communism."

The key concept launched by Kissinger and carried through even to the presidency of Jimmy Carter has been the insistence of the United States on *linkage* in any agreements with the U.S.S.R. Linkage means that any trade agreement, exchange program, credits—in effect, *any* concession to the U.S.S.R.—must be accompanied by (linked to) changes in Soviet policy. During the Kissinger years, the United States insisted on the elimination of ideology from Soviet foreign policy decisions—a vain hope. In negotiating the first Strategic Arms Limitation Treaties (SALT

I and II), the United States used its improved relations with Chairman Mao Tse-tung's China as leverage with Brezhnev's negotiators. In addition, the United States clearly obtained Soviet aid in ending the Vietnam War through negotiations by tying the negotiations to SALT's prospects.

In more recent years the United States has linked ties with the Soviets to human rights for peoples in the Soviet sphere; this linkage has had limited impact thus far. Despite the Helsinki Accords, Soviet suppression of dissidents continues unabated. President Carter's policy upholding and reaffirming human rights has been erratic and ineffective. Linkage, the cornerstone of *détente*, has been a failure. Clearly the Soviet Union has not and will not eliminate ideological considerations in the conduct of both its domestic and foreign policies. The concessions of *détente*, therefore, from the American viewpoint, have been a one-way street.

Pertinent Literature

LaFeber, Walter. *America, Russia, and the Cold War, 1945-1975*. New York: John Wiley and Sons, 1975.

Walter LaFeber is one of the leading diplomatic historians of the Cold War period. He teaches diplomatic history at Cornell University. This volume is part of a larger series of works in diplomatic history—"America in Crisis," edited by Robert A. Divine. The volume under consideration is singularly important for anyone interested in the Cold War and limited *détente*. It has run through three editions because of its extensive use as a text in college- and university-level history and political science courses.

LeFeber is one of the revisionist historians of the Cold War, and as such, he takes a much more evenhanded view of Cold War history than have many previous authors. He properly traces back the roots of the Cold War and of mutual Russian-American mistrust to the Bolshevik Revolution and to the American intervention in the Russian Civil War on behalf of the counter-revolutionary White Army. In his treatment, readers can follow the course of the Cold War years, with all of the nuances, through to the present stage of limited *détente*.

More than anything else, the longevity of Soviet-American mistrust militates against any quick reconciliation between Soviet and American interests. This is a comprehensive, well-documented, well-written account of a war of nerves that is yet to be resolved. LaFeber has produced a rare, objective account of Soviet-American relations.

Mazlish, Bruce. *Kissinger*. New York: Basic Books, 1976.

Bruce Mazlish is a Harvard historian (post-Kissinger in terms of Harvard's faculty) and an expert in the growing field of psychohistory. Psychohistory has involved, in recent years, the application of psychoanalytic analysis to important historical personages. In this book, Mazlish applies these techniques to Henry Kissinger.

There are distinct limits to Mazlish's book. First of all, the author does not know Henry Kissinger personally. Mazlish claims that this gives him greater objectivity in dealing with Kissinger's career since he has not been influenced by Kissinger's personal wit and charm. Yet Mazlish, had he interviewed Kissinger, would have strengthened his psychohistory immeasurably. One of the major criticisms of psychohistory is that psychoanalysis as a scientific mode of analysis is founded on information furnished by a living subject, while psychohistorians studying long-dead subjects, such as Adolf Hitler, are forced to "read back" their analysis through secondary and far from complete records. Mazlish has thus unnecessarily denied himself his most valuable source of information for a study such as this.

In any case, the book does provide coverage of Kissinger's career from childhood onward. Mazlish supplies a good portrait of Kissinger's childhood years, the trials of emigration, and the adaptations Kissinger made to American life. There is good descriptive coverage of Kissinger's academic career and accomplishments, followed by his career as a foreign policy activist. The relationship, often tentative, between Henry Kissinger and Richard Nixon is given impressive coverage also. Yet the whole is a mixture of factual information spun around a dubious psychohistorical approach. — *E.A.Z.*

Additional Recommended Reading

Kissinger, Henry A. *American Foreign Policy*. New York: W. W. Norton and Company, 1969. Kissinger's thought at first hand.

Nixon, Richard M. *RN: The Memoirs of Richard Nixon*. New York: Grosset and Dunlap, 1978. The sections on foreign policy and *détente* are the strongest points of Nixon's autobiography.

Landau, David. *Kissinger: The Uses of Power*. Boston: Houghton Mifflin Company, 1972. Sympathetic biography of Kissinger by a colleague and friend.

Kalb, Marvin and Bernard Kalb. *Kissinger*. Boston: Little, Brown and Company, 1974. Excellent journalistic account of Kissinger diplomacy, giving much detail on *détente*.

STRATEGIC ARMS LIMITATION TALKS (SALT) WITH THE SOVIET UNION

Type of event: Diplomatic: efforts to impose limits on strategic weapons
Time: 1969 to the present
Locale: The United States, the Soviet Union, and Europe

Principal personages:

RICHARD MILHOUS NIXON (1913-   ), thirty-seventh President of the United States, 1969-1974

GERALD RUDOLPH FORD (1913-   ), thirty-eighth President of the United States, 1974-1977

JIMMY (JAMES EARL) CARTER (1924-   ), thirty-ninth President of the United States, 1977-

HENRY ALFRED KISSINGER (1923-   ), Special Assistant for National Security Affairs, 1969-1973; United States Secretary of State, 1973-1977; American negotiator, SALT I, who helped prepare the way for SALT II

CYRUS ROBERTS VANCE (1917-   ), United States Secretary of State from 1977 and chief American negotiator, SALT II

LEONID ILICH BREZHNEV (1906-   ), First Secretary of the Communist Party of the Soviet Union, 1964-   ; and President of the Presidium of the Supreme Soviet, 1977-

ANDREI A. GROMYKO (1909-   ), Soviet Foreign Minister and arms negotiator

ANATOLY FEDOROVICH DOBRYNIN (1919-   ), Soviet Ambassador to the United States and arms negotiator

Summary of Event

The Strategic Arms Limitation Talks (SALT) must be understood as part of a process which, it is hoped, will eventually lead to world disarmament. Not that the SALT negotiations concern world disarmament: they are between two nations only—the Soviet Union and the United States—and they are not about all weapons, but only some nuclear weapons—those with an intercontinental range. The tactical nuclear arsenal (short-range weapons used in the battlefield) is not part of the negotiations at all. Nor are conventional (nonnuclear) weapons, all of which are presently tactical. In addition, SALT negotiations are not designed to eliminate even strategic weapons, but only to control their accumulation. Seen from this point of view, it might appear that the SALT talks lack real significance since their goals are specific and limited—if it were not for the awesome power of the weapons they discuss. A war that unleashed such weapons would last not years, but hours, and would end with both warring powers equally and vastly crippled.

1054

To deliver the atomic warheads of these frightening weapons, the United States and the Soviet Union have different systems which emphasize divergent priorities. The Americans have a system consisting of three components, a triad. The first component is the Intercontinental Ballistic Missile (ICBM), essentially a rocket launched from a concrete silo where it is stored. These missiles are or can be MIRVed (a reference to multiple independently targetable re-entry vehicles); that is, they can be fitted with multiple nuclear warheads which are individually targetable. The second American nuclear component is an intercontinental bomber force capable of delivering atomic bombs to the heart of the Soviet Union. This delivery system is considerably slower than the first, which is perhaps its advantage; bombers can be called back. The third component of the American force is the Submarine Launched Ballistic Missile (SLBM), which, although it is being improved, is not yet as accurate as the ICBM. SLBM's can also be MIRVed. They have the considerable advantage of being launched from platforms that move about in the open seas and are therefore much less vulnerable to attack than the stationary ICBM's or the slow-moving, exposed bombers. In addition, since SALT I, the Americans have developed a "cruise missile," essentially a pilotless plane that can be fitted with an atomic warhead. Finally, the United States has tactical weapons located in NATO countries. These conceivably could be targeted toward and could be a danger to the Soviet Union.

The Soviets do not have bombers as part of their strategic forces, but the United States has questioned the Soviet Backfire Bomber, calling it a strategic weapon because its one-way range includes the United States. So far, for strategic offense the Soviets have relied heavily on very large ICBM's which can also be MIRVed; they have enormous "throw-weight" (roughly equivalent to explosive force), but relatively poor accuracy, unlike American weapons which emphasize accuracy over "throw-weight." In addition, the Soviets have SLBM's that can be MIRVed, but their submarines are of poorer quality than the American ones. Furthermore, because of Soviet geography, the Russians need fifty percent more submarines than the United States to keep an equal number at sea.

Since the Soviets and the Americans have different weapons systems with divergent priorities, the concept of "parity," or equal force on both sides, becomes elusive. Is one American strategic bomber equal to one Soviet ICBM? No one really knows, since none of these weapons has been tried under actual combat conditions. Which is the more effective, Soviet power or American accuracy? Against cities, Soviet power is the more effective; against missile sites, American weapons have greater accuracy. Under such circumstances, parity can be questioned as a useful concept. In preventing an atomic war, it is probably the ability to retaliate after a preemptory first strike by the enemy that is the key. If this retaliation is sufficient to inflict unacceptable damage, what hostile power will strike first? Nevertheless, parity, however useless it may be as a military concept, has some use as a political counter. SALT I gave the Soviets more weapons with intercontinental range than the Americans. After SALT I there was a feeling that the Americans had sold out and that equality of weaponry was the only acceptable negotiating position. Here the argument was merely political: any other position interfered with American credibility as a super-power.

Talk about parity inevitably brings up the crucial matter of the theories of safety in a nuclear world. The first, and initially the most appealing, theory is that of "damage limitation." Certainly in a conventional war—and all previous wars were by definition conventional—it makes sense for a belligerent to protect its civilian population as well as its military forces. Over the long run, this insures its continued capacity to wage war, its morale, and its nationhood. In an all-out atomic war it still makes sense to protect military might for the retaliatory second strike that would inflict unacceptable damage on an enemy so foolhardy as to strike first. However, the protection of civilians is—in the view of the currently dominant theorists—"destabilizing." If a nation feels that a substantial part of its citizenry can survive a retaliatory second strike, then it might very well strike first. Only when both hostile nations feel sure that their citizens are wholly exposed to nuclear annihilation in the event of atomic attack will neither nation be willing to risk a first strike. This is called the doctrine of "assured destruction." To the theorists, this "balance of terror" offers the only peace possible in a nuclear age.

Whatever theories are espoused and whatever agreements are reached on the basis of these theories, there must be a means of monitoring compliance; this is the vexing problem of verification. For a long time, the United States and the Soviet Union disagreed on this matter—the Americans insisting on on-site inspection, the Soviets opting for national technical means only. The Soviet view has prevailed. For SALT I this was just as well. National technical means presently consist of satellite overflights and the use of newer, more sensitive, more versatile radars. SALT I concerned the kinds and numbers of weapons and excluded any qualitative improvements from control. Thus, filming the Soviet Union from satellites has proved a sufficient monitoring device. New film and cameras are remarkable, having ground resolutions of one to three feet; the film can be recovered in midair. Information is not only accurate; it is delivered with dispatch.

Finally, then, the matter of trust must be considered. Trust between nations, of course, is not the same as trust between individual human beings; it is more a feeling that a potentially hostile nation will behave rationally, and that rational self-interest and nuclear war are necessarily mutually exclusive. The United States and the Soviet Union, given their divergent historical backgrounds and their opposing political and social beliefs, do not inspire trust in each other. Despite their mutual distrust, however, the two nations began strategic arms limitation negotiations in 1969.

These negotiations, carried on in part by Henry Kissinger, Special Assistant for National Security Affairs and (from 1973) Secretary of State, and Soviet Ambassador to the United States, Anatoly Dobrynin, led to the SALT I agreement which President Richard Nixon and Soviet leader Leonid Brezhnev signed in Moscow on May 26, 1972. Subsequently, on August 3, 1972, the agreement was ratified by the United States Senate. Under SALT I, the United States and the Soviet Union agreed to abort Anti-Ballistic Missile systems designed to defend civilian populations and to freeze the number but not the sophistication of offensive weapons.

Two years later, President Gerald R. Ford and Soviet leader Brezhnev arrived at an understanding at Vladivostok which established basic guidelines for an eventual SALT II agreement. By this accord, both nations agreed to a limitation of no more than 2,400 strategic nuclear delivery systems of all types (including land-based and submarine missiles and bombers), of which no more than 1,320 of the missiles could be MIRVed. But there was a lack of clarity concerning the strategic status of the American Cruise Missile and the Soviet Backfire Bomber. Negotiations therefore continued with Secretary of State Henry Kissinger playing a leading role during the mid-1970's in representing the position of the United States.

Finally, in May, 1979, a SALT II agreement was concluded by Secretary of State Cyrus Vance, the chief negotiator for President Jimmy Carter, and the Soviet representatives, Foreign Minister Andrei Gromyko and Ambassador Anatoly Dobrynin. For both countries SALT II sets a limit of 2,250 strategic nuclear delivery systems of which no more than 1,320 can be MIRVed. It excludes the Soviet Backfire Bomber and certain American airplanes stationed in Europe. Bombers carrying Cruise Missiles are counted as MIRVed ICBM's. The treaty also restricts the number of MIRV's a missile may carry and imposes strict limitations on certain types of testing that are designed to improve delivery and payload. Verification is to be carried out by sophisticated technical means, including space satellites and electronic monitoring. On June 18, 1979, President Carter met with President Brezhnev in Vienna, where they formally signed the SALT II agreement.

It is clear that arms limitation itself is a worthwhile goal. Clearly such limitation reduces the risk of nuclear war by controlling the weapons by which war would be waged. Disarmament may be a preferable goal, but it is not at this time realistic. The "balance of terror," however distasteful, may be the only hope for peace in the near future. Moreover, arms control can do more than prevent wars: at least potentially, it reduces arms expenditures and releases funds for more worthwhile political goals. This result has not yet been achieved; nevertheless, it is obvious that escalation of the arms race is futile. Escalation is always mutual; it is always astronomically expensive; and it never increases mutual security in the slightest. For these reasons, then, the United States and the Soviet Union have pledged under the terms of the SALT II agreement to begin SALT III.

Pertinent Literature

Myrdal, Alva. *The Game of Disarmament: How the United States and Russia Run the Arms Race*. New York: Pantheon Books, 1977.

Alva Myrdal's book is a passionate plea for disarmament by a woman who was Sweden's former Minister of Disarmament and a leader of the neutralist block in the Conference of the Committee on Disarmament, which meets in Geneva. The author places the Strategic Arms Limitation Talks (SALT) in perspective by demonstrating the relationship between those talks and world political tensions, and by placing nuclear disarmament in the context of disarmament as a whole. In addition, *The Game of Disarmament* offers a plan for world disarmament based on Myrdal's years of experience as a negotiator.

Myrdal believes the blame for the escalation of the arms race must be placed squarely on the shoulders of the two superpowers—the United States and the Soviet Union. The title of the book refers to the purported insincerity of the efforts made by these two nations in the cause of disarmament. In this context, the SALT talks institutionalize the arms race rather than promote disarmament. In the first place, the concept of balance in the nuclear arms race makes no sense since both nations have extensive overkill capacity. Second, the emphasis on quantitative weapons control merely shifts national efforts toward qualitative improvement. Thus it makes little sense to limit the number of missiles if technology can increase the number of individually targetable warheads each missile can carry.

The author also attacks the partial nuclear test ban treaty which the United States, Great Britain, and the Soviet Union signed in 1963. She claims that a nuclear test ban is crucial in retarding the development of new weaponry, and she decries current agreements which place kilotonnage limits too high and allow for peaceful nuclear explosions which are of dubious value and cannot, in any case, be differentiated from those explosions used to test the military value of new weapons. Finally, she points out that nonproliferation of nuclear weapons does not work because nuclear materials are so readily available.

No attack on the slow progress of world disarmament negotiations could be complete without a critique of the stalemate in verification procedures. Here is a true point of contention between the United States and the Soviet Union. On the surface, the American contention that on-site inspections are necessary seems reasonable, while the Soviet avoidance of such inspections seems unnecessarily paranoid and obstructive. Although the Soviet position is worthy of criticism, Myrdal feels that American insistence on on-site inspection is misguided. In the first place, on-site inspection is not a very good system of verification; indirect systems such as satellite surveillance are actually better. Furthermore, superpower on-site inspection makes little sense because arms controls should be based on agreements monitored by an international verification agency and not on sanctions meted out by a superpower or the United Nations. If a nation is suspected of not living up to its agreements, it should be challenged and called upon to prove itself not guilty of the alleged violation.

As *The Game of Disarmament* makes clear, disarmament is not only a matter of nuclear weapons, but of all weapons. First, the author deals with conventional weapons, arguing that their continued production makes no economic sense. Second, she discusses cruel weapons such as napalm and dum-dum bullets; the first creates horrible burns, the second horrible wounds. She points out that even in war the purpose is to disable, not to maim the enemy; to destroy his military capability, not his population and countryside. Last, the author deals with biological and chemical weapons. The first are easier to control because they have limited military value. The second have proved more difficult because of their military value and the difficulty of determining whether a chemical is a weapon, since some chemicals have industrial as well as military uses, and others are harmless except in combination with additional chemicals.

The Game of Disarmament is strongest in attacking the alleged irresponsibility of the superpowers in what seems like a suicidal race for supremacy; it is weakest in analyzing the deep-seated causes for this race. To Myrdal, the race is an affront to rational self-interest; therefore, rational counterproposals and the actions of nonaligned, nonnuclear nations can stop it.

Newhouse, John. *Cold Dawn: The Story of SALT*. New York: Holt, Rinehart and Winston, 1973.

Cold Dawn is a masterpiece of diplomatic history. John Newhouse gives the reader an unparalleled objective insight into the complexities of the diplomatic process and negotiations necessarily shrouded in secrecy. In addition, he shows a firm grasp of the theoretical and technical issues. These are two considerable achievements for a topic as monumental and involved as the first round of the Strategic Arms Limitation Talks (SALT) between the United States and the Soviet Union.

Through his historical perspective, Newhouse answers the question of how such an irrational situation as a nuclear arms race came into being. Partly it was a matter of technology becoming an end in itself. First, there was the development of the German V-rockets into the Intercontinental Ballistic Missile (ICBM). Then the missile was fitted with multiple warheads; finally, these warheads were designed to be individually targetable (MIRVed). This sophistication in offense atomic weaponry led to the development of defensive weaponry equally sophisticated: complex and sensitive radars and the Anti-Ballistic Missile (ABM), capable of destroying the ICBM's in midflight. But technical sophistication is only part of the motive force behind the nuclear arms race. There is also the simple and virtually inevitable cycle of action and reaction: when one side develops a new invention, the other side feels obliged to come up with something one step better.

Between technology run wild and action and reaction cycles that became more and more intense, the arms race was clearly getting out of hand. In 1967, the Americans made an overture for arms control talks, but the Soviets were not ready; in 1968, the Soviet invasion of Czechoslovakia forstalled planned talks. It was not until November, 1969, when Richard Nixon consolidated SALT power in the White House, that the negotiations could begin. They were to last for more than two years.

In considering nuclear weapons of tremendous destructive power, the negotiators were faced with the question of what constitutes safety in an unsafe world. The author says that there were two theories. The first—"damage limitation"—was superficially the more reasonable view; it opted for the protection of population and the survival of as much of the nation as possible, and, on the evidence of previous wars, made the most sense. However, according to the currently reigning theorists, "damage limitation" is destabilizing because it creates a need for exotic systems of defense which never give real security. The safest situation, according to these theorists, will exist when the two superpowers are en-

tirely confident that they can completely destroy each other's population; this is called "assured destruction." Even "assured destruction" will not work, however, unless both nations have "second strike" capability: that is, each side must know incontrovertibly that an attack by its enemy would still leave it enough offensive strength to retaliate in equal measure. "Assured destruction" offends the ordinary instincts of human beings, but it is nevertheless the prevailing orthodoxy in arms negotiations and must be understood if SALT is to be understood. The ABM Treaty and the Interim Agreement that were the tangible products of SALT I are virtually meaningless outside of this theoretical context.

Also treated in detail by Newhouse is the actual negotiating process, which really consists of two processes: a front and a back channel. In the front channel were the official SALT negotiations in Finland and Austria, which were necessarily secret. Even more secret, and certainly more important, were the back channel negotiations between Henry Kissinger and Anatoly Dobrynin. These two sets of negotiations were carried on separately until they finally merged in a SALT treaty. Both sets were necessary—the official channel to provide the fullscale of traditional diplomacy, the back channel to add the necessary impetus of personal diplomacy.

The confluence of these channels resulted in the ABM treaty and the Interim Agreement. The basis of the ABM treaty was the orthodoxy that there would be no ABM's defending people and only limited ABM's defending missiles (national capitals were an exception, as a concession to the Soviets). The Interim Agreement put a freeze on the number of offensive weapons, but not on their sophistication. There were to be no exotic systems of defense. Verification of treaty provisions was to be by national technical means, not by inspection. In May, 1972, SALT I was over. Its results were inconclusive; SALT negotiations, like trade negotiations, would be continuous and only intermittently successful. But at least the United States and the Soviet Union had set up the machinery and begun the process of arms control.

— *A.G.G.*

Additional Recommended Reading

Aspin, Les. "SALT or No SALT," in *The Bulletin of the Atomic Scientists*. XXXIV (June, 1978), pp. 34-38. A cogent argument in favor of SALT II.

Drew, Elizabeth. "An Argument over Survival," in *New Yorker*. LIII (April 4, 1977), pp. 99-117. An analysis of the domestic politics behind the SALT negotiations.

Greenwood, Ted. "Reconnaissance and Arms Control," in *Scientific American*. CCXXVIII (February, 1973), pp. 14-25. Provides technical background on the verification controversy.

Lodal, Jan M. "Assuring Strategic Stability: An Alternative View," in *Foreign Affairs*. LIV (April, 1976), pp. 462-481. An introduction to the current controversy on what constitutes safety in a nuclear world.

Ravenal, Earl C. "Toward Nuclear Stability: A Modest Proposal for Avoiding Armageddon," in *Atlantic*. CCXL (September, 1977), pp. 35-41. An interesting proposal for unilateral arms limitations.

Talbott, Strobe. "Who Concealed What to Whom," in *Time*. CXIII (May 21, 1979), pp. 25-35. A comprehensive analysis of the negotiations for SALT II.

THE ECONOMIC CRISIS OF STAGFLATION

Type of event: Economic: predicament of stagnation and inflation affecting economic
stability simultaneously
Time: The 1970's
Locale: The United States

Summary of Event

"Stagflation" is a new word to describe a new phenomenon: simultaneous economic stagnation and inflation. Inflation refers, of course, to rising average prices, and stagnation signifies the economy's inability to increase production at a rate sufficient to put unemployment rates at "normal" levels. Signs of stagflation existed in the 1950's and 1960's, but did not become serious enough to earn a special name until the deep recession (some say depression) of 1974-1975, when double-digit inflation and high unemployment placed many white middle-class suburban families on food stamps. In the mid-1950's, both unemployment and inflation rates had been generally low; from 1958 to 1965 there were high unemployment rates with low inflation rates; then during the remainder of the 1960's, unemployment rates were low again, but inflation was on the rise. Not until the 1970's did the United States fully experience stagflation.

In twenty-three of the twenty-six business cycles before World War II, prices rose in the expansion (cycle trough to cycle peak) and fell in the contraction. The same occurred in the cycle that peaked in 1948. And in all these cycles, unemployment declined during expansions and rose during contractions. The pattern during expansions of declining unemployment with rising prices has continued since 1948; but the pattern during contractions has changed drastically. No longer do prices fall. Indeed, in the deep recession of 1974-1975, prices increased at rates that exceeded those of the preceding expansion.

Worse yet, there has been no compensating reversal in the unemployment pattern: unemployment still goes up during contractions. Thus the officially reported maximum unemployment rate for 1974-1975, occurring in the second quarter of 1975, was 8.8 percent. This level is far from the corresponding figure of about twenty-five percent for the Great Depression. The eight million "unemployed" it stands for may not represent all the truly unemployed, however, for left out are those five million or more discouraged workers who have given up looking for a job and thus are not officially counted in the labor force. Also left out are those nearly four million persons who are, says the Department of Labor, "on part-time schedules for economic reasons." In other words, included in the so-called employed are all those who have part-time jobs only because they cannot get jobs full time. If these part-timers were counted as only half-employed and if only the "hard-core discouraged" workers (those million or more who are no longer looking for work because they think "they cannot get a job") were added, the official rate of unemployment would be some twelve percent. And if a less conservative adjustment were made, the figure would be considerably higher. In any event, to those completely or partly out of work, it matters little whether they are counted or not counted as officially unemployed.

What matters more to those out of work is the impact of inflation. It matters to others too, of course. All those whose pay falls short of the inflation rate lose purchasing power. But not all lose from inflation; nor do all those who do lose, suffer equally. The poor, for example, who spend disproportionately more of their budgets on food, frequently find that food prices rise faster than the average represented by the Consumer Price Index. One dramatic instance of how the CPI can fail to reflect the differential impact of inflation occurred during the first eight months of 1973, when the CPI registered an increase of only 6.6 percent while food prices rose a whopping 18.6 percent. This meant that for the very poor, who spend as much as one-third instead of the average of under one-fourth of their budgets on food, the overall price increase was almost eight percent. More recently, and of more concern to the middle class, during the first half of 1978 the prices for "the basic necessities" rose at an annual rate of 13.2 percent, whereas the CPI was reporting only the lower total rate of 10.4 percent.

Inflation and unemployment, however, are simply manifestations of the underlying economic crisis of the 1970's. Simultaneous inflation and unemployment have wreaked havoc with the traditional Keynesian prescriptions for economic ills. The well-known Phillips Curve plots the inverse relationship, the trade-off if you will, between inflation and unemployment: rates of unemployment above five percent correlate, on the curve, with price deflation, while price inflation exceeds four percent only when unemployment rates go below two percent. And from 1952 to 1967 the facts were reasonably in accord with such predictions. But 1968 and 1969 diverged markedly; and by 1974—when inflation hit 14.6 percent while official unemployment soared to above seven percent—the expected relationship between prices and jobs disappeared completely. Furthermore, according to the assumption expressed in Okun's Law, perpetually high rates of growth are what will maintain or decrease rates of unemployment. A growth rate of four percent would maintain unemployment at a given level, but to reduce it substantially from high levels would require several years of extraordinarily high rates of growth. According to this law, then, current levels of the real Gross National Product (the market value of the nation's total output of wares and services adjusted for inflation) are too low to do the unemployed any good. The Business Council and Conference Board, two major business advisory groups, predicted that the real GNP growth rate, which was slightly under four percent in 1978, would reach only 3.3 percent for 1979—putting the expected official unemployment rate at 6.4 percent, significantly above the 1978 rate. And the administration's more recent prediction for 1979 is an even lower growth rate, about 2.25 percent.

The real crisis behind having exceptionally low growth at just the time when the unemployment rate requires it to be exceptionally high, however, involves the economy's inability to sustain normal stockholder returns on profits without corporations going further and further into debt. The *Economic Report to the President, 1975* (Tables C-37 and C-76) shows that the relationship between rates of profit on stockholder's equity and rates of capacity utilization was different during the expansion of 1971-1973 than what it had been during 1954-1970. The direct relationship remained, but the ratio between both sets of rates changed: profit rates in the early 1970's were at a distinctly higher level *at each level of capacity utilization* than in the earlier period. The problem here is that these higher profit rates occurred while capacity utilization rates were in the seventy-five to eighty-five percent range—a reversal of the early 1950's, when similarly high profit rates were associated with utilization rates of ninety to ninety-five percent. In other words, high profits are not being matched by correspondingly high growth.

This changed relationship reflects the fact that profit rates on stockholders' equity fail to provide a true picture of investment flows and capital productivity. As Secretary William Simon pointed out during his July, 1975, testimony before the House Ways and Means Committee, "A good part of the erosion in profits in recent years has been concealed by what might be called 'public relations bookkeeping.'" Or, as a 1975 *Business Week* article more bluntly stated, "Present financial accounting does not reflect economic reality." What *has* been occurring, in fact, is that normal profit rates have been sustained only by pumping in disproportionately more funds that are borrowed than are obtained from the sale of stocks. Hence, whereas in 1940 the capital invested directly by the owners of all United States corporations (through stock purchases) was twice as much as that invested from long-term debt, bonds, and mortgages, it was only little more than a third as much in 1970. And in terms of the *short*-term debt of non-financial corporations, such debt represented only twelve percent of the GNP originating in such corporations in 1950, but by the first half of 1974 it represented twenty-five percent. Herein lies the real economic crisis behind the stagflation of the 1970's.

Pertinent Literature

Simon, William E. *A Time for Truth.* Preface by Milton Friedman. New York: Reader's Digest Press, 1978.

"A Distinguished Conservative Dissects the Economic and Political Policies that Threaten Our Liberty— and Points the Way to an American Renaissance," proclaims the dust jacket subtitle. Simon, former Secretary of the Treasury, describes himself as a free-market economist in the tradition of Milton Friedman and conveys his unorthodox position with passion. Nevertheless, readers, especially liberal intellectuals, should not let the presence of some unpleasant rhetoric obscure their recognition of some unpleasant truths the author has taken the time to tell.

Two themes dominate Simon's account of our current economic crisis. Each is given full treatment in a separate "microcosm" case-study chapter, and both are considered in "U.S.A.: The Macrocosm." The first theme devolves upon the free-market principle that "government planning and regulation of the economy will ultimately lead to shortages, crises, and . . . some form of economic dictatorship." Recounting his experiences as so-called energy czar immediately after the Arab oil embargo, Simon illustrates how his *anti*bureaucratic behavior ended the gas station lines. In effect, he *had* to act as a mini-dictator in order to eliminate the allocation shortages resulting from his own Federal Energy Office's planning. Aside from illustrating the pitfalls of energy regulation, the chapter on energy policy also introduces the book's other central theme: government spending on groups that do not really need such aid. In this case, Simon takes Nelson Rockefeller to task for his grandiose plan for a one hundred billion dollar energy corporation to lend funds to private industry for the development of new fuel technologies. The author calls the plan "a gargantuan welfare boondoggle for the energy industries, lifted right out of the taxpayer's wallet."

According to the free-market theory, of course, the energy industry should be able to pay for any necessary development out of its own profits.

The theme of excessive government expenditures is picked up again in the later chapter on New York City's mid-1970's economic crisis, which is regarded as a microcosm (in an advanced stage, to be sure) of the economic problems facing the United States itself. There are the municipal unions and the pragmatic politicians and the financial community—each more clearly visible and mutually dependent than in any other major city. The unions can cripple the city, so their demands must be met; the politicians compete vigorously for office, so they must promise to meet union demands; the financial community needs a stable political environment for healthy business, so it must support the politicians' deficit financing to pay for their promises. The unions then demand more, and the cycle of promise-borrow-spend escalates. As long as enough of the city's tax-exempt bonds were being bought, of course, the cycle of ever-increasing debt could be sustained, and immediate problems taken care of, for the moment at least. But in early 1975, investors stopped buying, and within a year the city had to declare a three-year "moratorium" on repayment to their noteholders. In effect, says Simon, New York City defaulted. And, he adds, it did so without the collapse of the international financial system that David Rockefeller (whose bank held the most city notes) had been predicting in his effort to get federal assistance for New York.

Throughout the city's financial crisis, her politicians as well as a number of resident liberals were claiming that the troubles had resulted from a deep concern for the poor and concomitant expenditures on welfare. Simon neatly, if not nicely, debunks this claim with statistics that reveal who got what. His conclusion: "New York's subsidies to the middle classes have been overwhelmingly greater than its subsidies to the poor." Not only do most of the city's tax revenues go to its middle-class employees, but the middle class also obtains much of the funds allegedly allotted to the poor class. It is these middle-class subsidies, both direct and indirect, that the author identifies as the main cause of New York's fiscal collapse.

At any rate, when Simon turns to the macrocosm itself, the United States, the themes of government spending and government regulation come together. Noting that most federal dollars go for so-called social programs, he tells us the bitter truth: more than half these dollars are benefiting the middle class. Realizing that this is so very different from what is commonly believed, Simon proceeds to present a carefully documented account of how little the Aid to Families with Dependent Children and programs for the disabled cost compared to pensions; how most of the Social Security money goes to middle-class and wealthier people; how food stamp, lunch, and day-care programs are used widely if not mainly by the middle class; how ten to twenty-five percent of welfare program budgets are siphoned off by the program administrators; and how business, labor, and professional groups have a vested interest in perpetuating programs of welfare. These last two points indicate the link between the author's principle themes. For government regulation is itself eating up money that the poor need, and too much of the money that is left is being expended on those who are not really in need. It is for these reasons that Simon calls for a cutback in bureaucracy. Only that way, he maintains, can we remove millions of middle-class citizens from the dole.

Sherman, Howard J. *Stagflation: A Radical Theory of Unemployment and Inflation.* New York: Harper & Row Publishers, 1976.

Sherman's general theory of the business cycle is "radical" because, he says, it encompasses both the liberal and conservative views regarding the causes of depressions. Depressions are caused by *both* limited demand (underconsumption) *and* high costs (overinvestment), which means that capitalist cycles of boom and bust are inevitable. The cycles cannot be mitigated by giving workers higher wages to increase demand, because that contributes to the problem of supply costs; the lowering of costs through wage cuts is similarly counterproductive, for it leads to lessened demand. True, most of the traditional economists now agree with the "radical" view that such cycles are inherent in capitalism, but they believe that the worst consequences (depressions) can be prevented by governmental monetary and fiscal policies. It is simply a matter of trade-offs: so much unemployment for price stability, so much inflation for job expansion. That, at least, was the traditional economic theory before the coming of stagflation.

Sherman's explanation of stagflation is "radical" presumably because he attributes the current inflation-unemployment crisis to the behavior of big business rather than to that of labor unions. But he backs up his view with facts that cannot be ignored, regardless of one's partisan preferences. Stagflation, notes the author, must be explained by some new variable or by a new rise in some old variable. Is union power the explanatory variable? If so, it must, of course, be shown to have recently risen sharply. In fact, however, it has significantly declined. Union membership, as a percentage of all employees in nonagricultural employment, has dropped from its high of 35.5 percent in 1945 to a low of 26.7 percent in 1972. Furthermore, union membership strength declined by 5.3 percentage points in all manufacturing from 1958 to 1972. Perhaps this lessened unionism is why labor cost per unit usually decreased during most of each period of expansion and also why, although money wages have risen somewhat in recent contractions, they have risen much less than prices. Regardless of the reason, though, there is no doubt that prices have outrun wages. In 1968 the worker's *real* pay (in dollars of constant 1967 purchasing power) was $99.44. By April, 1975, although money wages had continued to rise, real wages had fallen to their lowest point in a decade—$87.46. Thus Sherman concludes that it is difficult,

at best, to see how unions can be blamed for simultaneous inflation and unemployment when inflation itself cannot be attributed to higher wages.

Is corporate power the explanatory variable? Certainly corporations, unlike unions, have been growing. The author draws on data from the Federal Trade Commission to show that the share of the two hundred largest manufacturing corporations as a percentage of total manufacturing assets has steadily and markedly climbed from 45.8 percent in 1929 to 60.4 percent in 1968. But can it be maintained that this increased concentration has anything to do with stagflation? Using Gardiner Means's classic government-sponsored study of "administered" prices and production during the Depression, Sherman shows that from 1929 to 1932 the sector with the least concentrated industries in terms of market share (the dispersed sector) had no choice but to respond to competitive pressures by sharply reducing prices, not production, while the concentrated sector was able to favorably administer its prices. In other words, the dispersed sector was competitive and lost profits, while the concentrated sector behaved like a monopoly in that it more or less maintained its prices instead of retaining its workers.

A similar, though more dramatic, pattern is seen in recent contractions. Contrasting the prices between the dispersed and the concentrated sector reveals that the former had to reduce prices during the five contractions from 1948 to 1970, but the latter reduced prices *only* in the 1948-1949 contraction. Granted, these administered price rises never exceeded six percent, yet that is precisely what appears to account for the relatively mild stagflation that occurred during the 1950's and 1960's. For when we turn to the December, 1973, to May, 1975, deep recession, the price index rose an incredible twenty-seven percent. So great was the increase that the now-dominant concentrated sector was apparently the cause of the dispersed, competitive sector's raising its prices (1.8 percent) during a downturn for the first time ever recorded.

These, then, are the facts underlying stagflation as the author sees them. They can be logically separated from Sherman's radical recommendation for democratic socialism (which, he notes, exists in neither the Swedish system nor Soviet system), but they cannot be ignored merely because they do not accord with Keynesian economic theory. It must be remembered that Keynesianism was itself once an unorthodox theory that only the reality of an economic crisis made into the contemporary economic orthodoxy it is. — *E.G.D.*

Additional Recommended Reading

Blair, John. "Market Power and Inflation," in *Journal of Economic Issues*. VIII (June, 1974), pp. 453-478. Application of the theory linking monopoly power to administered prices as an explanation for recent inflation.

Galbraith, John K. *Economics and the Public Purpose*. Boston: Houghton Mifflin Company, 1973. A somewhat stilted and repetitive account of the ideological aspects of Keynesian economics, and how these aspects prevent it from recognizing the dominance of the market system by the largest corporations, the "planning" system.

Labor Research Association. *Research in Economic Trends*. I, no. 3 (September, 1975). Cites figures from First National City Bank on profit rates (on stockholders' equity) *after* taxes, notably showing a drop from an average of 14 percent in 1965 to a low of 10 percent in 1970 among all manufacturing, and then a steady surge yielding a 15 percent return in 1973 and 1974.

Mermelstein, David, ed. *The Economic Crisis Reader*. New York: Random House, 1975. A collection of articles from journals, magazines, and newspapers, some of which deal with stagflation.

U.S. Department of Commerce. *Survey of Current Business*. Washington, D.C.: U.S. Government Printing Office, August, 1971-August, 1975. Data on cyclical patterns of national income, consumption, profits, wages, prices, and unemployment.

U.S. Department of Labor, Bureau of Labor Statistics. *Employment and Earnings*. Washington, D.C.: U.S. Government Printing Office, January, 1973-September, 1975 (esp. July, 1975). Compilation of employment and earnings by race, sex, age, and other categories, with statistical breakdowns within the group of officially employed.

——————. *Handbook of Labor Statistics 1974*. Washington, D.C.: U.S. Government Printing Office, 1975. Most useful for the history of price movements and of union membership, by industry.

PHILOSOPHICAL EFFORTS TOWARD AN OBJECTIVE VIEW OF PLANET EARTH

Type of event: Philosophical: emphasis in thought on the need for conservation
Time: The 1970's
Locale: The world

Principal personages:

RACHEL LOUISE CARSON (1907-1964), author of the acclaimed book *Silent Spring* (1962), which exposes the overuse of pesticides, especially DDT

DR. PAUL RALPH EHRLICH (1932-   ), author of *The Population Bomb* (1968), a study in overpopulation

JACQUES COUSTEAU (1910-   ), undersea explorer who has crusaded extensively against exploitation of the world's waterways

HERBERT MARSHALL MCLUHAN (1911-   ), University of Toronto Professor who popularized the "global village" concept

JAMES LOVELL (1928-   ), *Apollo VIII* astronaut whose lunar observations of earth made humankind more appreciative of our life systems

Summary of Event

Concepts of global politics, global economics, and global ecology have become catch terms in the 1970's. The once monolithic national states have lost their isolation in a world of COMSAT (communication) satellites, interdependent world trade, and the constant threat of worldwide nuclear holocaust. Petty rivalries still reign and national ambitions are strong, but there is also a growing recognition of the vulnerability of planet earth, of its delicate life-sustaining processes that can be unredeemably destroyed. Armageddon or Apocalypse is viewed by philosophers, scientists, and writers as an inevitable consequence of twentieth century technology and outmoded politics if key global concerns do not dominate national and international affairs.

The student activist movements of the 1960's helped popularize and inspire a tremendous volume of literature on ecology (or "environmental studies.") Critics of government-condoned exploitation of the land and sea by private corporations in a world of diminishing natural resources awakened public concern over the threats to the environment. Rachel Carson condemned the overuse of pesticides, especially DDT, in her widely acclaimed book, *Silent Spring*, published in 1962. Six years later, Dr. Paul Ehrlich's book, *The Population Bomb*, warned of the threat of overpopulation. In a similar vein, Jacques Cousteau, the undersea explorer, cru-

1069

saded extensively against exploitation of the world's waterways. Often lyrical and usually sad in their descriptions, these writers have awakened an apathetic public to active concern for wildlife and wilderness area preservation, for reasonable limits on hunting and fishing, and for strict control of the many forms of pollution. The greatest fear now confronted is that the battle cry rang too late or will be acknowledged too late for those in power to reverse the dying of planet earth.

Earthwatch, a conscientious monitoring of the globe by private and public organizations dedicated to saving mankind, is an often overpowering task. The earth is filthy and her resources badly ravaged by overgrazing, strip mining, inadequate sewage disposal, widespread deforestation, dangerous pesticides, an insupportable population growth, and dying waterways. Much of the deterioration is irreversible, particularly in areas where whole ecosystems, such as delicately balanced desert ecologies, have been disrupted. Pollution of Lake Erie, the Rhine river, and other major waterways with chlorinated hydrocarbons plus massive human and industrial waste threatens not only indigenous life forms, but also the continuance of food chains which support birds, animals, and man. The danger is not confined to any part of the globe, but exists in crisis proportions wherever civilization dominates the landscape. Since very little virgin acreage remains, human exploitation of Mother Earth is an accomplished fact.

What is needed to avert ecotragedy is a willingness to live within limits, a difficult compromise for the Western affluent nations who since World War II have enjoyed the practical benefits of unimpeded technological progress. To effect this change, values and attitudes about consumerism must become less selfish and the public must be educated in a philosophy of human survival that embraces all people and future generations. Ecotactics, a method of living involving individual limitations on food consumption, energy use, family size, automobile transportation, and amount of litter as well as political activism to bring about suitable legislation to curb future excesses, has been well articulated by the Sierra Club, Environmental Action, and other spearhead groups. Their last ditch alarmist pleas have successfully mobilized public support resulting in government air and safety controls on industrial pollution. However, ecological ignorance and apathy are still widespread in the 1970's, a frightening reality to the exponents of all "Save the Earth" movements who constantly warn that human behavior must be tailored to the carrying capacity of the planet.

To be fair, the present generation of overconsumers is not entirely to blame for the present problems of the planet. A belief in the ability of the natural world to meet human needs and man's God-given right to conquer nature have been the dominant philosophies of human history. Man was regarded as master, entrepreneur, and sanctioned exploiter of the seemingly unlimited resources of the planet. If he ruined the fertility of a certain plot of land, he could simply move to another. If he deforested a large area and thereby destroyed the nutrients for soil fertility, no authority checked his wastefulness. In fact, he was free to repeat the process. Past generations did not realize that there is no abundance in nature, that centuries of trial and error leading to the extermination of certain species and the thriving of others left nature with a very interrelated, interdependent system of checks and balances. Various plant and animal ecosystems co-existed and fed one another so that monocultures, single species, could not dominate an area and destroy other life forms including, eventually, themselves.

Man in his ignorance has often eradicated beneficial predators and overfarmed single crops to the extent that pests overmultiply in time and reduce harvest yields and wild game. Many studies have been published on the deleterious effects of DDT, a lethal fertilizer that not only killed undesirable plant parasites, but deer, rabbit, cattle, and beneficial soil and plant bacteria all over the world. After prolonged application, DDT was discovered to be fat soluble and communicative in accumulated dosages all the way up the food chain to man. Until recently, humans could not eat Lake Michigan's coho salmon because the DDT concentrations were too high. More thorough testing of the chemical before marketing would have prevented such unnecessary catastrophe, but the added time would have cut into profits; also, the environment twenty-five to thirty years ago was not as depleted of food chains. Present and future generations cannot afford to be so heedless, since the great global challenge of fa-

mine is being currently faced in the United Nations and other world forums. To quote Marshall McLuhan, "the world is a global village," or a planetary community interrelated and interdependent as much as are the creatures and plants in the natural world.

A growing protective attitude toward planet earth has, to a great extent, been fueled by a cosmic perspective resulting from manned space missions as much as by the prophecies of conservationists. Since 1968, when James Lovell and fellow astronauts of *Apollo VIII* became the first men to see earth rise over another planetary body, the world has been awestruck by a description of the planet as an oasis and a beautiful blue diamond in a vast unknown universe. It is merely one small planet among many thousands, but the only one thus far detected that can support human life. If mankind destroys earth's food regeneration system, human survival will cease because there is nowhere else for humans to migrate feasibly. Earth is the best spaceship we have to sustain our species, and at the present time, there is approximately a fifty-fifty chance that its life support systems can be maintained.

While concerted efforts to improve the environment by recycling wastes, banning certain bio-nondegradable materials, seeking government enforcement of pollution controls, mounting massive efforts to reverse the stagnation and dying of waterways, promoting zero population growth, protecting endangered species, and urging more prudent use of chemicals are in widespread practice, not enough is being done. The major cities of the world are still plagued by disease and such high levels of pollution that ozone and other toxic air alerts are commonplace. The developing countries of the Third World prefer the evils of industrial development to environmental safeguards. Marine life is threatened by oil spills, increasing concentrations of human sewage that cannot be absorbed, chemicals that destroy plankton (the source of our atmosphere), and overfishing. Nuclear fallout destruction and severe climatic changes wrought from pollution are increasing perils. As more and more governments acquire nuclear weaponry and radioactive materials while national conflicts rage, the existence of the entire human race may depend on one individual's use of a teaspoonful of Strontium 90. A case clearly exists for a greater understanding of the problems of the less affluent and the dosage limits of lethal substances absorbable by living creatures.

Mankind may as yet be only in the first stages of a planetary crisis since destructive trends can still be reversed by this generation, which is more educated and more knowledgeable than all previous ones. Also, the multitudinous uses of space for observational coverage of global weather, war preparations, natural disasters, and traffic control—as well as a projected use for orbiting self-containing colonies—promise to change the ideology of groups. Fortunately, the advantages of such reconnaissance and technological development are available to everyone. While a nontyrannical, ecology-minded Central World Government may be a possibility only in science fiction, national governments will have to cooperate more with one another if they are to share the planet's limited resources. If our generation cannot lay the groundwork for such ties, the human species on Spaceship Earth may hurl toward extinction. The decision, as faced in the 1970's, is as political as it is moral.

Pertinent Literature

Falk, Richard A. *This Endangered Planet: Prospects and Proposals for Human Survival*. New York: Random House, 1971.

This Endangered Planet: Prospects and Proposals for Human Survival is written from the scholarly eyrie of eminent international law specialist Richard Falk, Albert G. Milbank Professor of International Law and Practice at Princeton University. Falk is well qualified to assess the seriousness of the threats to mankind's existence posed by environmental pollution, the destruction of natural habitats, and the inability of nations to forego nationalism in favor of internationalism. He demonstrates how poorly we in the West have managed our earthly inheritance ever since we allowed technology to supplant God, and the Gross National Product to outstrip all other barometers of national prestige.

Thus, Falk's image of earth is that of paradise nearly lost—of a future almost forsaken because of man's greed and indifference toward his fellow man and the generations to come (if, in fact, such generations will exist). Highly opinionated and persuasive, the author relates how little time is left to alter existing perceptions of earth, to stop thinking of short-term gain and start thinking of long-term effects, to come to a consciousness that human beings are denizens of a fragile planet whose ability to house and feed themselves is becoming alarmingly strained.

What is particularly arresting about Falk is his command of cold fact. For instance, one would truly be living in a fool's paradise if one were to believe that mankind can go on forever when confronted with the fact that "The balance sheet of evolution is largely negative. Most species of mammal do not survive longer than 600,000 years." Man, however, has gone far beyond the average earthly stay, having managed to survive for more than 1,000,000 years; the implication, of course, is that his time may well be up. As Falk observes: "Unless man can make some extraordinary changes in his pattern of social and political behavior, he may well soon follow the dodo and the dinosaur down the path of extinction. . . ."

Therefore, as Falk sees it, the sole hope man has is that an awareness of his plight will lead to constructive action. Nonetheless, we are spared no illusions: we are creatures who have, from time immemorial, used our greatest energies thinking about war, preparing for war, and warring. Our billions of dollars, francs, and marks, are kept from the poor and desperate and handed over to war-oriented industries. Moreover, nationalism, rather than receding, is a steadily growing phenomenon that works against the best efforts of ecologists to bring about a unified world response to threats posed by our poisoning of our environment. Falk offers the example that, if only some whalers are told that they must desist from whaling, those who are not placed under the antiwhaling ordinance will profit greatly, taking in huge amounts of whales in the absence of competition. Thus, laws must be formulated that will make environmental destruction illegal in *all* countries of the world, and the power must exist to enforce such laws or no nation will stop butchering seals or polluting the ocean.

Given the competitive nature of nations, Falk notes, the creation of a world court will be exceedingly difficult, yet something must be done—and very soon—if such things as the proliferation of nuclear technology and the destruction of streams and lands are to be stopped.

Falk has concocted seven goals for mankind which will prevent the twentieth century from being our last. First, people must begin to have a vision of the oneness of mankind. Violence must be minimized in international affairs (through such acts of nations as the Camp David Meeting in 1978 between Anwar Sadat of Egypt and Menachem Begin of Israel). Environmental quality must be maintained by means of an internationally sanctioned monitoring system. Minimum world welfare standards must be raised so that starvation and malnutrition are eliminated. A world order must be created that is built upon the notion of human dignity. The value and beauty of diversity among nations must be recognized and retained at the same time that the essential brotherhood of all peoples is emphasized; and finally, all countries must be allowed to enter into a worldwide discussion of the state of planet earth.

Having offered his seven goals for mankind, Falk turns to what he calls "world order activism" in the last third of *This Endangered Planet*. For, as he pointed out in earlier chapters, the ecological problems of our earth are many and the ways to deal with them are few; little time remains for man to do something to avert Armageddon.

The author calls upon his readers to "spread the word of truth" to those in power who can change laws and make new ones guaranteeing the survival of our environment. Specifically, Falk calls upon informed persons to "commit their careers, their resources, their energies, and, if necessary, their well-being to solving the problems of an endangered planet" by alerting leaders to our peril, by fostering "survival universities" wherein the planet's problems can be discussed by humanists and scientists alike, by speaking out for ecological awareness at corporate board meetings and gatherings of stockholders, and by helping to construct a World Political Party "dedicated to the design of world order."

In short, then, Richard Falk is one who believes that man is not doomed to annihilation: he can do something to stop the headlong rush into the abyss. Yet nothing short of a worldwide wave of political activism on the part of the ecology-minded will save the human race from an environmental breakdown of planetary proportion.

Ward, Barbara and René Dubos. *Only One Earth: The Care and Maintenance of a Small Planet*. New York: W. W. Norton and Company, 1972.

Only One Earth: The Care and Maintenance of a Small Planet offers the ecology-minded one of the most illuminating overviews of planet earth's time of crisis, written as it is by two highly regarded authorities on the subject. Barbara Ward, a political economist recently made Albert Schweitzer Professor of International Economic Development at Columbia University and author of such standard works as *Nationalism and Ideology* and *India and the West*, is joined by René Dubos, a microbiologist and experimental pathologist, a Nobel Prize-winner in 1969, and the author of *So Human an Animal*, a study of mankind. Together Ward and Dubos take as their subject the changing fortunes of earth, envisioning it as a lovely, bounteous planet long the victim of human negligence and outright abuse. In this study, commissioned by the United Nations Conference on Human Environment, the authors conjecture about why things are going wrong and how mankind might go about correcting the abuses in time to save itself.

As they see it, we are living in an era of astonishing, unprecedented change in which population, energy use, and food consumption have increased more rapidly than the earth can tolerate. Those who have benefited most (in the short run) are those persons living in the highly industrialized parts of the world; their standard of living, however, has been attained at the expense of their environment. In the midst of plenty, Western people have come to expect increasingly more consumer goods, and these expectations have drained away resources at an incredible rate. If such expectations continue, earth might indeed become the "late, great Planet Earth," a fouled, septic orb devoid of life. As of now, our Western consumerism has dealt wildlife a terrific blow, forcing some species of animals to become extinct and polluting many bodies of water so badly that they may never be clean again.

Briefly but probingly, Ward and Dubos chart how we arrived at our present state of affairs, sketching the contributions of such eminent thinkers as Sir Francis Bacon, René Descartes, and Sir Isaac Newton to the creation of a scientific, utilitarian outlook that paved the way for the consumer society that we know today. Specifically, it was the notion that the world is man's to manipulate that created the industrial and postindustrial ages, with their attendant ugliness, waste, and pollution.

Though Ward and Dubos summon forth a decidedly grim picture of the industrial/technological world we inherit, they are far from pessimistic about planet earth's chances for survival. "Wisdom" and "restraint" are their watchwords, wisdom coming after we have taken a searching look at our ravaged planet and restraint being the action taken after we have become wise.

Rather than dismiss science as the force behind the rape of the earth and therefore something unworthy of trust, the authors maintain that a restrained use of science for the betterment of life is to be hoped for. But science must be turned from such deadly pursuits as weapons research and toward helping the environment recover from man-incurred wounds. Science cannot continue to be used to find new consumer goods for which no genuine need exists; instead, it must help "provide man with better, more reliable and wiser means of working with his environment."

What man needs to cultivate (if he is not to go the way of dodos and dinosaurs) is a sense of modesty—the sense that he is a part of nature, rather than something outside of nature, and as such is inextricably bound up in the destinies of all other creatures in nature. People must, argue Dubos and Ward, stop trying to be God: they must give up their cherished image as maker and mover and shifter of the world if they are to continue to exist. Otherwise, a terrible fate awaits them. — *A.C.R.*

Additional Recommended Reading

Clarke, Arthur C. *Report on Planet Three and Other Speculations.* New York: Harper & Row Publishers, 1972. Clarke's imaginative, lighthearted, and often serious collection of essays is woven around the theme that man is no longer earthbound.

Milne, Lorus J. *Ecology Out of Joint.* New York: Charles Scribner's Sons, 1977. A case history study of the effects of civilization on the natural world.

Mitchell, John G. and Constance Stallings, eds. *Ecotactics: The Sierra Club Handbook for Environment Activists*. New York: Pocket Books, 1969. A practical guide on how to mobilize political support for ecological concerns, as well as a comprehensive anthology of environmental problems; includes a useful bibliography and listing of professional conservation organizations.

Owen, Denis Frank. *What Is Ecology?* New York: Oxford University Press, 1974. Geared to help the layman think as an ecologist in order to understand the balance of nature in communities and how ecology effects all living things.

Wagner, Richard H. *Environment and Man*. New York: W. W. Norton and Company, 1974. An updating of Wagner's 1971 systematic study, this work is an objective treatment of key environmental concerns including urban ills and population control.

Ward, Barbara. *Spaceship Earth*. New York: Columbia University Press, 1966. Explains and appraises how the impact of technology on society impels mankind toward a world community ethos.

THE POPULATION SHIFT TO THE SUNBELT

Type of event: Sociological: America's population abandons the North in favor of the
  South and the Southwest
Time: The 1970's
Locale: America's Southern and Southwestern states

Summary of Event

America's population has been undergoing many drastic changes during the last two decades. Senior citizens account for an ever-increasing percent of our population, thanks to a dramatically longer life span; and there are also more young people, due in large measure to a decreasing infant mortality rate.

However, the most far-reaching change has been not in the composition of America's population, but in the shifting attitudes of that population. Demographers try to decide what is occurring to Americans, but their efforts can only partially explain the restless wandering of America's population. Nevertheless, they do agree on one thing: America's population is a mobile one; people pack up and move at a moment's notice. Nowhere has this been more evident than in the shift of America's population to the "Sunbelt," that collection of states with a predominantly warm climate, stretching from the Deep Southern States of the old Confederacy across the desert Southwest to California.

Once exclusively the mecca of retirees, the Sunbelt is rapidly becoming the population center and economic center of this country. Today, retirees comprise a mere twenty-five percent of the Sunbelt population. The nation's economic growth center has been shifting southward for decades, but during the fourth quarter of 1976, nonagricultural employment in the South and West passed that of the rest of the nation. Further, it is estimated that within a few years, more than fifty percent of the nation's goods and services will be provided by the Sunbelt. Such tremendous economic growth is partially the result of industrial expansion which took place in the mid-1960's, when the Sunbelt's population grew large enough to provide sufficient consumers to make industrial construction economically feasible.

Expansion was made possible by a "pro-business" atmosphere and by choice industrial sites which were well planned in every detail. The Sunbelt states were the first to develop state offices of economic development. Their energetic approach to attracting new industry, including the hard sell, paid off in new construction. Tax incentives also abound. Texas, for example, has no state income tax, either personal or corporate. Lower operating costs are automatic in the Sunbelt since factories do not require heat. While raw materials such as water and energy are not universally abundant in the Sunbelt, some states, such as Texas, are able to offer the added inducements of both water and energy. This is true

1077

for many Gulf Coast states. A final inducement is a willing and productive labor force which still gives a day's work for a day's pay, and while it is not antiunion *per se*, labor unions have made little progress in the Sunbelt.

Ultimately, the Sunbelt story is a story about people. People make industrial expansion work; they produce the goods and services. And people have been flocking to the Sunbelt in spectacular fashion. From 1970 to mid-1976, the Sunbelt population rose by 7,400,000 people, or sixty-three percent of the total national increase. In Florida alone, the population increased by 1,630,000; this increase is more than the combined total increase of the twenty-one Northeast and North Central states. This growth has been the result of more than "in-migration." For the first time since the Civil War, more people born in the South stayed in the South than moved North.

Something in the Sunbelt is attractive enough to keep people there as well as to lure newcomers. Obviously, one of these attractions is employment; however, other forces are also at work. People come seeking a refuge from the decaying Northern cities, from crime, pollution, and waste. They come seeking a way of life that never existed in the North, lured to a way of life that is part reality, part myth, and part media hype. It is a slower-paced, less pretentious life that they seek; the executive and the assembly line worker alike can come home to a more relaxed way of living. Recreation abounds, and for the more adventurous, the wilderness is only a few miles outside town. The South-

erner's gregariousness, his love of good conversation, good companionship, and good food, typified, of course, by that Texas tradition, the barbeque, have universal appeal for the new arrival.

However, such rapid growth is not without profound problems, and carries with it serious repercussions for both people and the land. For example, the rapid influx of non-Southern people to the Sunbelt poses a threat to the existence of the very qualities that make the Sunbelt attractive—namely, an easy-gaited pace of life, uncrowded surroundings, and a respect for traditional values such as patriotism, self-reliance, and a strong work ethic.

Both economic and population growth are expected to continue. By 1990 it is predicted that the Sunbelt will increase its population by twenty-two percent; jobs will increase by thirty-eight percent as compared to a twenty-eight percent increase for the rest of the nation, and per capita income will rise fifty-five percent as compared to forty-eight percent nationally.

Faced with such an increase in people, it is doubtful that the Sunbelt can survive without drastic changes. The population of Arizona doubled from 1950 to 1970 and is expected to double again by 1990; yet, 715 billion gallons of water, more than are replaced by rainfall, are used each year by Arizona citizens. No one is certain how long such depletion of the water table can go on, and no one has even begun to imagine the consequences of a major water shortage in Arizona. Texas and Oklahoma have thousands of acres of productive land now turning to dust because the falling water table has made irrigation too costly.

Unrestricted growth and poor planning have resulted in situations which may eventually cause the decline of the Sunbelt. Sunbelt cities are just beginning to develop the tell-tale signs of decay that their northern counterparts are now experiencing. Atlanta, once a model of industrial development, now finds itself surrounded by a white, suburban ring. The inner city is being abandoned and ghetto formation is certain to occur unless preventive steps are taken soon. Houston, now the fifth largest city in America, and growing by one thousand people a week, has four hundred miles of highways, but no mass transit system. Lubbock, Texas; Montgomery, Alabama; and Savannah, Georgia have the three highest murder rates in the nation. The Sunbelt has people problems that threaten to make it less attractive than the refuge it is reputed to be.

Environmental concerns pose the greatest threat to the population of the Sunbelt. The Environmental Pro-

tection Agency has ruled that no area in which pollution exceeds the 1970 Clean Air Act standards may add any new source of pollution without removing more than equivalent amounts of the same pollutants. This ruling hits the Sunbelt states because there are few older factories to close down, whereas in the North, industrial expansion consists of building new factories to replace old factories. For the North, compliance is relatively simple.

If demographers are correct, the Sunbelt will continue to experience rapid, economic growth and population increases. This will place unprecedented pressures upon the land and its people, for it is their survival which is at stake. The question to be answered is whether the people of the Sunbelt can learn from the mistakes of the past and preserve a way of living that is unique and different from that of their Northern neighbors. The alternative is to become a copy of the Northern metropolises, from which so many Sunbelt dwellers escaped long ago.

Pertinent Literature

"The South Today," in *Time*. CVIII (September 27, 1976), pp. 29-99.

Marble statues of Confederate soldiers in virtually every town square in the South attest to the Southerner's love of lost causes. Today, the dominant mood in the eleven states of the old Confederacy is not defeat, but confidence—in victory over an often tragic past and over the challenges of the future.

Spurred by an economic resurgence, the South is finally undergoing

a true revival, one that encompasses politics, education, and the arts, as well as finance. The basis for this revival is what has been termed the "non-stop Texas gusher." Since January 10, 1901, when oil was discovered, Texas has led the South on an economic binge that has changed the region from the nation's poorest to the nation's fastest developing area. Texas offers great inducements to the company seeking a new building site. Water and power are plentiful and taxes are low or nonexistent. Other Southern states were quick to pick up on Texas' lead; they formed Offices of Economic Development which got the word out to the business community that the South was the place to go. Ad campaigns and a hard sell paid off; industrial growth in the South has been spectacular.

But this growth is a mixed blessing, for it carries with it the seeds of self-destruction. The unparalleled economic growth of the South has been largely responsible for the dramatic increase in the Southern population. This unrestricted, unplanned-for growth has brought with it air pollution, traffic jams, and the beginning of decay in many Southern cities. In short, the things that make the South attractive are the things that are threatened with extinction.

The economic upsurge has spawned a basic change in the Southerner: he now has something to be proud of. This newfound pride could be the most far-reaching aspect of the Southern revival, for it touches all aspects of Southern life, which in the past was often characterized as barren, without intellectual culture. But that image is changing, as best typified, perhaps, by the new Southern politics. Typical of the new breed of politicians were the progressive governors elected in the early 1970's, such as Florida's Rueben Askew and Georgia's Jimmy Carter. These politicians sensed and responded to the signs of change in the South. They especially felt the rising importance of the black vote and understood the sentiment that, in the South, person-

ality counts more than issues. With the election of Jimmy Carter to the presidency, Southern politicians now flex new muscle nationally. This, combined with its rising economic strength, makes the South a force to be reckoned with.

What may make the South an even greater force is a burgeoning intellectual force which is being felt in all the arts. There was a time when the South was a victim of a "brain drain": when the constraints placed upon anyone who held divergent views became too frustrating, large numbers of the South's truly talented people fled North to write, to teach, to paint.

Today, the mobility of the population in general is bringing a mixture of people to the South. Economic growth is attracting others, while a greatly improved racial situation is allowing more talented Southerners to stay in the South. These developments portend good things for the Southern intellectual community. Playwright Preston Jones has given the South its first important native playwright in decades; in the music field, the larger cities now boast symphonic orchestras and original opera theaters; and intellectual life generally is on the upswing.

All this is not to imply that the South is without problems. As mentioned earlier, Houston, a teeming metropolis, has no mass transit system. Atlanta has surrounded itself with a belt of white suburbs, much like many northern cities, thus perhaps spelling doom for its inner city. Water shortages could present problems in some states.

However, for the first time since the Civil War, Southerners are confident that they have the solutions to reduce their problems. Even if the economic boom should stop, the feel-ing would prevail that the course of the future could easily be turned with a little Southern ingenuity.

Bell, Oliver, ed. *America's Changing Population.* New York: H. W. Wilson Company, 1974.

This collection of newspaper and magazine articles is a significant contribution to a study of the Sunbelt. The importance of the volume lies in the fact that it presents America's history of demographic change as well as a prognosis for America's later years. Not a narrow study of migration to the Sunbelt, *America's Changing Population* offers essays on related subjects such as the significance of the declining birthrate and the importance of increased age of the average American. It seeks to answer the question, "How fast is America growing?" It also studies the moral, social, and economic ramifications of the question.

As women's birth expectations decrease and zero population growth gains supporters, a byproduct is increased age for the average American. In a society that is more "adult" than ever before, Americans can become a little more selfish, not appeasing just the juvenile palate. Less concerned with a suburban environment that breeds Little League and Brownies, the adult American can consider his personal interests. Thus, appeal of a geographical area may revolve around an entirely new set of criteria. Freedom from snow shoveling, a climate conducive to year-round adult recreation, and a location perfect for retirement may be at the top of the list of priorities of a Northerner considering a move. This is not to imply that the Sunbelt is only for the adult, but merely to observe that the adult without children or with few children may be seeking different qualities in an area to call "home." Furthermore, Americans are more than ever before free to be mobile. Less family means fewer family ties. A decision to move to a new locale, to move into a new home, may be only interim decisions in a lifelong plan. Americans are free to "try" new areas.

It is only reasonable that the tremendous climate appeal of the Sunbelt will draw an increasing number of these "floating Americans" to the South and the Southwest. Once they arrive, less pollution, a lower crime rate, and a more relaxed pace of living will be immediately evident, most likely resulting in a permanent home.

A major problem exists, however, in this vast migration to the Sunbelt. Problems indigenous to major cities are common to all major cities, regardless of the climate. As the population rises, new metropolises are created, and with them, the resultant concerns. Crime, ghettos with satellite suburbs, and pollution may all destroy the Sunbelt, a present refuge from these urban crises. One need only read the essays in this collection by Jesse Jackson, Shirley Chisholm, and Lawrence Feinberg to be reminded of urban problems that Sunbelt dwellers have largely escaped.
— *D.W.T.*

Additional Recommended Reading

Breckenfeld, Gurney. "Business Loves the Sunbelt (and Vice Versa)," in *Fortune*. XCV (June, 1977), pp. 132-146. A major study of the rising industrial strength of the Sunbelt area.

"A New Milestone in the Shift to the Sunbelt," in *Nation's Business*. LXV (May, 1977), p. 69. A comparison of economic trends at work in the Sunbelt and the Snowbelt.

Proffitt, Nicholas. "Texas! The Superstate," in *Newsweek*. XC (December 12, 1977), pp. 36-50. Surveys Texas as an economic and cultural giant.

THE UNITED STATES INVADES CAMBODIA

Type of event: Military: expansion of a war
Time: April-June, 1970
Locale: Vietnam-Cambodia border

Principal personages:

RICHARD MILHOUS NIXON (1913-   ), thirty-seventh President of the United States, 1969-1974

HENRY ALFRED KISSINGER (1923-   ), Assistant to the President for National Security Affairs, 1969-1973; United States Secretary of State, 1973-1977

PRINCE NORODOM SIHANOUK (1922-   ), Cambodian monarch and deposed head of state

LON NOL (1913-   ), Cambodian chief of state following anti-Sihanouk *coup*

GENERAL CREIGHTON WILLIAMS ABRAMS (1914-   ), Commander of United States military forces in Vietnam

Summary of Event

In 1968, when Richard M. Nixon was voted into office on the basis of his promise to bring peace to Vietnam, Cambodia was at peace. Its ruler, Prince Norodom Sihanouk, had successfully maneuvered to keep his country separate from the Vietnam War by allowing the North Vietnamese to utilize border provinces as sanctuaries and also to channel supplies destined for South Vietnam through Cambodian territory. For Sihanouk, the decision to aid the Vietnamese Communists in this manner was more one of expediency than sympathy. In his eyes the choices were few; he must either help the Communists or accept "American imperialism."

The key to Nixon's plan for ending the war was "Vietnamization," a program calling for the gradual extrication of Americans and their replacement by Vietnamese. In essence, it was a solution to the American problem of disengaging from the war rather than a solution to the war. In the same way, the prospect of invading Cambodia was viewed only as a means to ease disengagement. That it would actually widen the war and introduce a previously neutral country to the conflict were possibilities that remained secondary considerations.

The American military leadership had for some time sought permission to invade Cambodia. President Nixon's immediate predecessor, Lyndon B. Johnson, had rejected several requests on the grounds that the impact of such an invasion on the course of the war would be negligible. In February of 1969, however, less than a month after Nixon assumed office, General Creighton W. Abrams, Commander of United States forces in Vietnam, requested that B-52 bombers be used against sanctuaries and supply routes. Nixon, in concurrence with his National Security Adviser Henry A. Kissinger, agreed, and in March, 1969, the bombing of Cambodia began. As the American Constitution specifically holds that only Congress can decide to wage war, this act to widen the war was almost certainly illegal. To prevent the issue of legality from arising, however, Nixon ordered that the bombing be kept secret. In this manner, without the knowledge of Congress or the American people, Cambodia was introduced to the war one year prior to the American invasion.

Although the bombing in itself achieved limited success in interdicting North Vietnamese supply routes and storage areas, it had a significant impact on the Cambodian political situation and was primarily responsible for initiating a series of events that would lead to Cambodia's present circumstances. First, it pushed the Communists out of the border sanctuary areas and deeper into Cambodia. This in turn irritated rightist elements in Sihanouk's government who, already dissatisfied with his permissiveness in allowing Vietnamese Communists access to Cambodian territory, became even more so as they witnessed the Communists usurp still more. Sihanouk, aware of the discord, took measures to allay it. By not protesting the B-52 raids which he strongly opposed, he felt he was making a significant concession to these same rightist elements who supported them.

In March, 1970, as tensions continued to mount within his government, Sihanouk departed Phnom Penh on a diplomatic mission to Moscow and Peking. Again, motivated by the need

to settle the unrest among his ministers, he intended to urge both governments to restrain the North Vietnamese from encroaching further into Cambodian territory. However, he had failed to assess accurately how far the crisis in his capital had actually advanced. While still in Moscow he learned he had been deposed by his pro-American defense minister, Lon Nol. Although there is no evidence that the United States or any other foreign power promoted the *coup*, it precipitated crucial policy changes on both sides of the Vietnam War. For the struggling Cambodian Communist movement (Khmer Rouge), previously judged by Hanoi to be too small to be effective, Sihanouk's downfall suddenly thrust it into a position where it could make a serious attempt at gaining power. As a result, Vietnamese assistance increased dramatically, and the Khmer Rouge received the support it needed eventually to achieve power. For those among the American leadership who supported an invasion plan, Sihanouk's downfall was a fortuitous event, since he alone among Cambodia's leaders had remained strongly opposed. With his removal all Cambodian opposition to an invasion attempt ended.

On April 29-30, 1970, an invasion was mounted with thirty thousand American and South Vietnamese crossing into Cambodia. Secrecy had so pervaded the operation's planning that no one in Cambodia, including the United States mission and least of all Lon Nol, learned of it until after it had occurred. Although Nixon spoke of the invasion as a decisive victory, the military regarded it as having attained at best a temporary advantage. While uncovering enormous stores of supplies it encountered few enemy troops. In effect, military planners had failed to take into account the Communists' move westward under the impact of the bombing. Thus, while temporarily disrupting the Communists' logistics, the invasion made little impact on their long-term conduct of the war. Pentagon estimates suggested that North Vietnamese plans for an offensive had been set back by no more than a year; and, in keeping with this assessment, the North Vietnamese, within two months of the withdrawal of United States invasion forces, had reestablished their supply trails and sanctuaries.

Within the United States the effect of the invasion was devastating. The antiwar movement reacted with intensified demonstrations and student strikes, while the death of four students at Kent State University as the result of a confrontation between National Guardsmen and protesters enraged the nation. The extent of the reaction engendered by the invasion surprised President Nixon. Although he defended his action to the American people, his arguments appeared flimsy and misrepresentative. Claiming that the United States had for five years respected Cambodian neutrality, he neglected to mention the bombing. Declaring further that the invasion was intended to destroy the headquarters for the entire Communist military operation in South Vietnam, he ignored overwhelming evidence offered by the military proving that no such target existed. Additionally depicting the invasion as a nec-

essary step taken against the North Vietnamese to preclude the possibility of attack on Americans withdrawing from the war, he hid the fact that during the course of negotiations for peace the North Vietnamese had already offered to refrain from such attacks once a withdrawal date was determined. Finally, referring to his decision as crucial to the maintenance of United States prestige abroad, Nixon contradicted evidence indicating a substantial fall in America's prestige following the invasion. Both internationally and domestically, the feeling prevailed that the President had succeeded only in expanding an already wearisome war.

For Cambodia, the invasion completed the destruction of a tenuous neutrality already severely damaged for more than a year by the bombing campaign. It precipitated an internal war which had not existed before American forces crossed the border and which subsequently enveloped Cambodia in a prolonged conflict between United States supported anti-Communist forces and Vietnam-supported Khmer Rouge insurgents, thereby subjecting the country to still further devastation and eventual Communist rule.

In this way the fate of Cambodia was decided. American policymakers, interested only in exploiting Cambodia's territory as an adjunct to the Vietnam War, held the welfare of Cambodians and their land in small regard. President Nixon made this clear when in December, 1970, he stated that the Cambodians were "tying down 40,000 North Vietnamese regulars (in Cambodia and) if those North Vietnamese weren't in

Cambodia they'd be over killing Americans. . . ." The Cambodians were thus reduced to acting as surrogate American targets for North Vietnamese guns. The tragedy of the American invasion was that so much was suffered for so little reason.

Pertinent Literature

Poole, Peter A. *The Expansion of the Vietnam War into Cambodia: Action and Response by the Governments of North Vietnam, South Vietnam, Cambodia, and the United States.* Athens: Ohio University Center for International Studies, 1970.

In the introduction to his work, Peter Poole suggests that his study of the events leading to the American invasion of Cambodia was not intended to be a definitive analysis. Writing in 1970, shortly after the invasion occurred, he was not permitted access to the classified government documents available to later researchers. Instead, he derived his account solely from open sources and personal interviews. Despite the limitations under which he worked, his analysis is an illuminating interpretation of the origins of the invasion and the subsequent immersion of Cambodia into the Vietnam War. Government documents since made public, although capable of providing greater detail, have not deviated substantially from his original assessment and have, for the most part, corroborated his conclusions.

Poole first provides a lengthy discussion of the origins of the *coup* which deposed Prince Norodom Sihanouk as Cambodian head of state. He then devotes the balance of the study to chronicling the actions of the various governments involved as they directly or indirectly responded to the change. Apparently the *coup* took all foreign governments, including the United States, by surprise. The au-

thor is careful to note that he was unable to find evidence linking the United States or any other foreign power to the *coup*; on the contrary, each government, without exception, had been acting under the assumption that conditions in Cambodia would never change. Consequently, they were not prepared to respond or to even anticipate the responses of one another once the *coup* occurred.

In the case of the United States, Poole observes that, like all political appointees in every administration, those under President Richard M. Nixon lacked a comprehensive understanding of the areas they were called upon to administer. Those responsible for keeping abreast of activity in Cambodia conformed to the pattern. Lacking an in-depth knowledge of Cambodia's social and political history, policy planners in both the Pentagon and the White House tended to let events as they occurred dictate policy. Poole points out that they were not only unprepared for a *coup*; they were also unprepared to deal with a government from which Sihanouk was absent. The possibility of having to face a post-Sihanouk era had never been seriously addressed.

President Nixon, Poole suggests, may have regarded the *coup* as a possible means to achieving his own ends. Since the beginning of 1970 he had been seeking a way in which to demonstrate to Communist leaders that he was not hindered by antiwar sentiment in the United States and was capable of summoning massive force should the need arise. The *coup* removed, in Prince Sihanouk, a long-time opponent of American intervention in Cambodia and provided Nixon with an unexpected opening to proceed with his plan. Few people other than his top advisers, however, were even aware of what he was contemplating.

Nixon's announcement on April 30 that an invasion of Cambodia was under way created surprise and outrage among the American public as well as among the members of Congress. Poole writes that not even President Lyndon B. Johnson's decision in 1965 to escalate the war generated so much opposition. Not ten days before, Nixon had announced in a televised speech a plan to withdraw 150,000 more American military personnel from Vietnam by the following spring. The speech conveyed a sense of hope as well as relief that he was indeed progressing toward disengagement from the war. The Cambodian invasion abruptly shattered these hopes. Poole attributes the massive reaction it inspired as opposition to an act expanding a war long since discredited. Although opposition in Congress was equally impressive, Poole writes that a good part of it stemmed from a completely different premise. Because the President had not bothered to consult with Congress concerning his deci-

sion, many members looked upon his omission as a sign that he intended to continue to override their powers and abuse the democratic system. Thus the invasion of Cambodia rapidly assumed the stature of a constitutional issue, and Poole suggests that, for many, this particular aspect soon took precedence over any other.

Apparently Nixon wrote the April 30 speech himself, without consulting his staff. The reasons for his decision, which he presented in the text, disturbed many of his advisers, who recognized them to be misleading if not wholly false. Poole, in examining the President's criteria, cites ample evidence to support Nixon's staff's assessment. He concludes that the invasion was a failure, not only for President Nixon and his questionable criteria, but for Cambodia and its future.

Although Poole makes only brief references to Cambodia's future, it is clear from his discussion of Congress' reasons for opposing Nixon's decision that the fate of Cambodia received little, if any, consideration from the United States, either before the *coup* or subsequently. He himself has little faith in United States postinvasion support of the Lon Nol regime, suggesting at one point that Lon Nol's armies were surviving not because of United States aid, but because of their own persistence. In this way Peter Poole displays throughout his work a certain skepticism concerning United States intentions in Cambodia. Writing in 1970, he is one of the first to question Cambodia's chances for survival following the American invasion.

The United States Invades Cambodia

Shawcross, William. "Cambodia: The Verdict Is Guilty on Nixon and Kissinger," in *Far Eastern Economic Review*. XXXIX (January 7, 1977), pp. 18-24.
—————————— . "Cambodia: When the Bombing Finally Stopped," in *Far Eastern Economic Review*. XXXIX (January 14, 1977), pp. 30-35.

William Shawcross' two-part series on United States intervention in Cambodia is a well-researched piece of journalism that reviews United States involvement in Cambodia from the beginning of the secret bombing campaign in March, 1969, to the collapse of the Lon Nol regime six years later. It is particularly revealing because the author chooses to view the entire affair as a moral issue and devotes a large part of the article to condemning President Nixon and his National Security Adviser (later Secretary of State) Henry Kissinger for the moral laxity they displayed in devising a Cambodian policy with little consideration for its consequences on the Cambodian nation. Shawcross enjoys the advantage of someone who writes several years after the event in that he is able to place United States intervention in Cambodia in context with events that occurred later—most importantly, the Watergate scandal and Nixon's subsequent resignation. According to Shawcross, Watergate actually began when Nixon decided to expand the Vietnam War into Cambodia. The decision to begin bombing Cambodia was made in secret and kept secret from Congress and the American people because it was illegal and overstepped constitutional limitations on presidential war-making powers. When it was reported in *The New York Times* in May, 1969, the Nixon Administration resorted to the illegal wiretapping of aides' telephones to determine the source of the leak. The author infers these particular wiretaps to have possibly been the first in a series of domestic crimes comprising Watergate, and finds it ironic that Nixon's decisions which clearly led to Cambodia's destruction also led to his own.

Perhaps Shawcross' most serious charge against Nixon and Kissinger is that they never allotted Cambodia anything more than adjunctive status to their greater concern, the Vietnam War. Kissinger, in a meeting with White House staffers on April 30, 1970, is quoted as saying "Look, we're not interested in Cambodia. We're only interested in it not being used as a base." Nixon inadvertently expressed the same lack of concern in a speech on December 10 when he argued that Cambodians were at that moment engaging North Vietnamese who might otherwise have been free to kill Americans. Both instances successfully illustrate the author's contention that Cambodians amounted to little more than "cannon fodder" in the Nixon Administration's plan to extricate itself from Vietnam without damaging its global prestige.

The Administration's apparent obsession with its global image and the need to demonstrate its strength to Communist powers is held by Shawcross to have contributed significantly to policy in Cambodia. In the same April 30 meeting, Kissinger justified the invasion by stating, "we're trying to shock the Soviets into calling a conference and we can't promote this by appearing weak." Nixon, in his April 30 speech to the nation announcing the invasion, seemed to dwell on the same theme. "It's not our power but our will and character that is being tested tonight. . . . If we fail to meet this challenge, all other nations will be on notice that despite its overwhelming power the United States, when a real crisis comes, will be found wanting."

Shawcross further examines Nixon's penchant for appearing tough by giving credence to the much-reported story that Nixon, on the night he made his decision to invade Cambodia, viewed *Patton*, a newly released film about the unyielding World War II general, twice. Although it is anyone's conjecture as to the effect the film had on his decision, Shawcross infers that, if nothing more, it influenced his state of mind.

For Cambodia, the first few days following the invasion were crucial. According to Shawcross there yet remained the choice of allowing Cambodia to regain its peace, or of pushing it further into the war. An option apparently favored by the State Department was to deny the Lon Nol regime any further aid and thus force it to make some accommodation with the Communists. The result would have incorporated a Communist faction in the government, but might have saved the country from the devastation of continued war. Nixon and Kissinger, however, believed it served United States objectives to preserve the Lon Nol regime, and thus they made the choice which prolonged the war.

The author discerns a strong resemblance between the course of action taken in Cambodia and that originally taken to involve the United States in Vietnam. Once again a United States administration had committed itself to a weak and corrupt regime and once again, as the regime deteriorated, the strength of that commitment was regarded as increasingly critical to the regime's survival. Indeed, for the United States, the transition in Cambodia from isolated invasion to massive military support occurred rather quickly. By November of 1970, Nixon was able to claim that the war in Cambodia was "a vital element in the continued success of Vietnamization."

The irony of creating a war to end a war is not lost on the author. Kissinger's acceptance of the Nobel Peace Prize for negotiating the extrication of United States troops from Vietnam while Cambodia's conflict continued unabated is viewed as particularly paradoxical. Shawcross caustically writes that, "in the world of superpowers you get the Nobel Peace Prize for leaving a country at war." It is the lack of morality behind United States decisionmaking that troubles the author throughout. It is clear from his discussion, however, that a similar concern was apparently never a consideration for either Nixon or Kissinger. — *R.J.C.*

Additional Recommended Reading

Allman, T. D. "Ever Wider," in *Far Eastern Economic Review.* XXXII (July 9, 1970), pp. 5-6. The article details America's deepening commitment to Cambodia following the invasion and estimates that United States military aid to Cambodia will reach five hundred million dollars in the fiscal year beginning July 1, 1970.

—————— . "Cambodia: Into an Iceberg War," in *Far Eastern Economic Review*. XXXII (July 23, 1970), pp. 16-17. The author reflects on the deepening involvement of the United States in Cambodia and the optimism of the Lon Nol regime in believing the United States to be fundamentally committed to its cause.

Caldwell, Malcolm and Lek Tan. *Cambodia in the Southeast Asian War*. New York: Monthly Review Press, 1973. A comprehensive record of recent Cambodian history which is severely critical of United States policy in Cambodia.

Chanda, Nayan. "The Four Year Coup," in *Far Eastern Economic Review*. XXXII (June 25, 1970), pp. 26-28. Summarizes the internal political conflicts in Cambodia which led to Sihanouk's deposal and concludes that the *coup* was the result of a protracted struggle entirely of Cambodia's own making.

Grant, Jonathan S., *et al*. *Cambodia: The Widening War in Indochina*. New York: Washington Square Press, 1971. A compendium of articles concerned with the Cambodian invasion and the expansion of the Vietnam War, written by Asia scholars opposed to America's role in Asia.

Langguth, A. J. "Dear Prince: Since You Went Away," in *The New York Times Magazine*. (August 2, 1970), pp. 4, 44, 46, and 49. Lamenting both the passing of Prince Sihanouk from power and the ensuing deterioration of the country under Lon Nol.

Roberts, Chalmers M. "Planning of Asia Thrust Began in Late March," in *The Washington Post*. (May 26, 1970), p. A14. Examines Nixon's reasons for deciding to invade Cambodia.

Smith, Hedrick. "Cambodian Decision: Why President Acted," in *The New York Times*. (June 30, 1970), pp. 1 and 14. Focuses on Nixon's decision to invade Cambodia and summarizes the various contributing factors.

Weber, William T. "Kissinger as Historian: A Historiographical Approach to Statesmanship," in *World Affairs, A Quarterly Review of International Problems*. CXLI, no. 1 (Summer, 1978). A cogent analysis of Kissinger's conception of global politics and statesmanship which, although not specifically concerned with Cambodia, substantially clarifies the Secretary of State's fundamental intentions in devising policy and thus provides an illuminating glimpse of United States motives in Cambodia.

THE INDIA-PAKISTAN WAR
AND THE CREATION OF BANGLADESH

Type of event: Military: armed intervention in another country's internal affairs and
the establishment of a new state
Time: January-December, 1971
Locale: South Asia (the Indian subcontinent)

Principal personages:

SHEIK MUJIBUR RAHMAN (1922-   ), Bengali politician and
first President of Bangladesh

YAHYA KHAN (1917-   ), Dictator of Pakistan, 1969-1971

ZULFIKAR ALI BHUTTO (1928-1979), President of Pakistan
after December, 1971

INDIRA GANDHI (1917-   ), Prime Minister of India, 1965-
1977

RICHARD MILHOUS NIXON (1913-   ), thirty-seventh President of the United States, 1969-1974

Summary of Event

The year 1971 witnessed the disintegration of Pakistan, a state of South Asia, and its replacement by two new states: Pakistan, consisting of the former West Pakistan, and Bangladesh, the former East Pakistan. Disintegration occurred as a result of a rebellion in East Pakistan, the success of which was guaranteed by the powerful assistance of the army of the neighboring state of India. The roots of these events go far back in history.

In August of 1947, Great Britain finally relinquished control over the Indian Empire, which she had ruled since the early nineteenth century. Because of the irreconcilable conflict between the Hindu and Muslim communities, however, the old Empire was split into two new states: India, with a Hindu majority, and Pakistan, with a Muslim majority. Pakistan itself consisted of two parts: West Pakistan, carved out of the old Western

province of the Indian Empire, and East Pakistan, which comprised the greater part of the former province of Bengal. The largest city in Bengal, Calcutta, was given to India. Even so, a sizable minority of the population of East Pakistan, about ten percent, was and would remain Hindu. The two wings of Pakistan were geographically separated by miles and miles of Indian territory.

The new state of India managed to establish a parliamentary democracy. Pakistan, however, was governed by a succession of military dictatorships. Both Pakistan and India were abysmally poor and underdeveloped, but they both managed to find enough money to conduct a ruinous arms race with each other. They fought two wars, one in 1949, the other in 1965, over Kashmir, a province which India insisted on holding by force despite its Muslim majority.

In the meantime, however, the

1091

unity of the State of Pakistan was slowly being eroded from within. The root of the problem was the incompatibility between the West Pakistanis and the East Pakistanis. The only thing the two widely separated halves of the country had in common was their Islamic religion.

In the thirteenth century, Muslim warrior conquerors, riding in from the plains of Western India, had overrun Bengal, bringing their religion with them. Under Muslim rule until the coming of the British, many of the Bengalis (especially those of the lower Hindu castes) had been converted to Islam. Though many Bengalis had converted to the religion of the Muslim conquerors, few had been converted to their language. By 1947, Urdu (the Indian-derived language of the West Pakistani Muslims, interspersed with Persian loanwords and written in Arabic characters) was spoken in Bengal only by a tiny minority, the aristocratic descendants of the original Muslim conquerors. To these were added, after 1947, a new and larger group of Urdu-speakers, the Muslim refugees from the state of Bihar, which had remained part of India. The overwhelming majority of the East Pakistani Muslims, however, spoke the Bengali language, as did the Hindus of East Pakistan. Attempts by the West Pakistanis to impose Urdu on the East provoked bitter resistance.

There were other problems, of course, though the cultural difference was the most basic reason for the disharmony between the two sections. Many East Pakistanis felt that they were economically exploited by the Western wing, and they complained also of inequality of representation in the higher levels of the administration. Thus, almost all the officers of the Pakistani Army were Urdu-speaking West Pakistanis. Finally, there was a "racial" aspect to the quarrel between the sections. The Bengalis are, in general, shorter and darker-complexioned than the people of West Pakistan.

In the year 1971, the accumulating tension between East and West Pakistan finally led to Civil War. On December 7, 1970, Yahya Khan, who had ruled as military dictator since March, 1969, ordered national elections held to provide for a return to democratic, parliamentary government. In these elections, the eastern seats were all won by the Awami League of Sheik Mujibur Rahman, the leading advocate of greater political autonomy for East Pakistan. There ensued three months of frantic but fruitless talks between Zulfikar Ali Bhutto, whose Pakistan People's Party had won most of the seats in the West, and Sheik Mujibur Rahman. Ever since his resignation from the government in 1966, Bhutto had urged a return to democracy. He could not, however, agree on a common program with the Bengali leader, whose strong insistence on immediate autonomy for the East made compromise difficult.

By March, 1971, President Yahya Khan sensed a plot against the unity of Pakistan. He ordered Sheik Mujibur Rahman placed under arrest, and had him forcibly taken to West Pakistan. On March 25-26, 1971, Yahya Khan dispatched large numbers of Pakistani Army troops, all of them West Pakistanis, to the East.

Soon these soldiers began to engage in atrocities against leading Bengali politicians and intellectuals, and also against the still sizable Hindu minority. Streams of refugees, both Hindu and Muslim, poured across the border from East Pakistan into India, and bands of guerrillas, the so-called Mukti Bahini, began to harass the Pakistani forces. After the beginning of May, these Bengali guerrillas used the territory of India as a base, and received covert aid from the Indian government. By late October, the Indian Army was steadily increasing its support of the Mukti Bahini. As a result, shooting incidents began to erupt between Indian and Pakistani troops along the border of East Pakistan. Tension between India and Pakistan steadily increased.

By the summer of 1971, Indira Gandhi, the Prime Minister of India, was getting ready to face the probability of yet another Indo-Pakistani conflict. On August 9, 1971, Mrs. Gandhi signed a treaty of friendship with the Soviet Union, assuring the benevolent neutrality of that country in the event of war.

If the friendship of Russia was assured, the good will of Communist China was not. Communist China, the northern neighbor of India, continued to have friendly relations with the Pakistani government of Yahya Khan. Thus, any Indian decision to risk war with Pakistan was still a gamble. In the end, however, it was a gamble which paid off.

On the night of December 3, 1971, the Pakistani Army began to attack at various points along the western border of India; India retaliated by launching a full-scale invasion of East Pakistan. By December 16, the Commander of Pakistani forces in East Pakistan had been forced to surrender to the Indian Army. On the Western front, however, the Indian Army confined itself to purely defensive operations. China, which needed West Pakistan as a buffer state between Russia and India, might conceivably have gone to war to save the Western wing.

In the end, no major power was willing to go to war to prevent the secession of East Pakistan. China did nothing. Henry Kissinger, who was then the chief foreign policy adviser to United States President Richard M. Nixon, did, it is true, verbally deplore the Indian action. Richard M. Nixon, faced with a Congress that was sympathetic to the Indian position, was unwilling to do anything more forceful than that. On December 17, 1971, President Yahya Khan, whose country was now almost completely isolated diplomatically ordered all Pakistani troops to cease fire. India had won the war.

On December 20, 1971, Yahya Khan, humiliated by the disastrous defeat, resigned as President of Pakistan. Zulfikar Ali Bhutto, the former leader of the West Pakistani opposition, now became President of what was left of Pakistan. It was not until the Indo-Pakistani Agreement of August, 1973, that Bhutto formally recognized the independence of Bangladesh.

As the 1970's drew to a close, the future stability of rump Pakistan was still in doubt. It was not certain that the Pathans, Sindhis, Baluchis, and Punjabis would be able to bury their quarrels in a common patriotism. As the result of the 1971 war, India had become the strongest state on the South Asian subcontinent. Her people, however, still suffered from widespread poverty. After 1971, independent Bangladesh, like her neighbor India, continued to face the problem of too many people and too few resources. She also faced problems of recurring political instability. Now, however, there was no foreign oppressor who could be blamed for these problems.

Pertinent Literature

Choudhury, G. W. *The Last Days of United Pakistan*. Bloomington: Indiana University Press, 1974.

This account of the 1971 crisis was written by a man who had once been a high official in the government of the old united Pakistan. The book does, therefore, have a definite point of view. Despite the inevitable bias, the author's firsthand experience of the crisis makes the book a mine of information on the origins of the civil war. Choudhury does not cover in any detail the Indian military campaign of December 3-17, 1971, nor does he treat the diplomatic prelude to the war in any great depth; instead, he focuses on political developments within Pakistan during the crucial years 1969 to 1971.

The first chapter gives the historical background of the rise of Bengali separatism; the second chapter attempts to explain the fall of Ayub Khan in 1969 and the ascent to power of Yahya Khan. Chapters Three to Seven deal with the fateful elections of December, 1970, and the frantic political dickering which ensued. Chapter Eight tells the story of how civil war erupted in March, 1971, and Chapter Nine discusses the international implications of the breakup of Pakistan. In Chapter Ten, the author sets out his conclusion.

Choudhury disagrees with the notion that the disintegration of united Pakistan in 1971 was in any sense inevitable. Instead, he believes that responsibility for this event, which he sees as a disaster, must be placed on the shoulders of two men: the West Pakistani politician Zulfikar Ali Bhutto, and the East Pakistani politician Mujibur Rahman. He accuses them both of having behaved like irresponsible demagogues. He sees Yahya Khan, on the other hand, as a tragic figure who sincerely desired both the restoration of constitutional government and the conciliation of the Bengalis.

As sources, the author uses newspapers, published documents, and his own memory of conversations held with various key military and political figures during his own years as a Pakistani public official. There are no photographs or maps in the book, nor is there any separate bibliography. Instead, there are reference notes at the end of each chapter. In the back of the volume, there is an exchange of letters dated December 11, 1970, and January 21, 1971, between Yahya Khan, the then-President of Pakistan, and the author.

The India-Pakistan War and the Creation of Bangladesh

Jackson, Robert Victor. *South Asian Crisis: India, Pakistan and Bangladesh. A Political and Historical Analysis of the 1971 War*. New York: Frederick A. Praeger, 1975.

This is an insightful, scholarly work, written by a British political scientist. Fair and objective, it is a contribution not only to the historiography of the 1971 War, but also to the development of more general theories concerning international crises.

In the first chapter, Jackson gives the reader the historical background to the crisis. First, he narrates the history of Islam in India from its beginnings in the thirteenth century to the formation of Pakistan in 1947. Then he goes on to trace the growth of Bengali separatism within the new Pakistani state from 1947 to 1971. Jackson attempts to show why, in his opinion, the Bengali rebellion of 1971 was inevitable.

Even through Jackson believes that the outbreak of the Bengali rebellion was inevitable, he does not believe that the success of the rebellion was equally inevitable. In Chapters Two through Five, Jackson shows how, during the months of March through November, 1971, the astute diplomatic maneuvers of Indian Prime Minister Indira Gandhi managed to ward off the threat of intervention by one of the Great Powers in favor of Pakistan. With the threat of such intervention averted, the local military superiority of India assured the quick defeat of the Pakistani Army and the triumph of the Bengali rebellion. In the concluding chapter, Jackson tries to interpret and summarize the story which he told in the previous narrative chapters.

This work is based chiefly on the Indian and Pakistani press, and on published documentary sources; the author's discussion of United States policy makes use of the so-called "Anderson Papers," which consisted of the minutes of Henry Kissinger's Washington Special Action Group, published by newspaper columnist Jack Anderson in *The New York Times* on January 5, 1972, and January 14, 1972. The book contains several excellent maps of the military fronts during the 1971 War. There is a complete bibliography of books, articles, and documents, as well as an appendix which contains a full selection and citation of documents relative to the 1971 crisis. There are no photographs. — *P.D.M.*

Additional Recommended Reading

Siddiqui, Kalim. *Conflict, Crisis, and War in Pakistan*. New York: Frederick A. Praeger, 1972. A detailed, informative work on the disintegration of Pakistan written by a Pakistani political scientist living in exile.

Loshak, David. *Pakistan Crisis*. New York: McGraw-Hill Book Company, 1971. An account written by an English journalist and published at the very time the war broke out, which shows a strong pro-Bengali bias.

Donaldson, Robert H. *Soviet Policy Toward India: Ideology and Strategy*. Cambridge, Mass.: Harvard University Press, 1974. Chapter 6, "From Mediation to Alliance," gives the background of the Soviet-Indian friendship treaty of August 9, 1971.

Ziring, Lawrence. *The Ayub Khan Era: Politics in Pakistan, 1958-1969*. Syracuse, N.Y.: Syracuse University Press, 1971. Sheds much light on the causes of the collapse of the old united Pakistan.

Choudhury, G. W. *India, Pakistan, Bangladesh, and the Major Powers: Politics of a Divided Subcontinent*. New York: The Free Press, 1975. Part IV discusses briefly both the attitudes of the Great Powers towards the 1971 War and the relations among the three South Asian countries after the war.

Verghese, B. G. *An End to Confrontation: Bhutto's Pakistan: Restructuring the Sub-Continent*. New Delhi, India: S. Chand and Company, 1972. An Indian journalist who visited rump Pakistan in May, 1972, tries to spell out the basis for a just and lasting peace between India and rump Pakistan in the wake of the 1971 War.